Practical Business Math Procedures

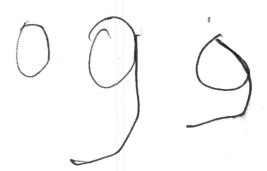

Practical Business Math Procedures

JEFFREY SLATER
North Shore Community College
Danvers, Massachusetts

SEVENTH EDITION

McGraw-Hill Irwin

Boston Burr Ridge, IL Dubuque, IA Madison, WI New York
San Francisco St. Louis Bangkok Bogotá Caracas Kuala Lumpur
Lisbon London Madrid Mexico City Milan Montreal New Delhi
Santiago Seoul Singapore Sydney Taipei Toronto

McGraw-Hill Higher Education

A Division of The **McGraw-Hill** Companies

Chapter opening photos:
Chapter 1: Felicia Martinez/PhotoEdit. Chapter 2: Rhoda Sidney/Stock Boston. Chapter 3: Michele Burgress/Stock Boston. Chapter 4: Tony Freeman/PhotoEdit. Chapter 5: Bill Bachmann/PhotoEdit. Chapter 6: David Young Wolff/PhotoEdit. Chapter 7: AFP/Corbis. Chapter 8: © Jeff Greenberg/PhotoEdit/PictureQuest. Chapter 9: Spencer Grant/PhotoEdit. Chapter 10: Robert Brenner/PhotoEdit. Chapter 11: Mark Richards/PhotoEdit. Chapter 12: Courtesy of Conseco, Inc. Chapter 13: David Young Wolff/PhotoEdit. Chapter 14: Mark Burnett/Stock Boston. Chapter 15: Tony Freeman/PhotoEdit. Chapter 16: William Jonson/Stock Boston. Chapter 17: Michael Newman/PhotoEdit. Chapter 18: Michael Newman/PhotoEdit. Chapter 19: John Coletti/Stock Boston. Chapter 20: Michael Newman/PhotoEdit. Chapter 21: Jim Pickerell/Stock Connection/PictureQuest. Chapter 22: Najlah Feanny/Stock Boston.

The Wall Street Journal articles republished by permission of Dow Jones, Inc. All Rights Reserved Worldwide.

Kiplinger's articles reprinted by permission of *Kiplinger's Personal Finance* magazine. Chapter 1: November 2000. Chapter 2: May 2000. Chapter 3: September 2001. Chapter 4: May 2001. Chapter 5: January 2000. Chapter 6: January 2001. Chapter 7: September 2001. Chapter 8: November 2001. Chapter 9: June 2001. Chapter 10: February 2001. Chapter 11: February 2001. Chapter 12: February 2001. Chapter 13: July 2001. Chapter 14: November 2001. Chapter 15: December 2000. Chapter 16: October 2001. Chapter 17: August 2001. Chapter 18: November 2001. Chapter 19: February 2000. Chapter 20: November 2001. Chapter 21: November 2001. Chapter 22: November 2001.

PRACTICAL BUSINESS MATH PROCEDURES

Published by McGraw-Hill/Irwin, a business unit of The McGraw-Hill Companies, Inc., 1221 Avenue of the Americas, New York, NY, 10020. Copyright © 2003, 2000, 1997, 1994, 1991, 1987, 1983 by The McGraw-Hill Companies, Inc. All rights reserved. No part of this publication may be reproduced or distributed in any form or by any means, or stored in a database or retrieval system, without the prior written consent of The McGraw-Hill Companies, Inc., including, but not limited to, in any network or other electronic storage or transmission, or broadcast for distance learning. Some ancillaries, including electronic and print components, may not be available to customers outside the United States.

This book is printed on acid-free paper.

3 4 5 6 7 8 9 0 DOW/DOW 0 9 8 7 6 5 4 3

ISBN 0-07-246856-4 (student edition)
ISBN 0-07-253741-8 (teacher's edition)
ISBN 0-07-253747-7 (brief student edition)
ISBN 0-07-253736-1 (brief teacher's edition)

Publisher: *Brent Gordon*
Executive editor: *Richard T. Hercher, Jr.*
Developmental editor: *Christina A. Sanders*
Freelance developmental editor: *Loretta Scholten*
Senior marketing manager: *Zina Craft*
Producer, Media technology: *Anthony Sherman*
Lead project manager: *Susan Trentacosti*
Manager, new book production: *Melonie Salvati*
Senior designer: *Jennifer McQueen*
Photo research coordinator: *David A. Tietz/Ira C. Roberts*
Photo researcher: *Connie Gardner*
Lead supplement producer: *Cathy L. Tepper*
Cover and interior design: *Michael Warrell*
Cover photographer: *Sharon Hoogstraten*
Typeface: *10/12 Times Roman*
Compositor: *GAC Indianapolis*
Printer: *R. R. Donnelley & Sons Company*

Library of Congress Control Number: 2002103318

www.mhhe.com

Just for Gracie

PREVIEW OF SPECIAL FEATURES

Before looking at how to succeed in each chapter, let's look at some special features.

1. **The toll-free, 24-hour hotline.** This toll-free number for students allows you to call anytime and get extra help on any of the 22 summary practice tests located at the end of each chapter. As the author, I have recorded messages on how you should solve each problem. Think of this hotline as a pre-exam tune-up. The toll-free number is 1-800-338-9708.

2. **Group activity: Personal Finance, a Kiplinger Approach.** In each chapter you can debate a business math issue I raise based on a *Kiplinger's Personal Finance* magazine article that is presented. This is great for critical thinking, as well as improving your writing skills.

3. *The Wall Street Journal* **newspaper.** This newspaper insert helps explain how to read *The Wall Street Journal,* as well as show how business math relates to it. The newspaper is page-referenced to the text and is helpful for those who have never followed stocks, bonds, and mutual funds.

4. *Business Math Handbook and Study Guide.* This reference guide contains all the tables found in the text. It makes homework, exams, etc. easier to deal with than flipping back and forth through the text. The *Handbook* also features a built-in study guide that provides self-paced worksheets that review each chapter's vocabulary, theory, and math applications. A set of 10 extra word problems for each chapter is included. Also included is a calculator reference guide with advice on how to use different calculators.

5. **Blueprint aid boxes.** For the first eight chapters (not in Chapter 4), blueprint aid boxes are available to help you map out a plan to solve a word problem.

6. **The Business Math Tutorial.** This software is a tutorial that guides you through the entire text. It is highly visual and user friendly.

7. **Spreadsheet templates.** Excel® templates are available for selected end-of-chapter problems. You can run these templates as is or enter your own data. The templates also include an interest table feature that enables you to input any percentage rate and any terms. The program will then generate table values for you.

8. **Business Math Internet Resource Guide.** This Guide lists websites covering topics from each chapter, as well as descriptions of what you can expect to find at each site. It is referenced on the Scrapbook page in the text and includes group projects you can work on using the exciting possibilities of the Web.

9. **New DVD-ROM.** The DVD packaged with the text includes practice quizzes, business math tutorial software links to websites listed in the Business Math Internet Resource Guide, the Excel® templates, PowerPoint, videocases, and videos—which feature tutorials by Jeff Slater of all Learning Unit Practice Quizzes.

10. **The Slater Business Math website.** Visit the site at www.mhhe.com/slater7e and find the Internet Resource Guide with hot links, tutorials, practice quizzes, and other materials useful for the course.

HOW TO READ AND USE THE BOOK

The colors in this text have a purpose. You should read the description below, then look at several pages to see how it works.

Blue: Movement, cancellations, steps to solve, arrows, blueprints

Gold: Formulas and steps

Green: Tables and forms

Red: Key items we are solving for

CHAPTERS

Each chapter is broken down into learning units. Each learning unit covers a key concept or a small group of concepts.

LEARNING OBJECTIVES

At the beginning of each chapter you'll find a list of learning objectives. Each is page referenced.

PRACTICE QUIZZES

At the end of each learning unit is a practice quiz, followed by solutions. These provide you with immediate feedback on your understanding of the unit. These are all solved on the DVD. Check with your instructor for availability.

CHAPTER ORGANIZER

At the end of each chapter is a quick reference guide called the Chapter Organizer. Key points, formulas, and examples are provided. A list of vocabulary terms is also included. All have page references. (A complete glossary is found at the end of the text.) Think of the chapter organizer as your set of notes.

CRITICAL THINKING DISCUSSION QUESTIONS

Factual, as well as thought-provoking, questions appear after the chapter organizer.

PROBLEMS

At the end of each chapter is a complete set of drill and word problems. Check figures for the odd-numbered problems are located in Appendix B.

CHALLENGE PROBLEMS

The last two word problems in each chapter let you "stretch" your business math skills. These are harder and require more effort.

ADDITIONAL HOMEWORK ASSIGNMENTS BY LEARNING UNIT

At the end of the text in Appendix A is a complete set of drill and word problems arranged by learning unit. These can be used for additional reinforcement. Your instructor may ask you to turn these in. Check figures for the odd-numbered problems are shown in Appendix B. On the inside back cover of the book is a table showing page references for each assignment.

SUMMARY PRACTICE TEST

This is a test before the test. All questions are page referenced back to the topic so you can check your methods. The test is a combination of drill and word problems. Check figures for *all* practice tests are in Appendix B. Remember: There is a toll-free hotline to review these tests at 1-800-338-9708.

BUSINESS MATH SCRAPBOOK

At the end of each chapter you will find actual clippings from *The Wall Street Journal* and various other publications. These articles will give you a chance to use the theory provided in the chapter to apply to the real world. It allows you to put your math skills to work.

CUMULATIVE REVIEWS

At the end of Chapters 3, 8, and 13 are word problems that test your retention of business math concepts and procedures. Check figures for *all* cumulative review problems are in Appendix B.

VIDEO CASES ON DVD

There are six new video cases applying business math concepts to real companies such as American President Lines, Washburn Guitars, Online Banking, Saturn Corporation, McDonald's, and Federal Signal Corporation. Video clips are included on the student DVD. Some background case information and assignment problems incorporating information on the companies are included at the end of Chapters 6, 9, 11, 14, 16, and 21 (pages 161, 240, 277, 341, 385, and 478).

COMPOUNDING/ PRESENT VALUE OVERLAYS

A set of color overlays are inserted in Chapter 13. These color graphics are intended to demonstrate for students the concepts of present value and future value and, even more important, the basic relationship between the two.

Jeffrey Slater

A C K N O W L E D G M E N T S

ACADEMIC EXPERTS, CONTRIBUTORS

Ellen Benowitz

Nancy Billows

Yvonne Block

Donald F. Boyer

Ronald Cooley

Patricia Dennis

Guy Devitt

Jacqueline Dlatt

Douglas Dorsey

Patricia Dumoulin

Thomas R. Etling

Stephen J. Feins

Bob Gronowski

Andrew Haaland

Rob Herman

Ron Holm

Janice Jenny

Lolita Keck

Bharat Kolluri

Dawn Kutz

Kathy Lewis-Payne

Gwendolyn Loftis

Kelly Luchtman

Bruce MacLean

Leland Mansuetti

Paul Martin

Jean McArthur, Jr.

Sharon Meyer

Daniel Pacheco

Joanne Salas

Ellen Sawyer

Loretta Scholten

Jim Setterstrom

Carl Sonntag

Steven Teeter

Jann Underwood

Yvonne Wabbington

Keith Weidkamp

Harold Zarr, Jr.

COMPANY/APPLICATION(S)

H. J. Heinz—*Whole numbers*

McDonald's Corp.—*General problem solving, Sweatshops, Financial reports, Product liability*

Southwest Airlines—*Reading, Writing, Whole numbers*

United Airlines—*Reading, Writing, Whole numbers*

American Airlines—*Reading, Writing, Whole numbers*

Delta—*Reading, Writing, Whole numbers, Percent decrease and increase, Pay scales*

US Airways—*Reading, Writing, Whole numbers*

Tootsie Roll Industries—*Dissecting word problems*

Continental Airlines—*Adding and subtracting whole numbers*

Ford—*Subtracting whole numbers*

Hershey—*Dissecting word problems*

Subway—*Whole numbers*

M&M Mars—*Fractions*

Wal-Mart—*Types of fractions, Discounts*

AltaVista—*Addition and subtraction of fractions*

AMC Theatres—*Addition and subtraction of fractions*

Lowes Theatres—*Addition and subtraction of fractions*

Regal Cinemas—*Addition and subtraction of fractions*

Showcase Cinemas—*Addition and subtraction of fractions*

United Artists Theatres—*Addition and subtraction of fractions*

United Air—*Adding and subtracting decimals*

Carmines, New York—*Subtracting decimals*

Heaven on Seven, Chicago—*Subtracting decimals*

Grill 23, Boston —*Subtracting decimals*

Docks, New York—*Subtracting decimals*

E*Trade—*Rounding, Web trading commissions*

Ipswich Bank—*Banking*

Bank One—*Trends in banking*

Wells Fargo—*Trends in banking*

Citigroup—*Trends in banking*

First Union—*Trends in banking*

Washington Mutual—*Trends in banking*

Chase—*Trends in banking*

Fleet Bank—*Trends in banking*

Visa USA—*Banking*

UPS—*Solving for the unknown*

Disney Co.—*Solving word problems, Theme parks, Financial reports*

Unilever—*Solving for the unknown*

Procter & Gamble—*Solving for the unknown*

Goodyear—*Solving for the unknown*

Sumitomo Rubber Industries—*Solving for the unknown*

Zipcar.com—*Kiplinger's*

Bank of America—*Kiplinger's*

Orbitz—*Kiplinger's*

Expedia—*Kiplinger's*

Sidestep—*Kiplinger's*

Travelocity—*Kiplinger's, Trade discounts*

Bb&T—*Kiplinger's*

U.S. Small Business—*Kiplinger's*

Wendy's—*Introduction to percents*

Coca-Cola Co.—*Converting percents to decimals, Solving for the unknown*

PepsiCo, Inc.—*Converting percents to decimals*

Wm. Wrigley Jr., Co.—*Percents*

American President's Lines—*Video case*

Jones Apparel Group—*Introduction to trade discounts*

Nine West—*Introduction to trade discounts*

Kodak—*Introduction to trade discounts*

Federal Express—*Freight*

CVS—*Kiplinger's*

Eckerd—*Kiplinger's*

Walgreens—*Kiplinger's*

Taco Bell—*Discounts*

True Value—*Introduction to retailing*

Bluefly, Inc.—*Markup*

JCPenney Co.—*Markdowns*

Sears—*Kiplinger's*

Family Dollar Store—*Kiplinger's*

UAL Corp.—*Pay scales*

Universal Pictures—*Work for hire*

Washburn Guitars—*Video case*

AT&T Corp.—*Interest introduction*

Cisco Systems—*Promissory notes*

Treasury Department—*Online sales*

Xerox—*Lines of credit*

Home Depot—*Loans, Kiplinger's*

Conseco—*Introduction to compounding*

Upromise—*Rebates, Kiplinger's*

Hewitt Associates—*Kiplinger's, 401K*

American Express—*Tax payment, Online security*

Debt. Solutions—*Settling debt, Kiplinger's*

Europay–MasterCard—*Smart Card*
Saturn Corp—*Video case*
Fannie Mae—*Jumbo mortgage*
Freddie Mac—*Jumbo mortgage*
Eloan—*Mortgage*
Lendingtree.com—*Mortgages*
Homespace.com—*Mortgages*
DIC Entertainment Holdings—*Financial reports*
Golden Books Family Entertainment—*Financial reports*
Rent-Way Inc.—*Financial reports*
Kimberly-Clark—*Income statement, Inventory control*
Motorola—*Trend analysis*
GemStar–T.V. Guide International—*Business models, Kiplinger's*
Show Boats International—*Floating condominium*
Land Rover—*Depreciation*

Campbell Soup Co.—*Inventory*
Amazon.com—*Perpetual inventory*
Circuit City—*Inventory strategy*
America Online—*Tax on Internet*
MCI World.com—*Tax on Internet*
Time Warner—*Tax on Internet*
Gateway—*Tax on Internet*
Bed Bath & Beyond—*Profit margins*
GE Financial—*Nursing home care*
Savings Bank Life—*Level premium*
Insurance (Massachusetts)—*Level premium*
Royal Caribbean Cruises, Ltd.—*Earnings per share*
Land O' Lakes—*Buyout*
Purina Mills Inc.—*Buyout*
Krispy Kreme—*Stock price*
Charles Schwab—*Web trading commissions, Tax on Internet*

Fidelity Investments—*Web trading commissions*
TD Waterhouse—*Web trading commissions*
Ameritrade—*Web trading commissions*
DLG Direct—*Web trading commissions*
Datek Online—*Web trading commissions*
National Discount Brokers—*Web trading commissions*
Federal Signal Corporation—*Video case*
BMW—*Median age*
Internal Revenue Service—*E-filing*
Ford Motor—*India car market*
Toys "R" Us—*New marketing strategy, Kiplinger's*
Kiplinger's Personal Finance—*Group projects*
Dow Jones & Company Inc.—*Clippings and Scrapbooks*

CONTENTS

BECAUSE MONEY MATTERS . . .
SUBSCRIBE TO *KIPLINGER'S*
AT SPECIAL STUDENT RATES!

Every month, more than three million Americans turn to *Kiplinger's Personal Finance* magazine for advice and information about how to manage their money. How to save it. Spend it. Invest it. Protect it. Insure it. And make more of it.

If it affects you and your money, then you'll find it in the pages of *Kiplinger's*. From our annual ranking of the nation's best mutual funds to our yearly rating of new automobiles we provide you with a different kind of investment publication.

We make it easy for you to subscribe with the lowest rates available to students and educators. Just provide your name and address below. Make checks payable to *Kiplinger's Personal Finance*. Or, if you prefer we will bill you later.

Aliae Mohader
Student's Name

_____   _____
Address   Apt. #

_____   _____   _____
City   State   Zip

(___)_____
Phone

Term: One year for $14.97

After completing the form, please mail it to: *Kiplinger's Personal Finance*, P.O. Box 3291, Harlan, Iowa 51593-2471.

CODE: J2MCGRAW

Case of Not Enough Ketchup for Meatloaf Squeezes H.J. Heinz

* * *

Company Agrees to Overfill Products in California, Pay $180,000 After Investigation

———

By Christina Binkley
Staff Reporter of The Wall Street Journal

LOS ANGELES—H.J. Heinz Co. has some catching up to do after two California district attorneys found it had been underfilling millions of ketchup bottles sold in this bastion of consumer protection.

Caught red-handed after a four-year investigation, the Pittsburgh-based ketchup manufacturer agreed yesterday to make up for shorting its customers by overfilling its 18- to 64-ounce bottles in California. So for the next year, California ketchup buyers can anticipate getting a tiny freebie—a little less air and about one extra ounce of ketchup in a bottle of Heinz. "We're going to return about 10 million ounces to the people," said Thomas A. Papageorge, head of the Los Angeles district attorney's consumer-protection division. That is expected to cost Heinz about $650,000.

1

Whole Numbers; How to Dissect and Solve Word Problems

People of all ages make personal business decisions based on the answers to number questions. Numbers also determine most of the business decisions of companies. For example, click on your computer and go to the website of a company such as eBay and note the importance of numbers in the company's business decision-making process.

The following *Wall Street Journal* clipping illustrates how McDonald's fast-food chain plans to increase its profit numbers by changing its business strategy.

Will Big Mac Find New Sizzle In Shoes, Videos?

By JENNIFER ORDONEZ
Staff Reporter of THE WALL STREET JOURNAL

McDonald's Corp. wants to supersize its brand name.

Led by a new brand-extension executive, the burger giant is quietly developing or expanding several lines of McDonald's-brand consumer goods. Already, German consumers are buying McDonald's-brand ketchup, and for some time American parents have been picking up McKids clothing and shoes at Wal-Mart **stores.** Under consideration now are McDonald's-brand snacks and other packaged goods, as well as a line of McDonald's books and videos.

"A few years from now, people will say, 'I remember when McDonald's was a restaurant,'" says Peter Oakes, a restaurant analyst for Merrill Lynch Global Securities who has caught wind of the strategy and is preparing a report on it. "Why not do something more than just sponsor Saturday morning cartoons?"

McDonald's has yet to announce the strategy, whose initial thrust will likely be overseas. But a year ago it created a new executive position—vice president for corporate strategy—to explore ways of extending the McDonald's brand. Mats Lederhausen, who holds the title, reports directly to Chief Executive Jack Greenberg.

Jack Greenberg

Companies often follow a general problem-solving procedure to arrive at a change in company policy. Using McDonald's as an example, the following steps illustrate this procedure:

Step 1.	State the problem(s).	The restaurant business is very competitive. A new strategy is needed that broadens the scope of sales and results in a continued increase in profits.
Step 2.	Decide on the best method(s) to solve the problem(s).	Create new products (ketchup; McKids clothing and shoes) with McDonald's brand name.
Step 3.	Does the solution make sense?	Test market new products overseas (ketchup). Sell McKids clothing and shoes at Wal-Mart.
Step 4.	Evaluate results.	All test markets will be evaluated before worldwide distribution begins.

Have you seen the new H. L. Heinz Company's green ketchup? McDonald's-brand ketchup was introduced in Germany to compete with the Heinz ketchup—the No. 1 seller of ketchup in Germany. How well is McDonald's-brand ketchup performing in the Heinz market? As you may expect, a spokesman for Heinz answers, "Not very well, consumers tell us ours is better." The driving force behind McDonald's desire to add new products such as ketchup to its brand name is higher profit numbers.

Your study of numbers begins with a review of basic computation skills that focuses on speed and accuracy. You may think, "But I can use my calculator." Even if your instructor allows you to use a calculator, you still must know the basic computation skills. You need these skills to know what to calculate, how to interpret your calculations, how to make estimates to recognize errors you made in using your calculator, and how to make calculations when you do not have a calculator. (How to use a calculator is explained in the *Business Math Handbook* and on the Slater website.)

The United States' numbering system is the **decimal system** or *base 10 system.* Your calculator gives the 10 single-digit numbers of the decimal system—0, 1, 2, 3, 4, 5, 6, 7, 8, and 9. The center of the decimal system is the **decimal point.** When you have a number with a decimal point, the numbers to the left of the decimal point are **whole numbers** and the numbers to the right of the decimal point are decimal numbers (discussed in Chapter 3). When you have a number *without* a decimal, the number is a whole number and the decimal is assumed to be after the number.

This chapter discusses reading, writing, and rounding whole numbers; adding and subtracting whole numbers; and multiplying and dividing whole numbers.

LEARNING UNIT 1–1 ❘ READING, WRITING, AND ROUNDING WHOLE NUMBERS

Click and Soar

The top 10 U.S. airlines, ranked by Internet revenue.

AIRLINE	1999	2000*
Southwest	$877,000,000	$1,280,000,000
United	505,000,000	1,190,000,000
American	416,000,000	1,060,000,000
Delta	671,000,000	1,040,000,000
US Airways	450,000,000	800,000,000

*Estimated.   © 2001 Dow Jones & Company, Inc.

We often use whole numbers in business calculations. For example, look at *The Wall Street Journal* clipping "Click and Soar." Note that in 2000 the Internet revenue of Southwest airline increased to $1,280,000,000. From the information in this unit, you will learn that you can read this numeric whole number as one billion, two hundred eighty million. Now let's begin our study of whole numbers.

Reading and Writing Numeric and Verbal Whole Numbers

The decimal system is a *place-value system* based on the powers of 10. Any whole number can be written with the 10 digits of the decimal system because the position, or placement, of the digits in a number gives the value of the digits.

To determine the value of each digit in a number, we use a place-value chart (Figure 1.1) that divides numbers into named groups of three digits, with each group separated by a comma. To separate a number into groups, you begin with the last digit in the number and insert commas every three digits, moving from right to left. This divides the number into the named groups (units, thousands, millions, billions, trillions) shown in the place-value chart. Within each group, you have a ones, tens, and hundreds place.

In Figure 1.1, the numeric number 1,605,743,891,412 illustrates place values. When you study the place-value chart, you can see that the value of each place in the chart is 10 times the value of the place to the right. We can illustrate this by analyzing the last four digits in the number 1,605,743,891,412 :

$$1,412 = (1 \times 1,000) + (4 \times 100) + (1 \times 10) + (2 \times 1)$$

So we can also say that in the number 745, the "7" means seven hundred (700); in the number 75, the "7" means 7 tens (70).

To read and write a numeric number in verbal form, you begin at the left and read each group of three digits as if it were alone, adding the group name at the end (except the last units group and groups of all zeros). Using the place-value chart in Figure 1.1, the

FIGURE 1.1

Whole number place-value chart

Whole Number Groups

Trillions				Billions				Millions				Thousands				Units			
Hundred trillions	Ten trillions	Trillions	Comma	Hundred billions	Ten billions	Billions	Comma	Hundred millions	Ten millions	Millions	Comma	Hundred thousands	Ten thousands	Thousands	Comma	Hundreds	Tens	Ones	Decimal Point
		1	,	6	0	5	,	7	4	3	,	8	9	1	,	4	1	2	.

number 1,605,743,891,412 is read as one trillion, six hundred five billion, seven hundred forty-three million, eight hundred ninety-one thousand, four hundred twelve. You do not read zeros. They fill vacant spaces as placeholders so that you can correctly state the number values. Also, the numbers twenty-one to ninety-nine must have a hyphen. And most important, when you read or write whole numbers in verbal form, do not use the word *and.* In the decimal system, *and* indicates the decimal, which we discuss in Chapter 3.

By reversing the above process of changing a numeric number to a verbal number, you can use the place-value chart to change a verbal number to a numeric number. Remember that you must keep track of the place value of each digit. The place values of the digits in a number determine its total value.

Rounding Whole Numbers

Many of the whole numbers you read and hear are rounded numbers. Government statistics are usually rounded numbers. The financial reports of companies also use rounded numbers. All rounded numbers are *approximate* numbers. The more rounding you do, the more you approximate the number.

Rounded whole numbers are used for many reasons. With rounded whole numbers you can quickly estimate arithmetic results, check actual computations, report numbers that change quickly such as population numbers, and make numbers easier to read and remember.

Numbers can be rounded to any identified digit place value, including the first digit of a number (rounding all the way). To round whole numbers, use the following three steps:

Rounding Whole Numbers

Step 1. Identify the place value of the digit you want to round.

Step 2. If the digit to the right of the identified digit in Step 1 is 5 or more, increase the identified digit by 1 (round up). If the digit to the right is less than 5, do not change the identified digit.

Step 3. Change all digits to the right of the rounded identified digit to zeros.

EXAMPLE 1   Round 9,362 to the nearest hundred.

Step 1.   9,362   The digit 3 is in the hundreds place value.

Step 2.   → The digit to the right of 3 is 5 or more (6). Thus, 3, the identified digit in Step 1, is now rounded to 4. You change the identified digit only if the digit to the right is 5 or more.

9,462

Step 3.   9,400   Change digits 6 and 2 to zeros, since these digits are to the right of 4, the rounded number.

McDonald's Restaurants
In selected cities

Chicago	440
New York	339
Dallas	336
Los Angeles	331
Miami	255
Sao Paulo	182
Mexico City	60

Source: the company

By rounding 9,362 to the nearest hundred, you can see that 9,362 is closer to 9,400 than to 9,300.

We can use *The Wall Street Journal* clipping "McDonald's Restaurants in Selected Cities" to illustrate rounding to the nearest hundred. Note that the number of restaurants in Chicago is 440 and in Sao Paulo, 182. Round these numbers to the nearest hundred as shown above and you can say, "Chicago has 400 McDonald's restaurants; Sao Paulo has 200 restaurants." Numbers rounded to the nearest hundred can either be relatively less than the actual number, as in the Chicago restaurants, or a little more than the actual number, as in the Sao Paulo restaurants. Next we show you how to round to the nearest thousand.

EXAMPLE 2 Round 67,951 to the nearest thousand.

Step 1. 67,951 The digit 7 is in the thousands place value.

Step 2. ⌐———→ Digit to the right of 7 is 5 or more (9). Thus, 7, the identified digit in Step 1, is now rounded to 8.

68,951

Step 3. 68,000 Change digits 9, 5, and 1 to zeros, since these digits are to the right of 8, the rounded number.

By rounding 67,951 to the nearest thousand, you can see that 67,951 is closer to 68,000 than to 67,000.

Now let's look at **rounding all the way.** To round a number all the way, you round to the first digit of the number (the leftmost digit) and have only one nonzero digit remaining in the number.

EXAMPLE 3 Round 7,843 all the way.

Step 1. 7,843 Identified leftmost digit is 7.

Step 2. ⌐———→ Digit to the right of 7 is greater than 5, so 7 becomes 8.

8,843

Step 3. 8,000 Change all other digits to zeros.

Rounding 7,843 all the way gives 8,000.

Remember that rounding a digit to a specific place value depends on the degree of accuracy you want in your estimate. For example, 24,800 rounds all the way to 20,000 because the digit to the right of 2 is less than 5. This 20,000 is 4,800 less than the original 24,800. You would be more accurate if you rounded 24,800 to the place value of the identified digit 4, which is 25,000.

Before concluding this unit, let's look at how to dissect and solve a word problem.

How to Dissect and Solve a Word Problem

As a student, your author found solving word problems difficult. Not knowing where to begin after reading the word problem caused the difficulty. Today, students still struggle with word problems as they try to decide where to begin.

Solving word problems involves *organization* and *persistence*. Recall how persistent you were when you learned to ride a two-wheel bike. Do you remember the feeling of success you experienced when you rode the bike without help? Apply this persistence to word problems. Do not be discouraged. Each person learns at a different speed. Your goal must be to FINISH THE RACE and experience the success of solving word problems with ease.

To be organized in solving word problems, you need a plan of action that tells you where to begin—a blueprint aid. Like a builder, you will refer to this blueprint aid constantly until you know the procedure. The blueprint aid for dissecting and solving a word problem looks like this:

Blueprint Aid for Dissecting and Solving a Word Problem

The facts	Solving for?	Steps to take	Key points

Now let's study this blueprint aid. The first two columns require that you *read* the word problem slowly. Think of the third column as the basic information you must know or calculate before solving the word problem. Often this column contains formulas that provide the foundation for the step-by-step problem solution. The last column reinforces the key points you should remember.

It's time now to try your skill at using the blueprint aid for dissecting and solving a word problem.

Michael Newman/PhotoEdit

The Word Problem   On the 100th anniversary of Tootsie Roll Industries, the company reported sharply increased sales and profits. Sales reached one hundred ninety-four million dollars and a record profit of twenty-two million, five hundred fifty-six thousand dollars. The company president requested that you round the sales and profit figures all the way.

Study the following blueprint aid and note how we filled in the columns with the information in the word problem. You will find the organization of the blueprint aid most helpful. Be persistent! You *can* dissect and solve word problems! When you are finished with the word problem, make sure the answer seems reasonable.

The facts	Solving for?	Steps to take	Key points
Sales: One hundred ninety-four million dollars. *Profit:* Twenty-two million, five hundred fifty-six thousand dollars.	Sales and profit rounded all the way.	Express each verbal form in numeric form. Identify leftmost digit in each number.	Rounding all the way means only the leftmost digit will remain. All other digits become zeros.

Steps to solving problem

1.   Convert verbal to numeric.

One hundred ninety-four million dollars ——————————————→ $194,000,000

Twenty-two million, five hundred fifty-six thousand dollars ——————→ $ 22,556,000

2.   Identify leftmost digit of each number.

$194,000,000 $22,556,000

3.   Round.   ↓   ↓

$200,000,000 $20,000,000

Note that in the final answer, $200,000,000 and $20,000,000 have only one nonzero digit.

Remember that you cannot round numbers expressed in verbal form. You must convert these numbers to numeric form.

Now you should see the importance of the information in the third column of the blueprint aid. When you complete your blueprint aids for word problems, do not be concerned if the order of the information in your boxes does not follow the order given in the text boxes. Often you can dissect a word problem in more than one way.

LU 1–1 PRACTICE QUIZ

At the end of each learning unit, you can check your progress with a Practice Quiz. If you had difficulty understanding the unit, the Practice Quiz will help identify your area of weakness. Work the problems on scrap paper. Check your answers with the worked-out solutions that follow the quiz. Ask your instructor about specific assignments and the videos available on your DVD for each chapter Practice Quiz. A complete set of drill and word problems follows each chapter.

Appendix A at the end of the text contains additional drill and word problems for the learning units. In the inside back cover of the text is a page reference guide you can use to find the additional learning unit drill and word problems in Appendix A.

1.   Write in verbal form:

a.   7,948   **b.**   48,775   **c.**   814,410,335,414

2.   Round the following numbers as indicated:

Nearest ten	Nearest hundred	Nearest thousand	Rounded all the way
a. 92	**b.** 745	**c.** 8,341	**d.** 4,752

3.   Kellogg's reported its sales as five million, one hundred eighty-one thousand dollars. The company earned a profit of five hundred two thousand dollars. What would the sales and profit be if each number were rounded all the way? (*Hint:* You might want to draw the blueprint aid since we show it in the solution.)

✓ **SOLUTIONS**

1. **a.** Seven thousand, nine hundred forty-eight
   b. Forty-eight thousand, seven hundred seventy-five
   c. Eight hundred fourteen billion, four hundred ten million, three hundred thirty-five thousand, four hundred fourteen

2. **a.** 92 = 90   **b.** 745 = 700   **c.** 8,341 = 8,000   **d.** 4,752 = 5,000

3. Kellogg's sales and profit:

The facts	Solving for?	Steps to take	Key points
Sales: Five million, one hundred eighty-one thousand dollars. *Profit:* Five hundred two thousand dollars.	Sales and profit rounded all the way.	Express each verbal form in numeric form. Identify leftmost digit in each number.	Rounding all the way means only the leftmost digit will remain. All other digits become zeros.

Steps to solving problem

1. Convert verbal to numeric.
   Five million, one hundred eighty-one thousand ⟶ $5,181,000
   Five hundred two thousand ⟶ $ 502,000

2. Identify leftmost digit of each number.
   $5,181,000 $502,000

3. Round.   ↓   ↓
   $5,000,000 $500,000

LEARNING UNIT 1–2 | ADDING AND SUBTRACTING WHOLE NUMBERS

Higher Fares for Fido Have Pet Owners Chasing Airline's Tail

By JANE COSTELLO
WSJ.com

Some pet lovers have a bone to pick with Continental Airlines.

Starting today, passengers with pets can no longer check Fido as baggage. Pets that aren't eligible to ride in the cabin must now travel via Continental's Quickpak priority service or via cargo.

So what used to cost $50 will now average $170 for a medium-sized dog traveling via Quickpak. Mileage-based cargo rates can range from $100 for a little kennel to $400 for the St. Bernard size. In-flight amenities, however, won't be any better. Pets will still be packed away with passenger luggage—just no longer considered checked bags.

© 2000 Dow Jones & Company, Inc.

If you are a pet owner and plan to fly with your pet, *The Wall Street Journal* clipping "Higher Fares for Fido Have Pet Owners Chasing Airline's Tail" has some important information for you. Pets no longer can fly as baggage but must fly via Continental's Quickpak or via cargo. The cost for a medium-size dog via Quickpak has increased $120 .

Difference in new price and old price

New price $170
Old price   − 50
               $120

Note from the clipping how much cargo rates have increased if your dog is the size of a St. Bernard.

This unit teaches you how to manually add and subtract whole numbers. When you least expect it, you will catch yourself automatically using this skill.

Addition of Whole Numbers

To add whole numbers, you unite two or more numbers called **addends** to make one number called a **sum,** *total,* or *amount.* The numbers are arranged in a column according to their place values—units above units, tens above tens, and so on. Then, you add the columns of numbers from top to bottom. To check the result, you re-add the columns from bottom to top.

Adding Whole Numbers
Step 1. Align the numbers to be added in columns according to their place values, beginning with the units place at the right and moving to the left (Figure 1.1).
Step 2. Add the units column. Write the sum below the column. If the sum is more than 9, write the units digit and carry the tens digit.
Step 3. Moving to the left, repeat Step 2 until all place values are added.

EXAMPLE

Adding top to bottom

$$
\begin{array}{r}
{}^{2\ 1\,1} \\
1,362 \\
5,913 \\
8,924 \\
+\ 6,594 \\
\hline
22,793
\end{array}
$$

Checking bottom to top

Alternate check

Add each column as a separate total and then combine. The end result is the same.

$$
\begin{array}{r}
1,362 \\
5,913 \\
8,924 \\
+\ 6,594 \\
\hline
13 \\
18 \\
2\,6 \\
20 \\
\hline
22,793
\end{array}
$$

How to Quickly Estimate Addition by Rounding All the Way

In Learning Unit 1–1, you learned that rounding whole numbers all the way gives quick arithmetic estimates. Using *The Wall Street Journal* clipping "Expat Expenses," note how you can round each number all the way and the total will not be rounded all the way. Remember that rounding all the way does not replace actual computations, but it is helpful in making quick commonsense decisions.

Expat Expenses

Overseas locales with highest living costs*

LOCATION:	ANNUAL COST OF LIVING
Seoul	$190,158
Tokyo	$185,181
London	$122,168
Singapore	$119,040
Moscow	$118,548
Buenos Aires	$105,551
Shanghai	$100,833

*Assumes U.S. family of three with a base salary of $100,000

Source: analysis by Runzheimer International, Rochester, Wisconsin

Rounded all the way

$$
\begin{array}{r}
\$200,000 \\
200,000 \\
100,000 \\
100,000 \\
100,000 \\
100,000 \\
+\ 100,000 \\
\hline
\$900,000
\end{array}
$$

← Rounding all the way means each number has only one nonzero digit.

Note: Final answer could have more than one nonzero since total is not rounded all the way.

*Assumes U.S. family of three with a base salary of $100,000.
© 2000 Dow Jones & Company, Inc.

Horizontal and Vertical Addition

Frequently, companies must use both horizontal and vertical additions. For example, manufacturers often need weekly production figures of individual products and a weekly total of all products. Today, many companies use computer spreadsheets to determine various manufacturing figures. The following example shows you how to do horizontal and vertical addition manually.

EXAMPLE

Production report: Units produced						
	Monday	**Tuesday**	**Wednesday**	**Thursday**	**Friday**	**Total**
Sneakers	400 +	300 +	170 +	70 +	450 =	1,390
Boots	650 +	180 +	190 +	210 +	220 =	1,450
Loafers	210 +	55 +	98 +	112 +	310 =	785
Totals	1,260 +	535 +	458 +	392 +	980 =	3,625

Besides production reports, payroll records often require horizontal and vertical addition.

The totals of the vertical and horizontal columns check to the grand total of 3,625.

Subtraction of Whole Numbers

Subtraction is the opposite of addition. Addition unites numbers; subtraction takes one number away from another number. In subtraction, the top (largest) number is the **minuend.** The number you subtract from the minuend is the **subtrahend,** which gives you the **difference** between the minuend and the subtrahend.

Subtracting Whole Numbers

Step 1. Align the minuend and subtrahend according to their place values.

Step 2. Begin the subtraction with the units digits. Write the difference below the column. If the units digit in the minuend is smaller than the units digit in the subtrahend, borrow 1 from the tens digit in the minuend. One tens digit is 10 units.

Step 3. Moving to the left, repeat Step 2 until all place values in the subtrahend are subtracted.

EXAMPLE   The following item from *The Wall Street Journal* clipping "Consumer Purchases" is used to illustrate the subtraction of whole numbers:

Consumer Purchases

	1998	**1999**	**2000**
Ford Taurus Sticker price, plus destination charge, for base model	$17,995	$18,245	**$18,860**

© 2000 Dow Jones & Company, Inc.

In the year 2000, a Ford Taurus cost $865 more than the 1998 model. You can use subtraction to arrive at the $865 difference.

$$
\begin{array}{r}
{}^{17}_{}\,{}^{15}_{} \\
7\ \ 7\ 5\,10 \\
\$18,860 \\
-\ 17,995 \\
\hline
\$\ \ \ \ 865
\end{array}
$$

← Minuend (the larger number)
← Subtrahend
← Difference

Check $17,995
            +   865
            ———————
            $18,860

Note how borrowing occurs in the example above. Starting at the rightmost column of the minuend and subtrahend, you can see that you cannot subtract 5 in the subtrahend from 0 in the minuend. You must borrow from the 6 to the left in the minuend. The 6 becomes 5 and you must borrow again from the 8 to the left so you can subtract 9 in the subtrahend from 15 to get 6 in the difference. This means that the first 8 to the left in the minuend becomes 7 and you must borrow from the second 8 to the left to get 17 so you can subtract the second 9 to the left in the subtrahend from 17 in the minuend. This gives 8 in the difference—$865 is the difference between the subtrahend $17,995 and the minuend $18,860, as proved in the check at the right. Checking subtraction requires adding the difference ($865) to the subtrahend ($17,995) to arrive at the minuend ($18,860). The Ford Taurus cost $865 more in 2000.

How to Dissect and Solve a Word Problem

Accurate subtraction is important in many business operations. In Chapter 4 we discuss the importance of keeping accurate subtraction in your checkbook balance. Now let's check your progress by dissecting and solving a word problem.

The Word Problem   Hershey's produced 25 million Kisses in one day. The same day, the company shipped 4 million to Japan, 3 million to France, and 6 million throughout the United States. At the end of that day, what is the company's total inventory of Kisses? What is the inventory balance if you round the number all the way?

The facts	Solving for?	Steps to take	Key points
Produced: 25 million. *Shipped:* Japan, 4 million; France, 3 million; United States, 6 million.	Total Kisses left in inventory. Inventory balance rounded all the way.	Total Kisses produced − Total Kisses shipped = Total Kisses left in inventory.	Minuend − Subtrahend = Difference. Rounding all the way means rounding to last digit on the left.

Steps to solving problem

1. Calculate the total Kisses shipped.

$$\begin{array}{r} 4,000,000 \\ 3,000,000 \\ +\ 6,000,000 \\ \hline 13,000,000 \end{array}$$

2. Calculate the total Kisses left in inventory.

$$\begin{array}{r} 25,000,000 \\ -\ 13,000,000 \\ \hline 12,000,000 \end{array}$$

3. Rounding all the way.

Identified digit is 1. Digit to right of 1 is 2, which is less than 5. *Answer:* 10,000,000 .

LU 1–2 PRACTICE QUIZ

1. Add by totaling each separate column:

$$\begin{array}{r} 8,974 \\ 6,439 \\ +6,941 \end{array}$$

2. Estimate by rounding all the way (do not round the total of estimate) and then do the actual computation:

$$\begin{array}{r} 4,241 \\ 8,794 \\ +3,872 \end{array}$$

3. Subtract and check your answer:

$$\begin{array}{r} 9,876 \\ -4,967 \end{array}$$

4. Jackson Manufacturing Company projected its year 2003 furniture sales at $900,000. During 2003, Jackson earned $510,000 in sales from major clients and $369,100 in sales from the remainder of its clients. What is the amount by which Jackson over- or underestimated its sales? Use the blueprint aid, since the answer will show the completed blueprint aid.

✓ SOLUTIONS

1.
$$\begin{array}{r} 1\!\!\!/4 \\ \!\!/4 \\ 2\,2 \\ \!/20 \\ \hline 22,354 \end{array}$$

2.

Estimate	Actual
4,000	4,241
9,000	8,794
+ 4,000	+ 3,872
17,000	16,907

3.
$$\begin{array}{r} 8\ \ 18\,6\,16 \\ 9,8\!\!\!/7\!\!\!/6 \\ -4,967 \\ \hline 4,909 \end{array}$$

Check
$$\begin{array}{r} 4,909 \\ +4,967 \\ \hline 9,876 \end{array}$$

4. Jackson Manufacturing Company over- or underestimated sales:

The facts	Solving for?	Steps to take	Key points
Projected 2003 sales: $900,000. *Major clients:* $510,000. *Other clients:* $369,100.	How much were sales over- or underestimated?	Total projected sales − Total actual sales = Over- or underestimated sales.	Projected sales (minuend) − Actual sales (subtrahend) = Difference.

Steps to solving problem

1. Calculate total actual sales.

$$\begin{array}{r} \$510,000 \\ +\ 369,100 \\ \hline \$879,100 \end{array}$$

2. Calculate over- or underestimated sales.

$$\begin{array}{r} \$900,000 \\ -\ 879,100 \\ \hline \$\ 20,900 \text{ (overestimated)} \end{array}$$

LEARNING UNIT 1–3 | MULTIPLYING AND DIVIDING WHOLE NUMBERS

A. Ramey/PhotoEdit

Recall from Learning Unit 1–2 that the annual cost of living in London was $122,168. The difference between living in London and living in Singapore is $3,128 ($122,168 − $119,040). If you lived in London for 3 years, it would cost you $9,384 more to live in London. You can get this number by multiplying $3,128 times 3. If you take the $9,384 and divide it by 3, you will get $3,128.

This unit will sharpen your skills in two important arithmetic operations—multiplication and division. These two operations frequently result in knowledgeable business decisions.

Multiplication of Whole Numbers—Shortcut to Addition

From calculating your 3-year living expenses in London, you know that multiplication is a *shortcut to addition:*

$$\$3,128 \times 3 = \boxed{\$9,384} \qquad or \qquad \$3,128 + \$3,128 + \$3,128 = \boxed{\$9,384}$$

Before learning the steps used to multiply whole numbers with two or more digits, you must learn some multiplication terminology.

Note in the following example that the top number (number we want to multiply) is the **multiplicand.** The bottom number (number doing the multiplying) is the **multiplier.** The final number (answer) is the **product.** The numbers between the multiplier and the product are **partial products.** Also note how we positioned the partial product 2090. This number is the result of multiplying 418 by 50 (the 5 is in the tens position). On each line in the partial products, we placed the first digit directly below the digit we used in the multiplication process.

EXAMPLE

$$\begin{array}{r} 418 \\ \times\ \ 52 \\ \hline 836 \\ 20\ 90 \\ \hline 21{,}736 \end{array}$$

    418 ⟵ Top number (multiplicand)
    × 52 ⟵ Bottom number (multiplier)
Partial products — 836, 20 90
21,736 ⟵ Product answer

$$\begin{array}{r} 2 \times 418 = \quad 836 \\ 50 \times 418 = +20{,}900 \\ \hline 21{,}736 \end{array}$$

We can now give the following steps for multiplying whole numbers with two or more digits:

Multiplying Whole Numbers with Two or More Digits

Step 1. Align the multiplicand (top number) and multiplier (bottom number) at the right. Usually, you should make the smaller number the multiplier.

Step 2. Begin by multiplying the right digit of the multiplier with the right digit of the multiplicand. Keep multiplying as you move left through the multiplicand. Your first partial product aligns at the right with the multiplicand and multiplier.

Step 3. Move left through the multiplier and continue multiplying the multiplicand. Your partial product right digit or first digit is placed directly below the digit in the multiplier that you used to multiply.

Step 4. Continue Steps 2 and 3 until you have completed your multiplication process. Then add the partial products to get the final product.

Checking and Estimating Multiplication

We can check the multiplication process by reversing the multiplicand and multiplier and then multiplying. Let's first estimate 52 × 418 by rounding all the way.

EXAMPLE

$$
\begin{array}{r}
50 \longleftarrow \quad 52 \\
\times\ 400 \longleftarrow \times\ 418 \\
\hline
20{,}000 \qquad 416 \\
52 \\
20\ 8 \\
\hline
21{,}736 \\
\end{array}
$$

By estimating before actually working the problem, we know our answer should be about 20,000. When we multiply 52 by 418, we get the same answer as when we multiply 418 × 52—and the answer is about 20,000. Remember, if we had not rounded all the way, our estimate would have been closer. If we had used a calculator, the rounded estimate would have helped us check the calculator's answer. Our commonsense estimate tells us our answer is near 20,000—not 200,000.

Before you study the division of whole numbers, you should know (1) the multiplication shortcut with numbers ending in zeros and (2) how to multiply a whole number by a power of 10.

Multiplication Shortcut with Numbers Ending in Zeros

Step 1. When zeros are at the end of the multiplicand or the multiplier, or both, disregard the zeros and multiply.

Step 2. Count the number of zeros in the multiplicand and multiplier.

Step 3. Attach the number of zeros counted in Step 2 to your answer.

EXAMPLE

$$
\begin{array}{r}
65{,}000 \\
\times\ 420 \\
\hline
\end{array}
\qquad
\begin{array}{r}
65 \\
\times\ 42 \\
\hline
1\ 30 \\
26\ 0 \\
\hline
27{,}300{,}000 \\
\end{array}
\qquad
\begin{array}{l}
\text{3 zeros} \\
+\ \text{1 zero} \\
\hline
\text{4 zeros} \\
\end{array}
$$

No need to multiply rows of zeros.

$$
\begin{array}{r}
65{,}000 \\
\times\ 420 \\
\hline
00\ 000 \\
1\ 300\ 00 \\
26\ 000\ 0 \\
\hline
27{,}300{,}000 \\
\end{array}
$$

Multiplying a Whole Number by a Power of 10

Step 1. Count the number of zeros in the power of 10 (a whole number that begins with 1 and ends in one or more zeros such as 10, 100, 1,000, and so on).

Step 2. Attach that number of zeros to the right side of the other whole number to obtain the answer. Insert comma(s) as needed every three digits, moving from right to left.

EXAMPLE 99×10 $= 99\underline{0}$ $= \boxed{990}$ $\longleftarrow$ Add 1 zero

99×100 $= 9,9\underline{00}$ $= \boxed{9,900}$ $\longleftarrow$ Add 2 zeros

$99 \times 1,000 = 99,\underline{000} = \boxed{99,000}$ $\longleftarrow$ Add 3 zeros

When a zero is in the center of the multiplier, you can do the following:

EXAMPLE

$$
\begin{array}{r}
658 \\
\times \quad 403 \\
\hline
1\,974 \\
263\,2\square \\
\hline
\boxed{265,174}
\end{array}
$$

$3 \times 658 = \quad\ \ 1,974$
$400 \times 658 = +263,200$
$\qquad\qquad\boxed{265,174}$

Division of Whole Numbers

Division is the reverse of multiplication and a timesaving shortcut related to subtraction. For example, in the introduction to this learning unit, you determined that it would cost $9,384 more to live 3 years in London compared to living 3 years in Singapore. If you subtract $3,128 (the difference between living 3 years in London and 3 years in Singapore) three times from $9,384, you would get zero. You can also multiply $3,128 times 3 to get $9,384. Since division is the reverse of multiplication, you can say that $9,384 ÷ 3 = $3,128.

Division can be indicated by the common symbols $\div$ and $\overline{)}$, or by the bar — in a fraction and the forward slant / between two numbers, which means the first number is divided by the second number. Division asks how many times one number (**divisor**) is contained in another number (**dividend**). The answer, or result, is the **quotient.** When the divisor (number used to divide) doesn't divide evenly into the dividend (number we are dividing), the result is a **partial quotient,** with the leftover amount the **remainder** (expressed as fractions in later chapters). The following example illustrates *even division* (this is also an example of *long division* because the divisor has more than one digit).

EXAMPLE

$$
\begin{array}{r}
\boxed{18} \quad \longleftarrow \text{Quotient} \\
15\overline{)270} \quad \longleftarrow \text{Dividend} \\
\underline{15} \\
120 \\
\underline{120}
\end{array}
$$

Divisor $\longrightarrow$

This example divides 15 into 27 once with 12 remaining. The 0 in the dividend is brought down to 12. Dividing 120 by 15 equals 8 with no remainder; that is, even division. The following example illustrates *uneven division with a remainder* (this is also an example of *short division* because the divisor has only one digit).

EXAMPLE

$$
\begin{array}{r}
\boxed{24\,\text{R1}} \quad \longleftarrow \text{Remainder} \\
7\overline{)169} \\
\underline{14} \\
29 \\
\underline{28} \\
1
\end{array}
$$

Check

$(7 \quad \times \quad 24) \quad + \quad 1 \quad = \quad 169$
Divisor $\times$ Quotient $+$ Remainder $=$ Dividend

Note how doing the check gives you assurance that your calculation is correct. When the divisor has one digit (short division) as in this example, you can often calculate the division mentally as illustrated in the following examples:

EXAMPLES

$$
\begin{array}{cc}
\boxed{108} & \boxed{16\,\text{R6}} \\
8\overline{)864} & 7\overline{)118}
\end{array}
$$

Next, let's look at the value of estimating division.

Estimating Division

Before actually working a division problem, estimate the quotient by rounding. This estimate helps check the answer. The example that follows is rounded all the way. After you make an estimate, work the problem and check your answer by multiplication.

EXAMPLE

$$
\begin{array}{r}
36\ \text{R}111 \\
138\overline{)5{,}079} \\
4\ 14 \\
\hline
939 \\
828 \\
\hline
111
\end{array}
$$

Estimate

$$
\begin{array}{r}
50 \\
100\overline{)5{,}000}
\end{array}
$$

Check

$$
\begin{array}{r}
138 \\
\times\ 36 \\
\hline
828 \\
4\ 14 \\
\hline
4{,}968 \\
+\ 111 \quad \longleftarrow \text{Add remainder}\\
\hline
5{,}079
\end{array}
$$

Now let's turn our attention to division shortcuts with zeros.

*Division Shortcuts
with Zeros*

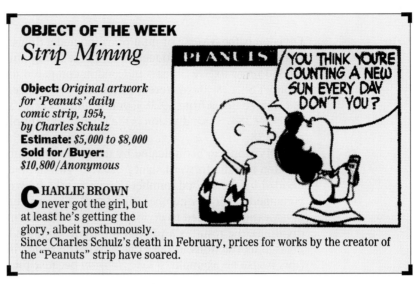

OBJECT OF THE WEEK
Strip Mining

Object: *Original artwork
for 'Peanuts' daily
comic strip, 1954,
by Charles Schulz*
Estimate: *$5,000 to $8,000*
Sold for/Buyer:
$10,800/Anonymous

CHARLIE BROWN never got the girl, but
at least he's getting the
glory, albeit posthumously.
Since Charles Schulz's death in February, prices for works by the creator of
the "Peanuts" strip have soared.

For many years the "Peanuts" daily comic strip has been a favorite of comic strip readers. *The Wall Street Journal* clipping "Object of the Week, Strip Mining," states that the original artwork for a 1954 "Peanuts" daily comic strip sold for $10,800.

If a group of 10 investors paid $10,800 for the comic strip artwork, what did each investor pay?

$$
\begin{array}{r}
\$1{,}080 \quad \longleftarrow \text{Amount each investor pays} \\
10\overline{)\$10{,}800}
\end{array}
$$

The steps that follow explain the shortcut used in the above division.

Division Shortcut with Numbers Ending in Zeros

Step 1. When the dividend and divisor have ending zeros, count the number of ending zeros in the divisor.

Step 2. Drop the same number of zeros in the dividend as in the divisor, counting from right to left.

Note the following examples of division shortcut with numbers ending in zeros. Since two of the symbols used for division are $\div$ and $\overline{)}$, our first examples show the zero shortcut method with the $\div$ symbol.

EXAMPLES

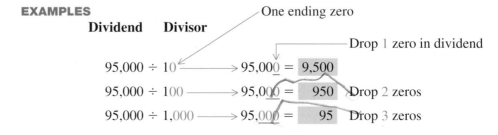

One ending zero

Dividend   Divisor

Drop 1 zero in dividend

$95{,}000 \div 10 \longrightarrow 95{,}000 = \boxed{9{,}500}$

$95{,}000 \div 100 \longrightarrow 95{,}000 = \boxed{950}$ Drop 2 zeros

$95{,}000 \div 1{,}000 \longrightarrow 95{,}000 = \boxed{95}$ Drop 3 zeros

In a long division problem with the $\overline{)}$ symbol, you again count the number of ending zeros in the divisor. Then drop the same number of ending zeros in the dividend and divide as usual.

EXAMPLE $6,5\underline{00})\overline{88,0\underline{00}}$ ⟵ Drop 2 zeros

$$
\begin{array}{r}
13 \text{ R35} \\
65)\overline{880} \\
\underline{65} \\
230 \\
\underline{195} \\
35
\end{array}
$$

$65)\overline{880}$ ⟵

You are now ready to practice what you learned by dissecting and solving a word problem.

How to Dissect and Solve a Word Problem

The blueprint aid that follows will be your guide to dissecting and solving the following word problem.

The Word Problem   Dunkin' Donuts sells to four different companies a total of $3,500 worth of doughnuts per week. What is the total annual sales to these companies? What is the yearly sales per company? (Assume each company buys the same amount.) Check your answer to show how multiplication and division are related.

The facts	Solving for?	Steps to take	Key points
Sales per week: $3,500. *Companies:* 4.	Total annual sales to all four companies. Yearly sales per company.	Sales per week × Weeks in year (52) = Total annual sales. Total annual sales ÷ Total companies = Yearly sales per company.	Division is the reverse of multiplication.

Steps to solving problem

1. Calculate total annual sales. $3,500 × 52 weeks = $182,000

2. Calculate yearly sales per company. $182,000 ÷ 4 = $45,500

Check
$45,500 × 4 = $182,000

It's time to try the Practice Quiz.

LU 1–3 PRACTICE QUIZ

1. Estimate the actual problem by rounding all the way, work the actual problem, and check:

Actual	Estimate	Check
3,894		
× 18		

2. Multiply: 3. Multiply by shortcut method:
   77,000   95 × 10,000
   × 1,800

4. Divide by rounding all the way, complete the actual calculation, and check, showing remainder as a whole number.
   $26)\overline{5,325}$

5. Divide by shortcut method:
   $4,000)\overline{96,000}$

6. Assume General Motors produces 960 Chevrolets each workday (Monday through Friday). If the cost to produce each car is $6,500, what is General Motors' total cost for the year? Check your answer.

✓ SOLUTIONS

1.

Estimate	Actual	Check
4,000	3,894	$8 \times 3{,}894 = 31{,}152$
$\times 20$	$\times 18$	$10 \times 3{,}894 = +38{,}940$
80,000	31 152	70,092
	38 94	
	70,092	

2. $77 \times 18 = 1{,}386 + 5$ zeros $= \boxed{138{,}600{,}000}$

3. $95 + 4$ zeros $= \boxed{950{,}000}$

4.

Rounding

$$\begin{array}{r} 166 \text{ R20} \\ 30\overline{)5{,}000} \\ \underline{3\,0} \\ 2\,00 \\ \underline{1\,80} \\ 200 \\ \underline{180} \\ 20 \end{array}$$

Actual

$$\begin{array}{r} 204 \text{ R21} \\ 26\overline{)5{,}325} \\ \underline{5\,2} \\ 125 \\ \underline{104} \\ 21 \end{array}$$

Check

$$26 \times 204 = \begin{array}{r} 5{,}304 \\ + 21 \\ \hline 5{,}325 \end{array}$$

5. Drop 3 zeros $= 4\overline{)96}\,^{24}$

6. General Motors' total cost per year:

The facts	Solving for?	Steps to take	Key points
Cars produced each workday: 960. *Workweek:* 5 days. *Cost per car:* $6,500.	Total cost per year.	Cars produced per week × 52 = Total cars produced per year. Total cars produced per year × Total cost per car = Total cost per year.	Whenever possible, use multiplication and division shortcuts with zeros. Multiplication can be checked by division.

Steps to solving problem

1. Calculate total cars produced per week. $5 \times 960 = 4{,}800$ cars produced per week

2. Calculate total cars produced per year. $4{,}800$ cars $\times 52$ weeks $= 249{,}600$ total cars produced per year

3. Calculate total cost per year. $249{,}600$ cars $\times \$6{,}500 = \boxed{\$1{,}622{,}400{,}000}$ (multiply $2{,}496 \times 65$ and add zeros)

Check

$\$1{,}622{,}400{,}000 \div 249{,}600 = \$6{,}500$ (drop 2 zeros before dividing)

Chapter Organizer and Reference Guide

Topic	Key point, procedure, formula	Example(s) to illustrate situation
Reading and writing numeric and verbal whole numbers, p. 5	Placement of digits in a number gives the value of the digits (Figure 1.1). Commas separate every three digits, moving from right to left. Begin at left to read and write number in verbal form. Do not read zeros or use *and.* Hyphenate numbers twenty-one to ninety-nine. Reverse procedure to change verbal number to numeric.	462 ⟶ Four hundred sixty-two 6,741 ⟶ Six thousand, seven hundred forty-one
Rounding whole numbers, p. 6	1. Identify place value of the digit to be rounded. 2. If digit to the right is 5 or more, round up; if less than 5, do not change. 3. Change all digits to the right of rounded identified digit to zeros.	643 to nearest ten 4 in tens place value. 3 is not 5 or more. Thus, 643 rounds to 640.
Rounding all the way, p. 7	Round to first digit of number. One nonzero digit remains. In estimating, you round each number of the problem to one nonzero digit. The final answer is not rounded.	468,451 ⟶ 500,000 The 5 is the only nonzero digit remaining.

(continues)

Chapter Organizer and Reference Guide (concluded)

Topic	Key point, procedure, formula	Example(s) to illustrate situation
Adding whole numbers, p. 9	1. Align numbers at the right. 2. Add units column. If sum more than 9, carry tens digit. 3. Moving left, repeat Step 2 until all place values are added. Add from top to bottom. Check by adding bottom to top or adding each column separately and combining.	$\begin{array}{r}1\\65\\+\ 47\\\hline 112\end{array}$ $\begin{array}{r}12\\+10\\\hline 112\end{array}$ Checking sum of each digit
Subtracting whole numbers, p. 11	1. Align minuend and subtrahend at the right. 2. Subtract units digits. If necessary, borrow 1 from tens digit in minuend. 3. Moving left, repeat Step 2 until all place values are subtracted. Minuend less subtrahend equals difference.	**Check** $\begin{array}{r}{}^{5\ 18}\\\cancel{685}\\-492\\\hline 193\end{array}$ $\begin{array}{r}193\\+492\\\hline 685\end{array}$
Multiplying whole numbers, p. 13	1. Align multiplicand and multiplier at the right. 2. Begin at the right and keep multiplying as you move to the left. First partial product aligns at the right with multiplicand and multiplier. 3. Move left through multiplier and continue multiplying multiplicand. Partial product right digit or first digit is placed directly below digit in multiplier. 4. Continue Steps 2 and 3 until multiplication is complete. Add partial products to get final product. **Shortcuts:** (a) When multiplicand or multiplier, or both, end in zeros, disregard zeros and multiply; attach same number of zeros to answer. If zero in center of multiplier, no need to show row of zeros. (b) If multiplying by power of 10, attach same number of zeros to whole number multiplied.	$\begin{array}{r}223\\\times\ 32\\\hline 446\\6\ 69\\\hline 7{,}136\end{array}$ a. $\begin{array}{r}48{,}000\\\times\ \ \ \ 40\end{array}$ $\begin{array}{r}48\\4\\\hline 1{,}920{,}000\end{array}$ $\begin{array}{r}3\ \text{zeros}\\+1\ \text{zero}\\\hline \leftarrow 4\ \text{zeros}\end{array}$ $\begin{array}{r}524\\\times\ 206\\\hline 3\ 144\\104\ 8\\\hline 107{,}944\end{array}$ b. $14 \times 10 \ \ = \boxed{140}$ (attach 1 zero) $14 \times 1{,}000 = \boxed{14{,}000}$ (attach 3 zeros)
Dividing whole numbers, p. 15	1. When divisor is divided into the dividend, the remainder is less than divisor. 2. Drop zeros from dividend right to left by number of zeros found in the divisor. Even division has no remainder; uneven division has a remainder; divisor with one digit is short division; and divisor with more than one digit is long division.	1. $\begin{array}{r}5\ \text{R6}\\14\overline{)76}\\70\\\hline 6\end{array}$ 2. $5{,}000 \div 100 \ \ = 50 \div 1 = \boxed{50}$ $5{,}000 \div 1{,}000 = 5 \div 1 = \boxed{5}$
Key terms	Addends, *p. 9* Decimal point, *p. 5* Decimal system, *p. 5* Difference, *p. 11* Dividend, *p. 15* Divisor, *p. 15*	Minuend, *p. 11* Multiplicand, *p. 13* Multiplier, *p. 13* Partial products, *p. 13* Partial quotient, *p. 15* Product, *p. 13* Quotient, *p. 15* Remainder, *p. 15* Rounding all the way, *p. 7* Subtrahend, *p. 11* Sum, *p. 9* Whole number, *p. 5*

Critical Thinking Discussion Questions

1. List the four steps of the decision-making process. Do you think all companies should be required to follow these steps? Give an example.

2. Explain the three steps used to round whole numbers. Pick a whole number and explain why it should not be rounded.

3. How do you check subtraction? If you were to attend a movie, explain how you might use the subtraction check method.

4. Explain how you can check multiplication. If you visit a local supermarket, how could you show multiplication as a shortcut to addition?

5. Explain how division is the reverse of multiplication. Using the supermarket example, explain how division is a timesaving shortcut related to subtraction.

END-OF-CHAPTER PROBLEMS

Name _____ Date _____

DRILL PROBLEMS

Add the following:

1–1.   79
     + 33

1–2.   820
     + 491

1–3.   99
     + 99

1–4.   66
     + 92

1–5.   6,251
     + 7,329

1–6.   59,481
     51,411
     + 70,821

1–7.   78,159
     15,850
     + 19,681

Subtract the following:

1–8.   87
     − 19

1–9.   80
     − 42

1–10.   287
     − 199

1–11.   8,900
     − 7,200

1–12.   9,800
     − 8,900

1–13.   1,622
     − 548

Multiply the following:

1–14.   55
     × 8

1–15.   510
     × 61

1–16.   900
     × 300

1–17.   677
     × 503

1–18.   309
     × 850

1–19.   450
     × 280

Divide the following by short division:

1–20. $4\overline{)324}$

1–21. $9\overline{)810}$

1–22. $4\overline{)164}$

Divide the following by long division. Show work and remainder.

1–23. $6\overline{)520}$

1–24. $62\overline{)8,915}$

Add the following without rearranging:

1–25. 78 + 109

1–26. 1,055 + 88

1–27. 666 + 950

1–28. 1,011 + 17

1–29. Add the following and check by totaling each column individually without carrying numbers:

Check

8,539
6,842
+ 9,495

Estimate the following by rounding all the way and then do actual addition:

	Actual	**Estimate**			**Actual**	**Estimate**
1–30.	7,700			**1–31.**	6,980	
	9,286				3,190	
	+ 3,900				+ 7,819	

Subtract the following without rearranging:

1–32. 190 − 66   **1–33.** 950 − 870

1–34. Subtract the following and check answer:

591,001
−375,956

Multiply the following horizontally:

1–35. 13 × 8   **1–36.** 84 × 8   **1–37.** 27 × 8   **1–38.** 17 × 6

Divide the following and check by multiplication:

1–39.   **Check**   **1–40.**   **Check**

45)876   46)1,950

1–41. Add the following columns horizontally and vertically:

Production Report					
	Monday	**Tuesday**	**Wednesday**	**Thursday**	**Friday**
Software packages	450	92	157	24	40
Laptops	490	75	44	77	30
Video	325	82	22	44	18
Computer monitors	66	24	51	66	50

Using data in Problem 1–41, answer the following:

1–42. What was the total difference in production on Monday versus Friday:

1–43. If two weeks ago production was 7 times the total of this report, what was total production?

Complete the following:

1–44.   9,200   **1–45.**   3,000,000
          −1,510   − 769,459

          − 700   − 68,541

1–46. Estimate the following problem by rounding all the way and then do the actual multiplication:

Actual   **Estimate**
   870
$\times$ 81

Divide the following by the shortcut method:

1–47. $1,000 \overline{)850,000}$

1–48. $100 \overline{)70,000}$

1–49. Estimate actual problem by rounding all the way and do actual division:

Actual   **Estimate**

$695 \overline{)8,950}$

WORD PROBLEMS

1–50. On June 30, 2000, *USA Today* ran an article titled "Keep Track of the Kids." This article reports that Walt Disney World Resort and United Vacations got together to create a special deal. The air-inclusive package features accommodations for three nights at Disney's All-Star Resort, hotel taxes, and a four-day unlimited Magic Pass. Prices are $609 per person traveling from Washington, DC and $764 per person traveling from Los Angeles. **(a)** What would be the cost for a family of four leaving from Washington, DC? **(b)** What would be the cost for a family of four leaving from Los Angeles? **(c)** How much more will it cost the family from Los Angeles?

1–51. On May 22, 2001, *USA Today* compared the amount of money Americans spent on playing state lotteries. A total of thirty-eight billion dollars was spent in 2000. Massachusetts topped the list with lottery sales of three billion, seven hundred thousand dollars. Montana was at the bottom, spending twenty-nine million dollars. In numerical form, how much more did Massachusetts residents spend compared to Montana residents?

1–52. On May 27, 2001, the *Los Angeles Times* ran an article titled "Bargains Are Out There Waiting to Be Caught." A year ago, Pleasant Holidays advertised Los Angeles-to-Maui air fares as low as $349 and eight-day Waikiki air-hotel packages for as little as $464. This month, that discount Maui fare is down to $309, and the Waikiki package is down to $450. Five customers plan to take advantage of the Waikiki package. How much is their total savings?

1–53. On March 30, 2001, *The New York Times* reported that "The Producers" received the top Broadway rate for a ticket. To see Mel Brooks, fans pay $91 for orchestra and front mezzanine seats. If 265 tickets were sold for today's performance, what would be the total revenue from these sales?

1–54. Banking.com plans a company picnic. A pizza (provided by Pizza Hut) will serve 6 people. If the company expects 960 people to attend, how many pizzas will they need? Each pizza costs $10. What is the total cost of the pizzas?

1–55. NTB Tires bought 910 tires from its manufacturer for $36 per tire. What is the total cost of NTB's purchase? If the store can sell all the tires at $65 each, what will be the store's gross profit, or the difference between its sales and costs (Sales − Costs = Gross profit)?

1–56. Media Metrix (an Internet measurement firm) compared the visits to the top five retail websites for Thanksgiving week ending November 26, 2000, as follows:

Rank/site	Average daily unique visitors
1. Amazon.com	1,527,000
2. Mypoints.com	1,356,000
3. Americangreetings.com	745,000
4. Bizrate.com	503,000
5. Half.com	397,000

What was the average number of visits for the top five?

1–57. Jose Gomez bought 4,500 shares of Microsoft stock. He held the stock for 6 months. Then Jose sold 180 shares on Monday, 270 shares on Tuesday and again on Thursday, and 800 shares on Friday. How many shares does Jose still own? The average share of the stock Jose owns is worth $52 per share. What is the total value of Jose's stock?

1–58. On May 2, 2001, Associated Press Online stated that New York is going after the bank account of pardoned financier Marc Rich. The tax commissioner announced he was going after Marc Rich in the amount of twenty-six million, nine hundred thousand dollars in back taxes; thirteen million, five hundred thousand in penalties; and ninety-seven million, four hundred thousand in interest. In numerical terms, what is the total amount?

1–59. At Rose State College, Alison Wells received the following grades in her online accounting class: 90, 65, 85, 80, 75, and 90. Alison's instructor, Professor Clark, said he would drop the lowest grade. What is Alison's average?

1–60. Lee Wills, professor of business, has 18 students in Accounting I, 26 in Accounting II, 22 in Introduction to Computers, 23 in Business Law, and 29 in Introduction to Business. What is the total number of students in Professor Wills's classes? If 12 students withdraw, how many total students will Professor Wills have?

1–61. Ron Alf, owner of Alf's Moving Company, bought a new truck. On Ron's first trip, he drove 1,200 miles and used 80 gallons of gas. How many miles per gallon did Ron get from his new truck? On Ron's second trip, he drove 840 miles and used 60 gallons. What is the difference in miles per gallon between Ron's first trip and his second trip?

1–62. Staples reduced its $390 Palm Pilot by $45. What is the new selling price of the Palm Pilot? If Staples sold 1,200 Palm Pilots at the new price, what were the store's Palm Pilot's dollar sales?

1–63. Barnes and Noble.com has 289 business math texts in inventory. During one month, the online bookstore ordered and received 1,855 texts; it also sold 1,222 on the Web. What is the bookstore's inventory at the end of the month? If each text costs $59, what is the end-of-month inventory cost?

1–64. Cabot Company produced 2,115,000 cans of paint in August. Cabot sold 2,011,000 of these cans. If each can cost $18, what were Cabot's ending inventory of paint cans and its total ending inventory cost?

1–65. Long College has 30 faculty members in the business department, 22 in psychology, 14 in English, and 169 in all other departments. What is the total number of faculty at Long College? If each faculty member advises 30 students, how many students attend Long College?

1–66. Hometown Buffet had 90 customers on Sunday, 70 on Monday, 65 on Tuesday, and a total of 310 on Wednesday to Saturday. How many customers did Hometown Buffet serve during the week? If each customer spends $9, what were the total sales for the week?

If Hometown's Buffet had the same sales each week, what were the sales for the year?

1–67. Longview Agency projected its year 2004 sales at $995,000. During 2004, the agency earned $525,960 sales from its major clients and $286,950 sales from the remainder of its clients. How much did the agency overestimate its sales?

1–68. Jim Floyd works at US Airways and earned $61,000 last year before tax deductions. From Jim's total earnings, his company subtracted $1,462 for federal income taxes, $3,782 for Social Security, and $884 for Medicare taxes. What was Jim's actual, or net, pay for the year?

1–69. Macy's received the following invoice amounts from suppliers. How much does the company owe?

	Per item
22 paintings	$210
39 rockers	75
40 desk lamps	65
120 coffee tables	155

1–70. Jole Company produces beach balls and it operates three shifts. It produces 5,000 balls per shift on shifts 1 and 2. On shift 3, the company can produce 6 times as many balls as on shift 1. Assume a 5-day workweek. How many beach balls does Jole produce per week and per year?

1–71. On April 13, 2000, *The New York Times* reported on the changes in the prices of Disneyland tickets. Disneyland lowered the age for adult tickets from 12 years old to 10 years old. This raised the cost of admission from $31 to $41. If 125 children attending the park each day are in this age bracket, how much additional revenue will Disneyland receive each day?

1–72. Moe Brink has a $900 balance in his checkbook. During the week, Moe wrote the following checks: rent, $350; telephone, $44; food, $160; and entertaining, $60. Moe also made a $1,200 deposit. What is Moe's new checkbook balance?

1–73. MVP, an athletic sports shop, bought and sold the following merchandise:

	Cost	Selling price
Tennis rackets	$ 2,900	$ 3,999
Tennis balls	70	210
Bowling balls	1,050	2,950
Sneakers	+ 8,105	+ 14,888

What was the total cost of merchandise bought by MVP? If the shop sold all its merchandise, what were the sales and the resulting gross profit (Sales − Costs = Gross profit)?

1–74. John Purcell, the bookkeeper for Roseville Real Estate, and his manager are concerned about the company's telephone bills. Last year the company's average monthly phone bill was $34. John's manager asked him for an average of this year's phone bills. John's records show the following:

January	$ 34	July	$ 28
February	60	August	23
March	20	September	29
April	25	October	25
May	30	November	22
June	59	December	41

What is the average of this year's phone bills? Did John and his manager have a justifiable concern?

1–75. On May 24, 2001, The Associated Press reported that bankruptcy filings were up for the first three months of the year. Filings reached 366,841 in the January–March period, the highest ever for a first quarter, up from 312,335 a year earlier. How much was the increase in quarterly filings?

1–76. On Monday, Wang Hardware sold 15 paint brushes at $3 each, 6 wrenches at $5 each, 7 bags of grass seed at $3 each, 4 lawn mowers at $119 each, and 28 cans of paint at $8 each. What were Wang's total dollar sales on Monday?

1–77. While redecorating, Paul Smith went to Home Depot and bought 125 square yards of commercial carpet. The total cost of the carpet was $3,000. How much did Paul pay per square yard?

1–78. Washington Construction built 12 ranch houses for $115,000 each. From the sale of these houses, Washington received $1,980,000. How much gross profit (Sales − Costs = Gross profit) did Washington make on the houses?

The four partners of Washington Construction split all profits equally. How much will each partner receive?

 CHALLENGE PROBLEMS

1–79. On June 1, 2001, *USA Today* compared financial contributions that the tobacco industry gave to political parties in the 1999–2000 election. The total dollar amount was eight million, four hundred thousand, with the following companies in the top five:

1. Philip Morris—three million, four hundred fifty thousand, one hundred thirty-nine.
2. UST Inc.—one million, five hundred eighty-eight thousand, three hundred fifty-four.
3. RJ Reynolds Tobacco—nine hundred ninety-one thousand, four hundred twenty-seven.
4. Brown & Williamson Tobacco—nine hundred seventy-nine thousand, seven hundred thirty-two.
5. Loews Corp.—two hundred eighty-five thousand, fifty.

(a) In verbal form, what was the total dollar amount contributed by the top five tobacco companies? **(b)** In numerical form, what is the difference between the total dollar amount contributed by the tobacco industry and the dollar amount contributed by the top five tobacco companies? **(c)** What was Philip Morris's average monthly contribution? Round your answer to the nearest hundred thousands.

1–80. Pat Valdez is trying to determine her 2004 finances. Pat's actual 2003 finances were as follows:

Income:		Assets:	
Gross income	$69,000	Checking account	$ 1,950
Interest income	450	Savings account	8,950
Total	$69,450	Auto	1,800
		Personal property	14,000
Expenses:		Total	$26,700
Living	$24,500	Liabilities:	
Insurance premium	350	Note to bank	4,500
Taxes	14,800	Net worth	$22,200 ($26,700 − $4,500)
Medical	585		
Investment	4,000		
Total	$44,235		

Net worth = Assets − Liabilities
                        (own)   (owe)

Pat believes her gross income will double in 2004 and her interest income will decrease $150. She plans to reduce her 2004 living expenses by one-half. Pat's insurance company wrote a letter announcing that insurance premiums would triple in 2004. Her accountant estimates her taxes will decrease $250 and her medical costs will increase $410. Pat also hopes to cut her investment expenses by one-fourth. Pat's accountant projects that her savings and checking accounts will each double in value. On January 2, 2004, Pat sold her automobile and began to use public transportation. Pat forecasts that her personal property will decrease by one-seventh. She has sent her bank a $375 check to reduce her bank note. Could you give Pat an updated list of her 2004 finances? If you round all the way each 2003 and 2004 asset and liability, what will be the difference in Pat's net worth?

SUMMARY PRACTICE TEST

1. Translate the following verbal forms to numbers and add. *(p. 5)*

   a. Four thousand, five hundred ninety-four

   b. Eight million, twelve

   c. Seventeen thousand, five hundred ninety-four

2. Express the following number in verbal form. *(p. 5)*
   7,944,581

3. Round the following numbers. *(p. 6)*

Nearest ten	**Nearest hundred**	**Nearest thousand**	**Round all the way**
a. 58	**b.** 583	**c.** 8,280	**d.** 19,876

4. Estimate the following actual problem by rounding all the way, work the actual problem, and check by adding each column of digits separately. *(pp. 5, 10)*

Actual	**Estimate**	**Check**
2,251		
7,899		
+ 8,498		

5. Estimate the following actual problem by rounding all the way and then do the actual multiplication. *(pp. 14, 15)*

Actual	**Estimate**
8,492	
× 706	

6. Multiply the following by the shortcut method. *(p. 15)*
$844,582 \times 1,000 =$

7. Divide the following and check the answer by multiplication. *(p. 15)*

Check

$38\overline{)9,900}$

8. Divide the following by the shortcut method. *(p. 16)*
$3,000 \div 30$

9. Gracie Lee bought a $79 calculator that was reduced to $28. Gracie gave the clerk a $100 bill. What change will Gracie receive? *(p. 9)*

10. Joe Smith plans to buy a $19,900 P.T. Cruiser with an interest charge of $1,100. Joe figures he can afford a monthly payment of $650. If Joe must pay 30 equal monthly payments, can he afford the van? *(p. 17)*

11. Jon Ree has the propane tank at his home filled 14 times per year. The tank has a capacity of 150 gallons. Assume **(a)** the price of propane fuel is $2 per gallon and **(b)** the tank is completely empty each time Jon has it filled. What is Jon's average monthly propane bill? Complete the following blueprint aid for dissecting and solving the word problem. *(pp. 17, 18)*

The facts	Solving for?	Steps to take	Key points

Steps to solving problem

TRENDS | For city dwellers who need wheels once in a while, **CAR SHARING** is an alternative to owning your own. *By Kathy Jones*

DON'T RENT, BORROW

HARD-CORE urbanites prefer to get there on foot, by bike or via mass transit. But sometimes even such diehards need the convenience of a car. The solution? Now you can "borrow" a car to run a day of errands—and pay a lot less than it costs to rent one.

Car-share organizations in roughly a half-dozen cities provide their members with conveniently located wheels, off-street parking and even gas, as well as maintenance and insurance. Participants in such car-sharing groups are required to pay an initial insurance deposit and an annual fee, and are then charged an hourly rate to use the car and in some cases a mileage fee.

In Portland, Ore., for example, the use of a compact car for four hours and 25 miles would cost $16, in addition to the $10 monthly fee. In Boston, driving 15 hours a month would cost about $1,300 a year— less than the insurance premiums alone for many car owners there.

At Zipcar (www.zipcar.com) in Boston, you reserve a Volkswagen Beetle, Golf or Passat online, and then swipe a smart card to unlock the car. It's "as convenient as using an ATM card," says Zipcar CEO Robin Chase. To see if there's a group in your area, go to www.carsharing.net. K

Business Math Issue

The day of renting a car is over. Borrowing is the way to go.
1. List the key points of the article and information to support your position.
2. Write a group defense of your position using math calculations to support your view.

BUSINESS MATH SCRAPBOOK
WITH INTERNET APPLICATION

Putting Your Skills to Work

How does SUBWAY® measure up?

Choosing a SUBWAY® 6" 7 Under 6 Sub instead of one of these fast food favorites can **save at least 200 calories and 23 grams of fat** in just one meal.

RESTAURANT	CALORIES	FAT (GRAMS)
SUBWAY® 7 Under 6 Sub	200-311	2.5-6
Burger King **Whopper**	680	39
KFC **original recipe chicken** (1 Chicken breast, 1 wing)	540	34
Taco Bell **3 tacos**	510	30
Chinese **take out** (1 cup chicken & vegetable stir fry, 1 cup of fried rice)	545	29
McDonald's **Big Mac**	590	34

Nutritional information obtained 12/1/00 from www.burgerking.com, www.kentuckyfriedchicken.com, and www.tacobell.com.

PROJECT A

Show the mathematical advantage that Subway® has over one of its competitors.

Go to the Web to see how Subway® measures up today compared to the table above. Update the table.

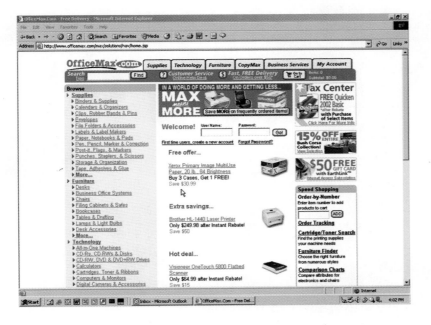

PROJECT B

Imagine as office manager for a company the budget for office furniture improvements this year is $11,300. The 24 employees (including you) have decided you should first replace the chairs in each of their offices. Go to www.officemax.com and select a chair from their catalog you'd like in your own office. Round prices to the nearest dollar—for instance use $280 for $279.99. Calculate how much 24 of those chairs would cost (ignore sales tax and delivery charges). Is $11,300 enough? If so, how much money do you have left? If not, how much more money do you need?

 Internet Projects: See text website (www.mhhe.com/slater7e) and *The Business Math Internet Resource Guide.*

Big Retailers Try to Speed Up Checkout Lines

By EMILY NELSON
Staff Reporter of THE WALL STREET JOURNAL

Imagine simply piling your groceries into a shopping cart, pushing it to a gate, swiping a credit-card and going on your way. Or having a store employee greet you with a portable scanner greet you in line, and hand you a tally while you wait.

Mass-market retailers are testing these and other technologies to bring their checkout lines into the 21st century. At a time when Internet rivals offer shopping with no lines at all, retailers face more pressure than ever to speed customers along and eliminate big bottlenecks that take up precious selling space.

Many are also realizing that "register rage" — customer irritation over long lines and slow clerks — can be a real threat to business.

Studies show that eighty-three out of a hundred ($\frac{83}{100}$) women and ninety-one out of a hundred ($\frac{91}{100}$) men say long lines prompted them to stop patronizing a particular store.

Fractions

Those M&M's® you have been calling "Plain" all these years have now received the name they deserve—Milk Chocolate M&M's®. These candies still come in different colors—yellow, red, blue, orange, brown, and green. Do you know how many of each color are in a bag of M&M's®? You probably have never stopped to sort the colors and count them.

The 1.69-ounce bag of M&M's® shown here contains 55 M&M's®. In this bag, you will find the following colors:[1]

18 yellow	9 blue	6 brown
10 red	7 orange	5 green

The number of yellow candies in a bag might suggest that yellow is the favorite color of many people. Since this is a business math text, however, let's look at the 55 M&M's® in terms of fractional arithmetic.

Of the 55 M&M's® in the 1.69-ounce bag, 5 of these M&M's® are green, so we can say that 5 parts of 55 represent green candies. We could also say that 1 out of 11 M&M's® is green. Are you confused?

For many people, fractions are difficult. If you are one of these people, this chapter is for you. First you will review the types of fractions and the fraction conversion procedures. Then you will gain a clear understanding of the addition, subtraction, multiplication, and division of fractions.

LEARNING UNIT 2–1 | TYPES OF FRACTIONS AND CONVERSION PROCEDURES

This chapter explains the parts of whole numbers called **fractions.** With fractions you can divide any object or unit—a whole—into a definite number of equal parts. For example, the bag of 55 M&M's® shown at the beginning of this chapter contains 6 brown candies. If you eat only the brown M&M's®, you have eaten 6 parts of 55, or 6 parts of the whole bag of M&M's®. We can express this in the following fraction:

$$\frac{6}{55}$$

6 is the **numerator,** or top of the fraction. The numerator describes the number of equal parts of the whole bag that you ate.

55 is the **denominator,** or bottom of the fraction. The denominator gives the total number of equal parts in the bag of M&M's®.

Before reviewing the arithmetic operations of fractions, you must recognize the three types of fractions described in this unit. You must also know how to convert fractions to a workable form.

---

[1]The color ratios currently given are a sample only used for educational purposes. They do not represent the manufacturer's color ratios.

Types of Fractions

> # Wal-Mart Fumes at Argentine Legislation
>
> ## Provincial Bills That Limit Size of Stores Threaten U.S. Retailer's Strategy
>
> By Ann Zimmerman
> And Matt Moffett
> *Staff Reporters of* The Wall Street Journal
>
> The legislatures of Buenos Aires and other Argentine provinces are considering bills limiting the size of retail stores, a move that would thwart **Wal-Mart Stores Inc.**'s plans to expand in the country.
>
> Prompted by owners of small and mid-size businesses, the Buenos Aires legislature is expected soon to vote on Bill 12088, which restricts the size of new hypermarkets to about 20,000 square feet, a tenth the size of a Wal-Mart Supercenter, which sell both food and general merchandise.

© 2000 Dow Jones & Company, Inc.

If you plan to visit Buenos Aires and other Argentine provinces in the future and shop at their new Wal-Mart Supercenters, you will be disappointed in the size of these supercenters. *The Wall Street Journal* clipping "Wal-Mart Fumes at Argentine Legislation" states that Argentine legislation plans to restrict the size of new hypermarkets to about 20,000 square feet.

In the United States, the average size of a Wal-Mart Supercenter is 200,000 square feet. Limiting the size of a Wal-Mart Supercenter in Argentine to 20,000 square feet means that the store is one-tenth ($\frac{1}{10}$) the size of the Wal-Mart Supercenters in the United States. The fraction $\frac{1}{10}$ is a proper fraction.

Proper Fractions

A **proper fraction** has a value less than 1; its numerator is smaller than its denominator.

EXAMPLES $\dfrac{1}{10}, \dfrac{1}{12}, \dfrac{1}{3}, \dfrac{4}{7}, \dfrac{9}{10}, \dfrac{12}{13}, \dfrac{18}{55}$

Improper Fractions

An **improper fraction** has a value equal to or greater than 1; its numerator is equal to or greater than its denominator.

EXAMPLES $\dfrac{13}{13}, \dfrac{7}{6}, \dfrac{15}{14}, \dfrac{22}{19}$

Mixed Numbers

A **mixed number** is the sum of a whole number greater than zero and a proper fraction.

EXAMPLES $4\frac{1}{7}, 5\frac{9}{10}, 8\frac{7}{8}, 33\frac{5}{6}, 139\frac{9}{11}$

Conversion Procedures

In Chapter 1 we worked with two of the division symbols ($\div$ and $\overline{)}\,$). The horizontal line (or the diagonal) that separates the numerator and the denominator of a fraction also indicates division. The numerator, like the dividend, is the number we are dividing into. The denominator, like the divisor, is the number we use to divide. Then, referring to the 6 brown M&M's® in the bag of 55 M&M's® ($\frac{6}{55}$) shown at the beginning of this unit, we can say that we are dividing 55 into 6, or 6 is divided by 55. Also, in the fraction $\frac{3}{4}$, we can say that we are dividing 4 into 3, or 3 is divided by 4.

Working with the smaller numbers of simple fractions such as $\frac{3}{4}$ is easier, so we often convert fractions to their simplest terms. In this unit we show how to convert improper fractions to whole or mixed numbers, mixed numbers to improper fractions, and fractions to lowest and highest terms.

Converting Improper Fractions to Whole or Mixed Numbers

Business situations often make it necessary to change an improper fraction to a whole number or mixed number. You can use the following steps to make this conversion:

Converting Improper Fractions to Whole or Mixed Numbers

Step 1. Divide the numerator of the improper fraction by the denominator.

Step 2. **a.** If you have no remainder, the quotient is a whole number.

  b. If you have a remainder, the whole number part of the mixed number is the quotient. The remainder is placed over the old denominator as the proper fraction of the mixed number.

EXAMPLES

$$\frac{15}{15} = 1 \qquad \frac{16}{5} = 3\frac{1}{5} \qquad \begin{array}{r} 3\,\text{R}1 \\ 5\overline{)16} \\ \underline{15} \\ 1 \end{array}$$

Converting Mixed Numbers to Improper Fractions

By reversing the procedure of converting improper fractions to mixed numbers, we can change mixed numbers to improper fractions.

Converting Mixed Numbers to Improper Fractions

Step 1. Multiply the denominator of the fraction by the whole number.

Step 2. Add the product from Step 1 to the numerator of the old fraction.

Step 3. Place the total from Step 2 over the denominator of the old fraction to get the improper fraction.

EXAMPLE $6\frac{1}{8} = \dfrac{(8 \times 6) + 1}{8} = \dfrac{49}{8}$ ↙ Note that the denominator stays the same.

Converting (Reducing) Fractions to Lowest Terms

When solving fraction problems, you always reduce the fractions to their lowest terms. This reduction does not change the value of the fraction. For example, in the bag of M&M's®, 5 out of 55 were green. The fraction for this is $\frac{5}{55}$. If you divide the top and bottom of the fraction by 5, you have reduced the fraction to $\frac{1}{11}$ without changing its value. Remember, we said in the chapter introduction that 1 out of 11 M&M's® in the bag of 55 M&M's® represents green candies. Now you know why this is true.

To reduce a fraction to its lowest terms, begin by inspecting the fraction, looking for the largest whole number that will divide into both the numerator and the denominator without leaving a remainder. This whole number is the **greatest common divisor,** which cannot be zero. When you find this largest whole number, you have reached the point where the fraction is reduced to its **lowest terms.** At this point, no number (except 1) can divide evenly into both parts of the fraction.

Reducing Fractions to Lowest Terms by Inspection

Step 1. By inspection, find the largest whole number (greatest common divisor) that will divide evenly into the numerator and denominator (does not change the fraction value).

Step 2. Now you have reduced the fraction to its lowest terms, since no number (except 1) can divide evenly into the numerator and denominator.

EXAMPLE $\dfrac{24}{30} = \dfrac{24 \div 6}{30 \div 6} = \dfrac{4}{5}$

Using inspection, you can see that the number 6 in the above example is the greatest common divisor. When you have large numbers, the greatest common divisor is not so obvious. For large numbers, you can use the following step approach to find the greatest common divisor:

Step Approach for Finding Greatest Common Divisor

Step 1. Divide the smaller number (numerator) of the fraction into the larger number (denominator).

Step 2. Divide the remainder of Step 1 into the divisor of Step 1.

Step 3. Divide the remainder of Step 2 into the divisor of Step 2. Continue this division process until the remainder is a 0, which means the last divisor is the greatest common divisor.

EXAMPLE

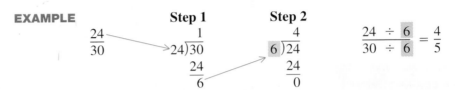

Reducing a fraction by inspection is to some extent a trial-and-error method. Sometimes you are not sure what number you should divide into the top (numerator) and bottom (denominator) of the fraction. The following reference table on divisibility tests will be helpful. Note that to reduce a fraction to lowest terms might result in more than one division.

	2	3	4	5	6	10
Will divide evenly into number if	Last digit is 0, 2, 4, 6, 8.	Sum of the digits is divisible by 3.	Last two digits can be divided by 4.	Last digit is 0 or 5.	The number is even and 3 will divide into the sum of the digits.	The last digit is 0.
Examples	$\dfrac{12}{14} = \dfrac{6}{7}$	$\dfrac{36}{69} = \dfrac{12}{23}$ $3 + 6 = 9 \div 3 = 3$ $6 + 9 = 15 \div 3 = 5$	$\dfrac{140}{160} = \dfrac{1(40)}{1(60)}$ $= \dfrac{35}{40} = \dfrac{7}{8}$	$\dfrac{15}{20} = \dfrac{3}{4}$	$\dfrac{12}{18} = \dfrac{2}{3}$	$\dfrac{90}{100} = \dfrac{9}{10}$

Converting (Raising) Fractions to Higher Terms

Later, when you add and subtract fractions, you will see that sometimes fractions must be raised to **higher terms.** Recall that when you reduced fractions to their lowest terms, you looked for the largest whole number (greatest common divisor) that would divide evenly into both the numerator and the denominator. When you raise fractions to higher terms, you do the opposite and multiply the numerator and the denominator by the same whole number. For example, if you want to raise the fraction $\frac{1}{4}$, you can multiply the numerator and denominator by 2.

EXAMPLE $\dfrac{1}{4} \times \dfrac{2}{2} = \dfrac{2}{8}$

The fractions $\frac{1}{4}$ and $\frac{2}{8}$ are **equivalent** in value. By converting $\frac{1}{4}$ to $\frac{2}{8}$, you only divided it into more parts.

Let's suppose that you have eaten $\frac{4}{7}$ of a pizza. You decide that instead of expressing the amount you have eaten in 7ths, you want to express it in 28ths. How would you do this?

To find the new numerator when you know the new denominator (28), use the steps that follow.

Raising Fractions to Higher Terms When Denominator Is Known

Step 1. Divide the *new* denominator by the *old* denominator to get the common number that raises the fraction to higher terms.

Step 2. Multiply the common number from Step 1 by the old numerator and place it as the new numerator over the new denominator.

EXAMPLE $\dfrac{4}{7} = \dfrac{?}{28}$

Step 1. Divide 28 by 7 = 4.

Step 2. Multiply 4 by the numerator 4 = 16.
Result:

$$\frac{4}{7} = \frac{16}{28} \quad \left(\textit{Note: } \text{This is the same as multiplying } \frac{4}{7} \times \frac{4}{4}.\right)$$

Note that the $\frac{4}{7}$ and $\frac{16}{28}$ are equivalent in value, yet they are different fractions.
Now try the following Practice Quiz to check your understanding of this unit.

LU 2–1 PRACTICE QUIZ

1. Identify the type of fraction—proper, improper, or mixed:

   a. $\dfrac{4}{5}$ **b.** $\dfrac{6}{5}$ **c.** $19\dfrac{1}{5}$ **d.** $\dfrac{20}{20}$

2. Convert to a mixed number (do not reduce):

   $\dfrac{160}{9}$

3. Convert the mixed number to an improper fraction:

   $9\dfrac{5}{8}$

4. Find the greatest common divisor by the step approach and reduce to lowest terms:

   a. $\dfrac{24}{40}$ **b.** $\dfrac{91}{156}$

5. Convert to higher terms:

   a. $\dfrac{14}{20} = \dfrac{}{200}$ **b.** $\dfrac{8}{10} = \dfrac{}{60}$

✓ SOLUTIONS

1. **a.** Proper
   b. Improper
   c. Mixed
   d. Improper

2.
$$
\begin{array}{r}
17\frac{7}{9} \\
9\overline{)160} \\
\underline{9} \\
70 \\
\underline{63} \\
7
\end{array}
$$

3. $\dfrac{(9 \times 8) + 5}{8} = \dfrac{77}{8}$

4. **a.**

$$
\begin{array}{r}
1 \\
24\overline{)40} \\
\underline{24} \\
16
\end{array}
\qquad
\begin{array}{r}
1 \\
16\overline{)24} \\
\underline{16} \\
8
\end{array}
\qquad
\begin{array}{r}
2 \\
8\,\overline{)16} \\
\underline{16} \\
0
\end{array}
$$

8 is greatest common divisor.

$$\frac{24 \div 8}{40 \div 8} = \frac{3}{5}$$

b.

$$
\begin{array}{r}
1 \\
91\overline{)156} \\
\underline{91} \\
65
\end{array}
\qquad
\begin{array}{r}
1 \\
65\overline{)91} \\
\underline{65} \\
26
\end{array}
\qquad
\begin{array}{r}
2 \\
26\,\overline{)65} \\
\underline{52} \\
13
\end{array}
\qquad
\begin{array}{r}
2 \\
13\,\overline{)26} \\
\underline{26} \\
0
\end{array}
$$

13 is greatest common divisor.

$$\frac{91 \div 13}{156 \div 13} = \frac{7}{12}$$

5. **a.** $\dfrac{10}{20\overline{)200}}$ $\quad 10 \times 14 = 140 \quad$ $\dfrac{14}{20} = \dfrac{\boxed{140}}{200}$

  b. $\dfrac{6}{10\overline{)60}}$ $\quad 6 \times 8 = 48 \quad$ $\dfrac{8}{10} = \dfrac{\boxed{48}}{60}$

LEARNING UNIT 2–2 | ADDITION AND SUBTRACTION OF FRACTIONS

AltaVista to Cut One-Fourth of Staff, Refocus Business

By JOHN HECHINGER
Staff Reporter of THE WALL STREET JOURNAL

AltaVista Co., retrenching in a drive to reach profitability, said it would lay off a quarter of its work force and refocus on its core Internet search-engine business.

The cutbacks at the Web pioneer underscore how New Economy companies, once content to report millions in losses, now feel intense pressure to shore up their bottom lines.

© 2000 Dow Jones & Company, Inc.

This clipping from *The Wall Street Journal* tells you that AltaVista will lay off one-fourth ($\frac{1}{4}$) of its work force. One-fourth of a staff of 840 employees is 210 employees. If you subtract 210 from 840, AltaVista will have a work force of 630.

Since a whole is $\frac{4}{4}$ ($\frac{4}{4} = 1$), you can determine how much of the work force remains by subtracting the numerator of the fraction $\frac{1}{4}$ from the numerator of the fraction $\frac{4}{4}$, which is $\frac{3}{4}$. You can make this subtraction because you are working with *like fractions*—fractions with the same denominators. Then you can prove that you are correct by adding the numerators of the fractions $\frac{1}{4}$ and $\frac{3}{4}$.

In this unit you learn how to add and subtract fractions with the same denominators (**like fractions**) and fractions with different denominators (**unlike fractions**). We have included how to add and subtract mixed numbers with the instructions for the addition and subtraction of fractions.

Addition of Fractions

When you add two or more quantities, they must have the same name or be of the same denomination. You cannot add 6 quarts and 3 pints unless you change the denomination of one or both quantities. You must either make the quarts into pints or the pints into quarts. The same principle also applies to fractions. That is, to add two or more fractions, they must have a **common denominator.**

Adding Like Fractions

In our AltaVista clipping at the beginning of this unit we stated that because the fractions had the same denominator, or a common denominator, they were *like fractions*. Adding like fractions is similar to adding whole numbers.

Adding Like Fractions

Step 1. Add the numerators and place the total over the original denominator.

Step 2. If the total of your numerators is the same as your original denominator, convert your answer to a whole number; if the total is larger than your original denominator, convert your answer to a mixed number.

EXAMPLE $\dfrac{1}{7} + \dfrac{4}{7} = \dfrac{\boxed{5}}{7}$

The denominator, 7, shows the number of pieces into which some whole was divided. The two numerators, 1 and 4, tell how many of the pieces you have. So if you add 1 and 4, you get 5, or $\frac{5}{7}$.

Adding Unlike Fractions

Since you cannot add *unlike fractions* because their denominators are not the same, you must change the unlike fractions to *like fractions*—fractions with the same denominators. To do this, find a denominator that is common to all the fractions you want to add. Then look for the **least common denominator (LCD).**[2] The LCD is the smallest nonzero whole number into which all denominators will divide evenly. You can find the LCD by inspection or with prime numbers.

Finding the Least Common Denominator (LCD) by Inspection   The example that follows shows you how to use inspection to find an LCD (this will make all the denominators the same).

EXAMPLE $\dfrac{3}{7} + \dfrac{5}{21}$

Inspection of these two fractions shows that the smallest number into which denominators 7 and 21 divide evenly is 21. Thus, $\boxed{21}$ is the LCD.

You may know that 21 is the LCD of $\frac{3}{7} + \frac{5}{21}$, but you cannot add these two fractions until you change the denominator of $\frac{3}{7}$ to 21. You do this by building (raising) the equivalent of $\frac{3}{7}$, as explained in Learning Unit 2–1. You can use the following steps to find the LCD by inspection:

Step 1.   Divide the new denominator (21) by the old denominator (7): $21 \div 7 = 3$.

Step 2.   Multiply the 3 in Step 1 by the old numerator (3): $3 \times 3 = 9$. The new numerator is 9.

Result:

$$\frac{3}{7} = \frac{9}{21}$$

Now that the denominators are the same, you add the numerators.

$$\frac{9}{21} + \frac{5}{21} = \frac{14}{21} = \frac{2}{3}$$

Note that $\frac{14}{21}$ is reduced to its lowest terms $\frac{2}{3}$. Always reduce your answer to its lowest terms.

You are now ready for the following general steps for adding proper fractions with different denominators. These steps also apply to the following discussion on finding LCD by prime numbers.

Adding Unlike Fractions

Step 1.   Find the LCD.
Step 2.   Change each fraction to a like fraction with the LCD.
Step 3.   Add the numerators and place the total over the LCD.
Step 4.   If necessary, reduce the answer to lowest terms.

Finding the Least Common Denominator (LCD) by Prime Numbers   When you cannot determine the LCD by inspection, you can use the prime number method. First you must understand prime numbers.

Prime Numbers

A **prime number** is a whole number greater than 1 that is only divisible by itself and 1. The number 1 is not a prime number.

EXAMPLES   2, 3, 5, 7, 11, 13, 17, 19, 23, 29, 31, 37, 41, 43

Note that the number 4 is not a prime number. Not only can you divide 4 by 1 and by 4, but you can also divide 4 by 2.

---

[2]Often referred to as the *lowest common denominator.*

> **Monster Prime Number Is Discovered by Scientists**
>
> EAGAN, Minn. (AP) — Computer scientists crunching numbers at the outer limits of numeration say they've stumbled on the largest-known prime number.
>
> Primes are whole numbers, like 3, 5, 17, 23 and so on, that are evenly divisible only by one and themselves. This one, at 378,632 digits, would fill up 12 newspaper pages in standard type. Mathematicians would express the number as two to the 1,257,787th power minus one.

The largest example of a prime number given in the list of examples above contains two digits. *The Wall Street Journal* clipping "Monster Prime Number Is Discovered by Scientists" states that computer scientists stumbled on the largest known prime number—a number with 378,632 digits.

Now let's see how to use prime numbers to find the LCD.

EXAMPLE $\dfrac{1}{3} + \dfrac{1}{8} + \dfrac{1}{9} + \dfrac{1}{12}$

Step 1. Copy the denominators and arrange them in a separate row.

3   8   9   12

Step 2. Divide the denominators in Step 1 by prime numbers. Start with the smallest number that will divide into at least two of the denominators. Bring down any number that is not divisible. Keep in mind that the lowest prime number is 2.

$$2\ \big/\ \underline{3 \quad 8 \quad 9 \quad 12}$$
$$3 \quad 4 \quad 9 \quad 6$$

Note: The 3 and 9 were brought down, since they were not divisible by 2.

Step 3. Continue Step 2 until no prime number will divide evenly into at least two numbers.

Note: The 3 is used, since 2 can no longer divide evenly into at least two numbers.

$$
\begin{array}{c|cccc}
2 & 3 & 8 & 9 & 12 \\
2 & 3 & 4 & 9 & 6 \\
3 & 3 & 2 & 9 & 3 \\
\hline
 & 1 & 2 & 3 & 1 \\
\end{array}
$$

Step 4. To find the LCD, multiply all the numbers in the divisors (2, 2, 3) and in the last row (1, 2, 3, 1).

$$\boxed{2 \times 2 \times 3} \times \boxed{1 \times 2 \times 3 \times 1} = \boxed{72}\ \text{(LCD)}$$
$$\underbrace{}_{\text{Divisors}} \times \underbrace{}_{\text{Last row}}$$

Step 5. Raise each fraction so that each denominator will be 72 and then add fractions.

$$\dfrac{1}{3} = \dfrac{?}{72} \qquad 72 \div 3 = 24$$
$$\qquad\qquad\qquad\quad 24 \times 1 = 24$$

$$\dfrac{24}{72} + \dfrac{9}{72} + \dfrac{8}{72} + \dfrac{6}{72} = \dfrac{47}{72}$$

$$\dfrac{1}{8} = \dfrac{?}{72} \qquad 72 \div 8 = 9$$
$$\qquad\qquad\qquad\quad 9 \times 1 = 9$$

The above five steps used for finding LCD with prime numbers are summarized as follows:

Finding LCD for Two or More Fractions

Step 1. Copy the denominators and arrange them in a separate row.

Step 2. Divide the denominators by the smallest prime number that will divide evenly into at least two numbers.

Step 3. Continue until no prime number divides evenly into at least two numbers.

Step 4. Multiply all the numbers in divisors and last row to find the LCD.

Step 5. Raise all fractions so each has a common denominator and then complete the computation.

Adding Mixed Numbers

The following steps will show you how to add mixed numbers:

> **Adding Mixed Numbers**
>
> **Step 1.** Add the fractions (remember that fractions need common denominators, as in the previous section).
>
> **Step 2.** Add the whole numbers.
>
> **Step 3.** Combine the totals of Steps 1 and 2. Be sure you do not have an improper fraction in your final answer. Convert the improper fraction to a whole or mixed number. Add the whole numbers resulting from the improper fraction conversion to the total whole numbers of Step 2. If necessary, reduce the answer to lowest terms.

Using prime numbers to find LCD of example

```
2 / 20   5   4
2 / 10   5   2
5 /  5   5   1
      1   1   1
2 × 2 × 5 = 20 LCD
```

EXAMPLE

$$4\frac{7}{20} \qquad 4\frac{7}{20} \qquad\qquad \frac{3}{5} = \frac{?}{20}$$

$$6\frac{3}{5} \qquad 6\frac{12}{20} \qquad\qquad 20 \div 5 = \quad 4$$

$$+\,7\frac{1}{4} \qquad +\,7\frac{5}{20} \qquad\qquad\qquad\quad \times 3$$

$$\qquad\qquad\qquad\qquad\qquad\qquad\qquad\quad 12$$

Step 1 → $\dfrac{24}{20} = 1\dfrac{4}{20}$

Step 2 → $= 17$

Step 3 → $= 18\dfrac{4}{20} = \boxed{18\dfrac{1}{5}}$

Subtraction of Fractions

The subtraction of fractions is similar to the addition of fractions. This section explains how to subtract like and unlike fractions and how to subtract mixed numbers.

Subtracting Like Fractions

To subtract like fractions, use the steps that follow.

> **Subtracting Like Fractions**
>
> **Step 1.** Subtract the numerators and place the answer over the common denominator.
>
> **Step 2.** If necessary, reduce the answer to lowest terms.

EXAMPLE $\quad \dfrac{9}{10} - \dfrac{1}{10} = \dfrac{8 \div 2}{10 \div 2} = \boxed{\dfrac{4}{5}}$

$$\qquad\qquad\qquad\qquad\qquad \uparrow \qquad \uparrow$$
$$\qquad\qquad\qquad\quad \textbf{Step 1} \quad \textbf{Step 2}$$

Subtracting Unlike Fractions

Now let's learn the steps for subtracting unlike fractions.

> **Subtracting Unlike Fractions**
>
> **Step 1.** Find the LCD.
>
> **Step 2.** Raise the fraction to its equivalent value.
>
> **Step 3.** Subtract the numerators and place the answer over the LCD.
>
> **Step 4.** If necessary, reduce the answer to lowest terms.

EXAMPLE

$$\frac{5}{8} \qquad \frac{40}{64} \qquad$$ By inspection, we see that LCD is 64.

$$\qquad\qquad\qquad\qquad$$ Thus $64 \div 8 = 8 \times 5 = 40$.

$$-\,\frac{2}{64} \qquad -\,\frac{2}{64}$$

$$\qquad\qquad\quad \frac{38}{64} = \boxed{\frac{19}{32}}$$

Subtracting Mixed Numbers

When you subtract whole numbers, sometimes borrowing is not necessary. At other times, you must borrow. The same is true of subtracting mixed numbers.

Subtracting Mixed Numbers	
When Borrowing Is Not Necessary	*When Borrowing Is Necessary*
Step 1. Subtract fractions, making sure to find the LCD.	**Step 1.** Make sure the fractions have the LCD.
Step 2. Subtract whole numbers.	**Step 2.** Borrow from the whole number.
Step 3. Reduce the fraction(s) to lowest terms.	**Step 3.** Subtract the whole numbers and fractions.
	Step 4. Reduce the fraction(s) to lowest terms.

EXAMPLE   Where borrowing is not necessary: Find LCD of 2 and 8. LCD is 8.

$$6\frac{1}{2}\qquad\qquad 6\frac{4}{8}$$
$$-\frac{3}{8}\qquad\qquad -\frac{3}{8}$$
$$\qquad\qquad\qquad 6\frac{1}{8}$$

EXAMPLE   Where borrowing is necessary:

$$3\frac{1}{2}=\qquad 3\frac{2}{4}=\qquad 2\frac{6}{4}\left(\frac{4}{4}+\frac{2}{4}\right)$$
$$-1\frac{3}{4}=\qquad -1\frac{3}{4}=\qquad -1\frac{3}{4}$$
$$\text{LCD is }4.\qquad\qquad 1\frac{3}{4}$$

Since $\frac{3}{4}$ is larger than $\frac{2}{4}$, we must borrow 1 from the 3. This is the same as borrowing $\frac{4}{4}$. A fraction with the same numerator and denominator represents a whole. When we add $\frac{4}{4}+\frac{2}{4}$, we get $\frac{6}{4}$. Note how we subtracted the whole number and fractions, being sure to reduce the final answer if necessary.

How to Dissect and Solve a Word Problem

Let's now look at how to dissect and solve a word problem involving fractions.

The Word Problem   The Albertson grocery store has $550\frac{1}{4}$ total square feet of floor space. Albertson's meat department occupies $115\frac{1}{2}$ square feet, and its deli department occupies $145\frac{7}{8}$ square feet. If the remainder of the floor space is for groceries, what square footage remains for groceries?

The facts	Solving for?	Steps to take	Key points
Total square footage: $550\frac{1}{4}$ sq. ft. *Meat department:* $115\frac{1}{2}$ sq. ft. *Deli department:* $145\frac{7}{8}$ sq. ft.	Total square footage for groceries.	Total floor space − Total meat and deli floor space = Total grocery floor space.	Denominators must be the same before adding or subtracting fractions. $\frac{8}{8}=1$ Never leave improper fraction as final answer.

Steps to solving problem

1. Calculate total square footage of the meat and deli departments.

Meat: $115\frac{1}{2}=\;\;115\frac{4}{8}$

Deli: $+145\frac{7}{8}=+145\frac{7}{8}$

$\qquad\qquad\qquad 260\frac{11}{8}=261\frac{3}{8}$ sq. ft.

2. Calculate total grocery square footage.　　　　　　　　　**Check**

$$550\tfrac{1}{4} = \quad 550\tfrac{2}{8} = \quad 549\tfrac{10}{8}$$

$$-261\tfrac{3}{8} = \quad -261\tfrac{3}{8} = \quad -261\tfrac{3}{8} \qquad \left(\tfrac{2}{8} + \tfrac{8}{8}\right)$$

$$\boxed{288\tfrac{7}{8}}\ \text{sq. ft.}$$

$$261\tfrac{3}{8}$$

$$+288\tfrac{7}{8}$$

$$549\tfrac{10}{8} = 550\tfrac{2}{8} = 550\tfrac{1}{4}\ \text{sq. ft.}$$

Note how the above blueprint aid helped to gather the facts and identify what we were looking for. To find the total square footage for groceries, we first had to sum the areas for meat and deli. Then we could subtract these areas from the total square footage. Also note that in Step 1 above, we didn't leave the answer as an improper fraction. In Step 2, we borrowed from the 550 so that we could complete the subtraction.

LU 2-2 PRACTICE QUIZ

1. Find LCD by the division of prime numbers:
12, 9, 6, 4

2. Add and reduce to lowest terms if needed:

　a. $\dfrac{3}{40} + \dfrac{2}{5}$ 　　　　　　**b.** $2\dfrac{3}{4} + 6\dfrac{1}{20}$

3. Subtract and reduce to lowest terms if needed:

　a. $\dfrac{6}{7} - \dfrac{1}{4}$ 　　　　**b.** $8\dfrac{1}{4} - 3\dfrac{9}{28}$ 　　　　**c.** $4 - 1\dfrac{3}{4}$

4. Computerland has $660\tfrac{1}{4}$ total square feet of floor space. Three departments occupy this floor space: hardware, $201\tfrac{1}{8}$ square feet; software, $242\tfrac{1}{4}$ square feet; and customer service, _____ square feet. What is the total square footage of the customer service area? You might want to try a blueprint aid, since the solution will show a completed blueprint aid.

✓ **SOLUTIONS**

1.
```
2 / 12  9  6  4
2 /  6  9  3  2
3 /  3  9  3  1
     1  3  1  1
```
$\text{LCD} = 2 \times 2 \times 3 \times 1 \times 3 \times 1 \times 1 = \boxed{36}$

2. **a.** $\dfrac{3}{40} + \dfrac{2}{5} = \dfrac{3}{40} + \dfrac{16}{40} = \boxed{\dfrac{19}{40}}$ 　　$\left(\begin{array}{l}\dfrac{2}{5} = \dfrac{?}{40} \\ 40 \div 5 = 8 \times 2 = 16\end{array}\right)$

　b.

$$2\tfrac{3}{4}$$
$$+6\tfrac{1}{20}$$

$$2\tfrac{15}{20}$$
$$+6\tfrac{1}{20}$$
$$8\tfrac{16}{20} = \boxed{8\tfrac{4}{5}}$$

$\dfrac{3}{4} = \dfrac{?}{20}$ 　　$20 \div 4 = 5 \times 3 = 15$

3. **a.**

$$\dfrac{6}{7} = \dfrac{24}{28}$$
$$-\dfrac{1}{4} = -\dfrac{7}{28}$$
$$\boxed{\dfrac{17}{28}}$$

　b.

$$8\tfrac{1}{4} = \quad 8\tfrac{7}{28} = \quad 7\tfrac{35}{28} \quad \left(\tfrac{28}{28} + \tfrac{7}{28}\right)$$
$$-3\tfrac{9}{28} = -3\tfrac{9}{28} = -3\tfrac{9}{28}$$
$$4\tfrac{26}{28} = \boxed{4\tfrac{13}{14}}$$

　c.

$$3\tfrac{4}{4}$$　　Note how we showed the 4 as $3\tfrac{4}{4}$.
$$-1\tfrac{3}{4}$$
$$\boxed{2\tfrac{1}{4}}$$

4. Computerland's total square footage for customer service:

The facts	Solving for?	Steps to take	Key points
Total square footage: $660\frac{1}{4}$ sq. ft. *Hardware:* $201\frac{1}{8}$ sq. ft. *Software:* $242\frac{1}{4}$ sq. ft.	Total square footage for customer service.	Total floor space − Total hardware and software floor space = Total customer service floor space.	Denominators must be the same before adding or subtracting fractions.

Steps to solving problem

1. Calculate the total square footage of hardware and software.

$$201\frac{1}{8} = \quad 201\frac{1}{8} \text{ (hardware)}$$
$$+242\frac{1}{4} = +242\frac{2}{8} \text{ (software)}$$
$$\overline{\qquad\qquad 443\frac{3}{8}}$$

2. Calculate the total square footage for customer service.

$$660\frac{1}{4} = \quad 660\frac{2}{8} = \quad 659\frac{10}{8} \text{ (total square footage)}$$
$$-443\frac{3}{8} = -443\frac{3}{8} = -443\frac{3}{8} \text{ (hardware plus software)}$$
$$\overline{\qquad\qquad 216\frac{7}{8} \text{ sq. ft. (customer service)}}$$

LEARNING UNIT 2–3 | MULTIPLICATION AND DIVISION OF FRACTIONS

The following recipe for Coconutty "M&M's"® Brownies makes 16 brownies. What would you need if you wanted to triple the recipe and make 48 brownies?

Coconutty "M&M's"® Brownies

6 squares (1 ounce each) semi-sweet chocolate
½ cup (1 stick) butter
¾ cup granulated sugar
2 large eggs
1 tablespoon vegetable oil
1 teaspoon vanilla extract
1¼ cups all-purpose flour
3 tablespoons unsweetened cocoa powder
1 teaspoon baking powder
½ teaspoon salt
1½ cups "M&M's"® Chocolate Mini Baking Bits, divided
Coconut Topping (recipe follows)

© 2000 Mars, Incorporated.

Preheat oven to 350°F. Grease 8 × 8 × 2-inch pan; set aside. In small saucepan combine chocolate, butter, and sugar over low heat; stir constantly until smooth. Remove from heat; let cool. In bowl beat eggs, oil, and vanilla; stir in chocolate mixture until blended. Stir in flour, cocoa powder, baking powder, and salt. Stir in 1 cup "M&M's"® Chocolate Mini Baking Bits. Spread batter in prepared pan. Bake 35 to 40 minutes or until toothpick inserted in center comes out clean. Cool. Prepare a coconut topping. Spread over brownies; sprinkle with $\frac{1}{2}$ cup "M&M's"® Chocolate Mini Baking Bits.

In this unit you learn how to multiply and divide **fractions.**

Multiplication of Fractions

Multiplying fractions is easier than adding and subtracting fractions because you do not have to find a common denominator. This section explains the multiplication of proper fractions and the multiplication of mixed numbers.

Multiplying Proper Fractions[3]

Step 1. Multiply the numerators and the denominators.

Step 2. Reduce the answer to lowest terms or use the cancellation method.

First let's look at an example that results in an answer that we do not have to reduce.

EXAMPLE $\dfrac{1}{7} \times \dfrac{5}{8} = \boxed{\dfrac{5}{56}}$

In the next example, note how we reduce the answer to lowest terms.

EXAMPLE $\dfrac{5}{1} \times \dfrac{1}{6} \times \dfrac{4}{7} = \dfrac{20}{42} = \boxed{\dfrac{10}{21}}$ Keep in mind $\dfrac{5}{1}$ is equal to 5.

We can reduce $\frac{20}{42}$ by the step approach as follows:

$$
\begin{array}{r}
2 \\
20\overline{)42} \\
40 \\
\hline
2
\end{array}
\qquad
\begin{array}{r}
10 \\
2\overline{)20} \\
20 \\
\hline
0
\end{array}
$$

We could also have found the
greatest common divisor
by inspection.

$$\dfrac{20 \div 2}{42 \div 2} = \boxed{\dfrac{10}{21}}$$

As an alternative to reducing fractions to lowest terms, we can use the **cancellation** technique. Let's work the previous example using this technique.

EXAMPLE $\dfrac{5}{1} \times \dfrac{1}{\cancel{6}} \times \dfrac{\overset{2}{\cancel{4}}}{7} = \boxed{\dfrac{10}{21}}$

2 divides evenly into 4 twice
and into 6 three times.

Note that when we cancel numbers, we are reducing the answer before multiplying. We know that multiplying or dividing both numerator and denominator by the same number gives an equivalent fraction. So we can divide both numerator and denominator by any number that divides them both evenly. It doesn't matter which we divide first. Note that this division reduces $\frac{10}{21}$ to its lowest terms.

Multiplying Mixed Numbers

The following steps explain how to multiply mixed numbers:

Multiplying Mixed Numbers

Step 1. Convert the mixed numbers to improper fractions.

Step 2. Multiply the numerators and denominators.

Step 3. Reduce the answer to lowest terms or use the cancellation method.

EXAMPLE

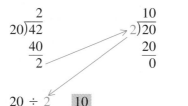

$$2\dfrac{1}{3} \times 1\dfrac{1}{2} = \dfrac{7}{\cancel{3}} \times \dfrac{\cancel{3}}{2} = \dfrac{7}{2} = \boxed{3\dfrac{1}{2}}$$

Step 1   **Step 2**   **Step 3**

Division of Fractions

When you studied whole numbers in Chapter 1, you saw how multiplication can be checked by division. The multiplication of fractions can also be checked by division, as you will see in this section on dividing proper fractions and mixed numbers.

Dividing Proper Fractions

The division of proper fractions introduces a new term—the **reciprocal.** To use reciprocals, we must first recognize which fraction in the problem is the divisor—the fraction

---

[3]You would follow the same procedure to multiply improper fractions.

that we divide by. Let's assume the problem we are to solve is $\frac{1}{8} \div \frac{2}{3}$. We read this problem as "$\frac{1}{8}$ divided by $\frac{2}{3}$." The divisor is the fraction after the division sign (or the second fraction). The steps that follow show how the divisor becomes a reciprocal.

Dividing Proper Fractions
Step 1. Invert (turn upside down) the divisor (the second fraction). The inverted number is the *reciprocal*.
Step 2. Multiply the fractions.
Step 3. Reduce the answer to lowest terms or use the cancellation method.

Do you know why the inverted fraction number is a reciprocal? Reciprocals are two numbers that when multiplied give a product of 1. For example, 2 (which is the same as $\frac{2}{1}$) and $\frac{1}{2}$ are reciprocals because multiplying them gives 1.

EXAMPLE $\frac{1}{8} \div \frac{2}{3}$ $\frac{1}{8} \times \frac{3}{2} = \boxed{\frac{3}{16}}$

Dividing Mixed Numbers

Now you are ready to divide mixed numbers by using improper fractions.

Dividing Mixed Numbers
Step 1. Convert all mixed numbers to improper fractions.
Step 2. Invert the divisor (take its reciprocal) and multiply. If your final answer is an improper fraction, reduce it to lowest terms. You can do this by finding the greatest common divisor or by using the cancellation technique.

EXAMPLE $8\frac{3}{4} \div 2\frac{5}{6}$

Step 1. $\frac{35}{4} \div \frac{17}{6}$

Step 2. $\frac{35}{\cancel{4}_2} \times \frac{\cancel{6}^3}{17} = \frac{105}{34} = 3\frac{3}{34}$ Here we used the cancellation technique.

How to Dissect and Solve a Word Problem

The Word Problem   Jamie Slater ordered $5\frac{1}{2}$ cords of oak. The cost of each cord is $150. He also ordered $2\frac{1}{4}$ cords of maple at $120 per cord. Jamie's neighbor, Al, said that he would share the wood and pay him $\frac{1}{5}$ of the total cost. How much did Jamie receive from Al?

Note how we filled in the blueprint aid columns. We first had to find the total cost of all the wood before we could find Al's share—$\frac{1}{5}$ of the total cost.

The facts	Solving for?	Steps to take	Key points
Cords ordered: $5\frac{1}{2}$ at $150 per cord; $2\frac{1}{4}$ at $120 per cord. *Al's cost share:* $\frac{1}{5}$ the total cost.	What will Al pay Jamie?	Total cost of wood × $\frac{1}{5}$ = Al's cost.	Convert mixed numbers to improper fractions when multiplying. Cancellation is an alternative to reducing fractions.

Steps to solving problem

1. Calculate the cost of oak. $5\frac{1}{2} \times \$150 = \frac{11}{2} \times \cancel{\$150}^{\$75} = \$825$

2. Calculate the cost of maple. $2\frac{1}{4} \times \$120 = \frac{9}{4} \times \cancel{\$120}^{\$30} = +270$

$\overline{\$1{,}095}$ (total cost of wood)

3. What Al pays. $\frac{1}{5} \times \cancel{\$1{,}095}^{\$219} = \boxed{\$219}$

(continues)

LU 2–3 PRACTICE QUIZ

1. Multiply (use cancellation technique):

   a. $\dfrac{4}{8} \times \dfrac{4}{6}$

   b. $35 \times \dfrac{4}{7}$

2. Multiply (do not use canceling; reduce by finding the greatest common divisor):

   $\dfrac{14}{15} \times \dfrac{7}{10}$

3. Complete the following. Reduce to lowest terms as needed.

   a. $\dfrac{1}{9} \div \dfrac{5}{6}$

   b. $\dfrac{51}{5} \div \dfrac{5}{9}$

4. Jill Estes bought a mobile home that was $8\frac{1}{8}$ times as expensive as the home her brother bought. Jill's brother paid $16,000 for his mobile home. What is the cost of Jill's new home?

✓ **SOLUTIONS**

1. a. $\dfrac{\overset{1}{\underset{\underset{1}{2}}{\cancel{4}}}}{\underset{\underset{1}{2}}{\cancel{8}}} \times \dfrac{\overset{1}{\cancel{4}}}{\underset{3}{\cancel{6}}} = \boxed{\dfrac{1}{3}}$

   b. $\overset{5}{\cancel{35}} \times \dfrac{4}{\underset{1}{\cancel{7}}} = \boxed{20}$

2. $\dfrac{14}{15} \times \dfrac{7}{10} = \dfrac{98 \div 2}{150 \div 2} = \boxed{\dfrac{49}{75}}$

   $98)\overline{150} \quad \begin{matrix}1\end{matrix} \qquad 52)\overline{98} \quad \begin{matrix}1\end{matrix} \qquad 46)\overline{52} \quad \begin{matrix}1\end{matrix} \qquad 6)\overline{46} \quad \begin{matrix}7\end{matrix} \qquad 4)\overline{6} \quad \begin{matrix}1\end{matrix} \qquad 2)\overline{4} \quad \begin{matrix}2\end{matrix}$

   $\dfrac{98}{52} \qquad \dfrac{52}{46} \qquad \dfrac{46}{6} \qquad \dfrac{42}{4} \qquad \dfrac{4}{2} \qquad \dfrac{4}{0}$

3. a. $\dfrac{1}{9} \times \dfrac{6}{5} = \dfrac{6 \div 3}{45 \div 3} = \boxed{\dfrac{2}{15}}$

   b. $\dfrac{51}{5} \times \dfrac{9}{5} = \dfrac{459}{25} = \boxed{18\dfrac{9}{25}}$

4. Total cost of Jill's new home:

The facts	Solving for?	Steps to take	Key points
Jill's mobile home: $8\frac{1}{8}$ as expensive as her brother's. *Brother paid:* $16,000.	Total cost of Jill's new home.	$8\frac{1}{8} \times$ Total cost of Jill's brother's mobile home = Total cost of Jill's new home.	Canceling is an alternative to reducing.

Steps to solving problem

1. Convert $8\frac{1}{8}$ to a mixed number. $\dfrac{65}{8}$

2. Calculate the total cost of Jill's home. $\dfrac{65}{\underset{1}{\cancel{8}}} \times \overset{\$2,000}{\cancel{\$16,000}} = \boxed{\$130,000}$

Chapter Organizer and Reference Guide

Topic	Key point, procedure, formula	Example(s) to illustrate situation
Types of fractions, p. 35	*Proper:* Value less than 1; numerator smaller than denominator.	$\dfrac{3}{5}, \dfrac{7}{9}, \dfrac{8}{15}$
	Improper: Value equal to or greater than 1; numerator equal to or greater than denominator.	$\dfrac{14}{14}, \dfrac{19}{18}$
	Mixed: Sum of whole number greater than zero and a proper fraction.	$6\dfrac{3}{8}, 9\dfrac{8}{9}$
Fraction conversions, p. 35	*Improper to whole or mixed:* Divide numerator by denominator; place remainder over *old* denominator.	$\dfrac{17}{4} = 4\dfrac{1}{4}$
	Mixed to improper: $\dfrac{\text{Whole number} \times \text{Denominator} + \text{Numerator}}{\text{Old denominator}}$	$4\dfrac{1}{8} = \dfrac{32 + 1}{8} = \boxed{\dfrac{33}{8}}$

Chapter Organizer and Reference Guide (continued)

Topic	Key point, procedure, formula	Example(s) to illustrate situation
Reducing fractions to lowest terms, p. 36	1. Divide numerator and denominator by largest possible divisor (does not change fraction value). 2. When reduced to lowest terms, no number (except 1) will divide evenly into both numerator and denominator.	$\dfrac{18 \div 2}{46 \div 2} = \dfrac{9}{23}$
Step approach for finding greatest common denominator, p. 37	1. Divide smaller number of fraction into larger number. 2. Divide remainder into divisor of Step 1. Continue this process until no remainder results. 3. The last divisor used is the greatest common divisor.	$\dfrac{15}{65} \longrightarrow 15\overline{)65}$ with 4, 60, 5; $\quad 5\overline{)15}$ with 3, 15, 0. $\quad 5$ is greatest common divisor.
Raising fractions to higher terms, p. 37	Multiply numerator and denominator by same number. Does not change fraction value.	$\dfrac{15}{41} = \dfrac{?}{410}$ $410 \div 41 = 10 \times 15 = 150$
Adding and subtracting like and unlike fractions, p. 39	When denominators are the same (like fractions), add (or subtract) numerators, place total over original denominator, and reduce to lowest terms. When denominators are different (unlike fractions), change them to like fractions by finding LCD using inspection or prime numbers. Then add (or subtract) the numerators, place total over LCD, and reduce to lowest terms.	$\dfrac{4}{9} + \dfrac{1}{9} = \dfrac{5}{9}$ $\dfrac{4}{9} - \dfrac{1}{9} = \dfrac{3}{9} = \dfrac{1}{3}$ $\dfrac{4}{5} + \dfrac{2}{7} = \dfrac{28}{35} + \dfrac{10}{35} = \dfrac{38}{35} = 1\dfrac{3}{35}$
Prime numbers, p. 40	Whole numbers larger than 1 that are only divisible by itself and 1.	2, 3, 5, 7, 11
LCD by prime numbers, p. 41	1. Copy denominators and arrange them in a separate row. 2. Divide denominators by smallest prime number that will divide evenly into at least two numbers. 3. Continue until no prime number divides evenly into at least two numbers. 4. Multiply all the numbers in the divisors and last row to find LCD. 5. Raise fractions so each has a common denominator and complete computation.	$\dfrac{1}{3} + \dfrac{1}{6} + \dfrac{1}{8} + \dfrac{1}{12} + \dfrac{1}{9}$ $2\,/\,3 \quad 6 \quad 8 \quad 12 \quad 9$ $2\,/\,3 \quad 3 \quad 4 \quad 6 \quad 9$ $3\,/\,3 \quad 3 \quad 2 \quad 3 \quad 9$ $\quad\; 1 \quad 1 \quad 2 \quad 1 \quad 3$ $2 \times 2 \times 3 \times 1 \times 1 \times 2 \times 1 \times 3 = 72$
Adding mixed numbers, p. 42	1. Add fractions. 2. Add whole numbers. 3. Combine totals of Steps 1 and 2. If denominators are different, a common denominator must be found. Answer cannot be left as improper fraction.	$1\dfrac{4}{7} + 1\dfrac{3}{7}$ Step 1: $\dfrac{4}{7} + \dfrac{3}{7} = \dfrac{7}{7}$ Step 2: $1 + 1 = 2$ Step 3: $2\dfrac{7}{7} = 3$
Subtracting mixed numbers, p. 43	1. Subtract fractions. 2. If necessary, borrow from whole numbers. 3. Subtract whole numbers and fractions if borrowing was necessary. 4. Reduce fractions to lowest terms. If denominators are different, a common denominator must be found.	$12\dfrac{2}{5} - 7\dfrac{3}{5}$ $11\dfrac{7}{5} - 7\dfrac{3}{5}$ $= 4\dfrac{4}{5}$ Due to borrowing $\dfrac{5}{5}$ from number 12 $\dfrac{5}{5} + \dfrac{2}{5} = \dfrac{7}{5}$ The whole number is now 11.
Multiplying proper fractions, p. 46	1. Multiply numerators and denominators. 2. Reduce answer to lowest terms or use cancellation method.	$\dfrac{4}{7} \times \dfrac{7}{9} = \dfrac{4}{9}$
Multiplying mixed numbers, p. 46	1. Convert mixed numbers to improper fractions. 2. Multiply numerators and denominators. 3. Reduce answer to lowest terms or use cancellation method.	$1\dfrac{1}{8} \times 2\dfrac{5}{8}$ $\dfrac{9}{8} \times \dfrac{21}{8} = \dfrac{189}{64} = 2\dfrac{61}{64}$

(continues)

Chapter Organizer and Reference Guide (concluded)

Topic	Key point, procedure, formula	Example(s) to illustrate situation
Dividing proper fractions, p. 47	1. Invert divisor. 2. Multiply. 3. Reduce answer to lowest terms or use cancellation method.	$\dfrac{1}{4} \div \dfrac{1}{8} = \dfrac{1}{\underset{1}{4}} \times \dfrac{\overset{2}{8}}{1} = 2$
Dividing mixed numbers, p. 47	1. Convert mixed numbers to improper fractions. 2. Invert divisor and multiply. If final answer is an improper fraction, reduce to lowest terms by finding greatest common divisor or using the cancellation method.	$1\dfrac{1}{2} \div 1\dfrac{5}{8} = \dfrac{3}{2} \div \dfrac{13}{8}$ $\quad = \dfrac{3}{\underset{1}{2}} \times \dfrac{\overset{4}{8}}{13}$ $\quad = \dfrac{12}{13}$
Key terms	Cancellation, *p. 46* Common denominator, *p. 39* Denominator, *p. 34* Equivalent, *p. 37* Fraction, *p. 45* Greatest common divisor, *p. 36*	Higher terms, *p. 37* Improper fraction, *p. 35* Least common denominator (LCD), *p. 40* Like fractions, *p. 39* Lowest terms, *p. 36* Mixed numbers, *p. 35* Numerator, *p. 34* Prime numbers, *p. 40* Proper fractions, *p. 35* Reciprocal, *p. 46* Unlike fractions, *p. 39*

Note: For how to dissect and solve a word problem, see page 43.

Critical Thinking Discussion Questions

1. What are the steps to convert improper fractions to whole or mixed numbers? Give an example of how you could use this conversion procedure when you eat at Pizza Hut.

2. What are the steps to convert mixed numbers to improper fractions? Show how you could use this conversion procedure when you order doughnuts at Dunkin' Donuts.

3. What is the greatest common divisor? How could you use the greatest common divisor to write an advertisement showing that 35 out of 60 people prefer MCI World-Com to AT&T?

4. Explain the step approach for finding the greatest common divisor. How could you use the MCI WorldCom–AT&T example in Question 3 to illustrate the step approach?

5. Explain the steps of adding or subtracting unlike fractions. Using a ruler, measure the heights of two different-size cans of food and show how to calculate the difference in height.

6. What is a prime number? Using the two cans in Question 5, show how you could use prime numbers to calculate the LCD.

7. Explain the steps for multiplying proper fractions and mixed numbers. Assume you went to Staples (a stationery superstore). Give an example showing the multiplying of proper fractions and mixed numbers.

DRILL PROBLEMS

Identify the following types of fractions:

2–1. $\dfrac{1}{9}$ **2–2.** $12\dfrac{5}{7}$ **2–3.** $\dfrac{16}{11}$

Convert the following to mixed numbers:

2–4. $\dfrac{58}{7}$ **2–5.** $\dfrac{921}{15}$

Convert the following to improper fractions:

2–6. $8\dfrac{9}{10}$ **2–7.** $19\dfrac{2}{3}$

Reduce the following to the lowest terms. Show how to calculate the greatest common divisor by the step approach.

2–8. $\dfrac{16}{38}$ **2–9.** $\dfrac{44}{52}$

Convert the following to higher terms:

2–10. $\dfrac{7}{8} = \dfrac{}{80}$

Determine the LCD of the following **(a)** by inspection and **(b)** by division of prime numbers:

2–11. $\dfrac{3}{4}, \dfrac{7}{12}, \dfrac{5}{6}, \dfrac{1}{5}$ **Check**

         Inspection

2–12. $\dfrac{5}{6}, \dfrac{7}{18}, \dfrac{5}{9}, \dfrac{2}{72}$ **Check**

         Inspection

2–13. $\dfrac{1}{4}, \dfrac{3}{32}, \dfrac{5}{48}, \dfrac{1}{8}$ **Check**

         Inspection

Add the following and reduce to lowest terms:

2–14. $\dfrac{4}{9} + \dfrac{2}{9}$ **2–15.** $\dfrac{3}{7} + \dfrac{4}{21}$

2–16. $6\dfrac{1}{8} + 4\dfrac{3}{8}$ **2–17.** $6\dfrac{3}{8} + 9\dfrac{1}{24}$

2–18. $9\dfrac{9}{10} + 6\dfrac{7}{10}$

Subtract the following and reduce to lowest terms:

2–19. $\dfrac{11}{12} - \dfrac{1}{12}$

2–20. $14\dfrac{3}{8} - 10\dfrac{5}{8}$

2–21. $12\dfrac{1}{9} - 4\dfrac{2}{3}$

Multiply the following and reduce to lowest terms. Do not use the cancellation technique for these problems.

2–22. $17 \times \dfrac{4}{2}$

2–23. $\dfrac{5}{6} \times \dfrac{3}{8}$

2–24. $8\dfrac{7}{8} \times 64$

Multiply the following. Use the cancellation technique.

2–25. $\dfrac{4}{10} \times \dfrac{30}{60} \times \dfrac{6}{10}$

2–26. $3\dfrac{3}{4} \times \dfrac{8}{9} \times 4\dfrac{9}{12}$

Divide the following and reduce to lowest terms. Use the cancellation technique as needed.

2–27. $\dfrac{12}{9} \div 4$

2–28. $18 \div \dfrac{1}{5}$

2–29. $4\dfrac{2}{3} \div 12$

2–30. $3\dfrac{5}{6} \div 3\dfrac{1}{2}$

WORD PROBLEMS

2–31. *Quilt World* magazine of July 2001 gave instructions on making a table topper. A partial list of material included $\frac{1}{3}$ yard red print, $\frac{1}{2}$ yard red/blue print, and $\frac{3}{4}$ yard blue print. What would be the total yards of material needed for this project?

2–32. Pete Rowe bought a new hand-held computer at Circuit City for $399. The manufacturer offers a rebate of 1/3 off the selling price. How much did Pete pay after the rebate?

2–33. U.S. Airways pays Paul Lose $125 per day to work in security at the airport. Paul became ill on Monday and went home after $\frac{1}{5}$ of a day. What did he earn on Monday? Assume no work, no pay.

2–34. Brian Summers visited Gold's Gym and lost $2\frac{1}{4}$ pounds in week 1, $1\frac{3}{4}$ pounds in week 2, and $\frac{5}{8}$ pound in week 3. What is the total weight loss for Brian?

2–35. Joy Wigens, who works at Putnam Investments, received a check for $1,600. She deposited $\frac{1}{4}$ of the check in her Citibank account. How much money does Joy have left after the deposit?

2–36. Pete Hall worked the following hours as a manager for News.com: $12\frac{1}{4}$, $5\frac{1}{4}$, $8\frac{1}{2}$, and $7\frac{1}{4}$. How many total hours did Pete work?

2–37. The June 2001 *Woodsmith* magazine tells how to build a country wall shelf. Two side panels are $\frac{3}{4} \times 7\frac{1}{2} \times 31\frac{5}{8}$ inches long. **(a)** What is the total length of board you will need? **(b)** If you have a board $74\frac{1}{3}$ inches long, how much of the board will remain after cutting?

2–38. Lester bought a piece of property in Vail, Colorado. The sides of the land measure $115\frac{1}{2}$ feet, $66\frac{1}{4}$ feet, $106\frac{1}{8}$ feet, and $110\frac{1}{4}$ feet. Lester wants to know the perimeter (sum of all sides) of his property. Can you calculate the perimeter for Lester?

2–39. According to an article in *The New York Times* on June 3, 2001, "Fuel Economy for New Cars Is at Lowest Level Since '80." The estimated average fuel economy of all cars and light trucks sold in the 2001 model year will be $24\frac{1}{2}$ miles a gallon. Your Mercedes-Benz CLK-Class has a $16\frac{1}{2}$-gallon tank. You have traveled 363 miles and are out of gas. How far below or above the average mileage was your Mercedes?

2–40. From Home Depot, Pete Wong ordered $\frac{6}{7}$ of a ton of crushed rock to make a patio. If Pete used only $\frac{3}{4}$ of the rock, how much crushed rock remains unused?

2–41. At a Wal-Mart store, a Coke dispenser held $19\frac{1}{4}$ gallons of soda. During working hours, $12\frac{3}{4}$ gallons were dispensed. How many gallons of Coke remain?

2–42. Katie Kaminski bought a home from Century 21 in San Antonio, Texas, that is $7\frac{1}{2}$ times as expensive as the home her parents bought. Katie's parents paid $16,000 for their home. What is the cost of Katie's new home?

2–43. Ajax Company charges $150 per cord of wood. If Bill Ryan orders $3\frac{1}{2}$ cords, what will his total cost be?

2–44. Learning.com bought 90 pizzas at Pizza Hut for their holiday party. Each guest ate $\frac{1}{6}$ of a pizza and there was no pizza left over. How many guests did Learning.com have for the party?

2–45. Marc, Steven, and Daniel entered into an Internet partnership. Marc owns $\frac{1}{9}$ of the Dot.com, and Steven owns $\frac{1}{4}$. What part does Daniel own?

2–46. Lionel Sullivan works for Burger King. He is paid time and one-half for Sundays. If Lionel works on Sunday for 6 hours at a regular pay of $8 per hour, what does he earn on Sunday?

2–47. Hertz pays Al Davis, an employee, $125 per day. Al decided to donate $\frac{1}{5}$ of a day's pay to his church. How much will Al donate?

2–48. A trip to New Hampshire from Boston will take you $2\frac{3}{4}$ hours. Assume you have traveled $\frac{1}{11}$ of the way. How much longer will the trip take?

2–49. Michael, who loves to cook, makes apple cobbler (serves 6) for his family. The recipe calls for $1\frac{1}{2}$ pounds of apples, $3\frac{1}{4}$ cups of flour, $\frac{1}{4}$ cup of margarine, $2\frac{3}{8}$ cups of sugar, and 2 teaspoons of cinnamon. Since guests are coming, Michael wants to make a cobbler that will serve 15 (or increase the recipe $2\frac{1}{2}$ times). How much of each ingredient should Michael use?

2–50. Mobil allocates $1,692\frac{3}{4}$ gallons of gas per month to Jerry's Service Station. The first week, Jerry sold $275\frac{1}{2}$ gallons; second week, $280\frac{1}{4}$ gallons; and third week, $189\frac{1}{8}$ gallons. If Jerry sells $582\frac{1}{2}$ gallons in the fourth week, how close is Jerry to selling his allocation?

2–51. A marketing class at North Shore Community College conducted a viewer preference survey. The survey showed that $\frac{5}{6}$ of the people surveyed preferred DVDs to videotapes. Assume 2,400 responded to the survey. How many favored using traditional tapes?

2–52. The price of a new Ford Explorer has increased to $1\frac{1}{4}$ times its earlier price. If the original price of the Ford Explorer was $28,000, what is the new price?

2–53. Chris Rong felled a tree that was 299 feet long. Chris decided to cut the tree into pieces $3\frac{1}{4}$ feet long. How many pieces can Chris cut from this tree?

2–54. Tempco Corporation has a machine that produces $12\frac{1}{2}$ baseball gloves each hour. In the last 2 days, the machine has run for a total of 22 hours. How many baseball gloves has Tempco produced?

2–55. McGraw-Hill/Irwin publishers stores some of its inventory in a warehouse that has 14,500 square feet of space. Each book requires $2\frac{1}{2}$ square feet of space. How many books can McGraw-Hill/Irwin keep in this warehouse?

2–56. Alicia, an employee of Dunkin' Donuts, receives $23\frac{1}{4}$ days per year of vacation time. So far this year she has taken $3\frac{1}{8}$ days in January, $5\frac{1}{2}$ days in May, $6\frac{1}{4}$ days in July, and $4\frac{1}{4}$ days in September. How many more days of vacation does Alicia have left?

2–57. Amazon.com offered a new portable color TV for $250 with a rebate of $\frac{1}{5}$ off the regular price. What is the final cost of the TV after the rebate?

2–58. Shelly Van Doren hired a contractor to refinish her kitchen. The contractor said the job would take $49\frac{1}{2}$ hours. To date, the contractor has worked the following hours:

Monday	$4\frac{1}{4}$
Tuesday	$9\frac{1}{8}$
Wednesday	$4\frac{1}{4}$
Thursday	$3\frac{1}{2}$
Friday	$10\frac{5}{8}$

How much longer should the job take to be completed?

ADDITIONAL SET OF WORD PROBLEMS

2–59. On July 2, 2001, you received a special ad from Home Depot stating that a $\frac{3}{4}$ inch $\times$ 10 feet piece of PVC piping is on sale for $1.39. You plan to install the PVC piping in your basement. The measurements you have calculated include pieces with a total length of $11\frac{3}{4}$ feet, $15\frac{3}{8}$ feet, and $8\frac{5}{16}$ feet. **(a)** What is the total length of piping needed? **(b)** If you purchased a total of 40 feet of piping, how much piping will you have left over?

2–60. Publics plans a big sale on apples and received 950 crates from the wholesale market. Publics will bag these apples in plastic. Each plastic bag holds $\frac{1}{8}$ of a crate. If Publics has no loss to perishables, how many bags of apples can be prepared?

2–61. Frank Puleo bought 6,625 acres of land in ski country. He plans to subdivide the land into parcels of $13\frac{1}{4}$ acres each. Each parcel will sell for $125,000. How many parcels of land will Frank develop? If Frank sells all the parcels, what will be his total sales?

If Frank sells $\frac{3}{5}$ of the parcels in the first year, what will be his total sales for the year?

2–62. A local Papa Gino's conducted a food survey. The survey showed that $\frac{1}{9}$ of the people surveyed preferred eating pasta to hamburger. If 5,400 responded to the survey, how many actually favored hamburger?

2–63. Tamara, Jose, and Milton entered into a partnership that sells men's clothing on the Web. Tamara owns $\frac{3}{8}$ of the company, and Jose owns $\frac{1}{4}$. What part does Milton own?

2–64. *Edmunds 2001 Buyer's Guide* lists the Honda Insight as getting 68 miles per gallon and having a gasoline tank capacity of $10\frac{6}{10}$ gallons. With a full tank, what is the maximum number of miles you could travel before you ran out of gas?

2–65. A trailer carrying supplies for a Taco Bell from Virginia to New York will take $3\frac{1}{4}$ hours. If the truck traveled $\frac{1}{5}$ of the way, how much longer will the trip take?

2–66. Land Rover has increased the price of a Discovery II by $\frac{1}{5}$ from the original price. The original price of the Discovery II was $30,000. What is the new price?

2–67. Norman Moen, an employee at Subway, prepared a 90-foot submarine sandwich for a party. Norman decided to cut the submarine into sandwiches of $1\frac{1}{2}$ feet. How many sandwiches can Norman cut from this submarine?

CHALLENGE PROBLEMS

2–68. Do+Able Products, Inc., of Chino, California, sent you a parts list for an entertainment center project. Included in the parts list were the following:

Two $\frac{3}{4} \times 15\frac{7}{8} \times 59\frac{1}{2}$ inch side panels

Three $\frac{3}{4} \times 15\frac{7}{8} \times 35\frac{7}{8}$ inch shelves

Two $\frac{3}{4} \times 15\frac{7}{8} \times 17\frac{9}{16}$ inch shelf/partition

The $\frac{3}{4} \times 15\frac{7}{8}$ inch wood comes in 7-foot lengths. **(a)** What is the total length of material needed? **(b)** How many 7-foot lengths must be purchased? **(c)** How many feet will be left over?

2–69. Jack MacLean has entered into a real estate development partnership with Bill Lyons and June Reese. Bill owns $\frac{1}{4}$ of the partnership, while June has a $\frac{1}{5}$ interest. The partners will divide all profits on the basis of their fractional ownership.

    The partnership bought 900 acres of land and plans to subdivide each lot into $2\frac{1}{4}$ acres. Homes in the area have been selling for $240,000. By time of completion, Jack estimates the price of each home will increase by $\frac{1}{3}$ of the current value. The partners sent a survey to 12,000 potential customers to see whether they should heat the homes with oil or gas. One-fourth of the customers responded by indicating a 5-to-1 preference for oil. From the results of the survey, Jack now plans to install a 270-gallon oil tank at each home. He estimates that each home will need 5 fills per year. Current price of home heating fuel is $1 per gallon. The partnership estimates its profit per home will be $\frac{1}{8}$ the selling price of each home.

    From the above, please calculate the following:

a. Number of homes to be built.

b. Selling price of each home.

c. **(1).** Number of people responding to survey.

    (2). Number of people desiring oil.

d. Average monthly cost to run oil heat per house.

e. Amount of profit Jack will receive from the sale of homes.

SUMMARY PRACTICE TEST

Identify the following types of fractions. *(p. 35)*

1. $7\frac{9}{10}$

2. $\frac{3}{7}$

3. $\frac{12}{11}$

4. Convert the following to a mixed number. *(p. 36)*

$\frac{138}{5}$

5. Convert the following to an improper fraction. *(p. 36)*

$7\frac{3}{4}$

6. Calculate the greatest common divisor of the following by the step approach and reduce to lowest terms. *(p. 37)*

$\frac{98}{140}$

7. Convert the following to higher terms. *(p. 37)*

$\frac{11}{33} = \frac{?}{264}$

8. Find the LCD of the following by using prime numbers. Show your work. *(p. 41)*

$\frac{1}{4} + \frac{1}{7} + \frac{1}{2} + \frac{1}{14}$

9. Subtract the following. *(p. 43)*

$14\frac{7}{9}$
$- 8\frac{5}{6}$

Complete the following using the cancellation technique. *(p. 46)*

10. $\frac{9}{14} \times \frac{2}{4} \times \frac{4}{6}$

11. $7\frac{3}{8} \times \frac{16}{19}$

12. $\frac{3}{4} \div 3$

13. A trip to Maryland from Boston will take you $8\frac{1}{2}$ hours. If you have traveled $\frac{1}{5}$ of the way, how much longer will the trip take? *(p. 46)*

14. Chairs.com produces 310 beanbag chairs per hour. If the machine runs $40\frac{1}{2}$ hours, how many chairs will the machine produce? *(p. 46)*

15. A taste-testing survey of Nature Foods showed that $\frac{2}{5}$ of the people surveyed preferred the taste of soy milk to regular milk. If 60,000 people were in the survey, how many favored soy milk? How many chose regular milk? *(p. 46)*

16. Lori Sharpe, an employee of Alamo Rent-A-Car, worked $7\frac{1}{4}$ hours on Monday, $4\frac{1}{4}$ hours on Tuesday, $8\frac{1}{2}$ hours on Wednesday, $8\frac{1}{4}$ hours on Thursday, and 8 hours on Friday. How many total hours did Lori work during the week? *(p. 42)*

17. Clairol offered a $\frac{1}{4}$ rebate on its $20 hair dryer. Melissa bought a Clairol hair dryer. What did Melissa pay after the rebate? *(p. 46)*

PERSONAL FINANCE

A Kiplinger Approach

Here's how to get one—fast. *By Catherine Siskos*

MAKING HISTORY

● After being turned down once, New York teacher Barbara Frailey, 27, finally got her first credit card—with a $200 limit.

BARBARA Frailey lives in an apartment in Brooklyn and is a full-time teacher. She pays her bills on time each month, and her only outstanding debt is a small amount on a student loan. Until recently, Frailey, 27, didn't even have a credit card—although not by choice. She once responded to a card offer through the mail but was turned down—ironically, because she had no history of repaying debt. "I was so discouraged that I didn't bother trying for a while," says Frailey. When she received a mail solicitation recently from Capital One Visa, she applied and got her first card—with a $200 credit line.

Credit card issuers can't seem to deal plastic fast enough to college students with no credit history and no income. It's estimated that more than two-thirds of college students have credit cards because banks and other issuers are willing to gamble that parents will bail out their kids if they get into trouble. But if you're among the one-third of students who resist the pressure to get a card while in school, once you graduate you may find that you're considered as risky a credit prospect as Bonnie or Clyde.

"The best way to get credit is to be in debt," says Todd Meagher, president of Credit.com, a consumer-educa-tion Web site, because card issuers can gauge how reliable you are when it comes to repaying. Credit card and mortgage payments are regularly reported to the three credit bureaus (Equifax, 888-532-0179; Trans Union, 800-888-4213; and Experian, 888-397-3742), but most consumer payments—including rent, insurance and even student loans—are not, unless there's a problem. "You could pay your rent and utilities for five years and be a good customer, and you won't get any credit for it," says Meagher. "But miss a payment once and—*bam*—it's on your credit report."

That doesn't mean you've missed the boat if you didn't get a credit card in college. Competition is so fierce among card issuers that you may be able to establish a satisfactory history in as little as six months—rather than the year or more it used to take. If you play your cards right, you might even be able to get credit immediately.

Winning strategies. Start by checking copies of your credit report. If you've been turned down for credit within the past 60 days, the credit bureaus will send you a copy of your report free; otherwise, you'll pay up to $8.50 for each report. Correct any errors and clear up any disputes before you apply for a card.

Apply first at the bank or credit union where you have a checking or savings account. As long as you're employed full-time and haven't bounced any checks, your bank will probably be willing to issue you a card with a low credit limit—say, $200—and gradually ratchet up that limit if you pay your bills on time. The longer you've lived at your current address or worked for the same employer, the safer a risk you are.

If your bank isn't willing to issue you a card right away, you can build a credit history over several months with a department-store or gasoline card (both of which are easier to get) or even with a small bank loan, as long as your payments are reported to the credit bureaus. Bank of America and other major banks often have programs to help you establish good credit, for instance, by making you a loan that you repay before getting the money. After repaying a $500 loan, for example, you'll have $500 plus a good payment record—and the rest will be credit history.

First-time cardholders with limited or no credit history rarely qualify for low interest rates. But you should take the card anyway, advises Meagher. "You can always renegotiate the rate after six months." If you pay your credit card bill in full each month,

---

Business Math Issue

Parents will bail out students if they get in credit card trouble.
1. List the key points of the article and information to support your position.
2. Write a group defense of your position using math calculations to support your view.

HOLLYWOOD JOURNAL / By Daniel Costello

Movie Seats: Thumbs Down?

*Fancy New Theaters Promise
Big Seats, but How Big?
Here's the Tale of the Tape*

NEXT TIME you fidget in your seat at the movies, don't blame the director. Blame the seats.

The past few years have seen the largest expansion in movie-theater history, a building binge that has nearly crippled some of the nation's biggest chains. So in an effort to stand out, theaters keep bragging about their big, comfy chairs. And while moviegoers clearly enjoy many of the improvements, some still say they feel a little uncomfortable in certain theaters.

That's because even with their new stadium and club seats, some movie-theater chains are doing everything from moving seats closer to the screen to simply not upgrading seats as much as they should. Legroom may be the biggest problem: To compensate for the new chairs, some theaters have been shaving off a few very noticeable inches.

So we went out with our tape measure in hand (and plenty of popcorn) and randomly sized up the seats at five chains in New York, Los Angeles and Boston. The Showcase Cinemas chain, for example, may brag about its "rocking recliners" and "plush cushioning" in ads, but we found these seats had only three inches of padding, and legroom—at 39 inches—that wasn't much better than competitors. Many of our measurements were all over the map.

"Some seats are still more like flying coach while others are more like first class," says Dana Wilson, a spokeswoman for Showcase. (She still insists, though, that the chain's new seats are "some of the best in the business.")

I liked the cushions

I thought the armrests were anticlimactic.

TICKETS

Gary Clement

Seating Chart

Movie theaters hype the seats in their new mall-size multiplexes, but all seats aren't created equal. Here's how they measured up at theaters we tried. (Theater chains confirmed these measurements are representative of their new theaters).

THEATER	SEAT WIDTH/ SEATBACK	LEGROOM	CUSHION	COMMENT
AMC Theatres	22"/ 41"	42"	3"	These seats were a toss-up: The width was among the smallest we tried, but the legroom was more generous than any in the bunch.
Loews Theaters	22½"/ 32.2"	39"	2.6"	Ouch! The cushioning here was the slimmest among the chains we tried, and there was no padding on the armrests. But a big plus: The front row was almost 14 feet from the screen.
Regal Cinemas	21½"/ 41"	38"	5"	Some of the comfiest seats around. They also have swing-up armrests, so moviegoers can snuggle if the mood hits.
Showcase Cinemas	24½"/ 34"	39"	3"	Chain boasts of having "the best seats in the business," but, sizewise, they fall somewhere in the middle.
United Artists Theaters	23"/ 42¼"	32½"	4"	Could be tough for the big guys: The legroom was considerably smaller here than at other theaters.

PROJECT A

What is the difference in the seatwidth/seatback between Regal Cinemas and Showcase Cinemas? Visit the website of your local theater chain and evaluate its presentation.

Internet Projects: See text website (www.mhhe.com/slater7e) and *The Business Math Internet Resource Guide.*

International Online Usage

Average Days Per Month Online

Japan	13.9
United States	12.7
Canada	12.0
Australia	11.1
Germany	9.9
United Kingdom	8.9
France	7.7

Average Minutes Spent Per Day

United States	70.6
Canada	54.2
Australia	52.4
Japan	44.9
Germany	39.7
United Kingdom	39.2
France	35.4

Source: Media Metrix (www.mediametrix.com)

Decimals

LU 3–1: Rounding Decimals; Fraction and Decimal Conversions

- Explain the place values of whole numbers and decimals; round decimals *(pp. 64–65).*

- Convert decimal fractions to decimals, proper fractions to decimals, mixed numbers to decimals, and pure and mixed decimals to decimal fractions *(pp. 66–68).*

LU 3–2: Adding, Subtracting, Multiplying, and Dividing Decimals

- Add, subtract, multiply, and divide decimals *(pp. 69–70).*

- Multiply and divide decimals by shortcut methods *(pp. 70–71).*

- Complete decimal applications in foreign currency *(pp. 71–72).*

© 2001 Dow Jones & Company, Inc.

In Chapter 2 you learned about fractions. As you probably know, prior to the year 2001, all stock exchange quotes were given in fractional terms. However, beginning in 2001, all stock exchange quotes are expressed in decimals. This means that a stock such as IBM will be now quoted at $110.55. This cartoon from *The Wall Street Journal* clipping "NYSE Adds Decimals, Subtracts Fractions" illustrates the end of the fraction in the stock market and the entrance of the decimal.

Chapter 2 introduced the 1.69-ounce bag of M&M's® shown in Table 3.1. Note that in Table 3.1 we give the fractional breakdown of the six colors in the 1.69-ounce bag of M&M's® and express the values in decimals. We have rounded the decimal equivalents to the nearest hundredths.

This chapter is divided into two learning units. The first unit discusses rounding decimals, converting fractions to decimals, and converting decimals to fractions. The second unit shows you how to add, subtract, multiply, and divide decimals, along with some shortcuts for multiplying and dividing decimals. Added to this unit is a global application of decimals dealing with foreign exchange rates.

One of the most common uses of decimals occurs when we spend dollars and cents, which is a *decimal number.* A **decimal,** then, is a decimal number with digits to the right of a *decimal point,* indicating that decimals, like fractions, are parts of a whole that are less than one. Thus, we can interchange the terms *decimals* and *decimal numbers.* Remembering this will avoid confusion between the terms *decimal, decimal number,* and *decimal point.*

LEARNING UNIT 3–1 | ROUNDING DECIMALS; FRACTION AND DECIMAL CONVERSIONS

Remember to read the decimal point as *and.*

In Chapter 1 we stated that the **decimal point** is the center of the decimal numbering system. So far we have studied the whole numbers to the left of the decimal point and the parts of whole numbers called fractions. We also learned that the position of the digits in

TABLE 3.1

Analyzing a bag of M&M's®

Sharon Hoogstraten.

Color*	Fraction	Decimal
Yellow	$\frac{18}{55}$	.33
Red	$\frac{10}{55}$	.18
Blue	$\frac{9}{55}$	.16
Orange	$\frac{7}{55}$	.13
Brown	$\frac{6}{55}$	.11
Green	$\frac{5}{55}$	.09
Total	$\frac{55}{55} = 1$	1.00

*The color ratios currently given are a sample used for educational purposes. They do not represent the manufacturer's color ratios.

FIGURE 3.1

Decimal place-value chart

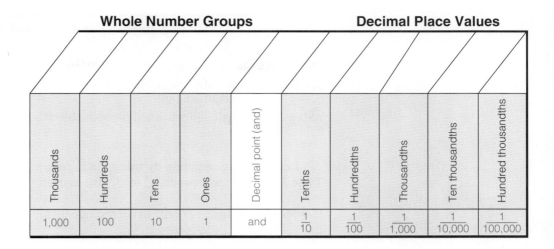

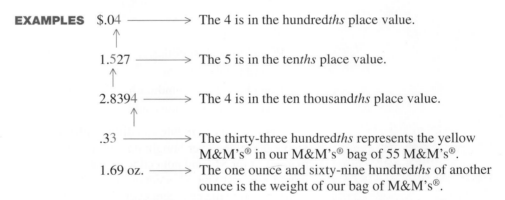

a whole number gives the place values of the digits (Figure 1.1). Now we will study the position (place values) of the digits to the right of the decimal point (Figure 3.1). Note that the words to the right of the decimal point end in *ths*.

You should understand the relationship of the place values of the digits on either side of the decimal point. If you move a digit to the left of the decimal point by place (ones, tens, and so on), you *increase* its value 10 times for each place. If you move a digit to the right of the decimal point by place (tenths, hundredths, and so on), you *decrease* its value 10 times for each place. This is why the decimal point is the center of the decimal system.

EXAMPLES $.04 ⟶ The 4 is in the hundred*ths* place value.

1.527 ⟶ The 5 is in the ten*ths* place value.

2.8394 ⟶ The 4 is in the ten thousand*ths* place value.

.33 ⟶ The thirty-three hundred*ths* represents the yellow M&M's® in our M&M's® bag of 55 M&M's®.

1.69 oz. ⟶ The one ounce and sixty-nine hundred*ths* of another ounce is the weight of our bag of M&M's®.

Do you recall from Chapter 1 how you used a place-value chart to read or write whole numbers in verbal form? To read or write decimal numbers, you read or write the decimal number as if it were a whole number. Then you use the name of the decimal place of the last digit as given in Figure 3.1. For example, you would read or write the decimal .0796 as seven hundred ninety-six ten thousandths (the last digit, 6, is in the ten thousandths place).

To read a decimal with four or fewer whole numbers, you can also refer to Figure 3.1. For larger whole numbers, refer to the whole-number place-value chart in Chapter 1 (Figure 1.1). For example, from Figure 3.1 you would read the number 126.2864 as one hundred twenty-six and two thousand eight hundred sixty-four ten thousandths. Remember that the *and* is the decimal point.

Now let's round decimals. Rounding decimals is similar to the rounding of whole numbers that you learned in Chapter 1.

Rounding Decimals

From Table 3.1, you know that the 1.69-ounce bag of M&M's® introduced in Chapter 2 contained $\frac{18}{55}$, or .33, yellow M&M's®. The .33 was rounded to the nearest hundredth. **Rounding decimals** involves the following steps:

Rounding Decimals to a Specified Place Value

Step 1. Identify the place value of the digit you want to round.

Step 2. If the digit to the right of the identified digit in Step 1 is 5 or more, increase the identified digit by 1. If the digit to the right is less than 5, do not change the identified digit.

Step 3. Drop all digits to the right of the identified digit.

Let's practice rounding by using the $\frac{18}{55}$ yellow M&M's® that we rounded to .33 in Table 3.1. Before we rounded $\frac{18}{55}$ to .33, the number we rounded was .3272727.

EXAMPLE Round .3272727 to nearest hundredth.

Step 1. .3272727   The identified digit is 2, which is in the hundredths place (two places to the right of the decimal point).

Step 2.   The digit to the right of 2 is more than 5 (7). Thus, 2, the identified digit in Step 1, is changed to 3.

.3372727

Step 3. .33   Drop all other digits to right of the identified digit 3.

We could also round the .3272727 M&M's® to the nearest tenth or thousandth as follows:

	Tenth		**or**		**Thousandth**
.3272727	→ .3		.3272727	→ .327	

OTHER EXAMPLES

Round to nearest dollar:	$166.39	→	$166
Round to nearest cent:	$1,196.885	→	$1,196.89
Round to nearest hundredth:	$38.563	→	$38.56
Round to nearest thousandth:	$1,432.9981	→	$1,432.998

The rules for rounding can differ with the situation in which rounding is used. For example, have you ever bought one item from a supermarket produce department that was marked "3 for $1" and noticed what the cashier charged you? One item marked "3 for $1" would not cost you $33\frac{1}{3}$ cents rounded to 33 cents. You will pay 34 cents. Many retail stores round to the next cent even if the digit following the identified digit is less than $\frac{1}{2}$ of a penny. In this text we round on the concept of 5 or more.

Fraction and Decimal Conversions

In business operations we must frequently convert fractions to decimal numbers and decimal numbers to fractions. This section begins by discussing three types of fraction-to-decimal conversions. Then we discuss converting pure and mixed decimals to decimal fractions.

Converting Decimal Fractions to Decimals

From Figure 3.1 you can see that a **decimal fraction** (expressed in the digits to the right of the decimal point) is a fraction with a denominator that has a power of 10, such as $\frac{1}{10}$, $\frac{17}{100}$, and $\frac{23}{1,000}$. To convert a decimal fraction to a decimal, follow these steps:

Converting Decimal Fractions to Decimals

Step 1. Count the number of zeros in the denominator.

Step 2. Place the numerator of the decimal fraction to the right of the decimal point the same number of places as you have zeros in the denominator. (The number of zeros in the denominator gives the number of digits your decimal has to the right of the decimal point.) Do not go over the total number of denominator zeros.

Now let's change $\frac{3}{10}$ and its higher multiples of 10 to decimals.

EXAMPLES

	Verbal form	Decimal fraction	Decimal	Number of decimal places to right of decimal point
a.	Three tenths	$\frac{3}{10}$	.3	1
b.	Three hundredths	$\frac{3}{100}$	.03	2
c.	Three thousandths	$\frac{3}{1,000}$	.003	3
d.	Three ten thousandths	$\frac{3}{10,000}$	.0003	4

Note how we show the different values of the decimal fractions above in decimals. The zeros after the decimal point and before the number 3 indicate these values. If you added zeros after the number 3, you do not change the value. Thus, the numbers .3 , .30 , and .300 have the same value. So 3 tenths of a pizza, 30 hundredths of a pizza, and 300 thousandths of a pizza are the same total amount of pizza. The first pizza is sliced into 10 pieces. The second pizza is sliced into 100 pieces. The third pizza is sliced into 1,000 pieces. Also, we didn't need to place a zero to the left of the decimal point.

Converting Proper Fractions to Decimals

Recall from Chapter 2 that proper fractions are fractions with a value less than 1. That is, the numerator of the fraction is smaller than its denominator. How can we convert these proper fractions to decimals? Since proper fractions are a form of division, it is possible to convert proper fractions to decimals by carrying out the division.

Converting Proper Fractions to Decimals

Step 1. Divide the numerator of the fraction by its denominator. (If necessary, add a decimal point and zeros to the number in the numerator.)

Step 2. Round as necessary.

EXAMPLES

$$\frac{3}{4} = 4\overline{)3.00} \quad \begin{array}{r} .75 \\ \hline \end{array}$$
$$\begin{array}{r} 2\ 8 \\ \hline 20 \\ 20 \\ \hline \end{array}$$

$$\frac{3}{8} = 8\overline{)3.000} \quad \begin{array}{r} .375 \\ \hline \end{array}$$
$$\begin{array}{r} 2\ 4 \\ \hline 60 \\ 56 \\ \hline 40 \\ 40 \\ \hline \end{array}$$

$$\frac{1}{3} = 3\overline{)1.000} \quad \begin{array}{r} .33\overline{3} \\ \hline \end{array}$$
$$\begin{array}{r} 9 \\ \hline 10 \\ 9 \\ \hline 10 \\ 9 \\ \hline 1 \end{array}$$

Note that in the last example 1/3, the 3 in the quotient keeps repeating itself (never ends). We call this a **repeating decimal.** The short bar over the last 3 means that the number endlessly repeats.

Converting Mixed Numbers to Decimals

A mixed number, you will recall from Chapter 2, is the sum of a whole number greater than zero and a proper fraction. To convert mixed numbers to decimals, use the following steps:

Converting Mixed Numbers to Decimals

Step 1. Convert the fractional part of the mixed number to a decimal (as illustrated in the previous section).

Step 2. Add the converted fractional part to the whole number.

EXAMPLE

$$8\frac{2}{5} = \textbf{(Step 1)} \quad 5\overline{)2.0} \quad \textbf{(Step 2)} \; 8 + .4 = \boxed{8.4}$$
$$\underline{2\,0}$$

Now that we have converted fractions to decimals, let's convert decimals to fractions.

Converting Pure and Mixed Decimals to Decimal Fractions

A **pure decimal** has no whole number(s) to the left of the decimal point (.43, .458, and so on). A **mixed decimal** is a combination of a whole number and a decimal. An example of a mixed decimal follows.

EXAMPLE 737.592 = Seven hundred thirty-seven and five hundred ninety-two
thousandths

Note the following conversion steps for converting pure and mixed decimals to decimal fractions:

Converting Pure and Mixed Decimals to Decimal Fractions

Step 1. Place the digits to the right of the decimal point in the numerator of the fraction. Omit the decimal point. (For a decimal fraction with a fractional part, see examples **c** and **d** below.)

Step 2. Put a 1 in the denominator of the fraction.

Step 3. Count the number of digits to the right of the decimal point. Add the same number of zeros to the denominator of the fraction. For mixed decimals, add the fraction to the whole number.

If desired, you can reduce the fractions in Step 3.

EXAMPLES

		Step 1	Step 2	Places	Step 3
a.	.3	$\underline{3}$	$\dfrac{3}{1}$	1	$\dfrac{3}{10}$
b.	.24	$\underline{24}$	$\dfrac{24}{1}$	2	$\dfrac{24}{100}$
c.	.24$\frac{1}{2}$	$\underline{245}$	$\dfrac{245}{1}$	3	$\dfrac{245}{1,000}$

Before completing Step 1 in example **c,** we must remove the fractional part, convert it to a decimal ($\frac{1}{2}$ = .5), and multiply it by .01 (.5 × .01 = .005). We use .01 because the 4 of .24 is in the hundredths place. Then we add .005 + .24 = .245 (three places to right of the decimal) and complete Steps 1, 2, and 3.

d.	.07$\frac{1}{4}$	$\underline{725}$	$\dfrac{725}{1}$	4	$\dfrac{725}{10,000}$

In example **d**, be sure to convert $\frac{1}{4}$ to .25 and multiply by .01. This gives .0025. Then add .0025 to .07, which is .0725 (four places), and complete Steps 1, 2, and 3.

e.	17.45	$\underline{45}$	$\dfrac{45}{1}$	2	$\dfrac{45}{100} = 17\dfrac{45}{100}$

Example **e** is a mixed decimal. Since we substitute *and* for the decimal point, we read this mixed decimal as seventeen and forty-five hundredths. Note that after we converted the .45 of the mixed decimals to a fraction, we added it to the whole number 17.

LU 3–1 PRACTICE QUIZ

Write the following as a decimal number.

  1. Four hundred eight thousandths

Name the place position of the identified digit:

  2. 6.8241   **3.** 9.3942
                              ↑

Round each decimal to place indicated:

		Tenth	**Thousandth**
4.	.62768	a.	b.
5.	.68341	a.	b.

Convert the following to decimals:

6. $\dfrac{9}{10,000}$ 7. $\dfrac{14}{100,000}$

Convert the following to decimal fractions (do not reduce):

8. .819   9. 16.93   10. $.05\dfrac{1}{4}$

Convert the following fractions to decimals and round answer to nearest hundredth:

11. $\dfrac{1}{6}$ 12. $\dfrac{3}{8}$ 13. $12\dfrac{1}{8}$

✓ SOLUTIONS

1. .408 (3 places to right of decimal)

2. Hundredths   3. Thousandths

4. a. .6 (identified digit 6—digit to right less than 5)   b. .628 (identified digit 7—digit to right greater than 5)

5. a. .7 (identified digit 6—digit to right greater than 5)   b. .683 (identified digit 3—digit to right less than 5)

6. .0009 (4 places)   7. .00014 (5 places)

8. $\dfrac{819}{1,000}\left(\dfrac{819}{1 + 3\ \text{zeros}}\right)$ 9. $16\dfrac{93}{100}$

10. $\dfrac{525}{10,000}\left(\dfrac{525}{1 + 4\ \text{zeros}}\ \dfrac{1}{4} \times .01 = .0025 + .05 = .0525\right)$

11. .16666 = .17   12. .375 = .38   13. 12.125 = 12.13

LEARNING UNIT 3–2 | ADDING, SUBTRACTING, MULTIPLYING, AND DIVIDING DECIMALS

$27.98 Air Fare To Paris, China? United: 'Oops'

By JANE COSTELLO
WSJ.com

Eric Bescher almost flew to Paris for less than $30.

An elite level United Airlines frequent flier from Los Angeles, Mr. Bescher visited United's Web site on Jan. 31 to search for a low fare to Europe in March. The deal he found was a lot better than he'd bargained for—passage to France for less than the price of a bottle of good burgundy. A technical glitch at the site listed the round-trip fare from San Jose to Paris as just $27.98. "I snapped it up right away," he says.

Have you flown from Los Angeles to Paris? If you have, you know the fare is expensive. Like Mr. Bescher in *The Wall Street Journal* clipping "$27.98 Air Fare to Paris, China? United: 'Oops,'" you may have also visited United's website looking for a bargain fare. The clipping states that Mr. Bescher did indeed find a bargain—$27.98 round-trip.

The regular price to fly to Paris is usually $573.00. With the website price of $27.98, Mr. Bescher saved $545.02 ($573.00 − $27.98). As you might expect, he "snapped it up right away" as did many other bargain seekers. However, United billed Mr. Bescher's credit card $573.00. According to United, a computer bug "zeroed out" the fare on a number of international flights so the amount shown reflected only a portion of the taxes and miscellaneous fees.

Mr. Bescher immediately contacted United's customer service office and complained that the charge was unauthorized. United replied by saying it would not honor the $27.98 fare. Eventually, United honored their Web $27.98 fare and kept the goodwill of many customers.

AP Photo/Paul Sakuma

Now you are ready to make calculations involving decimals.

Addition and Subtraction of Decimals

Since you know how to add and subtract whole numbers, to add and subtract decimal numbers you have only to learn about the placement of the decimals. The following steps will help you:

> **Adding and Subtracting Decimals**
>
> **Step 1.** Vertically write the numbers so that the decimal points align. You can place additional zeros to the right of the decimal point if needed without changing the value of the number.
>
> **Step 2.** Add or subtract the digits starting with the right column and moving to the left.
>
> **Step 3.** Align the decimal point in the answer with the above decimal points.

EXAMPLES Add 4 + 7.3 + 36.139 + .0007 + 8.22.

Whole number to the right of the last digit is assumed to have a decimal. →

$$
\begin{array}{r}
4.0000 \\
7.3000 \\
36.1390 \\
.0007 \\
8.2200 \\
\hline
55.6597
\end{array}
$$

← Extra zeros have been added to make calculation easier.

Subtract 45.3 − 15.273.

$$
\begin{array}{r}
{}^{2\,9\,10}\\
45.3\cancel{00} \\
-\ 15.273 \\
\hline
30.027
\end{array}
$$

Subtract 7 − 6.9.

$$
\begin{array}{r}
{}^{6\,10}\\
7.\cancel{0} \\
-\ 6.9 \\
\hline
.1
\end{array}
$$

Multiplication of Decimals

The multiplication of decimal numbers is similar to the multiplication of whole numbers except for the additional step of placing the decimal in the answer (product). The steps that follow simplify this procedure.

Multiplying Decimals

Step 1. Multiply the numbers as whole numbers ignoring the decimal points.

Step 2. Count and total the number of decimal places in the multiplier and multiplicand.

Step 3. Starting at the right in the product, count to the left the number of decimal places totaled in Step 2. Place the decimal point so that the product has the same number of decimal places as totaled in Step 2. If the total number of places is greater than the places in the product, insert zeros in front of the product.

EXAMPLES

$$
\begin{array}{r}
8.52 \ \ \text{(2 decimal places)} \\
\times \ \ 6.7 \ \ \text{(1 decimal place)} \\
\hline
5\ 964 \\
51\ 12 \\
\hline
57.084
\end{array}
$$

Step 1, Step 2, Step 3

$$
\begin{array}{r}
2.36 \ \ \text{(2 places)} \\
\times \ \ .016 \ \ \text{(3 places)} \\
\hline
1416 \\
236 \\
\hline
.03776
\end{array}
$$
Need to add zero

Division of Decimals

If the divisor in your decimal division problem is a whole number, first place the decimal point in the quotient directly above the decimal point in the dividend. Then divide as usual. If the divisor has a decimal point, complete the steps that follow.

Dividing Decimals

Step 1. Make the divisor a whole number by moving the decimal point to the right.

Step 2. Move the decimal point in the dividend to the right the same number of places that you moved the decimal point in the divisor (Step 1). If there are not enough places, add zeros to the right of the dividend.

Step 3. Place the decimal point in the quotient above the new decimal point in the dividend. Divide as usual.

EXAMPLE

Step 3 — Step 1 — Step 2

$$
\begin{array}{r}
1\ 3.12 \\
2.5\overline{)32.8.00} \\
25 \\
\hline
7\ 8 \\
7\ 5 \\
\hline
3\ 0 \\
2\ 5 \\
\hline
50 \\
50 \\
\hline
\end{array}
$$

Stop a moment and study the above example. Note that the quotient does not change when we multiply the divisor and the dividend by the same number. This is why we can move the decimal point in division problems and always divide by a whole number.

Decimal Applications in Foreign Currency

If you look at *The Wall Street Journal* clipping "Treading Water," you will see the total amount of bad-loan write-offs that Japanese banks had converted from the current rate of yen to U.S. dollars. The table that follows gives the key currency cross rates.

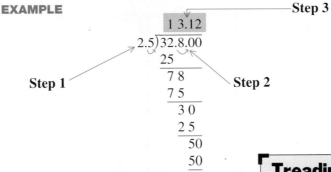

Treading Water

Total bad-loan liabilities and write-offs at Japanese banks, in billions of U.S. dollars converted from yen at current rate

Fiscal Years*	Bad-loan write-offs	Bad-loan balances
1996	$115.81	$246.31
1997	67.41	188.40
1998	114.94	257.54
1999	117.54	255.81
2000	59.63	262.73
2001 (First half)	19.88	274.82

*Fiscal years ending March 31

Source: Japan's Financial Services Agency

© 2001 Dow Jones & Company, Inc.

KEY CURRENCY CROSS RATES

	Dollar	Euro	Pound	SFranc	Gullder	Peso	Yen	Lira	D-Mark	FFranc	CdnDir
Canada............	1.5487	1.3573	2.2002	0.8848	.61588	.16814	.01264	.00070	.69392	.20690	....
France	7.4851	6.5599	10.6341	4.2765	2.9767	.81263	.06109	.00339	3.3538	....	4.8332
Germany	2.2318	1.9559	3.1707	1.2751	.88754	.24230	.01821	.00101	....	.29817	1.4411
Italy	2209.5	1936.4	3139.0	1262.3	878.65	239.87	18.032	....	989.99	295.18	1426.7
Japan..............	122.53	107.39	174.08	70.005	48.727	13.303	....	.05546	54.902	16.370	79.118
Mexico............	9.2110	8.0725	13.086	5.2625	3.6630	....	.07517	.00417	4.1272	1.2306	5.9476
Netherlands	2.5146	2.2038	3.5725	1.4367	....	.27300	.02052	.00114	1.1267	.33595	1.6237
Switzerland......	1.7503	1.5340	2.4867	....	.69606	.19002	.01428	.00079	.78425	.23384	1.1302
U.K.	.70390	.6169	....	.4021	.27992	.07642	.00574	.00032	.31539	.09404	.45450
*Euro..............	1.14100	....	1.6211	.65191	.45376	.12388	.00931	.00052	.51126	.15244	.73677
U.S.	....	.8764	1.4207	.57133	.39768	.10857	.00816	.00045	.44807	.13360	.64570

Source: Reuters

*12 countries in the European Economic Union are abandoning their local currencies in favor of Euro dollars. Those countries are: Germany, France, Italy, Austria, Spain, Portugal, Greece, Ireland, Belgium, Finland, Netherlands and Luxembourg.

From the first column in the table, you can see that in Canada the U.S. dollar is worth $1.5487. Let's assume that you want to buy a $3,500.00 Dell computer in Canada: What would it cost? If you multiply $3,500.00 by $1.5487, you can determine that in Canada the Dell computer would cost $5,420.45. How can you check this?

Look at the last item, $.64570, in the bottom far right column of the table. This number tells you that in the United States, the Canadian dollar is worth $.64570. Now multiply the $5,420.45 Canadian cost of the Dell computer by $.64570 and you get $3,500.00—the cost of the Dell computer in the United States.

$$\$3,500.00 \times \$1.5487 = \boxed{\$5,420.45} \longleftarrow \text{Cost in Canada}$$

Check* $\$5,420.45 \times \$.64570 = \$3,500.00 \longleftarrow$ Cost in United States

*Off 2 cents due to rounding.

Multiplication and Division Shortcuts for Decimals

The shortcut steps that follow show how to solve multiplication and division problems quickly involving multiples of 10.

Shortcuts for Multiples of 10

Multiplication

Step 1. Count the zeros in the multiplier.

Step 2. Move the decimal point in the multiplicand the same number of places to the right as you have zeros in the multiplier.

Division

Step 1. Count the zeros in the divisor.

Step 2. Move the decimal point in the dividend the same number of places to the left as you have zeros in the divisor.

In multiplication, the answers are *larger* than the original number.

EXAMPLE   If the art collector's average trip cost $252.59, what is the total value of 100 trips?

$$\$252.59 \times 100 = \boxed{\$25,259.} \qquad \text{(2 places to the right)}$$

OTHER EXAMPLES $6.89 \times 10 = \boxed{68.9}$ (1 place to the right)

$6.89 \times 100 = \boxed{689.}$ (2 places to the right)

$6.89 \times 1,000 = \boxed{6,890.}$ (3 places to the right)

In division, the answers are *smaller* than the original number.

EXAMPLES $6.89 \div 10 = \boxed{.689}$ (1 place to the left)

$6.89 \div 100 = \boxed{.0689}$ (2 places to the left)

$6.89 \div 1,000 = \boxed{.00689}$ (3 places to the left)

$6.89 \div 10,000 = \boxed{.000689}$ (4 places to the left)

Next, let's dissect and solve a word problem.

**How to Dissect and
Solve a Word Problem**

The Word Problem May O'Mally went to Sears to buy wall-to-wall carpet. She needs 101.3 square yards for downstairs, 16.3 square yards for the upstairs bedrooms, and 6.2 square yards for the halls. The carpet cost $14.55 per square yard. The padding cost $3.25 per square yard. Sears quoted an installation charge of $6.25 per square yard. What was May O'Mally's total cost?

By completing the following blueprint aid, we will slowly dissect this word problem. Note that before solving the problem, we gather the facts, identify what we are solving for, and list the steps that must be completed before finding the final answer, along with any key points we should remember. Let's go to it!

The facts	Solving for?	Steps to take	Key points
Carpet needed: 101.3 sq. yd.; 16.3 sq. yd.; 6.2 sq. yd. *Costs:* Carpet, $14.55 per sq. yd.; padding, $3.25 per sq. yd.; installation, $6.25 per sq. yd.	Total cost of carpet	Total square yards × Cost per square yard = Total cost.	Align decimals. Round answer to nearest cent.

Steps to solving problem

1. Calculate the total number of square yards.

$$\begin{array}{r} 101.3 \\ 16.3 \\ 6.2 \\ \hline 123.8 \text{ square yards} \end{array}$$

2. Calculate the total cost per square yard.

$$\begin{array}{r} \$14.55 \\ 3.25 \\ 6.25 \\ \hline \$24.05 \end{array}$$

3. Calculate the total cost of carpet.

$$123.8 \times \$24.05 = \boxed{\$2,977.39}$$

It's time to check your progress.

LU 3–2 PRACTICE QUIZ

1. Rearrange vertically and add:
   14, .642, 9.34, 15.87321

2. Rearrange and subtract:
   28.1549 − .885

3. Multiply and round the answer to the nearest tenth:
   28.53 × 17.4

4. Divide and round to the nearest hundredth:
   2,182 ÷ 2.83

Complete by the shortcut method:

5. 14.28 × 100   6. 9,680 ÷ 1,000   7. 9,812 ÷ 10,000

8. Could you help Mel decide which product is the "better buy"?

   Dog food A   **Dog food B**
   $9.01 for 64 ounces $7.95 for 50 ounces

   Round to the nearest cent as needed.

9. At Avis Rent-A-Car, the cost per day to rent a medium-size car is $39.99 plus 29 cents per mile. What is the charge to rent this car for 2 days if you drive 602.3 miles? You might want to complete a blueprint aid since the solution will show a completed one.

10. A trip to Mexico cost 6,000 pesos. What would this be in U.S. dollars? Check your answer.

✓ SOLUTIONS

1. 14.00000
      .64200
     9.34000
    15.87321
    $\boxed{39.85521}$

2. $\overset{\scriptstyle 7\ 10\ 14\ 14}{28.\cancel{1549}}$
    − .8850
    $\boxed{27.2699}$

Chapter 3 Decimals

3.
$$
\begin{array}{r}
28.53 \\
\times\ 17.4 \\
\hline
11\,412 \\
199\,71 \\
285\,3 \\
\hline
496{,}422 \\
\end{array}
$$
= 496.4

4.
$$
\begin{array}{r}
771.024 = 771.02 \\
2{,}83\overline{)218200{,}000} \\
1981 \\
\hline
2010 \\
1981 \\
\hline
290 \\
283 \\
\hline
7\,00 \\
5\,66 \\
\hline
1\,340 \\
1\,132 \\
\end{array}
$$

5. 14.28 = 1,428   **6.** 9,680 = 9.680   **7.** .9812 = .9812

8. A: $9.01 ÷ 64 = $.14   **B:** $7.95 ÷ 50 = $.16   Buy A.

9. Avis Rent-A-Car total rental charge:

The facts	Solving for?	Steps to take	Key points
Cost per day, $39.99. 29 cents per mile. Drove 602.3 miles. 2-day rental.	Total rental charge.	Total cost for 2 days' rental + Total cost of driving = Total rental charge.	In multiplication, count the number of decimal places. Starting from right to left in the product, insert decimal in appropriate place. Round to nearest cent.

Steps to solving problem

1. Calculate total costs for 2 days' rental. $39.99 × 2 = $79.98

2. Calculate the total cost of driving. $.29 × 602.3 = $174.667 = $174.67

3. Calculate the total rental charge.
$$
\begin{array}{r}
\$\ 79.98 \\
+\ 174.67 \\
\hline
\$254.65 \\
\end{array}
$$

10. 6,000 × $.10857 = $651.42

Check $651.42 × 9.2110 = 6,000.23 pesos due to rounding

Chapter Organizer and Reference Guide

Topic	Key point, procedure, formula	Example(s) to illustrate situation
Identifying place value, p. 65	$10, 1, \dfrac{1}{10}, \dfrac{1}{100}, \dfrac{1}{1{,}000}$, etc.	.439 in thousandths place value
Rounding decimals, p. 65	1. Identify place value of digit you want to round. 2. If digit to right of identified digit in Step 1 is 5 or more, increase identified digit by 1; if less than 5, do not change identified digit. 3. Drop all digits to right of identified digit.	.875 rounded to nearest tenth = .9 ↑ Identified digit
Converting decimal fractions to decimals, p. 66	1. Decimal fraction has a denominator with multiples of 10. Count number of zeros in denominator. 2. Zeros show how many places are in the decimal.	$\dfrac{8}{1{,}000}$ = .008 $\dfrac{6}{10{,}000}$ = .0006
Converting proper fractions to decimals, p. 67	1. Divide numerator of fraction by its denominator. 2. Round as necessary.	$\dfrac{1}{3}$ (to nearest tenth) = .3
Converting mixed numbers to decimals, p. 67	1. Convert fractional part of the mixed number to a decimal. 2. Add converted fractional part to whole number.	$6\dfrac{1}{4}$ $\dfrac{1}{4}$ = .25 + 6 = 6.25
Converting pure and mixed decimals to decimal fractions, p. 68	1. Place digits to right of decimal point in numerator of fraction. 2. Put 1 in denominator. 3. Add zeros to denominator, depending on decimal places of original number. For mixed decimals, add fraction to whole number.	.984 (3 places) 1. $\dfrac{984}{}$ 2. $\dfrac{984}{1}$ 3. $\dfrac{984}{1{,}000}$

(continues)

Chapter Organizer and Reference Guide (concluded)

Topic	Key point, procedure, formula	Example(s) to illustrate situation

Adding and subtracting decimals, p. 70	1. Vertically write and align numbers on decimal points.
	2. Add or subtract digits, starting with right column and moving to the left.
	3. Align decimal point in answer with above decimal points.
		Add 1.3 + 2 + .4
		
		1.3
		2.0
		.4
		‾‾‾
		3.7
		
		Subtract 5 − 3.9 4 10
		               5.0̸
		            − 3.9
		            ‾‾‾
		             1.1

Multiplying decimals, p. 70	1. Multiply numbers, ignoring decimal points. 2. Count and total number of decimal places in multiplier and multiplicand. 3. Starting at right in the product, count to the left the number of decimal places totaled in Step 2. Insert decimal point. If number of places greater than space in answer, add zeros.	2.48 (2 places) × .018 (3 places) ‾‾‾‾‾‾ 1 984 2 48 ‾‾‾‾‾ .04464

Dividing a decimal by a whole number, p. 71	1. Place decimal point in quotient directly above the decimal point in dividend.
	2. Divide as usual.
		1.1
		42)46.2
		  42
		  ‾‾
		  42
		  42
		  ‾‾

Dividing if the divisor is a decimal, p. 71	1. Make divisor a whole number by moving decimal point to the right.
	2. Move decimal point in dividend to the right the same number of places as in Step 1.
	3. Place decimal point in quotient above decimal point in dividend. Divide as usual.
		14.2
		2.9)41.39
		  29
		  ‾‾
		 123
		 116
		 ‾‾‾
		   79
		   58
		   ‾‾
		   21

Shortcuts on multiplication and division of decimals, p. 72	When multiplying by 10, 100, 1,000, and so on, move decimal point in multiplicand the same number of places to the right as you have zeros in multiplier. For division, move decimal point to the left.	4.85 × 100 = 485 4.85 ÷ 100 = .0485
Key terms	Decimal, *p. 64* Mixed decimal, *p. 68* Repeating decimal, *p. 67* Decimal fraction, *p. 66* Pure decimal, *p. 68* Rounding decimals, *p. 65* Decimal point, *p. 64*	

Note: For how to dissect and solve a word problem, see page 73.

Critical Thinking Discussion Questions

1. What are the steps for rounding decimals? Federal income tax forms allow the taxpayer to round each amount to the nearest dollar. Do you agree with this?

2. Explain how to convert fractions to decimals. If 1 out of 20 people buys a Land Rover, how could you write an advertisement in decimals?

3. Explain why .07, .70, and .700 are not equal. Assume you take a family trip to Disney World that covers 500 miles. Show that $\frac{8}{10}$ of the trip, or .8 of the trip, represents 400 miles.

4. Explain the steps in the addition or subtraction of decimals. Visit a car dealership and find the difference between two sticker prices. Be sure to check each sticker price for accuracy. Should you always pay the sticker price?

END-OF-CHAPTER PROBLEMS

DRILL PROBLEMS

Identify the place value for the following:

3–1. 9.55682
↑

3–2. 162.891
↑

Round the following as indicated;

	Tenth	Hundredth	Thousandth
3–3. .9482			
3–4. .7481			
3–5. 6.9245			
3–6. 6.8415			
3–7. 6.5555			
3–8. 75.9913			

Round the following to the nearest cent:

3–9. $2,011.669

3–10. $4,892.046

Convert the following types of decimal fractions to decimals (round to nearest hundredth as needed):

3–11. $\frac{7}{100}$

3–12. $\frac{4}{10}$

3–13. $\frac{91}{1,000}$

3–14. $\frac{910}{1,000}$

3–15. $\frac{64}{100}$

3–16. $\frac{979}{1,000}$

3–17. $14\frac{91}{100}$

Convert the following decimals to fractions. Do not reduce to lowest terms.

3-18. .6

3–19. .62

3–20. .006

3–21. .0125

3–22. .609

3–23. .825

3–24. .9999

3–25. .7065

Convert the following to mixed numbers. Do not reduce to lowest terms.

3–26. 8.2

3–27. 28.48

3–28. 6.025

Write the decimal equivalent of the following:

3–29. Four thousandths

3–30. Three hundred three and two hundredths

3–31. Eighty-five ten thousandths

3–32. Seven hundred seventy-five thousandths

Rearrange the following and add:

3–33. .115, 10.8318, 4.7, 802.4811

3–34. .005, 2,002.181, 795.41, 14.0, .184

Rearrange the following and subtract:

3–35. 9.2 − 5.8

3–36. 7 − 2.0815

3–37. 3.4 − 1.08

Estimate by rounding all the way and multiply the following (do not round final answer):

3–38. 6.24 × 3.9   **3–39.** .413 × 3.07

      Estimate   **Estimate**

3–40. 675 × 1.92   **3–41.** 4.9 × .825

      Estimate   **Estimate**

Divide the following and round to the nearest hundredth:

3–42. .8931 ÷ 3   **3–43.** 29.432 ÷ .0012

3–44. .0065 ÷ .07   **3–45.** 7,742.1 ÷ 48

3–46. 8.95 ÷ 1.18   **3–47.** 2,600 ÷ .381

Convert the following to decimals and round to the nearest hundredth:

3–48. $\dfrac{1}{8}$ **3–49.** $\dfrac{1}{25}$ **3–50.** $\dfrac{5}{6}$ **3–51.** $\dfrac{5}{8}$

Complete these multiplications and divisions by the shortcut method (do not do any written calculations):

3–52. 96.7 ÷ 10   **3–53.** 258.5 ÷ 100   **3–54.** 8.51 × 1,000

3–55. .86 ÷ 100   **3–56.** 9.015 × 100   **3–57.** 48.6 × 10

3–58. 750 × 10   **3–59.** 3,950 ÷ 1,000   **3–60.** 8.45 ÷ 10

3–61. 7.9132 × 1,000

WORD PROBLEMS

As needed, round answers to the nearest cent.

3–62. In preparation for a demonstration for a new Internet dot.com, 1,200 seats were set up. During the demonstration, 80 seats were vacant. In decimals to nearest hundredth, show how many seats were filled.

3–63. Al Fox got 6 hits out of 11 at bats. What was his batting average to the nearest thousandths place?

3–64. On May 22, 2001, the *Chicago Sun-Times* reported that Amazon.com dropped from its high for the last 52 weeks of $58.88 a share to $14.72 a share. You purchased 125 shares at the 52-week high. **(a)** What was your purchasing price? **(b)** What is the current selling price? **(c)** How much of a loss will you sustain if you sell your stock today?

3–65. Jane Lee purchased 18.49 yards of ribbon for the annual fair on the eBay auction site. Each yard cost 79 cents. What was the total cost of the ribbon before shipping charges?

3–66. Douglas Noel went to Home Depot and bought 4 doors at $42.99 each and 6 bags of fertilizer at $8.99 per bag. What was the total cost to Douglas? If Douglas had $300 in his pocket, what does he have left to spend?

3–67. The stock of Intel has a high of $30.25 today. It closed at $28.85. How much did the stock drop from its high?

3–68. Ed Weld is traveling by car to a comic convention in San Diego. His company will reimburse him $.39 per mile. If Ed travels 906.5 miles, how much will Ed receive from his company?

3–69. Mark Ogara rented a truck from Avis Rent-A-Car for the weekend (2 days). The base rental price was $29.95 per day plus $14\frac{1}{2}$ cents per mile. Mark drove 410.85 miles. How much does Mark owe?

3–70. On August 4, 2000, the *Daily Mail* wrote that Unilever had a sales profit of 1.16 billion in U.K. pounds and 10.3 billion in U.K. pounds in sales. How much would each be in U.S. dollars (use table in text)?

3–71. Pete Allan bought a scooter on the Web for $99.99. He saw the same scooter in the mall for $108.96. How much did Pete save by buying on the Web?

3–72. Russell is preparing the daily bank deposit for his coffee shop. Before the deposit, the coffee shop had a checking account balance of $3,185.66. The deposit contains the following checks:

| No. 1 | $ 99.50 | No. 3 | $8.75 |
| No. 2 | 110.35 | No. 4 | 6.83 |

Russell included $820.55 in currency with the deposit. What is the coffee shop's new balance, assuming Russell writes no new checks?

3–73. On July 23, 2000, *The New York Times* compared amusement park admission prices in Florida. The admission price to Orlando Science Center's planetarium, which includes a show, is $14.25 for adults, $13.25 for seniors, and $11 for children. You are visiting your grandparents and they plan to take the entire family to the planetarium. The members include 2 grandparents, 2 adults, and 2 children ages 4 and 10. What will be the total cost to attend the planetarium?

3–74. Randi went to Lowes to buy wall-to-wall carpeting. She needs 110.8 square yards for downstairs, 31.8 square yards for the halls, and 161.9 square yards for the bedrooms upstairs. Randi chose a shag carpet that costs $14.99 per square yard. She ordered foam padding at $3.10 per square yard. The carpet installers quoted Randi a labor charge of $3.75 per square yard. What will the total job cost Randi?

3–75. Art Norton bought 4 new Aquatred tires at Goodyear for $89.99 per tire. Goodyear charged $3.05 per tire for mounting, $2.95 per tire for valve stems, and $3.80 per tire for balancing. If Art paid no sales tax, what was his total cost for the 4 tires?

3–76. Shelly is shopping for laundry detergent, mustard, and canned tuna. She is trying to decide which of two products is the better buy. Using the following information, can you help Shelly?

Laundry detergent A	**Mustard A**	**Canned tuna A**
$2.00 for 37 ounces	$.88 for 6 ounces	$1.09 for 6 ounces

Laundry detergent B	**Mustard B**	**Canned tuna B**
$2.37 for 38 ounces	$1.61 for $12\frac{1}{2}$ ounces	$1.29 for $8\frac{3}{4}$ ounces

3–77. Roger bought season tickets to professional basketball games. The cost was $945.60. The season package included 36 home games. What is the average price of the tickets per game? Round to the nearest cent. Marcelo, Roger's friend, offered to buy 4 of the tickets from Roger. What is the total amount Roger should receive?

3–78. A nurse was to give her patients a 1.32-unit dosage of a prescribed drug. The total remaining units of the drug at the hospital pharmacy were 53.12. The nurse has 38 patients. Will there be enough dosages for all her patients?

3–79. Audrey Long went to Japan and bought an animation cell of Mickey Mouse. The price was 25,000 yen. What is the price in U.S. dollars? Check your answer.

ADDITIONAL SET OF WORD PROBLEMS

3–80. On Monday, the stock of IBM closed at $88.95. At the end of trading on Tuesday, IBM closed at $94.65. How much did the price of stock increase from Monday to Tuesday?

3–81. Tie Yang bought season tickets to the Boston Pops for $698.55. The season package included 38 performances. What is the average price of the tickets per performance? Round to nearest cent. Sam, Tie's friend, offered to buy 4 of the tickets from Tie. What is the total amount Tie should receive?

3–82. Morris Katz bought 4 new tires at Goodyear for $95.49 per tire. Goodyear also charged Morris $2.50 per tire for mounting, $2.40 per tire for valve stems, and $3.95 per tire for balancing. Assume no tax. What was Morris's total cost for the 4 tires?

3–83. *The New York Times*, dated June 3, 2001, compared a gallon of gasoline to a gallon of diesel. Diesel currently sells at an average of $1.45 a gallon as opposed to $1.70 for gasoline. What would be the cost of a fill-up of 12.6 gallons of **(a)** diesel, **(b)** gasoline, and **(c)** what is the difference?

3–84. Steven is traveling to a computer convention by car. His company will reimburse him $.29 per mile. If Steven travels 890.5 miles, how much will he receive from his company?

3–85. Gracie went to Home Depot to buy wall-to-wall carpeting for her house. She needs 104.8 square yards for downstairs, 17.4 square yards for halls, and 165.8 square yards for the upstairs bedrooms. Gracie chose a shag carpet that costs $13.95 per square yard. She ordered foam padding at $2.75 per square yard. The installers quoted Gracie a labor cost of $5.75 per square yard in installation. What will the total job cost Gracie?

3–86. The *National Mortgage News* dated March 5, 2001, revealed a month-by-month breakdown of business activity in private mortgage insurance (PMI). For the last six months of 2000, amounts expressed in millions were as follows: December, $16.8; November, $13.5; October, $12.9; September, $18.3; August, $15.1; and July $11.9. **(a)** What was the total dollar (in millions) activity? **(b)** What was the average per month? Round to the nearest million.

CHALLENGE PROBLEMS

3–87. The following items were charged in Canada to your bank credit card:

1.	Domino's Pizza, London, Canada	$15.32
2.	Shell 3001 Dougall Ave., Windsor, Canada	25.20
3.	Little Caesars, Ottawa, Canada	16.52
4.	Richmond Plaza Motel, Ottawa, Canada	79.08
5.	Petrocan Hwy. 401, Cambridge, Canada	14.90
6.	Mr. Gas #081, Kingston, Canada	14.39
7.	Days Inns, London, Canada	82.87

    a. Using the text exchange rates in your *Business Math Handbook,* find the amount you should be charged for each item.

    b. What should your total bill be? Check your answer.

3–88. Jill and Frank decided to take a long weekend in New York. City Hotel has a special getaway weekend for $79.95. The price is per person per night, based on double occupancy. The hotel has a minimum two-night stay. For this price, Jill and Frank will receive $50 credit toward their dinners at City's Skylight Restaurant. Also included in the package is a $3.99 credit per person toward breakfast for two each morning.

    Since Jill and Frank do not own a car, they plan to rent a car. The car rental agency charges $19.95 a day with an additional charge of $.22 a mile and $1.19 per gallon of gas used. The gas tank holds 24 gallons.

From the following facts, calculate the total expenses of Jill and Frank (round all answers to nearest hundredth or cent as appropriate). Assume no taxes.

Car rental (2 days):		Dinner cost at Skylight	$182.12
Beginning odometer reading	4,820	Breakfast for two:	
Ending odometer reading	4,940	Morning No. 1	24.17
Beginning gas tank: $\frac{3}{4}$ full.		Morning No. 2	26.88
Gas tank on return: $\frac{1}{2}$ full.			
Tank holds 24 gallons.			

SUMMARY PRACTICE TEST

1. Add the following by translating the verbal form to the decimal equivalent. *(p. 65)*

Five hundred thirty-eight and nine hundred three thousandths
Seventeen and fifty-eight hundredths
Three and three thousandths
Seventy-four hundredths
Two hundred three and nine tenths

Convert the following decimal fractions to decimals. *(p. 66)*

2. $\frac{6}{10}$ **3.** $\frac{6}{100}$ **4.** $\frac{6}{1,000}$

Convert the following to proper fractions or mixed numbers. Do not reduce to lowest terms. *(p. 67)*

5. .4   **6.** 8.95   **7.** .951

Convert the following fractions to decimals (or mixed decimals) and round to the nearest hundredth as needed. *(p. 68)*

8. $\frac{1}{7}$ **9.** $\frac{2}{7}$ **10.** $4\frac{5}{8}$ **11.** $\frac{1}{8}$

12. Rearrange the following and add. *(p. 70)*

6.4,   8.92,   9.481,   181.0832,   82.95

13. Subtract the following and round to the nearest tenth. *(p. 70)*

13.891 − 3.59

14. Multiply the following and round to the nearest hundredth. *(p. 71)*

7.3891 × 14.831

15. Divide the following and round to the nearest tenth. *(p. 71)*

118,555 ÷ 5.28

Complete the following by the shortcut method. *(p. 72)*

16. 86.33 × 1,000

17. 7,055,189.781 × 100

18. The average pay of employees is $610.99 per week. Garth earns $630.58 per week. How much is Garth's pay over the average? *(p. 70)*

19. Prudential reimburses Al $.33 per mile. Al submitted a travel log for a total of 1,610.8 miles. What will Prudential pay Al? Round to the nearest cent. *(p. 71)*

20. Jose Roy bought 2 new car tires from Goodyear for $99.55 per tire. Goodyear also charged Jose $3.88 per tire for mounting, $1.95 per tire for valve stems, and $5.10 per tire for balancing. What is Jose's final bill? *(p. 71)*

21. Could you help Bernie decide which of the following products is cheaper per ounce? *(p. 71)*

Canned fruit A	**Canned fruit B**
$.58 for 4 ounces	$.71 for $4\frac{3}{4}$ ounces

22. Bee Paul bought a watch in Italy for 15,000 lira. What is this in U.S. dollars? *(p. 72)*

23. Disney stock traded at a high of $42.85 and closed at $40.55. How much did the stock fall from its high? *(p. 70)*

TRAVEL | Check out this **AIRLINE WEB SITE** for cheap fares. *By Christopher Elliott*

ORBITZ TAKES FLIGHT

THE EARLY results are in, and the new and controversial online travel site, Orbitz, is mostly living up to its promise of low fares and customer-friendly service. Orbitz was spawned in the late 1990s, when airlines were struggling to reclaim some of the revenue earned by travel agents and Web sites for distributing tickets (commissions paid for domestic flights totaled $2.1 billion last year). Five carriers—American, Continental, Delta, Northwest and United—joined forces to create what became Orbitz.

The Orbitz edge: Its airline partners have agreed never to offer lower fares to competing sites and to sometimes offer the best deals exclusively through Orbitz. In theory, that would mean that no competitor could beat Orbitz—but in the convoluted world of airline fares, theories sometimes work as well as yesterday's boarding pass.

Check our chart at right. In some cases, Orbitz members offer lower fares on a competing site. How is that possible? Industry experts see a variety of explanations. For example, some sites may have access to ticket inventory that is sold through consolidators—essentially, tickets that are sold in bulk—which may be priced even lower than the ones offered directly by Orbitz members to the Orbitz site.

In addition, travel sites use different computer-reservation systems that have different inventory levels of certain tickets. So the tickets allotted to Orbitz at a certain low price may sell out more quickly than the tickets allotted to a competitor at the same or higher price. But once Orbitz's cheapest deals are gone, a competitor's price might slip below Orbitz's next-best offer. Finally, ticket prices change by the second, and no matter how fast a

HOW YOU'LL FARE ONLINE

Prices quoted are for a nonstop, 14-day-advance, round-trip economy-class ticket the week of June 20 to June 27, 2001. Other sites often beat or tied Orbitz (www.orbitz.com) on fares from Orbitz-member airlines.

FLIGHT	ORBITZ	EXPEDIA	SIDESTEP	TRAVELOCITY
New York (Kennedy) to Los Angeles	$426.50 (TWA)	$449.50 (American)	**$309.50 (American)**	$349.50 (TWA)
Chicago (O'Hare) to Dallas/Fort Worth	$263 (American)	$605 (American)	$254 (American)	**$227 (United)**
San Francisco (Intl) to Denver	**$312 (United)**	$328 (American)	$328 (United)	$328 (United)
Atlanta to Detroit	**$165 (Delta)**	$173 (Northwest/Delta)	**$165 (Delta)**	$173 (Northwest)

J.D. KING

computer system is, it can't update deals instantly.

So for now at least, the charge by competitors that Orbitz is anticompetitive—designed to use the airlines' power to set ticket prices and drive competing sites out of business—seems overblown. The U.S. Department of Transportation, which tentatively gave Orbitz a green light to launch this spring, plans to review it for antitrust concerns later this year.

Aside from pricing, Orbitz gets

high marks. Its Web site sports a simple, airy and almost minimalist look—a welcome change from the cluttered electronic storefronts run by Travelocity and Expedia. What's more, its booking mechanism is the best among online travel agencies. From fare search to purchase, buying travel on Orbitz is seamless and intuitive. But as our survey shows, Orbitz should be just one stop on your search for lower fares. **K** —*Reporter:* **DANIELLE GIOVANNELLI**

Business Math Issue

All ticket prices are basically the same. There is no need to shop around.
1. List the key points of the article and information to support your position.
2. Write a group defense of your position using math calculations to support your view.

BUSINESS MATH SCRAPBOOK
WITH INTERNET APPLICATION

Putting Your Skills to Work

Figuring Out the Tab

We asked five restaurants to tell us the ingredients of one of their entrees, and what they cost the restaurants wholesale. Then we bought the ingredients at the grocery store. The results:

RESTAURANT	DISH	INGREDIENTS	MENU PRICE	GROCERY STORE PRICE	WHOLESALE PRICE
Carmine's New York, NY	Zuppa di mussels	1 pound mussels with tomato sauce	$12	$3.15	$2.25–$2.50
Heaven on Seven Chicago, Ill.	Grilled Louisiana Gulf shrimp and Andouille sausage on bed of white rice (comes with a choice of cup of soup, gumbo or salad)	6 shrimp (about 6.5–7 ounces), 2.5 ounces andouille sausage, 6 ounces white rice, plus sauce and seasoning, and 1 cup of soup	$18.95	$9.00	$6.39
Grill 23 and Bar Boston, Mass.	Grilled swordfish	12 ounces swordfish	$24.50	$9.00	$4.50–$7.50
Docks New York, NY	Grilled tuna with steamed red potatoes and coleslaw	10 ounces tuna, 8 ounces potatoes, 5 ounces coleslaw	$20.50	$8.15	$6.55
Pinot Bistro Los Angeles, Calif.	Farm chicken with a roasted garlic glaze and Pinot fries	12 ounces chicken, 10 ounces french fries	$15.95	$3.00	$4.08

© 2000 Dow Jones & Company, Inc.

PROJECT A

For each restaurant, calculate the difference between the menu price and the grocery store price.

Go to the Web and find a restaurant of interest to you. Does the restaurant provide complete menus online?

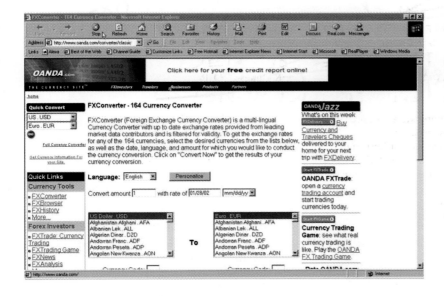

PROJECT B

Go to www.oanda.com/converter/classic. Find today's exchange rate from dollars to German marks by converting $1 to marks. Use this value to find how many marks $5,000 is worth. Confirm your answer by using the currency calculator.

Internet Projects: See text website (www.mhhe.com/slater7e) and *The Business Math Internet Resource Guide.*

CUMULATIVE REVIEW

A Word Problem Approach—Chapters 1, 2, 3

1. The top rate at the Waldorf Towers Hotel in New York is $390. The top rate at the Ritz Carlton in Boston is $345. If John spends 9 days at the hotel, how much can he save if he stays at the Ritz? *(p. 14)*

2. Robert Half Placement Agency was rated best by 4 to 1 in an independent national survey. If 250,000 responded to the survey, how many rated Robert Half the best? *(p. 44)*

3. Of the 63.2 million people who watch professional football, only $\frac{1}{5}$ watch the commercials. How many viewers do not watch the commercials? *(p. 44)*

4. AT&T advertised a 10-minute call for $2.27. MCI WorldCom's rate was $2.02. Assuming Bill Splat makes forty 10-minute calls, how much could he save by using MCI WorldCom? *(p. 70)*

5. A square foot of rental space in New York City, Boston, and Rhode Island costs as follows: New York City, $6.25; Boston, $5.75; and Rhode Island, $3.75. If Compaq Computer wants to rent 112,500 square feet of space, what will Compaq save by renting in Rhode Island rather than Boston? *(p. 70)*

6. American Airlines has a frequent-flier program. Coupon brokers who buy and sell these awards pay between 1 and $1\frac{1}{2}$ cents for each mile earned. Fred Dietrich earned a 50,000-mile award (worth two free tickets to any city). If Fred decided to sell his award to a coupon broker, approximately how much would he receive? *(p. 71)*

7. Lillie Wong bought 4 new Firestone tires at $82.99 each. Firestone also charged $2.80 per tire for mounting, $1.95 per tire for valves, and $3.15 per tire for balancing. Lillie turned her 4 old tires in to Firestone, which charged $1.50 per tire to dispose of them. What was Lillie's final bill? *(p. 14)*

8. Tootsie Roll Industries bought Charms Company for $65 million. Some analysts believe that in 4 years the purchase price could rise to 3 times as much. If the analysts are right, how much did Tootsie Roll save by purchasing Charms immediately? *(p. 14)*

9. Today the average business traveler will spend almost $50 a day on food. The breakdown is dinner, $22.26; lunch, $10.73; breakfast, $6.53; tips, $6.23; and tax, $1.98. If Clarence Donato, an executive for Honeywell, spends only $.3\overline{3}$ of the average, what is Clarence's total cost for food for the day? If Clarence wanted to spend $\frac{1}{3}$ more than the average on the next day, what would be his total cost on the second day? Round to the nearest cent. *(p. 71)*

Be sure you use the fractional equivalent in calculating $.3\overline{3}$.

It's Not in the Mail

Bounce a Check, and You Might Not Write Another for 5 Years

Banks Are Using Database To Blacklist Customers For Even Small Slip-Ups

Do the Poor Get Hurt More?

By Paul Beckett
Staff Reporter of The Wall Street Journal

Two years ago, Rebecca Cobos overdrew her checking account at a Bank of America branch in Los Angeles. When she couldn't immediately repay the bank, it not only closed her account, but also had her, in effect, banned for five years from opening a checking account at most other banks, too.

88

© 2000 Dow Jones & Company, Inc.

4

Banking

LU 4–1: The Checking Account; Credit Card Transactions

- Define and state the purpose of signature cards, checks, deposit slips, check stubs, check registers, and endorsements *(pp. 90–92)*.

- Correctly prepare deposit slips and write checks *(pp. 91–92)*.

- Explain how a merchant completes a credit card transaction for manual deposit or electronic deposit *(pp. 92–94)*.

LU 4–2: Bank Statement and Reconciliation Process; Trends in Online Banking

- Define and state the purpose of the bank statement *(pp. 95–96)*.

- Complete a check register and a bank reconciliation *(pp. 97–99)*.

- Explain the trends in online banking *(pp. 99–100)*.

An important fixture in today's banking is the **automatic teller machine (ATM).** The ability to get instant cash is a convenience many bank customers enjoy. The effect of using an ATM card is the same as using a **debit card**—both transactions result in money being immediately deducted from your checking account balance. As a result, debit cards have been called enhanced ATM cards or *check cards.* Often banks charge fees for these card transactions. However, the frequent complaints of bank customers have made many banks offer their ATMs as a free service, especially if you use an ATM that is in the same network of banks as your bank.

Have you ever found it necessary to use an ATM when you are away from home, say, on a vacation? Be warned that this convenience could be costly. A casino can charge from $3 to $5 for the use of an ATM, and cruises can charge as much as $9. Plan ahead for the amount of vacation money you will need. Travelers' checks can provide you with a money reserve at a lower cost—sometimes at no cost.

The use of debit cards also involves planning. As *check cards,* you must be aware of your bank balance every time you use a debit card. Also, if you use a credit card instead of a debit card, you can only be held responsible for $50 of illegal charges, and during the time the credit card company investigates the illegal charges, they are removed from your account. However, with a debit card, this legal limit only applies if you report your card lost or stolen within two business days.

We should add that debit cards are profitable for banks. When shopping, if you use a debit card that does not require a personal identification number, the store pays a fee to the bank that issued the card—usually from 1.4 to 2 cents on the dollar.

This chapter begins with a discussion of the checking account and credit card transactions. You will follow Molly Kate as she opens a checking account for Gracie's Natural Superstore and performs her banking and credit card transactions. Pay special attention to the procedure used by Gracie's to reconcile its checking account and bank statement. This information will help you reconcile your checkbook records with the bank's record of your account. Finally, the chapter discusses how the trends in online banking may affect your banking procedures.

Bachmann/PhotoEdit.

LEARNING UNIT 4–1 | THE CHECKING ACCOUNT; CREDIT CARD TRANSACTIONS

A **check** or **draft** is a written order instructing a bank, credit union, or savings and loan institution to pay a designated amount of your money on deposit to a person or an organization. Checking accounts are offered to individuals and businesses. The business checking account usually receives more services than the personal checking account.

Most small businesses depend on a checking account for efficient record keeping. In this chapter you will follow the checking account procedures of a newly organized small business. You can use many of these procedures in your personal check writing.

Elements of the Checking Account

Molly Kate, treasurer of Gracie's Natural Superstore, went to Ipswich Bank to open a business checking account. The bank manager gave Molly a **signature card.** The signature card contained space for the company's name and address, references, type of account, and the signature(s) of the person(s) authorized to sign checks. If necessary, the bank will use the signature card to verify that Molly signed the checks. Some companies authorize more than one person to sign checks or require more than one signature on a check.

Molly then lists on a **deposit slip** (or deposit ticket) the checks and/or cash she is depositing in her company's business account. The bank gave Molly a temporary checkbook to use until the company's printed checks arrived. Molly also will receive *preprinted* checking account deposit slips like the one shown in Figure 4.1. Since the deposit slips are in duplicate, Molly can keep a record of her deposit.

Writing business checks is similar to writing personal checks. Before writing any checks, however, you must understand the structure of a check and know how to write a check. Carefully study Figure 4.2. Note that the verbal amount written in the check should match the figure amount. If these two amounts are different, by law the bank uses the verbal amount. Also, note the bank imprint on the bottom right section of the check. When processing the check, the bank imprints the check's amount. This makes it easy to detect bank errors.

FIGURE 4.1   Deposit slip

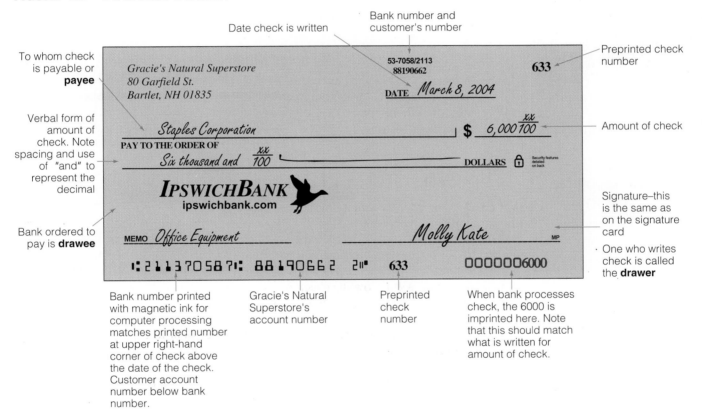

Preprinted numbers in magnetic ink identify bank number, routing and sorting of the check, and Gracie's Natural Superstore account number

DEPOSIT TICKET

Gracie's Natural Superstore
80 Garfield St.
Bartlet, NH 01835

DATE *March 4* 20 *04*
DEPOSITS MAY NOT BE AVAILABLE FOR IMMEDIATE WITHDRAWAL

IPSWICHBANK
ipswichbank.com

⑆211370587⑆ 88190662

CHECKS AND OTHER ITEMS ARE RECIEVED FOR DEPOSIT SUBJECT TO THE PROVISIONS OF THE UNIFORM COMMERCIAL CODE OR ANY APPLICABLE COLLECTION AGREEMENT.

CASH →		
LIST CHECK SINGLY		
53-7058	1,800	00
53-7058	200	00
TOTAL FROM OTHER SIDE		
TOTAL ITEMS TOTAL	2,000	00

USE OTHER SIDE FOR ADDITIONAL LISTING ◄ ENTER TOTAL HERE

BE SURE EACH ITEM IS PROPERLY ENDORSED.

The 53-7058 is taken from the upper right corner of the check from the top part of the fraction. This number is known as the American Bankers Association transit number. The 53 identifies the city or state where the bank is located and the 7058 identifies the bank.

FIGURE 4.2   The structure of a check

Date check is written

Bank number and customer's number

To whom check is payable or **payee**

Verbal form of amount of check. Note spacing and use of "and" to represent the decimal

Bank ordered to pay is **drawee**

Gracie's Natural Superstore
80 Garfield St.
Bartlet, NH 01835

53-7058/2113
88190662   **633**

DATE *March 8, 2004*

PAY TO THE ORDER OF *Staples Corporation* $ *6,000* *XX/100*

Six thousand and *XX/100*   DOLLARS

IPSWICHBANK
ipswichbank.com

MEMO *Office Equipment*   *Molly Kate*   MP

⑆211370587⑆ 88190662 ⑈ 633   0000006000

Preprinted check number

Amount of check

Signature–this is the same as on the signature card

· One who writes check is called the **drawer**

Bank number printed with magnetic ink for computer processing matches printed number at upper right-hand corner of check above the date of the check. Customer account number below bank number.

Gracie's Natural Superstore's account number

Preprinted check number

When bank processes check, the 6000 is imprinted here. Note that this should match what is written for amount of check.

Check Stub

It should be completed before the check is written.

No. 633	$ 6000 XX/100
March 8	20 04
To	Staples Corp.
For	Other Furniture

	DOLLARS	CENTS
BALANCE	14,416	24
AMT. DEPOSITED		
TOTAL	14,416	24
AMT. THIS CHECK	6,000	00
BALANCE FORWARD	8,416	24

Once the check is written, the writer must keep a record of the check. Knowing the amount of your written checks and the amount in the bank should help you avoid writing a bad check. Business checkbooks usually include attached **check stubs** to keep track of written checks. The sample check stub in the margin shows the information that the check writer will want to record. Some companies use a **check register** to keep their check records instead of check stubs. Figure 4.9 (p. 98) shows a check register with a ✓ column that is often used in balancing the checkbook with the bank statement (Learning Unit 4–2).

Gracie's Natural Superstore has had a busy week, and Molly must deposit its checks in the company's checking account. However, before she can do this, Molly must **endorse,** or sign, the back left side of the checks. Figure 4.3 explains the three types of check endorsements: **blank endorsement, full endorsement,** and **restrictive endorsement.** These endorsements transfer Gracie's ownership to the bank, which collects the money from the person or company issuing the check. Federal Reserve regulation limits

FIGURE 4.3

Types of common endorsements

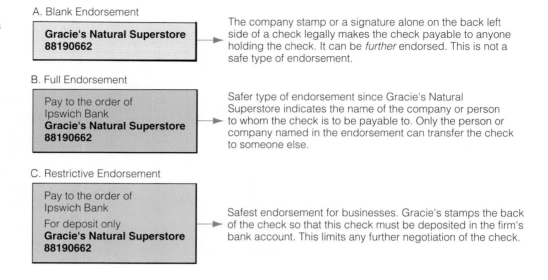

A. Blank Endorsement

> Gracie's Natural Superstore
> 88190662

The company stamp or a signature alone on the back left side of a check legally makes the check payable to anyone holding the check. It can be *further* endorsed. This is not a safe type of endorsement.

B. Full Endorsement

> Pay to the order of
> Ipswich Bank
> Gracie's Natural Superstore
> 88190662

Safer type of endorsement since Gracie's Natural Superstore indicates the name of the company or person to whom the check is to be payable to. Only the person or company named in the endorsement can transfer the check to someone else.

C. Restrictive Endorsement

> Pay to the order of
> Ipswich Bank
> For deposit only
> Gracie's Natural Superstore
> 88190662

Safest endorsement for businesses. Gracie's stamps the back of the check so that this check must be deposited in the firm's bank account. This limits any further negotiation of the check.

FIGURE 4.4

Charge slip

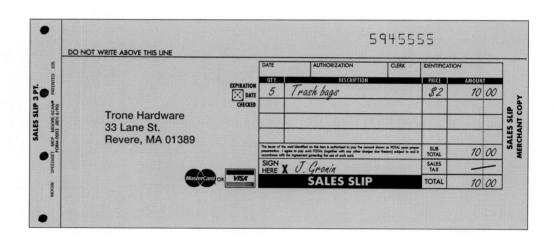

all endorsements to the top $1\frac{1}{2}$ inches of the trailing edge on the back left side of the check (Figure 4.3).

After the bank receives Molly's deposit slip, shown in Figure 4.1, it increases (or credits) Gracie's account by $2,000. Often Molly leaves the deposit in a locked bag in a night depository. Then the bank credits (increases) Gracie's account when it processes the deposit on the next working day.

Gracie's Natural Superstore handles many credit card transactions. Now let's see how the company records these transactions.

Depositing Credit Card Transactions

On April 1, 2004, Gracie's Natural Superstore will begin using MasterCard and Visa. This should increase its sales and avoid the collection of past-due accounts.

Ipswich Bank has given Gracie's two options for depositing **credit card** transactions—option 1, manual deposits, and option 2, electronic deposits. Note that although some very small companies still use the manual deposit system, most companies favor the electronic system. Now let's study these two systems. By looking at the old manual system, you will appreciate the technology that is in place today.

Option 1: Manual Deposits

When Gracie's makes a charge sale with the **manual deposit** option, the salesperson fills out a MasterCard or Visa charge slip similar to the one in Figure 4.4, which is for another company. Charge slips give the specific details of the sale.

At the end of *each business day,* Gracie's treasurer completes a **merchant batch header slip** and attaches copies of its charge slips. Figure 4.5 shows a sample batch header slip used by another company. Note that the company could list the slips on the form or provide an adding machine tape with the batch header slip. Also note that the to-

FIGURE 4.5

Merchant batch header slip

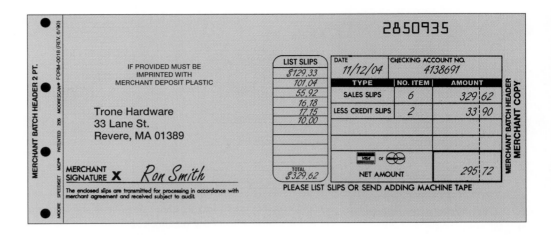

		2850935

IF PROVIDED MUST BE
IMPRINTED WITH
MERCHANT DEPOSIT PLASTIC

Trone Hardware
33 Lane St.
Revere, MA 01389

MERCHANT BATCH HEADER 2 PT.

MERCHANT SIGNATURE X *Ron Smith*

The enclosed slips are transmitted for processing in accordance with merchant agreement and received subject to audit.

LIST SLIPS
129.33
101.04
55.92
16.18
17.15
10.00
TOTAL 329.62

DATE 11/12/04	CHECKING ACCOUNT NO. 4138691	
TYPE	NO. ITEM	AMOUNT
SALES SLIPS	6	329 62
LESS CREDIT SLIPS	2	33 90
VISA or ⬤ NET AMOUNT		295 72

PLEASE LIST SLIPS OR SEND ADDING MACHINE TAPE

MERCHANT BATCH HEADER MERCHANT COPY

FIGURE 4.6

Electronic deposit statement

DEPOSIT DETAILS:	CARDHOLDER	DATE	TRAN	AMOUNT	CST–TIME	CODE
	361060558	11/14/04	SALE	15.00	11:55 :36	431011
	336808479		SALE	28.60	12:08 :30	673011
	633615209		SALE	11.28	12:34 :31	934440
	484383		SALE	7.77	14:03 :38	482360
	611445		SALE	17.57	14:12 :48	371224
	343103551		SALE	24.15	15:13 :50	694492
	000115629		SALE	14.74	15:16 :33	378823
	380057254		SALE	16.38	15:33 :18	213011
	288121723		SALE	23.08	16:21 :29	682011
	503999		SALE	9.96	16:27 :41	714593
	309021229		SALE	38.82	16:32 :29	891816
	005291394		SALE	19.93	16:42 :43	731020
	387076		SALE	15.62	16:51 :09	700644
	199011544		SALE	21.00	19:39 :08	001640

	-------- SALES --------		-------- RETURNS --------		NET DEPOSIT
	14	263.90	0	.00	263.90
MASTERCARD	7	147.90	0	.00	147.90
VISA	7	116.00	0	.00	116.00

tal of the charge slips is shown less the total of the credit slips (refunds). The **net deposit** (net amount) is the difference between the total sales and the total credits. At the *end of the statement period,* Ipswich Bank charges $3\frac{1}{4}\%$ (this means $3\frac{1}{4}$ cents per dollar) of the net deposit and subtracts this from Gracie's checking account.

Option 2: Electronic Deposits

Most retail stores use **electronic deposits.** If you use a MasterCard or Visa credit card, you have probably watched the salesperson run your card through an authorization terminal after you have made a purchase. You may also have noticed that some retail stores now use the cash register terminal as a credit card authorization terminal. These authorization terminals not only approve (or disapprove) the amount charged but also add this amount immediately to the store's bank balance—or in our example to Gracie's bank balance. Charge credits are also immediately subtracted from bank balances. The immediate authorizations and additions to a company's checking account are important advantages of the electronic transaction. Now we go back to Gracie's to continue the electronic deposit procedure.

Each day Ipswich Bank sends Gracie's a statement listing its MasterCard and Visa transactions. The bank charges Gracie's 2½% (2½ cents per dollar) since it wants to encourage the use of electronic deposits. The statement Gracie's receives is similar to the statement in Figure 4.6 for another company. When we work with percents in Chapter 6, you will see how to calculate the amount Gracie's pays for using MasterCard and Visa. For now, focus on calculating net deposits.

EXAMPLE From the following credit card sales and returns, calculate the net deposit for the day.

Credit card sales: $42.33, $16.88, $19.39, $47.66, $39.18.
Returns: $18.01, $13.04.
Solution:

Total credit cards sales	$165.44
Less returns	− 31.05
Net deposit	$134.39

---

1. Complete the following check and check stub for Long Company. Note the $9,500.60 balance brought forward on check stub No. 113. You must make a $690.60 deposit on May 3. Sign the check for Roland Small.

Date	Check no.	Amount	Payable to	For
June 5, 2004	113	$83.76	Angel Corporation	Rent

2. From the following information, complete Ryan Company's merchant batch header slip for August 19, 2004. Sign the slip for John Ryan, whose account number is 0139684.

Credit card sales	Credit card returns
$114.99	$14.07
21.15	15.19
72.80	
39.45	

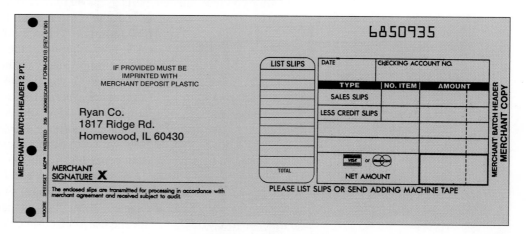

1.

2.

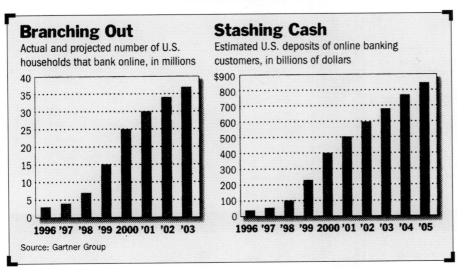

LEARNING UNIT 4–2 | BANK STATEMENT AND RECONCILIATION PROCESS; TRENDS IN ONLINE BANKING

Branching Out
Actual and projected number of U.S. households that bank online, in millions

Source: Gartner Group

Stashing Cash
Estimated U.S. deposits of online banking customers, in billions of dollars

© 2001 Dow Jones & Company, Inc.

In a survey by *The Wall Street Journal,* only one-half of the adults surveyed said they balanced their checkbook every month. Almost one-fourth said they never balanced their checkbook. The result of this survey is disappointing. Banks can make mistakes. This unit begins with a discussion on how Gracie's Natural Superstore reconciles its checkbook balance with the balance reported on its bank statement. You would use the same procedure in reconciling your personal checking account.

Also discussed in this learning unit is online banking. The accompanying *Wall Street Journal* clipping presents these interesting facts: more than 35 million households will be branching out and banking online; by the year 2005, online banking customers will be depositing cash estimated to be more than $800 billion.

Each month Ipswich Bank sends Gracie's Natural Superstore a **bank statement** (Figure 4.7). The statement gives different types of information. We are interested in the following:

Bank Statement

1. Beginning bank balance.
2. Total of all the account increases. Each time the bank increases the account amount, it *credits* the account.

3. Total of all account decreases. Each time the bank decreases the account amount, it *debits* the account.

4. Final ending balance.

Due to differences in timing, the bank balance on the bank statement frequently does not match the customer's checkbook balance. Also, the bank statement can show transactions that have not been entered in the customer's checkbook. Figure 4.8 tells you what to look for when comparing a checkbook balance with a bank balance.

FIGURE 4.7
Bank statement

Ipswich Bank
1 Pleasant St.
Bartlett, NH 01835

Account Statement

Gracie's Natural Superstore
80 Garfield St.
Bartlett, NH 01835

Checking Account: 881900662

Checking Account Summary as of 3/31/04

Beginning Balance	Total Deposits	Total Withdrawals	Service Charge	Ending Balance
$13,112.24	$8,705.28	$9,926.00	$28.50	$11,863.02

Checking Accounts Transactions

Deposits	Date	Amount
Deposit	3/05	2,000.00
Deposit	3/05	224.00
Deposit	3/09	389.20
EFT leasing: Bakery dept.	3/18	1,808.06
EFT leasing: Meat dept.	3/27	4,228.00
Interest	3/31	56.02

Charges	Date	Amount
Service charge: Check printing	3/31	28.50
EFT: Health insurance	3/21	722.00
NSF	3/21	104.00

Checks

Number	Date	Amount
301	3/07	200.00
633	3/13	6,000.00
634	3/13	300.00
635	3/11	200.00
636	3/18	200.00
637	3/31	2,200.00

Daily Balance

Date	Balance	Date	Balance
2/28	13,112.24	3/18	10,529.50
3/05	15,232.24	3/21	9,807.50
3/07	14,832.24	3/28	14,035.50
3/09	15,221.44	3/31	11,863.02
3/11	15,021.44		
3/13	8,721.44		

FIGURE 4.8
Reconciling checkbook with bank statement

Checkbook balance		Bank balance
+ EFT (electronic funds transfer)	− NSF check	+ Deposits in transit
+ Interest earned	− Online fees	− Outstanding checks
+ Notes collected	− Automatic payments*	± Bank errors
+ Direct deposits	− Overdrafts†	
− ATM withdrawals	− Service charges	
− Automatic withdrawals	− Stop payments‡	
− Check redeposits	± Book errors§	

*Preauthorized payments for utility bills, mortgage payments, insurance, etc.

†**Overdrafts** occur when the customer has no overdraft protection and a check bounces back to the company or person who received the check because the customer has written a check without enough money in the bank to pay for it.

‡A stop payment is issued when the writer of check does not want the receiver to cash the check.

§If a $60 check is recorded at $50, the checkbook balance must be decreased by $10.

Gracie's Natural Superstore is planning to offer to its employees the option of depositing their checks directly into each employee's checking account. This is accomplished through the **electronic funds transfer (EFT)**—a computerized operation that electronically transfers funds among parties without the use of paper checks. Gracie's, who sublets space in the store, receives rental payments by EFT. Gracie's also has the bank pay the store's health insurance premiums by EFT.

To reconcile the difference between the amount on the bank statement and in the checkbook, the customer should complete a **bank reconciliation.** Today, many companies and home computer owners are using software such as Quicken and QuickBooks to complete their bank reconciliation. However, you should understand the following steps for manually reconciling a bank statement.

Reconciling a Bank Statement

Step 1. Identify the outstanding checks (checks written but not yet processed by the bank). You can use the ✓ column in the check register (Figure 4.9) to check the canceled checks listed in the bank statement against the checks you wrote in the check register. The unchecked checks are the outstanding checks.

Step 2. Identify the deposits in transit (deposits made but not yet processed by the bank), using the same method in Step 1.

Step 3. Analyze the bank statement for transactions not recorded in the check stubs or check registers (like EFT).

Step 4. Check for recording errors in checks written, in deposits made, or in subtraction and addition.

Step 5. Compare the adjusted balances of the checkbook and the bank statement. If the balances are not the same, repeat Steps 1–4.

Molly uses a check register (Figure 4.9) to keep a record of Gracie's checks and deposits. By looking at Gracie's check register, you can see how to complete Steps 1 and 2 above. The explanation that follows for the first four bank statement reconciliation steps will help you understand the procedure.

Step 1. Identify Outstanding Checks

Outstanding checks are checks that Gracie's Natural Superstore has written but Ipswich Bank has not yet recorded for payment when it sends out the bank statement. Gracie's treasurer identifies the following checks written on 3/31 as outstanding:

No. 638	$572.00
No. 639	638.94
No. 640	166.00
No. 641	406.28
No. 642	917.06

Step 2. Identify Deposits in Transit

Deposits in transit are deposits that did not reach Ipswich Bank by the time the bank prepared the bank statement. The March 30 deposit of $3,383.26 did not reach Ipswich Bank by the bank statement date. You can see this by comparing the company's bank statement with its check register.

Step 3. Analyze Bank Statement for Transactions Not Recorded in Check Stubs or Check Register

The bank statement of Gracie's Natural Superstore (Figure 4.7, p. 96) begins with the deposits, or increases, made to Gracie's bank account. Increases to accounts are known as credits. These are the result of a **credit memo (CM).** Gracie's received the following increases or credits in March:

1. *EFT leasing:* $1,808.06 and $4,228.00.	Each month the bakery and meat departments pay for space they lease in the store.
2. *Interest credited:* $56.02.	Gracie's has a checking account that pays interest; the account has earned $56.02.

FIGURE 4.9

Gracie's Natural Superstore check register

NUMBER	DATE 2004	DESCRIPTION OF TRANSACTION	PAYMENT/DEBIT (−)	√	FEE (IF ANY) (−)	DEPOSIT/CREDIT (+)	BALANCE $ 12,912	24
		RECORD ALL CHARGES OR CREDITS THAT AFFECT YOUR ACCOUNT						
	3/04	Deposit	$		$	$ 2,000 00	+ 2,000	00
							14,912	24
	3/04	Deposit				224 00	+ 224	00
							15,136	24
633	3/08	Staples Company	6,000 00	✓			− 6,000	00
							9,136	24
634	3/09	Health Foods Inc.	1,020 00	✓			− 1,020	00
							8,116	24
	3/09	Deposit				389 20	+ 389	20
							8,505	44
635	3/10	Liberty Insurance	200 00	✓			− 200	00
							8,305	44
636	3/18	Ryan Press	200 00	✓			− 200	00
							8,105	44
637	3/29	Logan Advertising	2,200 00	✓			− 2,200	00
							5,905	44
	3/30	Deposit				3,383 26	+ 3,383	26
							9,288	70
638	3/31	Sears Roebuck	572 00				− 572	00
							8,716	70
639	3/31	Flynn Company	638 94				− 638	94
							8,077	76
640	3/31	Lynn's Farm	166 00				− 166	00
							7,911	76
641	3/31	Ron's Wholesale	406 28				− 406	28
							7,505	48
642	3/31	Grocery Natural, Inc.	917 06				− 917	06
							86,588	42

REMEMBER TO RECORD AUTOMATIC PAYMENTS/DEPOSITS ON DATE AUTHORIZED.

When Gracie's has charges against her bank account, the bank decreases, or debits, Gracie's account for these charges. Banks usually inform customers of a debit transaction by a **debit memo (DM).** The following items will result in debits to Gracie's account:

1. *Service charge:* $28.50   The bank charged $28.50 for printing Gracie's checks.

2. *EFT payment:* $722.   The bank made a health insurance payment for Gracie's.

3. *NSF check:* $104.   One of Gracie's customers wrote Gracie's a check for $104. Gracie's deposited the check, but the check bounced for **nonsufficient funds (NSF).** Thus, Gracie's has $104 less than it figured.

Step 4. Check for Recording Errors

The treasurer of Gracie's Natural Superstore, Molly Kate, recorded check No. 634 for the wrong amount—$1,020 (see the check register above). The bank statement showed that check No. 634 cleared for $300. To reconcile Gracie's checkbook balance with the bank balance, Gracie's must add $720 to its checkbook balance. Neglecting to record a deposit also results in an error in the company's checkbook balance. As you can see, reconciling the bank's balance with a checkbook balance is a necessary part of business and personal finance.

Step 5. Completing the Bank Reconciliation

Now we can complete the bank reconciliation on the back side of the bank statement as shown in Figure 4.10. This form is usually on the back of a bank statement. If necessary, however, the person reconciling the bank statement can construct a bank reconciliation form similar to Figure 4.11.

FIGURE 4.10
Reconciliation process

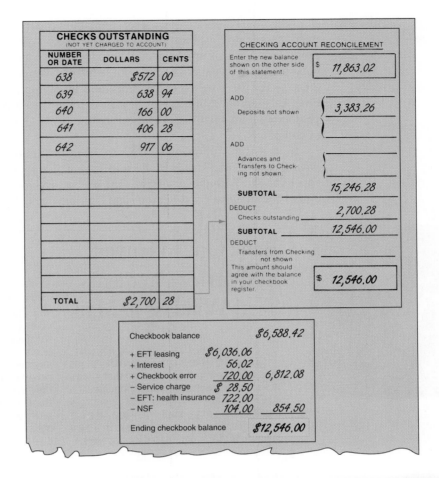

CHECKS OUTSTANDING (NOT YET CHARGED TO ACCOUNT)		
NUMBER OR DATE	**DOLLARS**	**CENTS**
638	8572	00
639	638	94
640	166	00
641	406	28
642	917	06
TOTAL	**$2,700**	**28**

CHECKING ACCOUNT RECONCILEMENT

Enter the new balance shown on the other side of this statement. $ 11,863.02

ADD
Deposits not shown　　3,383.26

ADD
Advances and Transfers to Checking not shown.

SUBTOTAL ____ 15,246.28

DEDUCT
Checks outstanding ____ 2,700.28

SUBTOTAL ____ 12,546.00

DEDUCT
Transfers from Checking not shown ____
This amount should agree with the balance in your checkbook register.　$ 12,546.00

Checkbook balance　　　　　　$6,588.42

\+ EFT leasing　　$6,036.06
\+ Interest　　　　56.02
\+ Checkbook error　720.00　6,812.08
− Service charge　$ 28.50
− EFT: health insurance　722.00
− NSF　　　　　104.00　854.50

Ending checkbook balance　$12,546.00

FIGURE 4.11
Bank reconciliation

GRACIE'S NATURAL SUPERSTORE
Bank Reconciliation as of March 31, 2004

Checkbook balance			Bank balance		
Gracie's checkbook balance		$ 6,588.42	Bank balance		$11,863.02
Add:			Add:		
EFT leasing: Bakery dept.	$ 1,808.06		Deposit in transit, 3/30		3,383.26
					$15,246.28
EFT leasing: Meat dept.	4,228.00				
Interest	56.02				
Error: Overstated check No. 634	720.00	$ 6,812.08			
		$13,400.50			
Deduct:			Deduct:		
Service charge	$28.50		Outstanding checks:		
NSF check	104.00		No. 638	$572.00	
EFT health insurance payment	722.00	854.50	No. 639	638.94	
			No. 640	166.00	
			No. 641	406.28	
			No. 642	917.06	2,700.28
Reconciled balance		$12,546.00	Reconciled balance		$12,546.00

Trends in Online Banking

DIRECT-DEPOSIT UPDATE: More taxpayers told the IRS to deposit their refunds directly into their bank accounts this year, rather than mailing a check to them. The IRS says about 26 million taxpayers chose direct deposit through April 14, up about 24% from a year earlier.

This *Wall Street Journal* clipping shows that online banking is becoming more popular. Instead of receiving a refund check in the mail, more taxpayers are requesting the IRS to directly deposit their refunds into their bank accounts.

Although banks are doing everything they can to get people to avoid writing checks, many people do not want to give up their check writing. In a recent Kansas City Bank presentation, it was emphasized that today more checks than ever are processed. To reduce the costs of paper checks, some banks no longer return canceled checks. Instead, these banks use a **safekeeping** procedure involving holding the checks for a period of time, keeping microfilm copies of checks for at least a year, and returning the check or a photocopy for a small fee. However, online banking will survive with the increased use of computers.

Note that the following *Wall Street Journal* clipping "Bank One to Unveil System for Payments That Will Use E-Mail" may have a plan for encouraging people to write fewer paper checks. With the new Bank One service, eMoneyMail, people can use the popular e-mail communication system to send their payments through an e-mail form.

David Young Wolfff/PhotoEdit

Bank One to Unveil System for Payments That Will Use E-Mail

By a WALL STREET JOURNAL *Staff Reporter*

CHICAGO—**Bank One** Corp. today plans to unveil a new payment system that allows individuals to settle payments among each other through a system that combines credit cards with e-mail, showing how big banks are now taking an interest in a new medium hitherto dominated by start-ups.

The new service, called eMoneyMail, will allow individuals to send money to other individuals merely by registering on the designated site, a process that initially takes about five minutes, then sending the payment through an e-mail form. Those receiving these payments can choose to have the payment credited to their **Visa International** credit or debit card, to have it sent into their bank account or have the service cut a check and mail it to the receiver's address.

In addition to the above *Wall Street Journal* clip, let's look at another trend in online banking.

Remember that online banking is in its infancy. Note, however, *The Wall Street Journal* clipping "Big Banks Rule the Net." Wells Fargo has the largest market share of Internet banking. This continued interest in Internet banking by big banks should result in a continued growth in online banking.

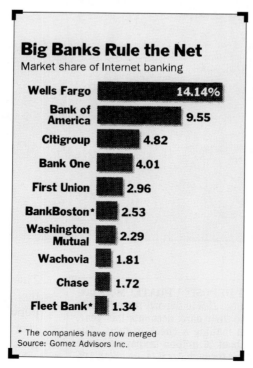

Big Banks Rule the Net
Market share of Internet banking

Bank	Market share
Wells Fargo	14.14%
Bank of America	9.55
Citigroup	4.82
Bank One	4.01
First Union	2.96
BankBoston*	2.53
Washington Mutual	2.29
Wachovia	1.81
Chase	1.72
Fleet Bank*	1.34

* The companies have now merged
Source: Gomez Advisors Inc.

For several years electronic bill paying has been available to bank customers. This method of bill paying has several advantages. You do not have to write checks, save the envelopes that come with bills, look for stamps, or be concerned that payments will not reach their destination in time to make a deadline. With the Internet, you can transfer money between accounts or checking balances. If you want to make deposits or withdraw funds, however, you must do this by wire, mail, or ATM.

LU 4–2 PRACTICE QUIZ

Rosa Garcia has received her February 3, 2004, bank statement, which has a balance of $212.80. Rosa's checkbook shows a balance of $929.15. The bank statement showed an ATM fee of $12 and a deposited check returned fee of $20. Rosa earned interest of $1.05. She had three outstanding checks: No. 300, $18.20; No. 302, $38.40; and No. 303, $68.12. A deposit for $810.12 was not on her bank statement. Prepare Rosa Garcia's bank reconciliation.

ROSA GARCIA
Bank Reconciliation as of February 3, 2004

Checkbook balance			Bank balance		
Rosa's checkbook balance		$929.15	Bank balance		$ 212.80
Add:			Add:		
Interest		1.05	Deposit in transit		810.12
		$930.20			$1,022.92
			Deduct:		
Deduct:			Outstanding checks:		
Deposited check			No. 300	$18.20	
returned fee	$20.00		No. 302	38.40	
ATM	12.00	32.00	No. 303	68.12	124.72
Reconciled balance		$898.20	Reconciled balance		$ 898.20

Chapter Organizer and Reference Guide

Topic	Key point, procedure, formula	Example(s) to illustrate situation
Types of endorsements, p. 92	*Blank:* Not safe; can be further endorsed.	Jones Co. 21-333-9
	Full: Only person or company named in endorsement can transfer check to someone else.	Pay to the order of Regan Bank Jones Co. 21-333-9
	Restrictive: Check must be deposited. Limits any further negotiation of the check.	Pay to the order of Regan Bank. For deposit only. Jones Co. 21-333-9
Credit card transactions, p. 92	*Manual deposit:* Need to calculate net deposit (credit card sales less returns). *Electronic deposit:* Eliminates deposit slips and summary batch header slip.	Calculate net deposit: Credit card sales $55.32 62.81 91.18 Credits − 10.16 − 8.15 $209.31 − 18.31 Net deposit = $191.00

(continues)

Chapter Organizer and Reference Guide (concluded)

Topic	Key point, procedure, formula		Example(s) to illustrate situation	
Bank reconciliation, p. 95	**Checkbook balance** + EFT (electronic funds transfer) + Interest earned + Notes collected + Direct deposits − ATM withdrawals − Check redeposits − NSF check − Online fees − Automatic withdrawals − Overdrafts − Service charges − Stop payments ± Book errors* CM—adds to balance DM—deducts from balance *If a $60 check is recorded as $50, we must decrease checkbook balance by $10.	**Bank balance** + Deposits in transit − Outstanding checks ± Bank errors	**Checkbook balance** Balance $800 − NSF 40 $760 − Service charge 4 $756	**Bank balance** Balance $ 632 + Deposits in transit 416 $1,048 − Outstanding checks 292 $ 756
Key terms	Automatic teller machine (ATM), p. 90 Bank reconciliation, p. 97 Bank statement, p. 96 Blank endorsement, p. 92 Check, p. 90 Check register, p. 98 Check stub, p. 98 Credit card, p. 92 Credit memo (CM), p. 97 Debit card, p. 90	Debit memo (DM), p. 98 Deposit slip, p. 90 Deposits in transit, p. 97 Draft, p. 90 Drawee, p. 91 Drawer, p. 91 Electronic deposit, p. 93 Electronic funds transfer (EFT), p. 97 Endorse, p. 91 Full endorsement, p. 92	Manual deposit, p. 92 Merchant batch header slip, p. 92 Net deposit, p. 93 Nonsufficient funds (NSF), p. 98 Outstanding checks, p. 97 Overdrafts, p. 96 Payee, p. 91 Restrictive endorsement, p. 92 Safekeeping, p. 100 Signature card, p. 90	

Critical Thinking Discussion Questions

1. Explain the structure of a check. The trend in bank statements is not to return the canceled checks. Do you think this is fair?
2. List the three types of endorsements. Endorsements are limited to the top $1\frac{1}{2}$ inches of the trailing edge on the back left side of your check. Why do you think the Federal Reserve made this regulation?
3. What is the difference between a manual and an electronic deposit of credit card transactions? Do you think credit cards should be used in supermarkets?
4. List the steps in reconciling a bank statement. Today, many banks charge a monthly fee for certain types of checking accounts. Do you think all checking accounts should be free? Please explain.
5. What are some of the trends in online banking? Will we become a cashless society in which all transactions are made with some type of credit card?

DRILL PROBLEMS

4–1. Fill out the check register that follows with this information:

2004

May	8	Check No. 611	Amazon.com	$ 81.96
	15	Check No. 612	Dell Computer	33.10
	19	Deposit		800.40
	20	Check No. 613	Sprint	110.22
	24	Check No. 614	Krispy Kreme	217.55
	29	Deposit		198.10

		RECORD ALL CHARGES OR CREDITS THAT AFFECT YOUR ACCOUNT						
NUMBER	DATE 2004	DESCRIPTION OF TRANSACTION	PAYMENT/DEBIT (−)	√	FEE (IF ANY) (−)	DEPOSIT/CREDIT (+)	BALANCE $ 1,017 20	
			$		$	$		

4–2. On November 1, 2004, Payroll.com, an Internet company, has a $9,482.10 checkbook balance. Record the following transactions for Payroll.com by completing the two checks and check stubs provided. Sign the checks Garth Scholten, controller.

  a. November 8, 2004, deposited $595.10.

  b. November 8, check No. 190 payable to Wal-Mart Corporation for office supplies—$750.10.

  c. November 15, check No. 191 payable to Compaq Corporation for computer equipment—$1,888.18.

No. _____ $ _____	PAYROLL.COM	No. 190
_____ 20 ____	1 LEDGER RD. ST. PAUL, MN 55113	
To _____		
For _____	PAY TO THE ORDER OF _____	_____ 20 ____ 5-13/110 $ _____
BALANCE · DOLLARS · CENTS		DOLLARS
AMT. DEPOSITED		
TOTAL	IpswichBank ipswichbank.com	
AMT. THIS CHECK		
BALANCE FORWARD	MEMO _____	⑆011000138⑆ 25 11103 190

No. _____ $ _____	PAYROLL.COM	No. 191
_____ 20 ____	1 LEDGER RD. ST. PAUL, MN 55113	
To _____		
For _____	PAY TO THE ORDER OF _____	_____ 20 ____ 5-13/110 $ _____
BALANCE · DOLLARS · CENTS		DOLLARS
AMT. DEPOSITED		
TOTAL	IpswichBank ipswichbank.com	
AMT. THIS CHECK		
BALANCE FORWARD	MEMO _____	⑆011000138⑆ 25 11103 191

4–3. You are the bookkeeper of Reese Company and must complete a merchant batch header for November 10, 2004, from the following credit card transactions. The company lost the charge slips and doesn't include an adding machine tape. Reese's checking account number is 3158062. The merchant's signature can be left blank. **Credit card sales** are $210.40, $178.99, $29.30, and $82.80. **Credit card returns** are $15.10 and $22.99.

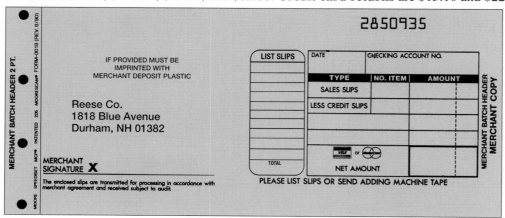

4–4. Using the check register in Problem 4–1 and the following bank statement, prepare a bank reconciliation for Lee.com.

Bank Statement			
Date·	**Checks**	**Deposits**	**Balance**
5/1 balance			$1,017.20
5/18	$ 81.96		935.24
5/19		$ 800.40	1,735.64
5/26	217.55		1,518.09
5/30	15.00 SC		1,503.09

WORD PROBLEMS

4–5. *The Record,* on January 21, 2001, ran a story on the rise in New Jersey bank fees. Some banks charge $20.00 or more a month, or $240.00 a year for checking account services. Anna Carmen, who banks in New Jersey, wants to balance her checkbook, which shows a balance of $1,018.25. The bank shows a balance of $210.20. The following checks have not cleared the bank: No. 85, $20.50; No. 87, $145.50; and No. 88, $215.10. Anna has a $20.00 service fee and a $24.00 NSF fee. The bank pays her $110.15 electric bill through automatic withdrawal. She also made a stop payment order with a fee of $20. A $1,015.00 deposit does not appear on the bank statement. Prepare Anna's bank reconciliation.

4–6. In the January 2001 issue of *Credit Card Management,* an article appeared on debit card fees and teller fees in Pittsburgh. A $2 fee kicks in after a certain number of teller visits. Jim Clinnin has an account in Pittsburgh. This month Jim was charged for four extra visits to a teller—a total $8.00 cost to him. Jim's bank statement shows a balance of

$35.56; his checkbook shows a $531.26 balance. He received $2.15 in interest. A $575.10 deposit was not recorded on his statement. The following checks were outstanding: No. 50, $16.50; No 52, $28.12; and No. 53, $40.63. Prepare Jim's bank reconciliation.

4–7. On June 8, 2004, Larson Company had the following MasterCard transactions (along with some returns). Sales were $28.96, $210.55, and $189.88. Returns were $11.10 and $29.85. As Larson's bookkeeper you must calculate the net deposit.

4–8. *The Record,* on April 3, 2001, reported on rising ATM fees. Consumers who used ATMs operated by banks paid an average of $2.86 per transaction. New Jersey banks were under the national average at $2.50 per transaction. Murray Mitchell banks at the Fleet Bank in New Jersey and received his bank statement on March 15, 2002. He had a $12.50 ATM charge. The bank statement showed a balance of $205.15. Murray's checkbook showed a balance of $1,612.20. Murray belongs to the YMCA and has his monthly membership fee of $28.00 paid through his bank. The bank also pays his monthly New York Life Insurance policy of $14.80. The following checks did not clear the bank: No. 512, $220.15; No. 514, $21.15; and No. 515, $123.60. On the 16th of March he made a $1,720.15 deposit that does not appear on his bank statement. Murray earned $3.50 in interest. Prepare Murray Mitchell's bank reconciliation.

4–9. The January 15, 2001, issue of the *Providence Journal* reported on Pennsylvania's banking fees. Sovereign Bancorp
Excel of Pennsylvania charges a $2.50 monthly checking fee, plus a 75-cent fee for each transaction over 10 per month. Judy Smejek has an account at Sovereign Bancorp and just received her April 3, 2002, bank statement. Included in the statement was a charge of 75 cents for 15 additional checks written. She was also charged a $2.50 service fee. The bank statement shows a $1,768.01 balance. Judy's checkbook has a $1,085.81 balance. The following checks have not cleared the bank: No. 113, $312.50; No. 114, $50.40; and No. 115, $16.80. Judy made a $650.25 deposit that is not shown on the bank statement. She has her $540 monthly mortgage payment paid through the bank. Her $1,506.50 IRS refund check was mailed to her bank. Prepare Judy Smejek's bank reconciliation.

4–10. On April 1, 2001, John D. Hawks, Jr., comptroller of the currency, delivered an address titled "Banks—Fees! Fees! Fees!" He points out that consumers who were unable to meet minimum balance requirements paid an average of $217 a year, or $18 a month, to maintain a checking account. Kameron Gibson has a hard time maintaining the minimum balance. He was having difficulty balancing his checkbook because he did not notice this fee on his bank statement. His bank statement showed a balance of $717.72. Kameron's checkbook had a balance of $209.50. Check No. 104 for $110.07 and check No. 105 for $15.55 were outstanding. A $620.50 deposit was not on the statement. He has his payroll check electronically deposited to his checking account—the payroll check was for $1,025.10. There was also a $4 teller fee and an $18 service charge. Prepare Kameron Gibson's bank reconciliation.

4–11. The *Arkansas Democrat-Gazette,* on October 29, 2000, reported that banks are finding more ways to charge fees, such as a $25 overdraft fee. Sue McVickers has an account in Fayetteville; she has received her bank statement with this $25 charge. Also, she was charged a $6.50 service fee; however, the good news is she had earned $5.15 interest. Her bank statement's balance was $315.65, but it did not show the $1,215.15 deposit she had made. Sue's checkbook balance shows $604.30. The following checks have not cleared: No. 250, $603.15; No. 253, $218.90; and No. 254, $130.80. Prepare Sue's bank reconciliation.

4–12. On February 5, 2001, the *Pittsburgh Post-Gazette* reported on miscellaneous checking account fees that are going up, including the bounced-check charge from $25 to $27 and the stop-payment fee from $25 to $30. Carol Stokke received her April 6, 2002, bank statement showing a balance of $859.75; her checkbook balance is $954.25. The bank statement shows an ATM charge of $25.00, NSF fee of $27.00, earned interest of $2.75, and Carol's $630.15 refund check, which was processed by the IRS and deposited to her account. Carol has two checks that have not cleared—No. 115 for $521.15 and No. 116 for $205.50. There is also a deposit in transit for $1,402.05. Prepare Carol's bank reconciliation.

4–13. Lowell Bank reported the following checking account fees: $2 to see a real-live teller, $20 to process a bounced check, and $1 to $3 if you need an original check to prove you paid a bill or made a charitable contribution. This past month you had to transact business through a teller 6 times—a total $12 cost to you. Your bank statement shows a $305.33 balance; your checkbook shows a $1,009.76 balance. You received $1.10 in interest. An $801.15 deposit was not recorded on your statement. The following checks were outstanding: No. 413, $28.30; No. 414, $18.60; and No. 418, $60.72. Prepare your bank reconciliation.

CHALLENGE PROBLEMS

4–14. Margaret Luna received her January 5, 2002, bank statement, which shows a $782.19 balance. Her checkbook shows $748.20 balance. The following transactions occurred: $2.50 check processing fee (25 checks at $.10), $159.36 automatic withdrawal to Nicor, $4.00 teller fee, NSF fee of $27.00, $8.50 ATM fee, $20.00 stop order payment order, $6.50 earned interest, $1,350.20 IRS refund check made to the bank, $7.00 service fee, $20.00 stop payment order, and $6.50 for check printing. A $1,430.50 deposit is not shown on the bank statement. The following checks were outstanding: No. 202, $216.12; No. 203, $58.40; No. 205, $29.50; and No. 206, $58.63. Prepare Margaret Luna's bank reconciliation.

4–15. Melissa Jackson, bookkeeper for Kinko Company, cannot prepare a bank reconciliation. From the following facts, can you help her complete the June 30, 2004, reconciliation? The bank statement showed a $2,955.82 balance. Melissa's checkbook showed a $3,301.82 balance.

Melissa placed a $510.19 deposit in the bank's night depository on June 30. The deposit did not appear on the bank statement. The bank included two DMs and one CM with the returned checks: $690.65 DM for NSF check, $8.50 DM for service charges, and $400.00 CM (less $10 collection fee) for collecting a $400.00 non-interest-bearing note. Check No. 811 for $110.94 and check No. 912 for $82.50, both written and recorded on June 28, were not with the returned checks. The bookkeeper had correctly written check No. 884, $1,000, for a new cash register, but she recorded the check as $1,069. The May bank reconciliation showed check No. 748 for $210.90 and check No. 710 for $195.80 outstanding on April 30. The June bank statement included check No. 710 but not check No. 748.

 SUMMARY PRACTICE TEST

1. Colonial Cleaners had the following MasterCard sales for a day: $114.18, $15.10, $76.80, and $19.99. The company also issued two credits for returned merchandise: $11.20 and $14.99. What would be the amount of the net deposit for Colonial Cleaners on its merchant batch summary slip? *(p. 93)*

2. Walgreen has a $10,198.55 beginning checkbook balance. Record the following transactions in the check stubs provided. *(p. 91)*

   a. November 4, 2004, check No. 191 payable to Merck Corporation, $2,185.99 for drugs.
   b. $1,500 deposit—November 24.
   c. November 24, 2004, check No. 192 payable to Gillette Corporation, $895.22 for merchandise.

No. _____ $ _____			No. _____ $ _____		
_____ 20 _____			_____ 20 _____		
To _____			To _____		
For _____			For _____		
	DOLLARS	CENTS		DOLLARS	CENTS
BALANCE			BALANCE		
AMT. DEPOSITED			AMT. DEPOSITED		
TOTAL			TOTAL		
AMT. THIS CHECK			AMT. THIS CHECK		
BALANCE FORWARD			BALANCE FORWARD		

3. On April 1, 2004, Gracemoll Company received a bank statement that showed a $9,200 balance. Gracemoll showed a $6,600 checking account balance. The bank did not return check No. 115 for $870 or check No. 118 for $1,345. A $700 deposit made on March 31 was in transit. The bank charged Gracemoll $40 for printing and $175 for NSF checks. The

bank also collected a $1,400 note for Gracemoll. Gracemoll forgot to record a $100 withdrawal at the ATM. Prepare a bank reconciliation. *(p. 99)*

4. Hal Bean banks at Chris Federal Bank. Today he received his March 31, 2004, bank statement showing a $1,842.33 balance. Hal's checkbook shows a balance of $645.15. The following checks have not cleared the bank: No. 140, $218.44; No. 149, $55.18; and No. 161, $88.51. Hal made a $615.35 deposit that is not shown on the bank statement. He has his $700 monthly mortgage payment paid through the bank. His $2,150.40 IRS refund check was mailed to his bank. Prepare Hal Bean's bank reconciliation. *(p. 99)*

5. On June 30, 2004, Andy Company's bank statement showed a $7,182.11 bank balance. The bank statement also showed that it collected a $1,200.10 note for the company. A $1,200.50 June 30 deposit was in transit. Check No. 119 for $950.12 and check No. 130 for $455.79 are outstanding. Andy's bank charges 30 cents per processed check. This month, Andy wrote 80 checks. Andy has a $5,800 checkbook balance. Prepare a reconciled statement. *(p. 99)*

ZOHAR LAZAR

BANKING | New technology will **DEDUCT YOUR CHECKS** from your bank account even before the store clerk hands you a receipt. *By Erin Burt*

LOSING THE FLOAT

WRITING a paper check will soon become more like using a debit card for customers of 11 large banks. If your bank is among them, it means you won't have the hassle of getting approval from the store manager to write a check. It also means you won't get the benefit of the float, because money will be deducted from your account as soon as you write a check.

The banks, which include Bank of America, Chase, Citibank, First Union and Wells Fargo, are linking their check-processing systems to ATM networks. When you write a check, the retailer will scan it to verify that your account has enough funds to cover your purchase. If it's accepted, your check will be voided and returned to you with your receipt, so you can't count on tomorrow's paycheck to cover it.

Despite the advent of debit cards, automatic transfers and online banking, consumers are actually writing a growing number of checks—an estimated 69 billion in 1999. Banks maintain that the new procedure will reduce the risk of check fraud and allow retailers to get their money faster. As with debit transactions, bank statements will list where each purchase took place.

BB&T, a bank in the Southeast, is already testing the checks-as-debits system, and Bank of America will begin in June. All 11 participating banks should have it under way by March of next year.

Business Math Issue

The consumer will be hurt if they lose float. Banks are in a win-win situation.

1. List the key points of the article and information to support your position.
2. Write a group defense of your position using math calculations to support your view.

Online Banks Fail to Realize Cyber-Goals

By PETER EDMONSTON
WSJ.com

In the beginning, online banks had a simple strategy: With the money they saved by not owning expensive, marble-clad branches, they could offer high-interest, low-fee bank accounts that would bring customers flocking to their virtual doors.

But things haven't worked out that way. Five years after the first Internet bank launched its Web site, online banks have failed to capture more than a sliver of the banking business. Meanwhile, their customers are demanding many of the conveniences associated with traditional banks—creating an added expense that Internet banks hadn't worked into their business plans.

These unexpected pressures have started to take a toll. Online banks are rolling back or abandoning the generous offers they once dangled in front of potential customers. BankDirect, a Dallas-based Internet bank, and WingspanBank.com, an online subsidiary of Chicago-based **Bank One** Corp., the nation's fourth-largest bank, are raising fees and cutting interest paid on deposits.

Meanwhile, other online banks have been bailing out of the business altogether. In November, a company called **X.com** Corp. decided to phase out its Internet-banking operations to focus on its person-to-person payment service, PayPal.

Also last year, financial-services giant **Citigroup** Inc. pulled the plug on citi f/i, its Internet-only banking subsidiary.

Many other Web banks will soon be forced to become more tightfisted or even shut down, analysts and industry executives say. Battling to offer the highest rates and the lowest fees to online banking customers "is a strategy for failure," says Paul Van Dyke, senior analyst for Jupiter Research, a unit of New York-based Jupiter Media Metrix. "And I think online banks are beginning to see that now."

PROJECT A
Do you agree with this article?

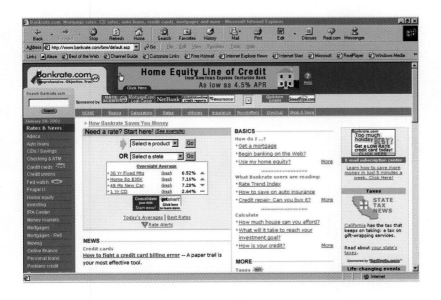

PROJECT B
Go to www.bankrate.com. Follow the link "Checking/ATM fees." Click the button marked Start. Select a city near where you live. Suppose you can only maintain a balance of $500 in your checking account and that you write 25 checks monthly. What is the most expensive and least expensive account for you to have?

Internet Projects: See text website (www.mhhe.com/slater7e) and *The Business Math Internet Resource Guide.*

Not Too Deep

India rates low in Internet penetration, compared with the rest of its region (in millions)

	NET USERS	ADULT POP.	USERS AS PCT. OF ADULT POP.
	1.2	3.4	36.2%
Singapore	4.1	15.4	26.3
Australia	4.0	17.7	22.8
Taiwan	1.2	5.9	19.7
Hong Kong	6.8	37.8	17.9
S. Korea	17.7	109.2	16.2
Japan	8.3	964.9	0.9
China	1.8	695.8	0.3
INDIA			

If Singapore increases its Net users by 3 times, will Singapore's users be more than Taiwan's users?

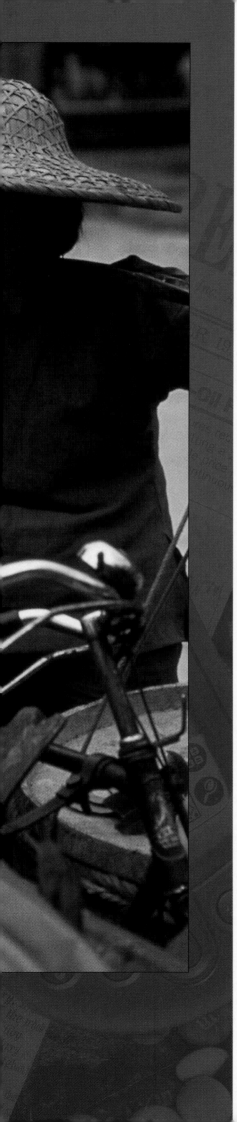

5

Solving for the Unknown: A How-to Approach for Solving Equations

LU 5–1:   Solving Equations for the Unknown

- Explain the basic procedures used to solve equations for the unknown *(pp. 115–19).*

- List the five rules and the mechanical steps used to solve for the unknown in seven situations; know how to check the answers *(pp. 116–19).*

LU 5–2:   Solving Word Problems for the Unknown

- List the steps for solving word problems *(p. 119).*

- Complete blueprint aids to solve word problems; check the solutions *(pp. 120–22).*

This letter is based on a true story.

Corbis Images/PictureQuest

> Rose Smith
> 15 Locust Street
> Lynn, MA 01915
>
> ## Flowers.net
> ### Decorating Service
>
> Dear Professor Slater,
>
>   Thank you for helping me get through your Business Math class. When I first started, my math anxiety level was real high. I felt I had no head for numbers. When you told us we would be covering the chapter on solving equations, I'll never forget how I started to shake. I started to panic. I felt I could never solve a word problem. I thought I was having an algebra attack.
>
>   Now that it's over (90 on the chapter on unknowns), I'd like to tell you what worked for me so you might pass this on to other students. It was your blueprint aids. Drawing boxes helped me to think things out. They were a <u>tool</u> that helped me more clearly understand how to dissect each word problem. They didn't solve the problem for me, but gave me the direction I needed. <u>Repetition</u> was the key to my success. At first I got them all wrong but after the third time, things started to click. I felt more confident. Your chapter organizers at the end of the chapter were great. Thanks for your patience – your repetition breeds success – now students are asking me to help them solve a word problem. Can you believe it!
>
> Best,
>
> *Rose*
>
> Rose Smith

The following *Wall Street Journal* clipping "UPS to Buy 60 Cargo Jets From Airbus" states that UPS agreed to buy 60 cargo jets with a total list value of about $6 billion. This is twice as big as its 1998 commitment to buy 30 wide-body planes. How much was the 1998 commitment? The calculation for this unknown uses the following equation:

$$\frac{\cancel{2}P}{\cancel{2}} = \frac{\$6,000,000,000}{2}$$

$$P = \$3,000,000,000$$

UPS to Buy 60 Cargo Jets From Airbus

By RICK BROOKS
And JEFF COLE
Staff Reporters of THE WALL STREET JOURNAL

ATLANTA—**United Parcel Service** Inc., anticipating big growth outside the U.S. far into the future, agreed to buy 60 cargo-carrying A300-600 aircraft from European plane maker **Airbus Industrie** with a total list value of about $6 billion.

The order is the largest in the parcel carrier's 93-year history and is twice as big as its previous commitment in 1998 to buy 30 of the wide-body planes. With the

Building Its Case

A filing suggests UPS might open a new hub in the Philippines if it wins Hong Kong delivery rights. Article on page A19.

latest order, UPS now says it will buy a total of 90 of the Airbus aircraft over nine years. The deal also gives the company options to buy 50 more of the A300-600s.

    Don't worry. Learning Unit 5–1 explains how to solve for unknowns in equations. In Learning Unit 5–2 you learn how to solve for unknowns in word problems. When you complete these learning units, you will not have to memorize as many formulas to solve business and personal math applications. Also, with the increasing use of computer software, a basic working knowledge of solving for the unknown has become necessary.

LEARNING UNIT 5–1 │ SOLVING EQUATIONS FOR THE UNKNOWN

The following heading appeared in a *Wall Street Journal* article:

Calculating Retirement?
It's No Simple Equation

© 2000 Dow Jones & Company, Inc.

Many of you are familiar with the terms *variables* and *constants*. If you are planning to prepare for your retirement by saving only what you can afford each year, your saving is a *variable*. However, if you plan to save the same amount each year, your saving is a *constant*. This unit explains the importance of mathematical variables and constants when solving equations.

Basic Equation-Solving Procedures

Do you know the difference between a mathematical expression, equation, and formula? A mathematical **expression** is a meaningful combination of numbers and letters called *terms*. Operational signs (such as $+$ or $-$) within the expression connect the terms to show a relationship between them. For example, $6 + 2$ or $6A - 4A$ are mathematical expressions. An **equation** is a mathematical statement with an equal sign showing that a mathematical expression on the left equals the mathematical expression on the right. An equation has an equal sign; an expression does not have an equal sign. A **formula** is an equation that expresses in symbols a general fact, rule, or principle. Formulas are shortcuts for expressing a word concept. For example, in Chapter 10 you will learn that the formula for simple interest is Interest (I) = Principal (P) × Rate (R) × Time (T). This means that when you see $I = P \times R \times T$, you recognize the simple interest formula. Now let's study basic equations.

As a mathematical statement of equality, equations show that two numbers or groups of numbers are equal. For example, $6 + 4 = 10$ shows the equality of an equation. Equations also use letters as symbols that represent one or more numbers. These symbols, usually a letter of the alphabet, are **variables** that stand for a number. We can use a variable even though we may not know what it represents. For example, $A + 2 = 6$. The variable A represents the number or **unknown** (4 in this example) for which we are solving. We distinguish variables from numbers, which have a fixed value. Numbers such as 3 or -7 are **constants** or **knowns,** whereas A and $3A$ (this means 3 times the variable A) are variables. So we can now say that variables and constants are *terms of mathematical expressions.*

Usually in solving for the unknown, we place variable(s) on the left side of the equation and constants on the right. The following rules for variables and constants are important.

Variables and Constants Rules
1. If no number is in front of a letter, it is a 1: $B = 1B$; $C = 1C$.
2. If no sign is in front of a letter or number, it is a $+$: $C = +C$; $4 = +4$.

You should be aware that in solving equations, the meaning of the symbols $+$, $-$, $\times$, and $\div$ has not changed. However, some variations occur. For example, you can also write $A \times B$ (A times B) as $A \cdot B$, $A(B)$, or AB. Also, A divided by B is the same as A/B. Remember that to solve an equation, you must find a number that can replace the unknown in the equation and make it a true statement. Now let's take a moment to look at how we can change verbal statements into variables.

Assume Dick Hersh, an employee of Nike, is 50 years old. Let's assign Dick Hersh's changing age to the symbol *A*. The symbol *A* is a variable.

Verbal statement	Variable *A* (age)
Dick's age 8 years ago	$A - 8$
Dick's age 8 years from today	$A + 8$
Four times Dick's age	$4A$
One-fifth Dick's age	$A/5$

FIGURE 5.1

Equality in equations

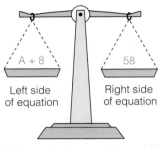

Left side of equation   Right side of equation

Dick's age in 8 years will equal 58.

To visualize how equations work, think of the old-fashioned balancing scale shown in Figure 5.1. The pole of the scale is the equals sign. The two sides of the equation are the two pans of the scale. In the left pan or left side of the equation, we have $A + 8$; in the right pan or right side of the equation, we have 58. To solve for the unknown (Dick's present age), we isolate or place the unknown (variable) on the left side and the numbers on the right. We will do this soon. For now, remember that to keep an equation (or scale) in balance, we must perform mathematical operations (addition, subtraction, multiplication, and division) to *both* sides of the equation.

Solving for the Unknown Rule

Whatever you do to one side of an equation, you must do to the other side.

How to Solve for Unknowns in Equations

This section presents seven drill situations and the rules that will guide you in solving for unknowns in these situations. We begin with two basic rules—the opposite process rule and the equation equality rule.

Opposite Process Rule

If an equation indicates a process such as addition, subtraction, multiplication, or division, solve for the unknown or variable by using the opposite process. For example, if the equation process is addition, solve for the unknown by using subtraction.

Equation Equality Rule

You can add the same quantity or number to both sides of the equation and subtract the same quantity or number from both sides of the equation without affecting the equality of the equation. You can also divide or multiply both sides of the equation by the same quantity or number *(except zero)* without affecting the equality of the equation.

To check your answer(s), substitute your answer(s) for the letter(s) in the equation. The sum of the left side should equal the sum of the right side.

Drill Situation 1: Subtracting Same Number from Both Sides of Equation

Example

$A + 8 = 58$
Dick's age *A* plus 8 equals 58.

Mechanical steps

$$A + 8 = 58$$
$$\underline{-8 \quad -8}$$
$$A \quad = \quad 50$$

Explanation

8 is subtracted from *both* sides of equation to isolate variable *A* on the left.

Check
$50 + 8 = 58$
$58 = 58$

Note: Since the equation process used *addition,* we use the opposite process rule and solve for variable *A* with *subtraction.* We also use the equation equality rule when we subtract the same quantity from both sides of the equation.

Drill Situation 2: Adding Same Number to Both Sides of Equation

Example

$B - 50 = 80$
Some number B
less 50 equals 80.

Mechanical steps

$B - 50 = \quad 80$
$\underline{+ 50 \qquad + 50}$
$B \qquad = \quad 130$

Explanation

50 is added to *both* sides to isolate variable B on the left.

Check
$130 - 50 = 80$
$\qquad \quad 80 = 80$

Note: Since the equation process used *subtraction,* we use the opposite process rule and solve for variable B with *addition.* We also use the equation equality rule when we add the same quantity to both sides of the equation.

Drill Situation 3: Dividing Both Sides of Equation by Same Number

Example

$7G = 35$
Some number G
times 7 equals 35.

Mechanical steps

$7G = 35$
$\dfrac{7G}{7} = \dfrac{35}{7}$
$G = 5$

Explanation

By dividing both sides by 7, G equals 5.

Check
$7(5) = 35$
$\quad \ 35 = 35$

Note: Since the equation process used *multiplication,* we use the opposite process rule and solve for variable G with *division.* We also use the equation equality rule when we divide both sides of the equation by the same quantity.

Drill Situation 4: Multiplying Both Sides of Equation by Same Number

Example

$\dfrac{V}{5} = 70$
Some number V
divided by 5
equals 70.

Mechanical steps

$\dfrac{V}{5} = 70$
$5\left(\dfrac{V}{5}\right) = 70(5)$
$V = 350$

Explanation

By multiplying both sides by 5, V is equal to 350.

Check
$\dfrac{350}{5} = 70$
$\quad 70 = 70$

Note: Since the equation process used *division,* we use the opposite process rule and solve for variable V with *multiplication.* We also use the equation equality rule when we multiply both sides of the equation by the same quantity.

Drill Situation 5: Equation That Uses Subtraction and Multiplication to Solve Unknown

Multiple Processes Rule

When solving for an unknown that involves more than one process, do the addition and subtraction before the multiplication and division.

Example

$\dfrac{H}{4} + 2 = 5$

When we divide unknown H by 4 and add the result to 2, the answer is 5.

Mechanical steps

$\dfrac{H}{4} + 2 = \quad 5$

$\dfrac{H}{4} + 2 = \quad 5$
$\underline{\quad - 2 \qquad - 2}$
$\dfrac{H}{4} \qquad = \quad 3$

$4\left(\dfrac{H}{4}\right) = 4(3)$
$H = 12$

Explanation

1. Move constant to right side by subtracting 2 from both sides.
2. To isolate H, which is divided by 4, we do the opposite process and multiply 4 times *both* sides of the equation.

Check
$\dfrac{12}{4} + 2 = 5$
$\quad 3 + 2 = 5$
$\qquad \quad 5 = 5$

Drill Situation 6: Using Parentheses in Solving for Unknown

> **Parentheses Rule**
>
> When equations contain parentheses (which indicate grouping together), you solve for the unknown by first multiplying each item inside the parentheses by the number or letter just outside the parentheses. Then you continue to solve for the unknown with the opposite process used in the equation. Do the additions and subtractions first; then the multiplications and divisions.

Example	**Mechanical steps**	**Explanation**
$5(P - 4) = 20$ The unknown P less 4, multiplied by 5 equals 20.	$5(P - 4) = 20$ $5P - 20 = 20$ $\underline{+ 20 \quad +20}$ $\dfrac{\cancel{5}P}{\cancel{5}} = \dfrac{40}{5}$ $P = \boxed{8}$	1. Parentheses tell us that everything inside parentheses is multiplied by 5. Multiply 5 by P and 5 by -4. 2. Add 20 to both sides to isolate $5P$ on left. 3. To remove 5 in front of P, divide both sides by 5 to result in P equals 8.

Check
$5(8 - 4) = 20$
$5(4) = 20$
$20 = 20$

Drill Situation 7: Combining Like Unknowns

> **Like Unknowns Rule**
>
> To solve equations with like unknowns, you first combine the unknowns and then solve with the opposite process used in the equation.

Example	**Mechanical steps**	**Explanation**
$4A + A = 20$	$4A + A = 20$ $\dfrac{\cancel{5}A}{\cancel{5}} = \dfrac{20}{5}$ $A = \boxed{4}$	To solve this equation: $4A + 1A = 5A$. Thus, $5A = 20$. To solve for A, divide both sides by 5, leaving A equals 4.

Before you go to Learning Unit 5–2, let's check your understanding of this unit.

LU 5–1 PRACTICE QUIZ

1. Write equations for the following (use the letter Q as the variable). Do not solve for the unknown.
    a. Nine less than one-half a number is fourteen.
    b. Eight times the sum of a number and thirty-one is fifty.
    c. Ten decreased by twice a number is two.
    d. Eight times a number less two equals twenty-one.
    e. The sum of four times a number and two is fifteen.
    f. If twice a number is decreased by eight, the difference is four.

2. Solve the following:
    a. $B + 24 = 60$ b. $D + 3D = 240$ c. $12B = 144$
    d. $\dfrac{B}{6} = 50$ e. $\dfrac{B}{4} + 4 = 16$ f. $3(B - 8) = 18$

✓ **SOLUTIONS**

1. **a.** $\frac{1}{2}Q - 9 = 14$ **b.** $8(Q + 31) = 50$ **c.** $10 - 2Q = 2$

    d. $8Q - 2 = 21$ **e.** $4Q + 2 = 15$ **f.** $2Q - 8 = 4$

2. **a.**
$$\begin{array}{rcl} B + 24 &=& 60 \\ -24 && -24 \\ \hline B &=& 36 \end{array}$$

    b.
$$\begin{array}{rcl} \dfrac{\cancel{4}D}{\cancel{4}} &=& \dfrac{240}{4} \\ D &=& 60 \end{array}$$

    c.
$$\begin{array}{rcl} \dfrac{\cancel{12}B}{\cancel{12}} &=& \dfrac{144}{12} \\ B &=& 12 \end{array}$$

    d.
$$\begin{array}{rcl} \cancel{6}\left(\dfrac{B}{\cancel{6}}\right) &=& 50(6) \\ B &=& 300 \end{array}$$

    e.
$$\begin{array}{rcl} \dfrac{B}{4} + 4 &=& 16 \\ -4 && -4 \\ \hline \dfrac{B}{4} &=& 12 \\ \cancel{4}\left(\dfrac{B}{\cancel{4}}\right) &=& 12(4) \\ B &=& 48 \end{array}$$

    f.
$$\begin{array}{rcl} 3(B - 8) &=& 18 \\ 3B - 24 &=& 18 \\ +24 && +24 \\ \hline \dfrac{\cancel{3}B}{\cancel{3}} &=& \dfrac{42}{3} \\ B &=& 14 \end{array}$$

LEARNING UNIT 5–2 | SOLVING WORD PROBLEMS FOR THE UNKNOWN

On the first day of your business math class, you count 29 students in the class. A week later, 11 additional students had joined the class. The semester ended with 35 students in attendance. How many students dropped out of class? You can solve this unknown as follows:

> 29 students started the class + 11 students joined the class = 40 total students
>
> 40 total students $-$ 35 students completed the class $=$ 5 students dropped the class

Whether you are in or out of class, you are continually solving word problems. In this unit we give you a road map showing you how to solve word problems with unknowns by using a blueprint aid. The five steps below will help you dissect and solve these word problems. In Chapters 1 through 3, we also presented blueprint aids for dissecting and solving word problems. Now the blueprint aid focuses on solving for the unknown.

We look at six different situations in this unit. Be patient and *persistent*. The more problems you work, the easier the process becomes. Note how we dissect and solve each problem in the blueprint aids. Do not panic! Repetition is the key. Now let's study the five steps.

Solving Word Problems for Unknowns

Step 1. Carefully read the entire problem. You may have to read it several times.

Step 2. Ask yourself: "What is the problem looking for?"

Step 3. When you are sure what the problem is asking, let a variable represent the unknown. If the problem has more than one unknown, represent the second unknown in terms of the same variable. For example, if the problem has two unknowns, Y is one unknown. The second unknown is $4Y$—4 times the first unknown.

Step 4. Visualize the relationship between unknowns and variables. Then set up an equation to solve for unknown(s).

Step 5. Check your result to see if it is accurate.

Word Problem Situation 1: Number Problems   From *The Wall Street Journal* clip "The Flagging Division," you can determine that Disney Stores reduced its product offerings by 1,600. Disney now has 1,800 product offerings. What was the original number of product offerings?

Bill Aron/PhotoEdit

The Flagging Division ...

A snapshot of the Disney Stores

● **NUMBER OF STORES:** 740

● **STORE VISITORS:** 250 million annually

● **LOCATIONS:** 11 countries including Britain, Australia and Japan

● **PRODUCTS:** Toys, costumes, apparel, jewelry, accessories, videos and games, among others

● **PRODUCT PLANS:** Each store will have 1,800 product offerings, down from 3,400 in the past. Focus on adults will be narrowed to sleepwear and parenting products.

© 2000 Dow Jones & Company, Inc.

Blueprint aid

Unknown(s)	Variable(s)	Relationship*
Original number of product offerings	P	$P - 1,600$ = New offerings New offerings = 1,800

*This column will help you visualize the equation before setting up the actual equation.

Mechanical steps

$$\begin{array}{rcr} P - 1,600 & = & 1,800 \\ + 1,600 & & + 1,600 \\ \hline P & = & \boxed{3,400} \end{array}$$

Explanation

The original offerings less 1,600 = 1,800. Note that we added 1,600 to both sides to isolate P on the left. Remember, $1P = P$.

Check

$$3,400 - 1,600 = 1,800$$
$$1,800 = 1,800$$

Word Problem Situation 2: Finding the Whole When Part Is Known   A local Burger King budgets $\frac{1}{8}$ of its monthly profits on salaries. Salaries for the month were \$12,000. What were Burger King's monthly profits?

Blueprint aid

Unknown(s)	Variable(s)	Relationship
Monthly profits	P	$\frac{1}{8}P$ Salaries = \$12,000

Mechanical steps

$$\frac{1}{8}P = \$12,000$$
$$8\left(\frac{P}{8}\right) = \$12,000(8)$$
$$P = \boxed{\$96,000}$$

Explanation

$\frac{1}{8}P$ represents Burger King's monthly salaries. Since the equation used division, we solve for P by multiplying both sides by 8.

Check

$$\frac{1}{8}(\$96,000) = \$12,000$$
$$\$12,000 = \$12,000$$

Word Problem Situation 3: Difference Problems   ICM Company sold 4 times as many computers as Ring Company. The difference in their sales is 27. How many computers of each company were sold?

Blueprint aid

Unknown(s)	Variable(s)	Relationship
ICM	$4C$	$4C$
Ring	C	$\dfrac{-\ C}{27}$

Note: If problem has two unknowns, assign the variable to smaller item or one who sells less. Then assign the other unknown using the same variable. *Use the same letter.*

Mechanical steps

$$4C - C = 27$$
$$\frac{3C}{3} = \frac{27}{3}$$
$$C = \boxed{9}$$

Ring = $\boxed{9}$ computers

ICM = 4(9)

= $\boxed{36}$ computers

Explanation

The variables replace the names ICM and Ring. We assigned Ring the variable C, since it sold fewer computers. We assigned ICM $4C$, since it sold 4 times as many computers.

Check

$$\begin{array}{r} 36 \text{ computers} \\ -\ 9 \\ \hline 27 \text{ computers} \end{array}$$

Word Problem Situation 4: Calculating Unit Sales   Together Barry Sullivan and Mitch Ryan sold a total of 300 homes for Regis Realty. Barry sold 9 times as many homes as Mitch. How many did each sell?

Blueprint aid

Unknown(s)	Variable(s)	Relationship
Homes sold:		
B. Sullivan	9H	9H
M. Ryan	H*	+ H
		300 homes

*Assign *H* to Ryan since he sold less.

Mechanical steps

$$9H + H = 300$$
$$\frac{\cancel{10}H}{\cancel{10}} = \frac{300}{10}$$
$$H = \boxed{30}$$

Ryan: $\boxed{30}$ homes

Sullivan: $9(30) = \boxed{270}$ homes

Explanation

We assigned Mitch *H*, since he sold fewer homes. We assigned Barry 9*H*, since he sold 9 times as many homes. Together Barry and Mitch sold 300 homes.

Check

$30 + 270 = 300$

Word Problem Situation 5: Calculating Unit and Dollar Sales (Cost per Unit) When Total Units Are Not Given   Andy sold watches ($9) and alarm clocks ($5) at a flea market. Total sales were $287. People bought 4 times as many watches as alarm clocks. How many of each did Andy sell? What were the total dollar sales of each?

Blueprint aid

Unknown(s)	Variable(s)	Price	Relationship
Unit sales:			
Watches	4C	$9	36C
Clocks	C	5	+ 5C
			$287 total sales

Mechanical steps

$$36C + 5C = 287$$
$$\frac{\cancel{41}C}{\cancel{41}} = \frac{287}{41}$$
$$C = \boxed{7}$$

$\boxed{7}$ clocks

$4(7) = \boxed{28}$ watches

Explanation

Number of watches times $9 sales price plus number of alarm clocks times $5 equals $287 total sales.

Check

$7(\$5) + 28(\$9) = \$287$
$\$35 + \$252 = \$287$
$\$287 = \$287$

Word Problem Situation 6: Calculating Unit and Dollar Sales (Cost per Unit) When Total Units Are Given   Andy sold watches ($9) and alarm clocks ($5) at a flea market. Total sales for 35 watches and alarm clocks were $287. How many of each did Andy sell? What were the total dollar sales of each?

Blueprint aid

Unknown(s)	Variable(s)	Price	Relationship
Unit sales:			
Watches	W*	$9	9W
Clocks	35 − W	5	+ 5(35 − W)
			$287 total sales

*The more expensive item is assigned to the variable first only for this situation to make the mechanical steps easier to complete.

Mechanical steps

$$9W + 5(35 - W) = 287$$
$$9W + 175 - 5W = 287$$
$$4W + 175 = 287$$
$$\frac{-175 \qquad\quad -175}{}$$
$$\frac{4W}{4} = \frac{112}{4}$$
$$W = \boxed{28}$$

Watches = $\boxed{28}$

Clocks = $35 - 28 = \boxed{7}$

Explanation

Number of watches (*W*) times price per watch plus number of alarm clocks times price per alarm clock equals $287. Total units given was 35.

Check

$28(\$9) + 7(\$5) = \$287$
$\$252 + \$35 = \$287$
$\$287 = \$287$

Why did we use $35 - W$? Assume we had 35 pizzas (some cheese, others meatball). If I said that I ate all the meatball pizzas (5), how many cheese pizzas are left? Thirty? Right, you subtract 5 from 35. Think of $35 - W$ as meaning one number.

Note in Word Problem Situations 5 and 6 that the situation is the same. In Word Problem Situation 5, we were not given total units sold (but we were told which sold better). In Word Problem Situation 6, we were given total units sold, but we did not know which sold better.

Now try these six types of word problems in the Practice Quiz. Be sure to complete blueprint aids and the mechanical steps for solving the unknown(s).

LU 5–2 PRACTICE QUIZ

Situations

1. An L. L. Bean sweater was reduced $30. The sale price was $90. What was the original price?
2. Kelly Doyle budgets $\frac{1}{8}$ of her yearly salary for entertainment. Kelly's total entertainment bill for the year is $6,500. What is Kelly's yearly salary?
3. Micro Knowledge sells 5 times as many computers as Morse Electronics. The difference in sales between the two stores is 20 computers. How many computers did each store sell?
4. Susie and Cara sell stoves at Elliott's Appliances. Together they sold 180 stoves in January. Susie sold 5 times as many stoves as Cara. How many stoves did each sell?
5. Pasquale's Pizza sells meatball pizzas ($6) and cheese pizzas ($5). In March, Pasquale's total sales were $1,600. People bought 2 times as many cheese pizzas as meatball pizzas. How many of each did Pasquale sell? What were the total dollar sales of each?
6. Pasquale's Pizza sells meatball pizzas ($6) and cheese pizzas ($5). In March, Pasquale's sold 300 pizzas for $1,600. How many of each did Pasquale's sell? What was the dollar sales price of each?

✓ SOLUTIONS

1.

Unknown(s)	Variable(s)	Relationship
Original price	P*	P − $30 = Sale price Sale price = $90

*P = Original price.

Mechanical steps

$$P - \$30 = \$90$$
$$\underline{+\ 30 \qquad +\ 30}$$
$$P \qquad = \boxed{\$120}$$

2.

Unknown(s)	Variable(s)	Relationship
Yearly salary	S*	$\frac{1}{8}S$ Entertainment = $6,500

*S = Salary.

Mechanical steps

$$\frac{1}{8}S = \$6,500$$
$$8\left(\frac{S}{8}\right) = \$6,500(8)$$
$$S = \boxed{\$52,000}$$

3.

Unknown(s)	Variable(s)	Relationship
Micro	5C*	5C
Morse	C	− C
		20 computers

*C = Computers.

Mechanical steps

$$5C - C = 20$$
$$\frac{4C}{4} = \frac{20}{4}$$
$$C = \boxed{5} \quad \text{(Morse)}$$
$$5C = \boxed{25} \quad \text{(Micro)}$$

4.

Unknown(s)	Variable(s)	Relationship
Stoves sold:		
Susie	5S*	5S
Cara	S	+ S
		180 stoves

*S = Stoves.

Mechanical steps

$$5S + S = 180$$
$$\frac{6S}{6} = \frac{180}{6}$$
$$S = \boxed{30} \quad \text{(Cara)}$$
$$5S = \boxed{150} \quad \text{(Susie)}$$

5.

Unknown(s)	Variable(s)	Price	Relationship
Meatball	M	$6	6M
Cheese	2M	5	+ 10M
			$1,600 total sales

Check

$$(100 \times \$6) + (200 \times \$5) = \$1,600$$
$$\$600 + \$1,000 = \$1,600$$
$$\$1,600 = \$1,600$$

Mechanical steps

$$6M + 10M = 1,600$$
$$\frac{16M}{16} = \frac{1,600}{16}$$
$$M = \boxed{100} \quad \text{(meatball)}$$
$$2M = \boxed{200} \quad \text{(cheese)}$$

6.

Unknown(s)	Variable(s)	Price	Relationship
Unit sales:			
Meatball	M*	$6	6M
Cheese	300 − M	5	+ 5(300 − M)
			$1,600 total sales

*We assign the variable to the most expensive to make the mechanical steps easier to complete.

Check

$$100(\$6) + 200(\$5) = \$600 + \$1,000$$
$$= \$1,600$$

Mechanical steps

$$6M + 5(300 - M) = 1,600$$
$$6M + 1,500 - 5M = 1,600$$
$$M + 1,500 = 1,600$$
$$\underline{-\ 1,500 \qquad\quad -\ 1,500}$$
$$M = 100$$

Meatball = $\boxed{100}$

Cheese = 300 − 100 = $\boxed{200}$

Chapter Organizer and Reference Guide

Solving for unknowns from basic equations	Mechanical steps to solve unknowns	Key point(s)
Situation 1: Subtracting same number from both sides of equation, p. 116	$D + 10 = 12$ $-10 = -10$ $D = 2$	Subtract 10 from both sides of equation to isolate variable D on the left. Since equation used addition, we solve by using opposite process—subtraction.
Situation 2: Adding same number to both sides of equation, p. 117	$L - 24 = 40$ $+24 = +24$ $L = 64$	Add 24 to both sides to isolate unknown L on left. We solve by using opposite process of subtraction—addition.
Situation 3: Dividing both sides of equation by same number, p. 117	$6B = 24$ $\dfrac{6B}{6} = \dfrac{24}{6}$ $B = 4$	To isolate B by itself on the left, divide both sides of the equation by 6. Thus, the 6 on the left cancels—leaving B equal to 4. Since equation used multiplication, we solve unknown by using opposite process—division.
Situation 4: Multiplying both sides of equation by same number, p. 117	$\dfrac{R}{3} = 15$ $3\left(\dfrac{R}{3}\right) = 15(3)$ $R = 45$	To remove denominator, multiply both sides of the equation by 3—the 3 on the left side cancels, leaving R equal to 45. Since equation used division, we solve unknown by using opposite process—multiplication.
Situation 5: Equation that uses subtraction and multiplication to solve for unknown, p. 117	$\dfrac{B}{3} + 6 = 13$ $-6 \quad -6$ $\dfrac{B}{3} = 7$ $3\left(\dfrac{B}{3}\right) = 7(3)$ $B = 21$	1. Move constant 6 to right side by subtracting 6 from both sides. 2. Isolate B by itself on left by multiplying both sides by 3.
Situation 6: Using parentheses in solving for unknown, p. 118	$6(A - 5) = 12$ $6A - 30 = 12$ $+30 \quad +30$ $\dfrac{6A}{6} = \dfrac{42}{6}$ $A = 7$	Parentheses indicate multiplication. Multiply 6 times A and 6 times -5. Result is $6A - 30$ on left side of the equation. Now add 30 to both sides to isolate $6A$ on left. To remove 6 in front of A, divide both sides by 6, to result in A equal to 7. Note that when deleting parentheses, we did not have to multiply the right side.
Situation 7: Combining like unknowns, p. 118	$6A + 2A = 64$ $\dfrac{8A}{8} = \dfrac{64}{8}$ $A = 8$	$6A + 2A$ combine to $8A$. To solve for A, we divide both sides by 8.

Solving for unknowns from word problems	Blueprint aid	Mechanical steps to solve unknown with check
Situation 1: Number problems, p. 119 U.S. Air reduced its airfare to California by $60. The sale price was $95. What was the original price?		**Unknown(s)**	**Variable(s)**	**Relationship**	 	Original price	P	$P - \$60 =$ Sale price Sale price $= \$95$		$P - \$60 = \$95$ $+60 \quad +60$ $P = \$155$ **Check** $\$155 - \$60 = \$95$ $\$95 = \$95$
Situation 2: Finding the whole when part is known, p. 120 K. McCarthy spends $\frac{1}{8}$ of her budget for school. What is the total budget if school costs $5,000?		**Unknown(s)**	**Variable(s)**	**Relationship**	 	Total budget	B	$\frac{1}{8}B$ School $= \$5,000$		$\frac{1}{8}B = \$5,000$ $8\left(\dfrac{B}{8}\right) = \$5,000(8)$ $B = \$40,000$ **Check** $\frac{1}{8}(\$40,000) = \$5,000$ $\$5,000 = \$5,000$

(continues)

Chapter Organizer and Reference Guide (concluded)

Solving for unknowns from word problems	Blueprint aid	Mechanical steps to solve unknown with check
Situation 3: Difference problems, p. 120 Moe sold 8 times as many suitcases as Bill. The difference in their sales is 280 suitcases. How many suitcases did each sell?	<table><tr><th>Unknown(s)</th><th>Variable(s)</th><th>Relationship</th></tr><tr><td>Suitcases sold: Moe Bill</td><td>8S S</td><td>8S – S <u>280 suitcases</u></td></tr></table>	$8S - S = 280$ (Bill) $\dfrac{7S}{7} = \dfrac{280}{7}$ $S = \boxed{40}$ (Bill) $8(40) = \boxed{320}$ (Moe) **Check** $320 - 40 = 280$ $280 = 280$
Situation 4: Calculating unit sales, p. 121 Moe sold 8 times as many suitcases as Bill. Together they sold a total of 360. How many did each sell?	<table><tr><th>Unknown(s)</th><th>Variable(s)</th><th>Relationship</th></tr><tr><td>Suitcases sold: Moe Bill</td><td>8S S</td><td>8S + S <u>360 suitcases</u></td></tr></table>	$8S + S = 360$ $\dfrac{9S}{9} = \dfrac{360}{9}$ $S = \boxed{40}$ (Bill) $8S = \boxed{320}$ (Moe) **Check** $320 + 40 = 360$ $360 = 360$
Situation 5: Calculating unit and dollar sales (cost per unit) when *total units not given*, p. 121 Blue Furniture Company ordered sleepers ($300) and nonsleepers ($200) that cost $8,000. Blue expects sleepers to outsell nonsleepers 2 to 1. How many units of each were ordered? What were dollar costs of each?	<table><tr><th>Unknown(s)</th><th>Variable(s)</th><th>Price</th><th>Relationship</th></tr><tr><td>Sleepers Nonsleepers</td><td>2N N</td><td>$300 200</td><td>600N + 200N <u>$8,000 total cost</u></td></tr></table>	$600N + 200N = 8,000$ $\dfrac{800N}{800} = \dfrac{8,000}{800}$ $N = \boxed{10}$ (nonsleepers) $2N = \boxed{20}$ (sleepers) **Check** $10 \times \$200 = \$2,000$ $20 \times \$300 = \underline{\ \ 6,000}$ $= \$8,000$
Situation 6: Calculating unit and dollar sales (cost per unit) when *total units given*, p. 121 Blue Furniture Company ordered 30 sofas (sleepers and nonsleepers) that cost $8,000. The wholesale unit cost was $300 for the sleepers and $200 for the nonsleepers. How many units of each were ordered? What were dollar costs of each?	<table><tr><th>Unknown(s)</th><th>Variable(s)</th><th>Price</th><th>Relationship</th></tr><tr><td>Unit cost: Sleepers Nonsleepers</td><td>S 30 – S</td><td>$300 200</td><td>300S + 200 (30 – S) <u>$8,000 total cost</u></td></tr></table> *When the total units are given, the higher-priced item (sleepers) is assigned to the variable first. This makes the mechanical steps easier to complete.	$\begin{aligned}300S + 200(30 - S) &= 8,000\\ 300S + 6,000 - 200S &= 8,000\\ 100S + 6,000 &= 8,000\\ -6,000 & \quad -6,000\end{aligned}$ $\dfrac{100S}{100} = \dfrac{2,000}{100}$ $S = \boxed{20}$ Nonsleepers $= 30 - 20$ $= \boxed{10}$ **Check** $20(\$300) + 10(\$200) = \$8,000$ $\$6,000 + \$2,000 = \$8,000$ $\$8,000 = \$8,000$
Key terms	Constants, *p. 115* Equation, *p. 115* Expression, *p. 115* Formula, *p. 115* Knowns, *p. 115*	Unknown, *p. 115* Variables, *p. 115*

Critical Thinking Discussion Questions

1. Explain the difference between a variable and a constant. What would you consider your monthly car payment—a variable or a constant?

2. How does the opposite process rule help solve for the variable in an equation? If a Mercedes costs 3 times as much as a Saab, how could the opposite process rule be used? The selling price of the Mercedes is $60,000.

3. What is the difference between Word Problem Situations 5 and 6 in Learning Unit 5–2? Show why the more expensive item in Word Problem Situation 6 is assigned to the variable first.

END-OF-CHAPTER PROBLEMS

Name _____ Date _____

DRILL PROBLEMS (First of Three Sets)

Solve the unknown from the following equations:

5–1. $H + 15 = 70$ **5–2.** $B + 29 = 75$ **5–3.** $N + 50 = 290$ **5–4.** $Q - 60 = 850$

5–5. $5Y = 75$ **5–6.** $\dfrac{P}{6} = 92$ **5–7.** $8Y = 96$ **5–8.** $\dfrac{N}{16} = 5$

5–9. $4(P - 9) = 64$ **5–10.** $3(P - 3) = 27$

WORD PROBLEMS (First of Three Sets)

5–11. The *Omaha World-Herald,* on January 23, 2001, ran an article titled "Lending Agency Convicted of Predatory Lending Practices." A loan company took the title to an elderly Bellevue widow's home by paying taxes of about $22,200. The market value of the house is $3\frac{1}{2}$ times the tax. What was the market value? Round to the nearest ten thousands.

5–12. Jim Mateja's article in the *Chicago Tribune,* dated May 27, 2001, compared the price of a 1955 Ford Thunderbird to the 2002 Ford Thunderbird. The 2002 Thunderbird's price is $34,595. This is 13 times as much as the selling price for the 1955 Thunderbird. What was the selling price of the 1955 Ford Thunderbird? (Round to the nearest hundred.)

5–13. Joe Sullivan and Hugh Kee sell cars for a Ford dealer. Over the past year, they sold 300 cars. Joe sells 5 times as many cars as Hugh. How many cars did each sell?

5–14. Nanda Yueh and Lane Zuriff sell homes for ERA Realty. Over the past 6 months they sold 120 homes. Nanda sold 3 times as many homes as Lane. How many homes did each sell?

5–15. Dots sells T-shirts ($2) and shorts ($4). In April, total sales were $600. People bought 4 times as many T-shirts as shorts. How many T-shirts and shorts did Dots sell? Check your answer.

5–16. Dots sells 250 T-shirts ($2) and shorts ($4). In April, total sales were $600. How many T-shirts and shorts did Dots sell? Check your answer. *Hint:* Let S = Shorts.

DRILL PROBLEMS (Second of Three Sets)

5–17. $6B = 420$

5–18. $7(A - 5) = 63$

5–19. $\dfrac{N}{9} = 7$

5–20. $18(C - 3) = 162$

5–21. $9Y - 10 = 53$

5–22. $7B + 5 = 26$

WORD PROBLEMS (Second of Three Sets)

5–23. On a flight from Boston to Los Angeles, American Airlines reduced its Internet price $130. The sale price was $299.50. What was the original price?

5–24. Fay, an employee at the Gap, budgets $\frac{1}{5}$ of her yearly salary for clothing. Fay's total clothing bill for the year is $8,000. What is her yearly salary?

5–25. Bill's Roast Beef sells 5 times as many sandwiches as Pete's Deli. The difference between their sales is 360 sandwiches. How many sandwiches did each sell?

5–26. *USA Today,* on June 1, 2001, ran an article entitled "Fast-Food Highway Hazards." The article compared the number of calories for the food sold by several fast-food chains. McDonald's "Big N' Tasty with Cheese" has almost 600 calories. This is 4 times as many as are in the "McSalad Shaker Chef Salad." How many calories are in the salad?

5–27. Computer City sells batteries ($3) and small boxes of pens ($5). In August, total sales were $960. Customers bought 5 times as many batteries as boxes of pens. How many of each did Computer City sell? Check your answer.

5–28. Staples sells cartons of pens ($10) and rubber bands ($4). Leona ordered a total of 24 cartons for $210. How many cartons of each did Leona order? Check your answer. *Hint:* Let P = Pens.

DRILL PROBLEMS (Third of Three Sets)
Solve the unknown from the following equations.

5–29. $B + 82 - 11 = 190$

5–30. $5Y + 15(Y + 1) = 35$

5–31. $3M + 20 = 2M + 80$

5–32. $20(C - 50) = 19,000$

WORD PROBLEMS (Third of Three Sets)

5–33. On December 7, 2000, the *Chicago Sun-Times* ran an article comparing major media ad outlays in the millions of dollars (TV, print, radio, outdoor). In the year 2003, the expected outlay in North America will be $168.6. This is $1\frac{1}{4}$ times more than was spent in 1999. What was the total dollar outlay (in millions) during 1999? Round to nearest tenth.

5–34. At General Electric, shift 1 produced 4 times as much as shift 2. General Electric's total production for July was 5,500 jet engines. What was the output for each shift?

5–35. Ivy Corporation gave 84 people a bonus. If Ivy had given 2 more people bonuses, Ivy would have rewarded $\frac{2}{3}$ of the workforce. How large is Ivy's workforce?

5–36. Jim Murray and Phyllis Lowe received a total of $50,000 from a deceased relative's estate. They decided to put $10,000 in a trust for their nephew and divide the remainder. Phyllis received $\frac{3}{4}$ of the remainder; Jim received $\frac{1}{4}$. How much did Jim and Phyllis receive?

5–37. The first shift of GME Corporation produced $1\frac{1}{2}$ times as many lanterns as the second shift. GME produced 5,600 lanterns in November. How many lanterns did GME produce on each shift?

5–38. Wal-Mart sells thermometers ($2) and hot-water bottles ($6). In December, Wal-Mart's total sales were $1,200. Customers bought 7 times as many thermometers as hot-water bottles. How many of each did Wal-Mart sell? Check your answer.

5–39. Ace Hardware sells cartons of wrenches ($100) and hammers ($300). Howard ordered 40 cartons of wrenches and hammers for $8,400. How many cartons of each are in the order? Check your answer.

 CHALLENGE PROBLEMS

5–40. Jack Barney and Michelle Denny sold a total of 450 home entertainment centers at Circuit City. Jack sold 2 times as many units as Michelle. Michelle had $97,500 in total sales, which was $1\frac{1}{2}$ times as much as Jack's sales. **(a)** How many units did Michelle sell? **(b)** How many units did Jack sell? **(c)** What was the total dollar amount Jack sold? **(d)** What was the average amount of sales for Jack? **(e)** What was the average amount of sales for Michelle? Round both averages to the nearest dollar.

5–41. Bessy has 6 times as much money as Bob, but when each earns $6, Bessy will have 3 times as much money as Bob. How much does each have before and after earning the $6?

SUMMARY PRACTICE TEST

1. United reduced its round-trip ticket price from Chicago to Boston by $95. The sale price was $205.99. What was the original price? *(p. 120)*

2. Al Ring is an employee at Amazon.com. He budgets $\frac{1}{6}$ of his salary for clothing. If Al's total clothing for the year is $9,000, what is his yearly salary? *(p. 120)*

3. A local Best Buy sells 6 times as many DVDs as Circuit City. The difference between their sales is 150 DVDs. How many DVDs did each sell? *(p. 120)*

4. Working at Sharper Image, Joy Allen and Flo Ring sold a total of 900 scooters. Joy sold 4 times as many scooters as Flo. How many did each sell? *(p. 121)*

5. Kitchen Etc. sells sets of pots ($19) and dishes ($13) at a local charity. On the July 4 weekend, Kitchen Etc.'s total sales were $1,780. People bought 4 times as many pots as dishes. How many of each did Kitchen Etc. sell? Check your answer. *(p. 121)*

6. Dominos sold a total of 1,300 small pizzas ($8) and hamburgers ($9) during the Super Bowl. How many of each did Dominos sell if total sales were $11,000? Check your answer. *(p. 121)*

JOHN DOLAN

LINDSAY FRUCCI'S next goal: $1 million in sales for her home-based fudge business.

SAVORING HER SWEET SUCCESS

Name: Lindsay Frucci, 48, Elkins, N.H.
Her goal: Running a successful business from her home.
What she did about it: Founded No-Pudge! Fudge Mixes Inc., in an office above her garage.
Sign of success: Sales in 1999 were $400,000. Stores now reorder her mixes, and she's attracting new outlets: "The other night I was in the office at 7:45 and the fax started to hum. It was confirmation from Blooming Prairie, my first distributor in the Midwest. Yes!"

How long it took: Four years
Total investment: $43,000
Lesson learned: "I was thinking small instead of big, so initially I focused on the wrong kinds of stores."
Best source of advice: Service Corps of Retired Executives (www.score.org), sponsored by the U.S. Small Business Administration.
Next goal: "Sales of $1 million by the end of 2000." ◄

Business Math Issue

In today's economy, starting a business is more risky than ever.
1. List the key points of the article and information to support your position.
2. Write a group defense of your position using math calculations to support your view.

BUSINESS MATH SCRAPBOOK
WITH INTERNET APPLICATION

Putting Your Skills to Work

Eager in the East

Top five advertisers in Vietnam, January through June.

COMPANY	PRODUCT	AD SPENDING (millions)
Unilever	Soap and shampoo	$10.70
Coca-Cola	Soft drinks	1.80
Procter & Gamble	Soap and shampoo	1.40
PepsiCo	Soft drinks	0.96
LG Group	Televisions	0.95

Source: ACNielsen estimates

© 2000 Dow Jones & Company, Inc.

PROJECT A

If Coca-Cola increases its advertising spending in Vietnam by 3 times for the next 6 months, what will it spend for the year?

Go to the Coca-Cola website and try to determine what Coca-Cola is spending on advertising today.

Goodyear to Cut Total of 650 Jobs At U.K. Facility

By PATRICIA DAVIS
Staff Reporter of THE WALL STREET JOURNAL

Goodyear Tire & Rubber Co. said it will discontinue commercial truck-tire and mold production at the Dunlop Tyres U.K. plant in Birmingham, England, resulting in the loss of 650 jobs there.

The Akron, Ohio, company will integrate truck-tire and mold production within its recently completed joint venture with Sumitomo Rubber Industries Ltd. in Europe, which makes the Dunlop brand. Truck-tire production will be moved to joint-venture plants in the U.K., Germany and France. Mold production will shift to Goodyear's facility in Luxembourg.

The company said the action will result in substantial cost savings and synergies for the Goodyear and Dunlop joint venture.

© 2000 Dow Jones & Company, Inc.

PROJECT B

If the total number of employees at Goodyear's Birmingham plant were 11,581 after the layoff, what was the total employment before the layoff?

Go to the Goodyear website to see how their business is doing today.

Juice Processors Make a Bet on India's Market

By RASUL BAILAY
Staff Reporter of THE WALL STREET JOURNAL

NEW DELHI—Breakfast in India rarely includes orange juice. Most people prefer their wake-up tea with milk and believe that citrus and milk mixed in the same meal are bad for the stomach and sour a person's mood. And later in the day, most Indians would rather stop at an open-air stall than buy a bottle or carton from a supermarket.

Despite these cultural hurdles, juice processors are betting they have identified a potentially profitable niche and their products, appearing in stores nationwide, are aimed at India's growing middle class.

"The market is in its infancy," says Abhay Manglik, country manager at Tropicana Beverages Co., the local unit of Bradenton, Fla.-based Tropicana Products Inc. "But the potentials are huge. We expect the Indian market to grow at least five times by the year 2002."

© 2000 Dow Jones & Company, Inc.

PROJECT C

If the total market for orange juice in India is $35 million, what should the Indian market grow to in the year 2002?

Go to the Web and look up New Delhi. Try to find other cultural differences that may affect business corporations.

Internet Projects: See text website (www.mhhe.com/slater7e) and *The Business Math Internet Resource Guide.*

131

It's Payback Time

MAYBE YOU SPENT a lot of money remodeling your house. But will you get it all back when it's time to sell? Below, a look at what percentage of their costs various remodeling jobs tend to pay back:

Michael Sloan

PROJECT	COST	AVERAGE PAYBACK
Add bathroom	$5,000 to $12,000	92%
Major kitchen remodeling	$9,000 to $25,000	90
Add a family room	$30,000	86
Add a fireplace	$1,500 to $3,000	75
Build a deck	$6,000	73
Remodel home office	$8,000	69
Replace windows	$6,000	68 to 74
Build a pool	$10,000 and up	44
Install or upgrade landscaping	$1,500 to $15,000	30 to 60
Finish basement	$3,000 to $7,000	15

Percents and Their Applications

LEARNING UNIT OBJECTIVES

LU 6–1: Conversions

- Convert decimals to percents (including rounding percents), percents to decimals, and fractions to percents *(pp. 134–37)*.

- Convert percents to fractions *(p. 137)*.

LU 6–2: Application of Percents—Portion Formula

- List and define the key elements of the portion formula *(pp. 138–39)*.

- Solve for one unknown of the portion formula when the other two key elements are given *(pp. 140–42)*.

- Calculate the rate of percent decreases and increases *(pp. 142–45)*.

Wendy's Net Falls 15% On One-Time Charge, But Tops Expectations

By a WALL STREET JOURNAL *Staff Reporter*

DUBLIN, Ohio—**Wendy's International Inc.**, buoyed by strong sales and a Christmas kid's-meal promotion, reported fourth-quarter earnings that beat Wall Street expectations but were hurt by a one-time charge from the closing of underperforming restaurants in Argentina.

The company that runs the Wendy's Old Fashioned Hamburger chain and Tim Hortons bakery restaurants said net income fell 15% to $34.4 million, or 29 cents a diluted share, from $40.6 million, or 33 cents a share, in the year-earlier period.

©2001 Dow Jones & Company, Inc.

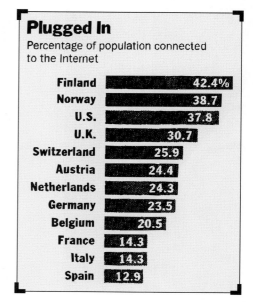

Plugged In
Percentage of population connected to the Internet

Finland	42.4%
Norway	38.7
U.S.	37.8
U.K.	30.7
Switzerland	25.9
Austria	24.4
Netherlands	24.3
Germany	23.5
Belgium	20.5
France	14.3
Italy	14.3
Spain	12.9

©2000 Dow Jones & Company, Inc.

Tom Wurl/Stock Boston

Companies frequently use percents to express various decreases and increases between two or more numbers, or to express only a decrease or increase. For example, note the two *Wall Street Journal* clippings "Wendy's Net Falls 15% On One-Time Charge, But Tops Expectations" and "Plugged In." Both clippings express business numbers in terms of percents. Wendy's reported that its fourth-quarter earnings beat Wall Street expectations, but the closing of underperforming restaurants in Argentina hurt Wendy's net income. The "Plugged In" clipping reported that Finland had the highest percentage of population connected to the Internet—42.4%. This means that in Finland, 42 people out of 100 people are connected to the Internet.

To understand percents, you should first understand the conversion relationship between decimals, percents, and fractions as explained in Learning Unit 6–1. Then, in Learning Unit 6–2, you will be ready to apply percents to personal and business events.

LEARNING UNIT 6–1 | CONVERSIONS

When we described parts of a whole in previous chapters, we used fractions and decimals. Percents also describe parts of a whole. The word *percent* means per 100. The percent symbol (%) indicates hundredths (division by 100). **Percents** are the result of expressing numbers as part of 100. Thus, the 15% reduction in Wendy's net income reported in the clipping above is 15 parts of 100 parts ($\frac{15}{100}$); and, as stated above, the 42.4% of the population in Finland connected to the Internet is 42 people out of 100 people ($\frac{42}{100}$).

Percents can provide some revealing information. Do you know how many people actually make purchases on the Internet? *The Wall Street Journal* clipping "Online Activities" answers this question. Note that 88.7%, or 89 out of 100 online users ($\frac{89}{100}$), send e-mail messages, but only 26.9%, or 27 online users out of 100 ($\frac{27}{100}$), make purchases.

Online Activities

Entertainment doesn't yet rank high among what Internet users do online. The percentage of users doing each at least three times in previous three months:

Send e-mail	**88.7%**	Visit reference sites	**40.7%**
Go to World Wide Web	**85.1%**	Read newspapers and magazines	**33.8%**
Use search-engine sites	**77.8%**	View stock quotes	**27.7%**
Visit company/product sites	**52.0%**	Make purchases	**26.9%**
Do research about product purchases	**47.4%**	Visit sports sites	**23.8%**
Look up weather information	**46.6%**	Participate in chat	**23.0%**

©2000 Dow Jones & Company, Inc.

TABLE 6.1

Analyzing a bag of M&M's®

Color	Fraction	Decimal (hundredth)	Percent (hundredth)
Yellow	$\frac{18}{55}$	.33	32.73%
Red	$\frac{10}{55}$	.18	18.18
Blue	$\frac{9}{55}$	.16	16.36
Orange	$\frac{7}{55}$	.13	12.73
Brown	$\frac{6}{55}$	.11	10.91
Green	$\frac{5}{55}$	.09	9.09
Total	$\frac{55}{55} = 1$	1.00	100.00%

Note: The color ratios currently given are a sample used for educational purposes. They do not represent the manufacturer's color ratios.

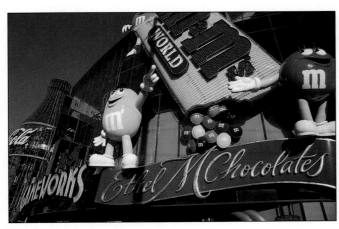

Michelle Burgess/Stock Boston

Let's return to the M&M's® example from earlier chapters. In Table 6.1, we use our bag of 55 M&M's® to show how fractions, decimals, and percents can refer to the same parts of a whole. For example, the bag of 55 M&M's® contained 18 yellow M&M's®. As you can see in Table 6.1, the 18 yellow candies in the bag of 55 can be expressed as a fraction $\left(\frac{18}{55}\right)$, decimal (.33), and percent (32.73%).

In this unit we discuss converting decimals to percents (including rounding percents), percents to decimals, fractions to percents, and percents to fractions. You will see when you study converting fractions to percents why you should first learn how to convert decimals to percents.

Converting Decimals to Percents

> **Some 65% of Online Shoppers Bolt at the Checkout Point; E-tailers Try to Keep Them**

This heading appeared above an article in *The Wall Street Journal*. Note that when making purchases online, 65 out of 100 online shoppers become discouraged and leave the purchase site. This means that only 35 out of 100 people complete their online shopping.

If the heading of the article stated the 65% as a decimal (.65), could you give its equivalent in percent? The decimal .65 in decimal fraction is $\frac{65}{100}$.[1] As you know, percents are the result of expressing numbers as a part of 100, so $65\% = \frac{65}{100}$. You can now conclude that $.65 = \frac{65}{100} = 65\%$. This leads to the following conversion steps:

Converting Decimals to Percents

Step 1. Move the decimal point two places to the right. You are multiplying by 100. If necessary, add zeros. This rule is also used for whole numbers and mixed decimals.

Step 2. Add a percent symbol at the end of the number.

EXAMPLES

$.65 = .65. = \boxed{65\%}$ $.8 = .80. = \boxed{80\%}$ $8 = 8.00. = \boxed{800\%}$

Add 1 zero to make two places.   Add 2 zeros to make two places.

[1]This is explained in Chapter 3.

$$.425 = .42.5 = \boxed{42.5\%} \qquad .007 = .00.7 = \boxed{.7\%} \qquad 2.51 = 2.51. = \boxed{251\%}$$

Caution: One percent means 1 out of every 100. Since .7% is less than 1%, it means $\frac{7}{10}$ of 1%—a very small amount. Less than 1% is less than .01. To show a number less than 1%, you must use more than two decimal places and add 2 zeros. Example: .7% = .007.

Rounding Percents

When necessary, percents should be rounded. Rounding percents is similar to rounding whole numbers. Use the following steps to round percents:

Rounding Percents
Step 1. When you convert from a fraction or decimal, be sure your answer is in percent before rounding.
Step 2. Identify the specific digit. If the digit to the right of the identified digit is 5 or greater, round up the identified digit.
Step 3. Delete digits to right of the identified digit.

For example, Table 6.1 shows that the 18 yellow M&M's® rounded to the nearest hundredth percent is 32.73% of the bag of 55 M&M's®. Let's look at how we arrived at this figure.

When using a calculator, you press $\boxed{18} \div \boxed{55} \boxed{\%}$. This allows you to go right to percent, avoiding the decimal step.

Step 1. $\frac{18}{55} = .3272727 = 32.72727\%$ Note that the number is in percent! Identify the hundredth percent digit.

Step 2. 32.73727% Digit to the right of the identified digit is greater than 5, so the identified digit is increased by 1.

Step 3. $\boxed{32.73\%}$ Delete digits to the right of the identified digit.

Converting Percents to Decimals

Colas Duke It Out

2000 Market Share

	Coke Classic	Pepsi-Cola
Market share	20.4%	13.6%
Unit cases sold (billions)	2.03	1.36
Volume growth	+0.5%	–1.0%

©2001 Dow Jones & Company, Inc.

The Wall Street Journal clipping "Colas Duke It Out" states that in 2000 the volume growth of Coke Classic increased +0.5%. This percent is less than 1%. You will learn in the paragraph and steps that follow how to convert percents to decimals. The first example below the steps shows you how to convert the +0.5% to a decimal. Our third example returns to the 65% of online shoppers that leave the checkout point and shows you how to state the 65% in decimal.

To convert percents to decimals, you reverse the process used to convert decimals to percents. The definition of percent states that $65\% = \frac{65}{100}$. The fraction $\frac{65}{100}$ can be written in decimal form as .65. You can conclude that $65\% = \frac{65}{100} = .65$. This leads to the following conversion steps:

Converting Percents to Decimals
Step 1. Drop the percent symbol.
Step 2. Move the decimal point two places to the left. You are dividing by 100. If necessary, add zeros.

EXAMPLES

Note that when a percent is less than 1%, the decimal conversion has at least two leading zeros before the whole number .005.

$$.5\% = .00.5 = \boxed{.005} \qquad 5\% = .05. = \boxed{.05} \qquad 65\% = .65. = \boxed{.65}$$

Add 2 zeros to make two places.   Add 1 zero to make two places.

$$82.4\% = .82.4 = \boxed{.824} \qquad 824.4\% = 8.24.4 = \boxed{8.244}$$

Now we must explain how to change fractional percents such as $\frac{1}{5}\%$ to a decimal. Remember that fractional percents are values less than 1%. For example, $\frac{1}{5}\%$ is $\frac{1}{5}$ of 1%. Fractional percents can appear singly or in combination with whole numbers. To convert them to decimals, use the following steps:

Converting Fractional Percents to Decimals

Step 1. Convert a single fractional percent to its decimal equivalent by dividing the numerator by the denominator. If necessary, round the answer.

Step 2. If a fractional percent is combined with a whole number (mixed fractional percent), convert the fractional percent first. Then combine the whole number and the fractional percent.

Step 3. Drop the percent symbol; move the decimal point two places to the left (this divides the number by 100).

EXAMPLES

$$\frac{1}{5}\% = .20\% = .00.20 = \boxed{.0020}$$

$$\frac{1}{4}\% = .25\% = .00.25 = \boxed{.0025}$$

$$7\frac{3}{4}\% = 7.75\% = .07.75 = \boxed{.0775}$$

$$6\frac{1}{2}\% = 6.5\% = .06.5 = \boxed{.065}$$

Think of $7\frac{3}{4}\%$ as

$$7\% = \quad .07$$

$$+ \ \frac{3}{4}\% = \ + .0075$$

$$7\frac{3}{4}\% = \quad .0775$$

Converting Fractions to Percents

When fractions have denominators of 100, the numerator becomes the percent. Other fractions must be first converted to decimals; then the decimals are converted to percents.

Converting Fractions to Percents

Step 1. Divide the numerator by the denominator to convert the fraction to a decimal.

Step 2. Move the decimal point two places to the right; add the percent symbol.

EXAMPLES

$$\frac{3}{4} = .75 = .75. = \boxed{75\%} \qquad \frac{1}{5} = .20 = .20. = \boxed{20\%} \qquad \frac{1}{20} = .05 = .05. = \boxed{5\%}$$

Converting Percents to Fractions

Using the definition of percent, you can write any percent as a fraction whose denominator is 100. Thus, when we convert a percent to a fraction, we drop the percent symbol and write the number over 100, which is the same as multiplying the number by $\frac{1}{100}$. This method of multiplying by $\frac{1}{100}$ is also used for fractional percents.

Converting a Whole Percent (or a Fractional Percent) to a Fraction

Step 1. Drop the percent symbol.

Step 2. Multiply the number by $\frac{1}{100}$.

Step 3. Reduce to lowest terms.

EXAMPLES

$$76\% = 76 \times \frac{1}{100} = \frac{76}{100} = \boxed{\frac{19}{25}} \qquad \frac{1}{8}\% = \frac{1}{8} \times \frac{1}{100} = \boxed{\frac{1}{800}}$$

$$156\% = 156 \times \frac{1}{100} = \frac{156}{100} = 1\frac{56}{100} = \boxed{1\frac{14}{25}}$$

Sometimes a percent contains a whole number and a fraction such as $12\frac{1}{2}\%$ or 22.5%. Extra steps are needed to write a mixed or decimal percent as a simplified fraction.

Converting a Mixed or Decimal Percent to a Fraction

Step 1. Drop the percent symbol.
Step 2. Change the mixed percent to an improper fraction.
Step 3. Multiply the number by $\frac{1}{100}$.
Step 4. Reduce to lowest terms.

Note: If you have a mixed or decimal percent, change the decimal portion to fractional equivalent and continue with Steps 1 to 4.

EXAMPLES $12\frac{1}{2}\% = \frac{25}{2} \times \frac{1}{100} = \frac{25}{200} = \boxed{\frac{1}{8}}$

$12.5\% = 12\frac{1}{2}\% = \frac{25}{2} \times \frac{1}{100} = \frac{25}{200} = \boxed{\frac{1}{8}}$

$22.5\% = 22\frac{1}{2}\% = \frac{45}{2} \times \frac{1}{100} = \frac{45}{200} = \boxed{\frac{9}{40}}$

LU 6–1 PRACTICE QUIZ

Convert to percents (round to the nearest tenth percent as needed);

1. .6666 _____   **2.** .832 _____
3. .004 _____   **4.** 8.94444 _____

Convert to decimals (remember, decimals representing less than 1% will have at least 2 leading zeros before the number):

5. $\frac{1}{4}\%$ _____   **6.** $6\frac{3}{4}\%$ _____
7. 87% _____   **8.** 810.9% _____

Convert to percents (round to the nearest hundredth percent):

9. $\frac{1}{7}$ _____   **10.** $\frac{2}{9}$ _____

Convert to fractions (remember, if it is a mixed number, first convert to an improper fraction):

11. 19% _____   **12.** $71\frac{1}{2}\%$ _____   **13.** 130% _____

14. $\frac{1}{2}\%$ _____   **15.** 19.9% _____

✓ **SOLUTIONS**

1. $.66.66 = \boxed{66.7\%}$ **2.** $.83.2 = \boxed{83.2\%}$

3. $.00.4 = \boxed{.4\%}$ **4.** $8.94.444 = \boxed{894.4\%}$

5. $\frac{1}{4}\% = .25\% = \boxed{.0025}$ **6.** $6\frac{3}{4}\% = 6.75\% = \boxed{.0675}$

7. $87\% = .87. = \boxed{.87}$ **8.** $810.9\% = 8.10.9 = \boxed{8.109}$

9. $\frac{1}{7} = .14.285 = \boxed{14.29\%}$ **10.** $\frac{2}{9} = .22.2\overline{2} = \boxed{22.22\%}$

11. $19\% = 19 \times \frac{1}{100} = \boxed{\frac{19}{100}}$ **12.** $71\frac{1}{2}\% = \frac{143}{2} \times \frac{1}{100} = \boxed{\frac{143}{200}}$

13. $130\% = 130 \times \frac{1}{100} = \frac{130}{100} = 1\frac{30}{100} = \boxed{1\frac{3}{10}}$ **14.** $\frac{1}{2}\% = \frac{1}{2} \times \frac{1}{100} = \boxed{\frac{1}{200}}$

15. $19\frac{9}{10}\% = \frac{199}{10} \times \frac{1}{100} = \boxed{\frac{199}{1,000}}$

LEARNING UNIT 6–2 | APPLICATION OF PERCENTS—PORTION FORMULA

The bag of M&M's® we have been studying contains Milk Chocolate M&M's®. M&M/Mars also makes Peanut M&M's® and some other types of M&M's®. To study the application of percents to problems involving M&M's®, we make two key assumptions:

1. Total sales of Milk Chocolate M&M's®, Peanut, and other M&M's® chocolate candies are $400,000.
2. Eighty percent of M&M's® sales are Milk Chocolate M&M's®. This leaves the Peanut and other M&M's® chocolate candies with 20% of sales (100% − 80%).

80% M&M's®	20% M&M's®	100%
Milk Chocolate +	Peanut and other	= Total sales
M&M's®	chocolate candies	($400,000)

Before we begin, you must understand the meaning of three terms—*base, rate,* and *portion.* These terms are the key elements in solving percent problems.

*   **Base (*B*).** The **base** is the beginning whole quantity or value (100%) with which you will compare some other quantity or value. Often the problems give the base after the word *of.* For example, the whole (total) sales of M&M's®—Milk Chocolate M&M's, Peanut, and other M&M's® chocolate candies—are $400,000.
*   **Rate (*R*).** The **rate** is a percent, decimal, or fraction that indicates the part of the base that you must calculate. The percent symbol often helps you identify the rate. For example, Milk Chocolate M&M's® currently account for 80% of sales. So the rate is 80%. Remember that 80% is also $\frac{4}{5}$, or .80.
*   **Portion (*P*).** The **portion** is the amount or part that results from the base multiplied by the rate. For example, total sales of M&M's® are $400,000 (base); $400,000 times .80 (rate) equals $320,000 (portion), or the sales of Milk Chocolate M&M's®. *A key point to remember is that portion is a number and not a percent. In fact, the portion can be larger than the base if the rate is greater than 100%.*

Solving Percents with the Portion Formula

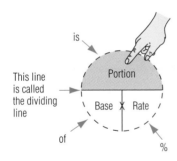

This line is called the dividing line

In problems involving portion, base, and rate, we give two of these elements. You must find the third element. Remember the following key formula:

$$\text{Portion } (P) = \text{Base } (B) \times \text{Rate } (R)$$

To help you solve for the portion, base, and rate, this unit shows pie charts. The shaded area in each pie chart indicates the element that you must solve for. For example, since we shaded *portion* in the pie chart at the left, you must solve for portion. To use the pie charts, put your finger on the shaded area (in this case portion). The formula that remains tells you what to do. So in the pie chart at the left, you solve the problem by multiplying base by the rate. Note the circle around the pie chart is broken since we want to emphasize that portion can be larger than base if rate is greater than 100%. The horizontal line in the pie chart is called the dividing line, and we will use it when we solve for base or rate.

The following example summarizes the concept of base, rate, and portion. Assume that you received a small bonus check of $100. This is a gross amount—your company did not withhold any taxes. You will have to pay 20% in taxes.

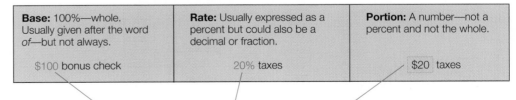

Base: 100%—whole. Usually given after the word *of*—but not always.	**Rate:** Usually expressed as a percent but could also be a decimal or fraction.	**Portion:** A number—not a percent and not the whole.
$100 bonus check	20% taxes	$20 taxes

First decide what you are looking for. You want to know how much you must pay in taxes—the portion. How do you get the portion? From the portion formula Portion (*P*) = Base (*B*) × Rate (*R*), you know that you must multiply the base ($100) by the rate (20%). When you do this, you get $100 × .20 = $20. So you must pay $20 in taxes.

Let's try our first word problem by taking a closer look at the M&M's® example to see how we arrived at the $320,000 sales of Milk Chocolate M&M's® given earlier. We will be using blueprint aids to help dissect and solve each word problem.

Solving for Portion

The Word Problem   Sales of Milk Chocolate M&M's® are 80% of the total M&M's® sales. Total M&M's® sales are $400,000. What are the sales of Milk Chocolate M&M's®?

The facts	Solving for?	Steps to take	Key points
Milk Chocolate M&M's® sales: 80%. *Total M&M's® sales: $400,000.*	Sales of Milk Chocolate M&M's®.	Identify key elements. *Base:* $400,000. *Rate:* .80. *Portion:* ? Portion = Base × Rate.	Amount or part of beginning Portion (?) Base ($400,000) × Rate (.80) Beginning whole quantity (often after "of") Percent symbol or word (here we put into decimal) Portion and rate must relate to same piece of base.

Steps to solving problem

1. Set up the formula.
2. Calculate portion (sales of Milk Chocolate M&M's®).

Portion = Base × Rate
$P = \$400,000 \times .80$
$P = \$320,000$

In the first column of the blueprint aid, we gather the facts. In the second column, we state that we are looking for sales of Milk Chocolate M&M's®. In the third column, we identify each key element and the formula needed to solve the problem. Review the pie chart in the fourth column. Note that the portion and rate must relate to the same piece of the base. In this word problem, we can see from the solution below the blueprint aid that sales of Milk Chocolate M&M's® are $320,000. The $320,000 does indeed represent 80% of the base. Note here that the portion ($320,000) is less than the base of $400,000 since the rate is less than 100%.

Now let's work another word problem that solves for the portion.

The Word Problem   Sales of Milk Chocolate M&M's® are 80% of the total M&M's® sales. Total M&M's® sales are $400,000. What are the sales of Peanut and other M&M's® chocolate candies?

The facts	Solving for?	Steps to take	Key points
Milk Chocolate M&M's® sales: 80%. *Total M&M's® sales: $400,000.*	Sales of Peanut and other M&M's® chocolate candies.	Identify key elements. *Base:* $400,000. *Rate:* .20 (100% − 80%). *Portion:* ? Portion = Base × Rate.	If 80% of sales are Milk Chocolate M&M's, then 20% are Peanut and other M&M's® chocolate candies. Portion (?) Base ($400,000) × Rate (.20) Portion and rate must relate to same piece of base.

Steps to solving problem

1. Set up the formula.
2. Calculate portion (sale of Peanut and other M&M's® chocolate candies).

Portion = Base × Rate
$P = \$400,000 \times .20$
$P = \$80,000$

In the previous blueprint aid, note that we must use a rate that agrees with the portion so the portion and rate refer to the same piece of the base. Thus, if 80% of sales are Milk Chocolate M&M's®, 20% must be Peanut and other M&M's® chocolate candies (100% − 80% = 20%). So we use a rate of .20.

In Step 2, we multiplied $400,000 × .20 to get a portion of $80,000. This portion represents the part of the sales that were *not* Milk Chocolate M&M's®. Note that the rate of

.20 and the portion of $80,000 relate to the same piece of the base—$80,000 is 20% of $400,000. Also note that the portion ($80,000) is less than the base ($400,000) since the rate is less than 100%.

Take a moment to review the two blueprint aids in this section. Be sure you understand why the rate in the first blueprint aid was 80% and the rate in the second blueprint aid was 20%.

Solving for Rate

The Word Problem Sales of Milk Chocolate M&M's® are $320,000. Total M&M's® sales are $400,000. What is the percent of Milk Chocolate M&M's® sales compared to total M&M's® sales?

The facts	Solving for?	Steps to take	Key points
Milk Chocolate M&M's® sales: $320,000. Total M&M's® sales: $400,000.	Percent of Milk Chocolate M&M's® sales to total M&M's® sales.	Identify key elements. Base: $400,000. Rate: ? Portion: $320,000 $$Rate = \frac{Portion}{Base}$$	Since portion is less than base, the rate must be less than 100% Portion ($320,000) Base × Rate ($400,000) (?) Portion and rate must relate to the same piece of base.

Steps to solving problem

1. Set up the formula. $$Rate = \frac{Portion}{Base}$$

2. Calculate rate (percent of Milk Chocolate M&M's® sales). $$R = \frac{\$320,000}{\$400,000}$$ $$R = \boxed{80\%}$$

Note that in this word problem, the rate of 80% and the portion of $320,000 refer to the same piece of the base.

The Word Problem Sales of Milk Chocolate M&M's® are $320,000. Total sales of Milk Chocolate M&M's, Peanut, and other M&M's® chocolate candies are $400,000. What percent of Peanut and other M&M's® chocolate candies are sold compared to total M&M's® sales?

The facts	Solving for?	Steps to take	Key points
Milk Chocolate M&M's® sales: $320,000. Total M&M's® sales: $400,000.	Percent of Peanut and other M&M's® chocolate candies sales compared to total M&M's® sales.	Identify key elements. Base: $400,000. Rate: ? Portion: $80,000 ($400,000 − $320,000). $$Rate = \frac{Portion}{Base}$$	Represents sales of Peanut and other M&M's® chocolate candies Portion ($80,000) Base × Rate ($400,000) (?) When portion becomes $80,000, the portion and rate now relate to same piece of base.

Steps to solving problem

1. Set up the formula. $$Rate = \frac{Portion}{Base}$$

2. Calculate rate. $$R = \frac{\$80,000}{\$400,000} \quad (\$400,000 - \$320,000)$$ $$R = \boxed{20\%}$$

The word problem asks for the rate of candy sales that are *not* Milk Chocolate M&M's. Thus, $400,000 of total candy sales less sales of Milk Chocolate M&M's®

($320,000) allows us to arrive at sales of Peanut and other M&M's® chocolate candies ($80,000). The $80,000 portion represents 20% of total candy sales. The $80,000 portion and 20% rate refer to the same piece of the $400,000 base. Compare this blueprint aid with the blueprint aid for the previous word problem. Ask yourself why in the previous word problem the rate was 80% and in this word problem the rate is 20%. In both word problems, the portion was less than the base since the rate was less than 100%.

Now we go on to calculate the base. Remember to read the word problem carefully so that you match the rate and portion to the same piece of the base.

Solving for Base

The Word Problem   Sales of Peanut and other M&M's® chocolate candies are 20% of total M&M's® sales. Sales of Milk Chocolate M&M's® are $320,000. What are the total sales of all M&M's®?

The facts	Solving for?	Steps to take	Key points
Peanut and other M&M's® chocolate candies sales: 20%. Milk Chocolate M&M's® sales: $320,000.	Total M&M's® sales.	Identify key elements. Base: ? Rate: .80 (100% − 20%) Portion: $320,000 Base = Portion / Rate	Portion ($320,000) Base (?) × Rate (.80) (100% − 20%) Portion ($320,000) and rate (.80) do relate to the same piece of base.

Steps to solving problem

1. Set up the formula. $Base = \dfrac{Portion}{Rate}$

2. Calculate the base. $B = \dfrac{\$320,000}{.80}$ ← $320,000 is 80% of base

$B = \$400,000$

Note that we could not use 20% for the rate. The $320,000 of Milk Chocolate M&M's® represents 80% (100% − 20%) of the total sales of M&M's®. We use 80% so that the portion and rate refer to same piece of the base. Remember that the portion ($320,000) is less than the base ($400,000) since the rate is less than 100%.

Calculating Percent Decreases and Increases

Worth the Grief?

WE RECENTLY CALLED THE AIRLINES to compare their so-called bereavement fares or compassion fares with other available last-minute discounts. Each time, we did better than the bereavement rate, sometimes simply by asking the carrier if it had a lower fare:

TRIP	BEREAVEMENT FARE	CHEAPER FARE	PERCENTAGE SAVED
Boston-Miami	$842.50/Delta	$312.50/Delta (posted on Expedia.com)	63%
New York-Dallas	$917/Continental	$462.95/ATA (quoted by 800-AIRFARE)	50%

©2000 Dow Jones & Company, Inc.

The Wall Street Journal clipping "Worth the Grief?" reports that customers should not assume that bereavement fares are cheaper than other last-minute discounts. The clipping states that for each bereavement fare checked, a lower fare could be found. For example, the Delta bereavement fare from Boston to Miami was $842.50. However, on the Internet, Delta had posted the fare from Boston to Miami as $312.50—a decrease of 63%.

Let's assume that we do not know the percent amount and see if we can use the portion formula to determine the percent decrease (the rate or *R*). The portion formula for solving the rate is as follows:

Rate of Percent Decrease

$$\text{Rate} = \frac{\text{Portion}}{\text{Base}} \xleftarrow{} \text{Difference between old and new fares} \\ \xleftarrow{} \text{Old fare}$$

$$R = \frac{\$530.00 \ (\$842.50 - \$312.50)}{\$842.50}$$

$$R = \boxed{.6290801, \text{ or } 63\%} \ \text{(rounded to nearest whole percent)}$$

As you can see, the 63% decrease in the Delta Airline fare on the Internet is correct. Let's prove the 63% decrease with a pie chart:

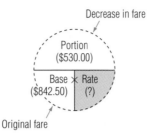

Using the trip of Boston to Miami, the formula for calculating Delta's **percent decrease** is given below at the left. To calculate **percent increase,** we use the formula at the right.

Percent decrease

Percent of decrease (R) = (63%)	$\dfrac{\text{Amount of decrease } (P) \ (\$530.00)}{\text{Original fare } (B) \ (\$842.50)}$

Percent increase

Percent of increase (R) =	$\dfrac{\text{Amount of increase } (P)}{\text{Original fare } (B)}$

Calculating Percent Decreases and Increases

Step 1. Find the difference between amounts (such as airline fares).

Step 2. Divide Step 1 by the original amount (the base): $R = P \div B$. Be sure to express your answer in percent.

Next you are ready for an example of calculating the rate of percent increase using M&M's®.

Rate of Percent Increase

The Word Problem   Sheila Leary went to her local supermarket and bought the bag of M&M's® shown in Figure 6.1. The bag gave its weight as 18.40 ounces, which was 15% more than a regular 1-pound bag of M&M's®. Sheila, who is a careful shopper, wanted to check and see if she was actually getting a 15% increase. Let's help Sheila dissect and solve this problem.

FIGURE 6.1
Bag of 18.40-ounce M&M's®

The facts	Solving for?	Steps to take	Key points
New bag of M&M's®: 18.40 oz. 15% increase in weight. *Original bag of M&M's®:* 16 oz. (1 lb.)	Checking percent increase of 15%.	Identify key elements. *Base:* 16 oz. *Rate:* ? *Portion:* 2.40 oz. $$\left(\begin{array}{r} 18.40 \text{ oz.} \\ -\ 16.00 \\ \hline 2.40 \text{ oz.} \end{array}\right)$$ $\text{Rate} = \dfrac{\text{Portion}}{\text{Base}}$	Difference between base and new weight — Portion (2.40 oz.) — Base × Rate (16 oz.) (?) — Original amount sold

Steps to solving problem

1. Set up the formula. $\text{Rate} = \dfrac{\text{Portion}}{\text{Base}}$

2. Calculate the rate. $R = \dfrac{2.40 \text{ oz.}}{16.00 \text{ oz.}}$ ⟵ Difference between base and new weight.
                                                                                                ⟵ Old weight equals 100%.

                                                        $R = 15\%$ increase

The new weight of the bag of M&M's® is really 115% of the old weight:

$$\begin{array}{rcl} 16.00 \text{ oz.} &=& 100\% \\ +\ 2.40 & & +\ 15 \\ \hline 18.40 \text{ oz.} &=& 115\% = 1.15 \end{array}$$

We can check this by looking at the following pie chart:

$$\text{Portion} = \text{Base} \times \text{Rate}$$

$$18.40 \text{ oz.} = 16 \text{ oz.} \times 1.15$$

Portion (18.40 oz.) — Base × Rate (16 oz.) (1.15) — 100%

Why is the portion greater than the base? Remember that the portion can be larger than the base only if the rate is greater than 100%. Note how the portion and rate relate to the same piece of the base—18.40 oz. is 115% of the base (16 oz.).

Let's see what could happen if M&M/Mars has an increase in its price of sugar. This is an additional example to reinforce the concept of percent decrease.

The Word Problem   The increase in the price of sugar caused the M&M/Mars company to decrease the weight of each 1-pound bag of M&M's® to 12 ounces. What is the rate of percent decrease?

The facts	Solving for?	Steps to take	Key points
16-oz. bag of M&M's®: reduced to 12 oz.	Rate of percent decrease.	Identify key elements. *Base:* 16 oz. *Rate:* ? *Portion:* 4 oz. (16 oz. − 12 oz.) $\text{Rate} = \dfrac{\text{Portion}}{\text{Base}}$	Amount of decrease — Portion (4 oz.) — Base × Rate (16 oz.) (?) — Old base 100%

Steps to solving problem

1. Set up the formula. $\text{Rate} = \dfrac{\text{Portion}}{\text{Base}}$

2. Calculate the rate. $R = \dfrac{4 \text{ oz.}}{16.00 \text{ oz.}}$

                                                        $R = 25\%$ decrease

The new weight of the bag of M&M's® is 75% of the old weight:

$$\begin{array}{rl} 16 \text{ oz.} & = \quad 100\% \\ -\ 4 & \quad -\ 25 \\ \hline 12 \text{ oz.} & = \quad 75\% \end{array}$$

We can check this by looking at the following pie chart:

Portion = Base × Rate

12 oz. = 16 oz. × .75

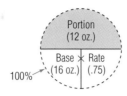

100%

Note that the portion is smaller than the base because the rate is less than 100%. Also note how the portion and rate relate to the same piece of the base—12 ounces is 75% of the base (16 oz.).

LU 6–2 PRACTICE QUIZ

Solve for portion:

1. 38% of 900. **2.** 60% of $9,000.

Solve for rate (round to nearest tenth percent as needed):

3. 430 is _____% of 5,000. **4.** 200 is _____% of 700.

Solve for base (round to the nearest tenth as needed):

5. 55 is 40% of _____. **6.** 900 is $4\frac{1}{2}$% of _____.

Solve the following (blueprint aids are shown in the solution; you might want to try some on scrap paper):

7. Five out of 25 students in Professor Ford's class received an "A" grade. What percent of the class *did not* receive the "A" grade?

8. Abby Biernet has yet to receive 60% of her lobster order. Abby received 80 lobsters to date. What was her original order?

9. In 2003, Dunkin' Donuts Company had $300,000 in doughnut sales. In 2004, sales were up 40%. What are Dunkin' Donuts sales for 2004?

10. The price of an Apple computer dropped from $1,600 to $1,200. What was the percent decrease?

11. In 1982, a ticket to the Boston Celtics cost $14. In 2003, a ticket cost $50. What is the percent increase to the nearest hundredth percent?

✓ **SOLUTIONS**

1. $\boxed{342} = 900 \times .38$
$\ (P)\ = (B) \times (R)$

2. $\boxed{\$5,400} = \$9,000 \times .60$
$\ (P)\ = \ (B)\ \times (R)$

3. $\dfrac{(P)430}{(B)5,000} = .086 = \boxed{8.6\% \ (R)}$

4. $\dfrac{(P)200}{(B)700} = .2857 = \boxed{28.6\% \ (R)}$

5. $\dfrac{(P)55}{(R).40} = \boxed{137.5 \ (B)}$

6. $\dfrac{(P)900}{(R).045} = \boxed{20,000 \ (B)}$

7. Percent of Professor Ford's class that did not receive the "A" grade:

The facts	Solving for?	Steps to take	Key points
5 "A"s. 25 in class.	Percent that did not receive "A."	Identify key elements. *Base:* 25 *Rate:* ? *Portion:* 20 (25 − 5). Rate = $\dfrac{\text{Portion}}{\text{Base}}$	Portion (20) Base × Rate (25) (?) The whole Portion and rate must relate to same piece of base.

Steps to solving problem

1. Set up the formula. $\text{Rate} = \dfrac{\text{Portion}}{\text{Base}}$

2. Calculate the rate. $R = \dfrac{20}{25}$

                 $R = 80\%$

8. Abby Biernet's original order:

The facts	Solving for?	Steps to take	Key points
60% of the order not in. 80 lobsters received.	Total order of lobsters.	Identify key elements. *Base:* ? *Rate:* 40 (100% − 60%) *Portion:* 80. $\text{Base} = \dfrac{\text{Portion}}{\text{Rate}}$	Portion (80) Base (?) × Rate (.40) 80 lobsters represent 40% of the order Portion and rate must relate to same piece of base.

Steps to solving problem

1. Set up the formula. $\text{Base} = \dfrac{\text{Portion}}{\text{Rate}}$

2. Calculate the base. $B = \dfrac{80}{.40}$ ⟵ 80 lobsters is 40% of base.

                 $B = 200$ lobsters

9. Dunkin' Donuts Company sales for 2004:

The facts	Solving for?	Steps to take	Key points
2003: $300,000 sales. *2004:* Sales up 40% from 2003.	Sales for 2004.	Identify key elements. *Base:* $300,000. *Rate:* 1.40. Old year 100% New year + 40 140% *Portion:* ? Portion = Base × Rate.	2004 sales Portion (?) Base ($300,000) × Rate (1.40) 2003 sales When rate is greater than 100%, portion will be larger than base.

Steps to solving problem

1. Set up the formula.   Portion = Base × Rate
2. Calculate the portion. $P = \$300{,}000 \times 1.40$

                 $P = \$420{,}000$

10. Percent decrease in Apple computer price:

The facts	Solving for?	Steps to take	Key points
Apple computer was $1,600; now, $1,200.	Percent decrease in price.	Identify key elements. *Base:* $1,600. *Rate:* ? *Portion:* $400 ($1,600 − $1,200). $\text{Rate} = \dfrac{\text{Portion}}{\text{Base}}$	Difference in price Portion ($400) Base ($1,600) × Rate (?) Original price

Steps to solving problem

1. Set up the formula. $\text{Rate} = \dfrac{\text{Portion}}{\text{Base}}$

2. Calculate the rate. $R = \dfrac{\$400}{\$1{,}600}$

                 $R = 25\%$

11. Percent increase in Boston Celtics ticket:

The facts	Solving for?	Steps to take	Key points
$14 ticket (old). $50 ticket (new).	Percent increase in price.	Identify key elements. *Base:* $14 *Rate:* ? *Portion:* $36 ($50 − $14) Rate = $\dfrac{\text{Portion}}{\text{Base}}$	Difference in price Portion ($36) Base × Rate ($14) (?) Original price When portion is greater than base, rate will be greater than 100%.

Steps to solving problem

1. Set up the formula.

$$\text{Rate} = \frac{\text{Portion}}{\text{Base}}$$

2. Calculate the rate.

$$R = \frac{\$36}{\$14}$$

$$R = 2.5714 = \boxed{257.14\%}$$

Chapter Organizer and Reference Guide

Topic	Key point, procedure, formula	Example(s) to illustrate situation
Converting decimals to percents, p. 135	1. Move decimal point two places to right. If necessary, add zeros. This rule is also used for whole numbers and mixed decimals. 2. Add a percent symbol at end of number.	.81 = .81. = $\boxed{81\%}$ .008 = .00.8 = $\boxed{.8\%}$ 4.15 = 4.15. = $\boxed{415\%}$
Rounding percents, p. 136	1. Answer must be in percent before rounding. 2. Identify specific digit. If digit to right is 5 or greater, round up. 3. Delete digits to right of identified digit.	Round to nearest hundredth percent. $\dfrac{3}{7}$ = .4285714 = 42.85714% = $\boxed{42.86\%}$
Converting percents to decimals, p. 136	1. Drop percent symbol. 2. Move decimal point two places to left. If necessary, add zeros. For fractional percents: 1. Convert to decimal by dividing numerator by denominator. If necessary, round answer. 2. If a mixed fractional percent, convert fractional percent first. Then combine whole number and fractional percent. 3. Drop percent symbol, move decimal point two places to left.	.89% = $\boxed{.0089}$ $8\frac{3}{4}\%$ = 8.75% = $\boxed{.0875}$ 95% = $\boxed{.95}$ $\frac{1}{4}\%$ = .25% = $\boxed{.0025}$ 195% = $\boxed{1.95}$ $\frac{1}{5}\%$ = .20% = $\boxed{.0020}$
Converting fractions to percents, p. 137	1. Divide numerator by denominator. 2. Move decimal point two places to right; add percent symbol.	$\dfrac{4}{5}$ = .80 = $\boxed{80\%}$
Converting percents to fractions, p. 137	Whole percent (or fractional percent) to a fraction: 1. Drop percent symbol. 2. Multiply number by $\frac{1}{100}$. 3. Reduce to lowest terms. Mixed or decimal percent to a fraction: 1. Drop percent symbol. 2. Change mixed percent to an improper fraction. 3. Multiply number by $\frac{1}{100}$. 4. Reduce to lowest terms. If you have a mixed or decimal percent, change decimal portion to fractional equivalent and continue with Steps 1 to 4.	$64\% \longrightarrow 64 \times \dfrac{1}{100} = \dfrac{64}{100} = \boxed{\dfrac{16}{25}}$ $\frac{1}{4}\% \longrightarrow \dfrac{1}{4} \times \dfrac{1}{100} = \boxed{\dfrac{1}{400}}$ $119\% \longrightarrow 119 \times \dfrac{1}{100} = \dfrac{119}{100} = \boxed{1\dfrac{19}{100}}$ $16\frac{1}{4}\% \longrightarrow \dfrac{65}{4} \times \dfrac{1}{100} = \dfrac{65}{400} = \boxed{\dfrac{13}{80}}$ $16.25\% \longrightarrow 16\frac{1}{4}\% = \dfrac{65}{4} \times \dfrac{1}{100}$ $= \dfrac{65}{400} = \boxed{\dfrac{13}{80}}$

(continues)

Chapter Organizer and Reference Guide (concluded)

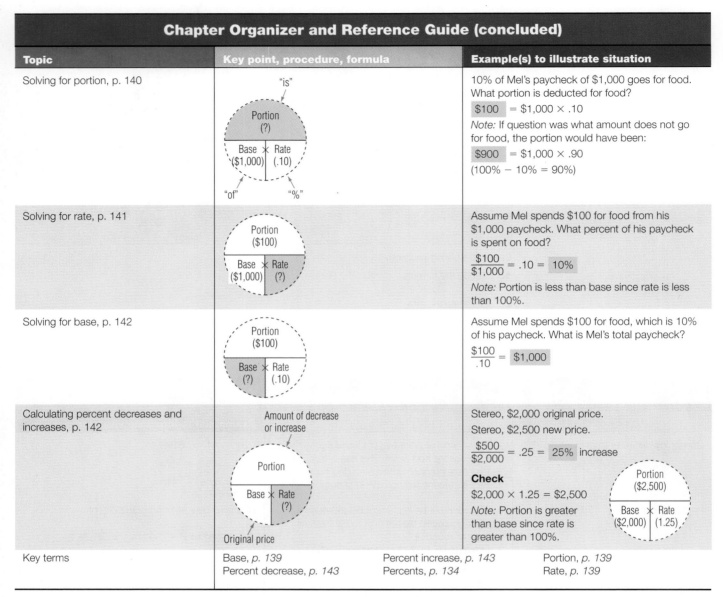

Topic	Key point, procedure, formula	Example(s) to illustrate situation
Solving for portion, p. 140	"is" Portion (?) Base × Rate ($1,000) (.10) "of" "%"	10% of Mel's paycheck of $1,000 goes for food. What portion is deducted for food? $100 = $1,000 × .10 *Note:* If question was what amount does not go for food, the portion would have been: $900 = $1,000 × .90 (100% − 10% = 90%)
Solving for rate, p. 141	Portion ($100) Base × Rate ($1,000) (?)	Assume Mel spends $100 for food from his $1,000 paycheck. What percent of his paycheck is spent on food? $\frac{\$100}{\$1,000} = .10 = 10\%$ *Note:* Portion is less than base since rate is less than 100%.
Solving for base, p. 142	Portion ($100) Base × Rate (?) (.10)	Assume Mel spends $100 for food, which is 10% of his paycheck. What is Mel's total paycheck? $\frac{\$100}{.10} = \$1,000$
Calculating percent decreases and increases, p. 142	Amount of decrease or increase Portion Base × Rate (?) Original price	Stereo, $2,000 original price. Stereo, $2,500 new price. $\frac{\$500}{\$2,000} = .25 = 25\%$ increase **Check** $2,000 × 1.25 = $2,500 *Note:* Portion is greater than base since rate is greater than 100%. Portion ($2,500) Base × Rate ($2,000) (1.25)
Key terms	Base, *p. 139* Percent decrease, *p. 143*	Percent increase, *p. 143* Portion, *p. 139* Percents, *p. 134* Rate, *p. 139*

Note: For how to dissect and solve a word problem, see page 140 or page 142.

Critical Thinking Discussion Questions

1. In converting from a percent to a decimal, when will you have at least 2 leading zeros before the whole number? Explain this concept, assuming you have 100 bills of $1.

2. Explain the steps in rounding percents. Count the number of students who are sitting in the back half of the room as a percent of the total class. Round your answer to the nearest hundredth percent. Could you have rounded to the nearest whole percent without changing the accuracy of the answer?

3. Define portion, rate, and base. Create an example using Walt Disney World to show when the portion could be larger than the base. Why must the rate be greater than 100% for this to happen?

4. How do we solve for portion, rate, and base? Create an example using IBM computer sales to show that the portion and rate do relate to the same piece of the base.

5. Explain how to calculate percent decreases or increases. Many years ago, comic books cost 10 cents a copy. Visit a bookshop or newsstand. Select a new comic book and explain the price increase in percent compared to the 10-cent comic. How important is the rounding process in your final answer?

END-OF-CHAPTER PROBLEMS

Name _____ Date _____

DRILL PROBLEMS

Convert the following decimals to percents:

6–1. .74   **6–2.** .861   **6–3.** .7

6–4. 8.00   **6–5.** 3.561   **6–6.** 6.006

Convert the following percents to decimals:

6–7. 4%   **6–8.** 14%   **6–9.** $64\frac{3}{10}\%$

6–10. 75.9%   **6–11.** 119%   **6–12.** 89%

Convert the following fractions to percents (round to the nearest tenth percent as needed):

6–13. $\frac{1}{12}$ **6–14.** $\frac{1}{400}$

6–15. $\frac{7}{8}$ **6–16.** $\frac{11}{12}$

Convert the following to fractions and reduce to lowest terms:

6–17. 5%   **6–18.** $18\frac{1}{2}\%$

6–19. $31\frac{2}{3}\%$ **6–20.** $61\frac{1}{2}\%$

6–21. 6.75%   **6–22.** 182%

Solve for the portion (round to the nearest hundredth as needed):

6–23. 6% of 120   **6–24.** 125% of 4,320   **6–25.** 25% of 410

6–26. 119% of 128.9   **6–27.** 17.4% of 900   **6–28.** 11.2% of 85

6–29. $12\frac{1}{2}\%$ of 919   **6–30.** 45% of 300

6–31. 18% of 90   **6–32.** 30% of 2,000

Solve for the base (round to the nearest hundredth as needed):

6–33. 170 is 120% of _____   **6–34.** 36 is .75% of _____

6–35. 50 is .5% of _____   **6–36.** 10,800 is 90% of _____

6–37. 800 is $4\frac{1}{2}\%$ of _____

Solve for rate (round to the nearest tenth percent as needed):

6–38. _____ of 80 is 50   **6–39.** _____ of 85 is 92

6–40. _____ of 250 is 65   **6–41.** 110 is _____ of 100

6–42. .09 is _____ of 2.25   **6–43.** 16 is _____ of 4

Solve the following problems. Be sure to show your work. Round to the nearest hundredth or hundredth percent as needed:

6–44. What is 180% of 310?

6–45. 66% of 90 is what?

6–46. 40% of what number is 20?

6–47. 770 is 70% of what number?

6–48. 4 is what percent of 90?

6–49. What percent of 150 is 60?

Complete the following table:

	Product	Sales in millions 2004	Sales in millions 2005	Amount of decrease or increase	Percent change (to nearest hundredth percent as needed)
6–50.	Scooters	$380	$410		
6–51.	DVD players	$ 50	$ 47		

WORD PROBLEMS (First of Four Sets)

6–52. At a local McDonald's, a survey showed that out of 6,000 customers eating lunch, 1,500 ordered Diet Coke with
Excel   their meal. What percent of customers ordered Diet Coke?

6–53. What percent of customers in Problem 6–52 did not order Diet Coke?
Excel

6–54. The August 7, 2000, issue of *U.S. News & World Report* informed readers of how to avoid the high cost of private mortgage insurance (PMI). Homebuyers who don't make a down payment of at least 20% may be required to take out PMI. On a $200,000 loan, the premiums can cost more than $100 per month. What would be the minimum down payment on a $200,000 loan?

6–55. Wally Chin, the owner of an Exxon station, bought a used Ford pickup truck, paying $2,000 as a down payment. He still owes 80% of the selling price. What was the selling price of the truck?

6–56. Maria Fay bought 4 Aquatread tires at a local Goodyear store. The salesperson told her that her mileage would increase by 6%. Before this purchase, Maria was getting 22 mpg. What should her mileage be with the new tires?

6–57. Pete Lavoie went to JCPenney and bought a Sony CD player. The purchase price was $350. He made a down payment of 30%. How much was Pete's down payment?

6–58. Assume that in the year 2003, 800,000 people attended the Christmas Eve celebration at Walt Disney World. In 2004, attendance for the Christmas Eve celebration is expected to increase by 35%. What is the total number of people expected at Walt Disney World for this event?

6–59. Pete Smith found in his attic a Woody Woodpecker watch in its original box. It had a price tag on it for $4.50. The watch was made in 1949. Pete brought the watch to an antiques dealer and sold it for $35. What was the percent of increase? Round to the nearest hundredth percent.

6–60. In 2004, the price of a Dell computer rose to $1,200. This is 8% more than the 2003 price. What was the old selling price? Check your answer.

6–61. Christie's Auction sold a painting for $24,500. It charges all buyers a 15% premium of the final bid price. How much did the bidder pay Christie's?

WORD PROBLEMS (Second of Four Sets)

6–62. Out of 6,000 college students surveyed, 600 responded that they do not eat breakfast. What percent of the students do not eat breakfast?

6–63. What percent of college students in Problem 6–62 eat breakfast?

6–64. Alice Hall made a $3,000 down payment on a new Ford Explorer wagon. She still owes 90% of the selling price. What was the selling price of the wagon?

6–65. On May 30, 2001, Associated Press Online provided information from a fiscal analyst stating that during the past 20 years, the average after-tax income of the wealthiest 1% of Americans had grown from $263,700 to $677,900. What was the percent increase? Round to the nearest percent.

6–66. Jim and Alice Lange, employees at Wal-Mart, have put themselves on a strict budget. Their goal at year's end is to buy a boat for $15,000 in cash. Their budget includes the following:

   40% food and lodging   20% entertainment   10% educational

Jim earns $1,900 per month and Alice earns $2,400 per month. After one year, will Alice and Jim have enough cash to buy the boat?

6–67. The price of a Fossil watch dropped from $49.95 to $30.00. What was the percent decrease in price? Round to the nearest hundredth percent.

6–68. The Museum of Science in Boston estimated that 64% of all visitors came from within the state. On Saturday, 2,500 people attended the museum. How many attended the museum from out of state?

6–69. Staples pays George Nagovsky an annual salary of $36,000. Today, George's boss informs him that he will receive a $4,600 raise. What percent of George's old salary is the $4,600 raise? Round to the nearest tenth percent.

6–70. In 2003, Dairy Queen had $550,000 in sales. In 2004, Dairy Queen's sales were up 35%. What were Dairy Queen's sales in 2004?

6–71. Blue Valley College has 600 female students. This is 60% of the total student body. How many students attend Blue Valley College?

6–72. Dr. Grossman was reviewing his total accounts receivable. This month, credit customers paid $44,000, which represented 20% of all receivables (what customers owe) due. What was Dr. Grossman's total accounts receivable?

6–73. Massachusetts has a 5% sales tax. Timothy bought a Toro lawn mower and paid $20 sales tax. What was the cost of the lawn mower before the tax?

6–74. The price of an antique doll increased from $600 to $800. What was the percent of increase? Round to the nearest tenth percent.

6–75. Borders bookstore ordered 80 marketing books but received 60 books. What percent of the order was missing?

WORD PROBLEMS (Third of Four Sets)

6–76. At a Christie's auction, the auctioneer estimated that 40% of the audience was from within the state. Eight hundred people attended the auction. How many out-of-state people attended?

6–77. Referring to increased mailing costs, the May 14, 2001, *Advertising Age* commented "Magazines Go Postal Over Rate Hike." The new rate will cost publishers $50 million; this is 12.5% more than they paid the previous year. How much did it cost publishers last year? Round to the nearest hundreds.

6–78. In 2004, Jim Goodman, an employee at Walgreens, earned $45,900, an increase of 17.5% over the previous year. What were Jim's earnings in 2003? Round to the nearest cent.

6–79. The *National Mortgage News,* dated February 5, 2001, reported on the number of applications received by Mortgage Insurance Companies of America. For the year 2000, application volume declined by 7% to 1,625,415. What had been the previous year's application volume?

6–80. In 2004, the price of a business math text rose to $80. This is 5% more than the 2003 price. What was the old selling price? Round to the nearest cent.

6–81. Web Consultants, Inc., pays Alice Rose an annual salary of $48,000. Today, Alice's boss informs her that she will receive a $6,400 raise. What percent of Alice's old salary is the $6,400 raise? Round to nearest tenth percent.

6–82. Earl Miller, a lawyer, charges Lee's Plumbing, his client, 25% of what he can collect for Lee from customers whose accounts are past due. The attorney also charges, in addition to the 25%, a flat fee of $50 per customer. This month, Earl collected $7,000 from 3 of Lee's past-due customers. What is the total fee due to Earl?

6–83. Petco ordered 100 dog calendars but received 60. What percent of the order was missing?

6-84. Blockbuster Video uses MasterCard. MasterCard charges $2\frac{1}{2}\%$ on net deposits (credit slips less returns). Blockbuster made a net deposit of $4,100 for charge sales. How much did MasterCard charge Blockbuster?

6-85. In 2003, Internet Access had $800,000 in sales. In 2004, Internet Access sales were up 45%. What are the sales for 2004?

WORD PROBLEMS (Fourth of Four Sets)

6-86. Saab Corporation raised the base price of its popular 900 series by $1,200 to $33,500. What was the percent increase? Round to the nearest tenth percent.

6-87. The sales tax rate is 8%. If Jim bought a new Buick and paid a sales tax of $1,920, what was the cost of the Buick before the tax?

6-88. Puthina Unge bought a new Compaq computer system on sale for $1,800. It was advertised as 30% off the regular price. What was the original price of the computer? Round to the nearest dollar.

6-89. John O'Sullivan has just completed his first year in business. His records show that he spent the following in advertising:

Newspaper	$600	Radio	$650
Yellow Pages	700	Local flyers	400

What percent of John's advertising was spent on the Yellow Pages? Round to the nearest hundredth percent.

6–90. In 2004, Levin Furniture plans to ship furniture overseas for a sales volume of $11.2 million, an increase of 40% from that in 2003. What was the sales volume in 2003?

6–91. Abby Kaminsky sold her ski house at Attitash Mountain in New Hampshire for $35,000. This sale represented a loss of 15% off the original price. What was the original price Abby paid for the ski house? Round your answer to the nearest dollar.

6–92. Out of 4,000 colleges surveyed, 60% reported that SAT scores were not used as a high consideration in viewing their applications. How many schools view the SAT as important in screening applicants?

6–93. On May 25, 2001, the *Chicago Sun-Times* had an article titled "What's Its Worth at Resale?" The article compared the resale benefit of various remodeling costs. Refinishing your basement at a cost of $45,404 would add $18,270 to the resale value of your home. What percent of your cost is recouped? Round to the nearest percent.

6–94. A major airline laid off 4,000 pilots and flight attendants. If this was a 12.5% reduction in the workforce, what was the size of the workforce after the layoffs?

6–95. Assume 450,000 people line up on the streets to see the Macy's Thanksgiving Parade in 2003. If attendance is expected to increase 30%, what will be the number of people lined up on the street to see the 2004 parade?

CHALLENGE PROBLEMS

6–96. On October 11, 2000, the *Milwaukee Journal Sentinel* reported that the third-quarter earnings of a Milwaukee-based mortgage insurance firm were up 19% from $122.9 million. For the first nine months of 2000, net income totaled $409.7 million, up 23%. On October 10, 2000, the firm's shares closed up 50 cents, at $60. **(a)** How much were the earnings in 2000? Round to the nearest hundred thousands. **(b)** What was the third-quarter amount of the previous year's net income? Round to the nearest hundred thousands. **(c)** What was the percent increase in shares? Round to the nearest hundredth percent.

6–97. A local Dunkin' Donuts shop reported that its sales have increased exactly 22% per year for the last 2 years. This year's sales were $82,500. What were Dunkin' Donuts sales 2 years ago? Round each year's sales to the nearest dollar.

SUMMARY PRACTICE TEST

Convert the following decimals to percents. *(p. 135)*

1. .682   **2.** .8   **3.** 15.47   **4.** 8.00

Convert the following percents to decimals. *(p. 136)*

5. 42%   **6.** 5.69%   **7.** 600%   **8.** $\frac{1}{4}$%

Convert the following fractions to percents. Round to the nearest tenth percent. *(p. 137)*

9. $\frac{1}{6}$ **10.** $\frac{1}{8}$

Convert the following percents to fractions and reduce to lowest terms as needed. *(p. 137)*

11. $15\frac{3}{4}$%   **12.** 7.2%

Solve the following problems for portion, base, or rate:

13. E.Site.com has a net income before taxes of $900,000. The company's treasurer estimates that 40% of the company's net income will go to federal and state taxes. How much will E.Site.com have left? *(p. 140)*

14. Papa Ginos projects a year-end net income of $650,000. The net income represents 30% of its projected annual sales. What are Papa Ginos's projected annual sales? Round to the nearest dollar. *(p. 142)*

15. Wal-Mart ordered 400 Sony Playstations. When Wal-Mart received the order, 20 Playstations were missing. What percent of the order did Wal-Mart receive? *(p. 141)*

16. Norma Maler, an employee at Putnam Investments, receives an annual salary of $80,000. Today, her boss informed her she would receive a $9,000 raise. What percent of her old salary is the $9,000 raise? Round to the nearest hundredth percent. *(p. 141)*

17. The price of a Delta airline ticket from San Diego to Boston increased to $550. This is a 30% increase. What was the old fare? Round to the nearest cent. *(p. 142)*

18. Al Ring earns a gross pay of $600 per week at Staples. Al's payroll deductions are 29%. What is Al's take-home pay? *(p. 140)*

19. Tom Bruce is reviewing the total accounts receivable of Rich's Department Store. Credit customers paid $60,000 this month. This represents 30% of all receivables due. What is Tom's total accounts receivable? *(p. 142)*

If you don't tip, don't plan on dining in that restaurant again because your server may try to exact revenge.

Slaves to culture

TIPPING IS also an American thing to do, as much a part of our culture as baseball and the Stars and Stripes. As a nation, we tip more occupations—33 in all (from shoeshiner to casino croupier)—than any other country. By comparison, New Zealanders tip just three jobs: waiter, cab driver and tour guide.

And good economic times have loosened our wallets so that we tip more generously than ever. Nationally, the average restaurant server's tip is nearly 18%, according to a recent Zagat survey, with many people reporting that they usually tip at least 20%. Bostonians, usually models of Yankee thrift, are either the best tippers or the biggest liars in the country, with 55%

of them claiming that they regularly tip servers 20% or more. Only 37% of the cheapskates in Los Angeles say they tip that generously on a regular basis.

Still, faced with abysmal service, most diners reserve the right to stiff a server. But unless you're prepared for the server to ambush you at the door, says etiquette expert Peggy Newfield, speak with the manager first and then leave only 10%.

If you don't tip, don't plan on dining in that restaurant again because servers have their own methods for exacting revenge against stingy patrons who return, says Debra Ginsberg, a former waitress and author of *Waiting: The True Confessions of a Waitress.* Ginsberg, who has waited tables in greasy diners and exclusive clubs, has seen angry servers in restaurant kitchens retrieve bread out of a garbage bin to serve to a customer or deliberately drop food on the floor before plopping it on a plate. Some patrons who don't tip are automatically given special dispensation, such as senior citizens on a fixed income. Those people, says Ginsberg, are a waiter's pro-bono cases.

VIP treatment

WHY ALL THE FUSS over a tip? In many states, restaurants may pay their servers less than minimum wage because they earn tips. Even people who work in other service-industry jobs, such as hotel personnel, depend on tips for a major part of their income.

What often works best is to subtly promise a good tip in exchange for a specific favor. Widzer does this when he travels, and sometimes the results astound him. Once, while making a hotel reservation over the phone for a trip to Puerto Rico, Widzer told the desk clerk that he appreciates good service and shows it. When Widzer arrived several days later, he had been given an upgraded room, ten free passes to use the hotel's golf course, two free passes for breakfast, and a bottle of champagne. In exchange for tipping the desk clerk $100, Widzer estimates he got more than $1,200 worth of VIP treatment.

Like any investment, tipping is all about timing. Usually, Widzer inquires about room upgrades when he first arrives at a hotel. He says the best technique is to take out money as if you were offering a tip but not hand it over until the employee has fulfilled his or her end of the bargain. (And you must deliver on your promise of a good tip once you've received the service.) Be specific about what you would like, such as a room with a view, but don't demand it.

FITTING TIPPING	Guidelines for giving	
OCCUPATION	**AMOUNT TO TIP**
Dog groomer	15% of the bill, or at least $2 per dog
Hotel manager	Write a letter
Hotel bellhop/desk clerk	$5 to $20 for a room upgrade; $1 to $2 for delivering messages and assisting with bags
Room service	15% to 20%; if bill includes service, 5% or $1 minimum
Chambermaid	$2 per night; leave it on your pillow
Hairstylist	10% to 15% of bill
Shampoo person at salon	$1 to $2
Doorman	$1 to $2 for cabs and assisting with baggage
Bartender	15% of liquor bill
Golf caddy	$20 to $30 per 18 holes
Casino croupier	At least $5 per session
Shoeshiner	$1 to $2
Tour guide	$1 to $2 per person per day

SOURCES: *The Penny Pincher's Passport to Luxury Travel,* by Joel Widzer; *Full House,* by Stephanie Horton; and The Original Tipping Page, at www.tipping.org.

Business Math Issue

Tipping in our culture should be eliminated.

1. List the key points of the article and information to support your position.
2. Write a group defense of your position using math calculations to support your view.

BUSINESS MATH SCRAPBOOK
WITH INTERNET APPLICATION

Putting Your Skills to Work

©2000 Dow Jones & Company, Inc.

PROJECT A

Your department at work needs a new fax machine. Go to www.bestbuy.com. Look under the pull-down Product Info menus for fax machines. Choose a fax machine you would like to purchase. Assume your organization is sales tax exempt in your state, but that your company's shipping and receiving department charges an 8% fee to handle all orders. How much will the fax machine cost before the surcharge? What is the amount of the surcharge?

PROJECT B

Calculate the entire candy-making workforce.

In Candy Making, Chicago Claims Title Of World Champion

* * *

With Tootsie Rolls, Brach's, Fannie Farmer and Gum, Windy City is the Sweetest

---

CHICAGO (AP)—Al Capone. Deep-dish pizza. Michael Jordan and Sammy Sosa. The Sears Tower. And . . . candy?

The title may be little-known outside the world of sweets, but the City of the Big Shoulders is indeed the candy capital of the world, the National Confectioners Association confirms.

"It's true," says Susan Fussell of the U.S. industry group. "Chicago has more confectioners and chocolate manufacturers within a small radius than any other place in the world."

Pennsylvania and Switzerland may rival Chicago for chocolate, officials acknowledge. But consider:

The candy industry employs 13,000 people in the Chicago area at about 100 companies. They manufacture $4 billion worth of candy every year, including chocolate and chewing gum—the city's **Wm. Wrigley Jr.** Co. makes a lot of the latter—and 16% of the national candy-making work force is employed in the Chicago area.

Internet Projects: See text website (www.mhhe.com/slater7e) and *The Business Math Internet Resource Guide.*

VIDEO CASE

American President Lines

American President Lines (APL) has automated its terminal so the average turnaround time for a trucker picking up a 40-foot container is only 17 minutes.

APL uses an automated wireless system to track containers parked across its recently remodeled 160-acre facility in Seattle.

The fast turnaround time gives customers who operate under the just-in-time mode the opportunity to make more trips. Independent truck drivers also benefit.

The international freight industry is plagued by red tape and inefficiency. APL has used its website to help clients like Excel Corporation, the country's second-largest beef packer and processor, speed up its billing time. Excel now wants to ask online for a place on a ship and for a call from APL when room will be available.

The shipping market is enormous, estimated anywhere from $100 billion to $1 trillion. Imports in the United States alone totaled 10 million containers, while exports totaled 6.5 million containers, together carrying $375 billion worth of goods. One of the most difficult transactions is to source goods from overseas and have them delivered with minimal paperwork all the way through to the end customer. Shipping lines must provide real-time information on the location of ships and goods.

Most significant are attempts to automate shipping transactions online. The industry's administrative inefficiencies, which account for 4% to 10% of international trade costs are targeted. Industry insiders peg error rates on documents even higher, at 25% to 30%. It's no secret that startups must overcome the reluctance of hidebound shipping lines, which have deep-seated emotional fears of dot-coms coming between them and their customers.

In conclusion, American President Lines needs to get on board by staying online, or it might go down with the ship.

PROBLEM 1

The $170 billion in international trade volume per year given in the video is expected to increase by 50% in 5 years and expected to double over the next 25 years. **(a)** What is the expected total dollar amount in 5 years? **(b)** What is the expected total dollar amount in 25 years?

PROBLEM 2

The video stated that thousands of containers arrive each day. Each 40-foot container will hold, for example, 16,500 boxes of running shoes, 132,000 videotapes, or 25,000 blouses. At an average retail price of $49.50 for a pair of running shoes, $14.95 for a videotape, and $26.40 for a blouse, what would be the total retail value of the goods in these three containers (assume different goods in each container)?

PROBLEM 3

APL spent $600 million to build a 230-acre shipping terminal in California. The terminal can handle 4 wide-body container ships. Each ship can hold 4,800 20-foot containers, or 2,400 40-foot containers. **(a)** What was the cost per acre to build the facility? **(b)** How many 20-foot containers can the terminal handle at one time? **(c)** How many 40-foot containers can the terminal handle at one time?

PROBLEM 4

According to *Shanghai Daily,* the recent decline in China's export container prices (which fell by 1.4%) has not taken its toll on the general interest in this sector. China's foreign trade grew by 35%, reaching $387.1 billion. APL reported that it would increase its services from Asia to Europe to take advantage of China's growth in exports. What was the dollar amount of China's foreign trade last year?

PROBLEM 5

APL has expanded its domestic fleet to 5,100 53-foot containers; it is expanding its global fleet to 253,000 containers. The 5,100 containers represent what percent of APL's total fleet? Round to the nearest hundredth percent.

PROBLEM 6

The cost of owning a shipping vessel is very high. Operating costs for large vessels can run between $75,000 and $80,000 per day. Using an average cost per day, what would be the operating costs for one week?

PROBLEM 7

The Port of Los Angeles financed new terminal construction through operating revenues and bonds. They will collect about $30 million a year in rent from APL, who signed a 30-year lease on the property. What is APL's monthly payment?

PROBLEM 8

According to port officials, APL expanded cargo-handling capabilities at the Los Angeles facility that are expected to generate 10,500 jobs, with $335 million in wages and annual industry sales of $1 billion. What would be the average wage received? Round to the nearest dollar.

PROBLEM 9

APL has disclosed that it ordered over 34,000 containers from a Chinese container manufacturer. With 253,000 containers in its possession, what will be the percent increase in containers owned by APL? Round to the nearest hundredth percent.

Stores Told To Lift Prices In Germany

Antitrust Office Says Wal-Mart and 2 Others Sold Food Below Cost

---

By ERNEST BECK
Staff Reporter of THE WALL STREET JOURNAL

Here's a new twist in consumer protection: forcing stores to raise prices. German antitrust authorities ordered the German unit of **Wal-Mart Stores Inc.** of the U.S. and two German rivals to increase prices on certain products.

The authorities last week accused Wal-Mart of starting a retail price war on basic food items, such as milk, sugar and flour, forcing its competitors to lower prices. It said the companies exploited their size and market share to sell the products below cost on a continuing basis, which violates German trade laws. While this benefits consumers in the short term, the office said, it would hurt small and medium-size rivals that can't match the lower prices.

Discounts: Trade and Cash

LU 7–1: Trade Discounts—Single and Chain (Includes Discussion of Freight)

• Calculate single trade discounts with formulas and complements *(pp. 164–65).*

• Explain the freight terms *FOB shipping point* and *FOB destination (pp. 165–66).*

• Find list price when net price and trade discount rate are known *(p. 168).*

• Calculate chain discounts with the net price equivalent rate and single equivalent discount rate *(pp. 168–70).*

LU 7–2: Cash Discounts, Credit Terms, and Partial Payments

• List and explain typical discount periods and credit periods that a business may offer *(pp. 172–78).*

• Calculate outstanding balance for partial payments *(p. 179).*

Jones Apparel Says It Settled Charges Against Nine West

By TERI AGINS

Staff Reporter of THE WALL STREET JOURNAL

NEW YORK—**Jones Apparel Group** Inc. said it agreed to pay $34 million to settle allegations that its Nine West footwear unit coerced stores to adhere to retail prices for its products for more than 10 years.

Jones said Nine West didn't admit any liability in the settlement reached with attorneys general of 50 states, five territories and the Federal Trade Commission.

©2000 Dow Jones & Company, Inc.

Kodak Co. Wins the Right To Be Sole Sam's Supplier

By a WALL STREET JOURNAL *Staff Reporter*

ROCHESTER, N.Y.—**Eastman Kodak** Co. has won the right to become the exclusive supplier of 35 millimeter film to **Sam's Club**, a 466-store chain that is a large seller of consumer film.

The contract, inked in May, could raise the Rochester, N.Y. photography concern's share of the film sold each year in the U.S. by 1.5 to two percentage points, to about 67%, said Jonathan Rosenzweig, an analyst at Salomon Smith Barney.

©2000 Dow Jones & Company, Inc.

The word *discount* makes buyers stop and listen. Buyers also stop and listen when a company can no longer force its retail stores to sell a particular product at retail prices. *The Wall Street Journal* clipping "Jones Apparel Says It Settled Charges Against Nine West" indicates that for more than 10 years, Jones Apparel may have coerced its Nine West footwear stores to adhere to retail prices. As a customer of Nine West footwear, you could have lost many discounts. It was also good news for Sam's Club customers who use Kodak 35-millimeter film when they read in *The Wall Street Journal* that Kodak won the right to be Sam's exclusive supplier of 35-millimeter film. Can you imagine the amount of discount Kodak had to give Sam's to earn this exclusive right? Sam's users of Kodak 35-millimeter film will now be checking the price of Kodak film at Sam's.

This chapter discusses two types of discounts taken by retailers—trade and cash. A **trade discount** is a reduction off the original selling price (list price) of an item and is not related to early payment. A **cash discount** is the result of an early payment based on the terms of the sale.

LEARNING UNIT 7–1 | TRADE DISCOUNTS—SINGLE AND CHAIN (INCLUDES DISCUSSION OF FREIGHT)

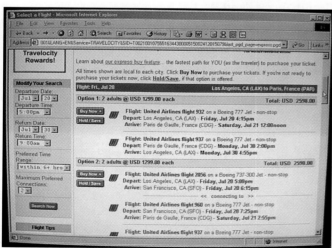

Tony Freeman/PhotoEdit.

United Airlines offers a 5% discount off the base sale price if you book a plane fare online. Why do Internet users often get lower prices? It costs less to sell services and products on the Internet. Many companies pass on some of these reduced costs to the Internet user. So before you buy a service or product, be sure to check the Internet for discount prices only available on the Internet.

Where do retailers such as the Internet get their merchandise? The merchandise sold by retailers is bought from manufacturers and wholesalers who sell only to retailers and not to customers. These manufacturers and wholesalers offer retailer discounts so they can resell the merchandise at a profit. The discounts are off the manufacturers' and wholesalers' **list price** (suggested retail price), and the amount of discount that retailers receive off the list price is the **trade discount amount.**

When you make a purchase, the retailer (seller) gives you a purchase **invoice.** Invoices are important business documents that help sellers keep track of sales transactions and buyers keep track of purchase transactions. North Shore Community College Bookstore is a retail seller of textbooks to students. The bookstore usually purchases its textbooks directly from publishers. Figure 7.1 shows a textbook invoice from McGraw-Hill/Irwin Publishing

FIGURE 7.1

Bookstore invoice showing a trade discount

Invoice No.: 5582

McGraw-Hill/Irwin Publishing Co.
1333 Burr Ridge Parkway
Burr Ridge, Illinois 60527

Date: July 8, 2004
Ship: Two-day UPS
Terms: 2/10, n/30

Sold to: North Shore Community College Bookstore
1 Ferncroft Road
Danvers, MA 01923

Description	Unit list price	Total amount
50 Managerial Accounting–Garrison/Noreen	$59.99	$2,999.50
10 Marketing–McCarthy	58.66	586.60
	Total List Price	$3,586.10
	Less: Trade Discount 25%	– 896.53
	Net Price	$2,689.57
	Plus: Prepaid Shipping Charge	65.50
	Total Invoice Amount	$2,755.07

Company to the North Shore Community College Bookstore. Note that the trade discount amount is given in percent. This is the **trade discount rate,** which is a percent off the list price that retailers can deduct. The following formula for calculating a trade discount amount gives the numbers from the Figure 7.1 invoice in parentheses:

Trade Discount Amount Formula

Trade discount amount = List price × Trade discount rate

($896.53)   ($3,586.10)   (25%)

The price that the retailer (bookstore) pays the manufacturer (publisher) or wholesaler is the **net price.** The following formula for calculating the net price gives the numbers from the Figure 7.1 invoice in parentheses:

Net Price Formula

Net price = List price − Trade discount amount

($2,689.57)   ($3,586.10)   ($896.53)

Frequently, manufacturers and wholesalers issue catalogs to retailers containing list prices of the seller's merchandise and the available trade discounts. To reduce printing costs when prices change, these sellers usually update the catalogs with new *discount sheets.* The discount sheet also gives the seller the flexibility of offering different trade discounts to different classes of retailers. For example, some retailers buy in quantity and service the products. They may receive a larger discount than the retailer who wants the manufacturer to service the products. Sellers may also give discounts to meet a competitor's price, to attract new retailers, and to reward the retailers who buy product-line products. Sometimes the ability of the retailer to negotiate with the seller determines the trade discount amount.

Retailers cannot take trade discounts on freight, returned goods, sales tax, and so on. Trade discounts may be single discounts or a chain of discounts. Before we discuss single trade discounts, let's study freight terms.

Freight Terms

The most common **freight terms** are *FOB shipping point* and *FOB destination.* These terms determine how the freight will be paid. The key words in the terms are *shipping point* and *destination.*

Chris Thatcher/Tony Stone Images

FOB shipping point means free on board at shipping point; that is, the buyer pays the freight cost of getting the goods to the place of business.

For example, assume that IBM in San Diego bought goods from Argo Suppliers in Boston. Argo ships the goods FOB Boston by plane. IBM takes title to the goods when the aircraft in Boston receives the goods, so IBM pays the freight from Boston to San Diego. Frequently, the seller (Argo) prepays the freight and adds the amount to the buyer's (IBM) invoice. When paying the invoice, the buyer takes the cash discount off the net price and adds the freight cost. FOB shipping point can be illustrated as follows:

FOB shipping point (Boston)

Boston | San Diego
Argo Suppliers (IBM takes title here) → **IBM** (Buyer pays the freight costs)
Buyer pays the freight

FOB destination means the seller pays the freight cost until it reaches the buyer's place of business. If Argo ships its goods to IBM FOB destination or FOB San Diego, the title to the goods remains with Argo. Then it is Argo's responsibility to pay the freight from Boston to IBM's place of business in San Diego. FOB destination can be illustrated as follows:

FOB destination (San Diego)

Boston
Argo Suppliers (Has title) → **IBM** (Get title on arrival of goods)
Seller pays the freight

The following *Wall Street Journal* clipping "Why Shoppers Are Wary" lists reasons why Internet users do not shop online. One of the leading reasons is that often the shipping charges are FOB shipping point—the buyer pays the freight. Another important reason is the difficulty in returning items. If you prefer to shop offline, is your reason for not shopping online listed in the clipping?

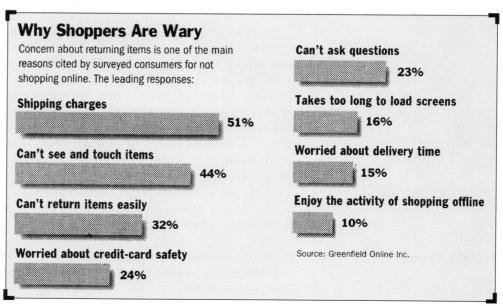

Why Shoppers Are Wary

Concern about returning items is one of the main reasons cited by surveyed consumers for not shopping online. The leading responses:

Shipping charges — 51%
Can't see and touch items — 44%
Can't return items easily — 32%
Worried about credit-card safety — 24%

Can't ask questions — 23%
Takes too long to load screens — 16%
Worried about delivery time — 15%
Enjoy the activity of shopping offline — 10%

Source: Greenfield Online Inc.

Now you are ready for the discussion on single trade discounts.

Single Trade Discount

In the introduction to this unit, we showed how to use the trade discount amount formula and the net price formula to calculate the McGraw-Hill/Irwin Publishing Company textbook sale to the North Shore Community College Bookstore. Since McGraw-Hill/Irwin gave the bookstore only one trade discount, it is a **single trade discount.** In the following word problem, we use the formulas to solve another example of a single trade discount. Again, we will use a blueprint aid to help dissect and solve the word problem.

The Word Problem   The list price of a Macintosh computer is $2,700. The manufacturer offers dealers a 40% trade discount. What are the trade discount amount and the net price?

The facts	Solving for?	Steps to take	Key points
List price: $2,700. Trade discount rate: 40%.	Trade discount amount. Net price.	Trade discount amount = List price × Trade discount rate. Net price = List price − Trade discount amount.	Trade discount amount Portion (?) Base × Rate ($2,700) (.40) List price Trade discount rate

Steps to solving problem

1. Calculate the trade discount amount. $2,700 × .40 = $1,080
2. Calculate the net price. $2,700 − $1,080 = **$1,620**

Now let's learn how to check the dealers' net price of $1,620 with an alternate procedure using a complement.

How to Calculate the Net Price Using Complement of Trade Discount Rate

The **complement** of a trade discount rate is the difference between the discount rate and 100%. The following steps show you how to use the complement of a trade discount rate:

Calculating Net Price Using Complement of Trade Discount Rate

Step 1.   To find the complement, subtract the single discount rate from 100%.
Step 2.   Multiply the list price times the complement (from Step 1).

Think of a complement of any given percent (decimal) as the result of subtracting the percent from 100%.

Step 1.   100%
      $\underline{- 40}$ ← Trade discount rate
         60% or .60

Portion (?)

Base × Rate
($2,700) (.60)

List price

The complement means that we are spending 60 cents per dollar because we save 40 cents per dollar. Since we planned to spend $2,700, we multiply .60 by $2,700 to get a net price of $1,620.

Step 2.   **$1,620** = $2,700 × .60

Note how the portion ($1,620) and rate (.60) relate to the same piece of the base ($2,700). The portion ($1,620) is smaller than the base, since the rate is less than 100%.

Be aware that some people prefer to use the trade discount amount formula and the net price formula to find the net price. Other people prefer to use the complement of the trade discount rate to find the net price. The result is always the same.

Finding List Price When You Know Net Price and Trade Discount Rate

The following formula has many useful applications:

> **Calculating List Price When Net Price and Trade Discount Rate Are Known**
>
> $$\text{List price} = \frac{\text{Net price}}{\text{Complement of trade discount rate}}$$

Next, let's see how to dissect and solve a word problem calculating list price.

The Word Problem   A Macintosh computer has a $1,620 net price and a 40% trade discount. What is its list price?

The facts	Solving for?	Steps to take	Key points
Net price: $1,620. *Trade discount rate:* 40%.	List price.	List price = $\dfrac{\text{Net price}}{\text{Complement of trade discount rate}}$	Net price Portion ($1,620) Base (?) × Rate (.60) List price 100% − 40%

Steps to solving problem

1. Calculate the complement of the trade discount.

$$\begin{array}{r} 100\% \\ -\ \ 40 \\ \hline 60\% = .60 \end{array}$$

2. Calculate the list price.

$$\frac{\$1,620}{.60} = \boxed{\$2,700}$$

Note that the portion ($1,620) and rate (.60) relate to the same piece of the base.

Let's return to the McGraw-Hill/Irwin invoice in Figure 7.1 and calculate the list price using the formula for finding list price when net price and trade discount rate are known. The net price of the textbooks is $2,689.57. The complement of the trade discount rate is 100% − 25% = 75% = .75. Dividing the net price $2,689.57 by the complement .75 equals $3,586.09,[1] the list price shown in the McGraw-Hill/Irwin invoice. We can show this as follows:

$$\frac{\$2,689.57}{.75} = \$3,586.09, \text{ the list price}$$

Chain Discounts

Frequently, manufacturers want greater flexibility in setting trade discounts for different classes of customers, seasonal trends, promotional activities, and so on. To gain this flexibility, some sellers give **chain** or **series discounts**—trade discounts in a series of two or more successive discounts.

Sellers list chain discounts as a group, for example, 20/15/10. Let's look at how Mick Company arrives at the net price of office equipment with a 20/15/10 chain discount.

EXAMPLE   The list price of the office equipment is $15,000. The chain discount is 20/15/10. The long way to calculate the net price is as follows:

Step 1	Step 2	Step 3	Step 4
$15,000	$15,000	$12,000	$10,200
× .20	− 3,000	− 1,800	− 1,020
$ 3,000	$12,000	$10,200	$ 9,180 net price
	× .15	× .10	
	$ 1,800	$ 1,020	

---

[1]Off by 1 cent due to rounding.

Never add the 20/15/10 together.

Note how we multiply the percent (in decimal) times the new balance after we subtract the previous trade discount amount. For example, in Step 3, we change the last discount, 10%, to decimal form and multiply times $10,200. Remember that each percent is multiplied by a successively *smaller* base. You could write the 20/15/10 discount rate in any order and still arrive at the same net price. Thus, you would get the $9,180 net price if the discount were 10/15/20 or 15/20/10. However, sellers usually give the larger discounts first. *Never try to shorten this step process by adding the discounts.* Your net price will be incorrect because, when done properly, each percent is calculated on a different base.

Net Price Equivalent Rate

In the example above, you could also find the $9,180 net price with the **net price equivalent rate**—a shortcut method. Let's see how to use this rate to calculate net price.

Calculating Net Price Using Net Price Equivalent Rate

Step 1. Subtract each chain discount rate from 100% (find the complement) and convert each percent to a decimal.

Step 2. Multiply the decimals. Do not round off decimals, since this number is the net price equivalent rate.

Step 3. Multiply the list price times the net price equivalent rate (Step 2).

The following word problem with its blueprint aid illustrates how to use the net price equivalent rate method.

The Word Problem   The list price of office equipment is $15,000. The chain discount is 20/15/10. What is the net price?

The facts	Solving for?	Steps to take	Key points
List price: $15,000. *Chain discount:* 20/15/10	Net price.	Net price equivalent rate. Net price = List price × Net price equivalent rate.	Do not round net price equivalent rate.

Steps to solving problem

1. Calculate the complement of each rate and convert each percent to a decimal.

$$\begin{array}{ccc} 100\% & 100\% & 100\% \\ -\ 20 & -\ 15 & -\ 10 \\ \hline 80\% & 85\% & 90\% \end{array}$$

$$\downarrow \qquad \downarrow \qquad \downarrow$$

$$.8 \qquad .85 \qquad .9$$

2. Calculate the net price equivalent rate. (Do not round.)

$.8 \times .85 \times .9 = .612$ Net price equivalent rate For each $1, you are spending about 61 cents.

3. Calculate the net price (actual cost to buyer).

$15,000 \times .612 = \boxed{\$9,180}$

Next we see how to calculate the trade discount amount with a simpler method.

In the previous word problem, we could calculate the trade discount amount as follows:

$$\begin{array}{ll} \$15,000 & \leftarrow \text{List price} \\ -\ 9,180 & \leftarrow \text{Net price} \\ \hline \boxed{\$\ 5,820} & \leftarrow \text{Trade discount amount} \end{array}$$

Single Equivalent Discount Rate

You can use another method to find the trade discount by using the **single equivalent discount rate.**

> **Calculating Trade Discount Amount Using Single Equivalent Discount Rate**
>
> **Step 1.** Subtract the net price equivalent rate from 1. This is the single equivalent discount rate.
>
> **Step 2.** Multiply the list price times the single equivalent discount rate. This is the trade discount amount.

Let's now do the calculations.

Step 1.   1.000   ← If you are using a calculator, just press 1.
          − .612
          .388   ← This is the single equivalent discount rate.

Step 2. $15,000 × .388 = $5,820   → This is the trade discount amount.

Remember that when we use the net price equivalent rate, the buyer of the office equipment pays $.612 on each $1 of list price. Now with the single equivalent discount rate, we can say that the buyer saves $.388 on each $1 of list price. The .388 is the single equivalent discount rate for the 20/15/10 chain discount. Note how we use the .388 single equivalent discount rate as if it were the only discount.

Have you noticed the display of magazines before you get to the supermarket cash register? Did you know that magazine companies pay for these valuable spaces that entice customers to buy their magazines? According to *The Wall Street Journal* clipping "Supermarkets Face Scrutiny Over Fees," food retailers also collect so-called slotting fees on everything from soup cans to vegetables. This is why you see, for example, Coca-Cola displayed at a prominent place at the end slot of a grocery isle. The Federal Trade Commission is looking into the sale of shelf space by retailers because this threatens the profitability and future of the family produce farmer.

Supermarkets Face Scrutiny Over Fees

By JERRY GUIDERA
And SHELLY BRANCH
Staff Reporters of THE WALL STREET JOURNAL

WASHINGTON—Senators blasted food retailers for levying so-called slotting fees on everything from soup cans to vegetables, and put supermarkets on notice that they are determined to step up scrutiny of the industry.

The fees, which retailers routinely charge suppliers to guarantee shelf space, are "threatening the profitability and the future of the family produce farmer," said Missouri Republican Sen. Christopher "Kit" Bond, chairman of the Senate Small Business Committee, which held a hearing on the matter yesterday.

Federal antitrust regulators have also taken a renewed interest in the way retailers will accept discounts from large manufacturers, while demanding upfront payments from smaller ones, to secure prime shelf space.

The Federal Trade Commission is expected to issue a report examining slotting fees by the end of the year. Beginning next year, $900,000 will be earmarked for the agency to cover legal fees to force companies to cooperate with its probe.

©2000 Dow Jones & Company, Inc.

It's time to try the Practice Quiz.

LU 7–1 PRACTICE QUIZ[2]

1. The list price of a dining room set with a 40% trade discount is $12,000. What are the trade discount amount and net price (use complement method for net price)?

2. The net price of a video system with a 30% trade discount is $1,400. What is the list price?

3. Lamps Outlet bought a shipment of lamps from a wholesaler. The total list price was $12,000 with a 5/10/25 chain discount. Calculate the net price and trade discount amount. (Use the net price equivalent rate and single equivalent discount rate in your calculation.)

---

[2]For all three problems we will show blueprint aids. You might want to draw them on scrap paper.

✓ **SOLUTIONS**

1. Dining room set trade discount amount and net price:

The facts	Solving for?	Steps to take	Key points
List price: $12,000. *Trade discount rate:* 40%.	Trade discount amount. Net price.	Trade discount amount = List price × Trade discount rate. Net price = List price × Complement of trade discount rate.	Trade discount amount / Portion (?) / Base × Rate ($12,000) (.40) / List price / Trade discount rate

Steps to solving problem

1. Calculate the trade discount. $12,000 × .40 = **$4,800** Trade discount amount

2. Calculate the net price. $12,000 × .60 = **$7,200** (100% − 40% = 60%)

2. Video system list price:

The facts	Solving for?	Steps to take	Key points
Net price: $1,400. *Trade discount rate:* 30%.	List price.	List price = Net price / Complement of trade discount	Net price / Portion ($1,400) / Base × Rate (?) (.70) / List price / 100% −30%

Steps to solving problem

1. Calculate the complement of trade discount.
100%
− 30
70% = .70

2. Calculate the list price. $\frac{\$1,400}{.70}$ = **$2,000**

3. Lamps Outlet's net price and trade discount amount:

The facts	Solving for?	Steps to take	Key points
List price: $12,000. *Chain discount:* 5/10/25.	Net price. Trade discount amount.	Net price = List price × Net price equivalent rate. Trade discount amount = List price × Single equivalent discount rate.	Do not round off net price equivalent rate or single equivalent discount rate.

Steps to solving problem

1. Calculate the complement of each chain discount.
100%   100%   100%
− 5   − 10   − 25
95%   90%   75%

2. Calculate the net price equivalent rate. .95 × .90 × .75 = .64125

3. Calculate the net price. $12,000 × .64125 = **$7,695**

4. Calculate the single equivalent discount rate.
1.00000
− .64125
.35875

5. Calculate the trade discount amount. $12,000 × .35875 = **$4,305**

LEARNING UNIT 7–2 | CASH DISCOUNTS, CREDIT TERMS, AND PARTIAL PAYMENTS

Invoice No.: 5582

McGraw-Hill/Irwin Publishing Co.
1333 Burr Ridge Parkway
Burr Ridge, Illinois 60527

Date: July 8, 2004
Ship: Two-day UPS
Terms: 2/10, n/30

Sold to: North Shore Community College Bookstore
1 Ferncroft Road
Danvers, MA 01923

	Description	Unit list price	Total amount
50	Managerial Accounting–Garrison/Noreen	$59.99	$2,999.50
10	Marketing–McCarthy	58.66	586.60
	Total List Price		$3,586.10
	Less: Trade Discount 25%		− 896.53
	Net Price		$2,689.57
	Plus: Prepaid Shipping Charge		65.50
	Total Invoice Amount		$2,755.07

NSCC Bookstore
1 Ferncroft Road
Danvers, MA 01923

4418
22-70/960

July 12 20 *04*

PAY TO THE
ORDER OF *McGraw-Hill/Irwin Publishing Co.* $ *2,701 28/100*
Two thousand, seven hundred one and 28/100 ———————— DOLLARS

PARK BANK
2254 Como Avenue
Danvers, MA 01924

James Casley

⑆096000700⑆ 23593100 ⑈ 0650

To introduce this learning unit, we return to the McGraw-Hill/Irwin Publishing Company textbook invoice shown in Figure 7.1. For your convenience, we have repeated the invoice.

As you can see, the terms of the McGraw-Hill/Irwin invoice are 2/10, n/30. This means that if North Shore Community College Bookstore pays the invoice within 10 days, it may deduct 2% from the net price before adding the prepaid shipping charge (FOB shipping point). The check below the invoice shows that the bookstore paid McGraw-Hill/Irwin $2,701.28.

Net price	$2,689.57
Less: Cash discount	− 53.79 ($2,689.57 × .02)
Plus: Freight	+ 65.50
	$2,701.28

In this unit we will see why the bookstore pays McGraw-Hill/Irwin $2,701.28. Before we discuss the common credit terms offered by sellers, let's look at cash discounts and how they are determined.

Cash Discounts

In the McGraw-Hill/Irwin Publishing Company invoice, the bookstore received a cash discount of $53.79. This amount is determined by the **terms of the sale,** which include the credit period, cash discount, discount period, and freight terms.

Buyers can often benefit from buying on credit. The time period that sellers give buyers to pay their invoices is the **credit period.** Frequently, buyers can sell the goods bought during this credit period. Then, at the end of the credit period, buyers can pay sellers with the funds from the sales of the goods. When buyers can do this, they can use the consumer's money to pay the invoice instead of their money.

A cash discount is for prompt payment. A trade discount is not.

Sellers can also offer a cash discount, or reduction from the invoice price, if buyers pay the invoice within a specified time. This time period is the **discount period,** which is part of the total credit period. Sellers offer this cash discount because they can use the dollars to better advantage sooner than later. Buyers who are not short of cash like cash discounts because the goods will cost them less and, as a result, provide an opportunity for larger profits.

Trade discounts should be taken before cash discounts.

Remember that buyers do not take cash discounts on freight, returned goods, sales tax, and trade discounts. Buyers take cash discounts on the *net price* of the invoice. Before we discuss how to calculate cash discounts, let's look at some aids that will help you calculate credit **due dates** and **end of credit periods.**

Aids in Calculating Credit Due Dates

Sellers usually give credit for 30, 60, or 90 days. Not all months of the year have 30 days. So you must count the credit days from the date of the invoice. The trick is to remember the number of days in each month. You can choose one of the following three options to help you do this.

Years divisible by 4 are leap years. Leap years occur in 2004 and 2008.

Option 1: Days-in-a-Month Rule   You may already know this rule. Remember that every 4 years is a leap year.

> Thirty days has September, April, June, and November; all the rest have 31 except February has 28, and 29 in leap years.

Option 2: Knuckle Months   Some people like to use the knuckles on their hands to remember which months have 30 or 31 days. Note in the following diagram that each knuckle represents a month with 31 days. The short months are in between the knuckles.

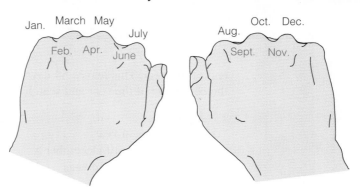

31 days: Jan., March, May, July, Aug., Oct., Dec.

Option 3: Days-in-a-Year Calendar   The days-in-a-year calendar (excluding leap year) is another tool to help you calculate dates for discount and credit periods (Table 7.1). For example, let's use Table 7.1 to calculate 90 days from August 12.

EXAMPLE   By Table 7.1: August 12 = $\begin{array}{r} 224 \text{ days} \\ + \ 90 \\ \hline 314 \text{ days} \end{array}$

Search for day 314 in Table 7.1. You will find that day 314 is November 10. In this example, we stayed within the same year. Now let's try an example in which we overlap from year to year.

EXAMPLE   What date is 80 days after December 5?

Table 7.1 shows that December 5 is 339 days from the beginning of the year. Subtracting 339 from 365 (the end of the year) tells us that we have used up 26 days by the

TABLE 7.1 Exact days-in-a-year calendar (excluding leap year)

Day of month	31 Jan.	28 Feb.	31 Mar.	30 Apr.	31 May	30 June	31 July	31 Aug.	30 Sept.	31 Oct.	30 Nov.	31 Dec.
1	1	32	60	91	121	152	182	213	244	274	305	335
2	2	33	61	92	122	153	183	214	245	275	306	336
3	3	34	62	93	123	154	184	215	246	276	307	337
4	4	35	63	94	124	155	185	216	247	277	308	338
5	5	36	64	95	125	156	186	217	248	278	309	339
6	6	37	65	96	126	157	187	218	249	279	310	340
7	7	38	66	97	127	158	188	219	250	280	311	341
8	8	39	67	98	128	159	189	220	251	281	312	342
9	9	40	68	99	129	160	190	221	252	282	313	343
10	10	41	69	100	130	161	191	222	253	283	314	344
11	11	42	70	101	131	162	192	223	254	284	315	345
12	12	43	71	102	132	163	193	224	255	285	316	346
13	13	44	72	103	133	164	194	225	256	286	317	347
14	14	45	73	104	134	165	195	226	257	287	318	348
15	15	46	74	105	135	166	196	227	258	288	319	349
16	16	47	75	106	136	167	197	228	259	289	320	350
17	17	48	76	107	137	168	198	229	260	290	321	351
18	18	49	77	108	138	169	199	230	261	291	322	352
19	19	50	78	109	139	170	200	231	262	292	323	353
20	20	51	79	110	140	171	201	232	263	293	324	354
21	21	52	80	111	141	172	202	233	264	294	325	355
22	22	53	81	112	142	173	203	234	265	295	326	356
23	23	54	82	113	143	174	204	235	266	296	327	357
24	24	55	83	114	144	175	205	236	267	297	328	358
25	25	56	84	115	145	176	206	237	268	298	329	359
26	26	57	85	116	146	177	207	238	269	299	330	360
27	27	58	86	117	147	178	208	239	270	300	331	361
28	28	59	87	118	148	179	209	240	271	301	332	362
29	29	—	88	119	149	180	210	241	272	302	333	363
30	30	—	89	120	150	181	211	242	273	303	334	364
31	31	—	90	—	151	—	212	243	—	304	—	365

end of the year. This leaves 54 days in the new year. Go back in the table and start with the beginning of the year and search for 54 (80 − 26) days. The 54th day is February 23.

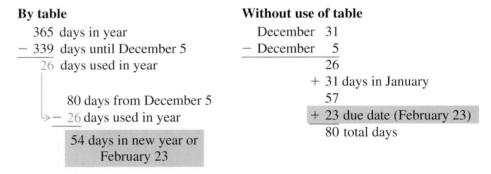

By table	**Without use of table**
365 days in year	December 31
− 339 days until December 5	− December 5
26 days used in year	26
	+ 31 days in January
80 days from December 5	57
↳− 26 days used in year	+ 23 due date (February 23)
54 days in new year or February 23	80 total days

When you know how to calculate credit due dates, you can understand the common business terms sellers offer buyers involving discounts and credit periods. Remember that discount and credit terms vary from one seller to another.

Common Credit Terms Offered by Sellers

The common credit terms sellers offer buyers include *ordinary dating, receipt of goods (ROG), and end of month (EOM).* In this section we examine these credit terms. To determine the due dates, we used the exact days-in-a-year calendar (Table 7.1).

Ordinary Dating

Today, businesses frequently use the **ordinary dating** method. It gives the buyer a cash discount period that begins with the invoice date. The credit terms of two common ordinary dating methods are 2/10, n/30 and 2/10, 1/15, n/30.

2/10, n/30 Ordinary Dating Method   The 2/10, n/30 is read as "two ten, net thirty." Buyers can take a 2% cash discount off the gross amount of the invoice if they pay the bill within 10 days from the invoice date. If buyers miss the discount period, the net amount—without a discount—is due between day 11 and day 30. *Freight, returned goods, sales tax, and trade discounts must be subtracted from the gross before calculating a cash discount.*

EXAMPLE $400 invoice dated July 5: terms 2/10, n/30; no freight; paid on July 11.

Step 1.   Calculate end of 2% discount period:

> July   5 date of invoice
> <u>+ 10</u> days
> July 15 end of 2% discount period

Step 2.   Calculate end of credit period:

> July 5 by Table 7.1
> 186 days
> <u>+ 30</u>
> 216 days

Search in Table 7.1 for 216 ⟶ August 4 ⟶ end of credit period

Step 3.   Calculate payment on July 11:

> .02 × $400 = $8 cash discount
> $400 − $8 = $392 paid

> *Note:* A 2% cash discount means that you save 2 cents on the dollar and pay 98 cents on the dollar. Thus, $.98 × $400 = $392.

The following time line illustrates the 2/10, n/30 ordinary dating method beginning and ending dates of the above example:

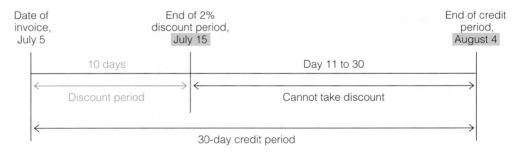

2/10, 1/15, n/30 Ordinary Dating Method   The 2/10, 1/15, n/30 is read "two ten, one fifteen, net thirty." The seller will give buyers a 2% (2 cents on the dollar) cash discount if they pay within 10 days of the invoice date. If buyers pay between day 11 and day 15 from the date of the invoice, they can save 1 cent on the dollar. If buyers do not pay on day 15, the net or full amount is due 30 days from the invoice date.

EXAMPLE $600 invoice dated May 8; $100 of freight included in invoice price; paid on May 22.

Step 1.   Calculate the end of the 2% discount period:

> May   8 date of invoice
> <u>+ 10</u> days
> May 18 end of 2% discount period

Step 2.   Calculate end of 1% discount period:

> May 18 end of 2% discount period
> <u>+   5</u> days
> May 23 end of 1% discount period

Step 3. Calculate end of credit period:

> May 8 by Table 7.1⌐
>   128 days ←———┘
> + 30
> ————
>   158 days

> Search in Table 7.1 for 158 —→ June 7 —→ end of credit period

Step 4. Calculate payment on May 22 (14 days after date of invoice):

> $600 invoice
> − 100 freight
> ————
> $500
> × .01
> ————
> $5.00

$500 − $5.00 + $100 freight = $595 ————————————┐

> A 1% discount means we pay $.99 on the dollar or
> $500 × $.99 = $495 + $100 freight = $595. ←
> *Note:* Freight is added back since no cash discount is taken on freight.

The following time line illustrates the 2/10, 1/15, n/30 ordinary dating method beginning and ending dates of the above example:

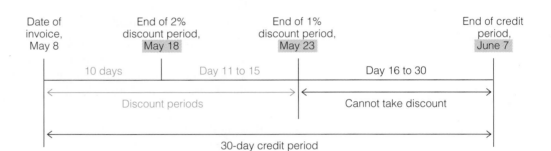

Date of invoice, May 8	End of 2% discount period, May 18	End of 1% discount period, May 23	End of credit period, June 7
	10 days	Day 11 to 15	Day 16 to 30
	Discount periods		Cannot take discount
	30-day credit period		

Receipt of Goods (ROG)

3/10, n/30 ROG   With the **receipt of goods (ROG),** the cash discount period begins when buyer receives goods, *not* the invoice date. Industry often uses the ROG terms when buyers cannot expect delivery until a long time after they place the order. Buyers can take a 3% discount within 10 days *after* receipt of goods. Full amount is due between day 11 and day 30 if cash discount period is missed.

EXAMPLE $900 invoice dated May 9; no freight or returned goods; the goods were received on July 8; terms 3/10, n/30 ROG; payment made on July 20.

Step 1. Calculate the end of the 3% discount period:

> July 8 date goods arrive
> + 10 days
> ————
> July 18 end of 3% discount period

Step 2. Calculate the end of the credit period:

> July 8 by Table 7.1⌐
>   189 days ←———┘
> + 30
> ————
>   219 days

> Search in Table 7.1 for 219 —→ August 7 —→ end of credit period

Step 3. Calculate payment on July 20:

> Missed discount period and paid net or full amount of $900.

The following time line illustrates 3/10, n/30 ROG beginning and ending dates of the above example:

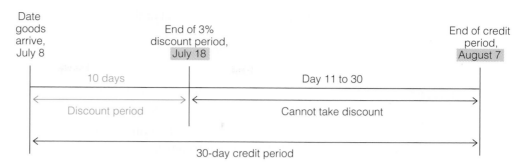

End of Month (EOM)[3]

In this section we look at terms involving **end of the month (EOM).** If an invoice is dated the *25th or earlier* of a month, we follow one set of rules. If an invoice is dated after the 25th of the month, a new set of rules is followed. Let's look at each situation.

Invoice Dated 25th or Earlier in Month, 1/10 EOM   If sellers date an invoice on the 25th or earlier in the month, buyers can take the cash discount if they pay the invoice by the first 10 days of the month following the sale (next month). If buyers miss the discount period, the full amount is due within 20 days after the end of the discount period.

EXAMPLE $600 invoice dated July 6; no freight or returns; terms 1/10 EOM; paid on August 8.

Step 1.   Calculate the end of the 1% discount period: ─┐
      August 10 ◄──────────────────────────┘   First 10 days of month
                                           following sale.

Step 2.   Calculate the end of the credit period: ──►
      August 10
          + 20 days
      August 30 ─► Credit period is 20 days after discount period.

Step 3.   Calculate payment on August 8:
      .99 × $600 = $594

The following time line illustrates the beginning and ending dates of the EOM invoice of the above example:

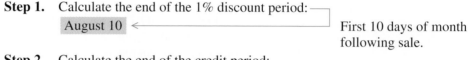

*Even though the discount period begins with the next month following the sale, if buyers wish, they can pay before the discount period (date of invoice until the discount period).

Invoice Dated after 25th of Month, 2/10 EOM   When sellers sell goods *after* the 25th of the month, buyers gain an additional month. The cash discount period ends on the 10th day of the second month that follows the sale. Why? This occurs because the seller guarantees the 15 days' credit of the buyer. If a buyer bought goods on August 29, September 10 would be only 12 days. So the buyer gets the extra month.

EXAMPLE $800 invoice dated April 29; no freight or returned goods; terms 2/10 EOM; payment made on June 18.

Step 1.   Calculate the end of the 2% discount period: ─┐
      June 10 ◄──────────────────────────────┘   First 10 days of second
                                           month following sale

---

[3]Sometimes the Latin term *proximo* is used. Other variations of EOM exist, but the key point is that the seller guarantees the buyer 15 days' credit. We assume a 30-day month.

Step 2. Calculate the end of the credit period:

June 10

+ 20 days

June 30   Credit period is 20 days after discount period.

Step 3. Calculate the payment on June 18:

No discount; $800 paid.

The following time line illustrates the beginning and ending dates of the EOM invoice of the above example:

Date of invoice, April 29	2nd month following sale, June*	End of 2% discount period, June 10	End of credit period, June 30
		10 days	20 days
		Discount period	Cannot take discount

*Even though the discount period begins with the second month following the sale, if buyers wish, they can pay before the discount date (date of invoice until the discount period)

Solving a Word Problem with Trade and Cash Discount

Now that we have studied trade and cash discounts, let's look at a combination that involves both a trade and a cash discount.

The Word Problem   Hardy Company sent Regan Corporation an invoice for office equipment with a $10,000 list price. Hardy dated the invoice July 29 with terms of 2/10 EOM (end of month). Regan receives a 30% trade discount and paid the invoice on September 6. Since terms were FOB destination, Regan paid no freight charge. What was the cost of office equipment for Regan?

The facts	Solving for?	Steps to take	Key points
List price: $10,000. *Trade discount rate:* 30%. *Terms:* 2/10 EOM. *Invoice date:* 7/29. *Date paid:* 9/6.	Cost of office equipment.	Net price = List price × Complement of trade discount rate. After 25th of month for EOM. Discount period is 1st 10 days of second month that follows sale.	Trade discounts are deducted before cash discounts are taken. Cash discounts are not taken on freight or returns.

Steps to solving problem

1. Calculate the net price. $10,000 × .70 = $7,000   ⌐ 100%
                                                        └ − 30% (trade discount)

2. Calculate the discount period.   Sale: 7/29 Month 1: Aug. Month 2: Sept 10 ⟶ Paid on Sept. 6—is
                                                                                        entitled to 2% off.

3. Calculate the cost of office equipment. $7,000 × .98 = $6,860   If you save 2 cents on a dollar, you are spending 98 cents.

                                                        100%
                                                        − 2%

Partial Payments

Often buyers cannot pay the entire invoice before the end of the discount period. To calculate partial payments and outstanding balance, use the following steps:

Calculating Partial Payments and Outstanding Balance

Step 1. Calculate the complement of a discount rate.

Step 2. Divide partial payments by the complement of a discount rate (Step 1). This gives the amount credited.

Step 3. Subtract Step 2 from the total owed. This is the outstanding balance.

EXAMPLE   Molly McGrady owed $400. Molly's terms were 2/10, n/30. Within 10 days, Molly sent a check for $80. The actual credit the buyer gave Molly is as follows:

Step 1. $100\% - 2\% = 98\% \longrightarrow .98$

Step 2. $\dfrac{\$80}{.98} = \$81.63$ $\dfrac{\$80}{1 - .02} \longleftarrow$ Discount rate

Step 3. $400.00
$\underline{-\ \ 81.63}$ partial payment—although sent in $80
$\boxed{\$318.37}$ outstanding balance

Note: We do not multiply .02 × $80 because the seller did not base the original discount on $80. When Molly makes a payment within the 10-day discount period, 98 cents pays each $1 she owes. Before buyers take discounts on partial payments, they must have permission from the seller. Not all states allow partial payments.

LU 7–2 PRACTICE QUIZ

Complete the following table:

	Date of invoice	Date goods received	Terms	Last day* of discount period	End of credit period
1.	July 6		2/10, n/30		
2.	February 19	June 9	3/10, n/30 ROG		
3.	May 9		4/10, 1/30, n/60		
4.	May 12		2/10 EOM		
5.	May 29		2/10 EOM		

*If more than one discount, assume date of last discount.

6.   Metro Corporation sent Vasko Corporation an invoice for equipment with an $8,000 list price. Metro dated the invoice May 26. Terms were 2/10 EOM. Vasco receives a 20% trade discount and paid the invoice on July 3. What was the cost of equipment for Vasko? (A blueprint aid will be in the solution to help dissect this problem.)

7.   Complete amount to be credited and balance outstanding:
   Amount of invoice: $600
   Terms: 2/10, 1/15, n/30
   Date of invoice: September 30
   Paid October 3: $400

✓ SOLUTIONS

1.   End of discount period: July 6 + 10 days = $\boxed{\text{July 16}}$
   End of credit period: By Table 7.1, July 6 =   187   days
                                                   $\underline{+\ 30}$ days
                                                      217   $\longrightarrow$ search $\longrightarrow$ $\boxed{\text{Aug. 5}}$

2.   End of discount period: June 9 + 10 days = $\boxed{\text{June 19}}$
   End of credit period: By Table 7.1, June 9 =   160   days
                                                   $\underline{+\ 30}$ days
                                                      190   $\longrightarrow$ search $\longrightarrow$ $\boxed{\text{July 9}}$

3.   End of discount period: By Table 7.1, May 9 =   129   days
                                                   $\underline{+\ 30}$ days
                                                      159   $\longrightarrow$ search $\longrightarrow$ $\boxed{\text{June 8}}$

   End of credit period: By Table 7.1, May 9 =   129   days
                                               $\underline{+\ 60}$ days
                                                  189   $\longrightarrow$ search $\longrightarrow$ $\boxed{\text{July 8}}$

4.   End of discount period: $\boxed{\text{June 10}}$
   End of credit period: June 10 + 20 = $\boxed{\text{June 30}}$

5.   End of discount period: $\boxed{\text{July 10}}$
   End of credit period: July 10 + 20 = $\boxed{\text{July 30}}$

6. Vasko Corporation's cost of equipment:

The facts	Solving for?	Steps to take	Key points
List price: $8,000. *Trade discount rate:* 20%. *Terms:* 2/10 EOM. *Invoice date:* 5/26. *Date paid:* 7/3.	Cost of equipment.	Net price = List price × Complement of trade discount rate. *EOM before 25th:* Discount period is 1st 10 days of month that follows sale.	Trade discounts are deducted before cash discounts are taken. Cash discounts are not taken on freight or returns.

Steps to solving problem

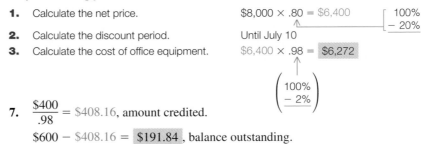

1. Calculate the net price. $8,000 × .80 = $6,400   ⌐ 100%
                                                                        └ − 20%

2. Calculate the discount period.   Until July 10

3. Calculate the cost of office equipment. $6,400 × .98 = $6,272

$$\left(\begin{array}{c} 100\% \\ -\ 2\% \end{array} \right)$$

7. $\dfrac{\$400}{.98} = \$408.16$, amount credited.

$600 − $408.16 = **$191.84** , balance outstanding.

Chapter Organizer and Reference Guide

Topic	Key point, procedure, formula	Example(s) to illustrate situation
Trade discount amount, p. 164	$\dfrac{\text{Trade discount}}{\text{amount}} = \dfrac{\text{List}}{\text{price}} \times \dfrac{\text{Trade discount}}{\text{rate}}$	$600 list price 30% trade discount rate Trade discount amount = $600 × .30 = **$180**
Calculating net price, p. 165	Net price = $\dfrac{\text{List}}{\text{price}} - \dfrac{\text{Trade discount}}{\text{amount}}$ or $\dfrac{\text{List}}{\text{price}} \times \dfrac{\text{Complement of trade}}{\text{discount price}}$	$600 list price 30% trade discount rate Net price = $600 × .70 = **$420** 1.00 − .30 .70
Freight, p. 166	FOB shipping point—buyer pays freight. FOB destination—seller pays freight.	Moose Company of New York sells equipment to Agee Company of Oregon. Terms of shipping are FOB New York. Agee pays cost of freight since terms are FOB shipping point.
Calculating list price when net price and trade discount rate are known, p. 168	List price = $\dfrac{\text{Net price}}{\text{Complement of trade discount rate}}$	40% trade discount rate Net price, $120 $\dfrac{\$120}{.60} = $ **$200** list price (1.00 − .40)
Chain discounts, p. 168	successively lower base.	5/10 on a $100 list item $100 $95 $95.00 × .05 × .10 ⌐(running − 9.50 $5.00 $9.50⌐ balance) **$85.50** net price
Net price equivalent rate, p. 169	$\dfrac{\text{Actual cost}}{\text{to buyer}} = \dfrac{\text{List}}{\text{price}} \times \dfrac{\text{Net price}}{\text{equivalent rate}}$ Take complement of each chain discount and multiply—do not round. $\dfrac{\text{Trade discount}}{\text{amount}} = \dfrac{\text{List}}{\text{price}} - \dfrac{\text{Actual cost}}{\text{to buyer}}$	Given: 5/10 on $1,000 list price Take complement: .95 × .90 = .855 (net price equivalent) $1,000 × .855 = **$855** (actual cost or net price) $1,000 − 855 **$ 145** trade discount amount

(continues)

Chapter Organizer and Reference Guide (concluded)		
Topic	**Key point, procedure, formula**	**Example(s) to illustrate situation**
Single equivalent discount rate, p. 169	$\dfrac{\text{Trade discount}}{\text{amount}} = \dfrac{\text{List}}{\text{price}} \times \dfrac{1 - \text{Net price}}{\text{equivalent rate}}$	See preceding example for facts: $1 - .855 = .145 \qquad .145 \times \$1,000 =$ $\boxed{\$145}$
Cash discounts, p. 172	Cash discounts, due to prompt payment, are not taken on freight, returns, etc.	Gross $\quad$ \$1,000 (includes freight) Freight $\quad$ \$25 $\qquad\qquad$ Terms, 2/10, n/30 Returns $\quad$ \$25 $\qquad\qquad$ Purchased: Sept. 9; $\qquad\qquad\qquad\qquad\qquad\qquad$ paid Sept 15 $\qquad$ Cash discount = \$950 $\times$ .02 = $\boxed{\$19}$
Calculating due dates, p. 173	*Option 1:* Thirty days has September, April, June, and November; all the rest have 31 except February has 28, and 29 in leap years. *Option 2:* Knuckles—31-day month; in between knuckles are short months. *Option 3:* Days-in-a-year table.	Invoice \$500 on March 5; terms 2/10, n/30. $\qquad\qquad\qquad\qquad\qquad\qquad$ March $\;$ 5 *End of discount* $\qquad\qquad\qquad\quad$ $+\;10$ *period:* $\longrightarrow$ $\boxed{\text{March 15}}$ *End of credit* $\quad$ March 5 = 64 days *period by* $\qquad\qquad\qquad$ $+\;30$ *Table 7.1:* $\longrightarrow$ 94 days $\qquad$ Search in Table 7.1 $\quad$ $\boxed{\text{April 4}}$
Common terms of sale **a.** Ordinary dating, p. 174	Discount period begins from date of invoice. Credit period ends 20 days from the end of the discount period unless otherwise stipulated; example, 2/10, n/60—the credit period ends 50 days from end of discount period.	Invoice \$600 (freight of \$100 included in price) dated March 8; payment on $\qquad\qquad$ March $\;$ 8 March 16; 3/10, n/30. $\qquad\qquad\qquad$ $+\;10$ *End of discount period:* $\longrightarrow$ $\boxed{\text{March 18}}$ *End of credit* $\quad$ March 8 = 67 days *period by* $\qquad\qquad\qquad$ $+\;30$ *Table 7.1:* $\longrightarrow$ 97 days $\qquad$ Search in Table 7.1 $\quad$ $\boxed{\text{April 7}}$ *If paid on March 16:* .97 $\times$ \$500 = \$485 $\qquad\qquad\quad$ $+\;100$ freight $\qquad\qquad\quad$ $\boxed{\$585}$
b. Receipt of goods (ROG), p. 176	Discount period begins when goods are received. Credit period ends 20 days from end of discount period.	4/10, n/30, ROG. \$600 invoice; no freight; dated August 5; goods received October 2, $\qquad\qquad$ October $\;$ 2 payment made October 20. $\qquad\qquad$ $+\;10$ *End of discount period:* $\longrightarrow$ $\boxed{\text{October 12}}$ *End of credit* $\qquad\qquad$ October 2 = 275 *period by* $\qquad\qquad\qquad\qquad$ $+\;30$ *Table 7.1:* $\longrightarrow$ 305 $\qquad\qquad\qquad\qquad\qquad\qquad$ $\downarrow$ Search in Table 7.1 $\qquad$ $\boxed{\text{November 1}}$ *Payment on October 20:* No discount, pay $\boxed{\$600}$
c. End of month (EOM), p. 177	On or before 25th of the month, discount period is 10 days after month following sale. After 25th of the month, an additional month is gained.	\$1,000 invoice dated May 12; no freight or returns; terms 2/10 EOM. *End of discount period* $\longrightarrow$ $\boxed{\text{June 10}}$ *End of credit period* $\longrightarrow$ $\boxed{\text{June 30}}$
Partial payments, p. 178	$\text{Amount credited} = \dfrac{\text{Partial payment}}{1 - \text{Discount rate}}$	\$200 invoice, terms 2/10, n/30, dated March 2, paid \$100 on March 5. $\dfrac{\$100}{1 - .02} = \dfrac{\$100}{.98} = \boxed{\$102.04}$
Key terms	Cash discount, *p. 164* Chain discounts, *p. 168* Complement, *p. 167* Credit period, *p. 172* Discount period, *p. 173* Due dates, *p. 173* End of credit period, *p. 173* End of month (EOM), *p. 177* FOB destination, *p. 166*	FOB shipping point, *p. 166* Freight terms, *p. 165* Invoice, *p. 165* List price, *p. 164* Net price, *p. 165* Net price equivalent rate, *p. 169* Ordinary dating, *p. 174* Receipt of goods (ROG), *p. 176* Series discounts, *p. 168* Single equivalent discount $\quad$ rate, *p. 169* Single trade discount, *p. 167* Terms of the sale, *p. 172* Trade discount, *p. 164* Trade discount amount, *p. 165* Trade discount rate, *p. 165*

**Critical Thinking
Discussion Questions**

1. What is the net price? June Long bought a jacket from a catalog company. She took her trade discount off the original price plus freight. What is wrong with June's approach? Who would benefit from June's approach—the buyer or the seller?

2. How do you calculate the list price when the net price and trade discount rate are known? A publisher tells the bookstore its net price of a book along with a suggested trade discount of 20%. The bookstore uses a 25% discount rate. Is this ethical when textbook prices are rising?

3. Explain FOB shipping point and FOB destination. Think back to your last major purchase. Was it FOB shipping point or FOB destination? Did you get a trade or a cash discount?

4. What are the steps to calculate the net price equivalent rate? Why is the net price equivalent rate *not* rounded?

5. What are the steps to calculate the single equivalent discount rate? Is this rate off the list or net price? Explain why this calculation of a single equivalent discount rate may not always be needed.

6. What is the difference between a discount and credit period? Are all cash discounts taken before trade discounts. Agree or disagree? Why?

7. Explain the following credit terms of sale:
   a. 2/10, n/30.
   b. 3/10, n/30 ROG.
   c. 1/10 EOM (on or before 25th of month).
   d. 1/10 EOM (after 25th of month).

8. Explain how to calculate a partial payment. Whom does a partial payment favor—the buyer or the seller?

DRILL PROBLEMS

For all problems, round your final answer to the nearest cent. Do not round net price equivalent rates or single equivalent discount rates.

Complete the following:

	Item	List price	Chain discount	Net price equivalent rate (in decimals)	Single equivalent discount rate (in decimals)	Trade discount	Net price
7–1.	Sony Playstation	$399	7/2				
7–2.	DVD player	$349	20/10/10				
7–3.	IBM scanner	$269	7/3/1				

Complete the following:

	Item	List price	Chain discount	Net price	Trade discount
7–4.	Trotter treadmill	$3,000	9/4		
7–5.	Maytag dishwasher	$450	8/5/6		
7–6.	Hewlett-Packard scanner	$320	3/5/9		
7–7.	Land Rover roofrack	$1,850	12/9/6		

7–8. Which of the following companies, A or B, gives a higher discount? Use the single equivalent discount rate to make your choice (convert your equivalent rate to the nearest hundredth percent).

Company A	Company B
8/10/15/3	10/6/16/5

Complete the following:

	Invoice	Dates when goods received	Terms	Last day* of discount period	Final day bill is due (end of credit period)
7–9.	June 18		1/10, n/30		
7–10.	Nov. 27		2/10 EOM		
7–11.	May 15	June 5	3/10, n/30, ROG		
7–12.	April 10		2/10, 1/30, n/60		
7–13.	June 12		3/10 EOM		
7–14.	Jan. 10	Feb. 3 (no leap year)	4/10, n/30, ROG		

*If more than one discount, assume date of last discount.

Complete the following by calculating the cash discount and net amount paid:

	Gross amount of invoice (freight charge already included)	Freight charge	Date of invoice	Terms of invoice	Date of payment	Cash discount	Net amount paid
7–15.	$7,000	$100	4/8	2/10, n/60	4/15		
7–16.	$600	None	8/1	3/10, 2/15, n/30	8/13		
7–17.	$200	None	11/13	1/10 EOM	12/3		
7–18.	$500	$100	11/29	1/10 EOM	1/4		

Complete the following:

	Amount of invoice	Terms	Invoice date	Actual partial payment made	Date of partial payment	Amount of payment to be credited	Balance outstanding
7–19.	$700	2/10, n/60	5/6	$400	5/15		

7–20. $600   4/10, n/60   7/5 $400   7/14

WORD PROBLEMS (Round to Nearest Cent as Needed)

7–21. The list price of a Fossil watch is $120.95. Jim O'Sullivan receives a trade discount of 40%. Find the trade discount amount and the net price.

7–22. A Radio Shack weather station lists for $699 with a trade discount of 20%. What is the net price of the weather station?

7–23. The November 2000 issue of *Business Horizons* featured an article titled "Discovering Hidden Pricing Power." Sharper Image Company asked for and received a discount from its suppliers. The discount was in the form of a $750 rebate. If Sharper Image Company placed an order of $7,650, what percent discount did they receive? Round to the nearest hundredth percent.

7–24. Levin Furniture buys a living room set with a $4,000 list price and a 55% trade discount. Freight (FOB shipping point) of $50 is not part of the list price. What is the delivered price (including freight) of the living room set, assuming a cash discount of 2/10, n/30, ROG? The invoice had an April 8 date. Levin received the goods on April 19 and paid the invoice on April 25.

7–25. A manufacturer of skateboards offered a 5/2/1 chain discount to many customers. Bob's Sporting Goods ordered 20 skateboards for a total $625 list price. What was the net price of the skateboards? What was the trade discount amount?

7–26. Home Depot wants to buy a new line of shortwave radios. Manufacturer A offers a 21/13 chain discount. Manufacturer B offers a 26/8 chain discount. Both manufacturers have the same list price. What manufacturer should Home Depot buy from?

7–27. Maplewood Supply received a $5,250 invoice dated 4/15/00. The $5,250 included $250 freight. Terms were 4/10, 3/30, n/60. **(a)** If Maplewood pays the invoice on April 27, what will it pay? **(b)** If Maplewood pays the invoice on May 21, what will it pay?

7–28. Sport Authority ordered 50 pairs of tennis shoes from Nike Corporation. The shoes were priced at $85 for each pair with the following terms: 4/10, 2/30, n/60. The invoice was dated October 15. Sports Authority sent in a payment on October 28. What should have been the amount of the check?

7–29. Macy of New York sold Marriott of Chicago office equipment with a $6,000 list price. Sale terms were 3/10, n/30 FOB New York. Macy agreed to prepay the $30 freight. Marriott pays the invoice within the discount period. What does Marriott pay Macy?

7–30. Royal Furniture bought a sofa for $800. The sofa had a $1,400 list price. What was the trade discount rate Royal received? Round to the nearest hundredth percent.

7–31. Amazon.com paid a $6,000 net price for textbooks. The publisher offered a 30% trade discount. What was the publisher's list price? Round to the nearest cent.

7–32. Bally Manufacturing sent Intel Corporation an invoice for machinery with a $14,000 list price. Bally dated the invoice July 23 with 2/10 EOM terms. Intel receives a 40% trade discount. Intel pays the invoice on August 5. What does Intel pay Bally?

7–33. On August 1, Intel Corporation (Problem 7–32) returns $100 of the machinery due to defects. What does Intel pay Bally on August 5? Round to nearest cent.

7–34. Stacy's Dress Shop received a $1,050 invoice dated July 8 with 2/10, 1/15, n/60 terms. On July 22, Stacy's sent a $242 partial payment. What credit should Stacy's receive? What is Stacy's outstanding balance?

7–35. On March 11, Jangles Corporation received a $20,000 invoice dated March 8. Cash discount terms were 4/10, n/30. On March 15, Jangles sent an $8,000 partial payment. What credit should Jangles receive? What is Jangles' outstanding balance?

ADDITIONAL SET OF WORD PROBLEMS

7–36. Prudential Life wants to buy a new line of high-speed computers. Manufacturer A offers a 10/5 chain discount. Manufacturer B offers a 9/6 chain discount. Both manufacturers have the same list price. Which manufacturer should Prudential buy from?

7–37. Borders.com paid a $79.99 net price for each calculus textbook. The publisher offered a 20% trade discount. What was the publisher's list price?

7–38. Home Office.com buys a computer from Compaq Corporation. The computers have a $1,200 list price with a 30% trade discount. What is the trade discount amount? What is the net price of the computer? Freight charges are FOB destination.

7–39. Vail Ski Shop received a $1,201 invoice dated July 8 with 2/10, 1/15, n/60 terms. On July 22, Vail sent a $485 partial payment. What credit should Vail receive? What is Vail's outstanding balance?

7–40. True Value received an invoice dated 4/15/02. The invoice had a $5,500 balance that included $300 freight. Terms were 4/10, 3/30, n/60. True Value pays the invoice on April 29. What amount does True Value pay?

7–41. Staples purchased seven new computers for $850 each. It received a 15% discount because it purchased more than five and an additional 6% discount because it took immediate delivery. Terms of payment were 2/10, n/30. Staples pays the bill within the cash discount period. How much should the check be? Round to the nearest cent.

7–42. On May 14, Talbots of Boston sold Forrest of Los Angeles $7,000 of fine clothes. Terms were 2/10 EOM FOB Boston. Talbots agreed to prepay the $80 freight. If Forrest pays the invoice on June 8, what will Forrest pay? If Forrest pays on June 20, what will Forrest pay?

7–43. Sam's Ski Boards.com offers 5/4/1 chain discounts to many of its customers. The Ski Hut ordered 20 ski boards with a total list price of $1,200. What is the net price of the ski boards? What was the trade discount amount? Round to the nearest cent.

7–44. Majestic Manufacturing sold Jordans Furniture a living room set for an $8,500 list price with 35% trade discount. The $100 freight (FOB shipping point) was not part of the list price. Terms were 3/10, n/30 ROG. The invoice date was May 30. Jordans received the goods on July 18 and paid the invoice on July 20. What was the final price (include cost of freight) of the living room set?

7–45. Boeing Truck Company received an invoice showing 8 tires at $110 each, 12 tires at $160 each, and 15 tires at $180 each. Shipping terms are FOB shipping point. Freight is $400; trade discount is 10/5; and a cash discount of 2/10, n/30 is offered. Assuming Boeing paid within the discount period, what did Boeing pay?

7–46. The March 2000 issue of *Business Credit* discussed customers who pay less than the invoice amount to suppliers. A company received an invoice with terms 3/10, n/ 30. The bill was $13,450. The company is short of cash and sends in a partial payment of $6,400 within 10 days. **(a)** What credit should the company receive? **(b)** What is the outstanding balance? Round to the nearest cent.

7–47. Verizon offers to sell cellular phones listing for $99.99 with a chain discount of 15/10/5. Cellular Company offers to sell its cellular phones that list at $102.99 with a chain discount of 25/5. If Irene is to buy 6 phones, how much could she save if she buys from the lower-priced company?

7–48. Bryant Manufacture sells its furniture to wholesalers and retailers. It offers to wholesalers a chain discount of 15/10/5 and to retailers a chain discount of 15/10. If a sofa lists for $500, how much would the wholesaler and retailer pay?

CHALLENGE PROBLEMS

7–49. In the October 9, 2000, issue of *Crain's New York Business,* a story appeared describing firms saving money by taking a plunge into online buying pools. Karen Curry was eager to find seven dozen soft-sided drink coolers for a company promotion. She found a good price, $24 each. However, through Mercata.com, a group purchasing website that offers volume discounts to smaller companies who electronically pool their orders, she found a lower price of $21. **(a)** What was Karen's final total net purchase price? **(b)** What was her total discount amount using the website? **(c)** What was the percent discount using the online buying pool? **(d)** If Karen meets the cash discount period of 2/10 net 30, what would be her final price?

7–50. On March 30, Century Television received an invoice dated March 28 from ACME Manufacturing for 50 televisions at a cost of $125 each. Century received a 10/4/2 chain discount. Shipping terms were FOB shipping point. ACME prepaid the $70 freight. Terms were 2/10 EOM. When Century received the goods, 3 sets were defective. Century returned these sets to ACME. On April 8, Century sent a $150 partial payment. Century will pay the balance on May 6. What is Century's final payment on May 6? Assume no taxes.

SUMMARY PRACTICE TEST

Complete the following: *(p. 180)*

	Item	List price	Single trade discount	Net price
1.	Michelin tires	$300	30%	
2.	DVD player		30%	$210

Calculate the net price and trade discount (use net price equivalent rate and single equivalent discount rate) for the following: *(p. 169)*

	Item	List price	Chain discount	Net price	Trade discount
3.	Computer scanner	$299	3/2		

4. From the following, what is the last date for each discount period and credit period? *(p. 174)*

	Date of invoice	Terms	End of discount period	End of credit period
a.	Oct. 7	2/10, n/30		
b.	Nov. 12, 2004	3/10, n/30 ROG (Goods received Aug. 6, 2005)		
c.	May 8	2/10 EOM		
d.	March 28	2/10 EOM		

5. JCPenney buys a television from a wholesaler with a $900 list price and a 30% trade discount. What is the trade discount amount? What is the net price of the television? *(p. 164)*

6. Ron Company of Boston sold Long Company of New York computer equipment with a $12,000 list price. Sale terms were 2/10, n/30 FOB Boston. Ron agreed to prepay the $200 freight. Long pays the invoice within the discount period. What does Long pay Ron? *(p. 174)*

7. Pat Manin wants to buy a new line of dolls for her shop. Manufacturer A offers a 16/10 chain discount. Manufacturer B Excel offers a 20/9 chain discount. Both manufacturers have the same list price. Which manufacturer should Pat buy from? *(p. 169)*

8. Kurck Copy received a $6,000 invoice dated June 10. Terms were 3/10, 2/15, n/60. On June 23, Kurck Copy sent a $1,500 partial payment. What credit should Kurck Copy receive? What is Kurck Copy's outstanding balance? Round to the nearest cent. *(p. 178)*

9. Angel Company received from Woody Company an invoice dated September 28. Terms were 2/10 EOM. List price on the invoice was $8,000 (freight not included). Angel receives a 12/7 chain discount. Freight charges are Angel's responsibility, but Woody agreed to prepay the $150 freight. Angel pays the invoice on November 6. What does Angel Company pay Woody? *(p. 169)*

PRESCRIPTIONS | Rx for high drug prices:

SHOP ONLINE for maintenance meds. *By Ronaleen R. Roha*

POTENT SAVINGS

KATY McHugh White of Seattle knew her parents were unhappy about the high cost of their many maintenance medications. The $10,000 annual cost was a mighty burden for the retired couple, who are on a fixed income and have no prescription-drug coverage. So White did a quick price comparison for one prescription at online pharmacy Drugstore.com. Then another. Then there was no going back. White found ordering online easy and convenient, and her parents now save about $2,000 a year.

Using the Internet won't work for the drugs you need in an emergency, of course, and lower prices won't affect your fixed co-payments under an employer's plan. But if you don't have prescription coverage or if your plan requires that you pay a percentage of the cost—as more and more employer plans are doing—the savings will find their way to your pocket.

Who's legit? To demonstrate the potential savings, we compared prices for a one-month supply of four brand-name drugs—Lipitor, Propecia, Vasotec and Zyrtec—at six online pharmacies: CVS (www.cvs.com), Drugstore.com, Eckerd.com, Family-meds.com, Prescriptiononline.com and Walgreens (www.walgreens.com). We also checked prices for similar supplies of the same medicines at major retail drugstores in Chicago, Dallas, Miami, New York City and San Francisco.

Web sites that dispense drugs without a prescription or those that do so based on a physician review of a simple online health-history questionnaire get lots of attention, but should not get your business. Each online phar-

RANDALL SCOTT

● Ordering online saves White's parents $2,000 a year.

macy we compared has the Verified Internet Pharmacy Practice Sites (VIPPS) seal issued by the National Association of Boards of Pharmacy. VIPPS pharmacies meet all licensing requirements where they do business plus 16 other criteria.

Prices worth booting up for. None of the online pharmacies we checked always delivered the best or worst price. But every online price was lower than the lowest price charged by the traditional pharmacies we checked. In addition, the *lowest* online price was consistently 20% to 30% lower than the *lowest* off-line price. For example, the cheapest price we found for 30 ten-milligram Vasotec tablets was $27.90 at Prescriptiononline.com, 30% less than the lowest off-line price of $39.99 at Duane Reade Pharmacy, in New York City, and Walgreens, in Chicago.

Most online drugstores will verify prescription orders with your doctor (so you don't have to send in the prescription) and all will arrange for transfer of prescriptions from other pharmacies. Walgreens charges $1.95 for shipping prescriptions, but the others we looked at ship free (with delivery generally within ten days) unless you choose overnight service. With CVS, Eckerd, Walgreens and Drugstore.com (through its affiliation with Rite Aid), you can pick up your order at a local pharmacy and pay the online price. If you regularly use one of those stores, it may pay to order online rather than by phone or in person. **K**
—*Reporter:* **ALISON STEVENSON**

Business Math Issue

Ordering online is an example of a cash discount. Online discounts are only for the wealthy.
1. List the key points of the article and information to support your position.
2. Write a group defense of your position using math calculations to support your view.

Spanish Officials Raid Coca-Cola Office

By BETSY McKAY
Staff Reporter of THE WALL STREET JOURNAL

Spanish antitrust regulators raided the offices of **Coca-Cola** Co. and three of its bottlers, seeking evidence that the soft-drink giant has abused its strong market position to squelch competitors.

The unannounced visits were conducted in response to complaints filed last year by the Spanish division of **PepsiCo** Inc., and a Spanish beverage company, **La Casera**. In a statement from its Spanish division, PepsiCo accused Coke of "illegal" marketing and sales practices "for the purpose of obtaining a monopolistic control of the sector." Such practices include discounts for large-volume purchases and exclusivity agreements between Coke, its bottlers, and retailers, which encourage retailers to cut back on Coke competitors' stocks, PepsiCo said.

Antitrust officials targeted Coke's regional corporate headquarters and one bottler in Madrid, as well as the offices of two other bottlers in Seville and Vizcaya. The bottlers are all independently owned.

The probe is the latest of several Coke is facing around the world, most of which were also prompted by complaints from PepsiCo. The European Union is already examining the practices of Coke and its bottlers in five European countries—the United Kingdom, Belgium, Germany, Austria and Denmark. Coke also recently began talks with Mexican antitrust officials with the hope of avoiding a legal tussle over the same issues there.

Coke Chairman Douglas Daft has said mending fences with regulators is a priority. He has made personal calls on several officials in Europe, and declared that Coke will play by the "house rules." The continued interest from regulators suggests that some have yet to be convinced.

A Coke executive said the company and its bottlers are cooperating. "The beverages market in Spain is very competitive," said Marcos de Quinto, president of Coke's Iberian division. "Coca-Cola is committed to operating in a very competitive environment. Coca-Cola Spain carries out its operations in compliance with Spanish and European law. We understand that the preference consumers and customers show for our brands is due to several decades of effort and investment by the company and its local bottlers, which are all local Spanish companies."

Spain is one of the most important soft-drink markets in the world because of its high per-capita consumption. It is Coke's second-largest market in Europe, and the company's Spanish unit has a reputation for posting consistent growth. Mr. Daft has singled out marketing programs drafted by Coke's executives in Spain as the kind of marketing he would like to see the rest of the company replicate.

Coke holds a 57% share of the carbonated soft-drinks market in Spain, Pepsi holds 16% and La Casera holds 10%, according to Beverage Digest, an industry publication.

©2000 Dow Jones & Company, Inc.

PROJECT A
Do think that the Spanish division of PepsiCo Inc. has a legitimate complaint? Check out PepsiCo Inc.'s website.

Taco Bell Franchisees Get Early 'Rebates' From PepsiCo Inc.

Dow Jones Newswires

DES MOINES, Iowa—**PepsiCo** Inc., responding to a call for financial help from one of its biggest customers, has sent out "soda rebate" checks six months early to Taco Bell franchisees across the U.S.

The accelerated payments—which are believed to total millions of dollars—are among multipronged efforts by **Tricon Global Restaurants** Inc. to alleviate a financial squeeze on franchisees suffering from a sales slump and a recent taco-shell recall.

A Dec. 20 memorandum from PepsiCo President and Chief Executive-designate Steve S. Reinemund, addressed to franchisees of the Mexican fast-food chain, said he had been made aware of "your difficult business environment." It said PepsiCo would "like to help resolve the near-term challenges that you face. ... Rest assured, we will expedite this funding as quickly as possible, but certainly by Jan. 15."

A PepsiCo spokesman had no comment on the memo, a copy of which was obtained by Dow Jones Newswires.

One large Taco Bell franchisee confirmed Tuesday that he had recently received his rebate check.

In addition to the beverage rebates, Tricon set up a $15 million loan pool—which it calls a "winter relief fund"—to assist Taco Bell franchisees strapped by what Tricon spokesman Jonathan Blum said were severe weather issues and the recall of taco shells containing StarLink, a genetically modified corn not approved for human consumption.

PepsiCo spun off Taco Bell and its two siblings, Pizza Hut and KFC, as Tricon in October 1997. There are about 4,000 franchised Taco Bell stores across the U.S. Nearly all dispense only Pepsi-made beverages.

©2001 Dow Jones & Company, Inc.

PROJECT B
Do you think rebate checks are ethical?

Internet Projects: See text website (www.mhhe.com/slater7e) and *The Business Math Internet Resource Guide.*

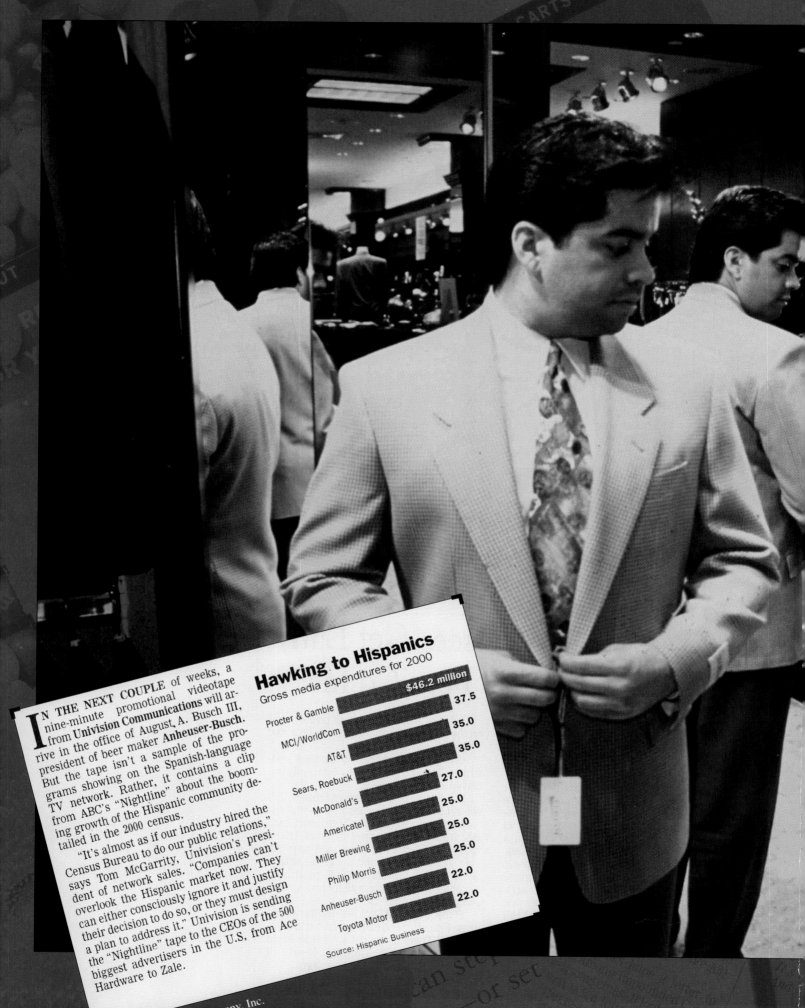

IN THE NEXT COUPLE of weeks, a nine-minute promotional videotape from **Univision Communications** will arrive in the office of August, A. Busch III, president of beer maker **Anheuser-Busch**. But the tape isn't a sample of the programs showing on the Spanish-language TV network. Rather, it contains a clip from ABC's "Nightline" about the booming growth of the Hispanic community detailed in the 2000 census.

"It's almost as if our industry hired the Census Bureau to do our public relations," says Tom McGarrity, Univision's president of network sales. "Companies can't overlook the Hispanic market now. They can either consciously ignore it and justify their decision to do so, or they must design a plan to address it." Univision is sending the "Nightline" tape to the CEOs of the 500 biggest advertisers in the U.S. from Ace Hardware to Zale.

Hawking to Hispanics
Gross media expenditures for 2000

Company	
Procter & Gamble	$46.2 million
MCI/WorldCom	37.5
AT&T	35.0
Sears, Roebuck	35.0
McDonald's	27.0
Americatel	25.0
Miller Brewing	25.0
Philip Morris	25.0
Anheuser-Busch	22.0
Toyota Motor	22.0

Source: Hispanic Business

Markups and Markdowns; Insight into Perishables

---

[1]Some texts use the term *markon* (selling price minus cost).

Photo courtesy of Cotter & Company, Chicago, which is the national headquarters for the more than 6,000 True Value hardware stores nationwide.

Nancy Ford is a retailer who owns a True Value hardware store. One of the most important business decisions Nancy must make concerns the selling price of her goods. She knows that her selling price must include the cost of bringing the goods into her store, her operating expenses, and a profit. To remain in business, Nancy's selling price must also be competitive with that of other hardware retailers.

Before we study the two pricing methods available to Nancy (percent markup on cost and percent markup on selling price), we must know the following terms:

- **Selling price:** The price retailers charge consumers. Sears Roebuck sells one-third of all the appliances sold in the United States. The total selling price of all the retailer's goods represents the retailer's total sales.
- **Cost:** The price retailers pay to a manufacturer or supplier to bring the goods into the store.
- **Markup, margin, or gross profit:** These three terms refer to the difference between the cost of bringing the goods into the store and the selling price of the goods.
- **Operating expenses or overhead:** The regular expenses of doing business such as wages, rent, utilities, insurance, and advertising.
- **Net profit or net income:** The profit remaining after subtracting the cost of bringing the goods into the store and the operating expenses from the sale of the goods (including any returns or adjustments).

From these definitions, we can conclude that **markup** represents the amount that retailers must add to the cost of the goods to cover their operating expenses and make a profit.[2]

To help you understand the basic selling price formula that follows, let's return to Nancy Ford and her True Value hardware store. Nancy has bought a Toro snowthrower from a supplier for $210. She plans to sell the snowthrower for $300.

Basic selling price formula

Selling price (S) =	Cost (C)	+	Markup (M)
$300 =	$210	+	$90
(snowthrower)	(price paid to bring snowthrower into store)		(amount in dollars to cover operating expenses and make a profit)

Bluefly's Goal: Raise Margins, But Keep Fans

By Rebecca Quick
Staff Reporter of The Wall Street Journal

This was the plan: Sell designer-label clothing online for less than it goes for in stores, and make up the difference through the promised efficiencies of an Internet-only business.

But a look at one key figure shows why **Bluefly Inc.** is struggling.

For retailers, profit begins with "markup," the amount they charge above what goods cost them wholesale. To tempt shoppers Bluefly has kept its markup low, below that of many other retailers. For every $10 that Bluefly marks up the Prada pants and Gucci shoes it sells, for example, catalog retailer Lands' End marks up its own-label clothes by roughly $17, and department store Macy's marks up its wares by $14 on average.

©2001 Dow Jones & Company, Inc.

Note that in this example, the markup is a dollar amount, or a **dollar markup**. Markup is also expressed in percent. When expressing markup in percent, retailers can choose a percent based on *cost* (Learning Unit 8–1) or a percent based on *selling price* (Learning Unit 8–2).

An example of a need for a change in markup strategy is reported by *The Wall Street Journal* in the clipping "Bluefly's Goal: Raise Margins, But Keep Fans." Bluefly's plan was to sell designer clothes online at a lower markup than Lands' End and Macy's. As "an outlet store in your home," shoppers received bargains when shopping at Bluefly.com.

[2]In this chapter we concentrate on the markup of retailers. Manufacturers and suppliers also use markup to determine selling price.

However, this low markup was a disaster for Bluefly's shareholders. After paying expenses, Bluefly has been running deep in red ink. The volume of Internet sales was not enough to make profit for Bluefly. Now Bluefly will have to determine how to raise its markup margin and also keep its customers.

LEARNING UNIT 8–1 | MARKUPS BASED ON COST (100%)

In Chapter 6 you were introduced to the portion formula, which we used to solve percent problems. We also used the portion formula in Chapter 7 to solve problems involving trade and cash discounts. In this unit you will see how we use the basic selling price formula and the portion formula to solve percent markup situations based on cost. We will be using blueprint aids to show how to dissect and solve all word problems in this chapter.

Many manufacturers mark up goods on cost because manufacturers can get cost information more easily than sales information. Since retailers have the choice of using percent markup on cost or selling price, in this unit we assume Nancy Ford has chosen percent markup on cost for her True Value hardware store. In Learning Unit 8–2 we show how Nancy Ford would determine her markup if she decided to use percent markup on selling price.

Businesses that use **percent markup on cost** recognize that cost is 100%. This 100% represents the base of the portion formula. All situations in this unit use cost as 100%.

To calculate percent markup on cost, let's use Nancy Ford's Toro snowthrower purchase and begin with the basic selling price formula given in the chapter introduction. When we know the dollar markup, we can use the portion formula to find the percent markup on cost.

Markup expressed in dollars:

Selling price ($300) = Cost ($210) + Markup ($90)

Markup expressed as percent markup on cost:

Cost	100.00% $\rightarrow$	Cost is 100%—the base. Dollar markup is the portion, and percent markup on cost is the rate.
+ Markup	+ 42.86	
= Selling price	142.86%	

In Situation 1 (p. 196) we show why Nancy has a 42.86% markup based on cost by presenting Nancy's snowthrower purchase as a word problem. We solve the problem with the blueprint aid used in earlier chapters. In the second column, however, you will see footnotes after two numbers. These refer to the steps we use below the blueprint aid to solve the problem. Throughout the chapter, the numbers that we are solving for are in red. Remember that cost is the base for this unit.

Situation 1: Calculating Dollar Markup and Percent Markup on Cost

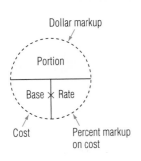

The dollar markup is calculated with the basic selling price formula $S = C + M$. When you know the cost and the selling price of the goods, you reverse the basic selling price formula to $M = S - C$. Subtract the cost from the selling price, and you have the dollar markup.

The percent markup on cost is calculated with the portion formula. For Situation 1 the *portion* (P) is the dollar markup, which you know from the selling price formula. In this unit the *rate* (R) is always the percent markup on cost and the *base* (B) is always the cost (100%). To find the percent markup on cost (R), use the portion formula $R = \frac{P}{B}$ and divide the dollar markup (P) by the cost (B). Convert your answer to a percent and round if necessary.

Now let's look at the Nancy Ford example to see how to calculate the 42.86% markup on cost.

The Word Problem   Nancy Ford bought a snowthrower that cost $210 for her True Value hardware store. She plans to sell the snowthrower for $300. What is Nancy's dollar markup? What is her percent markup on cost (round to the nearest hundredth percent)?

The facts	Solving for?			Steps to take	Key points
Snowthrower cost: $210.		%	S	Dollar markup = Selling price − Cost.	Dollar markup
Snowthrower selling price: $300.	C	100.00%	$210		Portion ($90)
	+ M	42.86[2]	90[1]	Percent markup on cost = $\dfrac{\text{Dollar markup}}{\text{Cost}}$	Base × Rate ($210) (?)
	= S	142.86%	$300		
	[1]Dollar markup.				Cost
	[2]Percent markup on cost.				

Steps to solving problem

1. Calculate the dollar markup.

$$\text{Dollar markup} = \text{Selling price} - \text{Cost}$$
$$\boxed{\$90} = \$300 - \$210$$

2. Calculate the percent markup on cost.

$$\text{Percent markup on cost} = \frac{\text{Dollar markup}}{\text{Cost}}$$
$$= \frac{\$90}{\$210} = \boxed{42.86\%}$$

To check the percent markup on cost, you can use the basic selling price formula $S = C + M$. Convert the percent markup on cost found with the portion formula to a decimal and multiply it by the cost. This gives the dollar markup. Then add the cost and the dollar markup to get the selling price of the goods.

You could also check the cost (B) by dividing the dollar markup (P) by the percent markup on cost (R).

Check

Selling price = Cost + Markup	**or**	Cost $(B) = \dfrac{\text{Dollar markup } (P)}{\text{Percent markup on cost } (R)}$

$$\$300 = \$210 + .4286(\$210) \longleftarrow$$
$$\$300 = \$210 + \$90*$$
$$\$300 = \$300$$

$$= \frac{\$90}{.4286} = \$209.99*$$

Parentheses mean that you multiply the percent markup on cost in decimal by the cost.

*Off 1 cent due to rounding of percent.

Situation 2: Calculating Selling Price When You Know Cost and Percent Markup on Cost

When you know the cost and the percent markup on cost, you calculate the selling price with the basic selling formula $S = C + M$. Remember that when goods are marked up on cost, the cost is the base (100%). So you can say that the selling price is the cost plus the markup in dollars (percent markup on cost times cost).

Now let's look at Mel's Furniture where we calculate Mel's dollar markup and selling price.

The Word Problem   Mel's Furniture bought a lamp that cost $100. To make Mel's desired profit, he needs a 65% markup on cost. What is Mel's dollar markup? What is his selling price?

The facts	Solving for?			Steps to take	Key points
Lamp cost: $100.		%	$	Dollar markup:	Selling price
Markup on cost: 65%.	C	100%	$100	$S = C + M.$ or	Portion (?)
	+ M	65	65[1]		Base × Rate ($100) (1.65)
	= S	165%	$165[2]	$S = \text{Cost} \times \left(1 + \begin{array}{c}\text{Percent}\\\text{markup}\\\text{on cost}\end{array}\right)$	
	[1]Dollar markup.				100%
	[2]Selling price.				Cost +65%

Steps to solving problem

1. Calculate the dollar markup.

$S = C + M$

$S = \$100 + .65(\$100)$ ←— Parentheses mean you multiply the percent markup in decimal by the cost.

$S = \$100 + \boxed{\$65}$ ←— Dollar markup

2. Calculate the selling price. $S = \boxed{\$165}$

You can check the selling price with the portion formula $P = B \times R$. You are solving for portion (P)—the selling price. Rate (R) represents the 100% cost plus the 65% markup on cost. Since in this unit the markup is on cost, the base is the cost. Convert 165% to a decimal and multiply the cost by 1.65 to get the selling price of $165.

Check

Selling price = Cost × (1 + Percent markup on cost)	
(P) (B) (R)	$= \$100 \times 1.65 = \boxed{\$165}$

Situation 3: Calculating Cost When You Know Selling Price and Percent Markup on Cost

When you know the selling price and the percent markup on cost, you calculate the cost with the basic selling formula $S = C + M$. Since goods are marked up on cost, the percent markup on cost is added to the cost.

Let's see how this is done in the following Jill Sport example.

The Word Problem Jill Sport, owner of Sports, Inc., sells tennis rackets for $50. To make her desired profit, Jill needs a 40% markup on cost. What do the tennis rackets cost Jill? What is the dollar markup?

The facts	Solving for?			Steps to take	Key points
Selling price: $50. Markup on cost: 40%.		%	$	$S = C + M.$ or $Cost = \dfrac{Selling\ price}{Percent}$ $1 + markup$ $on\ cost$ $M = S - C.$	Selling price, Portion ($50), Base × Rate (?) (1.40), 100% +40%, Cost
	C	100%	$35.71[1]		
	$+ M$	40	14.29[2]		
	$= S$	140%	$50.00		
	[1]Cost. [2]Dollar markup.				

Steps to solving problem

1. Calculate the cost.

$S = C + M$

$\$50.00 = C + .40C$ ←— This means 40% times cost. C is the same as $1C$. Adding $.40C$ to $1C$ gives the percent markup on cost of $1.40C$ in decimal.

$\dfrac{\$50.00}{1.40} = \dfrac{1.40C}{1.40}$

$\boxed{\$35.71} = C$

2. Calculate the dollar markup.

$M = S - C$

$M = \$50.00 - \$35.71$

$M = \boxed{\$14.29}$

You can check your cost answer with the portion formula $B = \frac{P}{R}$. Portion (P) is the selling price. Rate (R) represents the 100% cost plus the 40% markup on cost. Convert the percents to decimals and divide the portion by the rate to find the base, or cost.

Check

$$Cost\ (B) = \dfrac{Selling\ price\ (P)}{1 + Percent\ markup\ on\ cost\ (R)} = \dfrac{\$50.00}{1.40} = \boxed{\$35.71}$$

Now try the following Practice Quiz to check your understanding of this unit.

LU 8–1 PRACTICE QUIZ

Solve the following situations (markups based on cost):

1. Irene Westing bought a desk for $400 from an office supply house. She plans to sell the desk for $600. What is Irene's dollar markup? What is her percent markup on cost? Check your answer.

2. Suki Komar bought dolls for her toy store that cost $12 each. To make her desired profit, Suki must mark up each doll 35% on cost. What is the dollar markup? What is the selling price of each doll? Check your answer.

3. Jay Lyman sells calculators. His competitor sells a new calculator line for $14 each. Jay needs a 40% markup on cost to make his desired profit, and he must meet price competition. At what cost can Jay afford to bring these calculators into the store? What is the dollar markup? Check your answer.

✓ **SOLUTIONS**

1. Irene's dollar markup and percent markup on cost:

The facts	Solving for?	Steps to take	Key points
Desk cost: $400. Desk selling price: $600.	% $ C 100% $400 + M 50² 200¹ = S 150% $600 ¹Dollar markup. ²Percent markup on cost.	$\dfrac{\text{Dollar}}{\text{markup}} = \dfrac{\text{Selling}}{\text{price}} - \text{Cost.}$ $\dfrac{\text{Percent}}{\substack{\text{markup}\\\text{on cost}}} = \dfrac{\text{Dollar markup}}{\text{Cost}}$	Dollar markup Portion ($200) Base × Rate ($400) (?) Cost

Steps to solving problem

1. Calculate the dollar markup.

    Dollar markup = Selling price − Cost
    $200 = $600 − $400

2. Calculate the percent markup on cost.

    Percent markup on cost = $\dfrac{\text{Dollar markup}}{\text{Cost}}$

    $= \dfrac{\$200}{\$400} = 50\%$

Check

Selling price = Cost + Markup   **or**   Cost $(B) = \dfrac{\text{Dollar markup } (P)}{\text{Percent markup on cost } (R)}$

$600 = $400 + .50($400) $= \dfrac{\$200}{.50} = \$400$

$600 = $400 + $200

$600 = $600

2. Dollar markup and selling price of doll:

The facts	Solving for?	Steps to take	Key points
Doll cost: $12 each. Markup on cost: 35%.	% $ C 100% $12.00 + M 35 4.20¹ = S 135% $16.20² ¹Dollar markup. ²Selling price.	Dollar markup: $S = C + M.$ or $S = \text{Cost} \times \left(1 + \substack{\text{Percent}\\\text{markup}\\\text{on cost}}\right)$	Selling price Portion (?) Base × Rate ($12) (1.35) Cost 100% +35%

Steps to solving problem

1. Calculate the dollar markup.

    $S = \quad C \quad + M$
    $S = \$12.00 + .35(\$12.00)$
    $S = \$12.00 + \boxed{\$4.20} \longleftarrow \text{Dollar markup}$

2. Calculate the selling price.

    $S = \boxed{\$16.20}$

Check

Selling price = Cost × (1 + Percent markup on cost) = $12.00 × 1.35 = $16.20
    (P)   (B)   (R)

3. Cost and dollar markup:

The facts	Solving for?			Steps to take	Key points
Selling price: $14. *Markup on cost:* 40%.		%	$	$S = C + M.$ or $$Cost = \frac{Selling\ price}{Percent}$$ $$1 + markup\ on\ cost$$ $M = S - C.$	Selling price → Portion ($14) Base × Rate (?) (1.40) 100% +40% Cost
	C	100%	$10[1]		
	$+ M$	40	4[2]		
	$= S$	140%	$14		
	[1]Cost. [2]Dollar markup.				

Steps to solving problem

1. Calculate the cost.

$$S = C + M$$
$$\$14 = C + .40C$$
$$\frac{\$14}{1.40} = \frac{\cancel{1.40}C}{\cancel{1.40}}$$
$$\boxed{\$10} = C$$

2. Calculate the dollar markup.

$$M = S - C$$
$$M = \$14 - \$10$$
$$M = \boxed{\$4}$$

Check

$$Cost\ (B) = \frac{Selling\ price\ (P)}{1 + Percent\ markup\ on\ cost\ (R)} = \frac{\$14}{1.40} = \$10$$

LEARNING UNIT 8–2 | MARKUPS BASED ON SELLING PRICE (100%)

Many retailers mark up their goods on the selling price since sales information is easier to get than cost information. These retailers use retail prices in their inventory and report their expenses as a percent of sales.

Businesses that mark up their goods on selling price recognize that selling price is 100%. We begin this unit by assuming that Nancy Ford has decided to use percent markup based on selling price for her True Value hardware store. We repeat Nancy's selling price formula expressed in dollars.

Markup expressed in dollars:

Selling price ($300) = Cost ($210) + Markup ($90)

Markup expressed as **percent markup on selling price:**

Cost	70%
+ Markup	+ 30
= Selling price	100%

> Selling price is 100%—the base. Dollar markup is the portion, and percent markup on selling price is the rate.

In Situation 1 (below) we show why Nancy has a 30% markup based on selling price. In the last unit, markups were on cost. In this unit, markups are on *selling price.*

Situation 1: Calculating Dollar Markup and Percent Markup on Selling Price

The dollar markup is calculated with the selling price formula used in Situation 1, Learning Unit 8–1: $M = S - C$. To find the percent markup on selling price, use the portion formula $R = \frac{P}{B}$, where rate (the percent markup on selling price) is found by dividing the portion (dollar markup) by the base (selling price). Note that when solving for percent markup on cost in Situation 1, Learning Unit 8–1, you divided the dollar markup by the cost.

The Word Problem   Nancy Ford bought a snowthrower that cost $210 for her True Value hardware store. She plans to sell the snowthrower for $300. What is Nancy's dollar markup? What is her percent markup on selling price?

The facts	Solving for?			Steps to take	Key points
Snowthrower cost: $210. Snowthrower selling price: $300.		%	$	Dollar markup = Selling price − Cost.	Dollar markup
	C	70%	$210		
	+ M	30²	90¹	Percent markup on selling price = Dollar markup / Selling price	Portion ($90)
	= S	100%	$300		Base × Rate ($300) (?)
	¹Dollar markup. ²Percent markup on selling price.				Selling price

Steps to solving problem

1. Calculate the dollar markup.

$$\text{Dollar markup} = \text{Selling price} - \text{Cost}$$
$$\$90 = \$300 - \$210$$

2. Calculate the percent markup on selling price.

$$\frac{\text{Percent markup}}{\text{on selling price}} = \frac{\text{Dollar markup}}{\text{Selling price}}$$
$$= \frac{\$90}{\$300} = 30\%$$

You can check the percent markup on selling price with the basic selling price formula $S = C + M$. You can also use the portion formula by dividing the dollar markup (P) by the percent markup on selling price (R).

Check

Selling price = Cost + Markup	**or**	Selling price (B) = $\dfrac{\text{Dollar markup } (P)}{\text{Percent markup on selling price } (R)}$

$$\$300 = \$210 + .30(\$300)$$
$$\$300 = \$210 + \$90$$
$$\$300 = \$300$$

$$= \frac{\$90}{.30} = \$300$$

Parentheses mean you multiply the percent markup on selling price in decimal by the selling price.

Situation 2: Calculating Selling Price When You Know Cost and Percent Markup on Selling Price

When you know the cost and percent markup on selling price, you calculate the selling price with the basic selling formula $S = C + M$. Remember that when goods are marked up on selling price, the selling price is the base (100%). Since you do not know the selling price, the percent of markup is based on the unknown selling price. To find the dollar markup after you find the selling price, use the selling price formula $M = S - C$.

The Word Problem Mel's Furniture bought a lamp that cost $100. To make Mel's desired profit, he needs a 65% markup on selling price. What are Mel's selling price and his dollar markup?

The facts	Solving for?			Steps to take	Key points
Lamp cost: $100. Markup on selling price: 65%.		%	$	$S = C + M.$ or	Cost
	C	35%	$100.00		
	+ M	65	185.71²	$S = \dfrac{\text{Cost}}{1 - \text{Percent markup on selling price}}$	Portion ($100)
	= S	100%	$285.71¹		Base × Rate (?) (.35)
	¹Selling price. ²Dollar markup.				100% Selling price −65%

Steps to solving problem

1. Calculate the selling price.

$$S = C + M$$
$$S = \$100.00 + .65S$$
$$- .65S \quad - .65S$$
$$\frac{.35S}{.35} = \frac{\$100.00}{.35}$$
$$S = \$285.71$$

$$\begin{aligned} 1.00S \\ - .65S \\ = .35S \end{aligned}$$

Do not multiply the .65 times $100.00. The 65% is based on selling price not cost.

2. Calculate the dollar markup.

$$M = S - C$$
$$\$185.71 = \$285.71 - \$100.00$$

You can check your selling price with the portion formula $B = \frac{P}{R}$. To find the selling price (B), divide the cost (P) by the rate (100% − percent markup on selling price).

Check

$$\text{Selling price } (B) = \frac{\text{Cost } (P)}{1 - \text{Percent markup on selling price } (R)}$$

$$= \frac{\$100.00}{1 - .65} = \frac{\$100.00}{.35} = \$285.71$$

Situation 3: Calculating Cost When You Know Selling Price and Percent Markup on Selling Price

When you know the selling price and the percent markup on selling price, you calculate the cost with the basic formula $S = C + M$. To find the dollar markup, multiply the markup percent by the selling price. When you have the dollar markup, subtract it from the selling price to get the cost.

The Word Problem   Jill Sport, owner of Sports, Inc., sells tennis rackets for $50. To make her desired profit, Jill needs a 40% markup on the selling price. What is the dollar markup? What do the tennis rackets cost Jill?

The facts	Solving for?			Steps to take	Key points
Selling price: $50. Markup on selling price: 40%.		%	$	$S = C + M.$ or Cost = Selling price $\times$ $\left(1 - \dfrac{\text{Percent markup}}{\text{on selling price}}\right)$	Cost Portion (?) Base $\times$ Rate ($50) (.60) Selling price 100% −40%
	C	60%	$30[2]		
	$+ M$	40	20[1]		
	$= S$	100%	$50		
	[1]Dollar markup. [2]Cost.				

Steps to solving problem

1. Calculate the dollar markup.

$$S = C + M$$
$$\$50 = C + .40(\$50)$$

2. Calculate the cost.

$$\$50 = C + \boxed{\$20} \leftarrow \text{Dollar markup}$$
$$\underline{-20} \qquad \underline{-20}$$
$$\boxed{\$30} = C$$

To check your cost, use the portion formula Cost (P) = Selling price (B) $\times$ (100% selling price − Percent markup on selling price) (R).

Check

$$\underset{(P)}{\text{Cost}} = \underset{(B)}{\underset{\text{price}}{\text{Selling}}} \times \underset{(R)}{\left(1 - \frac{\text{Percent markup}}{\text{on selling price}}\right)} = \$50 \times .60 = \boxed{\$30}$$
$$(1.00 - .40)$$

In Table 8.1, we compare percent markup on cost with percent markup on retail (selling price). This table is a summary of the answers we calculated from the word problems in Learning Units 8–1 and 8–2. The word problems in the units were the same except in Learning Unit 8–1, we assumed markups were on cost, while in Learning Unit 8–2, markups were on selling price. Note that in Situation 1, the dollar markup is the same $90, but the percent markup is different.

Let's now look at how to convert from percent markup on cost to percent markup on selling price and vice versa. We will use Situation 1 from Table 8.1.

TABLE 8.1

Comparison of markup on cost versus markup on selling price

Markup based on cost—Learning Unit 8–1	Markup based on selling price—Learning Unit 8–2
Situation 1: Calculating dollar amount of markup and percent markup on cost. Snowthrower cost, $210. Snowthrower selling price, $300. $M = S - C$ $M = \$300 - \$210 = \boxed{\$90}$ markup (p. 196) $M \div C = \$90 \div \$210 = \boxed{42.86\%}$	*Situation 1: Calculating dollar amount of markup and percent markup on selling price.* Snowthrower cost, $210. Snowthrower selling price, $300. $M = S - C$ $M = \$300 - \$210 = \boxed{\$90}$ markup (p. 200) $M \div S = \$90 \div \$300 = \boxed{30\%}$
Situation 2: Calculating selling price on cost. Lamp cost, $100. 65% markup on cost $S = C \times (1 + \text{Percent markup on cost})$ $S = \$100 \times 1.65 = \boxed{\$165}$ (p. 197) $(100\% + 65\% = 165\% = 1.65)$	*Situation 2: Calculating selling price on selling price.* Lamp cost, $100. 65% markup on selling price $S = C \div (1 - \text{Percent markup on selling price})$ $S = \$100.00 \div .35$ $(100\% - 65\% = 35\% = .35)$ $S = \boxed{\$285.71}$ (p. 201)
Situation 3: Calculating cost on cost. Tennis racket selling price, $50. 40% markup on cost $C = S \div (1 + \text{Percent markup on cost})$ $C = \$50.00 \div 1.40$ $(100\% + 40\% = 140\% = 1.40)$ $C = \boxed{\$35.71}$ (p. 197)	*Situation 3: Calculating cost on selling price.* Tennis racket selling price, $50. 40% markup on selling price $C = S \times (1 - \text{Percent markup on selling price})$ $C = \$50 \times .60 = \boxed{\$30}$ (p. 201) $(100\% - 40\% = 60\% = .60)$

Formula for Converting Percent Markup on Cost to Percent Markup on Selling Price

To convert percent markup on cost to percent markup on selling price:

$$\frac{.4286}{1 + .4286} = \boxed{30\%}$$

$$\frac{\text{Percent markup on cost}}{1 + \text{Percent markup on cost}}$$

Formula for Converting Percent Markup on Selling Price to Percent Markup on Cost

To convert percent markup on selling price to percent markup on cost:

$$\frac{.30}{1 - .30} = \frac{.30}{.70} = \boxed{42.86\%}$$

$$\frac{\text{Percent markup on selling price}}{1 - \text{Percent markup on selling price}}$$

Key point: A 30% markup on selling price or a 42.86% markup on cost results in same dollar markup of $90.

Table 8.2 summarizes the calculations of these two formulas. As stated in the table, the rate of markup on selling price is always *lower* than the rate of markup on cost. Before you go on to the topic of markdowns and perishables, check your progress with the following Practice Quiz.

TABLE 8.2

Equivalent markup

Percent markup on selling price	Percent markup on cost (round to nearest tenth percent)
20	25.0
25	33.3
30	42.9
33	49.3
35	53.8
40	66.7
50	100.0

Note: Rate of markup on selling price is always lower than on cost because the cost base is always lower than the selling price base.

LU 8–2 PRACTICE QUIZ

Solve the following situations (markups based on selling price). Note numbers 1, 2, and 3 are parallel problems to those in Practice Quiz 8–1.

1. Irene Westing bought a desk for $400 from an office supply house. She plans to sell the desk for $600. What is Irene's dollar markup? What is her percent markup on selling price (round to the nearest tenth percent)? Check your answer. Selling price will be slightly off due to rounding.

2. Suki Komar bought dolls for her toy store that cost $12 each. To make her desired profit, Suki must mark up each doll 35% on the selling price. What is the selling price of each doll? What is the dollar markup? Check your answer.

3. Jay Lyman sells calculators. His competitor sells a new calculator line for $14 each. Jay needs a 40% markup on the selling price to make his desired profit, and he must meet price competition. What is Jay's dollar markup? At what cost can Jay afford to bring these calculators into the store? Check your answer.

4. Dan Flow sells wrenches for $10 that cost $6. What is Dan's percent markup at cost? Round to the nearest tenth percent. What is Dan's percent markup on selling price? Check your answer.

✓ **SOLUTIONS**

1. Irene's dollar markup and percent markup on selling price:

The facts	Solving for?			Steps to take	Key points
Desk cost: $400. Desk selling price: $600.		%	$	$\dfrac{\text{Dollar}}{\text{markup}} = \dfrac{\text{Selling}}{\text{price}} - \text{Cost}$	Markup
	C	66.7%	$400		Portion ($200)
	+ M	33.3²	200¹	$\dfrac{\text{Percent}}{\text{markup on}} = \dfrac{\text{Dollar markup}}{\text{Selling}}$ selling price price	Base × Rate ($600) (?)
	= S	100%	$600		
	¹Dollar markup.				Selling price
	²Percent markup on selling price.				

Steps to solving problem

1. Calculate the dollar markup.

    Dollar markup = Selling price − Cost

    $200 = $600 − $400

2. Calculate the percent markup on selling price.

    $\dfrac{\text{Percent markup}}{\text{on selling price}} = \dfrac{\text{Dollar markup}}{\text{Selling price}}$

    $= \dfrac{\$200}{\$600} = 33.3\%$

Check

Selling price = Cost + Markup   **or**   Selling price $(B) = \dfrac{\text{Dollar markup } (P)}{\text{Percent markup on selling price } (R)}$

  $600 = $400 + .333($600)

  $600 = $400 + $199.80 $= \dfrac{\$200}{.333} = \$600.60*$

  $600 = $599.80*   (not exactly $600 due to rounding)

*Off due to rounding.

2. Selling price of doll and dollar markup:

The facts	Solving for?			Steps to take	Key points
Doll cost: $12 each. Markup on selling price: $35%.		%	$	$S = C + M.$ or $S = \dfrac{\text{Cost}}{1 - \dfrac{\text{Percent markup}}{\text{on selling price}}}$	Cost
	C	65%	$12.00		Portion ($12)
	+ M	35	6.46²		Base × Rate (?) (.65)
	= S	100%	$18.46¹		100%
	¹Selling price.				−35%
	²Dollar markup.				Selling price

Steps to solving problem

1. Calculate the selling price.

    $\begin{aligned} S &= C + M \\ S &= \$12.00 + .35S \\ -.35S &\qquad\quad -.35S \\ \dfrac{.65S}{.65} &= \dfrac{\$12.00}{.65} \\ S &= \$18.46 \end{aligned}$

2. Calculate the dollar markup.

$$M = S - C$$
$$\$6.46 = \$18.46 - \$12.00$$

Check

$$\text{Selling price } (B) = \frac{\text{Cost } (P)}{1 - \text{Percent markup on selling price } (R)} = \frac{\$12.00}{.65} = \$18.46$$

3. Dollar markup and cost:

The facts	Solving for?			Steps to take	Key points
Selling price: $14.		%	$	$S = C + M$.	Cost
Markup on selling price: 40%.	C	60%	$ 8.40²	or	Portion (?)
	$+ M$	40	5.60¹	Cost = Selling price ×	Base × Rate ($14) (.60)
	$= S$	100%	$14.00	$\left(1 - \begin{array}{c}\text{Percent markup}\\\text{on selling price}\end{array}\right)$	100% −40%
	¹Dollar markup. ²Cost.				Selling price

Steps to solving problem

1. Calculate the dollar markup.

$$S = C + M$$
$$\$14.00 = C + .40(\$14.00)$$

2. Calculate the cost.

$$\$14.00 = C + \boxed{\$5.60} \longleftarrow \text{Dollar markup}$$
$$\underline{- 5.60 \qquad\qquad - 5.60}$$
$$\boxed{\$8.40} = C$$

Check

$$\underset{(P)}{\text{Cost}} = \underset{(B)}{\text{Selling price}} \times (1 - \underset{(R)}{\text{Percent markup on selling price}}) = \$14.00 \times .60 = \boxed{\$8.40}$$

$$(1.00 - .40)$$

4. $\text{Cost} = \dfrac{\$4}{\$6} = \boxed{66.7\%}$ $\dfrac{.40}{1 - .40} = \dfrac{.40}{.60} = \dfrac{2}{3} = 66.7\%$

   $\text{Selling price} = \dfrac{\$4}{\$10} = \boxed{40\%}$ $\dfrac{.667}{1 + .667} = \dfrac{.667}{1.667} = 40\% \text{ (due to rounding)}$

LEARNING UNIT 8–3 | MARKDOWNS AND PERISHABLES

David Young Wolff/PhotoEdit

J.C. PENNEY CO.

Price-Error Suit Settlement Will Mean Fine of $100,000

J.C. Penney Co. agreed to pay a $100,000 fine and to correct pricing and scanning errors in its Michigan stores as part of a settlement of a lawsuit filed by the Michigan Attorney General's office. Michigan sued the Plano, Texas, retailer in Ingham County, Mich., circuit court after finding that 33% of items purchased at four Michigan Penney stores in December rang up incorrectly at the register. As part of the settlement, the retailer also agreed to reimburse Michigan $9,200 in legal expenses. J.C. Penney said it will also designate on-site "pricing associates" to monitor and immediately correct errors and report them to store management and the company's headquarters. Half the $100,000 penalty will be waived if Penney maintains a 96% scanner accuracy rate, the attorney general's office said.

©2000 Dow Jones & Company, Inc.

You know that when you shop at a supermarket, you should check cash register clerks for errors as they scan your groceries. From *The Wall Street Journal* clipping "Price-Error Suit Settlement Will Mean Fine of $100,000," you also know that you should check all of your purchases for scanning errors at the cash register. The clipping reports that J.C. Penney Co. agreed to pay a $100,000 fine for scanning errors at four stores in Michigan. Penney agreed to have "pricing associates" monitor for errors and report them to store management. It was interesting to note that half of the $100,000 penalty would be waived if Penney maintains a 96% scanner accuracy rate.

Now let's focus our attention on how to calculate markdowns. Then we'll learn how a business prices perishable items that may spoil before customers buy them.

Markdowns

Dollar markdown

Portion
($7.20)

Base × Rate
($18)   (?)

Original selling price

Markdowns are reductions from the original selling price caused by seasonal changes, special promotions, style changes, and so on. We calculate the markdown percent as follows:

$$\text{Markdown percent} = \frac{\text{Dollar markdown}}{\text{Selling price (original)}}$$

Let's look at the following Kmart example:

EXAMPLE Kmart marked down an $18 video to $10.80. Calculate the **dollar markdown** and the markdown percent.

$18.00	Original selling price
− 10.80	Sale price
$ 7.20	Markdown

$$\frac{\text{Dollar markdown, \$7.20}}{\text{Selling price (original), \$18.00}} = \boxed{40\%}$$

Calculating a Series of Markdowns and Markups

Often the final selling price is the result of a series of markdowns (and possibly a markup in between markdowns). We calculate additional markdowns on the previous selling price. Note in the following example how we calculate markdown on selling price after we add a markup.

EXAMPLE Jones Department Store paid its supplier $400 for a TV. On January 10, Jones marked the TV up 60% on selling price. As a special promotion, Jones marked the TV down 30% on February 8 and another 20% on February 28. No one purchased the TV, so Jones marked it up 10% on March 11. What was the selling price of the TV on March 11?

January 10: Selling price = Cost + Markup

$$S = \$400 + .60S$$
$$-.60S \qquad\qquad -.60S$$
$$\frac{\cancel{.40}S}{\cancel{.40}} = \frac{\$400}{.40}$$
$$S = \$1,000$$

Check

$$S = \frac{\text{Cost}}{1 - \text{Percent markup on selling price}}$$

$$S = \frac{\$400}{1 - .60} = \frac{\$400}{.40} = \$1,000$$

February 8 markdown:	100% − 30 70%	→ .70 × $1,000 = $700 selling price
February 28 additional markdown:	100% − 20 80%	→ .80 × $700 = $560
March 11 additional markup:	100% + 10 110%	→ 1.10 × $560 = $616

Pricing Perishable Items

The following formula can be used to determine the price of goods that have a short shelf life such as fruit, flowers, and pastry. (We limit this discussion to obviously **perishable** items.)

$$\text{Selling price of perishables} = \frac{\text{Total dollar sales}}{\text{Number of units produced} - \text{Spoilage}}$$

The Word Problem Audrey's Bake Shop baked 20 dozen bagels. Audrey expects 10% of the bagels to become stale and not salable. The bagels cost Audrey $1.20 per dozen. Audrey wants a 60% markup on cost. What should Audrey charge for each dozen bagels so she will make her profit? Round to the nearest cent.

The facts	Solving for?	Steps to take	Key points
Bagels cost: $1.20 per dozen.	Price of a dozen bagels.	Total cost.	Markup is based on cost.
Not salable: 10%.		Total dollar markup.	
Baked: 20 dozen.		Total selling price.	
Markup on cost: 60%.		Bagel loss.	
		TS = TC + TM.	

Steps to solving problem

1. Calculate the total cost.

2. Calculate the total dollar markup.

3. Calculate the total selling price.

4. Calculate the bagel loss.

5. Calculate the selling price for a dozen bagels.

TC = 20 dozen × $1.20 = $24.00

$$\boxed{TS = TC + TM}$$

TS = $24.00 + .60($24.00)

TS = $24.00 + $14.40 ←— Total dollar markup

TS = $38.40 ←— Total selling price

20 dozen × .10 = 2 dozen

$\dfrac{\$38.40}{18}$ = $\boxed{\$2.13}$ per dozen $\begin{array}{r} 20 \\ -\ 2 \\ \hline 18 \end{array}$

It's time to try the Practice Quiz.

---

1. Sunshine Music Shop bought a stereo for $600 and marked it up 40% on selling price. To promote customer interest, Sunshine marked the stereo down 10% for one week. Since business was slow, Sunshine marked the stereo down an additional 5%. After a week, Sunshine marked the stereo up 2%. What is the new selling price of the stereo to the nearest cent? What is the markdown percent based on the original selling price to the nearest hundredth percent?

2. Alvin Rose owns a fruit and vegetable stand. He knows that he cannot sell all his produce at full price. Some of his produce will be markdowns, and he will throw out some produce. Alvin must put a high enough price on the produce to cover markdowns and rotted produce and still make his desired profit. Alvin bought 300 pounds of tomatoes at 14 cents per pound. He expects a 5% spoilage and marks up tomatoes 60% on cost. What price per pound should Alvin charge for the tomatoes?

✓ SOLUTIONS

1.

$S = C + M$

$S = \$600 + .40S$

$-.40S \qquad -.40S$

$\dfrac{.60S}{.60} = \dfrac{\$600}{.60}$

$S = \$1,000$

Check

$S = \dfrac{\text{Cost}}{1 - \text{Percent markup on selling price}}$

$S = \dfrac{\$600}{1 - .40} = \dfrac{\$600}{.60} = \$1,000$

First markdown: .90 × $1,000 = $900 selling price

Second markdown: .95 × $900 = $855 selling price

Markup: 1.02 × $855 = $\boxed{\$872.10}$ final selling price

$\$1,000 - \$872.10 = \dfrac{\$127.90}{\$1,000} = \boxed{12.79\%}$

2. Price of tomatoes per pound:

The facts	Solving for?	Steps to take	Key points
300 lb. tomatoes at $.14 per pound.	Price of tomatoes per pound.	Total cost.	Markup is based on cost.
Spoilage: 5%.		Total dollar markup.	
Markup on cost: 60%.		Total selling price.	
		Spoilage amount.	
		TS = TC + TM.	

Steps to solving problem

1. Calculate the total cost.

2. Calculate the total dollar markup.

$TC = 300$ lb. $\times$ \$.14 = \$42.00

$TS = TC + TM$

$TS = \$42.00 + .60(\$42.00)$

$TS = \$42.00 + \$25.20 \longleftarrow$ Total dollar markup

3. Calculate the total selling price.

$TS = \$67.20 \longleftarrow$ Total selling price

4. Calculate the tomato loss.

300 pounds $\times$ .05 = 15 pounds spoilage

5. Calculate the selling price per pound of tomatoes.

$\dfrac{\$67.20}{285} = \$.24$ per pound (rounded to nearest hundredth)

$(300 - 15)$

Chapter Organizer and Reference Guide

Topic	Key point, procedure, formula	Example(s) to illustrate situation
Markups based on cost: Cost is 100% (base), p. 195	Selling price (S) = Cost (C) + Markup (M)	$\$400 = \$300 + \$100$ $S \quad = \quad C \quad + \quad M$
Percent markup on cost, p. 195 Cost, p. 196	$\dfrac{\text{Dollar markup (portion)}}{\text{Cost (base)}} = \dfrac{\text{Percent markup}}{\text{on cost (rate)}}$ $C = \dfrac{\text{Dollar markup}}{\text{Percent markup on cost}}$	$\dfrac{\$100}{\$300} = \dfrac{1}{3} = 33\dfrac{1}{3}\%$ $\dfrac{\$100}{.33} = \$303$ Off slightly due to rounding
Calculating selling price, p. 196	$S = C + M$ **Check** $S = \text{Cost} \times (1 + \text{Percent markup on cost})$	Cost, \$6; percent markup on cost, 20% $S = \$6 + .20(\$6)$ **Check** $S = \$6 + \$1.20$ $S = \$7.20$ $\boxed{\$6 \times 1.20 = \$7.20}$

Calculating cost, p. 197	$S = C + M$
	Check
	$\text{Cost} = \dfrac{\text{Selling price}}{1 + \text{Percent markup on cost}}$
		$S = \$100;\ M = 70\%$ of cost
		    $S = C + M$
		    $\$100 = C + .70C$
		    $\$100 = 1.7C$ *(Remember, $C = 1.00C$)*
		    $\dfrac{\$100}{1.7} = C$ **Check**
		    $\$58.82 = C$ $\boxed{\dfrac{\$100}{1 + .70} = \$58.82}$

Markups based on selling price: selling price is 100% (Base), p. 199	Dollar markup = Selling price − Cost	$M = S - C$ $\$600 = \$1{,}000 - \$400$
Percent markup on selling price, p. 200 Selling price, p. 200	$\dfrac{\text{Dollar markup (portion)}}{\text{Selling price (base)}} = \dfrac{\text{Percent markup}}{\text{selling price (rate)}}$ $S = \dfrac{\text{Dollar markup}}{\text{Percent markup on selling price}}$	$\dfrac{\$600}{\$1{,}000} = 60\%$ $\dfrac{\$600}{.60} = \$1{,}000$
Calculating selling price, p. 200	$S = C + M$ **Check** $\text{Selling price} = \dfrac{\text{Cost}}{1 - \text{Percent markup on selling price}}$	Cost, \$400; percent markup on S, 60% $S = C + M$ $S = \$400 + .60S$ $S - .60S = \$400 + .60S - .60S$ $\dfrac{.40S}{.40} = \dfrac{\$400}{.40}$ $S = \$1{,}000$ **Check** $\longrightarrow$ $\boxed{\dfrac{\$400}{1 - .60} = \dfrac{\$400}{.40} = \$1{,}000}$
Calculating cost, p. 201	$S = C + M$ **Check** $\text{Cost} = \text{Selling price} \times \left(1 - \dfrac{\text{Percent markup}}{\text{on selling price}}\right)$	$\$1{,}000 = C + 60\%(\$1{,}000)$ $\$1{,}000 = C + \$600$ $\$400 = C$ **Check** $\longrightarrow$ $\boxed{\begin{array}{l}\$1{,}000 \times (1 - .60)\\ \$1{,}000 \times .40 = \$400\end{array}}$

(continues)

Chapter Organizer and Reference Guide (concluded)

Topic	Key point, procedure, formula	Example(s) to illustrate situation
Conversion of markup percent, p. 202	Percent markup on cost **to** Percent markup on selling price $\dfrac{\text{Percent markup on cost}}{1 + \text{Percent markup on cost}}$ Percent markup on selling price **to** Percent markup on cost $\dfrac{\text{Percent markup on selling price}}{1 - \text{Percent markup on selling price}}$	*Round to nearest percent:* 54% markup on cost ⟶ **35%** markup on selling price $\dfrac{.54}{1 + .54} = \dfrac{.54}{1.54} = 35\%$ 35% markup on selling price ⟶ **54%** markup on cost $\dfrac{.35}{1 - .35} = \dfrac{.35}{.65} = 54\%$
Markdowns, p. 205	Markdown percent $= \dfrac{\text{Dollar markdown}}{\text{Selling price (original)}}$	$40 selling price 10% markdown $40 × .10 = $4 markdown $\dfrac{\$4}{\$40} =$ **10%**
Pricing perishables, p. 205	1. Calculate total cost and total selling price. 2. Calculate selling price per unit by dividing total sales in Step 1 by units expected to be sold after taking perishables into account.	50 pastries cost 20 cents each; 10 will spoil before being sold. Markup is 60% on cost. 1. $TC = 50 × \$.20 = \$10$ $TS = TC + TM$ $TS = \$10 + .60(\$10)$ $TS = \$10 + \$6$ $TS = $ **$16** 2. $\dfrac{\$16}{40 \text{ pastries}} = $ **$.40** per pastry
Key terms	Cost, *p. 194* Dollar markdown, *p. 205* Dollar markup, *p. 194* Gross profit, *p. 194* Margin, *p. 194*	Markdowns, *p. 205* Markup, *p. 194* Net profit (net income), *p. 194* Operating expenses (overhead), *p. 194* Percent markup on cost, *p. 195* Percent markup on selling price, *p. 199* Perishables, *p. 205* Selling price, *p. 194*

Critical Thinking Discussion Questions

1. Assuming markups are based on cost, explain how the portion formula could be used to calculate cost, selling price, dollar markup, and percent markup on cost. Pick a company and explain why it would mark goods up on cost rather than on selling price.

2. Assuming markups are based on selling price, explain how the portion formula could be used to calculate cost, selling price, dollar markup, and percent markup on selling price. Pick a company and explain why it would mark up goods on selling price rather than on cost.

3. What is the formula to convert percent markup on selling price to percent markup on cost? How could you explain that a 40% markup on selling price, which is a 66.7% markup on cost, would result in the same dollar markup?

4. Explain how to calculate markdowns. Do you think stores should run one-day-only markdown sales? Would it be better to offer the best price "all the time"?

5. Explain the five steps in calculating a selling price for perishable items. Recall a situation where you saw a store that did *not* follow the five steps. How did it sell its items?

END-OF-CHAPTER PROBLEMS

Name _____ Date _____

DRILL PROBLEMS

Assume markups in Problems 8–1 to 8–6 are based on cost. Find the dollar markup and selling price for the following problems. Round answers to the nearest cent.

	Item	Cost	Markup percent	Dollar markup	Selling price
8–1.	Sony DVD player	$100	40%		
8–2.	Sharper Image Razor scooter	$65	40%		

Solve for cost (round to the nearest cent):

8–3. Selling price of office furniture at Staples, $6,000

Percent markup on cost, 40%

Actual cost?

8–4. Selling price of lumber at Home Depot, $4,000

Percent markup on cost, 30%

Actual cost?

Complete the following:

	Cost	Selling price	Dollar markup	Percent markup on cost*
8–5.	$15.10	$22.00	?	?
8–6.	?	?	$4.70	102.17%

*Round to the nearest hundredth percent.

Assume markups in Problems 8–7 to 8–12 are based on selling price.
Find the dollar markup and cost (round answers to the nearest cent):

	Item	Selling price	Markup percent	Dollar markup	Cost
8–7.	Kodak digital camera	$219	30%		
8–8.	IBM scanner	$80	30%		

Solve for the selling price (round to the nearest cent):

8–9. Selling price of a complete set of pots and pans at Wal-Mart?
40% markup on selling price
Cost, actual, $66.50

8–10. Selling price of a dining room set at Macy's?
55% markup on selling price
Cost, actual, $800

Complete the following:

	Cost	Selling price	Dollar markup	Percent markup on selling price (round to nearest tenth percent)
8–11.	$14.80	$49.00	?	?
8–12.	?	?	$4	20%

By conversion of the markup formula, solve the following (round to the nearest whole percent as needed):

	Percent markup on cost	Percent markup on selling price
8–13.	12.4%	?
8–14.	?	13%

Complete the following:

8–15. Calculate the final selling price to the nearest cent and markdown percent to the nearest hundredth percent:

Excel	Original selling price	First markdown	Second markdown	Markup	Final markdown
	$5,000	20%	10%	12%	5%

Item	Total quantity bought	Unit cost	Total cost	Percent markup on cost	Total selling price	Percent that will spoil	Selling price per brownie
8–16. Brownies	20	$.79	?	60%	?	10%	?

WORD PROBLEMS

8–17. On an eBay auction, Mike Kaminsky bought an old Walter Lantz Woody Woodpecker oil painting for $4,000. He plans to resell it at a toy show for $7,000. What are the dollar markup and the percent markup on cost? Check the cost figure.

8–18. Chin Yov, store manager for Best Buy, does not know how to price a GE freezer that cost the store $600. Chin knows his boss wants a 45% markup on cost. Help Chin price the refrigerator.

8–19. Cecil Green sells golf hats. He knows that most people will not pay more than $20 for a golf hat. Cecil needs a 40% markup on cost. What should Cecil pay for his golf hats? Round to the nearest cent.

8–20. On January 22, 2001, *U.S. News & World Report* informed readers on the results of after-Christmas sales. Macy's was selling Calvin Klein jeans shirts that were originally priced at $58.00 for $8.70. **(a)** What was the amount of the markdown? **(b)** Based on selling price, what is the percent markdown?

8–21. On March 15, 2001, *The Seattle Times* reported that Boeing would increase its prices for Jetliners. With a selling price of $201.5 million and a cost of $190.1 million, what was the percent markup based on cost? Round to the nearest percent.

8–22. The December 2000 issue of *Yahoo! Internet Life* reported that a 2001 Volkswagen New Beetle GLX with a dealer invoice price of $19,700 was retail priced at $23,000. **(a)** How much is the percent markup based on selling price? Round to the nearest hundredth percent. **(b)** How much is the markup percent if cost had been the base (use the equivalent markup formula)? Round to the nearest hundredth percent.

8–23. Misu Sheet, owner of the Bedspread Shop, knows his customers will pay no more than $120 for a comforter. Misu wants a 30% markup on selling price. What is the most that Misu can pay for a comforter?

8–24. Assume Misu Sheet (Problem 8–23) wants a 30% markup on cost instead of on selling price. What is Misu's cost? Round to the nearest cent.

8–25. Misu Sheet (Problem 8–23) wants to advertise the comforter as "percent markup on cost." What is the equivalent rate of percent markup on cost compared to the 30% markup on selling price? Check your answer. Is this a wise marketing decision? Round to the nearest hundredth percent.

8–26. DeWitt Company sells a kitchen set for $475. To promote July 4, DeWitt ran the following advertisement:

> Beginning each hour up to 4 hours we will mark down the kitchen
> set 10%. At the end of each hour, we will mark up the set 1%.

Assume Ingrid Swenson buys the set 1 hour 50 minutes into the sale. What will Ingrid pay? Round each calculation to the nearest cent. What is the markdown percent? Round to the nearest hundredth percent.

8–27. Angie's Bake Shop makes birthday chocolate chip cookies that cost $2 each. Angie expects that 10% of the cookies will crack and be discarded. Angie wants a 60% markup on cost and produces 100 cookies. What should Angie price each cookie? Round to the nearest cent.

8–28. Assume that Angie (Problem 8–27) can sell the cracked cookies for $1.10 each. What should Angie price each cookie?

ADDITIONAL SET OF WORD PROBLEMS

8–29. Sears bought a treadmill for $510. Sears has a 60% markup on selling price. What is the selling price of the treadmill?

8–30. Sachi Wong, store manager for Hawk Appliance, does not know how to price a GE dishwasher that cost the store $399. Sachi knows her boss wants a 40% markup on cost. Can you help Sachi price the dishwasher?

8–31. On September 26, 2000, the *Amarillo Globe-News* reported on the concept of "Furniture Clubs" selling to the public at wholesale prices on a cash-only, no-frills basis. Working off an 18% margin, with markups based on cost, the clubs boast they have 5,000 members and a 200% increase in sales. The markup is 36% based on cost. What would be their percent markup if selling price were the base? Round to the nearest hundredth.

8–32. At a local Bed and Bath Superstore, the manager, Jill Roe, knows her customers will pay no more than $300 for a bedspread. Jill wants a 35% markup on selling price. What is the most that Jill can pay for a bedspread?

8–33. On September 3, 2000, the *San Jose Mercury News* reported the difference between the cost and selling price of CDs. A rock band can make a batch of CDs for around $4 each. The record companies charge $18 for new releases. **(a)** What would be the markup amount? **(b)** What would be the percent markup on cost? **(c)** What would be the percent markup on selling price? Round to nearest hundredth percent.

8–34. Circuit City sells a hand-held personal planner for $199.99. Circuit City marked up the personal planner 35% on the selling price. What is the cost of the hand-held personal planner?

8–35. Arley's Bakery makes fat-free cookies that cost $1.50 each. Arley expects 15% of the cookies to fall apart and be discarded. Arley wants a 45% markup on cost and produces 200 cookies. What should Arley price each cookie? Round to the nearest cent.

8–36. Assume that Arley (Problem 8–35) can sell the broken cookies for $1.40 each. What should Arley price each cookie?

8–37. Ron's Computer Center sells computers for $1,258.60. Assuming the computers cost $10,788 per dozen, find for each computer the **(a)** dollar markup, **(b)** percent markup on cost, and **(c)** percent markup on selling price (nearest hundredth percent).

Prove **(b)** and **(c)** of the above problem using the equivalent formulas.

CHALLENGE PROBLEMS

8–38. On October 27, 2000, *WWD (Woman's Wear Daily)* reported on tackling the newsstand challenge. *Woman's Day* has raised its price from $1.29 to $1.69. *Elle* magazine has raised its original price of $3.00 by 14.28%. *George* magazine has raised its price to $3.50, a 15.71% markup. Using markup based on selling price: **(a)** How much is *Woman's Day*'s percent markup? **(b)** What was *Elle*'s new selling price? **(c)** What was *George*'s original price? Round all answers to the nearest hundredth percent as needed.

8–39. On July 8, 2004, Leon's Kitchen Hut bought a set of pots with a $120 list price from Lambert Manufacturing. Leon's receives a 25% trade discount. Terms of the sale were 2/10, n/30. On July 14, Leon's sent a check to Lambert for the pots. Leon's expenses are 20% of the selling price. Leon's must also make a profit of 15% of the selling price. A competitor marked down the same set of pots 30%. Assume Leon's reduces its selling price by 30%.

    a.   What is the sale price at Kitchen Hut?

    b.   What was the operating profit or loss?

SUMMARY PRACTICE TEST

1. Bayside Appliance marks up merchandise 40% on cost. A television costs Bayside $320. What is Bayside's selling price? Round to the nearest cent. *(p. 196)*

2. The Levi Shop sells jeans for $49.99 that cost $30.25. What is the percent markup on cost? Round to the nearest hundredth percent. Check the cost. *(p. 196)*

3. Best Buy sells a flat-screen TV for $1,250. Best Buy marks up the TV 60% on cost. What is the cost and dollar markup of the TV? *(p. 197)*

4. The Fitness Shop marks up Nike sneakers $35 and sells them for $125. Markup is on cost. What are the cost and percent markup to the nearest tenth percent? *(p. 196)*

5. The Boot Shop bought boots for $80 and marks up the boots 65% on the selling price. What is the selling price of the boots? Round to the nearest cent. *(p. 200)*

6. Office.com sells a desk for $599 and marks up the desk 30% on selling price. What did the desk cost Office.com? Round to the nearest cent. *(p. 201)*

7. Service Merchandise sells diamonds for $799 that cost $500. What is Service Merchandise's percent markup on selling price? Round to the nearest hundredth percent. Check the selling price. *(p. 201)*

8. Russell Amber, a customer of the Gap Company, will pay $200 for a new jacket. Gap has a 60% markup on selling price. What is the most that Gap can pay for this jacket? *(p. 201)*

9. Home Decorators marks up its merchandise 70% on cost. What is the company's equivalent markup on selling price? Round to the nearest tenth percent. *(p. 202)*

10. The Muffin Shop makes no-fat muffins that cost $.40 each. The Muffin Shop knows that 15% of the muffins will spoil. If Muffin wants 45% markup on cost and produces 600 muffins, what should Muffin Shop price each muffin? Round to the nearest cent. *(p. 206)*

Diana Maridi Salgado, who works at a Family Dollar store in Bayonne, N.J., says customers seem to want more personal attention.

RETAILING
LIKE INVESTORS, SHOPPERS ARE LOOKING FOR BARGAINS

RETAILERS were already being squeezed by a faltering economy before the terrorists struck. Consumer confidence was slumping and sales sagging. The attacks left Americans shellshocked and concerned about the future, adding momentum to the rolling snowball. The National Retail Federation says holiday-season sales, crucial to many retailers, will probably grow by a meager 3%. Beyond Christmas and Chanukah, the outlook is murkier than usual. "We can only speculate about what we think the government will do and how consumers will respond," says Rosalind Wells, the retail federation's chief economist.

What is clear is that in this environment, consumers are much more likely to spend money on what they need, rather than on what they want. They'll spend less on big-ticket items, such as refrigerators and washing machines, and luxury goods, such as expensive watches and fancy cars. They'll focus instead on getting good deals.

That plays into the strengths of bargain retailers like **Family Dollar Stores** (FDO). It sells detergents, beauty aids, candy, paper products, clothing and other items at low prices. Sales growth at stores open at least a year has been accelerating over the past eight months, says analyst Michael Baker of Deutsche Bank Alex. Brown. Family Dollar, which leads its peers in most measures of profitability, recently announced that sales are keeping pace with preattack goals. The stock, at $28, sells at 22 times 2002 earnings estimates.

Sears (S) sells both low-priced small household items and big-ticket major appliances. But its stock, at $39, selling at just nine times estimated 2002 earnings, is simply too cheap to pass up, says Susan Byrne, who runs Gabelli Westwood Equity fund. "Sears is a lot like Wal-Mart, only at one-third the price in terms of its price-earnings ratio," she says. Byrne adds that the kinds of basic services Sears offers, such as car tune-ups and tire changes, should hold up well in the economic downturn.

Stores that sell home-improvement tools and materials stand to benefit if lower interest rates spur homeowners to renovate. The obvious candidate is industry leader **Home Depot** (HD), which Robert Hagstrom, manager of Legg Mason Focus Trust, considers "one of the best retailers on the planet." The stock, recently $40, has rebounded smartly from a post-attack sell-off but is still 25% below its 52-week high. It sells at 27 times 2002 earnings estimates of $1.50 per share, a relatively low P/E ratio for this blue chip. —**BRIAN P. KNESTOUT**

PHOTOGRAPH BY DAVID BARRY

Business Math Issue

Terrorist attacks have had no long-term effect on retail sales.
1. List the key points of the article and information to support your position.
2. Write a group defense of your position using math calculations to support your view.

The Golden Arches: Burgers, Fries and 4-Star Rooms

McDonald's Plans to Open Two Hotels in Switzerland; Will Business Travelers Bite?

By Margaret Studer
And Jennifer Ordonez
Staff Reporters of The Wall Street Journal

ZURICH.—The room prices at the four-star hotel will be listed on electronic signs strangely reminiscent of McDonald's menu boards. The color scheme will be a softer version of the fast-food chain's famous red and yellow. And guests will spend their nights on a 'Big Mac' bed.

After decades of serving up Happy Meals around the globe, **McDonald's** Corp. is cooking up something new: the Golden Arch Hotels. In March, the company will open two hotels in Switzerland, aimed at business travelers during the week and families on the weekend. The hotels will offer 24-hour service and room service—amenities necessary to qualify for four-star status in Switzerland.

If the venture is successful, more hotels could follow in other parts of the world.

"Innovation is always on the menu at McDonald's," Jack Greenberg, McDonald's chairman and chief executive officer, said in a video shown at a press conference last week announcing the hotels. "Our passion for making customers smile extends very naturally to the hotel sector."

Back at McDonald's headquarters in Oak Brook, Ill., spokesman Jack Daly says that hotels are a concept that may never expand beyond Switzerland. "This is definitely a Swiss project," he says, attributing its genesis to Urs Hammer, a hotelier before he became chairman and CEO in 1980 of McDonald's Swiss Holding AG, a joint venture.

Yet the hotel test fits into a larger pattern of McDonald's experiments in Europe. In Germany, the company is selling McDonald's brand ketchup in grocery stores. In countries including Portugal and Austria, it is operating Mc-

A model of McDonald's Corp.'s Golden Arch Hotels opening in Switzerland next year.

Cafe, a coffee-bar concept that will be introduced in the U.S. next year.

The efforts represent the determination of Mr. Greenberg, chief executive since 1998, to leverage the McDonald's brand beyond hamburgers and french fries. In the U.S., where sales growth has been sluggish for years, that campaign has included the purchase of some or all of a Mexican restaurant chain, a pizza chain and Boston Chicken Inc.

Still, it is a bit of a leap to hotels. Mr. Greenberg said at the press conference that he believes clients will be attracted by the things they have come to expect from McDonald's: quality, service, cleanliness and value. A room will cost between 169 Swiss francs and 189 francs ($94.99 and $106.24), with 25 francs added for a second person.

"At a McDonald's, you have the security of knowing what you get," asserts Golden Arch Hotels Sales Director Mirjam von Zweden.

PROJECT A

Do you think this retailing strategy will work for McDonald's? Check out the McDonald's website to see if you can find any more updates on this strategy.

Internet Projects: See text website (www.mhhe.com/slater7e) and *The Business Math Internet Resource Guide.*

CUMULATIVE REVIEW

A Word Problem Approach—Chapters 6, 7, 8

1. Assume Kellogg's produced 715,000 boxes of Corn Flakes this year. This was 110% of the annual production last year. What was last year's annual production? (p. 142)

2. A new Sony camcorder has a list price of $420. The trade discount is 10/20 with terms of 2/10, n/30. If a retailer pays the invoice within the discount period, what is the amount the retailer must pay? (p. 167)

3. JCPenney sells loafers with a markup of $40. If the markup is 30% on cost, what did the loafers cost JCPenney? Round to the nearest dollar. (p. 196)

4. Aster Computers received from Ring Manufacturers an invoice dated August 28 with terms 2/10 EOM. The list price of the invoice is $3,000 (freight not included). Ring offers Aster a 9/8/2 trade chain discount. Terms of freight are FOB shipping point, but Ring prepays the $150 freight. Assume Aster pays the invoice on October 9. How much will Ring receive? (p. 178)

5. Runners World marks up its Nike jogging shoes 25% on selling price. The Nike shoe sells for $65. How much did the store pay for them? (p. 201)

6. Ivan Rone sells antique sleds. He knows that the most he can get for a sled is $350. Ivan needs a 35% markup on cost. Since Ivan is going to an antiques show, he wants to know the maximum he can offer a dealer for an antique sled. (p. 197)

7. Bonnie's Bakery bakes 60 loaves of bread for $1.10 each. Bonnie's estimates that 10% of the bread will spoil. Assume a 60% markup on cost. What is the selling price of each loaf? If Bonnie's can sell the old bread for one-half the cost, what is the selling price of each loaf? (p. 206)

Payroll

Delta's Pact With Pilots Will Be Costly, Bolstering Higher Industry Expectations

By RICK BROOKS
And MARTHA BRANNIGAN
Staff Reporters of THE WALL STREET JOURNAL

ATLANTA—**Delta Air Lines** averted a possibly crippling strike by reaching a tentative contract agreement with its pilots' union Sunday. But the price of peace at the nation's third-largest airline will be steep.

Delta hasn't disclosed an estimate of its projected pilot costs under the agreement, which would make Delta's 9,800 pilots the highest-paid in the industry by boosting their pay scale 1% above that of UAL Corp.'s United Airlines pilots, who concluded their labor pact in the summer. There is no doubt, though, that Delta's pilot paychecks are about to soar, as they did at United: Under Delta's five-year contract agreement, a Boeing 777 captain with 12 years of seniority would get annual base pay of roughly $287,600 starting in May 2004, up from $232,300 now. Raises would range between 24% and 34%, on a compound basis, depending on the aircraft type.

Flying High

Tentative pay pact puts Delta pilots at top of the industry.

Boeing 777 captain, (+23.8%)

Current annual base pay $232,300

Annual base pay as of May 2004 $287,600

Boeing 727 captain, (+32.6%)

$165,000

$218,800

Note: Base pay rate is for a captain with 12 years seniority.
Source: Air Line Pilots Association

©2001 Dow Jones & Company, Inc.

Most airline passengers agree that airline pilots deserve respect and excellent pay for the responsibility they assume. Do you wonder how much the captains of Boeing jets are paid for such a responsible position? *The Wall Street Journal* clipping "Delta's Pact With Pilots Will Be Costly, Bolstering Higher Industry Expectations" answers this question.

Note from the clipping that as of May 2004, the current annual base pay of a Boeing 777 captain will increase by 23.8% and the current annual pay of a Boeing 727 captain will increase 32.6%. As a result of a five-year contract, the paychecks of Boeing pilots are about to soar. This tentative pay pact would make Delta's 9,800 pilots the highest in the industry.

This chapter discusses (1) the type of pay people work for, (2) how employers calculate paychecks and deductions, and (3) what employers must report and pay in taxes.

LEARNING UNIT 9–1 | CALCULATING VARIOUS TYPES OF EMPLOYEES' GROSS PAY

Logan Company manufactures dolls of all shapes and sizes. These dolls are sold worldwide. We study Logan Company in this unit because of the variety of methods Logan uses to pay its employees.

Companies usually pay employees **weekly, biweekly, semimonthly,** or **monthly.** How often employers pay employees can affect how employees manage their money. Some employees prefer a weekly paycheck that spreads the inflow of money. Employees who have monthly bills may find the twice-a-month or monthly paycheck more convenient. All employees would like more money to manage.

Let's assume you earn $50,000 per year. The following table shows what you would earn each pay period. Remember that 13 weeks equals one quarter. Four quarters or 52 weeks equals a year.

Salary paid	Period (based on a year)	Earnings for period (dollars)
Weekly	52 times (once a week)	$ 961.54 ($50,000 ÷ 52)
Biweekly	26 times (every two weeks)	$1,923.08 ($50,000 ÷ 26)
Semimonthly	24 times (twice a month)	$2,083.33 ($50,000 ÷ 24)
Monthly	12 times (once a month)	$4,166.67 ($50,000 ÷ 12)

Now let's look at some pay schedule situations and examples of how Logan Company calculates its payroll for employees of different pay status.

Situation 1: Hourly Rate of Pay: Calculation of Overtime

The **Fair Labor Standards Act** sets minimum wage standards and overtime regulations for employees of companies covered by this federal law. The law provides that employees working for an hourly rate receive time-and-a-half pay for hours worked in excess of their regular 40-hour week. The current hourly minimum wage is $5.15, and it will probably increase in the future. Many managerial people, however, are exempt from the time-and-a-half pay for all hours in excess of a 40-hour week. *The Wall Street Journal* clipping "McDonald's Vows to Probe Report About Toy Factory" raises questions about the use of children as young as 14 employed in a mainland Chinese sweatshop.

Logan Company is calculating the weekly pay of Ramon Valdez who works in its manufacturing division. For the first 40 hours Ramon works, Logan calculates his **gross pay** (earnings before **deductions**) as follows:

Bill Bachmann/PhotoEdit

McDonald's Vows to Probe Report About Toy Factory

By a WALL STREET JOURNAL *Staff Reporter*
OAK BROOK, Ill.—**McDonald's** Corp. says it has "seen no evidence" supporting a Hong Kong newspaper's allegations that the toys accompanying McDonald's Happy Meals are packaged by children as young as 14 years old who are illegally employed by a mainland Chinese sweatshop.

The world's largest restaurant chain said it has dispatched its own auditors to inspect City Toys Ltd., a unit of **Pleasure Tech Holdings** Ltd., Hong Kong. The factory, which employs about 2,000 workers, is under contract for a McDonald's supplier, **Simon Marketing (Hong Kong)** Ltd.

©2000 Dow Jones & Company, Inc.

$$\text{Gross pay} = \frac{\text{Hours}}{\text{employee}} \times \frac{\text{Rate}}{\text{per}}$$
$$\text{worked} \qquad \text{hour}$$

Ramon works more than 40 hours in a week. For every hour over his 40 hours, Ramon must be paid an **overtime** pay of at least 1.5 times his regular pay rate. The following formula is used to determine Ramon's overtime:

Hourly overtime pay rate = Regular hourly pay rate × 1.5

Logan Company must include Ramon's overtime pay with his regular pay. To determine Ramon's gross pay, Logan uses the following formula:

Gross pay = Earnings for 40 hours + Earnings at time-and-a-half rate (1.5)

Let's calculate Ramon's gross pay from the following data:

EXAMPLE

Employee	M	T	W	Th	F	S	Total hours	Rate per hour
Ramon Valdez	13	$8\frac{1}{2}$	10	8	$11\frac{1}{4}$	$10\frac{3}{4}$	$61\frac{1}{2}$	$9

$61\frac{1}{2}$ total hours
$-\ 40\phantom{\frac{1}{2}}$ regular hours
$\overline{21\frac{1}{2}}$ hours overtime[1] Time-and-a-half pay: $9 × 1.5 = $13.50

Gross pay = (40 hours × $9) + ($21\frac{1}{2}$ hours × $13.50)

$ = 360$ + 290.25

$ = $650.25

---

[1]Some companies pay overtime for time over 8 hours in one day; Logan Company pays overtime for time over 40 hours per week.

Note that the $13.50 overtime rate came out even. However, throughout the text, *if an overtime rate is greater than two decimal places, do not round it. Round only the final answer. This gives greater accuracy.*

Situation 2: Straight Piece Rate Pay

Some companies, especially manufacturers, pay workers according to how much they produce. Logan Company pays Ryan Foss for the number of dolls he produces in a week. This gives Ryan an incentive to make more money by producing more dolls. Ryan receives $.96 per doll, less any defective units. The following formula determines Ryan's gross pay:

> Gross pay = Number of units produced × Rate per unit

Companies may also pay a guaranteed hourly wage and use a piece rate as a bonus. However, Logan uses straight piece rate as wages for some of its employees.

EXAMPLE During the last week of April, Ryan Foss produced 900 dolls. Using the above formula, Logan Company paid Ryan $864.

Gross pay = 900 dolls × $.96

= $864

Situation 3: Differential Pay Schedule

Some of Logan's employees can earn more than the $.96 straight piece rate for every doll they produce. Logan Company has set up a **differential pay schedule** for these employees. The company determines the rate these employees make by the amount of units the employees produce at different levels of production.

EXAMPLE Logan Company pays Abby Rogers on the basis of the following schedule:

	Units produced	Amount per unit
First 50 →	1–50	$ .50
Next 100 →	51–150	.62
Next 50 →	151–200	.75
	Over 200	1.25

Last week Abby produced 300 dolls. What is Abby's gross pay?
  Logan calculated Abby's gross pay as follows:

(50 × $.50) + (100 × $.62) + (50 × $.75) + (100 × $1.25)

$25 + $62 + $37.50 + $125 = $249.50

We are now ready to study some of the other types of employee commission payment plans.

Situation 4: Straight Commission with Draw

Companies frequently use **straight commission** to determine the pay of salespersons. This commission is usually a certain percentage of the amount the salesperson sells. Logan Company allows some of its salespersons to draw against this commission at the beginning of each month.

  A **draw** is an advance on the salesperson's commission. Logan subtracts this advance later from the employee's commission earned based on sales. When the commission does not equal the draw, the salesperson owes Logan the difference between the draw and the commission.

EXAMPLE Logan Company pays Jackie Okamoto a straight commission of 15% on her net sales (net sales are total sales less sales returns). In May, Jackie had net sales of $56,000. Logan gave Jackie a $600 draw in May. What is Jackie's gross pay?

Logan calculated Jackie's commission minus her draw as follows:

$56,000 × .15 = $8,400
                        −   600
                        ───────
                        $7,800

Logan Company pays some people in the sales department on a variable commission scale. Let's look at this, assuming the employee had no draw.

Situation 5: Variable Commission Scale

A company with a **variable commission scale** uses different commission rates for different levels of net sales.

EXAMPLE   Last month, Jane Ring's net sales were $160,000. What is Jane's gross pay based on the following schedule?

Up to $35,000   4%
Excess of $35,000 to $45,000   6%
Over $45,000   8%

Gross pay = ($35,000 × .04) + ($10,000 × .06) + ($115,000 × .08)
       = $1,400   + $600   + $9,200
       = $11,200

Situation 6: Salary Plus Commission

Logan Company pays Joe Roy a $3,000 monthly salary plus a 4% commission for sales over $20,000. Last month Joe's net sales were $50,000. Logan calculated Joe's gross monthly pay as follows:

Gross pay = Salary + (Commission × Sales over $20,000)
       = $3,000 +   ($.04 × $30,000)
       = $3,000 + $1,200
       = $4,200

Before you take the Practice Quiz, you should know that many managers today receive **overrides.** These managers receive a commission based on the net sales of the people they supervise.

LU 9–1 PRACTICE QUIZ

1. Jill Foster worked 52 hours in one week for Delta Airlines. Jill earns $10 per hour. What is Jill's gross pay, assuming overtime is at time-and-a-half?
2. Matt Long had $180,000 in sales for the month. Matt's commission rate is 9%, and he had a $3,500 draw. What was Matt's end-of-month commission?
3. Bob Meyers receives a $1,000 monthly salary. He also receives a variable commission on net sales based on the following schedule (commission doesn't begin until Bob earns $8,000 in net sales):

$8,000–$12,000   1%   Excess of $20,000 to $40,000   5%
Excess of $12,000 to $20,000   3%   More than $40,000   8%

Assume Bob earns $40,000 net sales for the month. What is his gross pay?

✓ **SOLUTIONS**

1.   40 hours × $10.00 = $400.00
      12 hours × $15.00 =   180.00 ($10.00 × 1.5 = $15.00)
                                       ─────────
                                       $580.00

2. $180,000 × .09 = $16,200
                                 −   3,500
                                 ─────────
                                 $12,700

3.   Gross pay = $1,000 + ($4,000 × .01) + ($8,000 × .03) + ($20,000 × .05)
             = $1,000 + $40   + $240   + $1,000
             = $2,280

LEARNING UNIT 9–2 | COMPUTING PAYROLL DEDUCTIONS FOR EMPLOYEES' PAY; EMPLOYERS' RESPONSIBILITIES

When you get your weekly paycheck, do you take the time to check all the numbers? Do you understand the difference between Social Security and Medicare? This unit begins by dissecting a paycheck. Then we give you an insight into the tax responsibilities of employers.

Computing Payroll Deductions for Employees

Companies often record employee payroll information in a multicolumn form called a **payroll register.** The increased use of computers in business has made computerized registers a timesaver for many companies.

Glo Company uses a multicolumn payroll register. Below is Glo's partial payroll register showing the payroll information for Alice Rey during week 41. Let's check each column to see if Alice's take-home pay of $1,340.83 is correct. Note how the circled letters in the register correspond to the explanations given below the register.

GLO COMPANY
Payroll Register
Week #41

								FICA taxable earnings		Deductions					
				Earnings						FICA					
Employee name	Allow. & marital status	Cum. earn.	Sal. per week	Reg.	Ovt.	Gross	Cum. earn.	S.S.	Med.	S.S.	Med.	FIT	SIT	Health ins.	Net pay
Rey, Alice	M-2	80,000	2,000	2,000	—	2,000	82,000	400	2,000	24.80	29	385.37	120	100	1,340.83
	Ⓐ	Ⓑ	Ⓒ		Ⓓ		Ⓔ	Ⓕ	Ⓖ	Ⓗ	Ⓘ	Ⓙ	Ⓚ	Ⓛ	Ⓜ

Payroll Register Explanations
Ⓐ—Allowance and marital status
Ⓑ, Ⓒ, Ⓓ—Cumulative earnings before payroll, salaries, earnings
Ⓔ—Cumulative earnings after payroll

When Alice was hired, she completed the **W-4 (Employee's Withholding Allowance Certificate)** form shown in Figure 9.1 stating that she is married and claims an allowance (exemption) of 2. Glo Company will need this information to calculate the federal income tax Ⓙ.

Before this pay period, Alice has earned $80,000 (40 weeks × $2,000 salary per week). Since Alice receives no overtime, her $2,000 salary per week represents her gross pay (pay before any deductions).

After this pay period, Alice has earned $82,000 ($80,000 + $2,000).

The **Federal Insurance Contribution Act (FICA)** funds the **Social Security** program. The program includes Old Age and Disability, Medicare, Survivor Benefits, and so

FIGURE 9.1
Employee's W-4 form

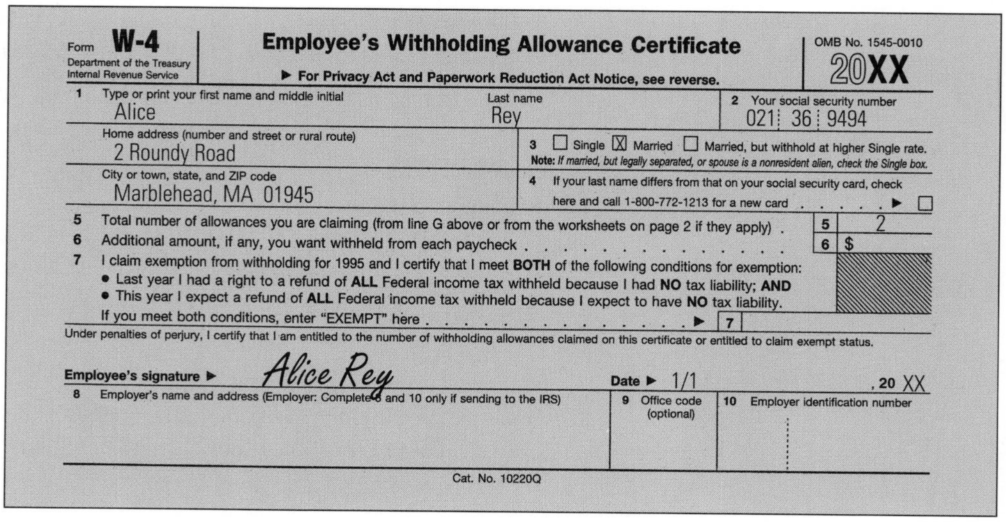
Form **W-4** Department of the Treasury Internal Revenue Service
Employee's Withholding Allowance Certificate
► For Privacy Act and Paperwork Reduction Act Notice, see reverse.
OMB No. 1545-0010 **20XX**

1 Type or print your first name and middle initial: Alice — Last name: Rey
2 Your social security number: 021 36 9494
Home address (number and street or rural route): 2 Roundy Road
3 ☐ Single ☒ Married ☐ Married, but withhold at higher Single rate.
Note: If married, but legally separated, or spouse is a nonresident alien, check the Single box.
City or town, state, and ZIP code: Marblehead, MA 01945
4 If your last name differs from that on your social security card, check here and call 1-800-772-1213 for a new card . . . . . ► ☐
5 Total number of allowances you are claiming (from line G above or from the worksheets on page 2 if they apply) . 5 | 2
6 Additional amount, if any, you want withheld from each paycheck . . . . 6 | $
7 I claim exemption from withholding for 1995 and I certify that I meet **BOTH** of the following conditions for exemption:
• Last year I had a right to a refund of **ALL** Federal income tax withheld because I had **NO** tax liability; **AND**
• This year I expect a refund of **ALL** Federal income tax withheld because I expect to have **NO** tax liability.
If you meet both conditions, enter "EXEMPT" here . . . . ► 7
Under penalties of perjury, I certify that I am entitled to the number of withholding allowances claimed on this certificate or entitled to claim exempt status.
Employee's signature ► Alice Rey **Date ►** 1/1 , 20 XX
8 Employer's name and address (Employer: Complete 8 and 10 only if sending to the IRS) 9 Office code (optional) 10 Employer identification number
Cat. No. 10220Q

on. The FICA tax requires separate reporting for Social Security and **Medicare.** We will use the following rates for Glo Company:

	Rate	Base
Social Security	6.20%	$80,400*
Medicare	1.45	No base

*The 2002 rate is 6.20% on a base of $84,900.

These rates mean that Alice Rey will pay Social Security taxes on the first $80,400 she earns this year. After earning $80,400, Alice's wages will be exempt from Social Security. Note that Alice will be paying Medicare taxes on all wages since Medicare has no base cutoff.

(F), (G)—Taxable earnings for Social Security and Medicare

To help keep Glo's record straight, the *taxable earnings column only shows what wages will be taxed. This amount is not the tax.* For example, in week 41, only $400 of Alice's salary will be taxable for Social Security.

$80,400 Social Security base
− 80,000 (B)
$ 400

(H)—Social Security

To calculate Alice's Social Security tax, we multiply $400 (F) by 6.2%:

$400 × .062 = $24.80

(I)—Medicare

Since Medicare has no base, Alice's entire weekly salary is taxed 1.45%, which is multiplied by $2,000.

$2,000 × .0145 = $29.00

(J)—FIT

Using the W-4 form Alice completed, Glo deducts **federal income tax withholding (FIT).** The more allowances an employee claims, the less money Glo deducts from the employee's paycheck. Glo uses the percentage method to calculate FIT.[2]

The Percentage Method[3]   Today, since many companies do not want to store the tax tables, they use computers for their payroll. These companies use the **percentage method.** For this method we use Table 9.1 and Table 9.2 from Circular E to calculate Alice's FIT.

Step 1.   In Table 9.1, locate the weekly withholding for one allowance. Multiply this number by 2.

$55.77 × 2 = $111.54

TABLE 9.1
Percentage method income tax withholding table

Payroll Period	One Withholding Allowance
Weekly	$ 55.77
Biweekly	111.54
Semimonthly	120.83
Monthly.	241.67
Quarterly	725.00
Semiannually.	1,450.00
Annually	2,900.00
Daily or miscellaneous (each day of the payroll period)	11.15

[2] The *Business Math Handbook* has a sample of the wage bracket method.
[3] An alternative method is called the wage bracket method that is shown in the *Business Math Handbook.*

Step 2.   Subtract $111.54 in Step 1 from Alice's total pay.

$$\begin{array}{r} \$2{,}000.00 \\ -\quad 111.54 \\ \hline \$1{,}888.46 \end{array}$$

Step 3.   In Table 9.2, locate the married person's weekly pay table. The $1,888.46 falls between $960 and $2,023. The tax is $125.40 plus 28% of the excess over $960.

$$\begin{array}{r} \$1{,}888.46 \\ -\quad 960.00 \\ \hline \$\ \ 928.46 \end{array}$$

Tax $125.40 + .28($928.46)

$125.40 + $259.97 = $385.37

Ⓚ—SIT

We assume a 6% **state income tax (SIT).**

$2,000 × .06 = $120.00

Ⓛ—Health insurance
Ⓜ—Net pay

Alice contributes $100 per week for health insurance.
Alice's **net pay** is her gross pay less all deductions.

$$\begin{array}{rl} \$2{,}000.00 & \text{gross} \\ -\quad\ \ 24.80 & \text{Social Security} \\ -\quad\ \ 29.00 & \text{Medicare} \\ -\quad 385.37 & \text{FIT} \\ -\quad 120.00 & \text{SIT} \\ -\quad 100.00 & \text{health insurance} \\ \hline =\ \$1{,}340.83 & \text{net pay} \end{array}$$

Employers' Responsibilities

In the first section of this unit, we saw that Alice contributed to Social Security and Medicare. Glo Company has the legal responsibility to match her contributions. Besides matching Social Security and Medicare, Glo must pay two important taxes that employees do not have to pay—federal and state unemployment taxes.

Federal Unemployment Tax Act (FUTA)

The federal government participates in a joint federal-state unemployment program to help unemployed workers. At this writing, employers pay the government a 6.2% **FUTA** tax on the first $7,000 paid to employees as wages during the calendar year. Any wages in excess of $7,000 per worker are exempt wages and are not taxed for FUTA. If the total cumulative amount the employer owes the government is less than $100, the employer can pay the liability yearly (end of January in the following calendar year). If the tax is greater than $100, the employer must pay it within a month after the quarter ends.

Companies involved in a state unemployment tax fund can usually take a 5.4% credit against their FUTA tax. *In reality, then, companies are paying .8% (.008) to the federal unemployment program.* In all our calculations, FUTA is .008.

Bob Daemmrich/Stock Boston

EXAMPLE   Assume a company had total wages of $19,000 in a calendar year. No employee earned more than $7,000 during the calendar year. The FUTA tax is .8% (6.2% minus the company's 5.4% credit for state unemployment tax). How much does the company pay in FUTA tax?

The company calculates its FUTA tax as follows:

$$\begin{array}{l} 6.2\%\ \text{FUTA tax} \\ -\ 5.4\%\ \text{credit for SUTA tax} \\ \hline =\ \ .8\%\ \text{tax for FUTA} \end{array}$$

.008 × $19,000 = $152 FUTA tax due to federal government

State Unemployment Tax Act (SUTA)

The current **SUTA** tax in many states is 5.4% on the first $7,000 the employer pays an employee. Some states offer a merit rating system that results in a lower SUTA rate for companies with a stable employment period. The federal government still allows 5.4% credit on FUTA tax to companies entitled to the lower SUTA rate. Usually states also

TABLE 9.2   Percentage method income tax withholding taxes

TABLE 1—WEEKLY Payroll Period

(a) SINGLE person (including head of household)—

If the amount of wages (after subtracting withholding allowances) is:		The amount of income tax to withhold is:	
Not over $51		$0	

Over—	But not over—		of excess over—
$51	—$552 . .	15%	—51
$552	—$1,196 . .	$75.15 plus 28%	—552
$1,196	—$2,662 . .	$255.47 plus 31%	—1,196
$2,662	—$5,750 . .	$709.93 plus 36%	—2,662
$5,750	. . . . . .	$1,821.61 plus 39.6%	—5,750

(b) MARRIED person—

If the amount of wages (after subtracting withholding allowances) is:		The amount of income tax to withhold is:	
Not over $124		$0	

Over—	But not over—		of excess over—
$124	—$960 . .	15%	—$124
$960	—$2,023 . .	$125.40 plus 28%	—$960
$2,023	—$3,292 . .	$423.04 plus 31%	—$2,023
$3,292	—$5,809 . .	$816.43 plus 36%	—$3,292
$5,809	. . . . . .	$1,722.55 plus 39.6%	—$5,809

TABLE 2—BIWEEKLY Payroll Period

(a) SINGLE person (including head of household)—

If the amount of wages (after subtracting withholding allowances) is:		The amount of income tax to withhold is:	
Not over $102		$0	

Over—	But not over—		of excess over—
$102	—$1,104 . .	15%	—$102
$1,104	—$2,392 . .	$150.30 plus 28%	—$1,104
$2,392	—$5,323 . .	$510.94 plus 31%	—$2,392
$5,323	—$11,500 . .	$1,419.55 plus 36%	—$5,323
$11,500	. . . . . .	$3,643.27 plus 39.6%	—$11,500

(b) MARRIED person—

If the amount of wages (after subtracting withholding allowances) is:		The amount of income tax to withhold is:	
Not over $248		$0	

Over—	But not over—		of excess over—
$248	—$1,919 . .	15%	—$248
$1,919	—$4,046 . .	$250.65 plus 28%	—$1,919
$4,046	—$6,585 . .	$846.21 plus 31%	—$4,046
$6,585	—$11,617 . .	$1,633.30 plus 36%	—$6,585
$11,617	. . . . . .	$3,444.82 plus 39.6%	—$11,617

TABLE 3—SEMIMONTHLY Payroll Period

(a) SINGLE person (including head of household)—

If the amount of wages (after subtracting withholding allowances) is:		The amount of income tax to withhold is:	
Not over $110		$0	

Over—	But not over—		of excess over—
$110	—$1,196 . .	15%	—$110
$1,196	—$2,592 . .	$162.90 plus 28%	—$1,196
$2,592	—$5,767 . .	$553.78 plus 31%	—$2,592
$5,767	—$12,458 . .	$1,538.03 plus 36%	—$5,767
$12,458	. . . . . .	$3,946.79 plus 39.6%	—$12,458

(b) MARRIED person—

If the amount of wages (after subtracting withholding allowances) is:		The amount of income tax to withhold is:	
Not over $269		$0	

Over—	But not over—		of excess over—
$269	—$2,079 . .	15%	—$269
$2,079	—$4,383 . .	$271.50 plus 28%	—$2,079
$4,383	—$7,133 . .	$916.62 plus 31%	—$4,383
$7,133	—$12,585 . .	$1,769.12 plus 36%	—$7,133
$12,585	. . . . . .	$3,731.84 plus 39.6%	—$12,585

TABLE 4—MONTHLY Payroll Period

(a) SINGLE person (including head of household)—

If the amount of wages (after subtracting withholding allowances) is:		The amount of income tax to withhold is:	
Not over $221		$0	

Over—	But not over—		of excess over—
$221	—$2,392 . .	15%	—$221
$2,392	—$5,183 . .	$325.65 plus 28%	—$2,392
$5,183	—$11,533 . .	$1,107.13 plus 31%	—$5,183
$11,533	—$24,917 . .	$3,075.63 plus 36%	—$11,533
$24,917	. . . . . .	$7,893.87 plus 39.6%	—$24,917

(b) MARRIED person—

If the amount of wages (after subtracting withholding allowances) is:		The amount of income tax to withhold is:	
Not over $538		$0	

Over—	But not over—		of excess over—
$538	—$4,158 . .	15%	—$538
$4,158	—$8,767 . .	$543.00 plus 28%	—$4,158
$8,767	—$14,267 . .	$1,833.52 plus 31%	—$8,767
$14,267	—$25,171 . .	$3,538.52 plus 36%	—$14,267
$25,171	. . . . . .	$7,463.96 plus 39.6%	—$25,171

charge companies with a poor employment record a higher SUTA rate. However, these companies cannot take any more than the 5.4% credit against the 6.2% federal unemployment rate.

EXAMPLE   Assume that a company has total wages of $20,000 and $4,000 of the wages are exempt from SUTA. What are the company's SUTA and FUTA taxes if the company's SUTA rate is 5.8% due to a poor employment record?

The exempt wages (over $7,000 earnings per worker) are not taxed for SUTA or FUTA. So the company owes the following SUTA and FUTA taxes:

$20,000
$-$ 4,000 (exempt wages)
$16,000 $\times$ .058 = $928 SUTA

Federal FUTA tax would then be:
$16,000 $\times$ .008 = $128

You can check your progress with the following Practice Quiz.

LU 9–2 PRACTICE QUIZ

1. Calculate Social Security taxes, Medicare taxes, and FIT for Joy Royce. Joy's company pays her a monthly salary of $9,500. She is single and claims 1 deduction. Before this payroll, Joy's cumulative earnings were $76,000. (Social Security maximum is 6.2% on $80,400, and Medicare is 1.45%.) Calculate FIT by the percentage method.

2. Jim Brewer, owner of Arrow Company, has three employees who earn $300, $700, and $900 a week. Assume a state SUTA rate of 5.1%. What will Jim pay for state and federal unemployment taxes for the first quarter?

✓ **SOLUTIONS**

1. **Social Security**

   $80,400
   $-$ 76,000
   $ 4,400 $\times$ .062 = $272.80

   FIT

   Percentage method: $9,500.00
   $241.67 $\times$ 1 = $-$ 241.67 (Table 9.1)
   $9,258.33

   $5,183 to $11,533 $\longrightarrow$ $1,107.13 plus 31% of excess over $5,183

   $9,258.33   (Table 9.2)
   $-$ 5,183.00
   $4,075.33 $\times$ .31 = $1,263.35
                          + 1,107.13
                          $2,370.48

   Medicare

   $9,500 $\times$ .0145 = $137.75

2. 13 weeks $\times$ $300 = $ 3,900
    13 weeks $\times$ $700 =   9,100 ($9,100 $-$ $7,000) $\longrightarrow$ $2,100 ⎫ Exempt wages
    13 weeks $\times$ $900 = 11,700 ($11,700 $-$ $7,000) $\longrightarrow$ 4,700 ⎬ (not taxed for
                             $24,700 $6,800 ⎭ FUTA or SUTA)

    $24,700 $-$ $6,800 = $17,900 taxable wages
    SUTA = .051 $\times$ $17,900 = $912.90
    FUTA = .008 $\times$ $17,900 = $143.20

    Note: FUTA remains at .008 whether SUTA rate is higher or lower than standard.

Chapter Organizer and Reference Guide		
Topic	**Key point, procedure, formula**	**Example(s) to illustrate situation**
Gross pay, p. 223	Hours employee worked $\times$ Rate per hour	$6.50 per hour at 36 hours Gross pay = 36 $\times$ $6.50 = $234
Overtime, p. 223	Gross earnings (pay) = Regular pay + Earnings at overtime rate ($1\frac{1}{2}$)	$6 per hour; 42 hours Gross pay = (40 $\times$ $6) + (2 $\times$ $9) = $240 + $18 = $258
Straight piece rate, p. 224	Gross pay = Number of units produced $\times$ Rate per unit	1,185 units; rate per unit, $.89 Gross pay = 1,185 $\times$ $.89 = $1,054.65

(continues)

Chapter Organizer and Reference Guide (concluded)		
Topic	**Key point, procedure, formula**	**Example(s) to illustrate situation**
Differential pay schedule, p. 224	Rate on each item is related to the number of items produced.	1–500 at \$.84; 501–1,000 at \$.96; 900 units produced. Gross pay = (500 × \$.84) + (400 × \$.96) = \$420 + \$384 = \$804
Straight commission, p. 224	Total sales × Commission rate Any draw would be subtracted from earnings.	\$155,000 sales; 6% commission \$155,000 × .06 = \$9,300
Variable commission scale, p. 225	Sales at different levels pay different rates of commission.	Up to \$5,000, 5%; \$5,001 to \$10,000, 8%; over \$10,000, 10% Sold: \$6,500 Solution: (\$5,000 × .05) + (\$1,500 × .08) = \$250 + \$120 = \$370
Salary plus commission, p. 225	Regular wages (fixed) + Commissions earned	Base \$400 per week + 2% on sales over \$14,000 Actual sales: \$16,000 \$400 (base) + (.02 × \$2,000) = \$440
Payroll register, p. 226	Multicolumn form to record payroll. Married and paid weekly. (Table 9.1) Claims 0 allowances. FICA rates from chapter.	(see table below)
FICA, p. 227 Social Security Medicare	6.2% on \$80,400 (S.S.) 1.45% (Med.) (Check IRS for latest rates.)	If John earns \$99,000, what did he contribute for the year to Social Security and Medicare? S.S.: \$80,400 × .062 = \$4,984.80 Med.: \$99,000 × .0145 = \$1,435.50

FIT calculation (percentage method), p. 227	*Facts:*
	  Al Doe: Married
	  Claims: 2
	  Paid weekly: \$1,600
		Use same example as above
		  \$1,600.00
		− 111.54 (\$55.77 × 2) Table 9.1
		  \$1,488.46
		By Table 9.2:
		  \$1,488.46
		− 960.00
		  \$ 528.46
		\$125.40 + .28(\$528.46)
		\$125.40 + \$147.97 = \$273.37

State and federal unemployment, p. 228	Employer pays these taxes. Rates are 6.2% on \$7,000 for federal and 5.4% for state on \$7,000. 6.2% − 5.4% = .8% federal rate after credit. If state unemployment rate is higher than 5.4%, no additional credit is taken. If state unemployment rate is less than 5.4%, the full 5.4% credit can be taken for federal unemployment.	Cumulative pay before payroll, \$6,400; this week's pay, \$800. What are state and federal unemployment taxes for employer, assuming a 5.2% state unemployment rate? State ⟶ .052 × \$600 = \$31.20 Federal ⟶ .008 × \$600 = \$4.80 (\$6,400 + \$600 = \$7,000 maximum)

Payroll register example table:

Earnings	Deductions			Net pay
Gross	FICA			
	S.S.	Med.	FIT	
1,100	68.20	15.95	174	841.85

Key terms

Biweekly, *p. 222*
Deductions, *p. 223*
Differential pay schedule, *p. 224*
Draw, *p. 224*
Employee's Withholding
  Allowance Certificate (W-4),
  p. 226
Fair Labor Standards
  Act, *p. 223*
Federal income tax withholding
  (FIT), *p. 227*

Federal Insurance Contribution
  Act (FICA), *p. 226*
Federal Unemployment Tax Act
  (FUTA), *p. 228*
Gross pay, *p. 223*
Medicare, *p. 227*
Monthly, *p. 227*
Net pay, *p. 228*
Overrides, *p. 225*
Overtime, *p. 223*
Payroll register, *p. 226*

Percentage method, *p. 227*
Semimonthly, *p. 222*
Social Security, *p. 226*
State income tax (SIT), *p. 228*
State Unemployment Tax Act
  (SUTA), *p. 228*
Straight commission, *p. 224*
Variable commission scale, *p. 225*
W-4, *p. 226*
Weekly, *p. 222*

**Critical Thinking
Discussion Questions**

1. Explain the difference between biweekly and semimonthly. Explain what problems may develop if a retail store hires someone on straight commission to sell cosmetics.

2. Explain what each column of a payroll register records (p. 226) and how each number is calculated. Social Security tax is based on a specific rate and base; Medicare tax is based on a rate but no base. Do you think this is fair to all taxpayers?

3. What taxes are the responsibility of the employer? How can an employer benefit from a merit-rating system for state unemployment?

END-OF-CHAPTER PROBLEMS

Name _____ Date _____

DRILL PROBLEMS

Complete the following table:

	Employee	M	T	W	Th	F	Hours	Rate per hour	Gross pay
9–1.	Jane Reese	9	7	6	8	5		$6.60	
9–2.	Pete Joll	7	9	8	8	8		$7.25	

Complete the following table (assume the overtime for each employee is a time-and-a-half rate after 40 hours):

	Employee	M	T	W	Th	F	Sa	Total regular hours	Total overtime hours	Regular rate	Overtime rate	Gross earnings
9–3.	Blue	12	9	9	9	9	3			$8.00		
9–4.	Tagney	14	8	9	9	5	1			$7.60		

Calculate gross earnings:

	Worker	Number of units produced	Rate per unit	Gross earnings
9–5.	Lang	510	$2.10	
9–6.	Swan	846	$ .58	

Calculate the gross earnings for each apple picker based on the following differential pay scale:

1–1,000:	$.03 each	1,001–1,600	$.05 each	over 1,600	$.07 each

	Apple picker	Number of apples picked	Gross earnings
9–7.	Ryan	1,600	
9–8.	Rice	1,925	

	Employee	Total sales	Commission rate	Draw	End-of-month commission received
9–9.	Reese	$300,000	7%	$8,000	

Ron Company has the following commission schedule:

Commission rate	Sales
2%	Up to $80,000
3.5%	Excess of $80,000 to $100,000
4%	More than $100,000

Calculate the gross earnings of Ron Company's two employees:

	Employee	Total sales	Gross earnings
9–10.	Bill Moore	$ 70,000	
9–11.	Ron Ear	$155,000	

Complete the following table, given that A Publishing Company pays its salespeople a weekly salary plus a 2% commission on all net sales over $5,000 (no commission on returned goods):

	Employee	Gross sales	Return	Net sales	Given quota	Commission sales	Commission rates	Total commission	Regular wage	Total wage
9–12.	Ring	$ 8,000	$25		$5,000		2%		$250	
9–13.	Porter	$12,000	$100		$5,000		2%		$250	

Calculate the Social Security and Medicare deductions for the following employees (assume a tax rate of 6.2% on $80,400 for Social Security and 1.45% for Medicare):

	Employee	Cumulative earnings before this pay period	Pay amount this period	Social Security	Medicare
9–14.	Miller	$70,000	$1,600		
9–15.	Long	$79,900	$1,900		
9–16.	Clancey	$100,000	$2,950		

Complete the following payroll register. Calculate FIT by the percentage method for this weekly period; Social Security and Medicare are the same rates as in the previous problems. No one will reach the maximum for FICA.

	Employee	Marital status	Allowances claimed	Gross pay	FIT	FICA S.S.	FICA Med.	Net pay
9–17.	Al Holland	M	2	$1,200				
9–18.	French	M	4	$1,900				

9–19. Given the following, calculate the state (assume 5.3%) and federal unemployment taxes that the employer must pay for each of the first two quarters. The federal unemployment tax is .8% on the first $7,000.

Payroll summary		
	Quarter 1	Quarter 2
Bill Adams	$4,000	$ 8,000
Rich Haines	8,000	14,000
Alice Smooth	3,200	3,800

WORD PROBLEMS

9–20. On November 7, 2000, the *Omaha World-Herald* reported on the hourly wages for building equipment operators. The top wage for union members will be $20.95, an increase of $1.25 or 6.3%. This week J. W. Masters worked 48 hours and is entitled to time-and-a-half overtime. How much did J. W. earn?

9–21. The March 13, 2001, issue of the *Chicago Tribune* reported that stagehands would be paid $22.40 per hour. Bill Crew, a stagehand, worked 33 hours. **(a)** How much will be deducted from Bill's pay for Social Security? **(b)** How much will be deducted for Medicare?

9–22. On December 10, 2000, the *Dallas Morning News* reported that retailers were attempting to entice workers to Dallas area stores with higher wages. Alex Healey is employed by Pier 1 and earns $6.25 per hour plus a 3% commission on sales. This week Alex worked 36 hours and sold $2,340 in merchandise. How much did Alex earn?

Excel

9–23. Dennis Toby is a salesclerk at Northwest Department Store. Dennis receives $8 per hour plus a commission of 3% on all sales. Assume Dennis works 30 hours and has sales of $1,900. What is his gross pay?

9–24. Blinn Corporation pays its employees on a graduated commission scale: 3% on first $40,000 sales, 4% on sales from $40,001 to $85,000, and 6% on sales greater than $85,000. Bill Burns had $87,000 sales. What commission did Bill earn?

9–25. Robin Hartman earns $600 per week plus 3% of sales over $6,500. Robin's sales are $14,000. How much does Robin earn?

9–26. Pat Maninen earns a gross salary of $2,100 each week. What are Pat's first week's deductions for Social Security and Medicare? Will any of Pat's wages be exempt from Social Security and Medicare for the calendar year? Assume a rate of 6.2% on $80,400 for Social Security and 1.45% for Medicare.

9–27. Richard Gaziano is a manager for Health Care, Inc. Health Care deducts Social Security, Medicare, and FIT (by percentage method) from his earnings. Assume the same Social Security and Medicare rates as in Problem 9–26. Before this payroll, Richard is $1,000 below the maximum level for Social Security earnings. Richard is married, is paid weekly, and claims 2 exemptions. What is Richard's net pay for the week if he earns $1,300?

9–28. Len Mast earned $2,200 for the last two weeks. He is married, is paid biweekly, and claims 3 exemptions. What is Len's income tax? Use the percentage method.

9–29. Westway Company pays Suzie Chan $2,200 per week. By the end of week 50, how much did Westway deduct for Suzie's Social Security and Medicare for the year? Assume Social Security is 6.2% on $80,400 and 1.45% for Medicare. What state and federal unemployment taxes does Westway pay on Suzie's yearly salary? The state unemployment rate is 5.1%. FUTA is .8%.

9–30. Morris Leste, owner of Carlson Company, has three employees who earn $400, $500, and $700 per week. What are the total state and federal unemployment taxes that Morris owes for the first 11 weeks of the year and for week 30? Assume a state rate of 5.6% and a federal rate of .8%.

CHALLENGE PROBLEMS

9–31. On January 14, 2001, the *Miami Herald* reported that a school psychologist earns $50,000 a year in the Miami-Dade public school system. She is single and claims one exemption. **(a)** What would be taken out of her check each month for Social Security? **(b)** What would be taken out each month for Medicare? **(c)** What would be taken out for FIT using the percentage method?

9–32. Bill Rose is a salesperson for Boxes, Inc. He believes his $1,460.47 monthly paycheck is in error. Bill earns a $1,400 salary per month plus a 9.5% commission on sales over $1,500. Last month, Bill had $8,250 in sales. Bill believes his traveling expenses are 16% of his weekly gross earnings before commissions. Monthly deductions include Social Security, $126.56; Medicare, $29.60; FIT, $239.29; union dues, $25.00; and health insurance, $16.99. Calculate the following: **(a)** Bill's monthly take-home pay, and indicate the amount his check was under- or overstated, and **(b)** Bill's weekly traveling expenses. Round your final answer to the nearest dollar.

SUMMARY PRACTICE TEST

1. Calculate Jeff's gross pay (he is entitled to time and a half). *(p. 223)*

M	T	W	Th	F	Total hours	Rate per hour	Gross pay
$9\frac{1}{2}$	$8\frac{1}{4}$	$10\frac{1}{2}$	$7\frac{1}{4}$	$11\frac{1}{2}$		$9.00	

2. Lee Winn sells shoes for JCPenney. JCPenney pays Lee $8 per hour plus a 3% commission on all sales. Assume Lee works 37 hours for the week and has $7,000 sales. What is Lee's gross pay? *(p. 224)*

3. Long Company pays its employees on a graduated commission scale: 4% on the first $30,000 sales; 6% on sales from $30,001 to $80,000; and 10% on sales of more than $80,000. Larry Felt, an employee of Long, has $180,000 in sales. What commission did Larry earn? *(p. 224)*

4. Bee Smith, an accountant for Aware.com, earned $70,000 from January to June. In July, Bee earned $15,000. Assume a tax rate of 6.2% for Social Security on $80,400 and 1.45% on Medicare. How much are the July taxes for Social Security and Medicare? *(p. 227)*

5. Maggie Kate earns $900 per week. She is married and claims 2 exemptions. What is Maggie's income tax? Use the percentage method. *(p. 227)*

6. John Jones pays his two employees $600 and $900 per week. Assume a state unemployment tax rate of 5.7% and a federal unemployment tax rate of .8%. What state and federal unemployment taxes will John pay at the end of quarter 1 and quarter 2? *(p. 228)*

Paul Hanlon hopes that his success story will inspire **UNDERACHIEVING STUDENTS**.

JUST YOUR AVERAGE MILLIONAIRE

Name: Paul Hanlon, 42, Largo, Fla.
Achievement: Went from a minimum-wage job to running his own company.
Sign of success: Retired at age 39 after selling his firm, Folio Inc., for about $20 million.
How he did it: A below-average student in school, Hanlon attended junior college and then took a job for minimum wage plus commissions selling pop-up displays for trade shows. At age 27, he borrowed $47,000 to buy out his divi-

sion for the cost of its inventory. Over time he created more-elaborate displays and acquired such big-name clients as GE, Oracle and Reebok.
Sources of help: His father, who encouraged him to think positively, and his employees, who helped him get across what he calls "the 99th yard line."
Lesson learned: Never believe that you are destined to fail.
Next goal: Go into schools and give motivational talks to students. ◀

PHOTOGRAPH BY MEREDITH HEUER

Business Math Issue

Underachieving students working for minimum wage will never have a success story to tell.
1. List the key points of the article and information to support your position.
2. Write a group defense of your position using math calculations to support your view.

Slater's

BUSINESS MATH SCRAPBOOK
WITH INTERNET APPLICATION
Putting Your Skills to Work

Veteran Comics Artist Fired Over Suit

DANIEL S. DECARLO, the principal cartoonist on "Betty and Veronica" for Archie Comics for the past 40 years, has been fired after filing a breach-of-contract lawsuit against the comic-book publisher.

The artist seeks $250,000 in damages because a coming Universal Pictures film, "Josie and the Pussycats," is based on characters Mr. DeCarlo created.

The groovy, fictional all-girl band may be familiar from the popular comic books and television cartoons. Mr. DeCarlo's suit, filed in New York State Supreme Court, alleges that Archie Comic Publications Inc. is using his characters, Josie, Melody and Pepper, for "purposes other than newsstand comic strips and comic books." A movie based on the comic begins filming in August, starring newcomer Rachel Leigh Cook (star of "She's All That") as Josie and Parker Posey as her nemesis, Alexandra.

The case goes to the heart of "work-for-hire" disputes that have shaken the comic-book industry in recent years.

*The creator of **Josie** (above) has sued Archie Comics.*

Archie Comic Publications, Inc.

Many artists signed away rights to characters they created only to see the characters become the center of lucrative film franchises such as "Superman" and "Batman."

Mr. DeCarlo, 80, says he invented Josie in 1957, basing her on his wife of the same name. His wife's spotted-cat outfit for a costume party inspired the group's outfits.

Archie Comics acknowledges that Mr. DeCarlo is the creator of Josie. But a prepared statement from the company notes that Archie Comics is the copyright owner and terms his claims "baseless."

Archie Comics informed Mr. DeCarlo earlier this month that his services were no longer needed. The company disputes the suit's contention that it is using the characters beyond what Mr. DeCarlo agreed to.

"He is making certain claims relating to ownership that we believe fail to actively portray the role that others had," says Charles Grimes, the company's legal counsel, who says that some characters were a collaboration with other cartoonists. Archie will be happy to "embrace" Mr. DeCarlo after the lawsuit is settled, he adds, but "it was hard on a day-to-day basis to interact with him, when he was allowing his attorney to pursue such an aggressive posture."

Universal Pictures Inc., which is producing the movie, said the company doesn't comment on pending lawsuits.

PROJECT A
Investigate the concept of work for hire. Does the artist have a case? Check out the Universal Pictures website.

Internet Projects: See text website (www.mhhe.com/slater7e) and *The Business Math Internet Resource Guide.*

239

VIDEO CASE
Washburn Guitars

Washburn International, founded in 1883, makes 80 models of instruments, both custom and for the mass market. Washburn is a privately held company with over 100 employees and annual sales of $48 million. This compares to its annual sales of $300,000 when Rudy Schlacher took over in 1976. When he acquired the company, about 250 guitars were produced per month; now 15,000 are produced each month.

The Washburn tradition of craftsmanship and innovation has withstood the tests of economics, brand competition, and fashion. Since its birth in Chicago, the name Washburn has been branded into the world's finest stringed instruments. To maintain quality, Washburn must have an excellent pool of qualified employees who are passionate about craftsmanship.

Washburn consolidated its four divisions in an expansive new 130,000 square foot plant in Mundelein, Illinois. The catalyst for consolidating operations in Mundelein was a chronic labor shortage in Elkhart and Chicago. The Mundelein plant was the ideal home for all Washburn operations because it had the necessary space, was cost effective, and gave Washburn access to a labor pool.

To grow profitably, Washburn must also sell its other products. To keep Washburn's 16 domestic salespeople tuned in to the full line, the company offers an override incentive. It is essential that to produce quality guitars, Washburn must keep recruiting dedicated, well-qualified, and team-oriented employees and provide them with profitable incentives.

PROBLEM 1
$120,000 was paid to 16 of Washburn's salespeople in override commissions. **(a)** What was the average amount paid to each salesperson? **(b)** What amount of the average sales commission will go toward the salesperson's Social Security tax? **(c)** What amount will go toward Medicare?

PROBLEM 2
Washburn is seeking a Sales and Marketing Coordinator with a bachelor's degree or equivalent experience, knowledgeable in Microsoft Office. This position pays $25,000 to $35,000, depending on experience. Assume a person is paid weekly and earns $32,500. Using the percentage method, what would be the taxes withheld for a married person who claims 3 exemptions?

PROBLEM 3
Guitarists hoping for a little country music magic in their playing can now buy an instrument carved out of oak pews from the former home of the Grand Ole Opry. Only 243 of the Ryman Limited Edition Acoustic Guitars are being made, each costing $6,250. Among the first customers were singers Vince Gill, Amy Grant, and Loretta Lynn. Ms. Lynn purchased two guitars. What would be the total revenue received by Washburn if all the guitars are sold?

PROBLEM 4
Under Washburn's old pay system, phone reps received a commission of 1.5% only on instruments they sold. Now the phone reps are paid an extra .75% commission on field sales made in their territory; the outside salespeople still get a commission up to 8%, freeing them to focus on introducing new products and holding in-store clinics. Assume sales were $65,500: **(a)** How much would phone reps receive? **(b)** How much would the outside salespeople receive?

PROBLEM 5
Washburn introduced the Limited Edition EA27 Gregg Allman Signature Series Festival guitar—only 500 guitars were produced with a selling price of $1,449.90. If Washburn's markup is 35% on selling price, what was Washburn's total cost for the 500 guitars?

PROBLEM 6
Retailers purchased $511 million worth of guitars from manufacturers—some 861,300 guitars—according to a study done by the National Association of Music Merchants. **(a)** What would be the average selling price of a guitar? **(b)** Based on the average selling price, if manufacturer's markup on cost is 40%, what would be the average cost?

PROBLEM 7
A Model NV 300 acoustic-electric guitar is being sold for a list price of $1,899.90, with a cash discount of 3/10, n/30. Sales tax is 7% and shipping is $30.40. How much is the final price if the cash discount period was met?

PROBLEM 8
A Model M3SWE mandolin has a list price of $1,299.90, with a chain discount of 5/3/2. **(a)** What would be the trade discount amount? **(b)** What would be the net price?

PROBLEM 9
A purchase was made of 2 Model J282DL six-string acoustic guitars at $799.90 each, with cases priced at $159.90, and 3 Model EA10 festival series acoustic-electric guitars at $729.90, with cases listed at $149.90. If sales tax is 6%, what is the total cost?

PROBLEM 10
Production of guitars has increased by what percent since Rudy Schlacher took over Washburn?

Central-Bank Watch

Interest rates, current and forecast for March 1

	CURRENT	FORECAST
Global*	5.06%	4.83%
U.S.	5.50	5.00
Brazil	15.25	14.25
Mexico	18.31	17.00
Chile	4.75	4.50
Euro	4.75	4.75
U.K.	5.75	5.75
Poland	19.00	17.00
Hong Kong	8.50	8.00
China	5.85	5.85
South Korea	5.00	5.00
India	8.00	8.00
Taiwan	4.38	4.13

*GDP-weighted average
Source: J.P. Morgan Chase & Co.

©2001 Dow Jones & Company, Inc.

You may want to check current interest rates on the Internet.

242

10

Simple Interest

LU 10–1: Calculation of Simple Interest and Maturity Value

- Calculate simple interest and maturity value for months and years *(p. 244)*.

- Calculate simple interest and maturity value by **(a)** exact interest and **(b)** ordinary interest *(pp. 245–46)*.

LU 10–2: Finding Unknown in Simple Interest Formula

- Using the interest formula, calculate the unknown when the other two (principal, rate, or time) are given *(pp. 247–48)*.

LU 10–3: U.S. Rule—Making Partial Note Payments before Due Date

- List the steps to complete the U.S. Rule *(pp. 249–50)*.

- Complete the proper interest credits under the U.S. Rule *(pp. 249–50)*.

William Johnson/Stock Boston

We live in a credit society. For various reasons many people and businesses use credit. An article in *The Wall Street Journal* titled "Loan Totaling $25 Billion Is Arranged to Repay Debt" reports on a $25 billion business loan of AT&T Corp. When you need a personal loan, you can get your loan from a single bank. There are three banks arranging the loan for AT&T; they are asking five banks to share in making the loan.

The price people and businesses must pay to get credit is **interest,** which is a rental charge for money. Can you imagine the interest that must be paid on a loan of $25 billion?

This chapter is about simple interest. The principles discussed apply whether you are paying interest or receiving interest. Let's begin by learning how to calculate simple interest.

LEARNING UNIT 10–1 | CALCULATION OF SIMPLE INTEREST AND MATURITY VALUE

Jan Carley, a young attorney, rented an office in a professional building. Since Jan recently graduated from law school, she was short of cash. To purchase office furniture for her new office, Jan went to her bank and borrowed $30,000 for 6 months at an 8% annual interest rate.

The original amount Jan borrowed ($30,000) is the **principal** (face value) of the loan. Jan's price for using the $30,000 is the interest rate (8%) the bank charges on a yearly basis. Since Jan is borrowing the $30,000 for 6 months, Jan's loan will have a **maturity value** of $31,200—the principal plus the interest on the loan. Thus, Jan's price for using the furniture before she can pay for it is $1,200 interest, which is a percent of the principal for a specific time period. To make this calculation, we use the following formula:

$$\text{Maturity value } (MV) = \text{Principal } (P) + \text{Interest } (I)$$

$$\$31,200 \quad = \quad \$30,000 \quad + \quad \$1,200$$

Jan's furniture purchase introduces **simple interest**—the cost of a loan, usually for 1 year or less. Simple interest is only on the original principal or amount borrowed. Let's examine how the bank calculated Jan's $1,200 interest.

Simple Interest Formula

To calculate simple interest, we use the following **simple interest formula:**

$$\text{Simple interest } (I) = \text{Principal } (P) \times \text{Rate } (R) \times \text{Time } (T)$$

In this formula, rate is expressed as a decimal, fraction, or percent; and time is expressed in years or a fraction of a year.

EXAMPLE   Jan Carley borrowed $30,000 for office furniture. The loan was for 6 months at an annual interest rate of 8%. What are Jan's interest and maturity value?

Using the simple interest formula, the bank determined Jan's interest as follows:

In your calculator, multiply $30,000 times .08 times 6. Divide your answer by 12. You could also use the % key—multiply $30,000 times 8% times 6 and then divide your answer by 12.

Step 1.   Calculate the interest.

$$I = \$30,000 \times .08 \times \frac{6}{12}$$
$$\qquad\quad (P) \qquad (R) \quad\ (T)$$
$$= \$1,200$$

Step 2.   Calculate the maturity value.

$$MV = \$30,000 + \$1,200$$
$$\qquad\quad\ (P) \qquad\quad (I)$$
$$= \boxed{\$31,200}$$

Now let's use the same example and assume Jan borrowed $30,000 for 1 year. The bank would calculate Jan's interest and maturity value as follows:

Step 1.   Calculate the interest.

$$I = \$30,000 \times .08 \times 1 \text{ year}$$
$$\qquad\quad (P) \qquad (R) \qquad (T)$$
$$= \$2,400$$

Step 2. Calculate the maturity value.

$$MV = \$30,000 + \$2,400$$
$$\quad\quad\quad\;\;\; (P) \quad\quad (I)$$
$$= \$32,400$$

Let's use the same example again and assume Jan borrowed $30,000 for 18 months. Then Jan's interest and maturity value would be calculated as follows:

Step 1. Calculate the interest.

$$I = \$30,000 \times .08 \times \frac{18}{12}^{1}$$
$$\quad\;\;\, (P) \quad\quad (R) \quad (T)$$
$$= \$3,600$$

Step 2. Calculate the maturity value.

$$MV = \$30,000 + \$3,600$$
$$\quad\quad\quad\;\;\; (P) \quad\quad (I)$$
$$= \$33,600$$

Next we'll turn our attention to two common methods we can use to calculate simple interest when a loan specifies its beginning and ending dates.

Two Methods for Calculating Simple Interest and Maturity Value

Method 1: Exact Interest (365 Days) The Federal Reserve banks and the federal government use the **exact interest** method. The *exact interest* is calculated by using a 365-day year. For **time,** we count the exact number of days in the month that the borrower has the loan. The day the loan is made is not counted, but the day the money is returned is counted as a full day. This method calculates interest by using the following fraction to represent time in the formula:

From the *Business Math Handbook*

July 6	187th day
March 4	− 63rd day
	124 days
	(exact time of loan)
March	31
	− 4
	27
April	30
May	31
June	30
July	+ 6
	124 days

$$\boxed{\text{Time} = \frac{\text{Exact number of days}}{365} \leftarrow}$$

Exact interest

For this calculation, we use the exact days-in-a-year calendar from the *Business Math Handbook.* You learned how to use this calendar in Chapter 7, pages 173–74.

EXAMPLE On March 4, Peg Carry borrowed $40,000 at 8% interest. Interest and principal are due on July 6. What is the interest cost and the maturity value?

Step 1. Calculate the interest.

$$I = P \times R \times T$$
$$= \$40,000 \times .08 \times \frac{124}{365}$$
$$= \$1,087.12 \text{ (rounded to nearest cent)}$$

Step 2. Calculate the maturity value.

$$MV = P + I$$
$$= \$40,000 + \$1,087.12$$
$$= \$41,087.12$$

Method 2: Ordinary Interest (360 Days) In the **ordinary interest** method, time in the formula $I = P \times R \times T$ is equal to the following:

$$\boxed{\text{Time} = \frac{\text{Exact number of days}}{360} \leftarrow}$$

Ordinary interest

Since banks commonly use the ordinary interest method, it is known as the **Banker's Rule.** Banks charge a slightly higher rate of interest because they use 360 days instead of 365 in the denominator. By using 360 instead of 365, the calculation is supposedly simplified. Consumer groups, however, are questioning why banks can use 360 days, since this benefits the bank and not the customer. The use of computers and calculators no longer makes the simplified calculation necessary. For example, after a court case in Oregon, banks began calculating interest on 365 days except in mortgages.

---

[1]This is the same as 1.5 years.

Now let's replay the Peg Carry example we used to illustrate Method 1 to see the difference in bank interest when we use Method 2.

EXAMPLE   On March 4, Peg Carry borrowed $40,000 at 8% interest. Interest and principal are due on July 6. What are the interest cost and the maturity value?

Step 1.   Calculate the interest.

$$I = \$40,000 \times .08 \times \frac{124}{360}$$
$$= \$1,102.22$$

Step 2.   Calculate the maturity value.

$$MV = P + I$$
$$= \$40,000 + \$1,102.22$$
$$= \boxed{\$41,102.22}$$

Note: By using Method 2, the bank increases its interest by $15.10.

$$
\begin{array}{ll}
\$1,102.22 & \longleftarrow \text{Method 2} \\
- \ 1,087.12 & \\
\hline
\$\quad 15.10 & \longleftarrow \text{Method 1}
\end{array}
$$

LU 10–1 PRACTICE QUIZ

Calculate simple interest (round to the nearest cent):
1. $14,000 at 4% for 9 months
2. $25,000 at 7% for 5 years
3. $40,000 at $10\frac{1}{2}$% for 19 months
4. On May 4, Dawn Kristal borrowed $15,000 at 8%. Dawn must pay the principal and interest on August 10. What are Dawn's simple interest and maturity value if you use the exact interest method?
5. What are Dawn Kristal's (Problem 4) simple interest and maturity value if you use the ordinary interest method?

✓ SOLUTIONS

1. $\$14,000 \times .04 \times \dfrac{9}{12} = \boxed{\$420}$

2. $\$25,000 \times .07 \times 5 = \boxed{\$8,750}$

3. $\$40,000 \times .105 \times \dfrac{19}{12} = \boxed{\$6,650}$

4. $\begin{array}{lr} \text{August 10} \longrightarrow & 222 \\ \text{May 4} \quad \longrightarrow & - \ 124 \\ \hline & 98 \end{array}$ $\$15,000 \times .08 \times \dfrac{98}{365} = \boxed{\$322.19}$

$MV = \$15,000 + \$322.19 = \boxed{\$15,322.19}$

5. $\$15,000 \times .08 \times \dfrac{98}{360} = \boxed{\$326.67}$ $MV = \$15,000 + \$326.67 = \boxed{\$15,326.67}$

LEARNING UNIT 10–2 | FINDING UNKNOWN IN SIMPLE INTEREST FORMULA

The Wall Street Journal clipping "Size of Loan Problem Is Debated in Japan" reports on the seriousness of Japan's loan problem. Many Japanese companies are having trouble paying the interest or the principal on their loans. For some of these companies, their loan problems are related to the amount of principal they borrowed. Think of the loan principal as its face value.

This unit begins with the formula used to calculate the principal of a loan. Then it discusses how to calculate the rate of interest and the time. In all the calculations, we use 360 days and round only final answers.

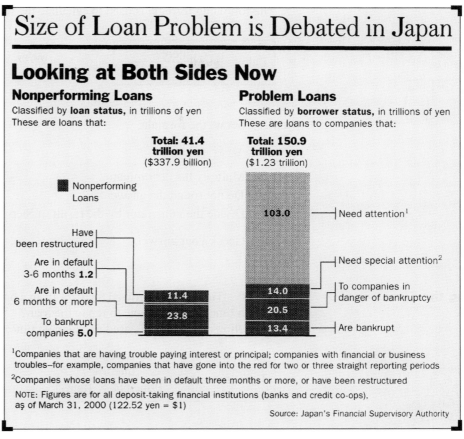

Looking at Both Sides Now

©2001 Dow Jones & Company, Inc.

Finding the Principal

EXAMPLE   Tim Jarvis paid the bank $19.48 interest at 9.5% for 90 days. How much did Tim borrow?

The following formula is used to calculate the principal of a loan:

$$\text{Principal} = \frac{\text{Interest}}{\text{Rate} \times \text{Time}}$$

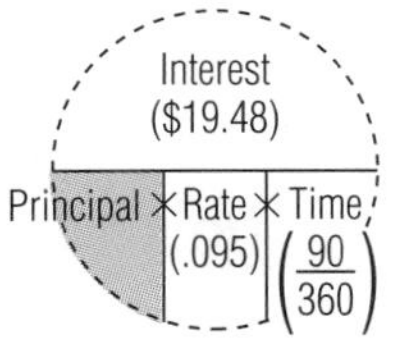

Note how we illustrated this in the margin. The shaded area is what we are solving for. When solving for principal, rate, or time, you are dividing. Interest will be in the numerator, and the denominator will be the other two elements multiplied by each other.

Step 1.   Set up the formula.

$$P = \frac{\$19.48}{.095 \times \frac{90}{360}}$$

Step 2.   Multiply the denominator.

.095 times 90 divided by 360 (do not round)

$$P = \frac{\$19.48}{.02375}$$

Step 3.   Divide the numerator by the result of Step 2. $P = \$820.21$

Step 4.   Check your answer.

$$\$19.48 = \$820.21 \times .095 \times \frac{90}{360}$$
$$\quad (I) \qquad\qquad (P) \qquad (R) \qquad (T)$$

Step 2. When using a calculator, press

.095 × 90 ÷ 360 M+.

Step 3. When using a calculator, press

19.48 ÷ MR =.

Finding the Rate

EXAMPLE   Tim Jarvis borrowed $820.21 from a bank. Tim's interest is $19.48 for 90 days. What rate of interest did Tim pay?

(margin figure)

Interest ($19.48)

Principal × Rate × Time
(.095) ($\frac{90}{360}$)

The following formula is used to calculate the rate of interest:

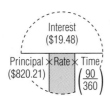

$$\text{Rate} = \frac{\text{Interest}}{\text{Principal} \times \text{Time}}$$

Step 1. Set up the formula.

$$R = \frac{\$19.48}{\$820.21 \times \frac{90}{360}}$$

Step 2. Multiply the denominator. Do not round the answer.

$$R = \frac{\$19.48}{\$205.0525}$$

Step 3. Divide the numerator by the result of Step 2. $R = 9.5\%$

Step 4. Check your answer.

$$\$19.48 = \$820.21 \times .095 \times \frac{90}{360}$$
$$\quad (I) \qquad (P) \qquad (R) \qquad (T)$$

Finding the Time

EXAMPLE Tim Jarvis borrowed $820.21 from a bank. Tim's interest is $19.48 at 9.5%. How much time does Tim have to repay the loan?

The following formula is used to calculate time:

$$\text{Time (in years)} = \frac{\text{Interest}}{\text{Principal} \times \text{Rate}}$$

Step 1. Set up the formula.

$$T = \frac{\$19.48}{\$820.21 \times .095}$$

Step 2. Multiply the denominator. Do not round the answer.

$$T = \frac{\$19.48}{\$77.91995}$$

Step 3. Divide the numerator by the result of Step 2. $T = .25$ years

Step 4. Convert years to days (assume 360 days). $.25 \times 360 = \boxed{90 \text{ days}}$

Step 5. Check your answer.

$$\$19.48 = \$820.21 \times .095 \times \frac{90}{360}$$
$$\quad (I) \qquad (P) \qquad (R) \qquad (T)$$

Step 2. When using a calculator, press

$\boxed{820.21}\ \boxed{\times}\ \boxed{.095}\ \boxed{M+}$.

Step 3. When using a calculator, press

$\boxed{19.48}\ \boxed{\div}\ \boxed{MR}\ \boxed{=}$.

Before we go on to Learning Unit 10–3, let's check your understanding of this unit.

LU 10–2 PRACTICE QUIZ

Complete the following (assume 360 days):

	Principal	Interest rate	Time (days)	Simple interest
1.	?	5%	90 days	$8,000
2.	$7,000	?	220 days	350
3.	$1,000	8%	?	300

✓ **SOLUTIONS**

1. $\dfrac{\$8,000}{.05 \times \dfrac{90}{360}} = \dfrac{\$8,000}{.0125} = \boxed{\$640,000} \qquad P = \dfrac{I}{R \times T}$

2. $\dfrac{\$350}{\$7,000 \times \dfrac{220}{360}} = \dfrac{\$350}{\$4,277.7777} = \boxed{8.18\%} \qquad R = \dfrac{I}{P \times T}$

   (do not round)

3. $\dfrac{\$300}{\$1,000 \times .08} = \dfrac{\$300}{\$80} = 3.75 \times 360 = \boxed{1,350 \text{ days}} \qquad T = \dfrac{I}{P \times R}$

LEARNING UNIT 10-3 | U.S. RULE—MAKING PARTIAL NOTE PAYMENTS BEFORE DUE DATE

Often a person may want to pay off a debt in more than one payment before the maturity date. The **U.S. Rule** allows the borrower to receive proper interest credits. This rule states that any partial loan payment first covers any interest that has built up. The remainder of the partial payment reduces the loan principal. Courts or legal proceedings generally use the U.S. Rule. The Supreme Court originated the U.S. Rule in the case of *Story v. Livingston.*

EXAMPLE   Joe Mill owes $5,000 on an 11%, 90-day note. On day 50, Joe pays $600 on the note. On day 80, Joe makes an $800 additional payment. Assume a 360-day year. What is Joe's adjusted balance after day 50 and after day 80? What is the ending balance due?

To calculate $600 payment on day 50:

Step 1.   Calculate interest on principal from date of loan to date of first principal payment. Round to nearest cent.

$$I = P \times R \times T$$
$$I = \$5{,}000 \times .11 \times \frac{50}{360}$$
$$I = \$76.39$$

Step 2.   Apply partial payment to interest due. Subtract remainder of payment from principal. This is the **adjusted balance** (principal).

```
   $600.00 payment
 −   76.39 interest
   $523.61            $5,000.00 principal
                    −   523.61
                      $4,476.39 adjusted
                                balance—
                                principal
```

To calculate $800 payment on day 80:

Step 3.   Calculate interest on adjusted balance that starts from previous payment date and goes to new payment date. Then apply Step 2.

Compute interest on $4,476.39 for 30 days (80 − 50)

$$I = \$4{,}476.39 \times .11 \times \frac{30}{360}$$
$$I = \$41.03$$

```
   $800.00 payment
 −   41.03 interest
   $758.97
                    $4,476.39
                  −   758.97
                    $3,717.42 adjusted
                              balance
```

Step 4.   At maturity, calculate interest from last partial payment. *Add* this interest to adjusted balance.

Ten days are left on note since last payment.

$$I = \$3{,}717.42 \times .11 \times \frac{10}{360}$$
$$I = \$11.36$$

Balance owed = $3,728.78 $\left(\begin{matrix} \$3{,}717.42 \\ + \quad 11.36 \end{matrix} \right)$

Note that when Joe makes two partial payments, Joe's total interest is $128.78 ($76.39 + $41.03 + $11.36). If Joe had repaid the entire loan after 90 days, his interest payment would have been $137.50—a total savings of $8.72.

LU 10-3 PRACTICE QUIZ

Polly Flin borrowed $5,000 for 60 days at 8%. On day 10, Polly made a $600 partial payment. On day 40, Polly made a $1,900 partial payment. What is Polly's ending balance due under the U.S. Rule (assume a 360-day year)?

✓ **SOLUTIONS**

$$\$5,000 \times .08 \times \frac{10}{360} = \$11.11$$

$$\begin{array}{r} \$600.00 \\ - \quad 11.11 \\ \hline \$588.89 \end{array} \qquad \begin{array}{r} \$5,000.00 \\ - \quad 588.89 \\ \hline \$4,411.11 \end{array}$$

$$\$4,411.11 \times .08 \times \frac{30}{360} = \$29.41$$

$$\begin{array}{r} \$1,900.00 \\ - \quad 29.41 \\ \hline \$1,870.59 \end{array} \qquad \begin{array}{r} \$4,411.11 \\ - \ 1,870.59 \\ \hline \$2,540.52 \end{array}$$

$$\$2,540.52 \times .08 \times \frac{20}{360} = \$11.29$$

$$\begin{array}{r} \$ \quad 11.29 \ \leftarrow \\ + \ 2,540.52 \\ \hline \boxed{\$2,551.81} \end{array}$$

Chapter Organizer and Reference Guide

Topic	Key point, procedure, formula	Example(s) to illustrate situation
Simple interest for months, p. 244	Interest = Principal × Rate × Time (I) $\quad$ (P) $\quad$ (R) $\quad$ (T)	$2,000 at 9% for 17 months $I = \$2,000 \times .09 \times \frac{17}{12}$ $I = \boxed{\$255}$
Exact interest, p. 245	$T = \dfrac{\text{Exact number of days}}{365}$ $I = P \times R \times T$	$1,000 at 10% from January 5 to February 20 $I = \$1,000 \times .10 \times \frac{46}{365}$ Feb. 20: $\quad$ 51 days Jan. 5: $\quad \underline{- \ 5}$ $\qquad\qquad$ 46 days $I = \boxed{\$12.60}$
Ordinary interest (Bankers Rule), p. 245	$T = \dfrac{\text{Exact number of days}}{360}$ $I = P \times R \times T$ $\boxed{\text{Higher interest costs}}$	$I = \$1,000 \times .10 \times \frac{46}{360}$ $\ (51 - 5)$ $I = \boxed{\$12.78}$
Finding unknown in simple interest formula (use 360 days), p. 246	$I = P \times R \times T$	Use this example for illustrations of simple interest formula parts: $1,000 loan at 9%, 60 days $I = \$1,000 \times .09 \times \frac{60}{360} = \boxed{\$15}$
Finding the principal, p. 247	$P = \dfrac{I}{R \times T}$	$P = \dfrac{\$15}{.09 \times \frac{60}{360}} = \dfrac{\$15}{.015} = \boxed{\$1,000}$
Finding the rate, p. 248	$R = \dfrac{I}{P \times T}$	$R = \dfrac{\$15}{\$1,000 \times \frac{60}{360}} = \dfrac{\$15}{166.66666} = .09$ $= \boxed{9\%}$ *Note:* We did not round the denominator.
Finding the time, p. 248	$T = \dfrac{I}{P \times R}$ (in years) Multiply answer by 360 days to convert answer to days for ordinary interest.	$T = \dfrac{\$15}{\$1,000 \times .09} = \dfrac{\$15}{\$90} = .1666666$ $.1666666 \times 360 = 59.99 = \boxed{60 \ \text{days}}$

(continues)

Chapter Organizer and Reference Guide (concluded)

Topic	Key point, procedure, formula	Example(s) to illustrate situation

U.S. Rule (use 360 days), p. 249	Calculate interest on principal from date of loan to date of first partial payment.	12%, 120 days, $2,000
		Partial payments:
		  On day 40; $250
		  On day 60; $200

	Calculate adjusted balance by subtracting from principal the partial payment less interest cost. The process continues for future partial payments with the adjusted balance used to calculate cost of interest from last payment to present payment.	*First payment:*
		$I = \$2,000 \times .12 \times \dfrac{40}{360}$
		$I = \$26.67$
		  $250.00 payment
		  − 26.67 interest
		  $223.33
		
		  $2,000.00 principal
		  − 223.33
		  $1,776.67 adjusted balance
		
		Second payment:
		$I = \$1,776.67 \times .12 \times \dfrac{20}{360}$
		$I = \$11.84$
		  $200.00 payment
		  − 11.84 interest
		  $188.16
		
		  $1,776.67
		  − 188.16
		  $1,588.51 adjusted balance

	Balance owed equals last adjusted balance plus interest cost from last partial payment to final due date.	*60 days left:*
		$\$1,588.51 \times .12 \times \dfrac{60}{360} = \$31.77$
		$1,588.51 + $31.77 = $1,620.28 balance due
		Total interest = $26.67
		        11.84
		      + 31.77
		        $70.28

Key terms	Adjusted balance, *p. 249* Banker's Rule, *p. 245* Exact interest, *p. 245* Interest, *p. 244*	Maturity value, *p. 244* Ordinary interest, *p. 245* Principal, *p. 244* Simple interest, *p. 244* Simple interest formula, *p. 244* Time, *p. 245* U.S. Rule, *p. 249*

Critical Thinking Discussion Questions

1. What is the difference between exact interest and ordinary interest? With the increase of computers in banking, do you think that the ordinary interest method is a dinosaur in business today?

2. Explain how to use the portion formula to solve the unknowns in the simple interest formula. Why would rounding the answer of the denominator result in an inaccurate final answer?

3. Explain the U.S. Rule. Why in the last step of the U.S. Rule is the interest added, not subtracted?

Name _____ Date _____

DRILL PROBLEMS

Calculate the simple interest and maturity value for the following problems. Round to the nearest cent as needed.

	Principal	Interest rate	Time	Simple interest	Maturity value
10–1.	$9,000	4%	13 mo.		
10–2.	$12,000	5%	$1\frac{3}{4}$ yr.		
10–3.	$7,000	$8\frac{1}{4}$%	7 mo.		

Complete the following, using ordinary interest:

	Principal	Interest rate	Date borrowed	Date repaid	Exact time	Interest	Maturity value
10–4. Excel	$1,000	8%	Mar. 8	June 9			
10–5. Excel	$585	9%	June 5	Dec. 15			
10–6. Excel	$1,200	12%	July 7	Jan. 10			

Complete the following, using exact interest:

	Principal	Interest rate	Date borrowed	Date repaid	Exact time	Interest	Maturity value
10–7.	$1,000	8%	Mar. 8	June 9			
10–8.	$585	9%	June 5	Dec. 15			
10–9.	$1,200	12%	July 7	Jan. 10			

Solve for the missing item in the following (round to the nearest hundredth as needed):

	Principal	Interest rate	Time (months years)	Simple interest
10–10.	$400	5%	?	$100
10–11.	?	7%	$1\frac{1}{2}$ years	$200
10–12.	$5,000	?	6 months	$300

10–13. Use the U.S. Rule to solve for total interest costs, balances, and final payments (use ordinary interest).

  Given   Principal: $10,000, 8%, 240 days
              Partial payments: On 100th day, $4,000
                                 On 180th day, $2,000

WORD PROBLEMS

10–14. The May 2001 issue of *Credit Union Magazine* stated that federal credit unions are limited to charging interest rates of no more than 18% per annum on any loan. A $2,500 loan is given to a member at 18%, and the interest is $225. When will the loan be due (assume 360 days)?

10–15. Rebecca Shore borrowed $80,000 to pay for her child's education at Ithaca College. Rebecca must repay the loan at the end of 8 months in one payment with $7\frac{1}{2}$% interest. How much interest must Rebecca pay? What is the maturity value?

10–16. On September 12, Jody Jansen went to Sunshine Bank to borrow $2,300 at 9% interest. Jody plans to repay the loan on January 27. Assume the loan is on ordinary interest. What interest will Jody owe on January 27? What is the total amount Jody must repay at maturity?

10–17. Kelly O'Brien met Jody Jansen (Problem 10–16) at Sunshine Bank and suggested she consider the loan on exact interest. Recalculate the loan for Jody under this assumption.

10–18. On May 3, 2001, Excellon Resources, Inc., negotiated a short-term loan of $685,000. On May 28, 2001, *Market News Publishing* reported that the loan is due October 1, 2001, and carries a 6.86% interest rate. Use ordinary interest to calculate the interest. What is the total amount Excellon would pay on the maturity date?

10–19. Gordon Rosel went to his bank to find out how long it will take for $1,200 to amount to $1,650 at 8% simple interest. Please solve Gordon's problem. Round time in years to the nearest tenth.

10–20. Bill Moore is buying a van. His April monthly interest at 12% was $125. What was Bill's principal balance at the beginning of April? Use 360 days.

10–21. On April 5, 2004, Janeen Camoct took out an $8\frac{1}{2}$% loan for $20,000. The loan is due March 9, 2005. Use ordinary interest to calculate the interest. What total amount will Janeen pay on March 9, 2005?

10–22. Sabrina Bowers took out the same loan as Janeen (Problem 10–21). Sabrina's terms, however, are exact interest. What is Sabrina's difference in interest? What will she pay on March 9, 2005?

10–23. Max Wholesaler borrowed $2,000 on a 10%, 120-day note. After 45 days, Max paid $700 on the note. Thirty days later, Max paid an additional $630. What is the final balance due? Use the U.S. Rule to determine the total interest and ending balance due. Use ordinary interest.

ADDITIONAL SET OF WORD PROBLEMS

10–24. On April 30, 2001, PR Newswire reported on a company that received a short-term loan. The loan was dated April 12, 2001, due April 30, 2001. The rate of interest was 6.5%. The interest earned was $162.50. Using ordinary interest, what was the original amount of the loan?

10–25. The January 2001 issue of *Consumer Reports* gave a report on interest charges. The article mentioned that with a good payment history you could be paying only 9% to 12% on credit cards. With a $560 charge, what would be the interest amount at 9% and at 12% for 1 month?

10–26. On September 14, Jennifer Rick went to Park Bank to borrow $2,500 at $11\frac{3}{4}$% interest. Jennifer plans to repay the loan on January 27. Assume the loan is on ordinary interest. What interest will Jennifer owe on January 27? What is the total amount Jennifer must repay at maturity?

10–27. Steven Linden met Jennifer Rick (Problem 10–26) at Park Bank and suggested she consider the loan on exact interest. Recalculate the loan for Jennifer under this assumption.

10–28. Lance Lopes went to his bank to find out how long it will take for $1,000 to amount to $1,700 at 12% simple interest. Can you solve Lance's problem? Round time in years to the nearest tenth.

10–29. Margie Pagano is buying a car. Her June monthly interest at $12\frac{1}{2}\%$ was $195. What was Margie's principal balance at the beginning of June? Use 360 days. Do not round the denominator before dividing.

10–30. Shawn Bixby borrowed $17,000 on a 120-day, 12% note. After 65 days, Shawn paid $2,000 on the note. On day 89, Shawn paid an additional $4,000. What is the final balance due? Determine total interest and ending balance due by the U.S. Rule. Use ordinary interest.

10–31. Carol Miller went to Europe and forgot to pay her $740 mortgage payment on her New Hampshire ski house. For her 59 days overdue on her payment, the bank charged her a penalty of $15. What was the rate of interest charged by the bank? Round to the nearest hundredth percent (assume 360 days).

10–32. Abe Wolf bought a new kitchen set at Sears. Abe paid off the loan after 60 days with an interest charge of $9. If Sears charges 10% interest, what did Abe pay for the kitchen set (assume 360 days)?

10–33. Joy Kirby made a $300 loan to Robinson Landscaping at 11%. Robinson paid back the loan with interest of $6.60. How long in days was the loan outstanding (assume 360 days)? Check your answer.

10–34. Molly Ellen, bookkeeper for Keystone Company, forgot to send in the payroll taxes due on April 15. She sent the payment November 8. The IRS sent her a penalty charge of 8% simple interest on the unpaid taxes of $4,100. Calculate the penalty. (Remember that the government uses exact interest.)

10–35. Oakwood Plowing Company purchased two new plows for the upcoming winter. In 200 days, Oakwood must make a single payment of $23,200 to pay for the plows. As of today, Oakwood has $22,500. If Oakwood puts the money in a bank today, what rate of interest will it need to pay off the plows in 200 days (assume 360 days)?

CHALLENGE PROBLEMS

10–36. On April 23, 2001, the *Philadelphia Inquirer* reported on mortgage interest. Debbie McAdams paid 8% interest on a $12,500 loan balance. Jan Burke paid $5,000 interest on a $62,500 loan. Based on 1 year: **(a)** What was the amount of interest paid by Debbie? **(b)** What was the interest rate paid by Jan? **(c)** Debbie and Jan are both in the 28% tax bracket. Since the interest is deductible, how much would Debbie and Jan each save in taxes?

10–37. Janet Foster bought a computer and printer at Computerland. The printer had a $600 list price with a $100 trade discount and 2/10, n/30 terms. The computer had a $1,600 list price with a 25% trade discount but no cash discount. On the computer, Computerland offered Janet the choice of (1) paying $50 per month for 17 months with the 18th payment paying the remainder of the balance or (2) paying 8% interest for 18 months in equal payments.

    a. Assume Janet could borrow the money for the printer at 8% to take advantage of the cash discount. How much would Janet save (assume 360 days)?

    b. On the computer, what is the difference in the final payment between choices 1 and 2?

SUMMARY PRACTICE TEST

1. Gracie Sullivan's real estate tax of $1,820.50 was due on December 10, 2004. Gracie lost her job and could not pay her tax bill until February 16, 2005. The penalty for late payment is $9\frac{1}{2}$% ordinary interest. *(p. 244)*

    a. What is the penalty Gracie must pay?

    b. What is the total amount Gracie must pay on February 16?

2. Damien Spaine borrowed $140,000 to pay for his child's education. He must repay the loan at the end of 8 years in one payment with $8\frac{1}{2}$% interest. What is the maturity value Damien must repay? *(p. 244)*

3. On May 11, Frank Soy borrowed $8,000 from Briar Bank at $9\frac{1}{2}\%$ interest. Frank plans to repay the loan on February 15. Assume the loan is on ordinary interest. How much will Frank repay on February 15? *(p. 245)*

4. Joy Blass met Frank Soy (Problem 3) at Briar Bank. After talking with Frank, Joy decided she would like to consider the same loan on exact interest. Can you recalculate the loan for Joy under this assumption? *(p. 245)*

5. Hing Hon is buying a car. Her September monthly interest was $180 at $9\frac{1}{4}\%$ interest. What is Hing's principal balance at the beginning of September? Use 360 days. Do not round the denominator in your calculation. *(p. 247)*

6. Baffour Silva borrowed $12,000 on an 8%, 60-day note. After 10 days, Baffour paid $4,000 on the note. On day 45, Baffour paid $3,000 on the note. What are the total interest and ending balance due by the U.S. Rule? Use ordinary interest. *(p. 249)*

PERSONAL FINANCE

A Kiplinger Approach

DON'T TAKE THIS RATE BAIT

ANTHONY LEO of Al-brightsville, Pa., puts his savings in certificates of deposit for one reason: safety. He says he's a "fellow who was never willing to take a risk." He has never bought a share of stock or a corporate bond. In fact, for a decade he routinely rolled over a $100,000 CD from East Stroudsburg Savings Association, in Stroudsburg, Pa.

But in February 1999 he balked at the skimpy 5% interest rate. That's when an employee told him about a CD paying 7.5% that was being offered through the bank by PrimeVest Financial Services, a brokerage in St. Cloud, Minn. The 7.5% rate was good for one year, after which it would fall to 6%—still better than the bank rate. Leo says he was told the CD would probably be called after a year and in the event that it wasn't, he could redeem it by paying a penalty of 1% or 1.5% of the principal.

Leo bit.

But when the year ended last February, the "one-year callable" CD was not called. When Leo tried to cash it in, he was horrified to learn that it was worth just $80,000. The $1,000 to $1,500 penalty he expected had soared to $20,000.

That's when, Leo says, he learned for the first time that his CD didn't mature for 20 years. He also discovered to his surprise that, because it was a brokered CD, its value could rise or fall based on changes in market interest rates. (PrimeVest won't comment specifically on Leo's complaint,

but says it makes both oral and written disclosures about its CDs.)

Protecting yourself. Leo is not the only saver to get such a rude awakening. Higher-than-market rates have been increasingly used to lure consumers into buying callable CDs. Many savers apparently think "one year" means they can redeem the CD after a year. In fact, such CDs can't be

redeemed until maturity, which could be 20 or more years down the road. The trick is that it is the issuing institution that can redeem the CD at any time after the first year. If rates have dropped, the bank will exercise that right and give savers back their cash to reinvest at lower yields.

But if rates have risen, the bank will keep the CD in force at what then amounts to a below-market rate. If the saver wants to go for a higher yield, he or she will face the same dilemma that confronted Leo. You can sell the CD back to the broker, but you may get back far less than

you originally invested.

In fact, buying a CD from a broker is similar to purchasing a bond. You are guaranteed the return of your principal at maturity. But if you want your money before then, the value of your investment depends on market interest rates. If rates have risen, the value of your CD may have plummeted. Susan Ferris Wyderko, director of the SEC's Office of Investor Education and Assistance, says, "We are seeing people who redeem early losing 20% to 30% of their principal."

Of course, with bonds this is a two-way street. If interest rates drop, the value of a bond rises and you can cash it in for more than you paid for it. Unfortunately, you don't have that opportunity with a callable CD.

When rates drop, the issuing institution can call the CD and issue a new one with a lower yield. "There is a limit on the upside, but not the downside," says Douglas Wilburn, securities commissioner of Missouri. "These savers are getting the worst of both worlds."

If you're offered a CD rate that seems too good to be true, check it out carefully. Be sure you know when the certificate matures and whether it can be called before that date. If you buy a CD from a broker and discover it's not what you expected, Wyderko recommends that you complain vociferously to the brokerage. If that fails, take your complaint to the SEC; there is a complaint form on its Web site, at www.sec.gov. The SEC has been successful in getting reimbursements for savers who were misled into buying callable CDs, says SEC spokesman John Nestor. **K** —*Reporter:* **COURTNEY MCGRATH**

ROXANNA BIKADOROFF

Business Math Issue

Interest rates have little effect on CD sales.
1. List the key points of the article and information to support your position.
2. Write a group defense of your position using math calculations to support your view.

BUSINESS MATH SCRAPBOOK
WITH INTERNET APPLICATION

Putting Your Skills to Work

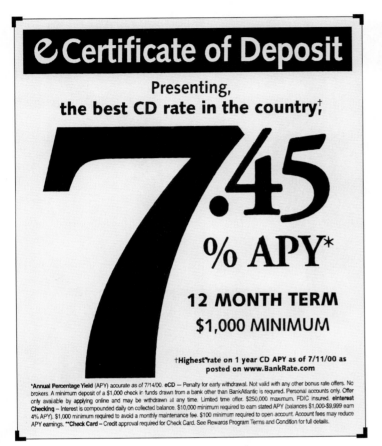

e Certificate of Deposit

Presenting,
the best CD rate in the country,†

7.45

% APY*

12 MONTH TERM

$1,000 MINIMUM

†Highest rate on 1 year CD APY as of 7/11/00 as
posted on www.BankRate.com

*Annual Percentage Yield (APY) accurate as of 7/14/00. eCD — Penalty for early withdrawal. Not valid with any other bonus rate offers. No brokers. A minimum deposit of a $1,000 check in funds drawn from a bank other than BankAtlantic is required. Personal accounts only. Offer only available by applying online and may be withdrawn at any time. Limited time offer. $250,000 maximum. FDIC insured. **einterest Checking** – Interest is compounded daily on collected balance. $10,000 minimum required to earn stated APY (balances $1,000-$9,999 earn 4% APY). $1,000 minimum required to avoid a monthly maintenance fee. $100 minimum required to open account. Account fees may reduce APY earnings. ****Check Card** – Credit approval required for Check Card. See Rewards Program Terms and Condition for full details.

Source: www.bankrate.com.

PROJECT A

If you buy a $3,000 CD from this institution, what would you earn on your money? Visit the website Bankrate.com for the latest CD rates.

PROJECT B

Go to http://ethanallen.com. Suppose you are moving in 8 months. Find a piece of furniture you would like to purchase when you move. If you find a savings account that pays 5% (annual rate) simple interest for 8 months, then how much would you have to invest today to purchase the furniture in 8 months?

Internet Projects: See text website (www.mhhe.com/slater7e) and *The Business Math Internet Resource Guide.*

11

Promissory Notes, Simple Discount Notes, and the Discount Process

LU 11–1: Structure of Promissory Notes; the Simple Discount Note

- Differentiate between interest-bearing and noninterest-bearing notes *(pp. 264–65)*.

- Calculate bank discount and proceeds for simple discount notes *(p. 265)*.

- Calculate and compare the interest, maturity value, proceeds, and effective rate of a simple interest note with a simple discount note *(p. 266)*.

- Explain and calculate the effective rate for a Treasury bill *(p. 266)*.

LU 11–2: Discounting an Interest-Bearing Note before Maturity

- Calculate the maturity value, bank discount, and proceeds of discounting an interest-bearing note before maturity *(p. 267)*.

- Identify and complete the four steps of the discounting process *(p. 268)*.

> *Treasury Beats Retailers With Highest Online Sales*
>
> *Dow Jones Newswires*
>
> NEW YORK—Is the Treasury Department, not **Amazon.com** Inc., the king of electronic retailers? It turns out that the Treasury Department's direct-sales site—which sells bonds, which are as bland as the paper they are printed on—is the largest dollar-volume online seller.
>
> Driven by $3.3 billion in online sales of Treasury securities during 2000, the Treasury Department's sales on its "Treasury Direct" Web site dwarfed most online retailers, includ-
>
> ing Amazon of Seattle, which had net sales of $2.8 billion for 2000. That finding was part of a larger study by the Federal Computer Week magazine and the Pew Internet & American Life Project in Washington.
>
> The dull, predictable qualities of Treasurys have propelled them to be the only real success story in the world of online-bond trading as well. Trading platforms such as **eSpeed**, **BrokerTech** and **TradeWeb**, and online-bond underwriters like **MuniAuction** and **BondBook** have found that, unlike Treasurys, the more variety of securities within a certain fixed-income sector, the less volume they tend to move.

©2001 Dow Jones & Company, Inc.

In this chapter we begin with a discussion of promissory notes and simple discount notes. We also look at the application of discounting with Treasury bills. As you can see from *The Wall Street Journal* clipping "Treasury Beats Retailers with Highest Online Sales," the Treasury Department's direct-sales site on the Web has a larger sales volume than Amazon.com Inc. The chapter concludes with an explanation of how to calculate the discounting of promissory notes.

LEARNING UNIT 11-1 | STRUCTURE OF PROMISSORY NOTES; THE SIMPLE DISCOUNT NOTE

Although businesses frequently sign promissory notes, customers also sign promissory notes. For example, some student loans may require the signing of promissory notes. Appliance stores often ask customers to sign a promissory note when they buy large appliances on credit. As you will see in this unit, promissory notes usually involve the payment of interest.

Structure of Promissory Notes

To borrow money, you must find a lender (a bank or a company selling goods on credit). You must also be willing to pay for the use of the money. In Chapter 10 you learned that interest is the cost of borrowing money for periods of time.

Money lenders usually require that borrowers sign a **promissory note.** This note states that the borrower will repay a certain sum at a fixed time in the future. The note often includes the charge for the use of the money, or the rate of interest. Figure 11.1 shows a sample promissory note with its terms identified and defined. Take a moment to look at each term.

FIGURE 11.1

Interest-bearing promissory note

> $10,000 **a.**   LAWTON, OKLAHOMA *October 2, 2004* **c.**
>
> *Sixty days* **b.**   AFTER DATE   we   PROMISE TO PAY TO
>
> THE ORDER OF   *G.J. Equipment Company* **d.**
>
> *Ten thousand and 00/100---------------------*DOLLARS.
>
> PAYABLE AT   *Able National Bank*
>
> VALUE RECEIVED WITH INTEREST AT *9%* **e.**   REGAL CORPORATION **f.**
>
> NO. *114*   DUE *December 1, 2004*   *J.M. Moore*
>   **g.**   TREASURER

a. Face value: Amount of money borrowed—$10,000. The face value is also the principal of the note.

b. Term: Length of time that the money is borrowed—60 days.

c. Date: The date that the note is issued—October 2, 2004.

d. Payee: The company extending the credit—G.J. Equipment Company.

e. Rate: The annual rate for the cost of borrowing the money—9%.

f. Maker: The company issuing the note and borrowing the money—Regal Corporation.

g. Maturity date: The date the principal and interest rate are due—December 1, 2004.

In this section you will learn the difference between interest-bearing notes and non-interest-bearing notes.

Interest-Bearing versus Noninterest-Bearing Notes

A promissory note can be interest bearing or noninterest bearing. To be **interest bearing,** the note must state the rate of interest. Since the promissory note in Figure 11.1 states that its interest is 9%, it is an interest-bearing note. When the note matures, Regal Corporation "will pay back the original amount (**face value**) borrowed plus interest. The simple interest formula (also known as the interest formula) and the maturity value formula from Chapter 10 are used for this transaction."

> Interest = Face value (principal) × Rate × Time
>
> Maturity value = Face value (principal) + Interest

If you sign a **noninterest-bearing** promissory note for $10,000, you pay back $10,000 at maturity. The maturity value of a noninterest-bearing note is the same as its face value. Usually, noninterest-bearing notes occur for short time periods under special conditions. For example, money borrowed from a relative could be secured by a non-interest-bearing promissory note.

Simple Discount Note

The total amount due at the end of the loan, or the **maturity value (MV),** is the sum of the face value (principal) and interest. Some banks deduct the loan interest in advance. When banks do this, the note is a **simple discount note.**

In the simple discount note, the **bank discount** is the interest that banks deduct in advance and the **bank discount rate** is the percent of interest. The amount that the borrower receives after the bank deducts its discount from the loan's maturity value is the note's **proceeds.** Sometimes we refer to simple discount notes as noninterest-bearing notes. Remember, however, that borrowers *do* pay interest on these notes.

In the example that follows, Pete Runnels has the choice of a note with a simple interest rate (Chapter 10) or a note with a simple discount rate (Chapter 11). Table 11.1 provides a summary of the calculations made in the example and gives the key points that you should remember. Now let's study the example, and then you can review Table 11.1.

EXAMPLE Pete Runnels has a choice of two different notes that both have a face value (principal) of $14,000 for 60 days. One note has a simple interest rate of 8%, while the other note has a simple discount rate of 8%. For each type of note, calculate **(a)** interest owed, **(b)** maturity value, **(c)** proceeds, and **(d)** effective rate.

Simple interest note—Chapter 10	Simple discount note—Chapter 11
Interest	**Interest**
a. I = Face value (principal) × R × T	**a.** I = Face value (principal) × R × T
$I = \$14,000 \times .08 \times \frac{60}{360}$	$I = \$14,000 \times .08 \times \frac{60}{360}$
$I = \$186.67$	$I = \$186.67$
Maturity value	**Maturity value**
b. MV = Face value + Interest	**b.** MV = Face value
$MV = \$14,000 + \$186.67$	$MV = \$14,000$
$MV = \$14,186.67$	
Proceeds	**Proceeds**
c. Proceeds = Face value	**c.** Proceeds = MV − Bank discount
= $14,000	= $14,000 − $186.67
	= $13,813.33
Effective rate	**Effective rate**
d. Rate = $\frac{\text{Interest}}{\text{Proceeds} \times \text{Time}}$	**d.** Rate = $\frac{\text{Interest}}{\text{Proceeds} \times \text{Time}}$
$= \frac{\$186.67}{\$14,000 \times \frac{60}{360}}$	$= \frac{\$186.67}{\$13,813.33 \times \frac{60}{360}}$
= 8%	= 8.11%

TABLE 11.1

Comparison of simple interest note and simple discount note (Calculations from the Pete Runnels example, p. 265)

Simple interest note (Chapter 10)	Simple discount note (Chapter 11)
1. A promissory note for a loan with a term of usually less than 1 year. *Example:* 60 days.	**1.** A promissory note for a loan with a term of usually less than 1 year. *Example:* 60 days.
2. Paid back by one payment at maturity. Face value equals actual amount (or principal) of loan (this is not maturity value).	**2.** Paid back by one payment at maturity. Face value equals maturity value (what will be repaid).
3. Interest computed on face value or what is actually borrowed. *Example:* $186.67.	**3.** Interest computed on maturity value or what will be repaid and not on actual amount borrowed. *Example:* $186.67.
4. Maturity value = Face value + Interest. *Example:* $14,186.67.	**4.** Maturity value = Face value. *Example:* $14,000.
5. Borrower receives the face value. *Example:* $14,000.	**5.** Borrower receives proceeds = Face value − Bank discount. *Example:* $13,813.33.
6. Effective rate (true rate is same as rate stated on note). *Example:* 8%.	**6.** Effective rate is higher since interest was deducted in advance. *Example:* 8.11%.
7. Used frequently instead of the simple discount note. *Example:* 8%.	**7.** Not used as much now because in 1969 congressional legislation required that the true rate of interest be revealed. Still used where legislation does not apply, such as personal loans.

Note that the interest of $186.67 is the same for the simple interest note and the simple discount note. The maturity value of the simple discount note is the same as the face value. In the simple discount note, interest is deducted in advance, so the proceeds are less than the face value. Note that the effective rate for a simple discount note is higher than the stated rate, since the bank calculated the rate on the face of the note and not on what Pete received.

Application of Discounting—Treasury Bills

Treasury Sets Offering Totaling $17 Billion In Short-Term Bills

Dow Jones Newswires

WASHINGTON—The Treasury plans to pay down $5.58 billion on the public debt with the sale Monday of about $17 billion in short-term bills. Maturing bills outstanding total $22.58 billion.

The offering will be divided between $9 billion 13-week and $8 billion 26-week bills maturing July 26, and Oct. 25, respectively. The Cusip number for the three-month bills is 912795HD6. The Cusip number for the six-month bills is 912795HT1.

Noncompetitive tenders for the bills, available in minimum $1,000 denominations, must be received by noon EDT on Monday. Competitive tenders for the bills must be received by 1 p.m. EDT.

©2001 Dow Jones & Company, Inc.

When the government needs money, it sells Treasury bills. A **Treasury bill** is a loan to the federal government for 91 days (13 weeks), or 1 year. Note that *The Wall Street Journal* clipping "Treasury Sets Offering Totaling $17 Billion in Short-Term Bills" states that the Treasury plans to pay down $5.58 billion of the public debt with the sale of about $17 billion in short-term bills.

Treasury bills can be bought over the phone or on the government website. The purchase price (or proceeds) of a Treasury bill is the value of the Treasury bill less the discount. For example, if you buy a $10,000, 13-week Treasury bill at 8%, you pay $9,800, since you have not yet earned your interest ($10,000 × .08 × $\frac{13}{52}$ = $200). At maturity—13 weeks—the government pays you $10,000. You calculate your effective yield (8.16% rounded to the nearest hundredth percent as follows:

$$(\$10,000 - \$200) \longrightarrow \$9,800 \times \frac{13}{52} \quad \frac{\$200}{} = 8.16\% \text{ effective rate}$$

Now it's time to try the Practice Quiz and check your progress.

LU 11–1 PRACTICE QUIZ

1. Warren Ford borrowed $12,000 on a noninterest-bearing, simple discount, $9\frac{1}{2}$%, 60-day note. Assume ordinary interest. What are (a) the maturity value, (b) the bank's discount, (c) Warren's proceeds, and (d) the effective rate to the nearest hundredth percent?

2. Jane Long buys a $10,000, 13-week Treasury bill at 6%. What is her effective rate? Round to the nearest hundredth percent.

✓ **SOLUTIONS**

1. **a.** Maturity value = Face value = $12,000$

    b. Bank discount = MV × Bank discount rate × Time

    $$= \$12,000 \times .095 \times \frac{60}{360}$$

    $$= \$190$$

    c. Proceeds = MV − Bank discount

    $$= \$12,000 - \$190$$

    $$= \$11,810$$

    d. Effective rate = $\dfrac{\text{Interest}}{\text{Proceeds} \times \text{Time}}$

    $$= \frac{\$190}{\$11,810 \times \dfrac{60}{360}}$$

    $$= 9.65\%$$

2. $\$10,000 \times .06 \times \dfrac{13}{52} = \$150$ interest

    $$\frac{\$150}{\$9,850 \times \dfrac{13}{52}} = 6.09\%$$

LEARNING UNIT 11–2 | DISCOUNTING AN INTEREST-BEARING NOTE BEFORE MATURITY

Manufacturers frequently deliver merchandise to retail companies and do not request payment for several months. For example, Roger Company manufactures outdoor furniture that it delivers to Sears in March. Payment for the furniture is not due until September. Roger will have its money tied up in this furniture until September. So Roger requests that Sears sign promissory notes.

If Roger Company needs cash sooner than September, what can it do? Roger Company can take one of its promissory notes to the bank, assuming the company that signed the note is reliable. The bank will buy the note from Roger. Now Roger has discounted the note and has cash instead of waiting until September when Sears would have paid Roger.

Remember that when Roger Company discounts the promissory note to the bank, the company agrees to pay the note at maturity if the maker of the promissory note fails to pay the bank. The potential liability that may or may not result from discounting a note is called a **contingent liability.**

Think of **discounting a note** as a three-party arrangement. Roger Company realizes that the bank will charge for this service. The bank's charge is a **bank discount.** The actual amount Roger receives is the **proceeds** of the note. The four steps below and the formulas in the example that follows will help you understand this discounting process.

Discounting a Note
Step 1. Calculate the interest and maturity value.
Step 2. Calculate the discount period (time the bank holds note).
Step 3. Calculate the bank discount.
Step 4. Calculate the proceeds.

EXAMPLE   Roger Company sold the following promissory note to the bank:

Date of note	Face value of note	Length of note	Interest rate	Bank discount rate	Date of discount
March 8	$2,000	185 days	10%	9%	August 9

What are Roger's (1) interest and maturity value (*MV*)? What are the (2) discount period and (3) bank discount? (4) What are the proceeds?

1. *Calculate Roger's interest and maturity value (MV):*

    $$MV = \text{Face value (principal)} + \text{Interest}$$

    $$\text{Interest} = \$2,000 \times .10 \times \frac{185}{360} \quad \text{Exact number of days over 360}$$

    $$= \$102.78$$
    $$MV = \$2,000 + \$102.78$$
    $$= \$2,102.78$$

Calculating days without table:

March	31
	$-\ 8$
	23
April	30
May	31
June	30
July	31
August	9
	154

185 days—length of note
$-$ 154 days Roger held note

 31 days bank waits

2. *Calculate **discount period:*** Determine the number of days that the bank will have to wait for the note to come due (discount period).

August 9	221 days
March 8	$-\ 67$
	154 days passed before note is discounted

    185 days
    $-$ 154

     31 days bank waits for note to come due

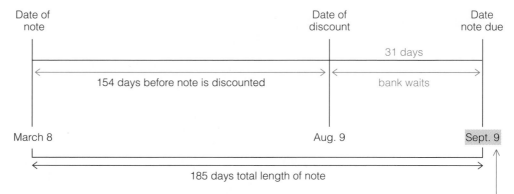

Date of note — March 8

Date of discount — Aug. 9

Date note due — Sept. 9

154 days before note is discounted

31 days bank waits

185 days total length of note

By table: March 8 = 67 days
+ 185
 252 search in table

3. *Calculate bank discount (bank charge):*

    $$\$2,102.78 \times .09 \times \frac{31}{360} = \$16.30$$

    $$\text{Bank discount} = MV \times \text{Bank discount rate} \times \frac{\text{Number of days bank waits for note to come due}}{360}$$

    Step 1

4. *Calculate proceeds:*

    $\$2,102.78$
    $-\quad 16.30$
    $\$2,086.48$

    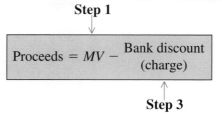

    $$\text{Proceeds} = MV - \text{Bank discount (charge)}$$

    Step 3

    If Roger had waited until September 9, it would have received $2,102.78. Now, on August 9, Roger received $2,000 plus $86.48 interest.

> # Xerox Taps $7 Billion Line of Bank Credit
>
> ## Firm Denies Cash Crunch, As It Responds to Surge In Its Trading Volume
>
> By JOHN HECHINGER
> And JOSEPH PEREIRA
> *Staff Reporters of* THE WALL STREET JOURNAL
> **Xerox** Corp. tapped a $7 billion line of bank credit for the first time after its borrowing was constrained in the commercial paper market.
>   The No. 1 copying-machine maker also issued a statement denying it was in a cash crunch and said that it had plenty of borrowing room. Xerox was responding to a surge in trading Friday that hurt its already struggling stock. The activity was touched off by speculation that it was headed toward a court filing to seek protection from creditors.

©2000 Dow Jones & Company, Inc.

Now let's assume Roger Company received a noninterest-bearing note. Then we follow the four steps for discounting a note except the maturity value is the amount of the loan. No interest accumulates on a noninterest-bearing note. Today, many banks use simple interest instead of discounting. Also, instead of discounting notes, many companies set up *lines of credit* so that additional financing is immediately available.

The Wall Street Journal clipping "Xerox Taps $7 Billion Line of Bank Credit" reports that for the first time, Xerox tapped a $7 billion line of credit. The company denies that tapping this line of credit was necessary because of a cash crunch

It is time to test your understanding of this unit with the following Practice Quiz.

LU 11–2 PRACTICE QUIZ

Date of note	Face value (principal) of note	Length of note	Interest rate	Bank discount rate	Date of discount
April 8	$35,000	160 days	11%	9%	June 8

From the above, calculate **(a)** interest and maturity value, **(b)** discount period, **(c)** bank discount, and **(d)** proceeds. Assume ordinary interest.

✓ SOLUTIONS

a. $I = \$35,000 \times .11 \times \dfrac{160}{360} =$ $\boxed{\$1,711.11}$

$MV = \$35,000 + \$1,711.11 =$ $\boxed{\$36,711.11}$

b.   Discount period = 160 − 61 = $\boxed{\text{99 days.}}$

April	30
	− 8
	22
May	+ 31
	53
June	+ 8
	61

Or by table:

June 8	159
April 8	− 98
	61

c.   Bank discount = $\$36,711.11 \times .09 \times \dfrac{99}{360} =$ $\boxed{\$908.60}$

d.   Proceeds = $36,711.11 − $908.60 = $\boxed{\$35,802.51}$

Chapter Organizer and Reference Guide

Topic	Key point, procedure, formula	Example(s) to illustrate situation
Simple discount note, p. 265	Bank discount (interest) = MV × Bank discount rate × Time Interest based on amount paid back and not what received.	$6,000 × .09 × $\frac{60}{360}$ = $90 Borrower receives $5,910 (the proceeds) and pays back $6,000 at maturity after 60 days. A Treasury bill is a good example of a simple discount note.
Effective rate, p. 266	$\dfrac{\text{Interest}}{\text{Proceeds} \times \text{Time}}$ ↑ What borrower receives (Face value − Discount)	*Example:* $10,000 note, discount rate 12% for 60 days. $I = \$10,000 \times .12 \times \dfrac{60}{360} = \$200$ Effective rate: $\dfrac{\$200}{\$9,800 \times \frac{60}{360}} = \dfrac{\$200}{\$1,633.3333} = $ 12.24% ↑ Amount borrower received

Discounting an interest-bearing note, p. 267	1. Calculate interest and maturity value.
	   I = Face value × Rate × Time
	   MV = Face value + Interest
	2. Calculate number of days bank will wait for note to come due (discount period).
	3. Calculate bank discount (bank charge).
	   MV × Bank discount rate × $\dfrac{\text{Number of days bank waits}}{360}$
	4. Calculate proceeds.
	   MV − Bank discount (charge)
		Example: $1,000 note, 6%, 60-day, dated November 1 and discounted on December 1 at 8%.
		
		1. $I = \$1,000 \times .06 \times \dfrac{60}{360} = \$10$
		    $MV = \$1,000 + \$10 = \$1,010$
		2. 30 days
		3. $\$1,010 \times .08 \times \dfrac{30}{360} = \$6.73$
		4. $\$1,010 − \$6.73 = \$1,003.27$

Key terms	Bank discount, *pp. 265, 267* Bank discount rate, *p. 265* Contingent liability, *p. 267* Discounting a note, *p. 267* Discount period, *p. 268* Effective rate, *p. 266*	Face value, *p. 265* Interest-bearing note, *p. 265* Maker, *p. 264* Maturity date, *p. 265* Maturity value (*MV*), *p. 264* Noninterest-bearing note, *p. 265* Payee, *p. 264* Proceeds, *pp. 265, 267* Promissory note, *p. 264* Simple discount note, *p. 265* Treasury bill, *p. 266*

Critical Thinking Discussion Questions

1. What are the differences between a simple interest note and a simple discount note? Which type of note would have a higher effective rate of interest? Why?

2. What are the four steps of the discounting process? Could the proceeds of a discounted note be less than the face value of the note?

3. What is a line of credit? What could be a disadvantage of having a large credit line?

END-OF-CHAPTER PROBLEMS

Name _____ Date _____

DRILL PROBLEMS

Complete the following table for these simple discount notes. Use the ordinary interest method.

	Amount due at maturity	Discount rate	Time	Bank discount	Proceeds
11–1.	$18,000	$4\frac{3}{4}\%$	190 days		
11–2.	$6,000	$7\frac{1}{4}\%$	240 days		

Calculate the discount period for the bank to wait to receive its money:

	Date of note	Length of note	Date note discounted	Discount period
11–3.	April 12	45 days	May 2	
11–4.	March 7	120 days	June 8	

Solve for maturity value, discount period, bank discount, and proceeds (assume for Problems 11–5 and 11–6 a bank discount rate of 9%).

	Face value (principal)	Rate of interest	Length of note	Maturity value	Date of note	Date note discounted	Discount period	Bank discount	Proceeds
11–5.	$50,000	11%	95 days		June 10	July 18			
11–6.	$25,000	9%	60 days		June 8	July 10			

11–7. Calculate the effective rate of interest (to the nearest hundredth percent) of the following Treasury bill. **Given:** $10,000 Treasury bill, 6% for 13 weeks.

WORD PROBLEMS

Use ordinary interest as needed.

11–8. Matt French borrowed $9,000 for 150 days from Lee Bank. The bank discounted the note at 7%. **(a)** What proceeds does Matt receive? **(b)** Calculate the effective rate to the nearest hundredth percent.

11–9. Jack Tripper signed a $9,000 note at Fleet Bank. Fleet charges a $9\frac{1}{4}\%$ discount rate. If the loan is for 200 days, find **(a)** the proceeds and **(b)** the effective rate charged by the bank (to the nearest tenth percent).

11–10. On June 19, 2001, the *Los Angeles Times* reported on short-term Treasury Department securities. The 3-month interest rate was the lowest in the past 7 years. The Treasury Department sold $14 billion in 3-month bills at a discount rate of 3.435%. An additional $12 billion were sold in 6-month bills at a rate of 3.38%. **(a)** What amount did the Treasury Department receive for the 3-month bills? **(b)** What amount did the Treasury Department receive for the 6-month bills?

11–11. On September 5, Sheffield Company discounted at Sunshine Bank a $9,000 (maturity value), 120-day note dated June 5. Sunshine's discount rate was 9%. What proceeds did Sheffield Company receive?

11–12. On May 16, 2001, the *Columbus Ledger-Enquirer* reported that Sun Trust Bank lowered interest from 7.5% to 7%. Joe Carter, a manufacturer of electric generators, sold $9,880 of goods to Browns Electronics. Browns signed a 90-day promissory note with a maturity value of $10,015.85. Browns decided to discount the note at Sun Trust. The loan has 40 days left to maturity. **(a)** What proceeds will Joe receive with the new rate? **(b)** What proceeds would Joe have received if Sun Trust hadn't lowered its interest rate?

11–13. Annika Scholten bought a $10,000, 13-week Treasury bill at 4%. What is her effective rate? Round to the nearest hundredth percent.

11–14. Ron Prentice bought goods from Shelly Katz. On May 8, Shelly gave Ron a time extension on his bill by accepting a $3,000, 8%, 180-day note. On August 16, Shelly discounted the note at Roseville Bank at 9%. What proceeds does Shelly Katz receive?

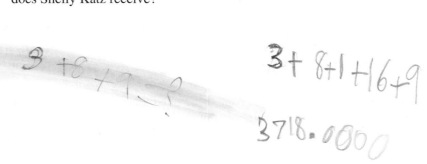

11–15. Rex Corporation accepted a $5,000, 8%, 120-day note dated August 8 from Regis Company in settlement of a past bill. On October 11, Rex discounted the note at Park Bank at 9%. What are the note's maturity value, discount period, and bank discount? What proceeds does Rex receive?

11–16. On May 12, Scott Rinse accepted an $8,000, 12%, 90-day note for a time extension of a bill for goods bought by Ron Prentice. On June 12, Scott discounted the note at Able Bank at 10%. What proceeds does Scott receive?

11–17. Hafers, an electrical supply company, sold $4,800 of equipment to Jim Coates Wiring, Inc. Coates signed a promissory note May 12 with 4.5% interest. The due date was August 10. Short of funds, Hafers contacted Charter One Bank on July 20; the bank agreed to take over the note at a 6.2% discount. What proceeds will Hafers receive?

CHALLENGE PROBLEMS

11–18. On May 30, 2001, the *Los Angeles Times* reported new discount rates for Treasury bills. Three-month Treasury bills totaling $12 billion were sold in $10,000 denominations at a discount rate of 3.605%. In addition, the Treasury Department sold 6-month bills totaling $10 billion at a discount rate of 3.55%. **(a)** What is the discount amount for 3-month bills? **(b)** What is the discount amount for 6-month bills? **(c)** What is the effective rate for 3-month bills? **(d)** What is the effective rate for 6-month bills? Round to nearest hundredth percent.

11–19. Tina Mier must pay a $2,000 furniture bill. A finance company will loan Tina $2,000 for 8 months at a 9% discount rate. The finance company told Tina that if she wants to receive exactly $2,000, she must borrow more than $2,000. The finance company gave Tina the following formula:

$$\text{What to ask for} = \frac{\text{Amount in cash to be received}}{1 - (\text{Discount rate} \times \text{Time of loan})}$$

Calculate Tina's loan request and the effective rate of interest to nearest hundredth percent.

SUMMARY PRACTICE TEST

1. On July 10, Sapient Corporation accepted a $130,000, 90-day, noninterest-bearing note from Link.com. What is the maturity value of the note? *(p. 270)*

2. The face value of a simple discount note is $7,000. The discount is 6% for 95 days. Calculate the following. *(p. 000)*

    Excel   **a.** Amount of interest charged for each note.

        b. Amount borrower would receive.

        c. Amount payee would receive at maturity.

        d. Effective rate (to nearest tenth percent).

3. On August 5, Jeff Jones accepted a $30,000, 8%, 160-day note from Dick Hercher. On October 5, Bill Flynn discounted the note at Roger Bank at 9%. What proceeds did Jeff receive? *(p. 267)*

4. Angle.com accepted a $40,000, $9\frac{1}{4}$%, 120-day note on August 18. Angle discounts the note on September 25 at Rio Bank at 9%. What proceeds did Angle receive? *(p. 267)*

5. The owner of Pete.com signed a $20,000 note at See Bank. See charges a $7\frac{1}{2}$% discount rate. If the loan is for 160 days, find **(a)** the proceeds and **(b)** the effective rate charged by the bank (to the nearest tenth percent). *(p. 266)*

6. John Tobey buys a $10,000, 13-week Treasury bill at $5\frac{1}{2}$%. What is the effective rate? Round to the nearest hundredth percent. *(p. 266)*

STARTING OUT | Building an **EMERGENCY FUND** should be your top savings priority. *By Catherine Siskos*

CASH IN A CRUNCH

BRIAN MACKIN'S 1994 Ford Bronco died abruptly one day last July. Then he got the really bad news: It would cost $3,000 to resuscitate the truck. With no savings and nothing close to three grand in his checking account, Mackin, 24, was forced to abandon the Bronco in his driveway until he could afford the repairs.

Deprived of his wheels, he hitched

Mackin decided to work out a financial fix, too. Instead of moving out of his father's home in Centreville, Va., to get a place of his own as he'd planned, he's taking extra time to pour money into a rainy-day fund.

Standard financial wisdom is to save enough cash to cover three to six months of living expenses—such as rent, food and utilities—in case you lose your job or, like Mackin, are unexpectedly hit with a large bill. But

and 35) has started saving for retirement earlier than previous generations. "But they don't take emergency funds seriously," says Nathan Dungan of Lutheran Brotherhood. One reason for the lack of motivation, Dungan believes, is the strong economy. Dotcoms may be laying people off in droves, but "when was the last time you heard someone say they had spent eight months without a job?" he says.

Credit cards and retirement accounts share the blame because both divert cash from emergency savings and create a false sense of security. "Young adults will tell you that their credit card or their 401(k) plan is their emergency fund," says Patti Houlihan, a financial planner in Oakton, Va.

But financing a calamity with a credit card that charges 19% or 20% interest only creates a vicious cycle of more debt and little savings. It's equally risky to borrow from your 401(k). If you lose or leave your job before you've repaid the money, the loan is considered a distribution. "By the time you pay the taxes and the 10% penalty, you're lucky if you get 50 cents on the dollar," says Houlihan.

Savings shortcut. Nevertheless, the prospect of stockpiling enough cash to cover three to six months' worth of living expenses can deter even the most dedicated saver. "If your income is low and you have a lot of debt, a big cushion may not be feasible," concedes Marianne Shine, a financial planner in Deerfield Beach, Fla.

The solution is to aim for a less-daunting alternative, say a month's worth of expenses. As your income rises, beef up your cash reserve to cover longer periods and to reflect any increases in your spending, such as higher rent. Your rainy-day fund should also cover the deductibles for your health and car insurance, says Shine.

STEVEN RUBIN

● Brian Mackin had to scare up $3,000 to fix his Bronco. Now he sets aside $250 to $300 a month.

rides with family members and friends to get to work, and even called a cab a few times. "I could have set emergency money aside in a savings account, but I just wasn't thinking ahead," admits Mackin, who works as an administrative assistant for, of all places, a financial-planning firm.

After three months of brown-bagging lunch and sacrificing his social life, Mackin had scraped together $2,100. His dad took pity on him and pitched in the rest of the money. And

only 38% of Americans actually keep that much savings on hand, according to a survey by Lutheran Brotherhood, a financial organization sponsored by the Lutheran Church. Young adults are especially short of cash, with just 30% of them reporting they have a cushion that would last at least three months.

It's not that young adults don't save. Because they have doubts about the future of social security, Generation X (adults between the ages of 24

Business Math Issue

Investing into Treasurys means no need to save additional cash for emergencies.
1. List the key points of the article and information to support your position.
2. Write a group defense of your position using math calculations to support your view.

Home Depot Plans Major Expansion Of Loan Program

By RICK BROOKS
Staff Reporter of THE WALL STREET JOURNAL

ATLANTA—**Home Depot** Inc., the giant retailer of supplies to do-it-yourself remodelers, plans a major expansion of a loan program for customers who want to finance a big project without leaving the store.

The company announced that it will expand a home-improvement loan program now being tested in about 65 stores to all 918 of its big-box Home Depot and upscale Expo stores in the U.S. by the fall.

The expansion of the loan program, offering customers on-the-spot approval for a credit line of up to $30,000, could help Home Depot widen its lead over rivals in the quickly consolidating home-improvement retail industry, analysts said.

"It could be meaningful" to Home Depot, said Wayne Hood, an analyst at Prudential Securities Inc. "The determining factor will be how well the stores get behind this program."

So far, Home Depot hasn't put all its muscle into encouraging customers to use the Home Depot credit card, the company's primary financial-services product. While ringing up items, cashiers often don't ask customers if they are carrying a Home Depot card or would like to apply for one. Home Depot cards were used to make purchases of about $6.5 billion in the fiscal year ended Jan. 30, or about 17% of the company's total sales of $38.4 billion.

Heather Wilson, Home Depot's home-improvement loan manager, said customers will be able to apply for a loan by filling out an application available throughout the store and then giving it to a Home Depot employee. The application details will be phoned in to GE Capital Financial Inc., which will decide which loans to approve by using credit-scoring formulas. Approved customers can use their loan to make purchases for up to six months.

Home Depot is considering putting the loan application on a souped-up Web site to be launched in late June or early July.

©2000 Dow Jones & Company, Inc.

PROJECT A

Discuss the pros and cons of the Home Depot's home-improvement loan program. Do you think the competition will imitate it? Visit Home Depot's website to see if any new marketing strategies have been started.

PROJECT B

Go to www.youcalc.com/cgi-bin/youcalc5. exe/tbillrate/youcalc. Assume that you paid $9,875 for a 91-day Treasury bill with a $10,000 face value. Use the T-bill rate calculator to find the effective yield rounded to the nearest hundredth percent. You should calculate the ratio of the price paid to the face value in decimal format.

Internet Projects: See text website (www.mhhe.com/slater7e) and *The Business Math Internet Resource Guide.*

VIDEO CASE
Online Banking

Online banking is very cost effective for the banking industry. Many customers enjoy the convenience; others, however, have doubts. For these individuals, online banking is a different way of thinking.

Banks want customers flocking online because it costs less after initial startup fees. A teller transaction typically costs a bank on average $1 to $1.50, while Internet transactions cost less than 5 cents. Less cost means more profit.

The Gartner Group, a research firm, says that 27 million Americans—one in 10—now do at least some of their banking online, up from 9 million a year earlier. According to a new Gallup poll, online banking services soared by 60% in the year 2000. CyberDialogue, an Internet consulting firm, predicted online banking will rise to 50.9 million customers by 2005. Most sites allow customers to view account information, transfer money, and pay bills online; some sites offer investment account data and transactions. Other applications are coming, including the ability to view and print account statements and canceled checks.

Pundits wrote off most Web banking because of all the things customers couldn't do—close on a loan, sign for a mortgage, or withdraw cash. The startups are applying increasingly innovative strategies to clear these hurdles. Security was, and still is, an issue for many people. According to a recent study, 85% of information technology staffs at corporations and government agencies had detected a computer security breach in the past 12 months, and 64% acknowledged financial losses as a result. Measures are being taken to improve security.

In addition to the usual conveniences of online banking, online banks can pay higher rates on deposits than branch-based banks. However, problems do exist in online banking, such as you can rack up late fees for bill paying and not even know it.

When picking an online banking service, look for the following: (1) 128-bit encryption, the standard in the industry; (2) written guarantees to protect from losses in case of online fraud or bank error; (3) automatic lockout if you wrongly enter your password more than three or four times; and (4) evidence that the bank is FDIC insured.

PROBLEM 1

In 2000, the number of households accessing their accounts through a computer increased to 12.5 million, an 81.42% increase from a year earlier. These numbers support the push for online banking. What was the number of online users last year? Round to the nearest million.

PROBLEM 2

Jupiter Media Metrix, an online research firm, estimated that banking online will increase from 12.5 million to about 43.3 million in 2005. CyberDialogue, an Internet consulting firm, predicted that by the end of 2000, 24.6 million people would bank online and by 2005, the number would rise to 50.9 million. **(a)** What percent increase is Jupiter Media Metrix forecasting? **(b)** What percent increase is CyberDialogue forecasting? Round to the nearest hundredth percent.

PROBLEM 3

E*Trade Bank pays at least 3.1% on checking accounts with balances of $1,000 or more. The national average is 0.78% for interest-bearing checking. If you have $2,300 in your account and bank at E*Trade based on simple interest: **(a)** How much interest would you earn at the end of 30 days (ordinary interest)? **(b)** How much interest would you earn at a non-online bank?

PROBLEM 4

Online banking users—people who do basic banking tasks such as occasionally transferring money between accounts online—jumped to an estimated 20 million in December 2000 from 15.9 million in September 2000. What was the percent increase? Round to the nearest hundredth percent.

PROBLEM 5

On January 9, 2001, Bank of America Corporation announced that it had more than 3 million online banking customers. If 130,000 customers are added in a month, what is the percent increase? Round to the nearest hundredth percent.

PROBLEM 6

The E*Trade Bank is an Internet bank in Menlo Park, California, owned by Internet brokerage company E*Trade Group. On January 4, 2001, E*Trade Bank said it had added more than $1 billion in net new deposits in its fourth quarter of 2000, bringing its total deposits to more than $5.7 billion. E*Trade had a total of $1.1 billion in deposits at the end of 1998. What is the percent increase in net deposits in the year 2000 compared to 1998? Round to the nearest hundredth percent.

PROBLEM 7

The research firm The Gartner Group says that in 2001, 27 million Americans—one in 10—do at least some of their banking online, up from 9 million a year ago. **(a)** How many were banking online last year? **(b)** What was the percent increase in online banking in 2001? Round to nearest hundredth percent.

PROBLEM 8

Industry experts expect that online banking and bill payment, like other forms of e-commerce, will continue to grow at a rapid pace. According to Killen & Associates, the number of bills paid online will rise to 11.7 billion by 2001, a 77% increase. What had been the amount of users in 2000? Round to the nearest tenth.

Conseco Removes Two Directors Who Failed to Pay Back Loans

By JOSEPH T. HALLINAN
Staff Reporter of THE WALL STREET JOURNAL

Conseco Inc. said it removed two of its directors after they failed to repay more than $130 million of company-backed loans used to buy Conseco stock.

The removals suggest new Conseco Chief Executive Gary C. Wendt is taking a tough stance in handling the effects of a disastrous stock-purchase program initiated under his predecessor, Stephen C. Hilbert. The program called for Conseco to guarantee $557.6 million of bank loans to 170 current and former directors, officers and employees to buy 19 million company shares. In addition, the Carmel, Ind., finance and insurance company provided $79.2 million of loans to participants to cover interest payments on the bank loans.

But a subsequent misguided acquisition and other bad moves sent Conseco
. . . . . . borrow . . .

cism from outsiders that board members found it difficult to function.

"It became a dysfunctional board when you had this kind of issue on the table," Mr. Mutz said. "We took the position that it was difficult for a director to be totally independent and still owe the company large sums of money." He said all directors who borrowed money under the program—including himself—were asked to repay their loans or leave the board.

Mr. Mutz, who paid his debt, said Dr. Decatur and Mr. Murray declined to do either. After a resolution was proposed by Mr. Wendt, the board voted to remove Dr. Decatur and Mr. Murray.

Asked if Dr. Decatur and Mr. Murray didn't pay off their loans because they couldn't afford to do so, Mr. Mutz said, "I think that's fair to say."

"Some of the people invol-
not have the assets . . .

12

Compound Interest and Present Value

Note: A complete set of plastic overlays showing the concepts of compound interest and present value is found in Learning Unit 13–2, p. 306.

LU 12–1: Compound Interest (Future Value)—The Big Picture

- Compare simple interest with compound interest *(pp. 280–82).*

- Calculate the compound amount and interest manually and by table lookup *(pp. 281–82).*

- Explain and compute the effective rate (APY) *(p. 284).*

LU 12–2: Present Value—The Big Picture

- Compare present value (PV) with compound interest (FV) *(p. 286).*

- Compute present value by table lookup *(pp. 287–88).*

- Check the present value answer by compounding *(p. 288).*

"Confused by Investing?" asks the following *Wall Street Journal* clipping. Read this clipping carefully. It explains how money increases when you invest. The important word is *compounding*.

Confused by Investing?

If there's something about your investment portfolio that doesn't seem to add up, maybe you should check your math.

Lots of folks are perplexed by the mathematics of investing, so I thought a refresher course might help. Here's a look at some key concepts:

■ **10 Plus 10 is 21**

Imagine you invest $100, which earns 10% this year and 10% next. How much have you made? If you answered 21%, go to the head of the class.

Here's how the math works. This year's 10% gain turns your $100 into $110. Next year, you also earn 10%, but you start the year with $110. Result? You earn $11, boosting your wealth to $121.

Thus, your portfolio has earned a *cumulative* 21% return over two years, but the *annualized* return is just 10%. The fact that 21% is more than double 10% can be attributed to the effect of investment compounding, the way that you earn money each year not only on your original investment, but also on earnings from prior years that you've reinvested.

■ **The Rule of 72**

To get a feel for compounding, try the rule of 72. What's that? If you divide a particular annual return into 72, you'll find out how many years it will take to double your money. Thus, at 10% a year, an investment will double in value in a tad over seven years.

© 1996, Dow Jones & Company, Inc.

In this chapter we look at the power of compounding—interest paid on earned interest. Let's begin by studying Learning Unit 12–1, which shows you how to calculate compound interest.

LEARNING UNIT 12–1 | COMPOUND INTEREST (FUTURE VALUE)—THE BIG PICTURE

So far we have discussed only simple interest, which is interest on the principal alone. Simple interest is either paid at the end of the loan period or deducted in advance. From the chapter introduction, you know that interest can also be compounded.

Check out the plastic overlays that appear within Chapter 13 to review these concepts.

Compounding involves the calculation of interest periodically over the life of the loan (or investment). After each calculation, the interest is added to the principal. Future calculations are on the adjusted principal (old principal plus interest). **Compound interest,** then, is the interest on the principal plus the interest of prior periods. **Future value (FV),** or the **compound amount,** is the final amount of the loan or investment at the end of the last period. In the beginning of this unit, do not be concerned with how to calculate compounding but try to understand the meaning of compounding.

Figure 12.1 shows how $1 will grow if it is calculated for 4 years at 8% annually. This means that the interest is calculated on the balance once a year. In Figure 12.1, we start with $1, which is the **present value (PV).** After year 1, the dollar with interest is

FIGURE 12.1
Future value of $1 at 8% for four periods

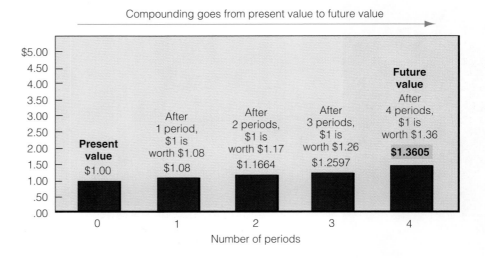

worth $1.08. At the end of year 2, the dollar is worth $1.17. By the end of year 4, the dollar is worth $1.36 . Note how we start with the present and look to see what the dollar will be worth in the future. *Compounding goes from present value to future value.*

Before you learn how to calculate compound interest and compare it to simple interest, you must understand the terms that follow. These terms are also used in Chapter 13.

- **Compounded annually:** Interest calculated on the balance once a year.
- **Compounded semiannually:** Interest calculated on the balance every 6 months or every $\frac{1}{2}$ year.
- **Compounded quarterly:** Interest calculated on the balance every 3 months or every $\frac{1}{4}$ year.
- **Compounded monthly:** Interest calculated on the balance each month.
- **Compounded daily:** Interest calculated on the balance each day.
- **Number of periods:**[1] Number of years multiplied by the number of times the interest is compounded per year. For example, if you compound $1 for 4 years at 8% annually, semiannually, or quarterly, the following periods will result:

  Annually: 4 years $\times$ 1 =   4 periods
  Semiannually: 4 years $\times$ 2 =   8 periods
  Quarterly: 4 years $\times$ 4 = 16 periods
- **Rate for each period:**[2] Annual interest rate divided by the number of times the interest is compounded per year. Compounding changes the interest rate for annual, semiannual, and quarterly periods as follows:

  Annually: 8% $\div$ 1 = 8%
  Semiannually: 8% $\div$ 2 = 4%
  Quarterly: 8% $\div$ 4 = 2%

Note that both the number of periods (4) and the rate (8%) for the annual example did not change. You will see later that rate and periods (not years) will always change unless interest is compounded yearly.

Now you are ready to learn the difference between simple interest and compound interest.

Simple versus Compound Interest

The following three situations of Bill Smith will clarify the difference between simple interest and compound interest.

Situation 1: Calculating Simple Interest and Maturity Value

EXAMPLE   Bill Smith deposited $80 in a savings account for 4 years at an annual interest rate of 8%. What is Bill's simple interest?

To calculate simple interest, we use the following simple interest formula:

$$\text{Interest } (I) = \text{Principal } (P) \times \text{Rate } (R) \times \text{Time } (T)$$

$$\$25.60 \quad = \quad \$80 \quad \times \quad .08 \quad \times \quad 4$$

In 4 years Bill receives a total of $105.60 ($80.00 + $25.60)—principal plus simple interest.

Now let's look at the interest Bill would earn if the bank compounded Bill's interest on his savings.

Situation 2: Calculating Compound Amount and Interest without Tables[3]

You can use the following steps to calculate the compound amount and the interest manually:

---

[1]Periods are often expressed with the letter N for number of periods.
[2]Rate is often expressed with the letter i for interest.
[3]For simplicity of presentation, round each calculation to nearest cent before continuing the compounding process. The compound amount will be off by 1 cent.

Calculating Compound Amount and Interest Manually
Step 1. Calculate the simple interest and add it to the principal. Use this total to figure next year's interest.
Step 2. Repeat for the total number of periods.
Step 3. Compound amount − Principal = Compound interest.

EXAMPLE Bill Smith deposited $80 in a savings account for 4 years at an annual compounded rate of 8%. What are Bill's compound amount and interest?

The following shows how the compounded rate affects Bill's interest:

	Year 1	**Year 2**	**Year 3**	**Year 4**
	$80.00	$86.40	$ 93.31	$100.77
	× .08	× .08	× .08	× .08
Interest	$ 6.40	$ 6.91	$ 7.46	$ 8.06
Beginning balance	+ 80.00	+ 86.40	+ 93.31	+ 100.77
Amount at year-end	$86.40	$93.31	$100.77	$108.83

Note that the beginning year 2 interest is the result of the interest of year 1 added to the principal. At the end of each interest period, we add on the period's interest. This interest becomes part of the principal we use for the calculation of the next period's interest. We can determine Bill's compound interest as follows[4]:

Compound amount	$108.83	
Principal	− 80.00	*Note:* In Situation 1 the interest was $25.60.
Compound interest	$ 28.83	

We could have used the following simplified process to calculate the compound amount and interest:

Year 1	**Year 2**	**Year 3**	**Year 4**
$80.00	$86.40	$ 93.31	$100.77
× 1.08	× 1.08	× 1.08	× 1.08
$86.40	$93.31	$100.77	$108.83 [5] ← Future value

When using this simplification, you do not have to add the new interest to the previous balance. Remember that compounding results in higher interest than simple interest. Compounding is the *sum* of principal and interest multiplied by the interest rate we use to calculate interest for the next period. So, 1.08 above is 108%, with 100% as the base and 8% as the interest.

Situation 3: Calculating Compound Amount by Table Lookup

To calculate the compound amount with a future value table, use the following steps:

Calculating Compound Amount by Table Lookup
Step 1. Find the periods: Years multiplied by number of times interest is compounded in 1 year.
Step 2. Find the rate: Annual rate divided by number of times interest is compounded in 1 year.
Step 3. Go down the Period column of the table to the number of periods desired; look across the row to find the rate. At the intersection of the two columns is the table factor for the compound amount of $1.
Step 4. Multiply the table factor by the amount of the loan. This gives the compound amount.

---

[4]The formula for compounding is $A = P(1 + i)^N$, where A equals compound amount, P equals the principal, i equals interest per period, and N equals number of periods. The calculator sequence would be as follows for Bill Smith: $1 \boxed{+} .08 \boxed{y^x} 4 \times 80 \boxed{=} 108.84$.

[5]Off 1 cent due to rounding.

TABLE 12.1   Future value of $1 at compound interest

Period	1%	1½%	2%	3%	4%	5%	6%	7%	8%	9%	10%
1	1.0100	1.0150	1.0200	1.0300	1.0400	1.0500	1.0600	1.0700	1.0800	1.0900	1.1000
2	1.0201	1.0302	1.0404	1.0609	1.0816	1.1025	1.1236	1.1449	1.1664	1.1881	1.2100
3	1.0303	1.0457	1.0612	1.0927	1.1249	1.1576	1.1910	1.2250	1.2597	1.2950	1.3310
4	1.0406	1.0614	1.0824	1.1255	1.1699	1.2155	1.2625	1.3108	1.3605	1.4116	1.4641
5	1.0510	1.0773	1.1041	1.1593	1.2167	1.2763	1.3382	1.4026	1.4693	1.5386	1.6105
6	1.0615	1.0934	1.1262	1.1941	1.2653	1.3401	1.4185	1.5007	1.5869	1.6771	1.7716
7	1.0721	1.1098	1.1487	1.2299	1.3159	1.4071	1.5036	1.6058	1.7138	1.8280	1.9487
8	1.0829	1.1265	1.1717	1.2668	1.3686	1.4775	1.5938	1.7182	1.8509	1.9926	2.1436
9	1.0937	1.1434	1.1951	1.3048	1.4233	1.5513	1.6895	1.8385	1.9990	2.1719	2.3579
10	1.1046	1.1605	1.2190	1.3439	1.4802	1.6289	1.7908	1.9672	2.1589	2.3674	2.5937
11	1.1157	1.1780	1.2434	1.3842	1.5395	1.7103	1.8983	2.1049	2.3316	2.5804	2.8531
12	1.1268	1.1960	1.2682	1.4258	1.6010	1.7959	2.0122	2.2522	2.5182	2.8127	3.1384
13	1.1381	1.2135	1.2936	1.4685	1.6651	1.8856	2.1329	2.4098	2.7196	3.0658	3.4523
14	1.1495	1.2318	1.3195	1.5126	1.7317	1.9799	2.2609	2.5785	2.9372	3.3417	3.7975
15	1.1610	1.2502	1.3459	1.5580	1.8009	2.0789	2.3966	2.7590	3.1722	3.6425	4.1772
16	1.1726	1.2690	1.3728	1.6047	1.8730	2.1829	2.5404	2.9522	3.4259	3.9703	4.5950
17	1.1843	1.2880	1.4002	1.6528	1.9479	2.2920	2.6928	3.1588	3.7000	4.3276	5.0545
18	1.1961	1.3073	1.4282	1.7024	2.0258	2.4066	2.8543	3.3799	3.9960	4.7171	5.5599
19	1.2081	1.3270	1.4568	1.7535	2.1068	2.5270	3.0256	3.6165	4.3157	5.1417	6.1159
20	1.2202	1.3469	1.4859	1.8061	2.1911	2.6533	3.2071	3.8697	4.6610	5.6044	6.7275
21	1.2324	1.3671	1.5157	1.8603	2.2788	2.7860	3.3996	4.1406	5.0338	6.1088	7.4002
22	1.2447	1.3876	1.5460	1.9161	2.3699	2.9253	3.6035	4.4304	5.4365	6.6586	8.1403
23	1.2572	1.4084	1.5769	1.9736	2.4647	3.0715	3.8197	4.7405	5.8715	7.2579	8.9543
24	1.2697	1.4295	1.6084	2.0328	2.5633	3.2251	4.0489	5.0724	6.3412	7.9111	9.8497
25	1.2824	1.4510	1.6406	2.0938	2.6658	3.3864	4.2919	5.4274	6.8485	8.6231	10.8347
26	1.2953	1.4727	1.6734	2.1566	2.7725	3.5557	4.5494	5.8074	7.3964	9.3992	11.9182
27	1.3082	1.4948	1.7069	2.2213	2.8834	3.7335	4.8223	6.2139	7.9881	10.2451	13.1100
28	1.3213	1.5172	1.7410	2.2879	2.9987	3.9201	5.1117	6.6488	8.6271	11.1672	14.4210
29	1.3345	1.5400	1.7758	2.3566	3.1187	4.1161	5.4184	7.1143	9.3173	12.1722	15.8631
30	1.3478	1.5631	1.8114	2.4273	3.2434	4.3219	5.7435	7.6123	10.0627	13.2677	17.4494

Note: For more detailed tables, see your reference booklet, the *Business Math Handbook.*

In Situation 2, Bill deposited $80 into a savings account for 4 years at an interest rate of 8% compounded annually. Bill heard that he could calculate the compound amount and interest by using tables. In Situation 3, Bill learns how to do this. Again, Bill wants to know the value of $80 in 4 years at 8%. He begins by using Table 12.1.

Looking at Table 12.1, Bill goes down the Period column to period 4, then across the row to the 8% column. At the intersection, Bill sees the number 1.3605. The marginal notes show how Bill arrived at the periods and rate. The 1.3605 table number means that $1 compounded at this rate will increase in value in 4 years to about $1.36. Do you recognize the $1.36? Figure 12.1 showed how $1 grew to $1.36. Since Bill wants to know the value of $80, he multiplies the dollar amount by the table factor as follows:

$80.00 × 1.3605 = $108.84

Principal × Table factor = Compound amount (future value)

Figure 12.2 illustrates this compounding procedure. We can say that compounding is a future value (FV) since we are looking into the future. Thus,

$108.84 − $80.00 = $28.84 interest for 4 years at 8%
compounded annually on $80.00

Now let's look at two examples that illustrate compounding more than once a year.

EXAMPLE Find the interest on $6,000 at 10% compounded semiannually for 5 years. We calculate the interest as follows:

Four Periods
No. of times
compounded × No. of years
in 1 year
1   ×   4

8% Rate
$\frac{8\%}{\text{rate}} = \frac{8\%}{1}$ → Annual rate
→ No. of times compounded in 1 year

FIGURE 12.2
Compounding (FV)

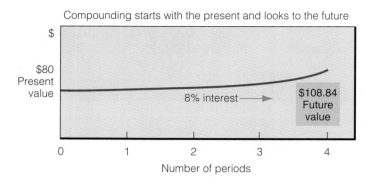

Compounding starts with the present and looks to the future

$80 Present value → 8% interest → $108.84 Future value

Number of periods (0, 1, 2, 3, 4)

Periods = 2 × 5 years = 10

Rate = 10% ÷ 2 = 5%

10 periods, 5%, in Table 12.1 = 1.6289 (table factor)

$6,000 × 1.6289 = $9,773.40
− 6,000.00
$3,773.40
interest

EXAMPLE Pam Donahue deposits $8,000 in her savings account that pays 6% interest compounded quarterly. What will be the balance of her account at the end of 5 years?

Periods = 4 × 5 years = 20

Rate = 6% ÷ 4 = $1\frac{1}{2}\%$

20 periods, $1\frac{1}{2}\%$, in Table 12.1 = 1.3469 (table factor)

$8,000 × 1.3469 = $10,775.20

Next, let's look at bank rates and how they affect interest.

Bank Rates—Nominal versus Effective Rates (Annual Percentage Yield, or APY)

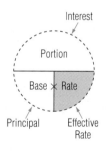

Banks often advertise their annual (nominal) interest rates and *not* their true or effective rate (annual percentage yield, or APY). This has made it difficult for investors and depositors to determine the actual rates of interest they were receiving. The Truth in Savings law forced savings institutions to reveal their actual rate of interest. The APY is defined in the Truth in Savings law as the percentage rate expressing the total amount of interest that would be received on a $100 deposit based on the annual rate and frequency of compounding for a 365-day period. As you can see from the following advertisement, banks now refer to the effective rate of interest as the annual percentage yield.

Let's study the rates of two banks to see which bank has the better return for the investor. Blue Bank pays 8% interest compounded quarterly on $8,000. Sun Bank offers 8% interest compounded semiannually on $8,000. The 8% rate is the **nominal rate,** or stated rate, on which the bank calculates the interest. To calculate the **effective rate (annual percentage yield,** or **APY),** however, we can use the following formula:

$$\text{Effective rate (APY)}^6 = \frac{\text{Interest for 1 year}}{\text{Principal}}$$

Now let's calculate the effective rate (APY) for Blue Bank and Sun Bank.

---

[6]Round to the nearest hundredth percent as needed. In practice, the rate is often rounded to the nearest thousandth.

Note the effective rates (APY) can
be seen from Table 12.1 for $1:
1.0824 ←— 4 periods, 2%
1.0816 ←— 2 periods, 4%

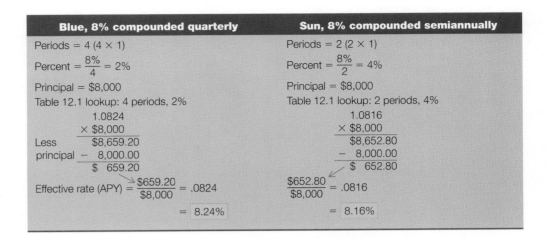

Blue, 8% compounded quarterly	Sun, 8% compounded semiannually
Periods = 4 (4 × 1)	Periods = 2 (2 × 1)
Percent = $\frac{8\%}{4}$ = 2%	Percent = $\frac{8\%}{2}$ = 4%
Principal = $8,000	Principal = $8,000
Table 12.1 lookup: 4 periods, 2%	Table 12.1 lookup: 2 periods, 4%
1.0824 × $8,000 $8,659.20	1.0816 × $8,000 $8,652.80
Less principal – 8,000.00 $ 659.20	– 8,000.00 $ 652.80
Effective rate (APY) = $\frac{\$659.20}{\$8,000}$ = .0824 = 8.24%	$\frac{\$652.80}{\$8,000}$ = .0816 = 8.16%

FIGURE 12.3

Nominal and effective rates
(APY) of interest compared

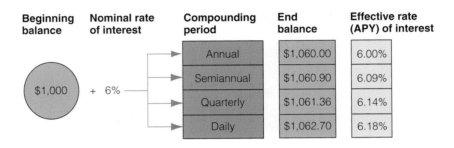

Beginning balance	Nominal rate of interest	Compounding period	End balance	Effective rate (APY) of interest
$1,000	+ 6%	Annual	$1,060.00	6.00%
		Semiannual	$1,060.90	6.09%
		Quarterly	$1,061.36	6.14%
		Daily	$1,062.70	6.18%

Figure 12.3 illustrates a comparison of nominal and effective rates (APY) of interest. This comparison should make you question any advertisement of interest rates before depositing your money.

Before concluding this unit, we briefly discuss compounding interest daily.

Compounding Interest Daily

Although many banks add interest to each account quarterly, some banks pay interest that is **compounded daily,** and other banks use *continuous compounding.* Remember that continuous compounding sounds great, but in fact, it yields only a fraction of a percent more interest over a year than daily compounding. Today, computers perform these calculations.

Table 12.2 (p. 286) is a partial table showing what $1 will grow to in the future by daily compounded interest, 360-day basis. For example, we can calculate interest compounded daily on $900 at 6% per year for 25 years as follows:

$900 × 4.4811 = $4,032.99 daily compounding

Now it's time to check your progress with the following Practice Quiz.

LU 12–1 PRACTICE QUIZ

1. Complete the following without a table (round each calculation to the nearest cent as needed):

Principal	Time	Rate of compound interest	Compounded	Number of periods to be compounded	Total amount	Total interest
$200	1 year	8%	Quarterly	a.	b.	c.

2. Solve the previous problem by using compound value (FV) Table 12.1.

3. Lionel Rodgers deposits $6,000 in Victory Bank, which pays 3% interest compounded semiannually. How much will Lionel have in his account at the end of 8 years?

4. Find the effective rate (APY) for the year: principal, $7,000; interest rate, 12%; and compounded quarterly.

5. Calculate by Table 12.2 what $1,500 compounded daily for 5 years will grow to at 7%.

TABLE 12.2   Interest on a $1 deposit compounded daily—360-day basis

Number of years	6.00%	6.50%	7.00%	7.50%	8.00%	8.50%	9.00%	9.50%	10.00%
1	1.0618	1.0672	1.0725	1.0779	1.0833	1.0887	1.0942	1.0996	1.1052
2	1.1275	1.1388	1.1503	1.1618	1.1735	1.1853	1.1972	1.2092	1.2214
3	1.1972	1.2153	1.2337	1.2523	1.2712	1.2904	1.3099	1.3297	1.3498
4	1.2712	1.2969	1.3231	1.3498	1.3771	1.4049	1.4333	1.4622	1.4917
5	1.3498	1.3840	1.4190	1.4549	1.4917	1.5295	1.5682	1.6079	1.6486
6	1.4333	1.4769	1.5219	1.5682	1.6160	1.6652	1.7159	1.7681	1.8220
7	1.5219	1.5761	1.6322	1.6904	1.7506	1.8129	1.8775	1.9443	2.0136
8	1.6160	1.6819	1.7506	1.8220	1.8963	1.9737	2.0543	2.1381	2.2253
9	1.7159	1.7949	1.8775	1.9639	2.0543	2.1488	2.2477	2.3511	2.4593
10	1.8220	1.9154	2.0136	2.1168	2.2253	2.3394	2.4593	2.5854	2.7179
15	2.4594	2.6509	2.8574	3.0799	3.3197	3.5782	3.8568	4.1571	4.4808
20	3.3198	3.6689	4.0546	4.4810	4.9522	5.4728	6.0482	6.6842	7.3870
25	4.4811	5.0777	5.7536	6.5195	7.3874	8.3708	9.4851	10.7477	12.1782
30	6.0487	7.0275	8.1645	9.4855	11.0202	12.8032	14.8747	17.2813	20.0772

✓ **SOLUTIONS**

1. **a.**   4 (4 × 1)   **b.** $216.48   **c.** $16.48 ($216.48 − $200)

    $200 × 1.02 = $204 × 1.02 = $208.08 × 1.02 = $212.24 × 1.02 = $216.48

2. $200 × 1.0824 = $216.48 (4 periods, 2%)

3. 16 periods, $1\frac{1}{2}$%, $6,000 × 1.2690 = $7,614

4. 4 periods, 3%,

    $7,000 × 1.1255 = $7,878.50 $\dfrac{\$878.50}{\$7,000.00} = 12.55\%$
                      − 7,000.00
                      ─────────────
                        $ 878.50

Check out the plastic overlays that appear within Chapter 13 to review these concepts.

5. $1,500 × 1.4190 = $2,128.50

LEARNING UNIT 12–2 | PRESENT VALUE—THE BIG PICTURE

Matthew Borkoski/Stock Boston

Figure 12.1 (p. 280) in Learning Unit 12–1 showed how by compounding, the *future value* of $1 became $1.36. This learning unit discusses *present value*. Before we look at specific calculations involving present value, let's look at the concept of present value.

Figure 12.4 shows that if we invested 74 cents today, compounding would cause the 74 cents to grow to $1 in the future. For example, let's assume you ask this question: "If I need $1 in 4 years in the future, how much must I put in the bank *today* (assume an 8% annual interest)?" To answer this question, you must know the present value of that $1 today. From Figure 12.4, you can see that the present value of $1 is .7350. Remember that the $1 is only worth 74 cents if you wait 4 periods to receive it. This is one reason why so many athletes get such big contracts—much of the money is paid in later years when it is not worth as much.

Relationship of Compounding (FV) to Present Value (PV)—The Bill Smith Example Continued

In Learning Unit 12–1, our consideration of compounding started in the *present* ($80) and looked to find the *future* amount of $108.84. Present value (PV) starts with the *future* and tries to calculate its worth in the *present* ($80). For example, in Figure 12.5, we assume Bill Smith knew that in 4 years he wanted to buy a bike that cost $108.84 (future). Bill's bank pays 8% interest compounded annually. How much money must Bill put in the bank *today* (present) to have $108.84 in 4 years? To work from the future to the present, we can use a present value (PV) table. In the next section you will learn how to use this table.

FIGURE 12.4

Present value of $1 at 8% for four periods

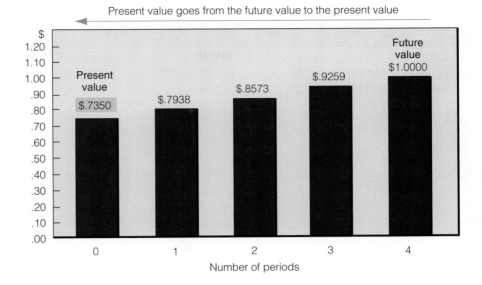

Present value goes from the future value to the present value

Present value
$.7350

$.7938

$.8573

$.9259

Future value
$1.0000

Number of periods

FIGURE 12.5

Present value

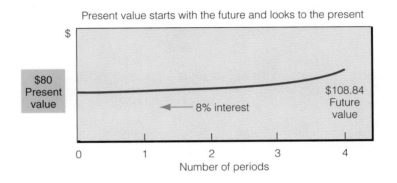

Present value starts with the future and looks to the present

$80
Present value

8% interest

$108.84
Future value

Number of periods

How to Use a Present Value (PV) Table[7]

To calculate present value with a present value table, use the following steps:

> **Calculating Present Value by Table Lookup**
>
> **Step 1.** Find the periods: Years multiplied by number of times interest is compounded in 1 year.
>
> **Step 2.** Find the rate: Annual rate divided by numbers of times interest is compounded in 1 year.
>
> **Step 3.** Go down the Period column of the table to the number of periods desired; look across the row to find the rate. At the intersection of the two columns is the table factor for the compound value of $1.
>
> **Step 4.** Multiply the table factor times the future value. This gives the present value.

Periods

$$4 \times 1 = 4$$

No. of years

No. of times compounded in 1 year

Table 12.3 is a present value (PV) table that tells you what $1 is worth today at different interest rates. To continue our Bill Smith example, go down the Period column in Table 12.3 to 4. Then go across to the 8% column. At 8% for 4 periods, we see a table factor of .7350. This means that $1 in the future is worth approximately 74 cents today. If Bill invested 74 cents today at 8% for 4 periods, Bill would have $1.

---

[7]The formula for present value is $PV = \dfrac{A}{(1 + i)^N}$, where A equals future amount (compound amount), N equals number of compounding periods, and i equals interest rate per compounding period. The calculator sequence for Bill Smith would be as follows: 1 [+] .08 [y^x] 4 [=] [M+] 108.84 [÷] [MR] [=] 80.03.

TABLE 12.3   Present value of $1 at end period

Period	1%	1½%	2%	3%	4%	5%	6%	7%	8%	9%	10%
1	.9901	.9852	.9804	.9709	.9615	.9524	.9434	.9346	.9259	.9174	.9091
2	.9803	.9707	.9612	.9426	.9246	.9070	.8900	.8734	.8573	.8417	.8264
3	.9706	.9563	.9423	.9151	.8890	.8638	.8396	.8163	.7938	.7722	.7513
4	.9610	.9422	.9238	.8885	.8548	.8227	.7921	.7629	.7350	.7084	.6830
5	.9515	.9283	.9057	.8626	.8219	.7835	.7473	.7130	.6806	.6499	.6209
6	.9420	.9145	.8880	.8375	.7903	.7462	.7050	.6663	.6302	.5963	.5645
7	.9327	.9010	.8706	.8131	.7599	.7107	.6651	.6227	.5835	.5470	.5132
8	.9235	.8877	.8535	.7894	.7307	.6768	.6274	.5820	.5403	.5019	.4665
9	.9143	.8746	.8368	.7664	.7026	.6446	.5919	.5439	.5002	.4604	.4241
10	.9053	.8617	.8203	.7441	.6756	.6139	.5584	.5083	.4632	.4224	.3855
11	.8963	.8489	.8043	.7224	.6496	.5847	.5268	.4751	.4289	.3875	.3505
12	.8874	.8364	.7885	.7014	.6246	.5568	.4970	.4440	.3971	.3555	.3186
13	.8787	.8240	.7730	.6810	.6006	.5303	.4688	.4150	.3677	.3262	.2897
14	.8700	.8119	.7579	.6611	.5775	.5051	.4423	.3878	.3405	.2992	.2633
15	.8613	.7999	.7430	.6419	.5553	.4810	.4173	.3624	.3152	.2745	.2394
16	.8528	.7880	.7284	.6232	.5339	.4581	.3936	.3387	.2919	.2519	.2176
17	.8444	.7764	.7142	.6050	.5134	.4363	.3714	.3166	.2703	.2311	.1978
18	.8360	.7649	.7002	.5874	.4936	.4155	.3503	.2959	.2502	.2120	.1799
19	.8277	.7536	.6864	.5703	.4746	.3957	.3305	.2765	.2317	.1945	.1635
20	.8195	.7425	.6730	.5537	.4564	.3769	.3118	.2584	.2145	.1784	.1486
21	.8114	.7315	.6598	.5375	.4388	.3589	.2942	.2415	.1987	.1637	.1351
22	.8034	.7207	.6468	.5219	.4220	.3418	.2775	.2257	.1839	.1502	.1228
23	.7954	.7100	.6342	.5067	.4057	.3256	.2618	.2109	.1703	.1378	.1117
24	.7876	.6995	.6217	.4919	.3901	.3101	.2470	.1971	.1577	.1264	.1015
25	.7798	.6892	.6095	.4776	.3751	.2953	.2330	.1842	.1460	.1160	.0923
26	.7720	.6790	.5976	.4637	.3607	.2812	.2198	.1722	.1352	.1064	.0839
27	.7644	.6690	.5859	.4502	.3468	.2678	.2074	.1609	.1252	.0976	.0763
28	.7568	.6591	.5744	.4371	.3335	.2551	.1956	.1504	.1159	.0895	.0693
29	.7493	.6494	.5631	.4243	.3207	.2429	.1846	.1406	.1073	.0822	.0630
30	.7419	.6398	.5521	.4120	.3083	.2314	.1741	.1314	.0994	.0754	.0573
35	.7059	.5939	.5000	.3554	.2534	.1813	.1301	.0937	.0676	.0490	.0356
40	.6717	.5513	.4529	.3066	.2083	.1420	.0972	.0668	.0460	.0318	.0221

Note: For more detailed tables, see your booklet, the *Business Math Handbook.*

Since Bill knows the bike will cost $108.84 in the future, he completes the following calculation:

$108.84 × .7350 = $80.00

This means that $108.84 in today's dollars is worth $80.00. Now let's check this.

Comparing Compound Interest (FV) Table 12.1 with Present Value (PV) Table 12.3

We know from our calculations that Bill needs to invest $80 for 4 years at 8% compound interest annually to buy his bike. We can check this by going back to Table 12.1 and comparing it with Table 12.3. Let's do this now.

Compound value Table 12.1			Present value Table 12.3		
Table 12.1	Present value	Future value	Table 12.3	Future value	Present value
1.3605 ×	$80.00 =	$108.84	.7350 ×	$108.84 =	$80.00
(4 per., 8%)			(4 per., 8%)		
We know the present dollar amount and find what the dollar amount is worth in the future.			We know the future dollar amount and find what the dollar amount is worth in the present.		

Note that the table factor for compounding is over 1 (1.3605) and the table factor for present value is less than 1 (.7350). The compound value table starts with the present and goes to the future. The present value table starts with the future and goes to the present. Let's look at another example before trying the Practice Quiz.

FIGURE 12.6

Present value

The present value is what we need *now* to have $20,000 in the future

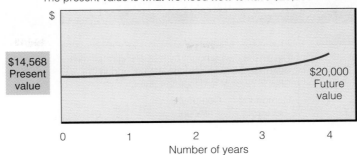

EXAMPLE Rene Weaver needs $20,000 for college in 4 years. She can earn 8% compounded quarterly at her bank. How much must Rene deposit at the beginning of the year to have $20,000 in 4 years?

Remember that in this example the bank compounds the interest *quarterly*. Let's first determine the period and rate on a quarterly basis:

$$\text{Periods} = 4 \times 4 \text{ years} = 16 \text{ periods} \qquad \text{Rate} = \frac{8\%}{4} = 2\%$$

Now we go to Table 12.3 and find 16 under the Period column. We then move across to the 2% column and find the .7284 table factor.

$$\underset{\text{(future value)}}{\$20{,}000} \times .7284 = \underset{\text{(present value)}}{\boxed{\$14{,}568}}$$

We illustrate this in Figure 12.6.

We can check the $14,568 present value by using the compound value Table 12.1:

16 periods, 2% column = 1.3728 × $14,568 = $19,998.95[8]

Let's test your understanding of this unit with the Practice Quiz.

LU 12–2 PRACTICE QUIZ

Use the present-value Table 12.3 to complete:

Future amount desired	Length of time	Rate compounded	Table period	Rate used	PV factor	PV amount
1. $ 7,000	6 years	6% semiannually	_____	_____	_____	_____
2. $15,000	20 years	10% annually	_____	_____	_____	_____

3. Bill Blum needs $20,000 6 years from today to attend V.P.R. Tech. How much must Bill put in the bank today (12% quarterly) to reach his goal?

4. Bob Fry wants to buy his grandson a Ford Taurus in 4 years. The cost of a car will be $24,000. Assuming a bank rate of 8% compounded quarterly, how much must Bob put in the bank today?

✓ **SOLUTIONS**

1. 12 periods (6 years × 2)   3% (6% ÷ 2)   .7014 $4,909.80   ($7,000 × .7014)

2. 20 periods (20 years × 1)   10% (10% ÷ 1)   .1486 $2,229.00   ($15,000 × .1486)

3. 6 years × 4 = 24 periods $\dfrac{12\%}{4} = 3\%$ .4919 × $20,000 = $9,838

4. 4 × 4 years = 16 periods $\dfrac{8\%}{4} = 2\%$ .7284 × $24,000 = $17,481.60

---

[8]Not quite $20,000 due to rounding of table factors.

Chapter Organizer and Reference Guide

Topic	Key point, procedure, formula	Example(s) to illustrate situation
Calculating compound amount without tables (future value),* p. 282	Determine new amount by multiplying rate times new balance (that includes interest added on). Start in present and look to future. $$\text{Compound interest} = \text{Compound amount} - \text{Principal}$$ ⊢— Compounding —⊣ PV FV	$100 in savings account, compounded annually for 2 years at 8%: $100 $108 × 1.08 × 1.08 —— —— $108 $116.64 (future value)
Calculating compound amount (future value) by table lookup, p. 282	$$\text{Periods} = \frac{\text{Number of times compounded}}{\text{per year}} \times \text{Years of loan}$$ $$\text{Rate} = \frac{\text{Annual rate}}{\text{Number of times compounded per year}}$$ Multiply table factor (intersection of period and rate) times amount of principal.	*Example:* $2,000 @ 12% 5 years compounded quarterly: Periods = 4 × 5 years = 20 $$\text{Rate} = \frac{12\%}{4} = 3\%$$ 20 periods, 3% = 1.8061 (table factor) $2,000 × 1.8061 = $3,612.20 (future value)
Effective rate (APY), p. 284	$$\text{Effective rate (APY)} = \frac{\text{Interest for 1 year}}{\text{Principal}}$$ or Rate can be seen in Table 12.1 factor.	$1,000 at 10% compounded semiannually for 1 year. By Table 12.1: 2 periods, 5% 1.1025 means at end of year investor has earned 110.25% of original principal. Thus the interest is 10.25%. $1,000 × 1.1025 = $1,102.50 − 1,000.00 —————— $ 102.50 $$\frac{\$102.50}{\$1,000} = 10.25\% \text{ effective rate (APY)}$$
Calculating present value (PV) with table lookup†, p. 287	Start with future and calculate worth in the present. Periods and rate computed like in compound interest. ⊢— Present value —⊣ PV FV Find periods and rate. Multiply table factor (intersection of period and rate) times amount of loan.	*Example:* Want $3,612.20 after 5 years with rate of 12% compounded quarterly: Periods = 4 × 5 = 20; % = 3% By Table 12.3: 20 periods, 3% = .5537 $3,612.20 × .5537 = $2,000.08 Invested today will yield desired amount in future
Key terms	Annual percentage yield (APY), p. 284 Compound amount, p. 280 Compounded annually, p. 281 Compounded daily, p. 285 Compounded monthly, p. 281	Compounded quarterly, p. 281 Compounded semiannually, p. 281 Compounding, p. 280 Compound interest, p. 280 Effective rate, p. 284	Future value (FV), p. 280 Nominal rate, p. 284 Number of periods, p. 281 Present value (PV), p. 280 Rate for each period, p. 281

*$A = P(1 + i)^N$.   †$\frac{A}{(1 + i)^N}$ if table not used.

Critical Thinking Discussion Questions

1. Explain how periods and rates are calculated in compounding problems. Compare simple interest to compound interest.

2. What are the steps to calculate the compound amount by table? Why is the compound table factor greater than $1?

3. What is the effective rate (APY)? Why can the effective rate be seen directly from the table factor?

4. Explain the difference between compounding and present value. Why is the present value table factor less than $1?

DRILL PROBLEMS

Complete the following without using Table 12.1 (round to the nearest cent for each calculation) and then check by Table 12.1 (check will be off one cent due to rounding).

	Principal	Time (years)	Rate of compound interest	Compounded	Periods	Rate	Total amount	Total interest
12–1.	$700	2	6%	Semiannually				

Complete the following using compound future value Table 12.1:

	Time	Principal	Rate	Compounded	Amount	Interest
12–2.	7 years	$8,000	4%	Semiannually		
12–3.	6 months	$10,000	8%	Quarterly		
12–4.	3 years	$2,000	12%	Semiannually		

Calculate the effective rate (APY) of interest for 1 year.

12–5. Principal: $15,500
Interest rate: 12%
Compounded quarterly
Effective rate (APY):

12–6. Using Table 12.2, calculate what $700 would grow to at $6\frac{1}{2}$% per year compounded daily for 7 years.

Complete the following using present value Table 12.3:

	Amount desired at end of period	Length of time	Rate	Compounded	On PV Table 12.3 Period used	On PV Table 12.3 Rate used	PV factor used	PV of amount desired at end of period
12–7.	$2,600	6 years	4%	Semiannually				
Excel								
12–8.	$7,650	2 years	12%	Monthly				
Excel								
12–9.	$17,600	7 years	12%	Quarterly				
Excel								
12–10.	$20,000	20 years	8%	Annually				
Excel								

12–11. Check your answer in Problem 12–9 by the compound value Table 12.1. The answer will be off due to rounding.

WORD PROBLEMS

12–12. On March 25, 2001, *The New York Times* reported on certificate of deposit rates. A savings account in the Emigrant Savings Bank in New York now earns 2.25% simple interest a year. Bank One pays 6% interest compounded semiannually on a certificate of deposit. Robert Wier wants to deposit $1,500 in his savings account, how much additional interest will he earn by placing the money in a certificate of deposit?

12–13. Jean Rich, owner of a local Dunkin' Donuts shop, loaned $14,000 to Mel Lyon to help him open an Internet business. Mel plans to repay Jean at the end of 6 years with 6% interest compounded semiannually. How much will Jean receive at the end of 6 years?

12–14. Molly Slate deposited $35,000 at Quazi Bank at 6% interest compounded quarterly. What is the effective rate (APY) to the nearest hundredth percent?

12–15. Melvin Indecision has difficulty deciding whether to put his savings in Mystic Bank or Four Rivers Bank. Mystic offers 10% interest compounded semiannually. Four Rivers offers 8% interest compounded quarterly. Melvin has $10,000 to invest. He expects to withdraw the money at the end of 4 years. Which bank gives Melvin the better deal? Check your answer.

12–16. Brian Costa deposited $20,000 in a new savings account at 12% interest compounded semiannually. At the beginning of year 4, Brian deposits an additional $30,000 at 12% interest compounded semiannually. At the end of 6 years, what is the balance in Brian's account?

12–17. Lee Wills loaned Audrey Chin $16,000 to open a hair salon. After 6 years, Audrey will repay Lee with 8% interest compounded quarterly. How much will Lee receive at the end of 6 years?

12–18. Financial planning for retirement was a topic in the July 31, 2000, issue of *Business Week*. Jim Fortunate received a large insurance settlement of $200,000. When Jim retires in 25 years, he would like to have at least $80,000 yearly income for 10 years. A local bank pays 6% interest compounded semiannually on a certificate of deposit. **(a)** How much of the settlement must Jim place in the bank to meet his retirement goal? **(b)** What amount would he receive if he invested the entire $200,000 in the bank?

12–19. John Roe, an employee of The Gap, loans $3,000 to another employee at the store. He will be repaid at the end of 4 years with interest at 6% compounded quarterly. How much will John be repaid?

12–20. An article in the June 21, 2001, *Sun Publications* mentioned the increasing cost of attending college. A child entering college 11 years from now can expect to pay more than $20,000 a year to attend a public institution and almost $60,000 a year for an Ivy League school. Assume you are planning your child's education and have received an inheritance that will cover the child's costs. You place the inheritance in a bank paying 6% interest compounded quarterly. **(a)** How much money should you put away to send your child to a public institution for 4 years? **(b)** How much money should you put away to send your child to a private institution? Use tables in the *Business Math Handbook*.

12–21. St. Paul Federal Bank is quoting 1-year Certificates of Deposits with an interest rate of 5% compounded semiannually. Joe Saver purchased a $5,000 CD. What is the CD's effective rate (APY) to the nearest hundredth percent? Use tables in the *Business Math Handbook*.

12–22. Jim Jones, an owner of a Burger King restaurant, assumes that his restaurant will need a new roof in 7 years. He estimates the roof will cost him $9,000 at that time. What amount should Jim invest today at 6% compounded quarterly to be able to pay for the roof? Check your answer.

12–23. Tony Ring wants to attend Northeast College. He will need $60,000 4 years from today. Assume Tony's bank pays 12% interest compounded semiannually. What must Tony deposit today so he will have $60,000 in 4 years?

12–24. Could you check your answer (to the nearest dollar) in Problem 12–23 by using the compound value Table 12.1? The answer will be slightly off due to rounding.

12–25. Pete Air wants to buy a used Jeep in 5 years. He estimates the Jeep will cost $15,000. Assume Pete invests $10,000 now at 12% interest compounded semiannually. Will Pete have enough money to buy his Jeep at the end of 5 years?

12–26. Lance Jackson deposited $5,000 at Basil Bank at 9% interest compounded daily. What is Lance's investment at the end of 4 years?

12–27. Paul Havlik promised his grandson Jamie that he would give him $6,000 8 years from today for graduating from high school. Assume money is worth 6% interest compounded semiannually. What is the present value of this $6,000?

12–28. Earl Ezekiel wants to retire in San Diego when he is 65 years old. Earl is now 50. He believes he will need $300,000 to retire comfortably. To date, Earl has set aside no retirement money. Assume Earl gets 6% interest compounded semiannually. How much must Earl invest today to meet his $300,000 goal?

12–29. Lorna Evenson would like to buy a $19,000 car in 4 years. Lorna wants to put the money aside now. Lorna's bank offers 8% interest compounded semiannually. How much must Lorna invest today?

12–30. John Smith saw the following advertisement. Could you show him how $88.77 was calculated?

9-Month CD   6.05% Annual* Percentage Yield

*As of January 31, 200X, and subject to change. Interest on the 9-month CD is credited on the maturity date and is not compounded. For example, a $2,000, 9-month CD on deposit for an interest rate of 6.00% (6.05% APY) will earn $88.77 at maturity. Withdrawals prior to maturity require the consent of the bank and are subject to a substantial penalty. There is $500 minimum deposit for IRA, SEP IRA, and Keogh CDs (except for 9-month CD for which the minimum deposit is $1,000). There is $1,000 minimum deposit for all personal CDs (except for 9-month CD for which the minimum deposit is $2,000). Offer not valid on jumbo CDs.

 CHALLENGE PROBLEMS

12–31. The U.S. government has ended 20 years of litigation by agreeing to pay $18 million to the estate of Richard M. Nixon. On June 14, 2000, the *Los Angeles Times* reported that the estate had demanded $35 million plus $8\frac{1}{2}\%$ interest compounded annually for items confiscated after Nixon resigned the presidency. **(a)** How much interest did the estate want? **(b)** What was the total amount the estate wanted? **(c)** How much did the government save by settling for $18 million?

12–32. You are the financial planner for Johnson Controls. Last year's profits were $700,000. The board of directors decided to forgo dividends to stockholders and retire high-interest outstanding bonds that were issued 5 years ago at a face value of $1,250,000. You have been asked to invest the profits in a bank. The board must know how much money you will need from the profits earned to retire the bonds in 10 years. Bank A pays 6% compounded quarterly, and Bank B pays $6\frac{1}{2}\%$ compounded annually. Which bank would you recommend, and how much of the company's profit should be placed in the bank? If you recommended that the remaining money not be distributed to stockholders but be placed in Bank B, how much would the remaining money be worth in 10 years? Use tables in the *Business Math Handbook.** Round final answer to nearest dollar.

*Check glossary for unfamiliar terms.

SUMMARY PRACTICE TEST

1. Joe Bayo, owner of Travel.com, loaned $13,000 to Jeff Line to help him open a flower shop online. Jeff plans to repay Joe at the end of 8 years with 6% interest compounded semiannually. How much will Joe receive at the end of 8 years? *(p. 282)*

2. Roy Hunter wants to attend Rose State College. Six years from today he will need $28,000. If Roy's bank pays 4% interest compounded semiannually, what must Roy deposit today to have $28,000 in 6 years? *(p. 287)*

3. Warren Ford deposited $18,000 in a savings account at 6% interest compounded semiannually. At the beginning of year 4, Warren deposits an additional $80,000 at 6% interest compounded semiannually. At the end of 6 years, what is the balance in Warren's account? *(p. 282)*

4. Joe Jones, owner of a Taco Bell, wants to buy a new delivery truck in 4 years. He estimates the truck will cost $17,000. If Joe invests $11,000 now at 10% interest compounded semiannually, will Joe have enough money to buy his delivery truck at the end of 4 years? *(p. 282)*

5. Abby Ellen deposited $12,000 in Street Bank at 9% interest compounded semiannually. What was the effective rate (APY)? Round to the nearest hundredth percent. *(p. 284)*

6. Paul Mahar, owner of Jeff's Lube, estimates that he will need $40,000 for new equipment in 8 years. Paul decided to put aside the money today so it will be available in 8 years. Lester Bank offers Paul 10% interest compounded semiannually. How much must Paul invest to have $40,000 in 8 years? *(p. 287)*

7. Gracie Lantz wants to retire to California when she is 65 years of age. Gracie is now 45. She believes that she will need $500,000 to retire comfortably. To date, Gracie has set aside no retirement money. If Gracie gets 8% compounded semiannually, how much must Gracie invest today to meet her $500,000 goal? *(p. 287)*

8. Bernie Sullivan deposited $12,000 in a savings account at 6% interest compounded daily. At the end of 20 years, what is the balance in Bernie's account? *(p. 285)*

SAVING | Here's a novel idea: Build a **COLLEGE FUND** by getting rebates on money you spend.

BUY A DEGREE

*I*NSTEAD OF frequent-flier miles that you're never able to use, why not have your credit card rebate go toward a higher calling—say, a college degree? That is the idea behind UPromise, a new service that will credit actual-dollar rebates on money you spend for all kinds of consumer products to a college-savings account set up for your family.

To participate, you will have to give UPromise information used to track your spending—for example, numbers for your credit cards and supermarket savings cards. Rebates may range from 1% for transactions on participating credit cards to 4% on long-distance calls to 10% on restaurant meals.

The savings are swept into a 529 plan—a state-sponsored college-savings plan in which money grows tax-deferred until it's used to pay tuition. You set up an account with a plan you select, and you can enlist friends and family members to have their rebates credited to your account.

UPromise will launch at the end of March, with a war chest of venture-capital funds and a brain trust of advisers that includes former governors, college presidents and CEOs, as well as former senator and presidential hopeful Bill Bradley. "I think UPromise could change the world," says Bradley.

What UPromise needs is companies willing to sign on to give rebates. It is courting the biggest players in every major consumer category, from automakers to long-distance services, supermarkets and restaurants. Citibank and Coca-Cola have already signed on.

UPromise's research indicates that families could accumulate "tens of thousands of dollars" over a 15-year period, an amount that depends on attracting a critical mass of participating companies, as well as consumer willingness to switch brands. Bradley, for one, thinks that won't be a problem. "One thing Americans do is shop wisely," he says.

SEAN KELLY

Business Math Issue

Compounding and present value are really not part of a 529 plan.

1. List the key points of the article and information to support your position.
2. Write a group defense of your position using math calculations to support your view.

BUSINESS MATH SCRAPBOOK
WITH INTERNET APPLICATION

Putting Your Skills to Work

	When you deposit	30-month C.D. interest rate	30-month interest at maturity	If 12% interest at maturity	Interest difference
A.	$100,000	12.28% 11.75% Annual percentage yield Interest rate	$33,578		
B.	$80,001	12.28% 11.75% Annual percentage yield Interest rate	$26,863		
C.	$60,001	12.28% 11.75% Annual percentage yield Interest rate	$20,147		
D.	$40,001	12.28% 11.75% Annual percentage yield Interest rate	$13,431		
E.	$20,001	12.28% 11.75% Annual percentage yield Interest rate	$6,716		
F.	$15,001	12.28% 11.75% Annual percentage yield Interest rate	$5,037		
G.	$10,001	12.28% 11.75% Annual percentage yield Interest rate	$3,358		

This yield assumes that principal and interest remain on deposit for a full year interest compounded quarterly

PROJECT A

Bill Smith saw this bank advertisement. He feels the interest rate may rise to 12% next month. If you use the compound interest Table 12.1 in the text, what would the interest be at maturity for each amount? By waiting until next month, how much interest could Bill gain over depositing now? Assume that Bill wants to work out the interest rate for each deposit shown. What would be the annual effective yield (APY) with an interest rate of 12%? Visit the Bank.com website. What are the current rates?

Internet Projects: See text website (www.mhhe.com/slater7e) and *The Business Math Internet Resource Guide.*

Year	Amount invested	
	Early investor	**Late investor**
		$0
1	$2,000	$0
2	$2,000	$0
3	$2,000	$0
4	$2,000	$0
5	$2,000	$0
6	$2,000	$0
7	$2,000	$0
8	$2,000	$2,000 every year
9-40	$0 every year	

515

16

64

378

☐ Total invested over 40 years
(In thousands of dollars)

■ Total earnings after 40 years
(In thousands of dollars)

SOURCE: www.financialfinesse.com;
www.netxclient.com; S&P's The Outlook

©2001 Dow Jones & Company, Inc.

FIGURE 13.1

Future value of an annuity of $1 at 8%

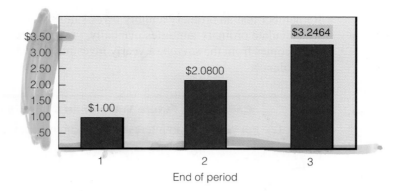

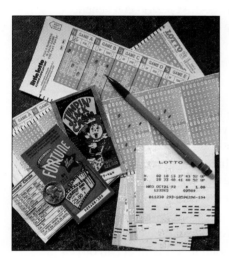

Sharon Hoogstraten

The continual growth of this sum through compound interest provides the lottery winner with a series of payments.

When we calculated the maturity value of a lump-sum payment in Chapter 12, the maturity value was the principal and its interest. Now we are looking not at lump-sum payments but at a series of payments (usually of equal amounts over regular **payment periods**) plus the interest that accumulates. So the **future value of an annuity** is the future *dollar amount* of a series of payments plus interest.[1] The **term of the annuity** is the time from the beginning of the first payment period to the end of the last payment period.

The concept of the future value of an annuity is illustrated in Figure 13.1. Do not be concerned about the calculations (we will do them soon). Let's first focus on the big picture of annuities. In Figure 13.1 we see the following:

At end of period 1:	The $1 is still worth $1 because it was invested at the *end* of the period.
At end of period 2:	An additional $1 is invested. The $2.00 is now worth $2.08. Note the $1 from period 1 earns interest but not the $1 invested at the end of period 2.
At end of period 3:	An additional $1 is invested. The $3.00 is now worth $3.25. Remember that the last dollar invested earns no interest.

Before learning how to calculate annuities, you should understand the two classifications of annuities.

How Annuities Are Classified

Annuities have many uses in addition to lottery payoffs. Some of these uses are insurance companies' pension installments, Social Security payments, home mortgages, businesses paying off notes, bond interest, and savings for a vacation trip or college education.

Annuities are classified into two major groups: contingent annuities and annuities certain. **Contingent annuities** have no fixed number of payments but depend on an uncertain event (e.g., life insurance payments that cease when the insured dies). **Annuities certain** have a specific stated number of payments (e.g., mortgage payments on a home). Based on the time of the payment, we can divide each of these two major annuity groups into the following:

1. **Ordinary annuity**—regular deposits (payments) made at the *end* of the period. Periods could be months, quarters, years, and so on. An ordinary annuity could be salaries, stock dividends, and so on.

2. **Annuity due**—regular deposits (payments) made at the *beginning* of the period, such as rent or life insurance premiums.

The remainder of this unit shows you how to calculate and check ordinary annuities and annuities due. Remember that you are calculating the *dollar amount* of the annuity at the end of the annuity term or at the end of the last period.

Ordinary Annuities: Money Invested at End of Period (Find Future Value)

Before we explain how to use a table that simplifies calculating ordinary annuities, let's first determine how to calculate the future value of an ordinary annuity manually.

---

[1]The term *amount of an annuity* has the same meaning as *future value of an annuity.*

Calculating Future Value of Ordinary Annuities Manually

Check out the plastic overlays that appear in Chapter 13 to review these concepts.

Remember that an ordinary annuity invests money at the *end* of each year (period). After we calculate ordinary annuities manually, you will see that the total value of the investment comes from the *stream* of yearly investments and the buildup of interest on the current balance.

Calculating Future Value of an Ordinary Annuity Manually

Step 1. For period 1, no interest calculation is necessary, since money is invested at the end of the period.

Step 2. For period 2, calculate interest on the balance and add the interest to the previous balance.

Step 3. Add the additional investment at the end of period 2 to the new balance.

Step 4. Repeat Steps 2 and 3 until the end of the desired period is reached.

EXAMPLE   Find the value of an investment after 3 years for a $3,000 ordinary annuity at 8%.

We calculate this manually as follows:

Step 1. ⟶ End of year 1: $3,000.00   ⟶ No interest, since this is put in at end of year 1. (Remember, payment is made at end of period.)

Year 2: $3,000.00   ⟶ Value of investment before investment at end of year 2.

Step 2. ⟶   +   240.00   ⟶ Interest (.08 × $3,000) for year 2.

$3,240.00   ⟶ Value of investment at end of year 2 before second investment.

Step 3. ⟶ End of year 2:   + 3,000.00   ⟶ Second investment at end of year 2.

Year 3: $6,240.00   ⟶ Investment balance going into year 3.

+   499.20   ⟶ Interest for year 3 (.08 × $6,240).

Step 4. ⟶ $6,739.20   ⟶ Value before investment at end of year 3.

+ 3,000.00   ⟶ Investment at end of year 3.

End of year 3: $9,739.20   ⟶ Total value of investment after investment at end of year 3.

Note: We totally invested $9,000 over three different periods. It is now worth $9,739.20

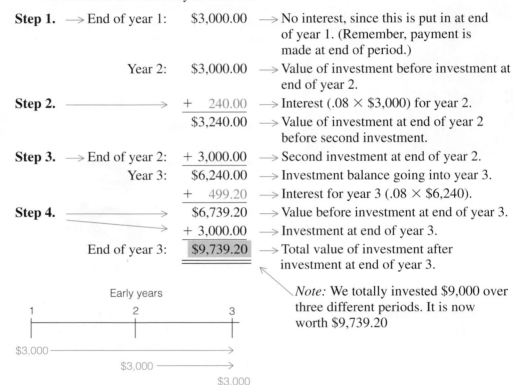

Early years

When you deposit $3,000 at the end of each year at an annual rate of 8%, the total value of the annuity is $9,739.20. What we called *maturity value* in compounding is now called the *future value of the annuity*. Remember that Interest = Principal × Rate × Time, with the principal changing because of the interest payments and the additional deposits. We can make this calculation easier by using Table 13.1 (p. 303).

Calculating Future Value of Ordinary Annuities by Table Lookup

Use the following steps to calculate the future value of an ordinary annuity by table lookup.[2]

---

[2]The formula for an ordinary annuity is $A = Pmt \times \dfrac{[(1 + i)^n - 1]}{i}$, where A equals future value of an ordinary annuity, Pmt equals annuity payment, i equals interest, and n equals number of periods. The calculator sequence for this example is: 1 [+] .08 = [yˣ] 3 [−] 1 [÷] .08 [×] 3,000 [=] 9,739.20.

TABLE 13.1 Ordinary annuity table: Compound sum of an annuity of $1

Period	2%	3%	4%	5%	6%	7%	8%	9%	10%	11%	12%	13%
1	1.0000	1.0000	1.0000	1.0000	1.0000	1.0000	1.0000	1.0000	1.0000	1.0000	1.0000	1.0000
2	2.0200	2.0300	2.0400	2.0500	2.0600	2.0700	2.0800	2.0900	2.1000	2.1100	2.1200	2.1300
3	3.0604	3.0909	3.1216	3.1525	3.1836	3.2149	3.2464	3.2781	3.3100	3.3421	3.3744	3.4069
4	4.1216	4.1836	4.2465	4.3101	4.3746	4.4399	4.5061	4.5731	4.6410	4.7097	4.7793	4.8498
5	5.2040	5.3091	5.4163	5.5256	5.6371	5.7507	5.8666	5.9847	6.1051	6.2278	6.3528	6.4803
6	6.3081	6.4684	6.6330	6.8019	6.9753	7.1533	7.3359	7.5233	7.7156	7.9129	8.1152	8.3227
7	7.4343	7.6625	7.8983	8.1420	8.3938	8.6540	8.9228	9.2004	9.4872	9.7833	10.0890	10.4047
8	8.5829	8.8923	9.2142	9.5491	9.8975	10.2598	10.6366	11.0285	11.4359	11.8594	12.2997	12.7573
9	9.7546	10.1591	10.5828	11.0265	11.4913	11.9780	12.4876	13.0210	13.5795	14.1640	14.7757	15.4157
10	10.9497	11.4639	12.0061	12.5779	13.1808	13.8164	14.4866	15.1929	15.9374	16.7220	17.5487	18.4197
11	12.1687	12.8078	13.4863	14.2068	14.9716	15.7836	16.6455	17.5603	18.5312	19.5614	20.6546	21.8143
12	13.4120	14.1920	15.0258	15.9171	16.8699	17.8884	18.9771	20.1407	21.3843	22.7132	24.1331	25.6502
13	14.6803	15.6178	16.6268	17.7129	18.8821	20.1406	21.4953	22.9534	24.5227	26.2116	28.0291	29.9847
14	15.9739	17.0863	18.2919	19.5986	21.0150	22.5505	24.2149	26.0192	27.9750	30.0949	32.3926	34.8827
15	17.2934	18.5989	20.0236	21.5785	23.2759	25.1290	27.1521	29.3609	31.7725	34.4054	37.2797	40.4174
16	18.6392	20.1569	21.8245	23.6574	25.6725	27.8880	30.3243	33.0034	35.9497	39.1899	42.7533	46.6717
17	20.0120	21.7616	23.6975	25.8403	28.2128	30.8402	33.7503	36.9737	40.5447	44.5008	48.8837	53.7390
18	21.4122	23.4144	25.6454	28.1323	30.9056	33.9990	37.4503	41.3014	45.5992	50.3959	55.7497	61.7251
19	22.8405	25.1169	27.6712	30.5389	33.7599	37.3789	41.4463	46.0185	51.1591	56.9395	63.4397	70.7494
20	24.2973	26.8704	29.7781	33.0659	36.7855	40.9954	45.7620	51.1602	57.2750	64.2028	72.0524	80.9468
25	32.0302	36.4593	41.6459	47.7270	54.8644	63.2489	73.1060	84.7010	98.3471	114.4133	133.3338	155.6194
30	40.5679	47.5754	56.0849	66.4386	79.0580	94.4606	113.2833	136.3077	164.4941	199.0209	241.3327	293.1989
40	60.4017	75.4012	95.0254	120.7993	154.7616	199.6346	259.0569	337.8831	442.5928	581.8260	767.0913	1013.7030
50	84.5790	112.7968	152.6669	209.3470	290.3351	406.5277	573.7711	815.0853	1163.9090	1668.7710	2400.0180	3459.5010

Note: This is only a sampling of tables available. The *Business Math Handbook* shows tables from $\frac{1}{2}$% to 15%.

Calculating Future Value of an Ordinary Annuity by Table Lookup

Step 1. Calculate the number of periods and rate per period.

Step 2. Look up the periods and rate in an ordinary annuity table. The intersection gives the table factor for the future value of $1.

Step 3. Multiply the payment each period by the table factor. This gives the future value of the annuity.

$$\frac{\text{Future value of}}{\text{ordinary annuity}} = \frac{\text{Annuity payment}}{\text{each period}} \times \frac{\text{Ordinary annuity}}{\text{table factor}}$$

EXAMPLE Find the value of an investment after 3 years for a $3,000 ordinary annuity at 8%.

Step 1. Periods = 3 years × 1 = 3   Rate = $\frac{8\%}{\text{Annually}}$ = 8%

Step 2. Go to Table 13.1, an ordinary annuity table. Look for 3 under the Period column. Go across to 8%. At the intersection is the table factor, 3.2464. (This was the example we showed in Figure 13.1.)

Step 3. Multiply $3,000 × 3.2464 = $9,739.20 (the same figure we calculated manually).

Annuities Due: Money Invested at Beginning of Period (Find Future Value)

In this section we look at what the difference in the total investment would be for an annuity due. As in the previous section, we will first make the calculation manually and then use the table lookup.

Calculating Future Value of Annuities Due Manually

Use the steps that follow to calculate the future value of an annuity due manually.

Calculating Future Value of an Annuity Due Manually

Step 1. Calculate the interest on the balance for the period and add it to the previous balance.

Step 2. Add additional investment at the *beginning* of the period to the new balance.

Step 3. Repeat Steps 1 and 2 until the end of the desired period is reached.

Remember that in an annuity due, we deposit the money at the *beginning* of the year and gain more interest. Common sense should tell us that the *annuity due* will give a higher final value. We will use the same example that we used before.

EXAMPLE Find the value of an investment after 3 years for a $3,000 annuity due at 8%. We calculate this manually as follows:

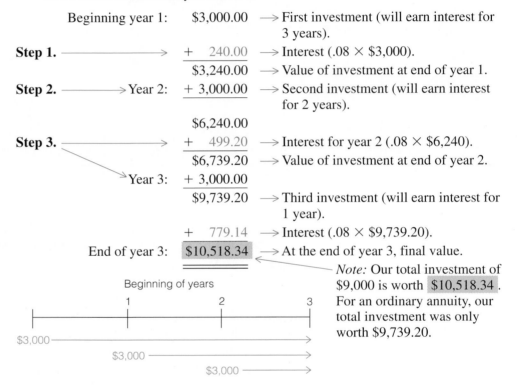

Beginning year 1:	$3,000.00	⟶	First investment (will earn interest for 3 years).
Step 1. ⟶	+ 240.00	⟶	Interest (.08 × $3,000).
	$3,240.00	⟶	Value of investment at end of year 1.
Step 2. ⟶ Year 2:	+ 3,000.00	⟶	Second investment (will earn interest for 2 years).
	$6,240.00		
Step 3. ⟶	+ 499.20	⟶	Interest for year 2 (.08 × $6,240).
	$6,739.20	⟶	Value of investment at end of year 2.
Year 3:	+ 3,000.00		
	$9,739.20	⟶	Third investment (will earn interest for 1 year).
	+ 779.14	⟶	Interest (.08 × $9,739.20).
End of year 3:	$10,518.34	⟶	At the end of year 3, final value.

Note: Our total investment of $9,000 is worth $10,518.34. For an ordinary annuity, our total investment was only worth $9,739.20.

Beginning of years

Calculating Future Value of Annuities Due by Table Lookup

To calculate the future value of an annuity due with a table lookup, use the steps that follow.

Calculating Future Value of an Annuity Due by Table Lookup[3]

Step 1. Calculate the number of periods and the rate per period. Add one extra period.

Step 2. Look up in an ordinary annuity table the periods and rate. The intersection gives the table *factor* for future value of $1.

Step 3. Multiply payment each period by the table factor.

Step 4. Subtract 1 payment from Step 3.

$$\text{Future value of an annuity due} = \left(\begin{array}{c} \text{Annuity} \\ \text{payment} \\ \text{each period} \end{array} \times \begin{array}{c} \text{Ordinary*} \\ \text{annuity} \\ \text{table factor} \end{array} \right) - 1 \text{ Payment}$$

*Add 1 period.

---

[3]The formula for an annuity due is $A = Pmt \times \dfrac{(1 + i)^n - 1}{i} \times (1 + i)$, where A equals future value of annuity due, Pmt equals annuity payment, i equals interest, and n equals number of periods. This formula is the same as that in footnote 2 except we multiply the future value of annuity by $1 + i$ since payments are made at the beginning of the period. The calculator sequence for this example is: 1 ⊞ .08 ⊟ ⊠ 9,739.20 ⊟ 10,518.34.

Let's check the $10,518.34 by table lookup.

Step 1. Periods = 3 years × 1 =   3 $\text{Rate} = \dfrac{8\%}{\text{Annually}} = 8\%$
                          + 1 extra
                          ———
                            4

Step 2. Table factor, 4.5061
Step 3. $3,000 × 4.5061 = $13,518.30
Step 4.   − 3,000.00 ← Be sure to subtract 1 payment.
                                      = $10,518.34 (off 4 cents due to rounding)

Note that the annuity due shows an ending value of $10,518.30, while the ending value of ordinary annuity was $9,739.20. We had a higher ending value with the annuity due because the investment took place at the beginning of each period.

Annuity payments do not have to be made yearly. They could be made semiannually, monthly, quarterly, and so on. Let's look at one more example with a different number of periods and rate.

Different Number of Periods and Rates

By using a different number of periods and rates, we will contrast an ordinary annuity with an annuity due in the following example:

EXAMPLE   Using Table 13.1, find the value of a $3,000 investment after 3 years made quarterly at 8%.

In the annuity due calculation, be sure to add one period and subtract one payment from the total value.

	Ordinary annuity	**Annuity due**	
Step 1.	Periods = 3 years × 4 = 12	Periods = 3 years × 4 = 12	**Step 1**
	Rate = 8% ÷ 4 = 2%	Rate = 8% ÷ 4 = 2%	
Step 2.	Table 13.1:	Table 13.1:	**Step 2**
	12 periods, 2% = 13.4120	13 periods, 2% = 14.6803	
Step 3.	$3,000 × 13.4120 = $40,236	$3,000 × 14.6803 = $44,040.90	**Step 3**
		− 3,000.00	**Step 4**
		$41,040.90	

Again, note that with annuity due, the total value is greater since you invest the money at the beginning of each period.

Now check your progress with the Practice Quiz.

LU 13–1 PRACTICE QUIZ

1. Using Table 13.1, **(a)** find the value of an investment after 4 years on an ordinary annuity of $4,000 made semiannually at 10%; and **(b)** recalculate, assuming an annuity due.

2. Wally Beaver won a lottery and will receive a check for $4,000 at the beginning of each 6 months for the next 5 years. If Wally deposits each check into an account that pays 6%, how much will he have at the end of the 5 years?

✓ **SOLUTIONS**

1. **a. Step 1.** Periods = 4 years × 2 = 8   **b.** Periods = 4 years × 2   **Step 1**
                                                          = 8 + 1 = 9

                        10% ÷ 2 = 5%   10% ÷ 2 = 5%
           Step 2. Factor = 9.5491   Factor = 11.0265   **Step 2**
           Step 3. $4,000 × 9.5491 $4,000 × 11.0265 = $44,106   **Step 3**
                        = $38,196.40   − 1 payment   − 4,000   **Step 4**
                                                                            $40,106

2. **Step 1.** 5 years × 2 =   10 $\dfrac{6\%}{2} = 3\%$
                              + 1
                              ———
                             11 periods

    Step 2. Table factor, 12.8078
    Step 3. $4,000 × 12.8078 = $51,231.20
    Step 4.   − 4,000.00
                                      $47,231.20

FIGURE 13.2

Present value of an annuity
of $1 at 8%

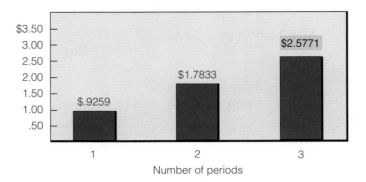

LEARNING UNIT 13-2 | PRESENT VALUE OF AN ORDINARY ANNUITY (FIND PRESENT VALUE)[4]

This unit begins by presenting the concept of present value of an ordinary annuity. Then you will learn how to use a table to calculate the present value of an ordinary annuity.

Concept of Present Value of an Ordinary Annuity— The Big Picture

Let's assume that we want to know how much money we need to invest *today* to receive a stream of payments for a given number of years in the future. This is called the **present value of an ordinary annuity.**

In Figure 13.2 you can see that if you wanted to withdraw $1 at the end of one period, you would have to invest 93 cents *today*. If at the end of each period for three periods, you wanted to withdraw $1, you would have to put $2.58 in the bank *today* at 8% interest. (Note that we go from the future back to the present.)

Now let's look at how we could use tables to calculate the present value of annuities and then check our answer.

Calculating Present Value of an Ordinary Annuity by Table Lookup

Use the following steps to calculate by table lookup the present value of an ordinary annuity.[5]

Calculating Present Value of an Ordinary Annuity by Table Lookup

Step 1. Calculate the number of periods and rate per period.

Step 2. Look up the periods and rate in the present value of an annuity table. The intersection gives the table factor for the present value of $1.

Step 3. Multiply the withdrawal for each period by the table factor. This gives the present value of an ordinary annuity.

$$\text{Present value of ordinary annuity payment} = \text{Annuity payment} \times \text{Present value of ordinary annuity table}$$

EXAMPLE   John Fitch wants to receive an $8,000 annuity in 3 years. Interest on the annuity is 8% annually. John will make withdrawals at the end of each year. How much must John invest today to receive a stream of payments for 3 years? Use Table 13.2. Remember that interest could be earned semiannually, quarterly, and so on, as shown in the previous unit.

Step 1.   3 years × 1 = 3 periods $\dfrac{8\%}{\text{Annually}} = 8\%$

Step 2.   Table factor, 2.5771   (we saw this in Figure 13.2)

Step 3. $8,000 × 2.5771 = $20,616.80

---

[4]For simplicity we omit a discussion of present value of annuity due that would require subtracting a period and adding a 1.

[5]The formula for the present value of an ordinary annuity is $P = Pmt \times \dfrac{1 - 1 \div (1 + i)^n}{i}$, where P equals present value of annuity, Pmt equals annuity payment, i equals interest, and n equals number of periods. The calculator sequence would be as follows for the John Fitch example: 1 [+] .08 [y^x] 3 [+/−] [=] [M+] 1 [−] [MR] [÷] .08 [×] 8,000 [=] 21,000.

Turn transparency over to see relationship of compounding to present value.

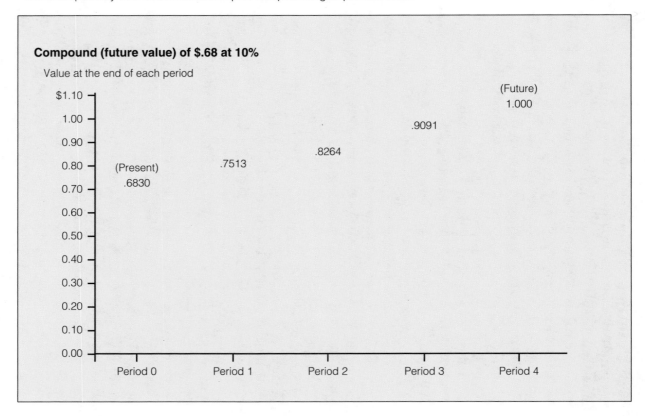

Compound (future value) of $.68 at 10%

Value at the end of each period

				(Future)
				1.000
			.9091	
		.8264		
	.7513			
(Present)				
.6830				

$1.10
1.00
0.90
0.80
0.70
0.60
0.50
0.40
0.30
0.20
0.10
0.00

Period 0   Period 1   Period 2   Period 3   Period 4

68¢ today will grow to $1.00 in the future.

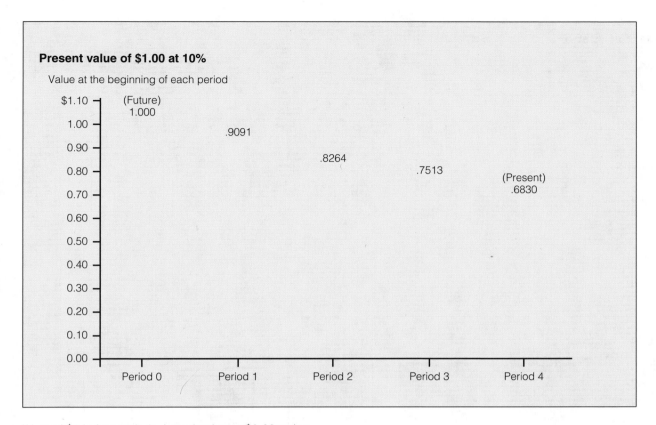

Present value of $1.00 at 10%

Value at the beginning of each period

	(Future) 1.000	.9091	.8264	.7513	(Present) .6830
$1.10					
1.00					
0.90					
0.80					
0.70					
0.60					
0.50					
0.40					
0.30					
0.20					
0.10					
0.00	Period 0	Period 1	Period 2	Period 3	Period 4

If I need $1 in four periods, I need to invest $0.68 today.

Present value of $1.00 at 10%

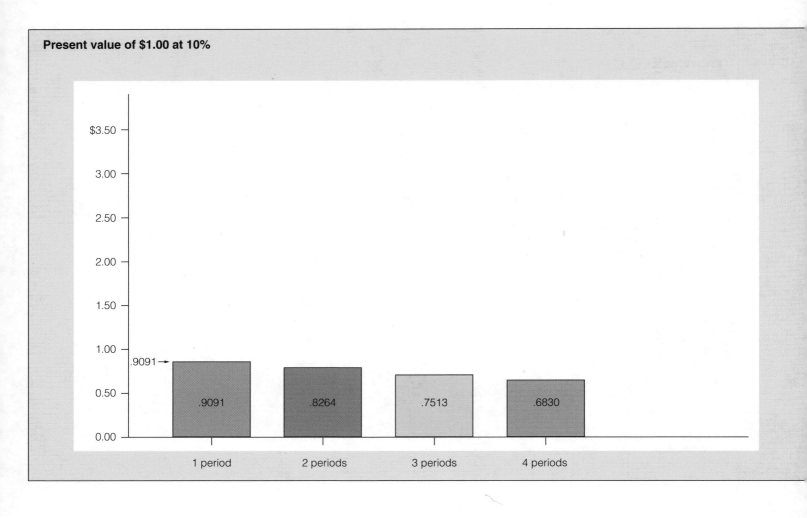

Future value of $1.00 at 10%

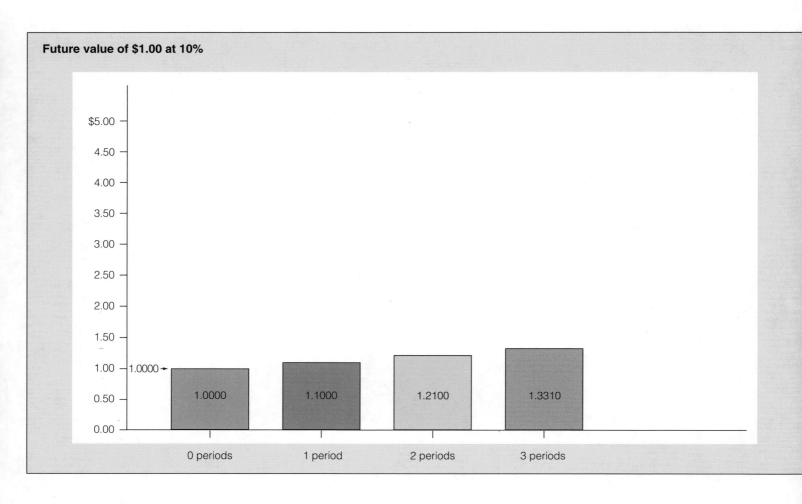

TABLE 13.2   Present value of an annuity of $1

Period	2%	3%	4%	5%	6%	7%	8%	9%	10%	11%	12%	13%
1	0.9804	0.9709	0.9615	0.9524	0.9434	0.9346	0.9259	0.9174	0.9091	0.9009	0.8929	0.8850
2	1.9416	1.9135	1.8861	1.8594	1.8334	1.8080	1.7833	1.7591	1.7355	1.7125	1.6901	1.6681
3	2.8839	2.8286	2.7751	2.7232	2.6730	2.6243	2.5771	2.5313	2.4869	2.4437	2.4018	2.3612
4	3.8077	3.7171	3.6299	3.5459	3.4651	3.3872	3.3121	3.2397	3.1699	3.1024	3.0373	2.9745
5	4.7134	4.5797	4.4518	4.3295	4.2124	4.1002	3.9927	3.8897	3.7908	3.6959	3.6048	3.5172
6	5.6014	5.4172	5.2421	5.0757	4.9173	4.7665	4.6229	4.4859	4.3553	4.2305	4.1114	3.9975
7	6.4720	6.2303	6.0021	5.7864	5.5824	5.3893	5.2064	5.0330	4.8684	4.7122	4.5638	4.4226
8	7.3255	7.0197	6.7327	6.4632	6.2098	5.9713	5.7466	5.5348	5.3349	5.1461	4.9676	4.7988
9	8.1622	7.7861	7.4353	7.1078	6.8017	6.5152	6.2469	5.9952	5.7590	5.5370	5.3282	5.1317
10	8.9826	8.5302	8.1109	7.7217	7.3601	7.0236	6.7101	6.4177	6.1446	5.8892	5.6502	5.4262
11	9.7868	9.2526	8.7605	8.3064	7.8869	7.4987	7.1390	6.8052	6.4951	6.2065	5.9377	5.6869
12	10.5753	9.9540	9.3851	8.8632	8.3838	7.9427	7.5361	7.1607	6.8137	6.4924	6.1944	5.9176
13	11.3483	10.6350	9.9856	9.3936	8.8527	8.3576	7.9038	7.4869	7.1034	6.7499	6.4235	6.1218
14	12.1062	11.2961	10.5631	9.8986	9.2950	8.7455	8.2442	7.7862	7.3667	6.9819	6.6282	6.3025
15	12.8492	11.9379	11.1184	10.3796	9.7122	9.1079	8.5595	8.0607	7.6061	7.1909	6.8109	6.4624
16	13.5777	12.5611	11.6523	10.8378	10.1059	9.4466	8.8514	8.3126	7.8237	7.3792	6.9740	6.6039
17	14.2918	13.1661	12.1657	11.2741	10.4773	9.7632	9.1216	8.5436	8.0216	7.5488	7.1196	6.7291
18	14.9920	13.7535	12.6593	11.6896	10.8276	10.0591	9.3719	8.7556	8.2014	7.7016	7.2497	6.8399
19	15.6784	14.3238	13.1339	12.0853	11.1581	10.3356	9.6036	8.9501	8.3649	7.8393	7.3658	6.9380
20	16.3514	14.8775	13.5903	12.4622	11.4699	10.5940	9.8181	9.1285	8.5136	7.9633	7.4694	7.0248
25	19.5234	17.4131	15.6221	14.0939	12.7834	11.6536	10.6748	9.8226	9.0770	8.4217	7.8431	7.3300
30	22.3964	19.6004	17.2920	15.3724	13.7648	12.4090	11.2578	10.2737	9.4269	8.6938	8.0552	7.4957
40	27.3554	23.1148	19.7928	17.1591	15.0463	13.3317	11.9246	10.7574	9.7790	8.9511	8.2438	7.6344
50	31.4236	25.7298	21.4822	18.2559	15.7619	13.8007	12.2335	10.9617	9.9148	9.0417	8.3045	7.6752

If John wants to withdraw $8,000 at the end of each period for 3 years, he will have to deposit $20,616.80 in the bank *today*.

$20,616.80
+   1,649.34 $\longrightarrow$ Interest at end of year 1 (.08 × $20,616.80)
$22,266.14
−   8,000.00 $\longrightarrow$ First payment to John
$14,266.14
+   1,141.29 $\longrightarrow$ Interest at end of year 2 (.08 × $14,266.14)
$15,407.43
−   8,000.00 $\longrightarrow$ Second payment to John
$ 7,407.43
+   592.59 $\longrightarrow$ Interest at end of year 3 (.08 × $7,407.43)
$ 8,000.02
−   8,000.00 $\longrightarrow$ After end of year 3 John receives his last $8,000
      .02[6]

Before we leave this unit, let's work out two examples that show the relationship of Chapter 13 to Chapter 12. Use the tables in your *Business Math Handbook*.

Lump Sum versus Annuities

EXAMPLE   John Sands made deposits of $200 semiannually to Floor Bank, which pays 8% interest compounded semiannually. After 5 years, John makes no more deposits. What will be the balance in the account 6 years after the last deposit?

Step 1.   Calculate amount of annuity: Table 13.1
         10 periods, 4% $200 × 12.0061 = $2,401.22

Step 2.   Calculate how much the final value of the annuity will grow by the compound interest table.   Table 12.1
         12 periods, 4% $2,401.22 × 1.6010 = $3,844.35

_____
[6]Off due to rounding.

For John, the stream of payments grows to $2,401.22. Then this *lump sum* grows for 6 years to $3,844.35. Now let's look at a present value example.

EXAMPLE   Mel Rich decided to retire in 8 years to New Mexico. What amount should Mel invest today so he will be able to withdraw $40,000 at the end of each year for 25 years *after* he retires? Assume Mel can invest money at 5% interest (compounded annually).

Step 1.   Calculate the present value of the annuity: Table 13.2

25 periods, 5% $40,000 × 14.0939 = $563,756

Step 2.   Find the present value of $563,756 since Mel will not retire for 8 years:

Table 12.3

8 periods, 5% (PV table) $563,756 × .6768 = $381,550.06

If Mel deposits $381,550 in year 1, it will grow to $563,756 after 8 years.

It's time to try the Practice Quiz and check your understanding of this unit.

LU 13–2 PRACTICE QUIZ

(Use tables in *Business Math Handbook*)

1.   What must you invest today to receive an $18,000 annuity for 5 years semiannually at a 10% annual rate? All withdrawals will be made at the end of each period.

2.   Rase High School wants to set up a scholarship fund to provide five $2,000 scholarships for the next 10 years. If money can be invested at an annual rate of 9%, how much should the scholarship committee invest today?

3.   Joe Wood decided to retire in 5 years in Arizona. What amount should Joe invest today so he can withdraw $60,000 at the end of each year for 30 years after he retires? Assume Joe can invest money at 6% compounded annually.

✓ SOLUTIONS

1.   **Step 1.**   Periods = 5 years × 2 = 10; Rate = 10% ÷ 2 = 5%
     Step 2.   Factor, 7.7217
     Step 3. $18,000 × 7.7217 = $138,990.60

2.   **Step 1.**   Periods = 10; Rate = 9%
     Step 2.   Factor, 6.4177
     Step 3. $10,000 × 6.4177 = $64,177

3.   **Step 1.**   Calculate present value of annuity: 30 periods, 6%.
                   $60,000 × 13.7648 = $825,888

     Step 2.   Find present value of $825,888 for 5 years: 5 periods, 6%.
                   $825,888 × .7473 = $617,186.10

LEARNING UNIT 13–3 | SINKING FUNDS (FIND PERIODIC PAYMENTS)

Michael Newman/PhotoEdit

A **sinking fund** is a financial arrangement that sets aside regular periodic payments of a particular amount of money. Compound interest accumulates on these payments to a specific sum at a predetermined future date. Corporations use sinking funds to discharge bonded indebtedness, to replace worn-out equipment, to purchase plant expansion, and so on.

A sinking fund is a different type of an annuity. In a sinking fund, you determine the amount of periodic payments you need to achieve a given financial goal. In the annuity, you know the amount of each payment and must determine its future value. Let's work with the following formula:

$$\text{Sinking fund payment} = \text{Future value} \times \text{Sinking fund table factor}^7$$

---

[7]Sinking fund table is the reciprocal of the ordinary annuity table.

TABLE 13.3

Sinking fund table based on $1

Period	2%	3%	4%	5%	6%	8%	10%
1	1.0000	1.0000	1.0000	1.0000	1.0000	1.0000	1.0000
2	0.4951	0.4926	0.4902	0.4878	0.4854	0.4808	0.4762
3	0.3268	0.3235	0.3203	0.3172	0.3141	0.3080	0.3021
4	0.2426	0.2390	0.2355	0.2320	0.2286	0.2219	0.2155
5	0.1922	0.1884	0.1846	0.1810	0.1774	0.1705	0.1638
6	0.1585	0.1546	0.1508	0.1470	0.1434	0.1363	0.1296
7	0.1345	0.1305	0.1266	0.1228	0.1191	0.1121	0.1054
8	0.1165	0.1125	0.1085	0.1047	0.1010	0.0940	0.0874
9	0.1025	0.0984	0.0945	0.0907	0.0870	0.0801	0.0736
10	0.0913	0.0872	0.0833	0.0795	0.0759	0.0690	0.0627
11	0.0822	0.0781	0.0741	0.0704	0.0668	0.0601	0.0540
12	0.0746	0.0705	0.0666	0.0628	0.0593	0.0527	0.0468
13	0.0681	0.0640	0.0601	0.0565	0.0530	0.0465	0.0408
14	0.0626	0.0585	0.0547	0.0510	0.0476	0.0413	0.0357
15	0.0578	0.0538	0.0499	0.0463	0.0430	0.0368	0.0315
16	0.0537	0.0496	0.0458	0.0423	0.0390	0.0330	0.0278
17	0.0500	0.0460	0.0422	0.0387	0.0354	0.0296	0.0247
18	0.0467	0.0427	0.0390	0.0355	0.0324	0.0267	0.0219
19	0.0438	0.0398	0.0361	0.0327	0.0296	0.0241	0.0195
20	0.0412	0.0372	0.0336	0.0302	0.0272	0.0219	0.0175
24	0.0329	0.0290	0.0256	0.0225	0.0197	0.0150	0.0113
28	0.0270	0.0233	0.0200	0.0171	0.0146	0.0105	0.0075
32	0.0226	0.0190	0.0159	0.0133	0.0110	0.0075	0.0050
36	0.0192	0.0158	0.0129	0.0104	0.0084	0.0053	0.0033
40	0.0166	0.0133	0.0105	0.0083	0.0065	0.0039	0.0023

EXAMPLE   To retire a bond issue, Moore Company needs $60,000 in 18 years from today. The interest rate is 10% compounded annually. What payment must Moore make at the end of each year? Use Table 13.3.

We begin by looking down the Period column in Table 13.3 until we come to 18. Then we go across until we reach the 10% column. The table factor is .0219.

Now we multiply $60,000 by the factor as follows:

$60,000 × .0219 = $1,314

This states that if Moore Company pays $1,314 at the end of each period for 18 years, then $60,000 will be available to pay off the bond issue at maturity.

We can check this by using Table 13.1 (the ordinary annuity table):

$1,314 × 45.5992 = $59,917.35[8]

It's time to try the following Practice Quiz.

LU 13–3 PRACTICE QUIZ

Today, Arrow Company issued bonds that will mature to a value of $90,000 in 10 years. Arrow's controller is planning to set up a sinking fund. Interest rates are 12% compounded semiannually. What will Arrow Company have to set aside to meet its obligation in 10 years? Check your answer. Your answer will be off due to the rounding of Table 13.3.

✓ SOLUTION

10 years × 2 = 20 periods $\frac{12\%}{2} = 6\%$ $90,000 × .0272 = $2,448

Check $2,448 × 36.7855 = $90,050.90

---
[8]Off due to rounding.

Chapter Organizer and Reference Guide

Topic	Key point, procedure, formula	Example(s) to illustrate situation
Ordinary annuities (find future value), p. 300	Invest money at end of each period. Find future value at maturity. Answers question of how much money accumulates. $$\begin{array}{l}\text{Future}\\\text{value of}\\\text{ordinary}\\\text{annuity}\end{array} = \begin{array}{l}\text{Annuity}\\\text{payment}\\\text{each}\\\text{period}\end{array} \times \begin{array}{l}\text{Ordinary}\\\text{annuity}\\\text{table}\\\text{factor}\end{array}$$	Use Table 13.1: 2 years, $4,000 ordinary annuity at 8% annually. Value = $4,000 × 2.0800 = $8,320 (2 periods, 8%)

Annuities due (find future value), p. 303	Invest money at beginning of each period. Find future value at maturity. Should be higher than ordinary annuity since it is invested at beginning of each period. Use Table 13.1, but add one period and subtract one payment from answer.
	
	$$\begin{array}{l}\text{Future}\\\text{value}\\\text{of an}\\\text{annuity}\\\text{due}\end{array} = \left(\begin{array}{l}\text{Annuity}\\\text{payment}\\\text{each}\\\text{period}\end{array} \times \begin{array}{l}\text{Ordinary*}\\\text{annuity}\\\text{table}\\\text{factor}\end{array}\right) - 1\,\text{Payment}$$
	*Add 1 period.
		Example: Same example as above but invest money at beginning of period.
		$4,000 × 3.2464 = $12,985.60
		     − 4,000.00
		     $ 8,985.60 (3 periods, 8%)

Present value of an ordinary annuity (find present value), p. 306	Calculate number of periods and rate per period. Use Table 13.2 to find table factor for present value of $1. Multiply withdrawal for each period by table factor to get present value of an ordinary annuity.
	
	$$\begin{array}{l}\text{Present}\\\text{value of an}\\\text{ordinary}\\\text{annuity}\\\text{payment}\end{array} = \begin{array}{l}\text{Annuity}\\\text{payment}\end{array} \times \begin{array}{l}\text{Present}\\\text{value of}\\\text{ordinary}\\\text{annuity}\\\text{table}\end{array}$$
		Example: Receive $10,000 for 5 years. Interest is 10% compounded annually.
		Table 13.2: 5 periods, 10%
		          3.7908
		       × $10,000
		What you put in today = $37,908

Sinking funds (find periodic payment), p. 308	Paying a particular amount of money for a set number of periodic payments to accumulate a specific sum. We know the future and must calculate the periodic payments needed. Answer can be proved by ordinary annuity table. $$\begin{array}{l}\text{Sinking}\\\text{fund}\\\text{payment}\end{array} = \begin{array}{l}\text{Future}\\\text{value}\end{array} \times \begin{array}{l}\text{Sinking}\\\text{fund table}\\\text{factor}\end{array}$$	*Example:* $200,000 bond to retire 15 years from now. Interest is 6% compounded annually. By Table 13.3: $200,000 × .0430 = $8,600 Check by Table 13.1: $8,600 × 23.2759 = $200,172.74
Key terms	Annuities certain, *p. 301* Annuity, *p. 300* Annuity due, *p. 301* Contingent annuities, *p. 301*	Future value of an annuity, *p. 301* Ordinary annuity, *p. 301* Payment periods, *p. 301* Present value of an annuity, *p. 306* Sinking fund, *p. 308* Term of the annuity, *p. 301*

Critical Thinking Discussion Questions

1. What is the difference between an ordinary annuity and an annuity due? If you were to save money in an annuity, which would you choose and why?

2. Explain how you would calculate ordinary annuities and annuities due by table lookup. Create an example to explain the meaning of a table factor from an ordinary annuity.

3. What is a present value of an ordinary annuity? Create an example showing how one of your relatives might plan for retirement by using the present value of an ordinary annuity. Would you ever have to use lump-sum payments in your calculation from Chapter 12?

4. What is a sinking fund? Why could an ordinary annuity table be used to check the sinking fund payment?

DRILL PROBLEMS

Complete the ordinary annuities for the following using tables in the *Business Math Handbook:*

	Amount of payment	Payment payable	Years	Interest rate	Value of annuity
13–1.	$5,000	Quarterly	5	4%	
13–2.	$3,000	Semiannually	10	10%	

Redo Problem 13–1 as an annuity due:

13–3.

Calculate the value of the following annuity due without a table. Check your results by Table 13.1 or the *Business Math Handbook* (they will be slightly off due to rounding):

	Amount of payment	Payment payable	Years	Interest rate
13–4.	$2,000	Annually	3	6%

Complete the following, using Table 13.2 or the *Business Math Handbook* for the present value of an ordinary annuity:

	Amount of annuity expected	Payment	Time	Interest rate	Present value (amount needed now to invest to receive annuity)
13–5.	$900	Annually	4 years	6%	
13–6.	$12,000	Quarterly	4 years	12%	

13–7. Check Problem 13–5 without the use of Table 13.2.

Using the sinking fund Table 13.3 or the *Business Math Handbook,* complete the following:

	Required amount	Frequency of payment	Length of time	Interest rate	Payment amount end of each period
13–8.	$25,000	Quarterly	6 years	8%	
13–9.	$15,000	Annually	8 years	8%	

13–10. Check the answer in Problem 13–9 by Table 13.1.

WORD PROBLEMS (Use Tables in the *Business Math Handbook*)

13–11. Ellen Sullivan, an employee at Wal-Mart, made deposits of $900 at the end of each year for 7 years. Interest is 7% compounded annually. What is the value of Sullivan's annuity at the end of 7 years?

13–12. Pete King promised to pay his son $300 semiannually for 9 years. Assume Pete can invest his money at 8% in an ordinary annuity. How much must Pete invest today to pay his son $300 semiannually for 9 years?

13–13. On April 12, 2001, Terry Savage of the *Chicago Sun-Times* wrote a column on saving for retirement. Assuming the stock market earns the historical market average return of 10.5%, you will have a nice retirement nest egg if you save $5,000 a year for 31 years. What is the value of this ordinary annuity?

13–14. On February 25, 2000, the *Journal Star* reported on the magic of compound interest. Alice Cooper begins saving at age 35 and wants to withdraw $25,000 at the end of each year for 10 years after she retires at age 65. At 8% interest compounded annually, how much should Alice invest today?

13–15. The October 2000 issue of *Black Enterprise* reported on compounding. If you were able to invest only $1,200 at the end of each quarter and placed it in a vehicle that produced an average annual return of 6% compounded quarterly, how much would you receive in 10 years?

13–16. Patricia and Joe Payne are divorced. The divorce settlement stipulated that Joe pay $525 a month for their daughter Suzanne until she turns 18 in 4 years. How much must Joe set aside today to meet the settlement? Interest is 6% a year.

13–17. Josef Company borrowed money that must be repaid in 20 years. The company wants to make sure the loan will be repaid at the end of year 20. So it invests $12,500 at the end of each year at 12% interest compounded annually. What was the amount of the original loan?

13–18. Jane Frost wants to receive yearly payments of $15,000 for 10 years. How much must she deposit at her bank today at 11% interest compounded annually?

13–19. Toby Martin invests $2,000 at the end of each year for 10 years in an ordinary annuity at 11% interest compounded annually. What is the final value of Toby's investment at the end of year 10?

13–20. Alice Longtree has decided to invest $400 quarterly for 4 years in an ordinary annuity at 8%. As her financial adviser, calculate for Alice the total cash value of the annuity at the end of year 4.

13–21. At the beginning of each period for 10 years, Merl Agnes invests $500 semiannually at 6%. What is the cash value of this annuity due at the end of year 10?

13–22. Jeff Associates borrowed $30,000. The company plans to set up a sinking fund that will repay the loan at the end of 8 years. Assume a 12% interest rate compounded semiannually. What must Jeff pay into the fund each period of time? Check your answer by Table 13.1.

13–23. On Joe's graduation from college, Joe Martin's uncle promised him a gift of $12,000 in cash or $900 every quarter
Excel   for the next 4 years after graduation. If money could be invested at 8% compounded quarterly, which offer is better for Joe?

13–24. An article appearing in the *Modesto Bee* on March 21, 2000, stated that the Institute of Certified Financial Planners recommends putting a minimum of 10% of your gross income toward retirement and as much as 20% if you are getting close to retiring. You are earning an average of $46,500 and will retire in 10 years. If you put 20% of your gross average income in an ordinary annuity compounded at 7% annually, what will be the value of the annuity when you retire?

13–25. GU Corporation must buy a new piece of equipment in 5 years that will cost $88,000. The company is setting up a sinking fund to finance the purchase. What will the quarterly deposit be if the fund earns 8% interest?

13–26. Mike Macaro is selling a piece of land. Two offers are on the table. Morton Company offered a $40,000 down payment and $35,000 a year for the next 5 years. Flynn Company offered $25,000 down and $38,000 a year for the next 5 years. If money can be invested at 8% compounded annually, which offer is better for Mike?

13–27. Al Vincent has decided to retire to Arizona in 10 years. What amount should Al invest today so that he will be able to withdraw $28,000 at the end of each year for 15 years *after* he retires? Assume he can invest the money at 8% interest compounded annually.

13–28. Victor French made deposits of $5,000 at the end of each quarter to Book Bank, which pays 8% interest compounded quarterly. After 3 years, Victor made no more deposits. What will be the balance in the account 2 years after the last deposit?

13–29. Janet Woo decided to retire to Florida in 6 years. What amount should Janet invest today so she can withdraw $50,000 at the end of each year for 20 years after she retires? Assume Janet can invest money at 6% compounded annually.

CHALLENGE PROBLEMS

13–30. *Sun Publications* dated March 21, 2001, reported that in 11 years it would cost approximately $80,000 for 4 years at a public university and $240,000 to send your child to a private university. Bank A quoted 6% interest compounded annually. Bank B quoted 7% interest compounded annually. **(a)** How much would you have to deposit in Bank A each year to pay for the public university? **(b)** How much would you have to deposit in Bank A each year to pay for the private university? **(c)** How much would you have to deposit in Bank B each year to pay for the public university? **(d)** How much would you have to deposit in Bank B each year to pay for the private university?

13–31. Ajax Corporation has hired Brad O'Brien as its new president. Terms included the company's agreeing to pay retirement benefits of $18,000 at the end of each semiannual period for 10 years. This will begin in 3,285 days. If the money can be invested at 8% compounded semiannually, what must the company deposit today to fulfill its obligation to Brad?

SUMMARY PRACTICE TEST (Use Tables in the *Business Math Handbook*)

1. Rio Sung plans to deposit $1,400 at the end of every 6 months for the next 15 years at 8% interest compounded semiannually. What is the value of Rio's annuity at the end of 15 years? *(p. 303)*

2. On Ray Long's graduation from law school, Ray's uncle, Paul Brown, promised him a gift of $24,000 or $2,400 every quarter for the next 4 years after graduating from law school. If the money could be invested at 6% compounded quarterly, which offer should Ray choose? *(p. 306)*

3. Ginny Kadu wants to receive $6,000 each year for 19 years. How much must Ginny invest today at 4% interest compounded annually? *(p. 306)*

4. In 7 years, Age.com will have to repay an $80,000 loan. Assume a 6% interest rate compounded quarterly. How much must Age.com. pay each period to have $80,000 at the end of 7 years? *(p. 309)*

5. Ron Enterprise borrowed $70,000. The company plans to set up a sinking fund that will repay the loan at the end of 10 years. Assume a 6% interest rate compounded semiannually. What amount must Ron Enterprise pay into the fund each period? Check your answer by Table 13.1. (*pp. 308, 309*)

6. Sachi Lee wants to receive $12,000 each year for the next 30 years. Assume a 7% interest rate compounded annually. How much must Sachi invest today? (*p. 307*)

7. Twice a year for 10 years, Wayne Burton invested $1,400 compounded semiannually at 6% interest. What is the value of this annuity due? (*p. 304*)

8. Scupper Rurse invested $1,200 semiannually for 20 years at 8% interest compounded semiannually. What is the value of this annuity due? (*p. 304*)

9. Morris Katz decided to retire to Mexico in 8 years. What amount should Morris deposit so that he will be able to withdraw $80,000 at the end of each year for 30 years after he retires? Assume Morris can invest money at 8% interest compounded annually. (*p. 306*)

10. Terri Swanson made deposits of $8,000 at the end of each quarter to Rio Bank, which pays 4% interest compounded quarterly. After 9 years, Terri made no more deposits. What will be the account's balance 4 years after the last deposit? (*p. 303*)

● Mike Reynolds is off to an early lead by sinking his savings into his 401(k).

KRISTINE LARSEN

STARTING OUT | Making the most of **YOUR 401(K)** early on gives you a better shot at retirement. *By Catherine Siskos*

POWER FORWARD

BY THE TIME he retires, Mike Reynolds expects to be a millionaire five times over. And that's just from the money he expects to have saved for retirement. Reynolds, 25, is determined not to repeat the mistakes that his parents made. "They didn't start saving for retirement right away and were extremely conservative with their investments," he says.

Reynolds wasted no time with his own savings. Two years ago, barely into his second month as a computer analyst for Towers Perrin in Philadelphia, he began stashing 12% of his salary—the maximum the company allows—into Towers Perrin's 401(k) plan. Not content to max out his employer-sponsored plan, Reynolds has also opened a Roth IRA, a plan that provides tax-free withdrawals in retirement. And still he wonders if there's more he could be doing.

Many young adults take the opposite approach and don't do nearly enough to save for a retirement 40 years hence. A study by benefits consulting firm Hewitt Associates found that 46% of people between the ages of 20 and 29 who earned less than $80,000 and were eligible to participate in their company's 401(k) plan chose not to. That's a shame, because they're passing up twin tax breaks as well as, in some cases, matching money from their employer.

When you contribute to a 401(k) plan, the money comes out of your paycheck *before* taxes. If, say, you're in the 28% federal bracket and have a state income-tax rate of 5%, you could make a $200-a-month contribution and find your take-home pay lighter by only $134. Plus, your contributions grow tax-deferred inside the plan. That means savings compound faster than they would if some of the earnings went to pay taxes.

Get in early. Invest as much of your salary as you can, within the range set by your employer (usually between 1% and 15% of your pay, up to the legal maximum in 2001 of $10,500 per year). You'll owe no taxes until you make withdrawals—but if you take your money before age 55, you'll owe taxes and a 10% penalty for early withdrawal.

Many employers make you wait up to a year before you can participate in a 401(k) plan. But with others, like Reynolds's company, you can hit the ground running. If you're forced to wait, don't just sit there: Take the money that you would have contributed to the 401(k) each month and save it in a bank account or money-market fund. Once you're eligible to participate, double your 401(k) contributions for the first year, and use your savings to make up the difference in your paycheck.

Business Math Issue

401K plans are a fad in the retirement process.*
1. List the key points of the article and information to support your position.
2. Write a group defense of your position using math calculations to support your view.

---

*401(K), 403(B), and 457 Plans New Contribution Limits.

Less than age 50		Age 50 and older	
Tax years	Maximum annual deferral	Tax years	Additional annual contribution
2001	$10,500	2001	Not available
2002	$11,000	2002	$1,000
2003	$12,000	2003	$2,000
2004	$13,000	2004	$3,000
2005	$14,000	2005	$4,000
2006	$15,000	2006	$5,000
2007–2010	Indexed for inflation	2007–2010	Indexed for inflation

*Source: Franklin Templeton Investments.

BUSINESS MATH SCRAPBOOK
WITH INTERNET APPLICATION

Putting Your Skills to Work

SMALL CHANGE IS BIG MONEY

How much does it cost for one large pizza a week? If you said $250,000, you obviously know a thing or two about investing. Financial planner Allyson Lewis, author of *The Million Dollar Car and $250,000 Pizza* (Dearborn Trade, 2000), says that if $20 spent on pizza were invested weekly in a mutual fund with a 9 percent annual return, it'd be worth a quarter of a million dollars in 30 years.

ITEM	COST	ANNUAL COST	YOU COULD'VE USED IT FOR ...	IF YOU INVESTED IT IN A 401(K), IN 2020 IT'D BE WORTH ...
ATM FEES	$2.50 per week (didn't use your own bank)	$130	Session with a financial planner	$7,280
SODA	$.75 per can, five times per week	$195	Limousine tour of Napa wineries	$10,192
PEDICURE	$35 per session, four times per year	$210	Donation to Habitat for Humanity	$11,595
LOTTERY TICKETS	$1 per ticket, five times per week	$260	Springsteen tickets (four)	$13,302
FROZEN YOGURT	$3 for a large (with sprinkles), two times per week	$312	Spring ski weekend at Vail	$15,962
CIGARS	$5 per stogie (box of 25), four boxes per year	$500	Autographed photo of Humphrey Bogart	$25,580

Source: *Modern Maturity,* July–August 2000.

PROJECT A

Can you add a new example to this table from your own experience? Go to the Internet and find a consumer website to add an additional example.

Harvesting Tax Breaks

Newly passed changes in maximum annual contributions to tax-deferred retirement plans and individual retirement accounts and Roth IRAs.

- IRAs
- Tax-deferred
- $500

$20,000
15,000
10,000
5,000
0

Under 50   50-plus

'01 '02 '03 '04 '05 '06   '01 '02 '03 '04 '05 '06

Notes: In 2008, the maximum IRA contribution rises to $5,000; after 2006, the retirement-plan catch-up contribution level for investors 50 years of age and older will be indexed to inflation.

Warren Gebert

Sources: Library of Congress; Deloitte & Touche

PROJECT B

Go to the IRS website to see if the IRA contributions have changed.

 Internet Projects: See text website (www.mhhe.com/slater7e) and *The Business Math Internet Resource Guide.*

CUMULATIVE REVIEW

A Word Problem Approach—Chapters 10, 11, 12, 13

1. Amy O'Mally graduated from high school. Her uncle promised her as a gift a check for $2,000 or $275 every quarter for 2 years. If money could be invested at 6% compounded quarterly, which offer is better for Amy? (Use the tables in the *Business Math Handbook*.) *(p. 310)*

2. Alan Angel made deposits of $400 semiannually to Sag Bank, which pays 10% interest compounded semiannually. After 4 years, Alan made no more deposits. What will be the balance in the account 3 years after the last deposit? (Use the tables in the *Business Math Handbook*.) *(p. 310)*

3. Roger Disney decides to retire to Florida in 12 years. What amount should Roger invest today so that he will be able to withdraw $30,000 at the end of each year for 20 years *after* he retires? Assume he can invest money at 8% interest compounded annually. (Use tables in the *Business Math Handbook*.) *(p. 306)*

4. On September 15, Arthur Westering borrowed $3,000 from Vermont Bank at $10\frac{1}{2}$% interest. Arthur plans to repay the loan on January 25. Assume the loan is based on exact interest. How much will Arthur totally repay? *(p. 245)*

5. Sue Cooper borrowed $6,000 on an $11\frac{3}{4}$%, 120-day note. Sue paid $300 toward the note on day 50. On day 90, Sue paid an additional $200. Using the U.S. Rule, Sue's adjusted balance after her first payment is the following. *(p. 249)*

6. On November 18, Northwest Company discounted an $18,000, 12%, 120-day note dated September 8. Assume a 10% discount rate. What will be the proceeds? Use ordinary interest. *(p. 245)*

7. Alice Reed deposits $16,500 into Rye Bank, which pays 10% interest compounded semiannually. Using the appropriate table, what will Alice have in her account at the end of 6 years? *(p. 290)*

8. Peter Regan needs $90,000 in 5 years from today to retire in Arizona. Peter's bank pays 10% interest compounded semiannually. What will Peter have to put in the bank today to have $90,000 in 5 years? *(p. 282)*

CHARGE IT: Paying taxes with a credit card attracts many more customers.
More than 16,750 people charged their federal income taxes to their American Express, MasterCard or Discover card as of March 31. That was more than triple the number a year earlier, during the first year of the program. Visa isn't participating. The average payment so far has been $1,362. American Express says the amount of taxes charged by its cardholders as of April 7 soared about 900% from a year earlier.

There have been more than 50 payments for more than $100,000, "a few" for more than $1 million — and one in excess of $7 million, says Bruce J. Zanca, senior vice president of Official Payments Corp., which processes the payments. For many people, the chief attractions are convenience and the lure of frequent-flier miles. But cardholders must pay a fee, based on the amount of taxes paid. For example, the fee to pay Uncle Sam $1,000 would be $35.

320 ©2000 Dow Jones & Company, Inc.

14

Installment Buying, Rule of 78, and Revolving Charge Credit Cards

LU 14–1: Cost of Installment Buying

- Calculate the amount financed, finance charge, and deferred payment *(p. 322).*

- Calculate the estimated APR by table lookup *(p. 323).*

- Calculate the monthly payment by formula and by table lookup *(p. 325).*

LU 14–2: Paying Off Installment Loans before Due Date

- Calculate the rebate and payoff for Rule of 78 *(p. 327).*

LU 14–3: Revolving Charge Credit Cards

- Calculate the finance charges on revolving charge credit card accounts *(pp. 329–30).*

American Express Unveils Online Card-Security Plan

By a WALL STREET JOURNAL *Staff Reporter*

NEW YORK—**American Express** Co., amid continued consumer concerns over online security, is proposing an answer: disposable credit-card numbers.

The travel and financial-services company announced a new technology allowing registered holders of any American Express card the ability to shop online with a random number, rather than their credit-card numbers. The card number would be good for one transaction only, and shoppers would no longer have to give their credit-card number to merchants over the Web. The service, to be called Private Payments, will be free for cardholders, and will cost nothing extra for merchants that accept American Express. The service will be available to holders of any American Express card within a month.

©2000 Dow Jones & Company, Inc.

Do you avoid shopping on the Web because you are concerned about online security when you give your credit card number over the Web? *The Wall Street Journal* clipping "American Express Unveils Online Card-Security Plan" may have a solution for you— disposable credit card numbers. These disposable numbers for online shopping may become as common as disposable diapers. To use the new free disposable credit card numbers, you must be a credit card holder of an American Express credit card.

Using credit for small and large purchases has become an important purchasing tool. This chapter discusses installment buying (closed-end credit) and the revolving credit card (open-end credit).

LEARNING UNIT 14–1 | COST OF INSTALLMENT BUYING

Installment buying, a form of *closed-end credit*, can add a substantial amount to the cost of big-ticket purchases. To illustrate this, we follow the procedure of buying a pickup truck, including the amount financed, finance charge, and deferred payment price. Then we study the effect of the Truth in Lending Act.

Amount Financed, Finance Charge, and Deferred Payment

Mary M. Steinbacher/PhotoEdit

Checking Calculations in Pickup Advertisement

This advertisement for the sale of a pickup truck appeared in a local paper. As you can see from this advertisement, after customers make a **down payment,** they can buy the truck with an **installment loan.** This loan is paid off with a series of equal periodic payments. These payments include both interest and principal. The payment process is called **amortization.** In the promissory notes of earlier chapters, the loan was paid off in one ending payment. Now let's look at the calculations involved in buying a pickup truck.

4X4 Pickup
9,345

$194³⁸ MONTH

With $300 down cash or trade for 60 months at Annual Percentage Rate of 10.5%. Amt. financed—$9,045.00. Finance chg.— $2,617.80. Total note—$11,662.80. Total deferred payment price—$11,962.80. Taxes, title, insurance additional.

Calculating Amount Financed   The **amount financed** is what you actually borrow. To calculate this amount, use the following formula:

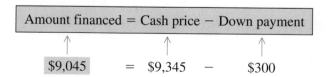

$$\text{Amount financed} = \text{Cash price} - \text{Down payment}$$

$$\$9,045 \quad = \quad \$9,345 \quad - \quad \$300$$

Calculating Finance Charge   The words **finance charge** in the advertisement represent the **interest** charge. The interest charge resulting in the finance charge includes the cost of credit reports, mandatory bank fees, and so on. You can use the following formula to calculate the total interest on the loan:

$$\boxed{\begin{array}{ccc} \text{Total finance charge} \\ \text{(interest charge)} \end{array} = \begin{array}{c} \text{Total of all} \\ \text{monthly payments} \end{array} - \begin{array}{c} \text{Amount} \\ \text{financed} \end{array}}$$

$$\$2,617.80 \quad = \quad \$11,662.80 \quad - \quad \$9,045$$
$$(\$194.38 \times 60 \text{ months})$$

Calculating Deferred Payment Price   The **deferred payment price** represents the total of all monthly payments plus the down payment. The following formula is used to calculate the deferred payment price:

$$\boxed{\text{Deferred payment price} = \begin{array}{c} \text{Total of all} \\ \text{monthly payments} \end{array} + \begin{array}{c} \text{Down} \\ \text{payment} \end{array}}$$

$$\$11,962.80 \quad = \quad \$11,662.80 \quad + \quad \$300$$
$$(\$194.38 \times 60)$$

Truth in Lending: APR Defined and Calculated

In 1969, the Federal Reserve Board established the **Truth in Lending Act** (Regulation Z). The law doesn't regulate interest charges; its purpose is to make the consumer aware of the true cost of credit.

The Truth in Lending Act requires that creditors provide certain basic information about the actual cost of buying on credit. Before buyers sign a credit agreement, creditors must inform them in writing of the amount of the finance charge and the **annual percentage rate (APR).** The APR represents the true or effective annual interest creditors charge. This is helpful to buyers who repay loans over different periods of time (1 month, 48 months, and so on).

To illustrate how the APR affects the interest rate, assume you borrow $100 for 1 year and pay a finance charge of $9. Your interest rate would be 9% if you waited until the end of the year to pay back the loan. Now let's say you pay off the loan and the finance charge in 12 monthly payments. Each month that you make a payment, you are losing some of the value or use of that money. So the true or effective APR is actually greater than 9%.

The APR can be calculated by formula or by tables. We will use the table method since it is more exact.

Calculating APR Rate by Table 14.1

Note the following steps for using a table to calculate APR:

Calculating APR by Table

Step 1.   Divide the finance charge by amount financed and multiply by $100 to get the table lookup factor.

Step 2.   Go to APR Table 14.1. At the left side of the table are listed the number of payments that will be made.

Step 3.   When you find the number of payments you are looking for, move to the right and look for the two numbers closest to the table lookup number. This will indicate the APR.

Now let's determine the APR for the pickup truck advertisement given earlier in the chapter.

As stated in Step 1 above, we begin by dividing the finance charge by the amount financed and multiply by $100:

$$\boxed{\frac{\text{Finance charge}}{\text{Amount financed}} \times \$100 = \begin{array}{c} \text{Table 14.1} \\ \text{lookup number} \end{array}}$$

We multiply by $100, since the table is based on $100 of financing.

$$\frac{\$2,617.80}{\$9,045.00} \times \$100 = \$28.94$$

TABLE 14.1   Annual percentage rate table per $100

NUMBER OF PAYMENTS	ANNUAL PERCENTAGE RATE														
	10.00%	10.25%	10.50%	10.75%	11.00%	11.25%	11.50%	11.75%	12.00%	12.25%	12.50%	12.75%	13.00%	13.25%	13.50%	13.75%
	(FINANCE CHARGE PER $100 OF AMOUNT FINANCED)														
1	0.83	0.85	0.87	0.90	0.92	0.94	0.96	0.98	1.00	1.02	1.04	1.06	1.08	1.10	1.12	1.15
2	1.25	1.28	1.31	1.35	1.38	1.41	1.44	1.47	1.50	1.53	1.57	1.60	1.63	1.66	1.69	1.72
3	1.67	1.71	1.76	1.80	1.84	1.88	1.92	1.96	2.01	2.05	2.09	2.13	2.17	2.22	2.26	2.30
4	2.09	2.14	2.20	2.25	2.30	2.35	2.41	2.46	2.51	2.57	2.62	2.67	2.72	2.78	2.83	2.88
5	2.51	2.58	2.64	2.70	2.77	2.83	2.89	2.96	3.02	3.08	3.15	3.21	3.27	3.34	3.40	3.46
6	2.94	3.01	3.08	3.16	3.23	3.31	3.38	3.45	3.53	3.60	3.68	3.75	3.83	3.90	3.97	4.05
7	3.36	3.45	3.53	3.62	3.70	3.78	3.87	3.95	4.04	4.12	4.21	4.29	4.38	4.47	4.55	4.64
8	3.79	3.88	3.98	4.07	4.17	4.26	4.36	4.46	4.55	4.65	4.74	4.84	4.94	5.03	5.13	5.22
9	4.21	4.32	4.43	4.53	4.64	4.75	4.85	4.96	5.07	5.17	5.28	5.39	5.49	5.60	5.71	5.82
10	4.64	4.76	4.88	4.99	5.11	5.23	5.35	5.46	5.58	5.70	5.82	5.94	6.05	6.17	6.29	6.41
11	5.07	5.20	5.33	5.45	5.58	5.71	5.84	5.97	6.10	6.23	6.36	6.49	6.62	6.75	6.88	7.01
12	5.50	5.64	5.78	5.92	6.06	6.20	6.34	6.48	6.62	6.76	6.90	7.04	7.18	7.32	7.46	7.60
13	5.93	6.08	6.23	6.38	6.53	6.68	6.84	6.99	7.14	7.29	7.44	7.59	7.75	7.90	8.05	8.20
14	6.36	6.52	6.69	6.85	7.01	7.17	7.34	7.50	7.66	7.82	7.99	8.15	8.31	8.48	8.64	8.81
15	6.80	6.97	7.14	7.32	7.49	7.66	7.84	8.01	8.19	8.36	8.53	8.71	8.88	9.06	9.23	9.41
16	7.23	7.41	7.60	7.78	7.97	8.15	8.34	8.53	8.71	8.90	9.08	9.27	9.46	9.64	9.83	10.02
17	7.67	7.86	8.06	8.25	8.45	8.65	8.84	9.04	9.24	9.44	9.63	9.83	10.03	10.23	10.43	10.63
18	8.10	8.31	8.52	8.73	8.93	9.14	9.35	9.56	9.77	9.98	10.19	10.40	10.61	10.82	11.03	11.24
19	8.54	8.76	8.98	9.20	9.42	9.64	9.86	10.08	10.30	10.52	10.74	10.96	11.18	11.41	11.63	11.85
20	8.98	9.21	9.44	9.67	9.90	10.13	10.37	10.60	10.83	11.06	11.30	11.53	11.76	12.00	12.23	12.46
21	9.42	9.66	9.90	10.15	10.39	10.63	10.88	11.12	11.36	11.61	11.85	12.10	12.34	12.59	12.84	13.08
22	9.86	10.12	10.37	10.62	10.88	11.13	11.39	11.64	11.90	12.16	12.41	12.67	12.93	13.19	13.44	13.70
23	10.30	10.57	10.84	11.10	11.37	11.63	11.90	12.17	12.44	12.71	12.97	13.24	13.51	13.78	14.05	14.32
24	10.75	11.02	11.30	11.58	11.86	12.14	12.42	12.70	12.98	13.26	13.54	13.82	14.10	14.38	14.66	14.95
25	11.19	11.48	11.77	12.06	12.35	12.64	12.93	13.22	13.52	13.81	14.10	14.40	14.69	14.98	15.28	15.57
26	11.64	11.94	12.24	12.54	12.85	13.15	13.45	13.75	14.06	14.36	14.67	14.97	15.28	15.59	15.89	16.20
27	12.09	12.40	12.71	13.03	13.34	13.66	13.97	14.29	14.60	14.92	15.24	15.56	15.87	16.19	16.51	16.83
28	12.53	12.86	13.18	13.51	13.84	14.16	14.49	14.82	15.15	15.48	15.81	16.14	16.47	16.80	17.13	17.46
29	12.98	13.32	13.66	14.00	14.33	14.67	15.01	15.35	15.70	16.04	16.38	16.72	17.07	17.41	17.75	18.10
30	13.43	13.78	14.13	14.48	14.83	15.19	15.54	15.89	16.24	16.60	16.95	17.31	17.66	18.02	18.38	18.74
31	13.89	14.25	14.61	14.97	15.33	15.70	16.06	16.43	16.79	17.16	17.53	17.90	18.27	18.63	19.00	19.38
32	14.34	14.71	15.09	15.46	15.84	16.21	16.59	16.97	17.35	17.73	18.11	18.49	18.87	19.25	19.63	20.02
33	14.79	15.18	15.57	15.95	16.34	16.73	17.12	17.51	17.90	18.29	18.65	19.08	19.47	19.87	20.26	20.66
34	15.25	15.65	16.05	16.44	16.85	17.25	17.65	18.05	18.46	18.86	19.27	19.67	20.08	20.49	20.90	21.31
35	15.70	16.11	16.53	16.94	17.35	17.77	18.18	18.60	19.01	19.43	19.85	20.27	20.69	21.11	21.53	21.95
36	16.16	16.58	17.01	17.43	17.86	18.29	18.71	19.14	19.57	20.00	20.43	20.87	21.30	21.73	22.17	22.60
37	16.62	17.06	17.49	17.93	18.37	18.81	19.25	19.69	20.13	20.58	21.02	21.46	21.91	22.36	22.81	23.25
38	17.08	17.53	17.98	18.43	18.88	19.33	19.78	20.24	20.69	21.15	21.61	22.07	22.52	22.99	23.45	23.91
39	17.54	18.00	18.46	18.93	19.39	19.86	20.32	20.79	21.26	21.73	22.20	22.67	23.14	23.61	24.09	24.56
40	18.00	18.48	18.95	19.43	19.90	20.38	20.86	21.34	21.82	22.30	22.79	23.27	23.76	24.25	24.73	25.22
41	18.47	18.95	19.44	19.93	20.42	20.91	21.40	21.89	22.39	22.88	23.38	23.88	24.38	24.88	25.38	25.88
42	18.93	19.43	19.93	20.43	20.93	21.44	21.94	22.45	22.96	23.47	23.98	24.49	25.00	25.51	26.03	26.55
43	19.40	19.91	20.42	20.94	21.45	21.97	22.49	23.01	23.53	24.05	24.57	25.10	25.62	26.15	26.68	27.21
44	19.86	20.39	20.91	21.44	21.97	22.50	23.03	23.57	24.10	24.64	25.17	25.71	26.25	26.79	27.33	27.88
45	20.33	20.87	21.41	21.95	22.49	23.03	23.58	24.12	24.67	25.22	25.77	26.32	26.88	27.43	27.99	28.55
46	20.80	21.35	21.90	22.46	23.01	23.57	24.13	24.69	25.25	25.81	26.37	26.94	27.51	28.08	28.65	29.22
47	21.27	21.83	22.40	22.97	23.53	24.10	24.68	25.25	25.82	26.40	26.98	27.56	28.14	28.72	29.31	29.89
48	21.74	22.32	22.90	23.48	24.06	24.64	25.23	25.81	26.40	26.99	27.58	28.18	28.77	29.37	29.97	30.57
49	22.21	22.80	23.39	23.99	24.58	25.18	25.78	26.38	26.98	27.59	28.19	28.80	29.41	30.02	30.63	31.24
50	22.69	23.29	23.89	24.50	25.11	25.72	26.33	26.95	27.56	28.18	28.80	29.42	30.04	30.67	31.29	31.92
51	23.16	23.78	24.40	25.02	25.64	26.26	26.89	27.52	28.15	28.78	29.41	30.05	30.68	31.32	31.96	32.60
52	23.64	24.27	24.90	25.53	26.17	26.81	27.45	28.09	28.73	29.38	30.02	30.67	31.32	31.98	32.63	33.29
53	24.11	24.76	25.40	26.05	26.70	27.35	28.00	28.66	29.32	29.98	30.64	31.30	31.97	32.63	33.30	33.97
54	24.59	25.25	25.91	26.57	27.23	27.90	28.56	29.23	29.91	30.58	31.25	31.93	32.61	33.29	33.98	34.66
55	25.07	25.74	26.41	27.09	27.77	28.44	29.13	29.81	30.50	31.18	31.87	32.56	33.26	33.95	34.65	35.35
56	25.55	26.23	26.92	27.61	28.30	28.99	29.69	30.39	31.09	31.79	32.49	33.20	33.91	34.62	35.33	36.04
57	26.03	26.73	27.43	28.13	28.84	29.54	30.25	30.97	31.68	32.39	33.11	33.83	34.56	35.28	36.01	36.74
58	26.51	27.23	27.94	28.66	29.37	30.10	30.82	31.55	32.27	33.00	33.74	34.47	35.21	35.95	36.69	37.43
59	27.00	27.72	28.45	29.18	29.91	30.65	31.39	32.13	32.87	33.61	34.36	35.11	35.86	36.62	37.37	38.13
60	27.48	28.22	28.96	29.71	30.45	31.20	31.96	32.71	33.47	34.23	34.99	35.75	36.52	37.29	38.06	38.83

Note: For a more detailed set of tables from 2% to 21.75%, see the reference tables in the *Business Math Handbook.*

To look up $28.94 in Table 14.1, we go down the left side of the table until we come to 60 payments (the advertisement states 60 months). Then, moving to the right, we look for $28.94 or the two numbers closest to it. The number $28.94 is between $28.22 and $28.96. So we look at the column headings and see a rate between 10.25% and 10.5%. The Truth in Lending Act requires that when creditors state the APR, it must be accurate to the nearest $\frac{1}{4}$ of 1%.[1]

Calculating the Monthly Payment by Formula and Table 14.2

The pickup truck advertisement showed a $194.38 monthly payment. We can check this by formula and by table lookup.

---

[1]If we wanted an exact reading of APR when the number is not exactly in the table, we would use the process of interpolating. We do not cover this method in this course.

TABLE 14.1 (concluded)

NUMBER OF PAYMENTS	ANNUAL PERCENTAGE RATE															
	14.00%	14.25%	14.50%	14.75%	15.00%	15.25%	15.50%	15.75%	16.00%	16.25%	16.50%	16.75%	17.00%	17.25%	17.50%	17.75%
	(FINANCE CHARGE PER $100 OF AMOUNT FINANCED)															
1	1.17	1.19	1.21	1.23	1.25	1.27	1.29	1.31	1.33	1.35	1.37	1.40	1.42	1.44	1.46	1.48
2	1.75	1.78	1.82	1.85	1.88	1.91	1.94	1.97	2.00	2.04	2.07	2.10	2.13	2.16	2.19	2.22
3	2.34	2.38	2.43	2.47	2.51	2.55	2.59	2.64	2.68	2.72	2.76	2.80	2.85	2.89	2.93	2.97
4	2.93	2.99	3.04	3.09	3.14	3.20	3.25	3.30	3.36	3.41	3.46	3.51	3.57	3.62	3.67	3.73
5	3.53	3.59	3.65	3.72	3.78	3.84	3.91	3.97	4.04	4.10	4.16	4.23	4.29	4.35	4.42	4.48
6	4.12	4.20	4.27	4.35	4.42	4.49	4.57	4.64	4.72	4.79	4.87	4.94	5.02	5.09	5.17	5.24
7	4.72	4.81	4.89	4.98	5.06	5.15	5.23	5.32	5.40	5.49	5.58	5.66	5.75	5.83	5.92	6.00
8	5.32	5.42	5.51	5.61	5.71	5.80	5.90	6.00	6.09	6.19	6.29	6.38	6.48	6.58	6.67	6.77
9	5.92	6.03	6.14	6.25	6.35	6.46	6.57	6.68	6.78	6.89	7.00	7.11	7.22	7.32	7.43	7.54
10	6.53	6.65	6.77	6.88	7.00	7.12	7.24	7.36	7.48	7.60	7.72	7.84	7.96	8.08	8.19	8.31
11	7.14	7.27	7.40	7.53	7.66	7.79	7.92	8.05	8.18	8.31	8.44	8.57	8.70	8.83	8.96	9.09
12	7.74	7.89	8.03	8.17	8.31	8.45	8.59	8.74	8.88	9.02	9.16	9.30	9.45	9.59	9.73	9.87
13	8.36	8.51	8.66	8.81	8.97	9.12	9.27	9.43	9.58	9.73	9.89	10.04	10.20	10.35	10.50	10.66
14	8.97	9.13	9.30	9.46	9.63	9.79	9.96	10.12	10.29	10.45	10.62	10.78	10.95	11.11	11.28	11.45
15	9.59	9.76	9.94	10.11	10.29	10.47	10.64	10.82	11.00	11.17	11.35	11.53	11.71	11.88	12.06	12.24
16	10.20	10.39	10.58	10.77	10.95	11.14	11.33	11.52	11.71	11.90	12.09	12.28	12.46	12.65	12.84	13.03
17	10.82	11.02	11.22	11.42	11.62	11.82	12.02	12.22	12.42	12.62	12.83	13.03	13.23	13.43	13.63	13.83
18	11.45	11.66	11.87	12.08	12.29	12.50	12.72	12.93	13.14	13.35	13.57	13.78	13.99	14.21	14.42	14.64
19	12.07	12.30	12.52	12.74	12.97	13.19	13.41	13.64	13.86	14.09	14.31	14.54	14.76	14.99	15.22	15.44
20	12.70	12.93	13.17	13.41	13.64	13.88	14.11	14.35	14.59	14.82	15.06	15.30	15.54	15.77	16.01	16.25
21	13.33	13.58	13.82	14.07	14.32	14.57	14.82	15.06	15.31	15.56	15.81	16.06	16.31	16.56	16.81	17.07
22	13.96	14.22	14.48	14.74	15.00	15.26	15.52	15.78	16.04	16.30	16.57	16.83	17.09	17.36	17.62	17.88
23	14.59	14.87	15.14	15.41	15.68	15.96	16.23	16.50	16.78	17.05	17.32	17.60	17.88	18.15	18.43	18.70
24	15.23	15.51	15.80	16.08	16.37	16.65	16.94	17.22	17.51	17.80	18.09	18.37	18.66	18.95	19.24	19.53
25	15.87	16.17	16.46	16.76	17.06	17.35	17.65	17.95	18.25	18.55	18.85	19.15	19.45	19.75	20.05	20.36
26	16.51	16.82	17.13	17.44	17.75	18.06	18.37	18.68	18.99	19.30	19.62	19.93	20.24	20.56	20.87	21.19
27	17.15	17.47	17.80	18.12	18.44	18.76	19.09	19.41	19.74	20.06	20.39	20.71	21.04	21.37	21.69	22.02
28	17.80	18.13	18.47	18.80	19.14	19.47	19.81	20.15	20.48	20.82	21.16	21.50	21.84	22.18	22.52	22.86
29	18.45	18.79	19.14	19.49	19.83	20.18	20.53	20.89	21.23	21.58	21.94	22.29	22.64	22.99	23.35	23.70
30	19.10	19.45	19.81	20.17	20.54	20.90	21.26	21.62	21.99	22.35	22.72	23.08	23.45	23.81	24.18	24.55
31	19.75	20.12	20.49	20.87	21.24	21.61	21.99	22.37	22.74	23.12	23.50	23.88	24.26	24.64	25.02	25.40
32	20.40	20.79	21.17	21.56	21.95	22.33	22.72	23.11	23.50	23.89	24.28	24.68	25.07	25.46	25.86	26.25
33	21.06	21.46	21.85	22.25	22.65	23.06	23.46	23.86	24.26	24.67	25.07	25.48	25.88	26.29	26.70	27.11
34	21.72	22.13	22.54	22.95	23.37	23.78	24.19	24.61	25.03	25.44	25.86	26.28	26.70	27.12	27.54	27.97
35	22.38	22.80	23.23	23.65	24.08	24.51	24.94	25.36	25.79	26.23	26.66	27.09	27.52	27.96	28.39	28.83
36	23.04	23.48	23.92	24.35	24.80	25.24	25.68	26.12	26.57	27.01	27.46	27.90	28.35	28.80	29.25	29.70
37	23.70	24.16	24.61	25.06	25.51	25.97	26.42	26.88	27.34	27.80	28.26	28.72	29.18	29.64	30.10	30.57
38	24.37	24.84	25.30	25.77	26.24	26.70	27.17	27.64	28.11	28.59	29.06	29.53	30.01	30.49	30.96	31.44
39	25.04	25.52	26.00	26.48	26.96	27.44	27.92	28.41	28.89	29.38	29.87	30.36	30.85	31.34	31.83	32.32
40	25.71	26.20	26.70	27.19	27.69	28.18	28.68	29.18	29.68	30.18	30.69	31.19	31.68	32.19	32.69	33.20
41	26.39	26.89	27.40	27.91	28.41	28.92	29.44	29.95	30.46	30.97	31.49	32.01	32.52	33.04	33.56	34.08
42	27.06	27.58	28.10	28.62	29.15	29.67	30.19	30.72	31.25	31.78	32.31	32.84	33.37	33.90	34.44	34.97
43	27.74	28.27	28.81	29.34	29.88	30.42	30.96	31.50	32.04	32.58	33.13	33.67	34.22	34.76	35.31	35.86
44	28.42	28.97	29.52	30.07	30.62	31.17	31.72	32.28	32.83	33.39	33.95	34.51	35.07	35.63	36.19	36.76
45	29.11	29.67	30.23	30.79	31.36	31.92	32.49	33.06	33.63	34.20	34.77	35.35	35.92	36.50	37.08	37.66
46	29.79	30.36	30.94	31.52	32.10	32.68	33.26	33.84	34.43	35.01	35.60	36.19	36.78	37.37	37.96	38.56
47	30.48	31.07	31.66	32.25	32.84	33.44	34.03	34.63	35.23	35.83	36.43	37.04	37.64	38.25	38.86	39.46
48	31.17	31.77	32.37	32.98	33.59	34.20	34.81	35.42	36.03	36.65	37.27	37.88	38.50	39.13	39.75	40.37
49	31.86	32.48	33.09	33.71	34.34	34.96	35.59	36.21	36.84	37.47	38.10	38.74	39.37	40.01	40.65	41.29
50	32.55	33.18	33.82	34.45	35.09	35.73	36.37	37.01	37.65	38.30	38.94	39.59	40.24	40.89	41.55	42.20
51	33.25	33.89	34.54	35.19	35.84	36.49	37.15	37.81	38.46	39.17	39.79	40.45	41.11	41.78	42.45	43.12
52	33.95	34.61	35.27	35.93	36.60	37.27	37.94	38.61	39.28	39.96	40.63	41.31	41.99	42.67	43.36	44.04
53	34.65	35.32	36.00	36.68	37.36	38.04	38.72	39.41	40.10	40.79	41.48	42.17	42.87	43.57	44.27	44.97
54	35.35	36.04	36.73	37.42	38.12	38.82	39.52	40.22	40.92	41.63	42.33	43.04	43.75	44.47	45.18	45.90
55	36.05	36.76	37.46	38.17	38.88	39.60	40.31	41.03	41.74	42.47	43.19	43.91	44.64	45.37	46.10	46.83
56	36.76	37.48	38.20	38.92	39.65	40.38	41.11	41.84	42.57	43.31	44.05	44.79	45.53	46.27	47.02	47.77
57	37.47	38.20	38.94	39.68	40.42	41.16	41.91	42.65	43.40	44.15	44.91	45.66	46.42	47.18	47.94	48.71
58	38.18	38.93	39.68	40.43	41.19	41.95	42.71	43.47	44.23	45.00	45.77	46.54	47.32	48.09	48.87	49.65
59	38.89	39.66	40.42	41.19	41.96	42.74	43.51	44.29	45.07	45.85	46.64	47.42	48.21	49.01	49.80	50.60
60	39.61	40.39	41.17	41.95	42.74	43.53	44.32	45.11	45.91	46.71	47.51	48.31	49.12	49.92	50.73	51.55

By Formula

$$\frac{\text{Finance charge} + \text{Amount financed}}{\text{Number of payments of loan}} = \frac{\$2{,}617.80 + \$9{,}045}{60} = \$194.38$$

By Table 14.2   The **loan amortization table** (many variations of this table are available) in Table 14.2 can be used to calculate the monthly payment for the pickup truck. To calculate a monthly payment with a table, use the following steps:

TABLE 14.2   Loan amortization table (monthly payment per $1,000 to pay principal and interest on installment loan)

Terms in months	7.50%	8%	8.50%	9%	10.00%	10.50%	11.00%	11.50%	12.00%
6	$170.34	$170.58	$170.83	$171.20	$171.56	$171.81	$172.05	$172.30	$172.55
12	86.76	86.99	87.22	87.46	87.92	88.15	88.38	88.62	88.85
18	58.92	59.15	59.37	59.60	60.06	60.29	60.52	60.75	60.98
24	45.00	45.23	45.46	45.69	46.14	46.38	46.61	46.84	47.07
30	36.66	36.89	37.12	37.35	37.81	38.04	38.28	38.51	38.75
36	31.11	31.34	31.57	31.80	32.27	32.50	32.74	32.98	33.21
42	27.15	27.38	27.62	27.85	28.32	28.55	28.79	29.03	29.28
48	24.18	24.42	24.65	24.77	25.36	25.60	25.85	26.09	26.33
54	21.88	22.12	22.36	22.59	23.07	23.32	23.56	23.81	24.06
60	20.04	20.28	20.52	20.76	21.25	21.49	21.74	21.99	22.24

Calculating Monthly Payment by Table Lookup

Step 1. Divide the loan amount by $1,000 (since Table 14.2 is per $1,000):

$$\frac{\$9,045}{\$1,000} = 9.045$$

Step 2. Look up the rate (10.5%) and number of months (60). At the intersection is the table factor showing the monthly payment per $1,000.

Step 3. Multiply quotient in Step 1 by the table factor in Step 2:

$$9.045 \times \$21.49 = \$194.38.$$

Remember that this $194.38 fixed payment includes interest and the reduction of the balance of the loan. As the number of payments increases, interest payments get smaller and the reduction of the principal gets larger.[2]

Now let's check your progress with the Practice Quiz.

LU 14–1 PRACTICE QUIZ

Courtesy Brunswick Corporation.

From the partial advertisement at the right calculate the following:

1. **a.** Amount financed.
   b. Finance charge.
   c. Deferred payment price.
   d. APR by Table 14.1.
   e. Monthly payment by formula.

$288 per month	
Sale price	$14,150
Down payment	$ 1,450
Term/Number of payments	60 months

2. Jay Miller bought a New Brunswick boat for $7,500. Jay put down $1,000 and financed the balance at 10% for 60 months. What is his monthly payment? Use Table 14.2.

✓ SOLUTIONS

1. **a.** $14,150 − $1,450 = $12,700

   b. $17,280 ($288 × 60) − $12,700 = $4,580

   c. $17,280 ($288 × 60) + $1,450 = $18,730

   d. $\dfrac{\$4,580}{\$12,700} \times 100 = \$36.06$; between 12.75% and 13%

   e. $\dfrac{\$4,580 + \$12,700}{60} = \$288$

2. $\dfrac{\$6,500}{\$1,000} = 6.5 \times \$21.25 = \$138.13$ (10%, 60 months)

---

[2]In Chapter 15 we give an amortization schedule for home mortgages that shows how much of each fixed payment goes to interest and how much reduces the principal. This repayment schedule also gives a running balance of the loan.

TABLE 14.2 (concluded)

Terms in months	12.50%	13.00%	13.50%	14.00%	14.50%	15.00%	15.50%	16.00%
6	$172.80	$173.04	$173.29	$173.54	$173.79	$174.03	$174.28	$174.53
12	89.08	89.32	89.55	89.79	90.02	90.26	90.49	90.73
18	61.21	61.45	61.68	61.92	62.15	62.38	62.62	62.86
24	47.31	47.54	47.78	48.01	48.25	48.49	48.72	48.96
30	38.98	39.22	39.46	39.70	39.94	40.18	40.42	40.66
36	33.45	33.69	33.94	34.18	34.42	34.67	34.91	35.16
42	29.52	29.76	30.01	30.25	30.50	30.75	31.00	31.25
48	26.58	26.83	27.08	27.33	27.58	27.83	28.08	28.34
54	24.31	24.56	24.81	25.06	25.32	25.58	25.84	26.10
60	22.50	22.75	23.01	23.27	23.53	23.79	24.05	24.32

LEARNING UNIT 14–2 | PAYING OFF INSTALLMENT LOANS BEFORE DUE DATE

In Learning Unit 10.3 (p. 249), you learned about the U.S. Rule. This rule applies partial payments to the interest *first,* and then the remainder of the payment reduces the principal. Many states and the federal government use this rule.

Some states use another method for prepaying a loan called the **Rule of 78.** It is a variation of the U.S. Rule. The Rule of 78 got its name because it bases the finance charge rebate and the payoff on a 12-month loan. (Any number of months can be used.) The Rule of 78 is used less today. However, GMAC says that about 50% of its auto loans still use the Rule of 78. For loans of 61 months or longer, the Rule of 78 is not allowed (some states have even shorter requirements).

With the Rule of 78, the finance charge earned the first month is $\frac{12}{78}$. The 78 comes from summing the digits of 12 months. The finance charge for the second month would be $\frac{11}{78}$, and so on. Table 14.3 simplifies these calculations.

TABLE 14.3

Rebate fraction table based on Rule of 78

Months to go	Sum of digits	Months to go	Sum of digits	
1	1	31	496	
2	3	32	528	
3	6	33	561	→ 33 months to go
4	10	34	595	
5	15	35	630	
6	21	36	666	
7	28	37	703	
8	36	38	741	
9	45	39	780	
10	55	40	820	
11	66	41	861	
12	78	42	903	
13	91	43	946	
14	105	44	990	
15	120	45	1,035	
16	136	46	1,081	
17	153	47	1,128	
18	171	48	1,176	
19	190	49	1,225	
20	210	50	1,275	
21	231	51	1,326	
22	253	52	1,378	
23	276	53	1,431	
24	300	54	1,485	
25	325	55	1,540	
26	351	56	1,596	
27	378	57	1,653	
28	406	58	1,711	
29	435	59	1,770	
30	465	60	1,830	→ 60 months = 1,830

When the installment loan is made, a larger portion of the interest is charged to the earlier payments. As a result, when a loan is paid off early, the borrower is entitled to a **rebate,** which is calculated as follows:

Calculating Rebate and Payoff for Rule of 78

Step 1. Find the balance of the loan outstanding.
Step 2. Calculate the total finance charge.
Step 3. Find the number of payments remaining.
Step 4. Set up the rebate fraction from Table 14.3.
Step 5. Calculate the rebate amount of the finance charge.
Step 6. Calculate the payoff.

Let's see what the rebate of the finance charge and payoff would be if the pickup truck loan were paid off after 27 months (instead of 60).

To find the finance charge rebate and the final payoff, we follow six specific steps listed below. Let's begin.

Step 1. Find the balance of the loan outstanding:

Total of monthly payments ($60 \times \$194.38$)	$\$11,662.80$
Payments to date: $27 \times \$194.38$	$-\ 5,248.26$
Balance of loan outstanding	$\$\ 6,414.54$

Step 2. Calculate the total finance charge:

$\$11,662.80$	Total of all payments ($60 \times \$194.38$)
$-\ 9,045.00$	Amount financed ($\$9,345 - \$300$)
$\$\ 2,617.80$	Total finance charge

Step 3. Find the number of payments remaining:

$$60 - 27 = 33$$

Step 4. Set up the **rebate fraction** from Table 14.3.[3]

$$\frac{\text{Sum of digits based on number of months to go}}{\text{Sum of digits based on total number of months of loan}} = \frac{561}{1,830} \quad \begin{array}{l} \leftarrow \text{33 months to go} \\ \leftarrow \text{60 months in loan} \end{array}$$

Note: If this loan were for 12 months, the denominator would be 78.

Step 5. Calculate the rebate amount of the finance charge:

Rebate fraction $\times$ Total finance charge $=$ Rebate amount

$$\underset{\textbf{(Step 4)}}{\frac{561}{1,830}} \quad \times \quad \underset{\textbf{(Step 2)}}{\$2,617.80} \quad = \quad \$802.51$$

Step 6. Calculate the payoff:

Balance of loan outstanding $-$ Rebate $=$ Payoff

$$\underset{\textbf{(Step 1)}}{\$6,414.54} \quad \underset{\textbf{(Step 5)}}{-\ \$802.51} = \boxed{\$5,612.03}$$

---

[3]If no table is available, the following formula is available:

$$\frac{\dfrac{N(N+1)}{2}}{\dfrac{T(T+1)}{2}} = \frac{\dfrac{33(33+1)}{2}}{\dfrac{60(60+1)}{2}} = \frac{561}{1,830}$$

In the numerator, N stands for number of months to go, and in the denominator, T is total months of the loan.

LU 14–2 PRACTICE QUIZ	Calculate the finance charge rebate and payoff (calculate all six steps):

Loan	Months of loan	End-of-month loan is repaid	Monthly payment	Finance charge rebate	Final payoff
$5,500	12	7	$510		

✓ **SOLUTIONS**

Step 1. $12 \times \$510 = \ \ \$6,120$
$\ \ \ \ \ \ \ \ \ 7 \times \$510 = -\ 3,570$
$\ \overline{\$2,550}$
$\ $ (balance outstanding)

Step 2. $12 \times \$510 = \ \ \$6,120$
$\ -\ 5,500$
$\ \overline{\$\ \ 620}$
$\ $ (total finance charge)

Step 3. $12 - 7 = 5$

Step 4. $\dfrac{15}{78}$ (by Table 14.3)

Step 5. $\dfrac{15}{78} \times \ \ \$620 = $ $\boxed{\$119.23 \text{ rebate}}$
$\ \ \ \ $ **(Step 4)   (Step 2)**

Step 6. Step 1 − Step 5
$\ \ \ \ \ \ \ \ \ \$2,550 - \$119.23$
$\ = \boxed{\$2,430.77 \text{ payoff}}$

LEARNING UNIT 14–3 | REVOLVING CHARGE CREDIT CARDS

Revolving charge credit cards are widely used today. Businesses find that consumers tend to buy more when they can use a credit card for their purchases. Consumers find credit cards convenient to use and valuable in establishing credit.

To protect consumers, Congress passed the **Fair Credit and Charge Card Disclosure Act of 1988.**[4] This act requires that for direct-mail application or solicitation, credit card companies must provide specific details involving all fees, grace period, calculation of finance charges, and so on.

We begin the unit by seeing how Moe's Furniture Store calculates the finance charge on Abby Jordan's previous month's credit card balance. Then we learn how to calculate the average daily balance on the partial bill of Joan Ring.

Calculating Finance Charge on Previous Month's Balance

Abby Jordan bought a dining room set for $8,000 on credit. She has a **revolving charge account** at Moe's Furniture Store. A revolving charge account gives a buyer **open-end credit.** Abby can make as many purchases on credit as she wants until she reaches her maximum $10,000 credit limit.

Often customers do not completely pay their revolving charge accounts at the end of a billing period. When this occurs, stores add interest charges to the customers' bills. Moe's furniture store calculates its interest using the *unpaid balance method.* It charges $1\frac{1}{2}$ % on the *previous month's balance,* or 18% per year. Moe's has no minimum monthly payment (many stores require $10 or $15, or a percent of the outstanding balance).

Abby has no other charges on her revolving charge account. She plans to pay $500 per month until she completely pays off her dining room set. Abby realizes that when she makes a payment, Moe's Furniture Store first applies the money toward the interest and then reduces the **outstanding balance** due. (This is the U.S. Rule we discussed in Chapter 10.) For her own information, Abby worked out the first 3-month schedule of payments, shown in Table 14.4. Note how the interest payment is the rate times the outstanding balance.

Today, most companies with credit card accounts calculate the finance charge, or interest, as a percentage of the average daily balance. Interest on credit cards can be very expensive for consumers; however, interest is a source of income for credit card companies. Note that Target and Best Buy moved their credit card headquarters to South Dakota, which made it possible for Target to raise its rate from 16% to 21% and Best Buy to raise its rate from 16% to 23%.

Calculating Average Daily Balance

Let's look at the following steps for calculating the **average daily balance.** Remember that a **cash advance** is a cash loan from a credit card company.

---

[4]An update to this act was made in 1997.

TABLE 14.4   Schedule of payments

Monthly payment number	Outstanding balance due	$1\frac{1}{2}$% interest payment	Amount of monthly payment	Reduction in balance due	Outstanding balance due
1	$8,000.00	$120.00 (.015 × $8,000.00)	$500	$380.00 ($500 − $120.00)	$7,620.00 ($8,000 − $380)
2	7,620.00	114.30 (.015 × 7,620.00)	500	385.70 ($500 − 114.30)	7,234.30 (7,620 − 385.70)
3	7,234.30	108.51 (.015 × 7,234.30)	500	391.49 ($500 − 108.51)	6,842.81 (7,234.30 − 391.49)

Calculating Average Daily Balance

Step 1. Calculate the daily balance or amount owed at the end of each day during the billing cycle:

$$\frac{\text{Daily}}{\text{balance}} = \frac{\text{Previous}}{\text{balance}} + \frac{\text{Cash}}{\text{advances}} + \text{Purchases} - \text{Payments}$$

Step 2. When the daily balance is the same for more than one day, multiply it by the number of days the daily balance remained the same, or the number of days of the current balance. This gives a cumulative daily balance.

Step 3. Add the cumulative daily balances.

Step 4. Divide the sum of the cumulative daily balances by the number of days in the billing cycle.

Following is the partial bill of Joan Ring and an explanation of how Joan's average daily balance was calculated. Note how we calculated each **daily balance** and then multiplied each daily balance by the number of days the balance remained the same. Take a moment to study how we arrived at 8 days. The total of the cumulative daily balances was $16,390. To get the average daily balance, we divided by the number of days in the billing cycle—30.

30-day billing cycle			
6/20	Billing date	Previous balance	$450
6/27	Payment		$ 50 cr.
6/30	Charge: JCPenney		200
7/9	Payment		40 cr.
7/12	Cash advance		60

7 days had a balance of $450

	No. of days of current balance	Current daily balance	Extension
Step 1 →	7	$450	$ 3,150 ← Step 2
	3	400 ($450 − $50)	1,200
	9	600 ($400 + $200)	5,400
	3	560 ($600 − $40)	1,680
	8	620 ($560 + $60)	4,960
	$\overline{30}$		$\overline{\$16{,}390}$ ← Step 3

30-day cycle − 22 (7 + 3 + 9 + 3) equals 8 days left with a balance of $620.

$$\text{Average daily balance} = \frac{\$16{,}390}{30} = \boxed{\$546.33} \leftarrow \textbf{Step 4}$$

Now try the following Practice Quiz to check your understanding of this unit.

LU 14–3 PRACTICE QUIZ

1. Calculate the balance outstanding at the end of month 2 (use U.S. Rule) given the following: purchased $600 desk; pay back $40 per month; and charge of $2\frac{1}{2}\%$ interest on unpaid balance.
2. Calculate the average daily balance from the following information:

31-day billing cycle			
8/20	Billing date	Previous balance	$210
8/27	Payment		$50 cr.
8/31	Charge: Staples		30
9/5	Payment		10 cr.
9/10	Cash advance		60

✓ **SOLUTIONS**

1.

Month	Balance due	Interest	Monthly payment	Reduction in balance	Balance outstanding
1	$600	$15.00 ($.025 × $600)	$40	$25.00 ($40 − $15)	$575.00
2	575	14.38 (.025 × $575)	40	25.62	$549.38

2. Average daily balance calculated as follows:

No. of days of current balance	Current balance	Extension
7	$210	$1,470
4	160 ($210 − $50)	640
5	190 ($160 + $30)	950
5	180 ($190 − $10)	900
10	240 ($180 + $60)	2,400
31		$6,360

31 − 21 (7 + 4 + 5 + 5) ⟶ $\frac{10}{31}$

$$\text{Average daily balance} = \frac{\$6,360}{31} = \boxed{\$205.16}$$

Chapter Organizer and Reference Guide

Topic	Key point, procedure, formula	Example(s) to illustrate situation
Amount financed, p. 322	$\frac{\text{Amount}}{\text{financed}} = \frac{\text{Cash}}{\text{price}} - \frac{\text{Down}}{\text{payment}}$	60 payments at $125.67 per month; cash price $5,295 with a $95 down payment Cash price　$5,295 − Down payment　− 95 = Amount financed　$5,200
Total finance charge (interest), p. 323	$\frac{\text{Total}}{\text{finance}} = \frac{\text{Total of}}{\text{all monthly}} - \frac{\text{Amount}}{\text{financed}}$ charge　payments	(continued from above) $\frac{\$125.67}{\text{per month}} \times \frac{60}{\text{months}} = \$7,540.20$ − Amount financed　− 5,200.00 = Finance charge　$2,340.20
Deferred payment price, p. 323	$\frac{\text{Deferred}}{\text{payment price}} = \frac{\text{Total of all}}{\text{monthly payments}} + \frac{\text{Down}}{\text{payment}}$	(continued from above) $7,540.20 + $95 = $7,635.20
Calculating APR by Table 14.1, p. 323	$\frac{\text{Finance charge}}{\text{Amount financed}} \times \$100 = \frac{\text{Table 14.1}}{\text{lookup number}}$	(continued from above) $\frac{\$2,340.20}{\$5,200.00} \times \$100 = \$45.004$ Search in Table 14.1 between 15.50% and 15.75% for 60 payments.
Monthly payment, p. 325	*By formula:* $\frac{\text{Finance charge} + \text{Amount financed}}{\text{Number of payments of loan}}$ *By table:* $\frac{\text{Loan}}{\$1,000} \times \frac{\text{Table}}{\text{factor}} \text{(rate, months)}$	(continued from above) $\frac{\$2,340.20 + \$5,200.00}{60} = \$125.67$ Given: 15.5% 　　60 months 　　$5,200 loan $\frac{\$5,200}{\$1,000} = 5.2 \times \$24.05 = \$125.06^*$ *Off due to rounding of rate.

(continues)

Chapter Organizer and Reference Guide (concluded)		
Topic	**Key point, procedure, formula**	**Example(s) to illustrate situation**

Paying off installment loan before due date, p. 327	1. Find balance of loan outstanding (Total of monthly payments − Payments to date).
	2. Calculate total finance charge.
	3. Find number of payments remaining.
	4. Set up rebate fraction from Table 14.3.
	5. Calculate rebate amount of finance charge.
	6. Calculate payoff.
		Example: Loan, $8,000; 20 monthly payments of $420; end of month repaid 7.
		1. $8,400 (20 × $420)
		   − 2,940 (7 × $420)
		   $5,460 (balance of loan outstanding)
		
		2. $8,400 (total payments)
		   − 8,000 (amount financed)
		   $ 400 (total finance charge)
		
		3. 20 − 7 = 13
		
		4 and 5. $\frac{91}{210}$ × $400 = $173.33
		
		6. $5,460.00 (Step 1)
		   − 173.33 rebate (Step 5)
		   $5,286.67 payoff

Open end credit, p. 329	Monthly payment applied to interest first before reducing balance outstanding.	$4,000 purchase $250 a month payment $2\frac{1}{2}$% interest on unpaid balance $4,000 × .025 = $100 interest $250 − $100 = $150 to lower balance $4,000 − $150 = $3,850 Balance outstanding after month 1.

Average daily balance, p. 330	$\text{Daily balance} = \text{Previous balance} + \text{Cash advances}$
	$+ \text{Purchases} - \text{Payments}$
	
	$\text{Average daily balance} = \dfrac{\text{Sum of cumulative daily balances}}{\text{Number of days in billing cycle}}$
	
	30-day billing cycle less the 8 and 14. ←
		30-day billing cycle:
		Example: 8/21 Balance $100
		        8/29 Payment $10
		        9/12 Charge 50
		Average daily balance equals:
		  8 days × $100 = $ 800
		14 days × 90 = 1,260
		  8 days × 140 = 1,120
		        $3,180 ÷ 30
		Average daily balance = $106

Key terms	Amortization, *p. 322* Amount financed, *p. 322* Annual percentage rate (APR), *p. 323* Average daily balance, *p. 330* Cash advance, *p. 329* Daily balance, *p. 330* Deferred payment price, *p. 323*	Down payment, *p. 322* Fair Credit and Charge Card Disclosure Act of 1988, *p. 329* Finance charge, *p. 322* Installment loan, *p. 322* Interest, *p. 322* Loan amortization table, *p. 325* Open-end credit, *p. 329* Outstanding balance, *p. 328* Rebate, *p. 328* Rebate fraction, *p. 328* Revolving charge account, *p. 329* Rule of 78, *p. 327* Truth in Lending Act, *p. 323*

Critical Thinking Discussion Questions

1. Explain how to calculate the amount financed, finance charge, and APR by table lookup. Do you think the Truth in Lending Act should regulate interest charges?

2. Explain how to use the loan amortization table. Check with a person who owns a home and find out what part of each payment goes to pay interest versus the amount that reduces the loan principal.

3. What are the six steps used to calculate the rebate and payoff for the Rule of 78? Do you think it is right for the Rule of 78 to charge a larger portion of the finance charges to the earlier payments?

4. What steps are used to calculate the average daily balance? Many credit card companies charge 18% annual interest. Do you think this is a justifiable rate? Defend your answer.

END-OF-CHAPTER PROBLEMS

Name _____ Date _____

DRILL PROBLEMS

Complete the following table:

	Purchase price of product	Down payment	Amount financed	Number of monthly payments	Amount of monthly payments	Total of monthly payments	Total finance charge
14–1.	Chrysler PT Cruiser $22,500	$6,000		60	$310		
14–2.	Magnavox DVD player $249	$50		15	$15.75		

Calculate **(a)** the amount financed, **(b)** the total finance charge, and **(c)** APR by table lookup.

	Purchase price of a used car	Down payment	Number of monthly payments	Amount financed	Total of monthly payments	Total finance charge	APR
14–3.	$5,673	$1,223	48		$5,729.76		
14–4.	$4,195	$95	60		$5,944.00		

Calculate the monthly payment for Problems 14–3 and 14–4 by table lookup and formula. (Answers will not be exact due to rounding of percents in table lookup.)

14–5. **(14–3)** (Use 13% for table lookup.)

14–6. **(14–4)** (Use 15.5% for table lookup.)

Calculate the finance charge rebate and payoff:

	Loan	Months of loan	End-of-month loan is repaid	Monthly payment	Finance charge rebate	Final payoff
14–7.	$7,000	36	10	$210		

Step 1.   **Step 2.**

Step 3.   **Step 4.**

Step 5.   **Step 6.**

	Loan	Months of loan	End-of-month loan is repaid	Monthly payment	Finance charge rebate	Final payoff
14–8.	$9,000	24	9	$440		
	Step 1.			Step 2.		
	Step 3.			Step 4.		
	Step 5.			Step 6.		

14–9. Calculate the average daily balance:

30-day billing cycle			
9/16	Billing date	Previous balance	$2,000
9/19	Payment	$ 60	
9/30	Charge: Home Depot	1,500	
10/3	Payment	60	
10/7	Cash advance	70	

WORD PROBLEMS

14–10. The January 2001 issue of *Consumer Guide* listed a Chrysler PT Cruiser LHS 4-door sedan at $28,680. Dan Sege-
Excel   barth wants to purchase this vehicle and is interested in knowing the finance charges. He plans to put $3,680 down and will finance the vehicle for 48 months. His monthly payments will be $610.32. What would be Dan's finance charges?

14–11. The *Edmunds 2001 Buyer's Guide* listed a 2001 Ford Taurus SE wagon at $18,646. Margaret Paine purchased the car with $1,900 down. The loan is for 48 months with monthly payments of $408.10. **(a)** What amount did Margaret finance? **(b)** What is her finance charge? **(c)** Calculate the deferred payment price. **(d)** What is Margaret's APR?

14–12. Ramon Hernandez saw the following advertisement for a used Volkswagen Bug and decided to work out the numbers to be sure the ad had no errors. Please help Ramon by calculating (**a**) the amount financed, (**b**) the finance charge, (**c**) APR by table lookup, (**d**) the monthly payment by formula, and (**e**) the monthly payment by table lookup (will be off slightly).

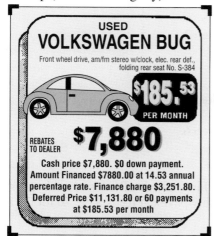

USED
VOLKSWAGEN BUG
Front wheel drive, am/fm stereo w/clock, elec. rear def., folding rear seat No. S-384

$185.⁵³
PER MONTH

REBATES TO DEALER **$7,880**

Cash price $7,880. $0 down payment. Amount Financed $7880.00 at 14.53 annual percentage rate. Finance charge $3,251.80. Deferred Price $11,131.80 or 60 payments at $185.53 per month

a. Amount financed:

b. Finance charge:

c. APR by table lookup:

d. Monthly payment by formula:

e. Monthly payment by table lookup (use 14.50%):

14–13. From this partial advertisement calculate:

$95.10 per month
#43892 Used car. Cash price $4,100. Down payment $50. For 60 months.

a. Amount financed. **b.** Finance charge.

c. Deferred payment price. **d.** APR by Table 14.1.

e. Check monthly payment (by formula).

14–14. Paula Westing borrowed $6,200 to travel to Sweden to see her son Arthur. Her loan was to be paid in 48 monthly installments of $170. At the end of 9 months, Paula's daughter Irene convinced her that she should pay off the loan early. What are Paula's rebate and her payoff amount?

Step 1.   **Step 2.**

Step 3.   **Step 4.**

Step 5.   **Step 6.**

14–15. The May 2001 issue of *Consumers' Research* commented on the price of a Jaguar XK8 convertible, which sells for $74,155. Bill Rich made a $15,000 down payment. The loan is for 48 months with a monthly payment of $1,465. From this information calculate (**a**) the amount financed, (**b**) the finance charges, (**c**) deferred payment price, and (**d**) APR using the table. Use the tables in the *Business Math Handbook*.

14–16. Joanne Flynn bought a new boat for $14,500. She put a $2,500 down payment on it. The bank's loan was for 48 months. Finance charges totaled $4,400.16. Assume Joanne decided to pay off the loan at the end of the 28th month. What rebate would she be entitled to and what would be the actual payoff amount?

Step 1.   Step 2.

Step 3.   Step 4.

Step 5.   Step 6.

14–17. On June 24, 2001, the *Bank Rate Monitor* reported on auto loan rates. First America Bank's monthly payment charge on a 48-month $20,000 loan is $488.26. The U.S. Bank's monthly payment fee is $497.70 for the same loan amount. What would be the APR for each of these banks?

14–18. From the following facts, Molly Roe has requested you to calculate the average daily balance. The customer believes the average daily balance should be $877.67. Respond to the customer's concern.

28-day billing cycle			
3/18	Billing date	Previous balance	$800
3/24	Payment	$ 60	
3/29	Charge: Sears	250	
4/5	Payment	20	
4/9	Charge: Macy's	200	

14–19. Jill bought a $500 rocking chair. The terms of her revolving charge are $1\frac{1}{2}\%$ on the unpaid balance from the previous month. If she pays $100 per month, complete a schedule for the first 3 months like Table 14.4. Be sure to use the U.S. Rule.

Monthly payment number	Outstanding balance due	$1\frac{1}{2}\%$ interest payment	Amount of monthly payment	Reduction in balance due	Outstanding balance due

CHALLENGE PROBLEMS

14–20. Jim Dawson purchased a 2001 Saturn for $16,666.67 with 10% down. He is paying $373.28 per month for 48 months. He has decided to make the payment in 36 months rather than 48 months. What is the amount of Jim's final payoff?

14–21. You have a $1,100 balance on your 15% credit card. You have lost your job and been unemployed for 6 months. You have been unable to make any payments on your balance. However, you received a tax refund and want to pay off the credit card. How much will you owe on the credit card, and how much interest will have accrued? What will be the effective rate of interest after the 6 months (to nearest hundredth percent)?

SUMMARY PRACTICE TEST

1. Paul Marciano bought a Land Rover Discovery for $36,500. Paul made a down payment of $12,000 and paid $450 monthly for 60 months. What are the total amount financed and the total finance charge that Paul paid at the end of the 60 months? *(p. 331)*

2. Lynn Brooks bought a Dell computer at Staples for $1,800. Lynn made a $500 down payment and financed the balance at 8% for 48 months. What is her monthly payment? (Use the loan amortization table.) *(p. 326)*

3. Ed Sloan read the following partial advertisement: price, $19,900; down payment, $1,100, cash or trade; and $375.88 per month for 60 months. Calculate **(a)** the total finance charge and **(b)** the APR by Table 14.1 (use the tables in *Business Math Handbook*) to the nearest hundredth percent. *(p. 323)*

4. Alvez Mooney bought a $4,000 desk at Furniture.com. Based on his income, Rich could only afford to pay back $400 per month. The charge on the unpaid balance is 3%. The U.S. Rule is used in the calculation. Calculate the balance outstanding at the end of month 2. *(p. 330)*

Month	Balance due	Interest	Monthly payment	Reduction in balance	Balance outstanding

5. George Mars borrowed $9,500 to travel to England to see his son Rich. George's loan was to be paid in 48 monthly installments of $250. At the end of 8 months, his daughter Fran convinced him that he should pay off the loan early. What are George's rebate and the payoff amount? *(p. 327)*

Step 1.   **Step 2.**

Step 3.   **Step 4.**

Step 5.   **Step 6.**

6. Calculate the average daily balance on the statement below. *(p. 330)*

30-day billing cycle		
9/9	Balance	$400
9/16	Payment	60
9/22	Charge Macy's	90

DEBT RELIEF | A growing number of services promise to lend a hand

WHERE TO GO FOR HELP

Need assistance to get out of debt? Credit counseling may be the answer—as it was for Deann Martinez and her husband (see the accompanying story). Check out groups that are members of the National Foundation for Credit Counseling (800-388-2227; www.nfcc.org) to find a program in your area, or the Association of Independent Consumer Credit Counseling Agencies (703-934-6118; www.aiccca.org). These agencies can usually get card companies to lower your interest rates and eliminate some late fees. You make one monthly payment and the agency distributes it to your creditors. A good program will also help you create a budget. It usually takes about five or six years to become debt-free.

These credit-counseling agencies charge debtors very little—an average of $11 per month, says Joy Thormodsgard, vice-president of the NFCC. They get paid primarily by the credit card companies—which typically pay them 9% to 15% of the money they collect.

A magic bullet? You are undoubtedly bombarded with e-mail messages touting debt-relief deals—some making grandiose claims such as being able to "cut your debt in half!" You are right to be skeptical. Here's how one commercial debt mediator works:

DebtSolution of Pasadena, Cal., negotiates with creditors to settle debts for 25 cents to 60 cents on the dollar. "We go to the creditor and say, 'This guy owes you $5,000; he can afford to pay you $2,000,'" says Duane Anderson, chief executive officer of DebtSolution. "We then ask 'Will you accept this as settlement in full?' and they say 'yes' or 'no.'" The firm keeps resubmitting the proposal until the creditor says yes. It usually takes about three years to settle with all of a client's creditors.

DebtSolution's fee? A 25% cut of the money they saved you. If DebtSolution settles a $10,000 debt for $4,000, for example, the charge would be $1,500—a hefty fee, but the total paid by the debtor is just a little more than half of what was actually owed.

In order to make this program work, you need to have enough money to pay the lump sums to the creditors. Most people who come to DebtSolution don't have such a stash. Instead, they accumulate the money by defaulting on their credit card payments. Rather than making the minimum payments to their credit card companies, they put the money in a savings account. After a few months they accumulate enough cash for the debt mediators to start making offers to the credit card companies.

This strategy isn't for those with a weak stomach. Defaulting on your credit card bills can ruin your credit record, and "probably about 10% of our clients

get sued" for defaulting, says Anderson. DebtSolution is affiliated with a law firm that handles the cases. Anderson admits that anyone who might make it through credit counseling should try that first. But his clients' only other option is to file for bankruptcy—which would look even worse on their credit record.

"I would be really wary" of any service that is urging you to default, warns Kathleen Michon, a lawyer who edits Nolo Press's bankruptcy books. "I find it hard to believe that people could come up with enough money" to pay off their creditors by defaulting for a few months—and if they could afford that, they should be in credit counseling instead. And before you work with any debt-mediation service, she urges, make sure you know about all fees and will be able to verify that the company is actually sending your money to the creditors. —**JOAN GOLDWASSER** and **KIMBERLY LANKFORD**

JONATHAN CARLSON

Business Math Issue

Getting out of debt is really a simple process.
1. List the key points of the article and information to support your position.
2. Write a group defense of your position using math calculations to support your view.

From Smart Cards to Video Goggles

Precocious Plastic

What It Is: A credit card with a computer chip that can remember all sorts of things about its owner and even carry electronic cash.

Where You'll Find It: All over Europe

Smart cards are just plain smart. Europeans use them everywhere to, in effect, tote crucial bits of information around in their wallets and to pay for everyday items you'd never be able to charge in the U.S.

In Amsterdam, you can stick them into parking meters. In Germany, you can use one to pay for your Big Mac. And in nearly every European country, people make calls from pay phones using smart cards charged up with calling minutes. Because chip-based security systems provide more protection, smart-card fraud is as little as one-fifth of that for traditional credit cards, according to Europay, MasterCard's European partner.

Smart cards–*like cash but better*

In Germany, nearly every citizen has a health-insurance smart card that holds an insurance ID number and other basic data. Doctors insert the cards into special readers to call up the information, eliminating much of the need for patients to fill out lengthy forms before each appointment.

Even the Pope is getting into the act. Organizers of the Catholic Church's Jubilee 2000 are using smart cards to help manage as many as 20 million religious pilgrims expected to flood Rome this year. Visitors can buy a single "Pilgrim" card before leaving home and then use it to gain entry to multiple Jubilee-related activities in the Vatican and Assisi.

When will the U.S. smarten up? American Express launched its Blue card last fall, and response has been encouraging. Analysts estimate about 1.5 million Blue cards have been issued. But attempts to roll out digital cash have mostly flopped. The problem: getting banks to agree on a standard. Smart cards aren't much good unless they're good almost everywhere.

©2000 Dow Jones & Company, Inc.

PROJECT A

Why do you think smart cards have not been well received in the United States? Visit the American Express website to see how smart cards are doing.

Internet Projects: See text website (www.mhhe.com/slater7e) and *The Business Math Internet Resource Guide.*

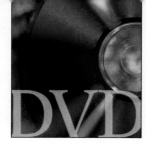

VIDEO CASE

Saturn Corporation

Personal finance is your responsibility. Remember, it's not how much you earn—it's how much you keep. Are you getting the most value for your money? Is it possible to both finance car payments and set aside savings? Purchasing a quality, yet value-priced car could be the answer.

For years we have known that American workers are not putting away enough money for retirement. Today, a growing number of workers are also not spending wisely.

Why are so many Americans depleting their savings and buying on credit? Some social critics blame schools, financial institutions, and even employers for failing to educate the public on the importance of savings. Others blame modern society, which places a premium on materialism and creature comfort.

In 1990, when the first Saturn automobile rolled off the Spring Hill, Tennessee, assembly line, the event was heralded as a landmark in both U.S. automotive manufacturing and union-management relations. The start-up plant had been nur-

tured under an agreement that called a tentative truce between General Motors and the UAW. The Saturn automobile had been manufactured with team-based processes—a radical departure from the assembly-line production of the American automakers.

Saturn is sold to the public with a "no-price-hassle" policy by sales teams trained to make car buying a "celebration." This works effectively for its customers because they know the next person in the door won't negotiate a better deal. In addition, Saturn's performance is so exceptional that in 2000, J.D. Power and Associates ranked Saturn first among all automakers in customer satisfaction. Also, Saturn remains the GM brand most likely to lure first-time buyers. Saturn has established its name on value and customer service. The Saturn automobile is regarded as more than simply a successful product; the company is seen as an embodiment of GM's vision of modern corporate ideals.

PROBLEM 1

Four years ago you planned to purchase a 2002 Saturn and anticipated the total cost would be $22,350. A sum of $18,500 was placed in a bank earning 4% compounded semiannually. **(a)** Was enough money placed in your account to purchase the Saturn? **(b)** How much will be in the account over or under the purchasing price? **(c)** What should you have placed in your account to have exactly what you would need?

PROBLEM 2

Saturn's first SUV, the VUE, has a price range of $23,000–$26,000 and features flexible, dent-resistant plastic body panels (as on Saturn cars). You were aware 3 years ago of the new VUE. The VUE has a total price of $25,590. You are worried about the cost of interest. To pay cash for the vehicle, how much money should you have set aside 3 years ago at your bank, which compounded interest quarterly at a rate of 4%?

PROBLEM 3

Bank One's Market Index Account compounds interest daily with a minimum deposit of $15,000. A 2002 Saturn 3-door coupe has a retail price of $16,080. Assume the purchasing price was placed in Bank One and interest rose to 6%: **(a)** How much would the account grow to in 3 years? **(b)** How much interest would have been earned?

PROBLEM 4

A 2002 Saturn L-Series Wagon has a $19,155 list price with a 10% down payment. A one-year certificate of deposit has an average effective yield of 5.25% interest compounded

annually. Without withdrawing any of the principal, how much would be required in the account to cover the down payment?

PROBLEM 5

A 2002 Saturn L-Series Sedan has a retail price of $19,500 with or without a down payment of 10%. Assume the down payment were to be placed in a Roth IRA for the next 10 years and the bank is compounding interest semiannually at 6%: **(a)** How much would be in the Roth IRA at the end of 10 years? **(b)** If the same amount were placed each period in an annuity with the same rate for the next 10 years, how much would the annuity be worth?

PROBLEM 6

A 2002 Saturn LS2 4-door 4-cylinder automatic lists for $18,495. The down payment is $3,495 with 48 monthly payments of $359.19. What would be the finance charge for the Saturn?

PROBLEM 7

A 2002 LS3 4-door V-6 automatic retails at $20,345 with $2,845 down. Bank A has an interest rate of 7% with 48 monthly payments of $419.06. Bank B has an interest rate of 8% with 48 monthly payments of $427.23. What is the total interest saved by obtaining the 7% loan?

PROBLEM 8

A 2002 Saturn S-Series Coupe retails for $14,000 with $1,500 down. The loan is for 48 months and payments are $299.33 per month. What is the annual percentage rate?

Your mortgage is a great investment

You can save considerable money over the life of your loan by prepaying part of your mortgage principal each month. Based on a $100,000 30-year mortgage at 8 percent.

Total interest cost

$164,149 $140,812 $124,243 $101,693 $88,260

$75,889

$62,456

Savings

$39,906

$23,337

$0 $25 $50 $100 $200

Monthly prepayment amount

SOURCE: www.investinyourself.com

©The Boston Sunday Globe, June 4, 2000.

342

The Cost of Home Ownership

FIGURE 15.1 Types of mortgages available

Loan types	Advantages	Disadvantages
30-year fixed rate mortgage	A predictable monthly payment.	If interest rates fall, you are locked in to higher rate unless you refinance. (Application and appraisal fees along with other closing costs will result.)
15-year fixed rate mortgage	Interest rate lower than 30-year fixed (usually $\frac{1}{4}$ to $\frac{1}{2}$ of a percent). Your equity builds up faster while interest costs are cut by more than one-half.	A larger down payment is needed. Monthly payment will be higher.
Graduated-payment mortgage (GPM)	Easier to qualify for than 30- or 15-year fixed rate. Monthly payments start low and increase over time.	May have higher APR than fixed or variable rates.
Biweekly mortgage	Shortens term loan; saves substantial amount of interest; 26 biweekly payments per year. Builds equity twice as fast.	Not good for those not seeking an early loan payoff.
Adjustable rate mortgage (ARM)	Lower rate than fixed. If rates fall, could be adjusted down without refinancing. Caps available that limit how high rate could go for each adjustment period over term of loan.	Monthly payment could rise if interest rates rise. Riskier than fixed rate mortgage in which monthly payment is stable.
Home equity loan	Cheap and reliable accessible lines of credit backed by equity in your home. Tax-deductible. Rates can be locked in. Reverse mortgages may be available to those 62 or older.	Could lose home if not paid. No annual or interest caps.

Chapter 15 could save you thousands of dollars! Read the following true story.

Purchasing a home usually involves paying a large amount of interest. Note how your author was able to save $70,121.40.

Over the life of a 30-year **fixed rate mortgage** (Figure 15.1) of $100,000, the interest would have cost $207,235. Monthly payments would have been $849.99. This would not include taxes, insurance, and so on.

Your author chose a **biweekly mortgage** (Figure 15.1). This meant that every two weeks (26 times a year) the bank would receive $425. By paying every two weeks instead of once a month, the mortgage would be paid off in 23 years instead of 30—a $70,121.40 *savings* on interest. Why? When a payment is made every two weeks, the principal is reduced more quickly, which substantially reduces the interest cost.

LEARNING UNIT 15–1 | TYPES OF MORTGAGES AND THE MONTHLY MORTGAGE PAYMENT

In the past several years, interest rates have been low, which has caused an increase in home sales. Today, more people are buying homes than are renting homes. The question facing prospective buyers concerns which type of **mortgage** will be best for them. Figure 15.1 lists the types of mortgages available to home buyers. Depending on how interest rates are moving when you purchase a home, you may find one type of mortgage to be the most advantageous for you.

TABLE 15.1 Amortization table (mortgage principal and interest per $1,000)

Term in years	Interest												
	$6\frac{1}{2}$%	7%	$7\frac{1}{2}$%	8%	$8\frac{1}{2}$%	9%	$9\frac{1}{2}$%	10%	$10\frac{1}{2}$%	11%	$11\frac{1}{2}$%	$11\frac{3}{4}$%	12%
10	11.36	11.62	11.88	12.14	12.40	12.67	12.94	13.22	13.50	13.78	14.06	14.21	14.35
12	10.02	10.29	10.56	10.83	11.11	11.39	11.67	11.96	12.25	12.54	12.84	12.99	13.14
15	8.72	8.99	9.28	9.56	9.85	10.15	10.45	10.75	11.06	11.37	11.69	11.85	12.01
17	8.12	8.40	8.69	8.99	9.29	9.59	9.90	10.22	10.54	10.86	11.19	11.35	11.52
20	7.46	7.76	8.06	8.37	8.68	9.00	9.33	9.66	9.99	10.33	10.67	10.84	11.02
22	7.13	7.44	7.75	8.07	8.39	8.72	9.05	9.39	9.73	10.08	10.43	10.61	10.78
25	6.76	7.07	7.39	7.72	8.06	8.40	8.74	9.09	9.45	9.81	10.17	10.35	10.54
30	6.33	6.66	7.00	7.34	7.69	8.05	8.41	8.78	9.15	9.53	9.91	10.10	10.29
35	6.05	6.39	6.75	7.11	7.47	7.84	8.22	8.60	8.99	9.37	9.77	9.96	10.16

Have you heard that elderly people who are house-rich and cash-poor can use their home to get cash or monthly income? The Federal Housing Administration makes it possible for older homeowners to take out a **reverse mortgage** on their homes. Under reverse mortgages, senior homeowners borrow against the equity in their property, often getting fixed monthly checks. The debt is repaid only when the homeowners or their estate sells the home.

Now let's learn how to calculate a monthly mortgage payment and the total cost of loan interest over the life of a mortgage. We will use the following example in our discussion.

EXAMPLE Gary bought a home for $200,000. He made a 20% down payment. The 9% mortgage is for 30 years (30 × 12 = 360 payments). What are Gary's monthly payment and total cost of interest?

Computing the Monthly Payment for Principal and Interest

You can calculate the principal and interest of Gary's **monthly payment** using the **amortization table** shown in Table 15.1 and the following steps. (Remember that this is the same type of amortization table used in Chapter 14 for installment loans.)

Computing Monthly Payment by Using an Amortization Table

Step 1. Divide the amount of the mortgage by $1,000.

Step 2. Look up the rate and term in the amortization table. At the intersection is the table factor.

Step 3. Multiply Step 1 by Step 2.

For Gary, we calculate the following:

$$\frac{\$160,000 \text{ (amount of mortgage)}}{\$1,000} = 160 \times \$8.05 \text{ (table rate)} = \boxed{\$1,288}$$

So $160,000 is the amount of the mortgage ($200,000 less 20%). The $8.05 is the table factor of 9% for 30 years per $1,000. Since Gary is mortgaging 160 units of $1,000, the factor of $8.05 is multiplied by 160. Remember that the $1,288 payment does not include taxes, insurance, and so on.

What Is the Total Cost of Interest?

We can use the following formula to calculate Gary's total interest cost over the life of the mortgage:

$$\begin{array}{ccc}
\text{Total cost} & = & \text{Total of all} & - & \text{Amount of} \\
\text{of interest} & & \text{monthly payments} & & \text{mortgage} \\
\uparrow & & \uparrow & & \uparrow \\
\boxed{\$303,680} & = & \$463,680 & - & \$160,000 \\
& & (\$1,288 \times 360) & &
\end{array}$$

TABLE 15.1 (concluded)

Term in years	Interest									
	$12\frac{1}{2}\%$	$12\frac{3}{4}\%$	13%	$13\frac{1}{2}\%$	$13\frac{3}{4}\%$	14%	$14\frac{1}{2}\%$	$14\frac{3}{4}\%$	15%	$15\frac{1}{2}\%$
10	14.64	14.79	14.94	15.23	15.38	15.53	15.83	15.99	16.14	16.45
12	13.44	13.60	13.75	14.06	14.22	14.38	14.69	14.85	15.01	15.34
15	12.33	12.49	12.66	12.99	13.15	13.32	13.66	13.83	14.00	14.34
17	11.85	12.02	12.19	12.53	12.71	12.88	13.23	13.41	13.58	13.94
20	11.37	11.54	11.72	12.08	12.26	12.44	12.80	12.99	13.17	13.54
22	11.14	11.33	11.51	11.87	12.06	12.24	12.62	12.81	12.99	13.37
25	10.91	11.10	11.28	11.66	11.85	12.04	12.43	12.62	12.81	13.20
30	10.68	10.87	11.07	11.46	11.66	11.85	12.25	12.45	12.65	13.05
35	10.56	10.76	10.96	11.36	11.56	11.76	12.17	12.37	12.57	12.98

TABLE 15.2   Effect of interest rates on monthly payments

	9%	11%	Difference
Monthly payment	$1,288	$1,524.80	$236.80 per month
	(160 × $8.05)	(160 × $9.53)	
Total cost of interest	$303,680	$388,928	$85,248
	($1,288 × 360) − $160,000	($1,524.80 × 360) − $160,000	($236.80 × 360)

Effects of Interest Rates on Monthly Payment and Total Interest Cost

Table 15.2 shows the effect that an increase in interest rates would have on Gary's monthly payment and his total cost of interest. Note that if Gary's interest rate rises to 11%, the 2% increase will result in Gary paying an additional $85,248 in total interest.

For most people, purchasing a home is a major lifetime decision. Many factors must be considered before this decision is made. One of these factors is how to pay for the home. The purpose of this unit is to tell you that being informed about the types of available mortgages can save you thousands of dollars.

In addition to the mortgage payment, buying a home can include the following costs:

- *Closing costs:* When property passes from seller to buyer, **closing costs** may include fees for credit reports, recording costs, lawyer's fees, points, title search, and so on. A **point** is a one-time charge that is a percent of the mortgage. Two points means 2% of the mortgage.

- *Escrow amount:* Usually, the lending institution, for its protection, requires that each month $\frac{1}{12}$ of the insurance cost and $\frac{1}{12}$ of the real estate taxes be kept in a special account called the **escrow account.** The monthly balance in this account will change depending on the cost of the insurance and taxes. Interest is paid on escrow accounts.

- *Repairs and maintenance:* This includes paint, wallpaper, landscaping, plumbing, electrical expenses, and so on.

As you can see, the cost of owning a home can be expensive. But remember that all interest costs of your monthly payment and your real estate taxes are deductible. For many, owning a home can have advantages over renting.

LU 15–1 PRACTICE QUIZ

Given: Price of home, $225,000; 20% down payment; 9% interest rate; 25-year mortgage.
Solve for:

1. Monthly payment and total cost of interest over 25 years.
2. If rate fell to 8%, what would be the total decrease in interest cost over the life of the mortgage?

✓ **SOLUTIONS**

1. $225,000 − $45,000 = $180,000

    $\dfrac{\$180,000}{\$1,000}$ = 180 × $8.40 = $1,512

    $273,600 = $453,600   − $180,000
                ($1,512 × 300)   25 years × 12 payments per year

2. 8% = $1,389.60   monthly payment
            (180 × $7.72)

    Total interest cost $236,880 = ($1,389.60 × 300) − $180,000
    Savings $36,720 = ($273,600 − $236,880)

LEARNING UNIT 15–2 | AMORTIZATION SCHEDULE—BREAKING DOWN THE MONTHLY PAYMENT

In Learning Unit 15–1, we saw that over the life of Gary's $160,000 loan, he would pay $303,680 in interest. Now let's use the following steps to determine what portion of Gary's first monthly payment reduces the principal and what portion is interest.

Calculating Interest, Principal, and New Balance of Monthly Payment

Step 1. Calculate the interest for a month (use current principal):
Interest = Principal × Rate × Time.

Step 2. Calculate the amount used to reduce the principal:
Principal reduction = Monthly payment − Interest (Step 1).

Step 3. Calculate the new principal: Current principal − Reduction of principal (Step 2) = New principal.

Step 1. Interest (I) = Principal (P) × Rate (R) × Time (T)

$$\$1,200 = \$160,000 \times .09 \times \frac{1}{12}$$

Step 2. The reduction of the $160,000 principal each month is equal to the payment less interest. So we can calculate Gary's new principal balance at the end of month 1 as follows:

Monthly payment at 9% (from Table 15.1)	$1,288 (160 × $8.05)
− Interest for first month	− 1,200
= Principal reduction	$ 88

Step 3. As the years go by, the interest portion of the payment decreases and the principal portion increases.

Principal balance	$160,000
Principal reduction	− 88
Balance of principal	$159,912

Let's do month 2:

Step 1. Interest = Principal × Rate × Time

$$= \$159,912 \times .09 \times \frac{1}{12}$$

$$= \$1,199.34$$

Step 2.
$1,288.00	monthly payment
− 1,199.34	interest for month 2
$ 88.66	principal reduction

Step 3.
$159,912.00	principal balance
− 88.66	principal reduction
$159,823.34	balance of principal

Note that in month 2, interest costs drop 66 cents ($1,200.00 − $1,199.34). So in 2 months, Gary has reduced his mortgage balance by $176.66 ($88.00 + $88.66). After 2 months, Gary has paid a total interest of $2,399.34 ($1,200.00 + $1,199.34).

Example of an Amortization Schedule

The partial **amortization schedule** given in Table 15.3 shows the breakdown of Gary's monthly payment. Note the amount that goes toward reducing the principal and toward payment of actual interest. Also note how the outstanding balance of the loan is reduced. After 7 months, Gary still owes $159,369.97. Often when you take out a mortgage loan, you will receive an amortization schedule from the company that holds your mortgage.

The Wall Street Journal clipping "Jumbo Mortgages? Not a Huge Problem" (p. 348) gives an option for how to work around the problem of large mortgages known as jumbo mortgages. Read the clipping and see how Mark Rosen and his wife plan to take out two smaller loans instead of a jumbo mortgage. These smaller loans will save $35,000 in interest by avoiding the increased interest charged for jumbo mortgages.

TABLE 15.3   Partial amortization schedule

| Payment number | Principal (current) | Monthly payment, $1,288 | | |
		Interest	Principal reduction	Balance of principal
1	$160,000.00	$1,200.00 $\left(\$160{,}000 \times .09 \times \frac{1}{12}\right)$	$88.00 ($1,288 − $1,200)	$159,912.00 ($160,000 − $88)
2	$159,912.00	$1,199.34 $\left(\$159{,}912 \times .09 \times \frac{1}{12}\right)$	$88.66 ($1,288 − $1,199.34)	$159,823.34 ($159,912 − $88.66)
3	$159,823.34	$1,198.68	$89.32	$159,734.02
4	$159,734.02	$1,198.01	$89.99	$159,644.03
5	$159,644.03	$1,197.33	$90.67	$159,553.36
6	$159,553.36	$1,196.65	$91.35	$159,462.01
7	$159,462.01	$1,195.97*	$92.04	$159,369.97

*Off 1 cent due to rounding.

Jumbo Mortgages? Not a Huge Problem

There Are Ways to Avoid These Expensive Loans

YOUR
MONEY
MATTERS

By Patrick Barta
Staff Reporter of The Wall Street Journal

M.E. Cohen

Mark Rosen and his wife had just found the perfect house in an up-and-coming Chicago neighborhood when their mortgage broker uttered a word they really didn't want to hear: jumbo.

To buy the three-bedroom house, Mr. Rosen and his wife, Dina Shiner, needed to borrow about $317,000, an amount considered too high for the buyers to qualify for a "plain vanilla" mortgage. So, like thousands of other higher-income couples, the couple was thrust into the bewildering world of the jumbo mortgage market, so called because the loans are bigger than average. In fact, any mortgage in excess of $252,700—$275,000 beginning Jan. 1—is considered a jumbo.

Such loans, which accounted for about 21% of the $1.1 trillion in mortgages issued last year, carry higher interest rates than ordinary mortgage loans and end up costing buyers thousands of dollars in extra interest payments. But as Mr. Rosen and his wife found, there are sometimes ways to work around the problem and avoid a jumbo. Instead of one big mortgage, they plan to take out two smaller loans that they expect will save them some $35,000 in interest over the life of their loans.

The cutoff "seemed to be so arbitrary," says Mr. Rosen, a 34-year-old software developer. "You're never going to be able to explain to me why a $300,000 loan is more expensive" than a similar—but smaller—one, he says.

Just why do jumbos cost so much more?

For years, the conventional wisdom has been that lenders had to charge more for jumbos because the loans aren't backed by Fannie Mae and Freddie Mac, the giant government-sponsored loan purchasers. The two companies exist to buy eligible mortgages from banks and other lenders, freeing up lenders to make more loans, and in the process, they're supposed to lower interest rates for the home buyers who qualify.

Fannie and Freddie, which are mandated to help low- and moderate-income homeowners, are prohibited from buying loans over a certain amount. That limit, which sets the cutoff between ordinary loans and jumbos, is adjusted every year using data from the Federal Housing Finance Board, an independent housing-related agency.

Lately, though, many of the old assumptions about the mortgage market have been called into question. A controversial study published by the Federal Reserve in October suggested that Fannie and Freddie don't necessarily affect the interest rates paid by home buyers. At the same time, many mortgage experts believe that factors unrelated to Fannie and Freddie contribute to jumbo loans' higher prices.

Despite the Fed study, though, the vast majority of mortgage experts still think Fannie and Freddie play some role in prices, although they don't know how much. For one thing, loans that fit Fannie's and Freddie's guidelines are easier to package and sell as securities to investors, and that allows lenders to charge lower rates for those loans. Mortgages that don't fit the companies' guidelines—like jumbos—are sometimes harder to sell, especially in times of economic stress.

LU 15–2 PRACTICE QUIZ

Prepare an amortization schedule for first three periods for the following: mortgage, $100,000; 11%; 30 years.

$100,000 mortgage; monthly payment, $953 (100 × $9.53)

✓ SOLUTIONS

Payment number	Principal (current)	Interest	Principal reduction	Balance of principal
		Portion to—		
1	$100,000	$916.67	$36.33	$99,963.67
		$\left(\$100{,}000 \times .11 \times \frac{1}{12}\right)$	($953 − $916.67)	($100,000 − $36.33)
2	$99,963.67	$916.33	$36.67	$99,927.00
		$\left(\$99{,}963.67 \times .11 \times \frac{1}{12}\right)$	($953 − $916.33)	($99,963.67 − $36.67)
3	$99,927	$916.00	$37.00	$99,890.00
		$\left(\$99{,}927 \times .11 \times \frac{1}{12}\right)$	($953 − $916)	($99,927 − $37)

Chapter Organizer and Reference Guide

Topic	Key point, procedure, formula	Example(s) to illustrate situation
Computing monthly mortgage payment, p. 345	Based on per $1,000 Table 15.1: $$\frac{\text{Amount of mortgage}}{\$1{,}000} \times \text{Table rate}$$	Use Table 15.1: 12% on $60,000 mortgage for 30 years. $$\frac{\$60{,}000}{\$1{,}000} = 60 \times \$10.29$$ $$= \$617.40$$
Calculating total interest cost, p. 345	$$\begin{array}{c}\text{Total of all} \\ \text{monthly payments}\end{array} - \begin{array}{c}\text{Amount of} \\ \text{mortgage}\end{array}$$	Using example above: 30 years = 360 (payments) × $617.40 $222,264 − 60,000 $162,264 (mortgage interest over life of mortgage)
Amortization schedule, p. 348	$I = P \times R \times T$ $$\left(I \text{ for month} = P \times R \times \frac{1}{12}\right)$$ $$\frac{\text{Principal}}{\text{reduction}} = \frac{\text{Monthly}}{\text{payment}} - \text{Interest}$$ $$\frac{\text{New}}{\text{principal}} = \frac{\text{Current}}{\text{principal}} - \frac{\text{Reduction of}}{\text{principal}}$$	Using same example: **Portion to—** <table><tr><td>Payment number</td><td>Interest</td><td>Principal reduction</td><td>Balance of principal</td></tr><tr><td>1</td><td>$600</td><td>$17.40</td><td>$59,982.60</td></tr><tr><td></td><td>$\left(\$60{,}000 \times .12 \times \frac{1}{12}\right)$</td><td>$\left(\begin{array}{c}\$617.40 \\ -\$600.00\end{array}\right)$</td><td>$\left(\begin{array}{c}\$60{,}000.00 \\ -\ \$17.40\end{array}\right)$</td></tr><tr><td>2</td><td>$599.83</td><td>$17.57</td><td>$59,965.03</td></tr><tr><td></td><td>$\left(\$59{,}982.60 \times .12 \times \frac{1}{12}\right)$</td><td>$\left(\begin{array}{c}\$617.40 \\ -\$599.83\end{array}\right)$</td><td>$\left(\begin{array}{c}\$59{,}982.60 \\ -\ \$17.57\end{array}\right)$</td></tr></table>
Key terms	Adjustable rate mortgage, (ARM), p. 344 Amortization schedule, p. 347 Amortization table, p. 345 Biweekly mortgage, p. 344	Closing costs, p. 346 Escrow account, p. 346 Fixed rate mortgage, p. 344 Graduated-payment mortgages (GPM), p. 344 Home equity loan, p. 344 Monthly payment, p. 345 Mortgages, p. 344 Points, p. 346 Reverse mortgage, p. 345

Critical Thinking Discussion Questions

1. Explain the advantages and disadvantages of the following loan types: 30-year fixed rate, 15-year fixed rate, graduated-payment mortgage, biweekly mortgage, adjustable rate mortgage, and home equity loan. Why might a bank require a home buyer to establish an escrow account?

2. How is an amortization schedule calculated? Is there a best time to refinance a mortgage?

3. What is a point? Is paying points worth the cost?

4. Would you ever consider a jumbo mortgage?

DRILL PROBLEMS

Complete the following amortization chart by using Table 15.1.

	Selling price of home	Down payment	Principal (loan)	Rate of interest	Years	Payment per $1,000	Monthly mortgage payment
15–1.	$159,000	$10,000		$6\frac{1}{2}\%$	25		
Excel							
15–2.	$70,000	$12,000		11%	30		
Excel							
15–3.	$275,000	$50,000		9%	35		
Excel							

15–4. What is total cost of interest in Problem 15–2?

15–5. If the interest rate rises to 13% in Problem 15–2, what is the total cost of interest?

Complete the following:

	Selling price	Down payment	Amount mortgage	Rate	Years	Monthly payment	First payment broken down into—		Balance at end of month
							Interest	Principal	
15–6.	$125,000	$5,000		7%	30				
15–7.	$199,000	$40,000		$12\frac{1}{2}\%$	35				

15–8. Bob Jones bought a new log cabin for $70,000 at 11% interest for 30 years. Please prepare an amortization schedule for first 3 periods.

Payment number	Portion to—		Balance of loan outstanding
	Interest	Principal	

WORD PROBLEMS

15–9. On March 23, 2000, the *Philadelphia Inquirer* reported on 15-year versus 30-year fixed rate mortgages. The total interest for 15 years would be $72,000 and $164,000 for 30 years; this is based on a $100,000 loan at 8%. Doug Tweeten wants to take advantage of this savings. **(a)** How much would his monthly payments be on a 15-year loan? **(b)** How much would his monthly payments be on a 30-year loan? **(c)** How much more would he pay each month on a 15-year loan?

15–10. On January 5, 2001, *USA Today* reported that million-dollar homes sold at a record pace during the year 2000. For example, Oprah Winfrey has closed on a 42-acre estate near Santa Barbara, California, for $50,000,000. If Oprah puts 20% down and finances at 7% for 30 years, what would her monthly payment be?

15–11. Bill Allen bought a home in Arlington, Texas, for $108,000. He put down 25% and obtained a mortgage for 30 years at 11%. What is Bill's monthly payment? What is the total interest cost of the loan?

15–12. If in Problem 15–11 the rate of interest is 14%, what is the difference in interest cost?

15–13. Mike Jones bought a new split-level home for $150,000 with 20% down. He decided to use Victory Bank for his mortgage. They were offering $13\frac{3}{4}\%$ for 25-year mortgages. Provide Mike with an amortization schedule for the first three periods.

Payment number	Portion to—		Balance of loan outstanding
	Interest	Principal	

15–14. Harriet Marcus is concerned about the financing of a home. She saw a small cottage that sells for $50,000. If she puts 20% down, what will her monthly payment be at **(a)** 25 years, $11\frac{1}{2}\%$; **(b)** 25 years, $12\frac{1}{2}\%$; **(c)** 25 years, $13\frac{1}{2}\%$; **(d)** 25 years, 15%? What is the total cost of interest over the cost of the loan for each assumption? **(e)** What is the savings in interest cost between $11\frac{1}{2}\%$ and 15%? **(f)** If Harriet uses 30 years instead of 25 for both $11\frac{1}{2}\%$ and 15%, what is the difference in interest?

15–15. On May 25, 2001, the *Chicago Sun-Times* reported a lowering of interest rates. Rates are being lowered with minimal points. Sandra Jordon will be able to obtain a $6\frac{1}{2}\%$ 25-year loan. The loan is for $180,000. However, she must pay 1 point. She is interested in knowing how much of her beginning payments will go toward interest and what will go toward the principal. **(a)** What must Sandra pay in points? **(b)** What will be the monthly payment? **(c)** Provide an amortization schedule for her first three payments.

15–16. The April 23, 2001, issue of *Business Week* reported on private mortgage insurance (PMI). Jesse Garza wants to avoid paying PMI and has to put 20% down. The most Jesse has for a down payment is $43,000. His bank is offering 15-year fixed loans at $6\frac{1}{2}\%$. **(a)** What is the most Jesse can pay for a home? **(b)** Based on what he can afford, what would be Jesse's monthly payments?

 CHALLENGE PROBLEMS

15–17. On December 21, 2000, the *Los Angeles Times* provided a chart to enable readers to figure out how refinancing would effect their mortgage payments. To use this chart, drop the last three zeros from your current mortgage amount and multiply that by the multiplier that most closely corresponds to your new interest rate and loan term. Subtract that number from your current loan payment, and that's your monthly savings.

Multipliers		
Loan rate	**30-year loan**	**15-year loan**
8.0%	7.3376	9.5565
7.9%	7.2680	9.4988
7.8%	7.1987	9.4414
7.7%	7.1296	9.3841
7.6%	7.0607	9.3270
7.5%	6.9921	9.2701
7.4%	6.9238	9.2134

Consider a $200,000 loan at 8% with a monthly payment of $1,467.53. Calculate refinancing at 7.4% for 30 years. **(a)** What would be the savings per month? **(b)** If the loan costs were $2,000, how many months would it take for refinancing to pay off?

15–18.   Sharon Fox decided to buy a home in Marblehead, Massachusetts, for $275,000. Her bank requires a 30% down payment. Sue Willis, an attorney, has notified Sharon that besides the 30% down payment there will be the following additional costs:

Recording of the deed	$ 30.00
A credit and appraisal report	155.00
Preparation of appropriate documents	48.00

A transfer tax of 1.8% of the purchase price and a loan origination fee of 2.5% of the mortgage amount

Assume a 30-year mortgage at a rate of 10%.

a.   What is the initial amount of cash Sharon will need?

b.   What is her monthly payment?

c.   What is the total cost of interest over the life of the mortgage?

SUMMARY PRACTICE TEST

1.   Patty Cole bought a home for $120,000 with a down payment of $5,000. Her rate of interest is $6\frac{1}{2}$% for 35 years. Calculate her **(a)** monthly payment; **(b)** first payment, broken down into interest and principal; and **(c)** balance of mortgage at the end of the month. *(pp. 345, 346)*

2.   Jay Miller bought a home in Alabama for $90,000. He put down 20% and obtained a mortgage for 25 years at 7%. What are Jay's monthly payment and the total interest cost of the loan? *(p. 345)*

3.   Christina Sanders is concerned about the financing of a home. She saw a small cape that sells for $80,000. If she puts 10% down, what will her monthly payment be at **(a)** 25 years, $6\frac{1}{2}$%; **(b)** 25 years, 7%; **(c)** 25 years, $7\frac{1}{2}$%; and **(d)** 25 years, 8%? What is the total cost of interest over the cost of the loan for each assumption? *(p. 345)*

4.   Katie Hercher bought a home for $125,000 with a down payment of $5,000. Her rate of interest is 9% for 25 years. Calculate Katie's payment per $1,000 and her monthly mortgage payment. *(p. 345)*

5.   Using Problem 4, calculate the total cost of interest for Katie Hercher. *(p. 345)*

HOME | Rising values may mean you can quit

paying **MORTGAGE INSURANCE**. *By Elizabeth Razzi*

BYE-BYE, PMI

YOU MIGHT WANT to write a little thank-you note to the folks who paid top dollar to move into your neighborhood over the past few years. Thanks to them, you may be able to scrap a mortgage insurance policy you no longer need and save a couple thousand dollars a year.

If you bought a home with less than 20% down within the past few years, the housing boom may have pushed your equity over the 20% threshold, making private mortgage insurance superfluous. A survey by HomeGain.com, a real estate Web site, shows that 95% of 61 cities surveyed had enough appreciation between 1997 and 2000 to justify dropping PMI. Improvements may bolster equity, too.

Dumping your PMI—which protects the lender from loss if a borrower with little equity quits paying the mortgage—won't be easy, but because it costs 0.5% to 1% of your loan balance each year, or $1,000 to $2,000 a year on a $200,000 mortgage, it may be worth the hassle. Nearly all lenders expect you to pay your mortgage faithfully for at least two years before you even ask to drop the insurance. And your lender will want to have its appraiser check out your home's value.

Before you shell out $250 to $300 for the appraisal, make sure the effort will be worthwhile. Look at your annual escrow-account statement to see how much you pay for PMI each month. Divide the appraisal fee by the PMI payment to see how many months it will take to recoup the appraisal cost. (If you're paying $1,000 a year, you'll recoup a $250 appraisal fee in just three months.)

You also don't want to spend money on an appraisal only to find that your equity is still shy of 20%. Take a few minutes to plug your address into a Web-based price calculator, such as at www.homegain.com, to see whether you're within shooting range. You can get a more accurate estimate by asking a real estate agent for an opinion based on sales of nearby homes similar to yours. Web sites don't take into account such factors as the number of bedrooms and bathrooms.

But one thing you don't want to do is rely on the government to get rid of your PMI. Although federal law now requires lenders to drop PMI automatically when it's no longer needed, those rules take only regularly scheduled monthly mortgage payments (not price appreciation) into account when figuring your equity. You could end up paying PMI for ten or 15 years, most of it needlessly. **K** —*Reporter:* **JOSEPHINE ROSSI**

Business Math Issue

Mortgage insurance really deals with depreciation.
1. List the key points of the article and information to support your position.
2. Write a group defense of your position using math calculations to support your view.

Their Presence Is Growing...

Although it's still relatively small, the market for online mortgages is growing. Meanwhile, thanks to improvements in the sites, customer satisfaction has improved significantly.

Total value of mortgage loans made each year...approximately $1 trillion

Loans closed through online providers in 2000 ....about $20 billion

Loans closed through online providers in 1999...about $10 billion

Loans closed through online providers in 1998 ....less than $5 billion

Estimated mortgage Web sites...more than 100

Borrowers satisfied with service at a major online lender, Q4 2000..92%

Borrowers satisfied with service at a major online lender, Q4 1999..50%

...But Many Are Still Struggling to Survive

Even though some sites are making profits, many others have closed or are struggling. Some of the most high-profile sites:

■ **E-LOAN.COM** One of the most widely recognized names in the business, E-Loan provides auto and other consumer loans in addition to mortgages. But it reported a $20.7 million loss in the fourth quarter of 2000*

■ **LENDINGTREE.COM** A popular marketplace for home loans through which loan requests are farmed out to other lenders, LendingTree nevertheless reported a $15 million loss in the third quarter of 2000.

■ **INDYMAC.COM** An online lender that receives high marks in consumer surveys for good service. The company is profitable, but much of its revenue comes from a second business that buys loans and sells them to other lenders or investors.

■ **COUNTRYWIDE.COM** One of the most popular "bricks-and-clicks" sites, serving as the online site for Countrywide Home Loans, a profitable traditional lender.

■ **HOMESPACE.COM** The online provider of mortgages and other real-estate services received lots of hype, but wound up selling its mortgage business to LendingTree last August.

■ **MORTGAGE.COM** A high-profile flameout. Originally designed to provide loans directly to consumers, the company switched to offer business-to-business services to banks and others. Announced plans to wind down its operations in October.

■ **iOWN.COM** Previously an online mortgage provider, the company stopped accepting new loan applications in August and laid off 140 people. It now operates as a referral service to help consumers find other lenders, compare rates and shop for houses.

■ **ONLOAN.COM** Once an online mortgage provider, the company exited the mortgage business last fall and shut down its Web site.

■ **LOANSDIRECT.COM** An online loan provider, recently acquired by E*Trade Group Inc., that gets high marks for service. Does not publicly disclose revenue or profits.

■ **KEYSTROKE.COM** Ranked as the cheapest online mortgage provider by Gomez Advisors this summer, the company soon after ended its consumer mortgage business and turned to developing software for the mortgage industry.

*E-Loan reported a pro-forma net loss of $6.5 million, which excludes compensation charges related to the company's stock-option plan, amortization of goodwill on the acquisition of CarFinance.com, and amortization of marketing costs related to warrants issued to purchase the company's common stock.

Source: Gomez Advisors, the companies

PROJECT A

Visit some of these websites to see how they are doing today.

 Internet Projects: See text website (www.mhhe.com/slater7e) and *The Business Math Internet Resource Guide.*

McDonald's Hen-Care Guidelines Lead Egg Producers to Warn of Higher Prices

By Jennifer Ordonez
Staff Reporter of The Wall Street Journal

The egg industry is warning that a McDonald's Corp. campaign to improve the treatment of chickens could drive up the price of eggs at the grocery store.

McDonald's this week sent a letter to the producers of the nearly two billion eggs it buys each year, ordering them to comply with strict guidelines for the humane treatment of hens or risk losing the company's business. Scientists and animal activists concerned about what they call inhumane and unsafe treatment of hens have been putting pressure on McDonald's, based in Oak Brook, Ill.

The industry and the Food and Drug Administration are developing guidelines that could improve the welfare of hens and egg safety. But McDonald's has stepped forward as the first company of its size to pressure producers to implement changes now. During the past few years, McDonald's also has taken steps to oversee and audit the animal-welfare practices of its beef and broiler-chicken producers.

An animal-welfare advisory committee recently formed by McDonald's established the guidelines, which require that each hen be allowed a minimum of 72 square inches of space by the end of 2001. The move probably will improve the mortality rates of the hens, say poultry specialists, but will increase by 50% the amount of space required to keep hens.

"It's premature for us to take a position" on the McDonald's mandate, said Ken Klippen, executive director of government relations for the United Egg Producers, which represents 80% of the nation's suppliers. He said, however, that the new space guidelines "will cause a substantial increase in the cost of production and that has to be passed on to the consumers."

Other new guidelines require that by early 2001, McDonald's egg suppliers must stop withholding food and water from chickens, a practice designed to induce molting, which restores a hen's ability to produce eggs.

Almost two billion of the 75 billion eggs the industry will produce this year will be served at McDonald's. While the new guidelines could drive up the price of eggs, the image of McDonald's will benefit.

"Essentially, McDonald's is responding to social pressure," said Bruce Webster, a poultry-science professor at the University of Georgia: "This is going to place a moral imperative on other producers."

A McDonald's spokesman said, "These directives will begin improving the lives of more than five million hens throughout the United States. It was the right thing to do." He said McDonald's will "work with" suppliers on increased expenses related to the guidelines, but wouldn't say how.

How to Read, Analyze, and Interpret Financial Reports

DIC Is Buying Assets of Golden Books For $80 Million, Assumption of Liabilities

By JONATHAN FRIEDLAND
And JOHN LIPPMAN
Staff Reporters of THE WALL STREET JOURNAL

LOS ANGELES—Frosty the Snowman and the Poky Little Puppy are moving in with Sabrina the Teenage Witch and Sonic the Hedgehog.

The closely held producer of children's television programming **DIC Entertainment Holdings** Inc. will announce today the purchase of the assets of **Golden Books Family Entertainment** Inc., the venerable but financially troubled publisher of books for the toddler and kindergarten set. DIC, Burbank, Calif., will pay $80 million and assume $90 million of Golden Books' liabilities. As part of the deal, Golden, whose shares trade over-the-counter, will be put into bankruptcy protection prior to being absorbed by DIC.

©2000 Dow Jones & Company, Inc.

Rent-Way Asks Its President to Resign After Probe of Accounting Irregularities

By QUEENA SOOK KIM
Staff Reporter of THE WALL STREET JOURNAL

Rent-Way Inc., an operator of rent-to-own stores, asked Jeffrey Conway, its president and chief operating officer, to resign after auditors found greater-than-expected accounting irregularities.

Between $55 million and $60 million of as much as $75 million in total accounting irregularities uncovered by the auditors are due in large part to "fictitious" entries, said Rent-Way Chief Executive William Morgenstern. "It was inaccurately entered with regards to timing and proper classification," he said.

©2000 Dow Jones & Company, Inc.

The Wall Street Journal clippings above illustrate the importance of accounting in today's reporting process. As you will see in this chapter, an understatement of expenses overstates the reported earnings or net income of a company. This overstatement presents a false picture of the company's financial position.

In this chapter we focus our attention on analyzing financial reports. Business owners must understand their financial statements to avoid financial difficulties. This includes knowing how to read, analyze, and interpret financial reports.

The two key financial reports that we discuss in this chapter are the *balance sheet* (shows a company's financial condition at a particular date) and the *income statement* (shows a company's profitability over a time period).[1]

LEARNING UNIT 16–1 | BALANCE SHEET—REPORT AS OF A PARTICULAR DATE

David Young Wolff/PhotoEdit

The **balance sheet** gives a financial picture of what a company is worth as of a particular date, usually at the end of a month or year. This report lists (1) how much the company owns (assets), (2) how much the company owes (liabilities), and (3) how much the owner (owner's equity) is worth. Note that assets and liabilities are divided into two groups: current (*short term*, usually less than one year); and *long term*, usually more than one year. The basic formula for a balance sheet is as follows:

$$\text{Assets} - \text{Liabilities} = \text{Owner's equity}$$

Like all formulas, the items on both sides of the equal sign must balance.

By reversing the above formula, we have the following common balance sheet layout:

$$\boxed{\text{Assets} = \text{Liabilities} + \text{Owner's equity}}$$

---

[1]The third key financial report is the statement of cash flows. We do not discuss this statement. For more information on the statement of cash flows, check your accounting text.

To introduce you to the balance sheet, let's assume that you collect baseball cards and decide to open a baseball card shop. As the owner of The Card Shop, your investment, or owner's equity, is called **capital.** Since your business is small, your balance sheet is short. After the first year of operation, The Card Shop balance sheet looks like this below. The heading gives the name of the company, title of the report, and date of the report. Note how the totals of both sides of the balance sheet are the same. This is true of all balance sheets.

Capital does not mean cash. It is the owner's investment in the company.

THE CARD SHOP
Balance Sheet
December 31, 2004

Report as of a particular date

Assets		Liabilities	
Cash	$ 3,000	Accounts payable	$ 2,500
Merchandise inventory (baseball cards)	4,000	**Owner's Equity**	
Equipment	3,000	E. Slott, capital	7,500
Total assets	$10,000	Total liabilities and owner's equity	$10,000

We can take figures from the balance sheet of The Card Shop and use our first formula to determine how much the business is worth:

$$\text{Assets} - \text{Liabilities} = \text{Owner's equity (capital)}$$
$$\$10,000 - \$2,500 = \$7,500$$

Since you are the single owner of The Card Shop, your business is a **sole proprietorship.** If a business has two or more owners, it is a **partnership.** A **corporation** has many owners or stockholders, and the equity of these owners is called **stockholders' equity.** Now let's study the balance sheet elements of a corporation.

Elements of the Balance Sheet

The format and contents of all corporation balance sheets are similar. Figure 16.1 shows the balance sheet of Mool Company. As you can see, the formula Assets = Liabilities + Stockholders' equity (we have a corporation in this example) is also the framework of this balance sheet.

FIGURE 16.1 Balance sheet

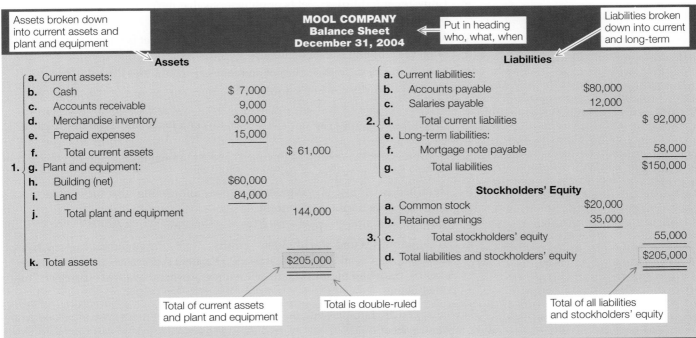

To help you understand the three main balance sheet groups (assets, liabilities, and stockholders' equity) and their elements, we have labeled them in Figure 16.1. An explanation of these groups and their elements follows. Do not try to memorize the elements. Just try to understand their meaning. Think of Figure 16.1 as a reference aid. You will find that the more you work with balance sheets, the easier it is for you to understand them.

1. **Assets:** Things of value *owned* by a company (economic resources of the company) that can be measured and expressed in monetary terms.

   a. **Current assets:** Assets that companies consume or convert to cash *within 1 year* or a normal operating cycle.

   b. **Cash:** Total cash in checking accounts, savings accounts, and on hand.

   c. **Accounts receivable:** Money *owed* to a company by customers from sales on account (buy now, pay later).

   d. **Merchandise inventory:** Cost of goods in stock for resale to customers.

   e. **Prepaid expenses:** The purchases of a company are assets until they expire (insurance or rent) or are consumed (supplies).

   f. **Total current assets:** Total of all assets that the company will consume or convert to cash within 1 year.

   g. **Plant and equipment:** Assets that will last longer than 1 year. These assets are used in the operation of the company.

   h. **Building (net):** The cost of the building minus the depreciation that has accumulated. Usually, balance sheets show this as "Building less accumulated depreciation." In Chapter 17 we discuss accumulated depreciation in greater detail.

   i. **Land:** An asset that does not depreciate, but it can increase or decrease in value.

   j. **Total plant and equipment:** Total of building and land, including machinery and equipment.

   k. **Total assets:** Total of current assets and plant and equipment.

2. **Liabilities:** Debts or obligations of the company.

   a. **Current liabilities:** Debts or obligations of the company that are *due within 1 year.*

   b. **Accounts payable:** A current liability that shows the amount the company owes to creditors for services or items purchased.

   c. **Salaries payable:** Obligations that the company must pay within 1 year for salaries earned but unpaid.

   d. **Total current liabilities:** Total obligations that the company must pay within 1 year.

   e. **Long-term liabilities:** Debts or obligations that the company does not have to pay within 1 year.

   f. **Mortgage note payable:** Debt owed on a building that is a long-term liability; often the building is the collateral.

   g. **Total liabilities:** Total of current and long-term liabilities.

3. **Stockholders' equity (owner's equity):** The rights or interest of the stockholders to assets of a corporation. If the company is not a corporation, the term *owner's equity* is used. The word *capital* follows the owner's name under the title *Owner's Equity.*

   a. **Common stock:** Amount of the initial and additional investment of corporation owners by the purchase of stock.

   b. **Retained earnings:** The amount of corporation earnings that the company retains, not necessarily in cash form.

   c. **Total stockholders' equity:** Total of stock plus retained earnings.

   d. **Total liabilities and stockholders' equity:** Total current liabilities, long-term liabilities, stock, and retained earnings. This total represents all the claims on assets—prior and present claims of creditors, owners' residual claims, and any other claims.

Now that you are familiar with the common balance sheet items, you are ready to analyze a balance sheet.

Vertical Analysis and the Balance Sheet

Often financial statement readers want to analyze reports that contain data for two or more successive accounting periods. To make this possible, companies present a statement showing the data from these periods side by side. As you might expect, this statement is called a **comparative statement.**

Comparative reports help illustrate changes in data. Financial statement readers should compare the percents in the reports to industry percents and the percents of competitors.

Figure 16.2 shows the comparative balance sheet of Roger Company. Note that the statement analyzes each asset as a percent of total assets for a single period. The statement then analyzes each liability and equity as a percent of total liabilities and stockholders' equity. We call this type of analysis **vertical analysis.**

The following steps use the portion formula to prepare a vertical analysis of a balance sheet.

Preparing a Vertical Analysis of a Balance Sheet

Step 1. Divide each asset (the portion) as a percent of total assets (the base). Round as indicated.

Step 2. Round each liability and stockholders' equity (the portions) as a percent of total liabilities and stockholders' equity (the base). Round as indicated.

FIGURE 16.2

Comparative balance sheet: Vertical analysis

We divide each item by the total of assets.

Portion
($8,000)

Base × Rate
($85,000)   (?)

We divide each item by the total of liabilities and stockholders' equity.

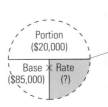

Portion
($20,000)

Base × Rate
($85,000)   (?)

ROGER COMPANY
Comparative Balance Sheet
December 31, 2003 and 2004

	2004		2003	
	Amount	**Percent**	**Amount**	**Percent**
Assets				
Current assets:				
Cash	$22,000	25.88	$18,000	22.22
Accounts receivable	8,000	9.41	9,000	11.11
Merchandise inventory	9,000	10.59	7,000	8.64
Prepaid rent	4,000	4.71	5,000	6.17
Total current assets	$43,000	50.59	$39,000	48.15*
Plant and equipment:				
Building (net)	$18,000	21.18	$18,000	22.22
Land	24,000	28.24	24,000	29.63
Total plant and equipment	$42,000	49.41*	$42,000	51.85
Total assets	$85,000	100.00	$81,000	100.00
Liabilities				
Current liabilities:				
Accounts payable	$14,000	16.47	$ 8,000	9.88
Salaries payable	18,000	21.18	17,000	20.99
Total current liabilities	$32,000	37.65	$25,000	30.86*
Long-term liabilities:				
Mortgage note payable	12,000	14.12	20,000	24.69
Total liabilities	$44,000	51.76*	$45,000	55.56*
Stockholders' Equity				
Common stock	$20,000	23.53	$20,000	24.69
Retained earnings	21,000	24.71	16,000	19.75
Total stockholders' equity	$41,000	48.24	$36,000	44.44
Total liabilities and stockholders' equity	$85,000	100.00	$81,000	100.00

Note: All percents are rounded to the nearest hundredth percent.

*Due to rounding.

FIGURE 16.3

Comparative balance sheet: Horizontal analysis

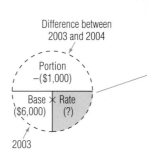

Difference between 2003 and 2004

Portion −($1,000)

Base ($6,000) × Rate (?)

2003

ABBY ELLEN COMPANY Comparative Balance Sheet December 31, 2003 and 2004				
			Increase (decrease)	
	2004	**2003**	**Amount**	**Percent**
Assets				
Current assets:				
Cash	$ 6,000	$ 4,000	$2,000	50.00*
Accounts receivable	5,000	6,000	(1,000)	− 16.67
Merchandise inventory	9,000	4,000	5,000	125.00
Prepaid rent	5,000	7,000	(2,000)	− 28.57
Total current assets	$25,000	$21,000	$4,000	19.05
Plant and equipment:				
Building (net)	$12,000	$12,000	−0−	−0−
Land	18,000	18,000	−0−	−0−
Total plant and equipment	$30,000	$30,000	−0−	−0−
Total assets	$55,000	$51,000	$4,000	7.84
Liabilities				
Current liabilities:				
Accounts payable	$ 3,200	$ 1,800	$1,400	77.78
Salaries payable	2,900	3,200	(300)	− 9.38
Total current liabilities	$ 6,100	$ 5,000	$1,100	22.00
Long-term liabilities:				
Mortgage note payable	17,000	15,000	2,000	13.33
Total liabilities	$23,100	$20,000	$3,100	15.50
Owner's Equity				
Abby Ellen, capital	$31,900	$31,000	$ 900	2.90
Total liabilities and owner's equity	$55,000	$51,000	$4,000	7.84

*The percents are not summed vertically in horizontal analysis.

We can also analyze balance sheets for two or more periods by using **horizontal analysis.** Horizontal analysis compares each item in one year by amount, percent, or both with the same item of the previous year. Note the Abby Ellen Company horizontal analysis shown in Figure 16.3. To make a horizontal analysis, we use the portion formula and the steps that follow.

Preparing a Horizontal Analysis of a Comparative Balance Sheet

Step 1. Calculate the increase or decrease (portion) in each item from the base year.

Step 2. Divide the increase or decrease in Step 1 by the old or base year.

Step 3. Round as indicated.

You can see the difference between vertical analysis and horizontal analysis by looking at the example of vertical analysis in Figure 16.2. The percent calculations in Figure 16.2 are for each item of a particular year as a percent of that year's total assets or total liabilities and stockholders' equity.

Horizontal analysis needs comparative columns because we take the difference *between* periods. In Figure 16.3, for example, the accounts receivable decreased $1,000 from 2003 to 2004. Thus, by dividing $1,000 (amount of change) by $6,000 (base year), we see that Abby's receivables decreased 16.67%.

Let's now try the following Practice Quiz.

1. Complete this partial comparative balance sheet by vertical analysis. Round percents to the nearest hundredth.

	2004		2003	
	Amount	**Percent**	**Amount**	**Percent**
Assets				
Current assets:				
a. Cash	$ 42,000		$ 40,000	
b. Accounts receivable	18,000		17,000	
c. Merchandise inventory	15,000		12,000	
d. Prepaid expenses	17,000		14,000	
	•	•	•	•
	•	•	•	•
	•	•	•	•
Total current assets	$160,000		$150,000	

2. What is the amount of change in merchandise inventory and the percent increase?

✓ **SOLUTIONS**

		2004		2003	

1.

a. Cash

$$\frac{\$42,000}{\$160,000} = 26.25\% \qquad\qquad \frac{\$40,000}{\$150,000} = 26.67\%$$

b. Accounts receivable

$$\frac{\$18,000}{\$160,000} = 11.25\% \qquad\qquad \frac{\$17,000}{\$150,000} = 11.33\%$$

c. Merchandise inventory

$$\frac{\$15,000}{\$160,000} = 9.38\% \qquad\qquad \frac{\$12,000}{\$150,000} = 8.00\%$$

d. Prepaid expenses

$$\frac{\$17,000}{\$160,000} = 10.63\% \qquad\qquad \frac{\$14,000}{\$150,000} = 9.33\%$$

2.

$$\begin{array}{r} \$15,000 \\ -\ 12,000 \\ \hline \end{array}$$

Amount = $ 3,000

$$\text{Percent} = \frac{\$3,000}{\$12,000} = 25\%$$

LEARNING UNIT 16-2 | INCOME STATEMENT—REPORT FOR A SPECIFIC PERIOD OF TIME

Michael Newman/PhotoEdit

Kimberly-Clark Has Plans to Restructure Operations in Europe

By a WALL STREET JOURNAL Staff Reporter

DALLAS—**Kimberly-Clark** Corp., in a move that underscores the growing power that retailers wield over suppliers, plans to consolidate and shuffle responsibilities in its European operations.

The consumer-products company, which makes Huggies diapers, Kleenex tissues and other products, is replacing its country-based organization in Europe with teams assigned to each major retailer. It said it began phasing in the teams in March.

The Wall Street Journal clipping "Kimberly-Clark Has Plans to Restructure Operations in Europe" shows the need to understand financial reports.

In this learning unit we look at the **income statement**—a financial report that tells how well a company is performing (its profitability or net profit) during a specific period of time (month, year, etc.). In general, the income statement reveals the inward flow of revenues (sales) against the outward or potential outward flow of costs and expenses.

The form of income statements varies depending on the company's type of business. However, the basic formula of the income statement is the same.

$$\boxed{\text{Revenues} - \text{Operating expenses} = \text{Net income}}$$

In a merchandising business like The Card Shop, we can enlarge on this formula:

Revenues (sales) ← After any returns, allowances, or discounts

− Cost of merchandise or goods ← Baseball cards

= Gross profit from sales

− Operating expenses

= Net income (profit)

THE CARD SHOP Income Statement For Month Ended December 31, 2004	
Revenues (sales)	$8,000
Cost of merchandise (goods) sold	3,000
Gross profit from sales	$5,000
Operating expenses	750
Net income	$4,250

Now let's look at The Card Shop's income statement to see how much profit The Card Shop made during its first year of operation. For simplicity, we assume The Card Shop sold all the cards it bought during the year. For its first year of business, The Card Shop made a profit of $4,250.

We can now go more deeply into the income statement elements as we study the income statement of a corporation.

Elements of the Corporation Income Statement

Figure 16.4 gives the format and content of the Mool Company income statement—a corporation. The five main items of an income statement are revenues, cost of merchandise (goods) sold, gross profit on sales, operating expenses, and net income. We will follow the same pattern we used in explaining the balance sheet and define the main items and the letter-coded subitems.

1. **Revenues:** Total earned sales (cash or credit) less any sales returns and allowances or sales discounts.
   a. **Gross sales:** Total earned sales before sales returns and allowances or sales discounts.
   b. **Sales returns and allowances:** Reductions in price or reductions in revenue due to goods returned because of product defects, errors, and so on. When the buyer keeps the damaged goods, an allowance results.
   c. **Sales (not trade) discounts:** Reductions in the selling price of goods due to early customer payment. For example, a store may give a 2% discount to a customer who pays a bill within 10 days.
   d. **Net sales:** Gross sales less sales returns and allowances less sales discounts.
2. **Cost of merchandise (goods) sold:** All the costs of getting the merchandise that the company sold. The cost of all unsold merchandise (goods) will be subtracted from this item (ending inventory).
   a. **Merchandise inventory, December 1, 2004:** Cost of inventory in the store that was for sale to customers at the beginning of the month.
   b. **Purchases:** Cost of additional merchandise brought into the store for resale to customers.
   c. **Purchase returns and allowances:** Cost of merchandise returned to the store due to damage, defects, errors, and so on. Damaged goods kept by the buyer result in a cost reduction called an *allowance.*
   d. **Purchase discounts:** Savings received by the buyer for paying for merchandise before a certain date. These discounts can result in a substantial savings to a company.
   e. **Cost of net purchases:** Cost of purchases less purchase returns and allowances less purchase discounts.

FIGURE 16.4 Income statement

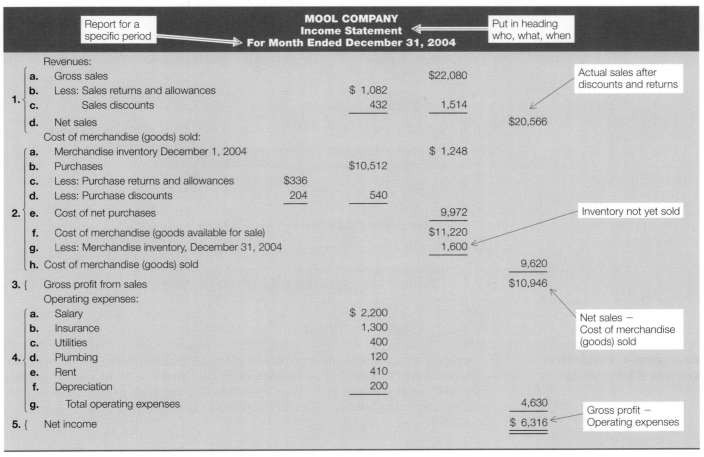

MOOL COMPANY
Income Statement
For Month Ended December 31, 2004

Report for a specific period →

Put in heading who, what, when →

	Revenues:			
a.	Gross sales		$22,080	
b.	Less: Sales returns and allowances	$ 1,082		
c.	Sales discounts	432	1,514	
d.	Net sales			$20,566

Actual sales after discounts and returns →

	Cost of merchandise (goods) sold:			
a.	Merchandise inventory December 1, 2004		$ 1,248	
b.	Purchases	$10,512		
c.	Less: Purchase returns and allowances	$336		
d.	Less: Purchase discounts	204	540	
e.	Cost of net purchases		9,972	
f.	Cost of merchandise (goods available for sale)		$11,220	
g.	Less: Merchandise inventory, December 31, 2004		1,600	
h.	Cost of merchandise (goods) sold			9,620

Inventory not yet sold →

	Gross profit from sales			$10,946
	Operating expenses:			
a.	Salary	$ 2,200		
b.	Insurance	1,300		
c.	Utilities	400		
d.	Plumbing	120		
e.	Rent	410		
f.	Depreciation	200		
g.	Total operating expenses			4,630
	Net income			$ 6,316

Net sales − Cost of merchandise (goods) sold →

Gross profit − Operating expenses →

Note: Numbers are subtotaled from left to right.

f. Cost of merchandise (goods available for sale): Sum of beginning inventory plus cost of net purchases.

g. Merchandise inventory, December 31, 2004: Cost of inventory remaining in the store to be sold.

h. Cost of merchandise (goods) sold: Beginning inventory plus net purchases less ending inventory.

3. Gross profit from sales: Net sales less cost of merchandise (goods) sold.

4. Operating expenses: Additional costs of operating the business beyond the actual cost of inventory sold.

   a.–f. Expenses: Individual expenses broken down.

   g. Total operating expenses: Total of all the individual expenses.

5. Net income: Gross profit less operating expenses.

In the next section you will learn some formulas that companies use to calculate various items on the income statement.

Calculating Net Sales, Cost of Merchandise (Goods) Sold, Gross Profit, and Net Income of an Income Statement

It is time to look closely at Figure 16.4 and see how each section is built. Use the previous vocabulary as a reference. We will study Figure 16.4 step by step.

Step 1. Calculate the net sales—what Mool earned:

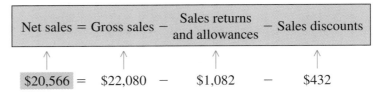

$$\text{Net sales} = \text{Gross sales} - \text{Sales returns and allowances} - \text{Sales discounts}$$

$$\$20,566 = \$22,080 - \$1,082 - \$432$$

Step 2.   Calculate the cost of merchandise (goods) sold:

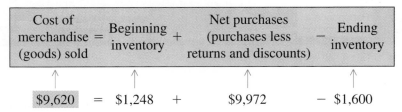

$$\text{Cost of merchandise (goods) sold} = \text{Beginning inventory} + \text{Net purchases (purchases less returns and discounts)} - \text{Ending inventory}$$

$$\$9,620 = \$1,248 + \$9,972 - \$1,600$$

Step 3.   Calculate the gross profit from sales—profit before operating expenses:

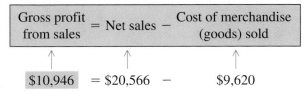

$$\text{Gross profit from sales} = \text{Net sales} - \text{Cost of merchandise (goods) sold}$$

$$\$10,946 = \$20,566 - \$9,620$$

Step 4.   Calculate the net income—profit after operating expenses:

$$\text{Net income} = \text{Gross profit} - \text{Operating expenses}$$

$$\$6,316 = \$10,946 - \$4,630$$

Analyzing Comparative Income Statements

We can apply the same procedures of vertical and horizontal analysis to the income statement that we used in analyzing the balance sheet. Let's first look at the vertical analysis for Royal Company, Figure 16.5. Then we will look at the horizontal analysis of Flint Company's 2003 and 2004 income statements shown in Figure 16.6. Note in the margin how numbers are calculated.

FIGURE 16.5
Vertical analysis

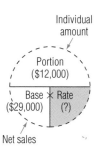

Individual amount
Portion ($12,000)
Base ($29,000) × Rate (?)
Net sales

ROYAL COMPANY
Comparative Income Statement
For Years Ended December 31, 2003 and 2004

	2004	Percent of net	2003	Percent of net
Net sales	$45,000	100.00	$29,000	100.00*
Cost of merchandise sold	19,000	42.22	12,000	41.38
Gross profit from sales	$26,000	57.78	$17,000	58.62
Operating expenses:				
Depreciation	$ 1,000	2.22	$500	1.72
Selling and advertising	4,200	9.33	1,600	5.52
Research	2,900	6.44	2,000	6.90
Miscellaneous	500	1.11	200	.69
Total operating expenses	$ 8,600	19.11†	$ 4,300	14.83
Income before interest and taxes	$17,400	38.67	$12,700	43.79
Interest expense	6,000	13.33	3,000	10.34
Income before taxes	$11,400	25.33†	$ 9,700	33.45
Provision for taxes	5,500	12.22	3,000	10.34
Net income	$ 5,900	13.11	$ 6,700	23.10†

*Net sales = 100%
†Off due to rounding.

FIGURE 16.6
Horizontal analysis

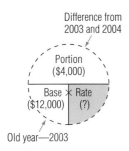

Difference from
2003 and 2004

Portion
($4,000)

Base × Rate
($12,000)   (?)

Old year—2003

FLINT COMPANY Comparative Income Statement For Years Ended December 31, 2003 and 2004				
			Increase (decrease)	
	2004	**2003**	**Amount**	**Percent**
Sales	$90,000	$80,000	$10,000	
Sales returns and allowances	2,000	2,000	–0–	
Net sales	$88,000	$78,000	$10,000	+ 12.82
Cost of merchandise (goods) sold	45,000	40,000	5,000	+ 12.50
Gross profit from sales	$43,000	$38,000	$ 5,000	+ 13.16
Operating expenses:				
Depreciation	$ 6,000	$ 5,000	$ 1,000	+ 20.00
Selling and administrative	16,000	12,000	4,000	+ 33.33
Research	600	1,000	(400)	− 40.00
Miscellaneous	1,200	500	700	+ 140.00
Total operating expenses	$23,800	$18,500	$ 5,300	+ 28.65
Income before interest and taxes	$19,200	$19,500	$ (300)	− 1.54
Interest expense	4,000	4,000	–0–	
Income before taxes	$15,200	$15,500	$ (300)	− 1.94
Provision for taxes	3,800	4,000	(200)	− 5.00
Net income	$11,400	$11,500	$ (100)	− .87

LU 16–2 PRACTICE QUIZ

From the following information, calculate:

a. Net sales.   **b.** Cost of merchandise (goods) sold.

c. Gross profit from sales.   **d.** Net income.

Given   Gross sales, $35,000; sales returns and allowances, $3,000; beginning inventory, $6,000; net purchases, $7,000; ending inventory, $5,500; operating expenses, $7,900.

   ✓ **SOLUTIONS**

a. $35,000 − $3,000 = $32,000 (Gross sales − Sales returns and allowances)

b. $6,000 + $7,000 − $5,500 = $7,500 (Beginning inventory + Net purchases − Ending inventory)

c. $32,000 − $7,500 = $24,500 (Net sales − Cost of merchandise sold)

d. $24,500 − $7,900 = $16,600 (Gross profit from sales − Operating expenses)

LEARNING UNIT 16–3 | TREND AND RATIO ANALYSIS

Motorola to Make Phone Chips in China

Deal Valued at $1.9 Billion Will Make Firm Largest Foreign Investor There

---

By Matt Forney
Staff Reporter of THE WALL STREET JOURNAL

BEIJING—**Motorola** Inc. is poised to become the largest foreign investor in China after confirming yesterday that it had won Chinese government approval for a $1.9 billion project to make silicon chips for its mobile phones.

The Wall Street Journal clipping "Motorola to Make Phone Chips in China" shows how Motorola is becoming a large investor in China. Analyzing financial reports of companies like Motorola can indicate various trends. The study of these trends is valuable to businesses, financial institutions, and consumers. We begin this unit with a discussion of trend analysis.

Trend Analysis

Many tools are available to analyze financial reports. When data cover several years, we can analyze changes that occur by expressing each number as a percent of the base year. The base year is a past period of time that we use to compare sales, profits, and so on, with other years. We call this **trend analysis.**

Using the following example of Rose Company, we complete a trend analysis with the following steps:

Completing a Trend Analysis
Step 1. Select the base year (100%).
Step 2. Express each amount as a percent of the base year amount (rounded to the nearest whole percent).

	Given (base year 2002)			
	2005	**2004**	**2003**	**2002**
Sales	$621,000	$460,000	$340,000	$420,000
Gross profit	182,000	141,000	112,000	124,000
Net income	48,000	41,000	22,000	38,000

	Trend analysis			
	2005	**2004**	**2003**	**2002**
Sales	148%	110%	81%	100%
Gross profit	147	114	90	100
Net income	126	108	58	100

How to Calculate Trend Analysis

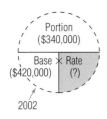

Portion
($340,000)

Base × Rate
($420,000)   (?)

2002

$$\frac{\text{Each item}}{\text{Base amount}} = \frac{\$340,000 \;\leftarrow \text{Sales for 2003}}{\$420,000 \;\leftarrow \text{Sales for 2002}} = 80.95\% = \boxed{81\%}$$

What Trend Analysis Means . Sales of 2003 were 81% of the sales of 2002. Note that you would follow the same process no matter which of the three areas you were analyzing. All categories are compared to the base year—sales, gross profit, or net income.

We now will examine **ratio analysis**—another tool companies use to analyze performance.

Ratio Analysis

A *ratio* is the relationship of one number to another. Many companies compare their ratios with those of previous years and with ratios of other companies in the industry. Companies can get ratios of the performance of other companies from their bankers, accountants, local small business center, libraries, and newspaper articles.

Percentage ratios are used by companies to determine the following:

1. How well the company manages its assets—*asset management ratios.*
2. The company's debt situation—*debt management ratios.*
3. The company's profitability picture—*profitability ratios.*

Each company must decide the true meaning of what the three types of ratios (asset management, debt management, and profitability) are saying. Table 16.1 gives a summary of the key ratios, their calculations (rounded to the nearest hundredth), and what they mean. All calculations are from Figures 16.1 and 16.4.

Now you can check your knowledge with the Practice Quiz that follows.

TABLE 16.1   Summary of key ratios: A reference guide*

Ratio	Formula	Actual calculations	What it says	Questions that could be raised
1. Current ratio†	$\dfrac{\text{Current assets}}{\text{Current liabilities}}$ (Current assets include cash, accounts receivable, and marketable securities.)	$\dfrac{\$61{,}000}{\$92{,}000} = .66{:}1$ Industry average, 2 to 1	Business has 66¢ of current assets to meet each $1 of current debt.	Not enough current assets to pay off current liabilities. Industry standard is $2 for each $1 of current debt.
2. Acid test (quick ratio) Top of fraction often ⟶ referred to as *quick assets*	$\dfrac{\substack{\text{Current assets}\\-\text{ Inventory}\\-\text{ Prepaid expenses}}}{\text{Current liabilities}}$ (Inventory and prepaid expenses are excluded because it may not be easy to convert these to cash.)	$\dfrac{\substack{\$61{,}000 - \$30{,}000\\-\ \$15{,}000}}{\$92{,}000}$ $= .17{:}1$ Industry average, 1 to 1	Business has only 17¢ to cover each $1 of current debt. This calculation excludes inventory and prepaid expenses.	Same as above but more severe.
3. Average day's collection	$\dfrac{\text{Accounts receivable}}{\dfrac{\text{Net sales}}{360}}$	$\dfrac{\$9{,}000}{\dfrac{\$20{,}566}{360}} = 158\text{ days}$ Industry average, 90–120 days	On the average, it takes 158 days to collect accounts receivable.	Could we speed up collection since industry average is 90–120 days?
4. Total debt to total assets	$\dfrac{\text{Total liabilities}}{\text{Total assets}}$	$\dfrac{\$150{,}000}{\$205{,}000} = 73.17\%$ Industry average, 50%–70%	For each $1 of assets, the company owes 73¢ in current and long-term debt.	73% is slightly higher than industry average.
5. Return on equity	$\dfrac{\text{Net income}}{\text{Stockholders' equity}}$	$\dfrac{\$6{,}316}{\$55{,}000} = 11.48\%$ Industry average, 15%–20%	For each $1 invested by the owner, a return of 11¢ results.	Could we get a higher return on money somewhere else?
6. Asset turnover	$\dfrac{\text{Net sales}}{\text{Total assets}}$	$\dfrac{\$20{,}566}{\$205{,}000} = 10\text{¢}$ Industry average, 3¢ to 8¢	For each $1 invested in assets, it returns 10¢ in sales.	Are assets being utilized efficiently?
7. Profit margin on net sales	$\dfrac{\text{Net income}}{\text{Net sales}}$	$\dfrac{\$6{,}316}{\$20{,}566} = 30.71\%$ Industry average, 25%–40%	For each $1 of sales, company produces 31¢ in profit.	Compared to competitors, are we showing enough profits versus our increased sales?

*Inventory turnover is discussed in Chapter 18.

†For example, Wal-Mart Stores, Inc., has a current ratio of 1.51.

LU 16–3 PRACTICE QUIZ

1. Prepare a trend analysis from the following sales, assuming a base year of 2002. Round to the nearest whole percent.

	2005	**2004**	**2003**	**2002**
Sales	$29,000	$44,000	$48,000	$60,000

2. **Given** Total current assets (CA), $15,000; accounts receivable (AR), $6,000; total current liabilities (CL), $10,000; inventory (Inv.), $4,000; net sales, $36,000; total assets, $30,000; net income (NI), $7,500.

   Calculate

   a. Current ratio.   b. Acid test.

   c. Average day's collection.   d. Profit margin on sales (round to the nearest hundredth percent).

✓ **SOLUTIONS**

		2005	2004	2003	2002
1.	Sales	48%	73%	80%	100%

$$\left(\frac{\$29,000}{\$60,000}\right) \quad \left(\frac{\$44,000}{\$60,000}\right) \quad \left(\frac{\$48,000}{\$60,000}\right)$$

2. **a.** $\dfrac{CA}{CL} = \dfrac{\$15,000}{\$10,000} = 1.5$ **b.** $\dfrac{CA - Inv}{CL} = \dfrac{\$15,000 - \$4,000}{\$10,000} = 1.1$

   c. $\dfrac{AR}{\dfrac{Net\ sales}{360}} = \dfrac{\$6,000}{\dfrac{\$36,000}{360}} = 60\ days$ **d.** $\dfrac{NI}{Net\ sales} = \dfrac{\$7,500}{\$36,000} = 20.83\%$

Chapter Organizer and Reference Guide

Topic	Key point, procedure, formula	Example(s) to illustrate situation
Balance sheet		
Vertical analysis, p. 363	Process of relating each figure on a financial report (down the column) to a total figure.	Current assets $ 520 52% Plant and equipment 480 48 Total assets $1,000 100%
Horizontal analysis, p. 364	Analyzing comparative financial reports shows rate and amount of change across columns item by item.	<table><tr><th>2004</th><th>2003</th><th>Change</th><th>%</th></tr><tr><td>Cash, $5,000</td><td>$4,000</td><td>$1,000</td><td>25% ← $\left(\dfrac{\$1,000}{\$4,000}\right)$</td></tr></table>
Income statement formulas, p. 366	(Horizontal and vertical analysis can also be done for income statements.)	
Net sales, p. 367	Gross sales − Sales returns and allowances − Sales discounts	$200 gross sales − 10 sales returns and allowances − 2 sales discounts $188 net sales
Cost of merchandise (goods) sold, p. 368	Beginning inventory + Net purchases − Ending inventory	$50 + $100 − $20 = $130 Beginning inventory + Net purchases − Ending inventory = Cost of merchandise (goods) sold
Gross profit from sales, p. 368	Net sales − Cost of merchandise (goods) sold	$188 − $130 = $58 gross profit from sales Net sales − Cost of merchandise (goods) sold = Gross profit from sales
Net income, p. 368	Gross profit − Operating expenses	$58 − $28 = $30 Gross profit from sales − Operating expenses = Net income
Trend analysis, p. 369	Each number expressed as a percent of the base year. $\dfrac{Each\ item}{Base\ amount}$	<table><tr><th></th><th>2005</th><th>2004</th><th>2003</th></tr><tr><td>Sales</td><td>$200</td><td>$300</td><td>$400 ← Base year</td></tr><tr><td></td><td>50%</td><td>75%</td><td>100%</td></tr></table>$\left(\dfrac{\$200}{\$400}\right) \quad \left(\dfrac{\$300}{\$400}\right)$
Ratios, p. 370	Tools to interpret items on financial reports.	Use this example for calculating the following ratios: current assets, $30,000; accounts receivable, $12,000; total current liabilities, $20,000; inventory, $6,000; prepaid expenses, $2,000; net sales, $72,000; total assets, $60,000; net income, $15,000; total liabilities, $30,000.
Current ratio, p. 371	$\dfrac{Current\ assets}{Current\ liabilities}$	$\dfrac{\$30,000}{\$20,000} = 1.5$
Acid test (quick ratio), p. 371	Called quick assets ↙ $\dfrac{Current\ assets - Inventory - Prepaid\ expenses}{Current\ liabilities}$	$\dfrac{\$30,000 - \$6,000 - \$2,000}{\$20,000} = 1.1$

(continues)

Chapter Organizer and Reference Guide (concluded)

Topic	Key point, procedure, formula	Example(s) to illustrate situation
Average day's collection, p. 371	$\dfrac{\dfrac{\text{Accounts receivable}}{\text{Net sales}}}{360}$	$\dfrac{\$12,000}{\dfrac{\$72,000}{360}} =$ 60 days
Total debt to total assets, p. 371	$\dfrac{\text{Total liabilities}}{\text{Total assets}}$	$\dfrac{\$30,000}{\$60,000} =$ 50%
Return on equity, p. 371	$\dfrac{\text{Net income}}{\text{Stockholders' equity (A} - \text{L)}}$	$\dfrac{\$15,000}{\$30,000} =$ 50%
Asset turnover, p. 371	$\dfrac{\text{Net sales}}{\text{Total assets}}$	$\dfrac{\$72,000}{\$60,000} =$ 1.2
Profit margin on net sales, p. 371	$\dfrac{\text{Net income}}{\text{Net sales}}$	$\dfrac{\$15,000}{\$72,000} = .2083 =$ 20.83%

Key terms			
	Accounts payable, *p. 362*	Gross profit from sales, *p. 366*	Purchase discounts, *p. 366*
	Accounts receivable, *p. 362*	Gross sales, *p. 366*	Purchase returns and allowances, *p. 366*
	Acid test, *p. 371*	Horizontal analysis, *p. 364*	Purchases, *p. 366*
	Assets, *p. 362*	Income statement, *p. 365*	Quick assets, *p. 371*
	Asset turnover, *p. 371*	Liabilities, *p. 362*	Quick ratio, *p. 371*
	Balance sheet, *p. 362*	Long-term liabilities, *p. 362*	Ratio analysis, *p. 370*
	Capital, *p. 361*	Merchandise inventory, *p. 366*	Retained earnings, *p. 362*
	Common stock, *p. 362*	Mortgage note payable, *p. 362*	Return on equity, *p. 371*
	Comparative statement, *p. 363*	Net income, *p. 367*	Revenues, *p. 366*
	Corporation, *p. 362*	Net purchases, *p. 366*	Salaries payable, *p. 362*
	Cost of merchandise (goods) sold, *p. 366*	Net sales, *p. 366*	Sales (not trade) discounts, *p. 366*
	Current assets, *p. 362*	Operating expenses, *p. 367*	Sales returns and allowances, *p. 366*
	Current liabilities, *p. 362*	Owner's equity, *p. 362*	Sole proprietorship, *p. 361*
	Current ratio, *p. 371*	Partnership, *p. 361*	Stockholders' equity, *p. 361*
	Expenses, *p. 366*	Plant and equipment, *p. 362*	Trend analysis, *p. 370*
		Prepaid expenses, *p. 362*	Vertical analysis, *p. 363*

Critical Thinking Discussion Questions

1. What is the difference between current assets and plant and equipment? Do you think land should be allowed to depreciate?

2. What items make up stockholders' equity? Why might a person form a sole proprietorship instead of a corporation?

3. Explain the steps to complete a vertical or horizontal analysis relating to balance sheets. Why are the percents not summed vertically in horizontal analysis?

4. How do you calculate net sales, cost of merchandise (goods) sold, gross profit, and net income? Why do we need two separate figures for inventory in the cost of merchandise (goods) sold section?

5. Explain how to calculate the following: current ratios, acid test, average day's collection, total debt to assets, return on equity, asset turnover, and profit margin on net sales. How often do you think ratios should be calculated?

6. What is trend analysis? Explain how the portion formula assists in preparing a trend analysis.

DRILL PROBLEMS

16–1. As the accountant for True Value Hardware, prepare a December 31, 2004, balance sheet like that for The Card Shop (LU 16–1) from the following: cash, $15,000; accounts payable, $18,000; merchandise inventory, $7,000; A. Long, capital, $18,000; and equipment, $14,000.

16–2. From the following, prepare a classified balance sheet for Rug Company as of December 31, 2004. Ending merchandise inventory was $3,000 for the year.

Cash	$1,000	Accounts payable	$1,200
Prepaid rent	1,200	Salaries payable	1,500
Prepaid insurance	2,000	Note payable (long term)	1,000
Office equipment (net)	3,000	B. Rug, capital*	6,500

*What the owner supplies to the business. Replaces common stock and retained earnings section.

16–3. Complete a horizontal analysis for Brown Company (round percents to the nearest hundredth):

Excel

BROWN COMPANY Comparative Balance Sheet December 31, 2003 and 2004			Increase (decrease)	
	2004	2003	Amount	Percent
Assets				
Current assets:				
Cash	$ 15,750	$ 10,500		
Accounts receivable	18,000	13,500		
Merchandise inventory	18,750	22,500		
Prepaid advertising	54,000	45,000		
Total current assets	$106,500	$ 91,500		
Plant and equipment:				
Building (net)	$120,000	$126,000		
Land	90,000	90,000		
Total plant and equipment	$210,000	$216,000		
Total assets	$316,500	$307,500		
Liabilities				
Current liabilities:				
Accounts payable	$132,000	$120,000		
Salaries payable	22,500	18,000		
Total current liabilities	$154,500	$138,000		
Long-term liabilities:				
Mortgage note payable	99,000	87,000		
Total liabilities	$253,500	$225,000		
Owner's Equity				
J. Brown, capital	63,000	82,500		
Total liabilities and owner's equity	$316,500	$307,500		

16–4. Prepare an income statement for Munroe Sauce for the year ended December 31, 2004. Beginning inventory was $1,248. Ending inventory was $1,600.

Sales	$34,900
Sales returns and allowances	1,092
Sales discount	1,152
Purchases	10,512
Purchase discounts	540
Depreciation expense	115
Salary expense	5,200
Insurance expense	2,600
Utilities expense	210
Plumbing expense	250
Rent expense	180

16–5. The following is a partial list of financial highlights from Motorola's 2000 annual report:

	2000	**1999**
	(dollars in millions)	
Net sales	$37,580	$33,075
Earnings before taxes	2,231	1,283
Net earnings	1,318	891

Complete a horizontal and vertical analysis from the above information. Round to the nearest hundredth percent.

16–6. From the Lowell Instrument Corporation second-quarter report ended 2004, do a vertical analysis for the second quarter of 2004.

LOWELL INSTRUMENT CORPORATION AND SUBSIDIARIES **Consolidated Statements of Operation** **(Unaudited) (In thousands of dollars, except share data)**			
	Second quarter		
	2004	**2003**	**Percent of net**
Net sales	$6,698	$6,951	
Cost of sales	4,089	4,462	
Gross margin	2,609	2,489	
Expenses:			
Selling, general and administrative	1,845	1,783	
Product development	175	165	
Interest expense	98	123	
Other (income), net	(172)	(99)	
Total expenses	1,946	1,972	
Income before income taxes	663	517	
Provision for income taxes	265	209	
Net income	$ 398	$ 308	
Net income per common share*	$ .05	$ .03	
Weighted average number of common shares and equivalents	6,673,673	6,624,184	

*Income per common share reflects the deduction of the preferred stock dividend from net income.

†Off due to rounding.

16–7. Complete the comparative income statement and balance sheet for Logic Company (round percents to the nearest hundredth):

LOGIC COMPANY
Comparative Income Statement
For Years Ended December 31, 2004 and 2005

	2005	2004	Increase (decrease) Amount	Percent
Gross sales	$19,000	$15,000		
Sales returns and allowances	1,000	100		
Net sales	$18,000	$14,900		
Cost of merchandise (goods) sold	12,000	9,000		
Gross profit	$ 6,000	$ 5,900		
Operating expenses:				
Depreciation	$ 700	$ 600		
Selling and administrative	2,200	2,000		
Research	550	500		
Miscellaneous	360	300		
Total operating expenses	$ 3,810	$ 3,400		
Income before interest and taxes	$ 2,190	$ 2,500		
Interest expense	560	500		
Income before taxes	$ 1,630	$ 2,000		
Provision for taxes	640	800		
Net income	$ 990	$ 1,200		

LOGIC COMPANY
Comparative Balance Sheet
December 31, 2004 and 2005

	2005 Amount	Percent	2004 Amount	Percent
Assets				
Current assets:				
Cash	$12,000		$ 9,000	
Accounts receivable	16,500		12,500	
Merchandise inventory	8,500		14,000	
Prepaid expenses	24,000		10,000	
Total current assets	$61,000		$45,500	
Plant and equipment:				
Building (net)	$14,500		$11,000	
Land	13,500		9,000	
Total plant and equipment	$28,000		$20,000	
Total assets	$89,000		$65,500	
Liabilities				
Current liabilities:				
Accounts payable	$13,000		$ 7,000	
Salaries payable	7,000		5,000	
Total current liabilities	$20,000		$12,000	
Long-term liabilities:				
Mortgage note payable	22,000		20,500	
Total liabilities	$42,000		$32,500	
Stockholders' Equity				
Common stock	$21,000		$21,000	
Retained earnings	26,000		12,000	
Total stockholders' equity	$47,000		$33,000	
Total liabilities and stockholders' equity	$89,000		$65,500	

*Due to rounding.

From Problem 16–7, your supervisor has requested that you calculate the following ratios (round to the nearest hundredth):

	2005	**2004**
16–8. Current ratio.		
16–9. Acid test.		
16–10. Average day's collection.		
16–11. Asset turnover.		
16–12. Total debt to total assets.		
16–13. Net income (after tax) to the net sales.		
16–14. Return on equity (after tax).		

16–8.

16–9.

16–10.

16–11.

16–12.

16–13.

16–14.

WORD PROBLEMS

16–15. An Internet magazine contained an article that stated the following: "The net income for 2004 was $800,000, and the return on equity was 20." What was the amount of equity to the nearest dollar?

16–16. On March 1, 2000, the *Saint Paul Pioneer Press* reported that Target's earnings topped Wal-Mart's for the quarter. Target reported this year that overall profit rose 15% to $522 million. Sales rose 8.7% to $10.8 billion. **(a)** How much were Target's profits last year? **(b)** How much were Target's sales last year?

16–17. Find the following ratios for Motorola Credit Corporation from the Motorola 2000 annual report: **(a)** total debt to total assets, **(b)** return on equity, **(c)** asset turnover, **(d)** profit margin on net sales. Round to the nearest hundredth.

	2000 **(dollars in millions)**
Net revenue (sales)	$ 265
Net earnings	147
Total assets	2,015
Total liabilities	1,768
Total stockholders' equity	427

16–18. On May 16, 2001, the *Chicago Sun-Times* reported that the meltdown in the dot-com economy has substantially trimmed the prices of Web development. The following are median prices for Web development:

	Small project	**Medium project**	**Large project**
Sept. 1999	$ 77,500	$150,000	$405,000
May 2000	113,500	119,500	606,000
May 2001	65,000	125,500	250,000

Complete a trend analysis for each project. Round to the nearest whole percent and use 1999 as the base year.

16–19. Don Williams received a memo requesting that he complete a trend analysis of the following numbers using 2003 as the base year and rounding each percent to the nearest whole percent. Could you help Don with the request?

	2006	**2005**	**2004**	**2003**
Sales	$340,000	$400,000	$420,000	$500,000
Gross profit	180,000	240,000	340,000	400,000
Net income	70,000	90,000	40,000	50,000

 CHALLENGE PROBLEMS

16–20. On March 20, 2001, the *Houston Chronicle* reported on the profits of Oshman's Sporting Goods. For the fourth quarter, Oshman's reported net income of $7.3 million. That compares with a net income of $1.5 million the same quarter a year earlier. Net sales for the quarter increased 12.5% to $105.4 million. **(a)** What was Oshman's profit margin on net sales this quarter? **(b)** What was the percent increase in net income? **(c)** What were last year's net sales? **(d)** What was last year's profit margin on net sales? Round to the nearest hundredth percent.

16–21. As the accountant for Tootsie Roll, you are asked to calculate the current ratio and the quick ratio for the following partial financial statement:

Assets		Liabilities	
Current assets:		Current liabilities:	
Cash and cash equivalents (Note 1)	$ 4,224,190	Notes payable to banks	$ 672,221
Investments (Note 1)	32,533,769	Accounts payable	7,004,075
Accounts receivable, less allowances of		Dividends payable	576,607
$748,000 and $744,000	16,206,648	Accrued liabilities (Note 5)	9,826,534
Inventories (Note 1):		Income taxes payable	4,471,429
Finished goods and work in progress	12,650,955		
Raw materials and supplies	10,275,858		
Prepaid expenses	2,037,710		

SUMMARY PRACTICE TEST

1. **Given:** Gross sales, $120,000; sales returns and allowances, $7,000; beginning inventory, $7,500; net purchases, $12,000; ending inventory, $2,200; and operating expenses, $39,000. Calculate **(a)** net sales, **(b)** cost of merchandise (goods) sold, **(c)** gross profit from sales, and **(d)** net income. *(p. 367)*

2. Complete the following partial comparative balance sheet by filling in the total current assets and the percent column; assume no plant and equipment (round to the nearest hundredth percent as needed). *(p. 365)*

	Amount	Percent	Amount	Percent
Assets				
Current assets:				
Cash	$ 6,000		$ 7,000	
Accounts receivable	3,000		5,500	
Merchandise inventory	7,000		3,300	
Prepaid expenses	9,000		6,000	
Total current assets				

3. Calculate the amount of increase or decrease and the percent change of each item (round to the nearest hundredth percent as needed). *(p. 363)*

	2005	2004	Amount	Percent
Cash	$14,000	$ 6,000		
Land	48,000	19,000		
Accounts payable	18,000	16,000		

4. Complete a trend analysis for sales (round to the nearest whole percent and use 2004 as the base year). *(p. 369)*

	2007	**2006**	**2005**	**2004**
Sales	$165,000	$210,000	$150,000	$190,000

5. From the following, prepare a balance sheet for Leslie Corporation as of December 31, 2005. *(p. 361)*

Building	$30,000	Mortgage note payable	$60,000
Merchandise inventory	12,000	Common stock	25,000
Cash	18,000	Retained earnings	16,000
Land	60,000	Accounts receivable	5,000
Accounts payable	25,000	Salaries payable	9,000
Prepaid rent	10,000		

6. Solve from the following facts (round to the nearest hundredth): *(p. 371)*

Current assets	$15,000	Net sales	$32,000
Accounts receivable	3,800	Total assets	31,000
Current liabilities	17,000	Net income	6,600
Inventory	4,600		

   a. Current ratio.

   b. Acid test.

   c. Average day's collection.

   d. Asset turnover.

   e. Profit margin on sales.

PERSONAL FINANCE

A Kiplinger Approach

STOCKS | **GEMSTAR-TV GUIDE** seeks to control

the technology of interactive TV. *By Mark McLaughlin*

THE BOOB TUBE'S HIGH-TECH SHERPA

YOU KNOW the old saying: If it sounds too good to be true, it probably is. But if you took that adage too literally, you might never even consider **Gemstar-TV Guide International**, whose own CEO admits that the company's business model may look a little *too* good to be true. And that could be a mistake.

Gemstar aims to be both the Sherpa and the sheriff of TV Land by controlling the technology of interactive TV. The company owns *TV Guide* magazine. But it's the highly profitable intellectual-property business of technology licensing that analysts say could turn the company into a media powerhouse. The driver of its strategy is interactive program guides, or IPGs, TV welcome screens that let you sort channels and record

shows, and will eventually allow you to order movies and other products.

Hot to trot. Cable operators are so anxious for the guide that they are willing to sign lopsided deals that guarantee Gemstar an 85% cut of future national advertising and a 50% cut of revenues generated by future TV commerce, such as pay-per-view movie orders. Microsoft and AOL Time Warner are so hot on interactive TV that they paid Gemstar a combined $85 million to incorporate the guide technology into their services.

For broadcasters, the IPG is so valuable because ads are seen at the moment viewers decide what to watch. Analysts project that total revenue from the guide will jump from $100 million this year to more

than $1 billion by the end of 2004, and perhaps to $10 billion by the end of the decade—all at a minimal cost to Gemstar once the systems are in place. "It has the potential to do billions of dollars of cash flow with almost no cost," says Mitch Rubin, manager of Baron iOpportunity fund.

Adds Gemstar CEO Henry Yuen: "We are not like other companies whose business models look good on spreadsheets. We are real. We are talking about an international, interactive platform without capital expenditure or inventory risk."

For now, Gemstar is focusing on expanding distribution, for its IPGs as well as its new electronic-book and TV horse-betting businesses. Its IPGs are in more than 13 million homes and should reach at least 46 million by the end of 2005, says Goldman Sachs. As it waits for IPG advertising to take off, the company receives licensing revenue from cable operators and certain manufacturers of VCRs, TVs, set-top boxes and electronic-book readers. But its greatest cash generator, *TV Guide*, is in decline because of rising costs and lagging sales.

Possible risks. Competition among IPGs may intensify. Already, set-top-box maker Scientific-Atlanta and TVGateway, an alliance of five companies, offer their own guides. Gemstar's distribution could be somewhat limited should it lose one of the patent-infringement and antitrust lawsuits now pending.

Perhaps the biggest concern is Gemstar's stock price. Despite a 60% decline over the past year, the shares, recently $34, still look expensive. With a market value of $14 billion, Gemstar, which is not yet profitable, sells at ten times revenues. Given investors' recent distaste for high-priced issues, the stock could fall into the $20s. But if shares drop any lower, get ready to click the buy button. **K**

—*Reporter:* **CHRISTINE PULFREY**

SPOTLIGHT | Gemstar–TV Guide International

The company's products and their reach at a glance

INTERACTIVE PROGRAM GUIDES
13 million+ homes

TV GUIDE
9.9 million weekly circulation

VCR PLUS+
Available in 40 countries

TVG NETWORK
6.9 million homes

ANDRÉ BARANOWSKI

Business Math Issue

Very few business models fail.
1. List the key points of the article and information to support your position.
2. Write a group defense of your position using math calculations to support your view.

Disney's Big California Gamble

*Power Crisis, High Fuel Prices,
Slowing Economy Will Test
Company's New Theme Park*

By BRUCE ORWALL
Staff Reporter of THE WALL STREET JOURNAL

WALT DISNEY CO.'S newest theme park in Anaheim, Calif. isn't even open yet and already it's faced with some unwanted gate crashers: a slowing economy, high gas prices and a full-blown power crisis in California.

The new park, called Disney's California Adventure, is set to open Feb. 8 adjacent to the company's original Disneyland park. Its theme is the quintessential California vacation, from the Golden Gate Bridge to the wine country and the beach. The park is part of a broader expansion in Anaheim that also includes a recently opened "Downtown Disney" retail and entertainment district and a new high-end hotel, the Grand Californian.

The $1.4 billion complex is the first of several ambitious moves meant to buttress the company's theme-park empire in coming years, with second Disney parks planned in Tokyo (later this year) and Paris (2002) and a park in Hong Kong slated for 2005. The theme park unit has been a dependable earner in past six or seven years, even as Disney has faced trouble in some of its other businesses.

But that durability will be put to a test in coming months, as Disney opens the new park into the teeth of an economic downturn of still-undetermined dimensions. The recession in the early 1990s, combined with the 1991 Gulf War, knocked Disney's theme parks for a loop.

The company's executives, including Chairman and Chief Executive Michael Eisner, remain confident the new park will be a hit. To prove it, Disney isn't wavering from its initial attendance goal of seven million annual visitors. Says Walt Disney Parks and Resorts Chairman Paul Pressler: "As I look at it today, we're excited and we don't believe there's anything in the economy that should affect us."

PROJECT A

Go to the Disney site on the Internet and see how this theme park is doing today.

Internet Projects: See text website (www.mhhe.com/slater7e) and *The Business Math Internet Resource Guide.*

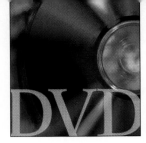

VIDEO CASE

McDonald's

During the mid-1990s, a new McDonald's store opened somewhere in America every few hours. In the rush to sell as many burgers and fries as possible, overworked employees churned out sandwiches in large batches and let them sit for 10 minutes or longer under heat lamps. To improve a business mired in slow sales, McDonald's created a "just-in-time" system called "Made for You."

The company's toughest sell on the "Made for You" system has been to its franchisees. The system is costly to install, sometimes as much as $100,000 per restaurant. McDonald's claims an average installment price of $25,000 with the corporation kicking in half. As of April 2000, "Made for You" was in place in all 13,755 U.S. and Canadian units. A consulting firm found that franchisees had grown frustrated with longer wait lines and began using a hybrid system that includes "Made for You."

In December 2000, a year into the program, customers sometimes faced an unwelcome trade-off: hotter, fresher food but longer waits at the counter. Even Alan Feldman, McDonald's U.S. chief, in November 2000 admitted service at the front counter had not been going as smoothly as the company wanted.

McDonald's is engaged in an intense food fight. It faces strong competition in the domestic quick-service restaurant market against the likes of Burger King, Wendy's, and Hardees. At 42%, McDonald's has the biggest share of the hamburger market, yet rates lowest for customer satisfaction among all other fast-food operations. To solve the problems, McDonald's operators need to work on executing the system. Operators have to spend a little more time in training and positioning their people.

PROBLEM 1

Improvements hadn't immediately registered with customers. Through the first nine months of 2000, sales at U.S. restaurants are up 3% to $14.40 billion. What were the sales for the same period in 1999? Round your answer to the nearest hundredth.

PROBLEM 2

Wall Street was also lukewarm to McDonald's market value. On Friday, January 21, 2000, stock stood at $33.56 a share, a 20% drop from the year before. What had been the trading price of the stock in 1999?

PROBLEM 3

Mediocre growth combined with international currency woes has made it a tough year for McDonald's investors. On November 7, 2000, shares fell to $31.75, well off their New York Stock Exchange 52-week high of $49.56. (a) What percent did the stock drop? Round to the nearest hundredth percent. (b) If the average "Big Mac" cost $2.29 in the United States, what would the cost be in Italy? Round to the nearest tenth. Use the exchange rate table in *Business Math Handbook*.

PROBLEM 4

As of April 2000, "Made for You" was in place in all 13,755 McDonald's units. The corporation claims the average installment price, of which they paid half, was $25,000. (a) What was the total cost of installment for all the units? (b) What was McDonald's dollar share for the installment?

PROBLEM 5

Quick-service chains have been focused on improving drive-through speed—60% of McDonald's business is at the drive-through. The chain has trimmed its average drive-through line by 23.5% to 130 seconds. What had been the average drive-through time? Round to the nearest whole second.

PROBLEM 6

Assuming a base year of 1997, McDonald's Corporation's Annual Report 2000 reported the following on its system sales. Dollars were in the millions.

	2000	1999	1998	1997
Sales	$40,181	$38,491	$35,979	$33,638

(a) Complete a trend analysis for the past four years. Round to the nearest whole percent. (b) What was the percent increase/decrease from 1999 to 2000? Round to the nearest hundredth percent. (c) What was the percent increase/decrease from 1998 to 1999? Round to the nearest hundredth percent.

PROBLEM 7

Based on McDonald's 2000 Annual Report, the corporation's average annual U.S. sales were $1,647,000 per traditional restaurant. With 13,755 restaurants, what would be the amount of total sales?

PROBLEM 8

The following is a partial balance sheet from McDonald's 2000 Annual Report (in millions).

Assets
Current assets:

Cash and equivalents	$421.7
Accounts and notes receivable	796.5
Inventories, at cost	99.3
Prepaid expenses	344.9

Liabilities

Notes payable	$275.5
Accounts payable	684.9
Income taxes	92.2
Other taxes	195.5

Calculate to the nearest hundredth the (a) Current ratio, and (b) Acid test ratio.

THE CURRENT DEPRECIATION schedule needs revamping.

Both the Treasury and accounting firm Deloitte & Touche conclude as much in separate reports. Treasury officials recently delivered their message to Congress, telling lawmakers the current schedule for all depreciable items fails to take into account new industries and technologies. But the agency cautions that a comprehensive change could lead to adverse tax-shelter pursuits.

The Deloitte & Touche study, commissioned for the real-estate industry, finds the current investment recovery periods—39 years for nonresidential property and 27.5 years for residential—are much too slow. The firm advocates a period of less than 20 years for property depreciation, arguing that structures "lose value quicker than the tax system recognizes."

Depreciation can affect both small-business people with home offices and the world's largest corporations.

17

Depreciation

This chapter concentrates on depreciation—a business operating expense. In Learning Units 17–1 to 17–4, we discuss methods of calculating depreciation for financial reporting. In Learning Unit 17–5, we look at how tax laws force companies to report depreciation for tax purposes. Financial reporting methods and the tax-reporting methods are both legal.

LEARNING UNIT 17–1 | CONCEPT OF DEPRECIATION AND THE STRAIGHT-LINE METHOD

Companies frequently buy assets such as equipment or buildings that will last longer than 1 year. As time passes, these assets depreciate, or lose some of their market value. The total cost of these assets cannot be shown in *1 year* as an expense of running the business. In a systematic and logical way, companies must estimate the asset cost they show as an expense of a particular period. This process is called **depreciation.**

Remember that depreciation *does not* measure the amount of deterioration or decline in the market value of the asset. Depreciation is simply a means of recognizing that these assets are depreciating. For example, *The Wall Street Journal* clipping "IRS to Allow Depreciation of Some Golf-Green Costs" reports that some golf greens are depreciated for tax purposes.

IRS to Allow Depreciation Of Some Golf-Green Costs

Dow Jones Newswires

WASHINGTON—Certain land-improvement costs associated with "modern" golf greens are depreciable for tax purposes, the Internal Revenue Service said.

In a ruling released yesterday, the IRS said old-fashioned "push up" or natural-soil greens will remain nondepreciable but that certain costs incurred in the original construction or reconstruction of "modern" golf-course greens, which feature substantial integrated drainage systems, will be depreciable.

According to the IRS's ruling, "push up or natural soil greens are essentially landscaping that involves some reshaping or regrading of the land." Those greens may have limited irrigation systems, such as hoses and sprinklers adjacent, but a subsurface drainage system isn't used.

The IRS said modern greens make use of technological changes in green design and construction and contain sophisticated drainage systems.

© 2000 Dow Jones & Company, Inc.

The depreciation process results in **depreciation expense** that involves three key factors: (1) **asset cost**—amount the company paid for the asset including freight and charges relating to the asset; (2) **estimated useful life**—number of years or time periods for which the company can use the asset; and (3) **residual value (salvage** or **trade-in value)**—expected cash value at the end of the asset's useful life.

Depreciation expense is listed on the income statement. The **accumulated depreciation** title on the balance sheet gives the amount of the asset's depreciation taken to date. Asset cost less accumulated depreciation is the asset's book value. The **book value** shows the unused amount of the asset cost that the company may depreciate in future accounting periods. At the end of the asset's life, the asset's book value is the same as its residual value—book value cannot be less than residual value.

Depending on the amount and timetable of an asset's depreciation, a company can increase or decrease its profit. If a company shows greater depreciation in earlier years, the company will have a lower reported profit and pay less in taxes. Thus, depreciation can be an indirect tax savings for the company.

Later in the chapter we will discuss the different methods of computing depreciation that spread the cost of an asset over specified periods of time. However, first let's look at some of the major causes of depreciation.

Causes of Depreciation

As assets, all machines have an estimated amount of usefulness simply because as companies use the assets, the assets gradually wear out. The cause of this depreciation is *physical deterioration.*

The growth of a company can also cause depreciation. Many companies begin on a small scale. As the companies grow, they often find their equipment and buildings

Bob Daemmrich/Stock Boston

inadequate. The use of depreciation enables these businesses to "write off" their old, inadequate equipment and buildings. Companies cannot depreciate land. For example, a garbage dump can be depreciated but not the land.

Another cause of depreciation is the result of advances in technology. The computers that companies bought a few years ago may be in perfect working condition but outdated. Companies may find it necessary to replace these old computers with more sophisticated, faster, and possibly more economical machines. Thus, *product obsolescence* is a key factor contributing to depreciation.

Now we are ready to begin our study of depreciation methods. The first method we will study is straight-line depreciation. It is also the most common of the four depreciation methods (straight line, units of production, sum-of-the-years' digits, and declining balance). In a survey of 600 corporations, 81% responded that they used straight-line depreciation.

Straight-Line Method

The **straight-line method** of depreciation is used more than any other method. It tries to distribute the same amount of expense to each period of time. Most large companies, such as Gillette Corporation, use the straight-line method. For example, let's assume Ajax Company bought equipment for $2,500. The company estimates that the equipment's period of "usefulness"—or *useful life*—will be 5 years. After 5 years the equipment will have a residual value (salvage value) of $500. The company decides to calculate its depreciation with the straight-line method and uses the following formula:

$$\frac{\text{Depreciation expense}}{\text{each year}} = \frac{\text{Cost} - \text{Residual value}}{\text{Estimated useful life in years}}$$

$$\frac{\$2,500 - \$500}{5 \text{ years}} = \$400 \text{ depreciation expense}$$
taken each year

Table 17.1 gives a summary of the equipment depreciation that Ajax Company will take over the next 5 years. Companies call this summary a **depreciation schedule.**

TABLE 17.1

Depreciation schedule for straight-line method

$$\frac{100\%}{\text{Number of years}} = \frac{100\%}{5} = 20\%$$

Thus, the company is depreciating the equipment at a 20% rate each year.

End of year	Cost of equipment	Depreciation expense for year	Accumulated depreciation at end of year	Book value at end of year (Cost − Accumulated depreciation)
1	$2,500	$400	$ 400	$2,100 ($2,500 − $400)
2	2,500	400	800	1,700
3	2,500	400	1,200	1,300
4	2,500	400	1,600	900
5	2,500	400	2,000	500
	↑	↑	↑	↑
	Cost stays the same.	Depreciation expense is same each year.	Accumulated depreciation increases by $400 each year.	Book value is lowered by $400 until residual value of $500 is reached.

Depreciation for Partial Years

If a company buys an asset before the 15th of the month, the company calculates the asset's depreciation for a full month. Companies do not take the full month's depreciation for assets bought after the 15th of the month. For example, assume Ajax Company (Table 17.1) bought the equipment on May 6. The company would calculate the depreciation for the first year as follows:

$$\frac{\$2,500 - \$500}{5 \text{ years}} = \$400 \times \frac{8}{12} = \$266.67$$

Now let's check your progress with the Practice Quiz before we look at the next depreciation method.

LU 17-1 PRACTICE QUIZ

1. Prepare a depreciation schedule using straight-line depreciation for the following:

Cost of truck	$16,000
Residual value	1,000
Life	5 years

2. If the truck were bought on February 3, what would the depreciation expense be in the first year?

✓ **SOLUTIONS**

1.

End of year	Cost of truck	Depreciation expense for year	Accumulated depreciation at end of year	Book value at end of year (Cost − Accumulated depreciation)
1	$16,000	$3,000	$ 3,000	$13,000 ($16,000 − $3,000)
2	16,000	3,000	6,000	10,000
3	16,000	3,000	9,000	7,000
4	16,000	3,000	12,000	4,000
5	16,000	3,000	15,000	1,000 ⟵ Note that we are down to residual value

2. $$\frac{\$16,000 - \$1,000}{5} = \$3,000 \times \frac{11}{12} = \boxed{\$2,750}$$

LEARNING UNIT 17-2 | UNITS-OF-PRODUCTION METHOD

Unlike in the straight-line depreciation method, in the **units-of-production method** the passage of time is not used to determine an asset's depreciation amount. Instead, the company determines the asset's depreciation according to how much the company uses the asset. This use could be miles driven, tons hauled, or units that a machine produces. For example, when a company such as Ajax Company (in Learning Unit 17–1) buys equipment, the company estimates how many units the equipment can produce. Let's assume the equipment has a useful life of 4,000 units. The following formulas are used to calculate the equipment's depreciation for the units-of-production method.

$$\frac{\text{Depreciation}}{\text{per unit}} = \frac{\text{Cost} - \text{Residual value}}{\text{Total estimated units produced}} = \frac{\$2,500 - \$500}{4,000 \text{ units}} = \frac{\$.50}{\text{per unit}}$$

$$\frac{\text{Depreciation}}{\text{amount}} = \frac{\text{Unit}}{\text{depreciation}} \times \frac{\text{Units}}{\text{produced}} = \$.50 \text{ times actual number of units}$$

Now we can complete Table 17.2. Note that the table gives the units produced each year. Let's check your understanding of this unit with the Practice Quiz.

TABLE 17.2   Depreciation schedule for units-of-production method

End of year	Cost of equipment	Units produced	Depreciation expense for year	Accumulated depreciation at end of year	Book value at end of year (Cost − Accumulated depreciation)
1	$2,500	300	$ 150 (300 × $.50)	$ 150	$2,350 ($2,500 − $150)
2	2,500	400	200	350	2,150
3	2,500	600	300	650	1,850
4	2,500	2,000	1,000	1,650	850
5	2,500	700	350	2,000	500

At the end of 5 years, the equipment produced 4,000 units. If in year 5 the equipment produced 1,500 units, only 700 could be used in the calculation, or it will go below the equipment's residual value.

Units produced per year times $.50 equals depreciation expense.

Residual value of $500 is reached. (Be sure depreciation is not taken below the residual value.)

LU 17-2 PRACTICE QUIZ

From the following facts prepare a depreciation schedule:

Machine cost $20,000
Residual value   4,000
Expected to produce 16,000 units over its expected life

	2004	**2005**	**2006**	**2007**	**2008**
Units produced:	2,000	8,000	3,000	1,800	1,600

✓ SOLUTIONS

$$\frac{\$20,000 - \$4,000}{16,000} = \$1$$

End of year	Cost of machine	Units produced	Depreciation expense for year	Accumulated depreciation at end of year	Book value at end of year (Cost − Accumulated depreciation)
1	$20,000	2,000	$2,000 (2,000 × $1)	$ 2,000	$18,000
2	20,000	8,000	8,000	10,000	10,000
3	20,000	3,000	3,000	13,000	7,000
4	20,000	1,800	1,800	14,800	5,200
5	20,000	1,600	1,200*	16,000	4,000

*Note that we only can depreciate 1,200 units since we cannot go below the residual value of $4,000.

LEARNING UNIT 17-3 | SUM-OF-THE-YEARS'-DIGITS METHOD[1]

Now we look at the **sum-of-the-years'-digits method.** This is an **accelerated depreciation method** that computes more depreciation expense in the early years of the asset's life than in the later years. The accelerated method may more closely match the way the assets lose their value.

To calculate depreciation expense for the sum-of-the-years'-digits method, we use the following formula:

$$\text{Depreciation expense} = (\text{Cost} - \text{Residual value}) \times \frac{\text{Remaining life}}{\text{Sum-of-the-years' digits}}$$

The fraction in the formula is the key to understanding the sum-of-the-years'-digits method. We can explain this fraction by assuming an asset has 5 years of remaining life.

---
[1]This method is seldom used today. In a recent survey of 600 companies, only 3% use the sum-of-the-years'-digits method.

TABLE 17.3   Depreciation schedule for sum-of-the-years'-digits method

End of year	Cost – Residual value	×	Fraction for year	=	Yearly depreciation expense	Accumulated depreciation at end of year	Book value at end of year (Cost – Accumulated depreciation)
1	$2,000 ($2,500 – $500)	×	$\frac{5}{15}$	=	$666.67	$ 666.67	$1,833.33 ($2,500 – $666.67)
2	2,000	×	$\frac{4}{15}$	=	533.33	1,200.00	1,300.00 ($2,500 – $1,200)
3	2,000	×	$\frac{3}{15}$	=	400.00	1,600.00	900.00
4	2,000	×	$\frac{2}{15}$	=	266.67	1,866.67	633.33
5	2,000	×	$\frac{1}{15}$	=	133.33	2,000.00	500.00
	↑ Cost *less* residual value is multiplied by fraction for year.		↑ Large numerator occurs in early years.		↑ *Note:* Depreciation of $666.67 in year 1 is highest.	↑ Accumulated depreciation increases more slowly in later years.	↑ *Note:* We used cost of $2,500 – $2,000 accumulated depreciation to equal book value of $500.

$\left(\dfrac{5}{15}\right)$ ⟵ Numerator of fraction is years remaining

⟵ Denominator of fraction is the sum of the asset's service life (5 + 4 + 3 + 2 + 1)

We can calculate the denominator of the fraction by this formula:

$$\frac{N(N+1)}{2} = \frac{5(5+1)}{2} = \frac{30}{2} = 15$$

where N is the estimated life of the asset. Remember that the numerator of the fraction—remaining years left—changes each year as the asset gets older. The denominator of the fraction—sum-of-the-years' digits—remains the same for the life of the asset.

Now let's use the sum-of-the-years'-digits method and prepare the depreciation schedule shown in Table 17.3 for Ajax Company in Learning Unit 17–2. Keep in mind that partial years for depreciation could result, as we showed in the straight-line method.

It's time for another Practice Quiz.

LU 17–3 PRACTICE QUIZ

Prepare a depreciation schedule for the sum-of-the-years'-digits method from the following:
Cost of machine, 5-year life $16,000
Residual value   1,000

✓ **SOLUTIONS**

End of year	Cost – Residual value	×	Fraction for year	=	Yearly depreciation expense	Accumulated depreciation at end of year	Book value at end of year (Cost – Accumulated depreciation)
1	$15,000	×	$\frac{5}{15}$	=	$5,000	$ 5,000	$11,000 ($16,000 – $5,000)
2	15,000	×	$\frac{4}{15}$	=	4,000	9,000	7,000
3	15,000	×	$\frac{3}{15}$	=	3,000	12,000	4,000
4	15,000	×	$\frac{2}{15}$	=	2,000	14,000	2,000
5	15,000	×	$\frac{1}{15}$	=	1,000	15,000	1,000

TABLE 17.4 Depreciation schedule for declining-balance method

End of year	Cost of equipment	Accumulated depreciation at beginning of year	Book value at beginning of year (Cost − Accumulated depreciation)	Depreciation (Book value at beginning of year × Rate)	Accumulated depreciation at end of year	Book value at end of year (Cost − Accumulated depreciation)
1	$2,500	—	$2,500	$1,000 ($2,500 × .40)	$1,000	$1,500 ($2,500 − $1,000)
2	2,500	$1,000	1,500	600 ($1,500 × .40)	1,600	900
3	2,500	1,600	900	360 ($900 × .40)	1,960	540
4	2,500	1,960	540	40	2,000	500
5	2,500	2,000	500		2,000	500
	↑ Original cost of $2,500 does not change. Residual value was not subtracted.	↑ Ending accumulated depreciation of 1 year becomes next year's beginning.	↑ Cost less accumulated depreciation	↑ *Note:* In year 4, only $40 is taken since we cannot depreciate below residual value of $500. In year 5, no depreciation is taken.	↑ Accumulated depreciation balance plus depreciation expense this year.	↑ Book value now equals residual value.

LEARNING UNIT 17-4 | DECLINING-BALANCE METHOD

In the declining-balance method, we cannot depreciate below the residual value.

The **declining-balance method** is another type of accelerated depreciation that takes larger amounts of depreciation expense in the earlier years of the asset. The straight-line method, you recall, estimates the life of the asset and distributes the same amount of depreciation expense to each period. To take larger amounts of depreciation expense in the asset's earlier years, the declining-balance method uses up to *twice* the **straight-line rate** in the first year of depreciation. A key point to remember is that the declining-balance method does not deduct the residual value in calculating the depreciation expense. Today, the declining-balance method is the basis of current tax depreciation.

For all problems, we will use double the straight-line rate unless we indicate otherwise. Today, the rate is often 1.5 or 1.25 times the straight-line rate. Again we use our $2,500 equipment with its estimated useful life of 5 years. As we build the depreciation schedule in Table 17.4, note the following steps:

Step 1. Rate is equal to $\dfrac{100\%}{5 \text{ years}} \times 2 = 40\%$.

Or another way to look at it is that the straight-line rate is $\frac{1}{5} \times 2 = \frac{2}{5} = 40\%$.

Step 2.

$$\dfrac{\text{Depreciation expense}}{\text{each year}} = \dfrac{\text{Book value of equipment}}{\text{at beginning of year}} \times \dfrac{\text{Depreciation}}{\text{rate}}$$

Step 3. We cannot depreciate the equipment below its residual value ($500). The straight-line method and the sum-of-the-years'-digits method automatically reduced the asset's book value to the residual value. This is not true with the declining-balance method. So you must be careful when you prepare the depreciation schedule.

Now let's check your progress again with another Practice Quiz.

LU 17-4 PRACTICE QUIZ

Prepare a depreciation schedule from the following:

Cost of machine: $16,000   Estimated life: 5 years

Rate: 40% (this is twice the straight-line rate)   Residual value: $1,000

✓ **SOLUTIONS**

End of year	Cost of machine	Accumulated depreciation at beginning of year	Book value at beginning of year (Cost − Accumulated depreciation)	Depreciation (Book value at beginning of year × Rate)	Accumulated depreciation at end of year	Book value at end of year (Cost − Accumulated depreciation)
1	$16,000	$ –0–	$16,000.00	$6,400.00	$ 6,400.00	$9,600.00
2	16,000	6,400.00	9,600.00	3,840.00	10,240.00	5,760.00
3	16,000	10,240.00	5,760.00	2,304.00	12,544.00	3,456.00
4	16,000	12,544.00	3,456.00	1,382.40	13,926.40	2,073.60
5	16,000	13,926.40	2,073.60	829.44*	14,755.84	1,244.16

*Since we do not reach the residual value of $1,000, another $244.16 could have been taken as depreciation expense to bring it to the estimated residual value of $1,000.

LEARNING UNIT 17–5 | MODIFIED ACCELERATED COST RECOVERY SYSTEM (MACRS) WITH INTRODUCTION TO ACRS

In Learning Units 17–1 to 17–4, we discussed the depreciation methods used for financial reporting. Since 1981, federal tax laws have been passed that state how depreciation must be taken for income tax purposes. Assets put in service from 1981 through 1986 fell under the federal **Accelerated Cost Recovery System (ACRS)** tax law enacted in 1981. The Tax Reform Act of 1986 established the **Modified Accelerated Cost Recovery System (MACRS)** for all property placed into service after December 31, 1986. Both these federal laws provide users with tables giving the useful lives of various assets and the depreciation rates. We look first at the MACRS and then at a 1989 update.

Depreciation for Tax Purposes Based on the Tax Reform Act of 1986 (MACRS)

Tables 17.5 and 17.6 give the classes of recovery and annual depreciation percentages that MACRS established in 1986. The key points of MACRS are:

1. It calculates depreciation for tax purposes.
2. It ignores residual value.
3. Depreciation in the first year (for personal property) is based on the assumption that the asset was purchased halfway through the year. (A new law adds a midquarter convention for all personal property if more than 40% is placed in service during the last 3 months of the taxable year.)
4. Classes 3, 5, 7, and 10 use a 200% declining-balance method for a period of years before switching to straight-line depreciation. You do not have to determine the year in which to switch since Table 17.6 builds this into the calculation.
5. Classes 15 and 20 use a 150% declining-balance method before switching to straight-line depreciation.
6. Classes 27.5 and 31.5 use straight-line depreciation.

EXAMPLE   Using the same equipment cost of $2,500 for Ajax, prepare a depreciation schedule under MACRS assuming the equipment is a 5-year class and not part of the tax bill of 1989. Use Table 17.6. Note that percent figures from Table 17.6 have been converted to decimals.

End of year	Cost	Depreciation expense	Accumulated depreciation	Book value at end of year
1	$2,500	$500 (.20 × $2,500)	$ 500	$2,000
2	2,500	800 (.32 × $2,500)	1,300	1,200
3	2,500	480 (.1920 × $2,500)	1,780	720
4	2,500	288 (.1152 × $2,500)	2,068	432
5	2,500	288 (.1152 × $2,500)	2,356	144
6	2,500	144 (.0576 × $2,500)	2,500	–0–

TABLE 17.5
Modified Accelerated Cost
Recovery System (MACRS) for
assets placed in service after
December 31, 1986

Class recovery period (life)	Asset types
3-year*	Racehorses more than 2 years old or any horse other than a racehorse that is more than 12 years old at the time placed into service; special tools of certain industries.
5-year*	Automobiles (not luxury); taxis; light general-purpose trucks; semiconductor manufacturing equipment; computer-based telephone central-office switching equipment; qualified technological equipment; property used in connection with research and experimentation.
7-year*	Railroad track; single-purpose agricultural (pigpens) or horticultural structures; fixtures; equipment; furniture.
10-year*	New law doesn't add any specific property under this class.
15-year†	Municipal wastewater treatment plants; telephone distribution plants and comparable equipment used for two-way exchange of voice and data communications.
20-year†	Municipal sewers.
27.5-year‡	Only residential rental property.
31.5-year‡	Only nonresidential real property.

*These classes use a 200% declining-balance method switching to the straight-line method.

†These classes use a 150% declining-balance method switching to the straight-line method.

‡These classes use a straight-line method.

TABLE 17.6   Annual recovery for MACRS

Recovery year	3-year class (200% D.B.)	5-year class (200% D.B.)	7-year class (200% D.B.)	10-year class (200% D.B.)	15-year class (150% D.B.)	20-year class (150% D.B.)
1	33.00	20.00	14.28	10.00	5.00	3.75
2	45.00	32.00	24.49	18.00	9.50	7.22
3	15.00*	19.20	17.49	14.40	8.55	6.68
4	7.00	11.52*	12.49	11.52	7.69	6.18
5		11.52	8.93*	9.22	6.93	5.71
6		5.76	8.93	7.37	6.23	5.28
7			8.93	6.55*	5.90*	4.89
8			4.46	6.55	5.90	4.52
9				6.55	5.90	4.46*
10				6.55	5.90	4.46
11				3.29	5.90	4.46
12					5.90	4.46
13					5.90	4.46
14					5.90	4.46
15					5.90	4.46
16					3.00	4.46

*Identifies when switch is made to straight line.

Update on MACRS: The 1989 Tax Bill

Before the 1989 tax bill (**Omnibus Budget Reconciliation Act of 1989**), cellular phones and similar equipment were depreciated under MACRS. Since cellular phones are subject to personal use, the 1989 act now treats them as "listed" property. This means that unless business use is greater than 50%, the straight-line method of depreciation is required.

Let's try another Practice Quiz.

LU 17–5 PRACTICE QUIZ

1. In 1991, Rancho Corporation bought semiconductor equipment for $80,000. Using MACRS, what is the depreciation expense in year 3?

2. What would depreciation be the first year for a wastewater treatment plant that cost $800,000?

✓ **SOLUTIONS**

1. $80,000 × .1920 = $15,360

2. $800,000 × .05 = $40,000

Chapter Organizer and Reference Guide

Topic	Key point, procedure, formula	Example(s) to illustrate situation
Straight-line method, p. 388	$$\text{Depreciation expense each year} = \frac{\text{Cost} - \text{Residual value}}{\text{Estimated useful life in years}}$$ For partial years if purchased before 15th of month depreciation is taken.	Truck, $25,000; $5,000 residual value, 4-year life. $$\text{Depreciation expense} = \frac{\$25,000 - \$5,000}{4}$$ $$= \boxed{\$5,000} \text{ per year}$$
Units-of-production method, p. 390	$$\text{Depreciation per unit} = \frac{\text{Cost} - \text{Residual value}}{\text{Total estimated units produced}}$$ Do not depreciate below residual value even if actual units are greater than estimate.	Machine, $5,000; estimated life in units, 900; residual value, $500. Assume first year produced 175 units. $$\text{Depreciation expense} = \frac{\$5,000 - \$500}{900}$$ $$= \frac{\$4,500}{900}$$ $$= \$5 \text{ depreciation per unit}$$ 175 units $\times$ \$5 = $\boxed{\$875}$ depreciation expense
Sum-of-the-years'-digits method, p. 391	$$\text{Depreciation expense} = \left(\begin{array}{c}\text{Cost} - \\ \text{Residual} \\ \text{value}\end{array}\right) \times \frac{\text{Remaining life}}{\substack{\text{Sum-of-the-years'} \\ \text{digits}}}$$ $\uparrow$ $$\frac{N(N+1)}{2}$$	Truck, $32,000; estimated life, 5 years; residual value, $2,000. **Year** / **Cost (less residual value)** $\times$ **Rate** = **Depreciation expense** 1 — \$30,000 $\times \frac{5}{15}$ = $\boxed{\$10,000}$ 2 — 30,000 $\times \frac{4}{15}$ = $\boxed{8,000}$
Declining-balance method, p. 393	An accelerated method. Residual value not subtracted from cost in depreciation schedule. Do not depreciate below residual value. $$\substack{\text{Depreciation} \\ \text{expense} \\ \text{each year}} = \substack{\text{Book value of} \\ \text{equipment at} \\ \text{beginning of year}} \times \substack{\text{Depreciation} \\ \text{rate}}$$	Truck, $50,000; estimated life, 5 years; residual value, $10,000. $\frac{1}{5} = 20\% \times 2 = 40\%$ (assume double the straight-line rate) **Year** / **Cost** / **Depreciation expense** / **Book value at end of year** 1 \$50,000 $\boxed{\$20,000}$ (\$50,000 $\times$ .40) \$30,000 (\$50,000 − \$20,000) 2 50,000 $\boxed{12,000}$ (\$30,000 $\times$ .40) 18,000 (\$50,000 − \$32,000)
MACRS/Tax Bill of 1989, p. 394	After December 31, 1986, depreciation calculation is modified. Tax Act of 1989 modifies way to depreciate cellular phones and similar equipment.	Auto: $8,000, 5 years. First year, .20 $\times$ \$8,000 = $\boxed{\$1,600}$ depreciation expense
Key terms	Accelerated Cost Recovery System (ACRS), *p. 394* Accelerated depreciation method, *p. 391* Accumulated depreciation, *p. 388* Asset cost, *p. 388* Book value, *p. 388* Declining-balance method, *p. 393*	Depreciation, *p. 388* Depreciation expense, *p. 388* Depreciation schedule, *p. 389* Estimated useful life, *p. 388* Modified Accelerated Cost Recovery System (MACRS), *p. 395* Omnibus Budget Reconciliation Act of 1989, *p. 395* · Residual value, *p. 388* Salvage value, *p. 388* Straight-line method, *p. 389* Straight-line rate, *p. 389* Sum-of-the-years'-digits method, *p. 391* Trade-in value, *p. 388* Units-of-production method, *p. 390*

Critical Thinking Discussion Questions

1. What is the difference between depreciation expense and accumulated depreciation? Why does the book value of an asset never go below the residual value?

2. Compare the straight-line method to the units-of-production method. Should both methods be based on the passage of time?

3. Explain the difference between the sum-of-the-years'-digits method and declining-balance method. Why is it possible in the declining-balance method for a person to depreciate below the residual value by mistake?

4. Explain the Modified Accelerated Cost Recovery System. Do you think this system will be eliminated in the future?

Name _____ Date _____

DRILL PROBLEMS

From the following facts, complete a depreciation schedule, using the straight-line method:

Given Cost of Range Rover $50,000
        Residual value   10,000
        Estimated life   8 years

End of year	Cost of Range Rover	Depreciation expense for year	Accumulated depreciation at end of year	Book value at end of year
17–1.				
17–2.				
17–3.				
17–4.				
17–5.				
17–6.				
17–7.				
17–8.				

Prepare a depreciation schedule using the sum-of-the-years'-digits method:

Given Ford pickup $11,000
        Residual value   1,000
        Estimated life   4 years

End of year	Cost − Residual value	Fraction for year	Depreciation expense for year	Accumulated depreciation at end of year	Book value at end of year
17–9.					
17–10.					
17–11.					
17–12.					

Prepare a depreciation schedule using the declining-balance method (twice the straight-line rate):

Given Volvo truck $25,000
        Residual value   5,000
        Estimated life   5 years

End of year	Cost of truck	Accumulated depreciation at beginning of year	Book value at beginning of year	Depreciation expense for year	Accumulated depreciation at end of year	Book value at end of year
17–13.						
17–14.						
17–15.						
17–16.						

For the first 2 years, calculate the depreciation expense for a $7,000 car under MACRS. This is a nonluxury car.

MACRS	**MACRS**
17–17. Year 1	**17–18.** Year 2

Complete the following table given this information:

Cost of machine	$94,000	Estimated units machine will produce		100,000
Residual value	4,000	Actual production:	**Year 1**	**Year 2**
Useful life	5 years		60,000	15,000

	Depreciation expense	
Method	**Year 1**	**Year 2**
17–19. Straight line		
17–20. Units of production		
17–21. Sum-of-the-years' digits		
17–22. Declining balance		
17–23. MACRS (5-year class)		

WORD PROBLEMS

17–24. Ace Corporation has just purchased a 2001 Dodge Intrepid for $24,975 with a residual value of $10,500. The vehicle will be used by the information systems manager to call on stores. The vehicle is used 80% for business and the rest for personal use. Using the modified accelerated cost recovery system (MACRS), how much would Ace Corporation deduct for depreciation during the first year?

17–25. Pat Brown bought a Chevy truck for $28,000 with an estimated life of 5 years. The residual value of the truck is $3,000. Assume a straight-line method of depreciation. **(a)** What will be the book value of the truck at the end of year 3? **(b)** If the Chevy truck was bought the first year on April 12, how much depreciation would be taken the first year?

17–26. Jim Company bought a machine for $36,000 with an estimated life of 5 years. The residual value of the machine is $6,000. Calculate **(a)** the annual depreciation and **(b)** the book value at the end of year 3. Assume straight-line depreciation.

17–27. Using Problem 17–26, calculate the first 2 years' depreciation, assuming the units-of-production method. This machine is expected to produce 120,000 units. In year 1, it produced 19,000 units, and in year 2, 38,000 units.

17–28. Assume Jim Company (Problem 17–26) used the sum-of-the-years'-digits method. How much more or less depreciation expense over the first 2 years would have been taken compared to straight-line depreciation?

17–29. Ray Kunz, owner of Ray's Auto Service, purchased a 2001 Corvette convertible listed in *Edmunds 2001 Buyer's Guide* at $46,605 with a residual value of $24,235. Ray uses the Corvette in his business. The life expectancy is 5 years. Using the declining-balance method, what would the depreciation expense be the first year?

17–30. The June 2001 issue of *Tax Adviser* explained the treatment of depreciation using MACRS. In January 2001, Irene Baldus purchased a warehouse (nonresidential real property) in La Porte, Indiana, for $200,000. Using the *Business Math Handbook,* what will the allowable depreciation be each year?

17–31. Mr. Fix Company bought a new Dodge Ram truck for $26,000 with an estimated life of 5 years. The residual value of the truck is $1,000. As Mr. Fix's accountant, prepare depreciation schedules for straight-line, sum-of-the-years'-digits, and declining-balance ($1\frac{1}{2}$ times the straight-line rate) methods.

Straight-line method:

End of year	Cost of truck	Depreciation expense	Accumulated depreciation

Sum-of-the-years'-digits method:

End of year	Cost of truck − Residual	Depreciation expense	Accumulated depreciation

Declining-balance method:

End of year	Cost of truck	Accumulated depreciation at beginning of year	Book value at beginning of year	Depreciation expense	Accumulated depreciation at end of year	Book value at end of year

 CHALLENGE PROBLEMS

17–32. The April 16, 2001, issue of *Auto Week* reported on a Mazda MPV minivan's original sticker price and trade-in value. The 2001 Mazda original sticker price was $29,325, and the trade-in value (per the National Association of Dealers of America) was $19,600. A driver had traveled 20,812 miles during the first year. The vehicle has a life expectancy of 4 years or 100,000 miles. **(a)** What would be the depreciation in the first year using the straight-line method? **(b)** What would be the depreciation in the first year using the declining-balance method? **(c)** What would be the depreciation for the first year using the sum-of-the years'-digits method? **(d)** What would be the depreciation expense for the first year if miles driven were used to calculate depreciation?

17–33. A piece of equipment was purchased July 26, 2003, at a cost of $72,000. The estimated residual value is $5,400 with a useful life of 5 years. Assume a production life of 60,000 units. Compute the depreciation for years 2003 and 2004 using **(a)** straight-line; **(b)** units-of-production (in 2003, 5,000 units produced and in 2004, 18,000 units produced); and **(c)** sum-of-the-years'-digits methods.

SUMMARY PRACTICE TEST

1. Lee Winn, owner of the Panda Express, bought a delivery truck for $30,000. The truck has an estimated life of 5 years with a residual value of $10,000. Lee wants to know which depreciation method will be best for his truck. He asks you to prepare a depreciation schedule using the declining-balance method at twice the straight-line rate. *(p. 393)*

2. Using MACRS, what is the depreciation for the first year on furniture costing $8,000? *(p. 394)*

3. Leah Wills bought a new Ford Explorer for $50,000. The Explorer has a life expectancy of 5 years with a residual value of $5,000. Prepare a depreciation schedule for the sum-of-the-years'-digits method. *(p. 391)*

4. Prestige.com bought a Range Rover for $60,000. The Rover has a life expectancy of 10 years with a residual value of Excel $10,000. After 2 years, the Rover was sold for $45,000. What was the difference between the book value and the amount received from selling the car if Prestige.com used the straight-line method of depreciation? *(p. 388)*

5. If Prestige.com (Problem 4) used the sum-of-the-years'-digits method, what was the difference between the book value and the price at which the Range Rover was sold? Round each calculation to the nearest dollar. *(p. 391)*

REAL ESTATE | This is no joke: First, you pay $7 million for a **FLOATING CONDOMINIUM**.

Then you're told you have to bring your own helicopter. *By Sean O'Neill*

SWELLS AMONG THE SWELLS

A NEW LUXURY cruise ship, *The World,* is putting a wildly upscale twist on the term "mobile home." For between $2 million and $7 million, you can own a piece of *The World* by buying one of the 24 remaining residences on the first cruise ship/condominium, which is scheduled to launch in December from Norway.

Making a succession of stops in celebrated ports of call, *The World* will anchor three-fourths of the year for events such as the Cannes film festival in France and the Grand Prix auto race in Monaco. The ship, which resembles a 12-deck wedding cake the length of two football fields and the width of an ice-hockey rink, will carry a battalion of 252 crew members and about 550 residents and guests. This is no crammed-to-the-gills party boat.

An oceangoing resort has been a real estate idea seeking venturesome capital since the 1980s, says Tom Ogg, editor of CruiseReviews.com. Skeptics doubted anyone would ever sink money into a floating mortgage. But the number of potential seafarers has finally reached critical mass: Since 1983, the number of Americans with a net worth greater than $5 million, adjusted for inflation, has tripled, to 500,000. The dozen penthouses on *The World* sold out the fastest, despite a hefty, $7-million price tag.

Driving range included. The least-expensive condo on *The World*—an 1,100-square-foot, two-bedroom unit—goes for about $2 million, which makes it roughly as pricey ($2,090 per square foot) as Bill Gates's mansion. For just $1.5 million more, says Jim Gilbert, editor of *Show-Boats International* magazine, you could buy an 80-foot yacht sufficiently seaworthy to sail the seven seas in style.

Here's what your money will buy: Every condo boasts an ocean view from its veranda. Each condo's entryway has interior double doors to permit a grand entrance to the living room, which features a wood or stone floor, coffered ceiling, designer furniture and three Internet connections. Your servants or guests may live in one of 88 less-sumptuous suites.

An annual fee of about 6% of the purchase price covers utilities, gratuities, daily housekeeping, concerts, cultural seminars, massages at the Clinique La Prairie spa, and use

MATTHEW MARTIN

Business Math Issue

Boats cannot depreciate.
1. List the key points of the article and information to support your position.
2. Write a group defense of your position using math calculations to support your view.

A Range Rover Depreciates* Faster than Most Luxury Vehicles.

Tax Depreciation Comparison

$58,000 Range Rover			$58,000 Luxury Car		
Year One	$	26,800	Year One	$	3,060
Year Two	$	9,984	Year Two	$	5,000
Year Three	$	4,073	Year Three	$	2,950
Year Four	$	4,937	Year Four	$	1,775

Tax depreciation comparison for individuals using their vehicles 100 percent for business. Owners of vehicles with GVW over 6,000 pounds are eligible for the first year expensing of $19,000, and can claim depreciation of 20% of the remaining cost basis in the first year, 32% of the remaining cost basis in the second year, 19.20% of the remaining cost basis in the third year and 28.80% of the remaining cost basis in the fourth year. Please consult a qualified tax attorney or accountant for details of IRS Code section 179.

PROJECT A

Go to Land Rover on the Web and see if you can find updated material on Range Rover tax depreciation comparison. You may also want to check with a tax attorney or consultant to find out more details.

Internet Projects: See text website (www.mhhe.com/slater7e) and *The Business Math Internet Resource Guide.*

Campbell Recalling Soup After Consumers Found Aluminum Bits

WASHINGTON (AP)—Campbell Soup Co. is recalling 109,000 pounds of soup after consumers found shards of a soft drink can that accidentally went through a vegetable dicer, the company said.

Five pieces of aluminum, ranging in length from an inch to almost 3 inches, have been found in three cans of the soup, said John Faulkner, a spokesman for the Camden, N.J., company. None of the metal was ingested, he said.

The aluminum can apparently was caught in a load of carrots or potatoes, he said.

The recalled product is labeled "Campbell's Healthy Request Vegetable Beef Condensed Soup." Some 168,000 cans of soup that was processed Sept. 27 are involved.

Each can is stamped with the code "SEP 01 09279" and "EST 4K DEAL," plus four digits that indicate military time.

The soup was distributed to stores in Arizona, Colorado, Iowa, Kansas, Louisiana, Missouri, Mississippi, Nebraska, New Mexico, Oklahoma and South Dakota, the Agriculture Department said.

Consumers should return the soup to the store where they bought it, Mr. Faulkner said. There is a toll-free telephone number on the label for consumers with questions about the recall.

Inventory and Overhead

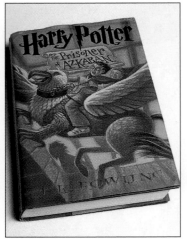

Amazon.com, Inc., promised its customers it would deliver copies of the fourth Harry Potter book to their doorstep on July 8, the day of the book's release. However, 3,800 customers did not receive their books on July 8. Amazon said its software failed to recognize the addresses of customers who did not fill out the first of three lines in the address box given on the Web.

Although the 3,800 disappointed customers represented only 1.5% of the orders for the fourth Harry Potter book, the disappointed customers made their disappointment heard on Web chat sites. Amazon refunded these customers the cost of the book and the shipping and sent them free books.

Amazon did not report the inventory method it used to keep track of their books. The company could have used either the *perpetual inventory system* or the *periodic inventory system.*

The perpetual inventory system should be familiar to most consumers. Today, it is common for cashiers to run scanners across the product code of each item sold. These scanners read pertinent information into a computer terminal, such as the item's number, department, and price. The computer then uses the **perpetual inventory system** as it subtracts outgoing merchandise from inventory and adds incoming merchandise to inventory. However, as you probably know, the computer cannot be completely relied on to maintain an accurate count of merchandise in stock. Since some products may be stolen or lost, periodically a physical count is necessary to verify the computer count.

With the increased use of computers, many companies are changing to a perpetual inventory system of maintaining inventory records. Some small stores, however, still use the **periodic inventory system.** This system usually does not keep a running account of its inventory but relies only on a physical inventory count taken at least once a year. The store then uses various accounting methods to value the cost of its merchandise. In this chapter we discuss the periodic method of inventory.

You may wonder why a company should know the status of its inventory. In Chapter 16 we introduced you to the balance sheet and the income statement. Companies cannot accurately prepare these statements unless they have placed the correct value on their inventory. To do this, a company must know (1) the cost of its ending inventory (found on the balance sheet) and (2) the cost of the goods (merchandise) sold (found on the income statement).

Frequently, the same type of merchandise flows into a company at different costs. The value assumptions a company makes about the merchandise it sells affects the cost assigned to its ending inventory. Remember that different costs result in different levels of profit on a firm's financial reports.

This chapter begins by using the Blue Company to discuss four common methods (specific identification, weighted average, FIFO, and LIFO) that companies use to calculate costs of ending inventory and the cost of goods sold. In these methods, the flow of costs does not always match the flow of goods. The chapter continues with a discussion of two methods of estimating ending inventory (retail and gross profit methods), inventory turnover, and the distribution of overhead.

LEARNING UNIT 18–1 | ASSIGNING COSTS TO ENDING INVENTORY—SPECIFIC IDENTIFICATION; WEIGHTED AVERAGE; FIFO; LIFO

Blue Company is a small artist supply store. Its beginning inventory is 40 tubes of art paint that cost $320 (at $8 a tube) to bring into the store. As shown in Figure 18.1, Blue made additional purchases in April, May, October, and December. Note that because of inflation and other competitive factors, the cost of the paint rose from $8 to $13 per tube. At the end of December, Blue had 48 unsold paint tubes. During the year, Blue had 120 paint tubes to sell. Blue wants to calculate (1) the cost of ending inventory (not sold) and (2) the cost of goods sold.

FIGURE 18.1

Blue Company—a case study

	Number of units purchased	Cost per unit	Total cost
Beginning inventory	40	$ 8	$ 320
First purchase (April 1)	20	9	180
Second purchase (May 1)	20	10	200
Third purchase (October 1)	20	12	240
Fourth purchase (December 1)	20	13	260
Goods (merchandise) available for sale	120		$1,200 ← **Step 1**
Units sold	72		
Units in ending inventory	48		

Specific Identification Method

Companies that sell high-cost items such as autos, jewelry, antiques, and so on, usually use the specific identification method.

Companies use the **specific identification method** when they can identify the original purchase cost of an item with the item. For example, Blue Company color codes its paint tubes as they come into the store. Blue can then attach a specific invoice price to each paint tube. This makes the flow of goods and flow of costs the same. Then, when Blue computes its ending inventory and cost of goods sold, it can associate the actual invoice cost with each item sold and in inventory.

To help Blue calculate its inventory with the specific identification method, use the steps that follow.

Calculating the Specific Identification Method

Step 1. Calculate the cost of goods (merchandise available for sale).
Step 2. Calculate the cost of the ending inventory.
Step 3. Calculate the cost of goods sold (Step 1 − Step 2).

First, Blue must actually count the tubes of paint on hand. Since Blue coded these paint tubes, it can identify the tubes with their purchase cost and multiply them by this cost to arrive at a total cost of ending inventory. Let's do this now.

	Cost per unit	Total cost
20 units from April 1	$ 9	$180
20 units from October 1	12	240
8 units from December 1	13	104
Cost of ending inventory		$524 ← **Step 2**

Blue uses the following cost of goods sold formula to determine its cost of goods sold:

$$\text{Cost of goods available for sale} - \text{Cost of ending inventory} = \text{Cost of goods sold} \quad \leftarrow \textbf{Step 3}$$

$$\underset{\text{(Figure 18.1)}}{\$1,200} - \$524 = \boxed{\$676}$$

Note that the $1,200 for cost of goods available for sale comes from Figure 18.1. Remember, we are focusing our attention on Blue's *purchase costs*. Blue's actual *selling price* does not concern us.

Now let's look at how Blue would use the weighted-average method.

Weighted-Average Method[1]

The **weighted-average method** prices the ending inventory by using an average unit cost. Let's replay Blue Company and use the weighted-average method to find the average unit cost of its ending inventory and its cost of goods sold. Blue would use the steps that follow.

Calculating the Weighted-Average Method

Step 1. Calculate the average unit cost.
Step 2. Calculate the cost of the ending inventory.
Step 3. Calculate the cost of goods sold.

In the table that follows, Blue makes the calculation.

	Number of units purchased	Cost per unit	Total cost
Beginning inventory	40	$ 8	$ 320
First purchase (April 1)	20	9	180
Second purchase (May 1)	20	10	200
Third purchase (October 1)	20	12	240
Fourth purchase (December 1)	20	13	260
Goods (merchandise) available for sale	120		$1,200
Units sold	72		
Units in ending inventory	48		

$$\text{Weighted average unit cost} = \frac{\text{Total cost of goods available for sale}}{\text{Total number of units available for sale}} = \frac{\$1,200}{120 \text{ units}} = \$10 \text{ average unit cost}$$ ← **Step 1**

Average cost of ending inventory: 48 units at $10 = $480 ← **Step 2**

$$\text{Cost of goods available for sale} - \text{Cost of ending inventory} = \text{Cost of goods sold}$$

$1,200   − $480   = $720 ← **Step 3**

Remember that some of the costs we used to determine the average unit cost were higher and others were lower. The weighted-average method, then, calculates an *average unit price* for goods. Companies with similar units of goods, such as rolls of wallpaper, often use the weighted-average method. Also, companies with homogeneous products such as fuels and grains may use the weighted-average method.

Now let's see how Blue Company would value its inventory with the FIFO method.

FIFO—First-In, First-Out Method[2]

The **first-in, first-out (FIFO)** inventory valuation method assumes that the first goods (paint tubes for Blue) brought into the store are the first goods sold. Thus, FIFO assumes that each sale is from the oldest goods in inventory. FIFO also assumes that the inventory remaining in the store at the end of the period is the most recently acquired goods. This cost flow assumption may or may not hold in the actual physical flow of the goods. An example of a corporation's using the FIFO method is Gillette Corporation.

Use the following steps to calculate inventory with the FIFO method.

---

[1] Virtually all countries permit the use of the weighted-average method.
[2] Virtually all countries permit the use of the FIFO method.

Calculating the FIFO Inventory

Step 1. List the units to be included in the ending inventory and their costs.
Step 2. Calculate the cost of the ending inventory.
Step 3. Calculate the cost of goods sold.

In the table that follows, we show how to calculate FIFO for Blue using the above steps.

FIFO (bottom up)	Number of units purchased	Cost per unit	Total cost
Beginning inventory	40	$ 8	$ 320
First purchase (April 1)	20	9	180
Second purchase (May 1)	20	10	200
Third purchase (October 1)	20	12	240
Fourth purchase (December 1)	20	13	260
Goods (merchandise) available for sale	120		$1,200
Units sold	72		
Units in ending inventory	48		

20 units from December 1 purchased at $13 $260
20 units from October 1 purchased at $12   ⟵ **Step 1** ⟶   240
 8 units from May 1 purchased at $10   80
48 units result in an ending inventory cost of $580 ⟵ **Step 2**

Cost of goods available for sale	−	Cost of ending inventory	=	Cost of goods sold
$1,200	−	$580	=	$620 ⟵ **Step 3**

In FIFO, the cost flow of goods tends to follow the physical flow. For example, a fish market could use FIFO because it wants to sell its old inventory first. Note that during inflation, FIFO produces a higher income than other methods. So companies using FIFO during this time must pay more taxes.

We conclude this unit by using the LIFO method to value Blue Company's inventory.

LIFO—Last-In, First-Out Method[3]

If Blue Company chooses the **last-in, first-out (LIFO)** method of inventory valuation, then the goods sold by Blue will be the last goods brought into the store. The ending inventory would consist of the old goods that Blue bought earlier.

You can calculate inventory with the LIFO method by using the steps that follow.

Calculating the LIFO Inventory

Step 1. List the units to be included in the ending inventory and their costs.
Step 2. Calculate the cost of the ending inventory.
Step 3. Calculate the cost of goods sold.

Now we use the above steps to calculate LIFO for Blue.

---

[3]Many countries, such as Australia, Hong Kong, South Africa, and the United Kingdom, do not permit the use of LIFO.

LIFO (top down)	Number of units purchased	Cost per unit	Total cost
Beginning inventory	40	$ 8	$ 320
First purchase (April 1)	20	9	180
Second purchase (May 1)	20	10	200
Third purchase (October 1)	20	12	240
Fourth purchase (December 1)	20	13	260
Goods (merchandise) available for sale	120		$1,200
Units sold	72		
Units in ending inventory	48		

40 units of beginning inventory at $8 $320
 8 units from April at $9   ← Step 1 →   72
48 units result in an ending inventory cost of $392 ← Step 2

Cost of goods available for sale	−	Cost of ending inventory	=	Cost of goods sold

$1,200 − $392 = $808 ← Step 3

Although LIFO doesn't always match the physical flow of goods, companies do still use it to calculate the flow of costs for products such as DVDs and computers, which have declining replacement costs. Also, during inflation, LIFO produces less income than other methods. This results in lower taxes for companies using LIFO.

Before we conclude this unit, let's make the following summary for the cost of ending inventory and cost of goods sold under the weighted-average, FIFO, and LIFO methods.

Inventory method	Cost of goods available for sale	Cost of ending inventory	Cost of goods sold
Weighted average	$1,200	$480 **Step 1:** Total goods, $1,200 Total units, $\frac{\$1,200}{120} = \$10$ **Step 2:** $10 × 48 = $480	$1,200 − $480 = $720
FIFO	$1,200	Bottom up to inventory level (48) 20 × $13 = $260 20 × $12 = 240 8 × $10 = 80 $580	$1,200 − $580 = $620
LIFO	$1,200	Top down to inventory level (48) 40 × $8 = $320 8 × $9 = 72 $392	$1,200 − $392 = $808

From this summary, you can see that in times of rising prices, LIFO gives the highest cost of goods sold ($808). This results in a tax savings for Blue. The weighted-average method tends to smooth out the fluctuations between LIFO and FIFO and falls in the middle.

The key to this discussion of inventory valuation is that different costing methods produce different results. So management, investors, and potential investors should understand the different inventory costing methods and should know which method a particular company uses. For example, Fruit of the Loom, Inc., changed its inventories from LIFO to FIFO due to cost reductions.

Let's check your understanding of this unit with a Practice Quiz.

LU 18–1 PRACTICE QUIZ

From the following, calculate **(a)** the cost of ending inventory and **(b)** the cost of goods sold under the assumption of (1) weighted-average method, (2) FIFO, and (3) LIFO (ending inventory shows 72 units):

	Number of books purchased for resale	Cost per unit	Total
January 1 inventory	30	$3	$ 90
March 1	50	2	100
April 1	20	4	80
November 1	60	6	360

✔ **SOLUTIONS**

1. **a.** 72 units of ending inventory × $3.94 = $283.68 cost of ending inventory
   ($630 ÷ 160)

   b.
Cost of goods available for sale	−	Cost of ending inventory	=	Cost of goods sold
↓		↓		↓
$630	−	$283.68	=	**$346.32**

2. **a.** 60 units from November 1 purchased at $6 $360
   12 units from April 1 purchased at $4   48
   72 units   Cost of ending inventory $408

   b.
Cost of goods available for sale	−	Cost of ending inventory	=	Cost of goods sold
↓		↓		↓
$630	−	$408	=	**$222**

3. **a.** 30 units from January 1 purchased at $3 $ 90
   42 units from March 1 purchased at $2   84
   72   Cost of ending inventory $174

   b.
Cost of goods available for sale	−	Cost of ending inventory	=	Cost of goods sold
↓		↓		↓
$630	−	$174	=	**$456**

LEARNING UNIT 18–2 | RETAIL METHOD; GROSS PROFIT METHOD; INVENTORY TURNOVER; DISTRIBUTION OF OVERHEAD

Amy C. Etra/PhotoEdit

SLIM JIMS and slim profit margins augur changes for convenience stores.

Gas and cigarettes account for more than 60% of a typical convenience store's sales and are expected to continue as leaders, says a study from the National Association of Convenience Stores, Alexandria, Va. But margins are shrinking and competition is growing. Smokers, for instance, are increasingly price-sensitive as cigarette taxes soar. Savvy stores are filling the margin gap by expanding food-service items like "portable" meals that go beyond snacks.

But growth in the next five years will involve "big, tough management decisions" on business strategy, not small changes in merchandise, the report says. Technology is key — both in trimming overhead and in offering new services, such as Internet access at gas pumps so consumers can check their stocks and such while filling up.

©2000 Dow Jones & Company, Inc.

The Wall Street Journal clipping "Slim Jims" discusses the shrinking profits of convenience stores and how technology can be used to trim overhead and offer new services that will increase profits. Controlling inventory is one way to increase profits.

Taking a physical inventory at convenience stores can be time-consuming and expensive. Some stores draw up monthly financial reports but do not want to spend the time or money to take a monthly physical inventory. Many stores estimate the amount of inventory on hand. Stores may also have to estimate their inventories when they have a loss of goods due to fire, theft, flood, and the like. This unit begins with two methods of estimating the value of ending inventory—the retail method and the gross profit method.

FIGURE 18.2

Estimating inventory with the retail method

	Cost	Retail	
Beginning inventory	$4,000	$6,000	
Net purchases during month	2,300	3,000	
Cost of goods available for sale **(Step 1)**	$6,300	$9,000	
Less net sales for month		4,000	**(Step 3)**
Ending inventory at retail		$5,000	
Cost ratio ($6,300 ÷ $9,000) **(Step 2)**		70%	
Ending inventory at cost (.70 × $5,000) **(Step 4)**		$3,500	

Retail Method

Many companies use the **retail method** to estimate their inventory. As shown in Figure 18.2, this method does not require that a company calculate an inventory cost for each item. To calculate the $3,500 ending inventory in Figure 18.2, Green Company used the steps that follow.

Calculating the Retail Method

Step 1. Calculate the cost of goods available for sale at cost and retail: $6,300; $9,000.

Step 2. Calculate a cost ratio using the following formula:

$$\frac{\text{Cost of goods available for sale at cost}}{\text{Cost of goods available for sale at retail}} = \frac{\$6,300}{\$9,000} = .70$$

Step 3. Deduct net sales from cost of goods available for sale at retail: $9,000 − $4,000.

Step 4. Multiply the cost ratio by the ending inventory at retail: .70 × $5,000.

Now let's look at the gross profit method.

Gross Profit Method

To use the **gross profit method** to estimate inventory, the company must keep track of (1) average gross profit rate, (2) net sales at retail, (3) beginning inventory, and (4) net purchases. You can use the following steps to calculate the gross profit method:

Calculating the Gross Profit Method

Step 1. Calculate the cost of goods available for sale (Beginning inventory + Net purchases).

Step 2. Multiply the net sales at retail by the complement of the gross profit rate. This is the estimated cost of goods sold.

Step 3. Calculate the cost of estimated ending inventory (Step 1 − Step 2).

EXAMPLE Assume Radar Company has the following information in its records:

Gross profit on sales	30%
Beginning inventory, January 1, 2004	$20,000
Net purchases	8,000
Net sales at retail for January	12,000

If you use the gross profit method, what is the company's estimated inventory?

The gross profit method calculates Radar's estimated cost of ending inventory at the end of January as follows:

Goods available for sale		
Beginning inventory, January 1, 2004		$20,000
Net purchases		8,000
Cost of goods available for sale		$28,000 ← **Step 1**
Less estimated cost of goods sold:		
Net sales at retail	$12,000	
Cost percentage (100% − 30%) **Step 2** →	.70	
Estimated cost of goods sold		8,400
Estimated ending inventory, January 31, 2004		$19,600 ← **Step 3**

Note that the cost of goods available for sale less the estimated cost of goods sold gives the estimated cost of ending inventory.

Since this chapter has looked at inventory flow, let's discuss inventory turnover—a key business ratio.

Inventory Turnover

Inventory turnover is the number of times the company replaces inventory during a specific time. Companies use the following two formulas to calculate inventory turnover:

$$\text{Inventory turnover at retail} = \frac{\text{Net sales}}{\text{Average inventory at retail}}$$

$$\text{Inventory turnover at cost} = \frac{\text{Cost of goods sold}}{\text{Average inventory at cost}}$$

You should note that inventory turnover at retail is usually lower than inventory turnover at cost. This is due to theft, markdowns, spoilage, and so on. Also, retail outlets and grocery stores usually have a higher turnover, but jewelry and appliance stores have a low turnover.

Now let's use an example to calculate the inventory turnover at retail and at cost.

EXAMPLE   The following facts are for Abby Company, a local sporting goods store (rounded to the nearest hundredth):

Net sales	$32,000	Cost of goods sold	$22,000
Beginning inventory at retail	11,000	Beginning inventory at cost	7,500
Ending inventory at retail	8,900	Ending inventory at cost	5,600

With these facts, we can make the following calculations:

$$\textbf{Average inventory} = \frac{\text{Beginning inventory} + \text{Ending inventory}}{2}$$

At retail: $\dfrac{\$32,000}{\dfrac{\$11,000 + \$8,900}{2}} = \dfrac{\$32,000}{\$9,950} = \boxed{3.22}$

At cost: $\dfrac{\$22,000}{\dfrac{\$7,500 + \$5,600}{2}} = \dfrac{\$22,000}{\$6,550} = \boxed{3.36}$

What Turnover Means

Inventory is often a company's most expensive asset. The turnover of inventory can have important implications. Too much inventory results in the use of needed space, extra insurance coverage, and so on. A low inventory turnover could indicate customer dissatisfaction, too much tied-up capital, and possible product obsolescence. A high inventory turnover might mean insufficient amounts of inventory causing stockouts that may lead to future lost sales. If inventory is moving out quickly, perhaps the company's selling price is too low compared to that of its competitors.

In recent years the **just-in-time (JIT) inventory system** from Japan has been introduced in the United States. Under ideal conditions, manufacturers must have suppliers that will provide materials daily as the manufacturing company needs them, thus eliminating inventories. The companies that are using this system, however, have often not been able to completely eliminate the need to maintain some inventory.

Distribution of Overhead

In Chapter 16 we studied the cost of goods sold and operating expenses shown on the income statement. The operating expenses included **overhead expenses**—expenses that are *not* directly associated with a specific department or product but that contribute indirectly to the running of the business. Examples of such overhead expenses are rent, taxes, and insurance.

Companies must allocate their overhead expenses to the various departments in the company. The two common methods of calculating the **distribution of overhead** are by (1) floor space (square feet) or (2) sales volume.

Calculations by Floor Space

To calculate the distribution of overhead by floor space, use the steps that follow.

> **Calculating the Distribution of Overhead by Floor Space**
>
> **Step 1.** Calculate the total square feet in all departments.
> **Step 2.** Calculate the ratio for each department based on floor space.
> **Step 3.** Multiply each department's floor space ratio by the total overhead.

EXAMPLE Roy Company has three departments with the following floor space:

Department A	6,000 square feet
Department B	3,000 square feet
Department C	1,000 square feet

The accountant's job is to allocate $90,000 of overhead expenses to the three departments. To allocate this overhead by floor space:

	Floor space in square feet	Ratio
Department A	6,000	$\frac{6,000}{10,000} = 60\%$
Department B	3,000	$\frac{3,000}{10,000} = 30\%$ ← **Steps 1 and 2**
Department C	$\frac{1,000}{10,000}$ total square feet	$\frac{1,000}{10,000} = 10\%$

Department A	$.60 \times \$90,000 =$	$54,000
Department B	$.30 \times \$90,000 =$	27,000 ← **Step 3**
Department C	$.10 \times \$90,000 =$	9,000
		$90,000

Calculations by Sales

To calculate the distribution of overhead by sales, use the steps that follow.

> **Calculating the Distribution of Overhead by Sales**
>
> **Step 1.** Calculate the total sales in all departments.
> **Step 2.** Calculate the ratio for each department based on sales.
> **Step 3.** Multiply each department's sales ratio by the total overhead.

EXAMPLE Morse Company distributes its overhead expenses based on the sales of its departments. For example, last year Morse's overhead expenses were $60,000. Sales of its two departments were as follows, along with its ratio calculation.

Since Department A makes 80% of the sales, it is allocated 80% of the overhead expenses.

	Sales	**Ratio**	
Department A	$ 80,000	$\dfrac{\$80,000}{\$100,000} = .80$	$\left.\rule{0pt}{2.5em}\right]$ ← **Steps 1 and 2**
Department B	20,000	$\dfrac{\$20,000}{\$100,000} = .20$	
Total sales	$100,000		

These ratios are then multiplied by the overhead expense to be allocated.

Department A   .80 × $60,000 = $48,000
Department B   .20 × $60,000 = 12,000 ← **Step 3**
                                 $60,000

It's time to try another Practice Quiz.

LU 18–2 PRACTICE QUIZ

1. From the following facts, calculate the cost of ending inventory using the retail method (round the cost ratio to the nearest tenth percent):

January 1—inventory at cost	$ 18,000
January 1—inventory at retail	$ 58,000
Net purchases at cost	$220,000
Net purchases at retail	$376,000
Net sales at retail	$364,000

2. Given the following, calculate the estimated cost of ending inventory using the gross profit method:

Gross profit on sales	40%
Beginning inventory, January 1, 2004	$27,000
Net purchases	$ 7,500
Net sales at retail for January	$15,000

3. Calculate the inventory turnover at cost and at retail from the following (round the turnover to the nearest hundredth):

Average inventory at cost	**Average inventory at retail**	**Net sales**	**Cost of goods sold**
$10,590	$19,180	$109,890	$60,990

4. From the following, calculate the distribution of overhead to Departments A and B based on floor space.

Amount of overhead expense to be allocated	**Square footage**
$70,000	10,000 Department A
	30,000 Department B

   ✓ **SOLUTIONS**

	Cost	**Retail**
1. Beginning inventory	$ 18,000	$ 58,000
Net purchases during the month	220,000	376,000
Cost of goods available for sale	$238,000	$434,000
Less net sales for the month		364,000
Ending inventory at retail		$ 70,000
Cost ratio ($238,000 ÷ $434,000)		54.8%
Ending inventory at cost (.548 × $70,000)		$ 38,360
2. Goods available for sale		
Beginning inventory, January 1, 2004		$ 27,000
Net purchases		7,500
Cost of goods available for sale		$ 34,500

Less estimated cost of goods sold:

Net sales at retail	$ 15,000	
Cost percentage (100% − 40%)	.60	
Estimated cost of goods sold		9,000
Estimated ending inventory, January 31, 2004		$ 25,500

3. $\text{Inventory turnover at cost} = \dfrac{\text{Cost of goods sold}}{\text{Average inventory at cost}} = \dfrac{\$60,900}{\$10,590} = 5.76$

$\text{Inventory turnover at retail} = \dfrac{\text{Net sales}}{\text{Average inventory at retail}} = \dfrac{\$109,890}{\$19,180} = 5.73$

4.

		Ratio		
Department A	10,000	$\dfrac{10,000}{40,000} = .25 \times \$70,000 =$	$17,500	
Department B	$\dfrac{30,000}{40,000}$	$\dfrac{30,000}{40,000} = .75 \times \$70,000 =$	52,500	
			$70,000	

Chapter Organizer and Reference Guide

Topic	Key point, procedure, formula	Example(s) to illustrate situation
Specific identification method, p. 407	Identification could be by serial number, physical description, or coding. The flow of goods and flow of costs are the same.	<table><tr><td></td><td>**Cost per unit**</td><td>**Total cost**</td></tr><tr><td>April 1, 3 units at</td><td>$7</td><td>$21</td></tr><tr><td>May 5, 4 units at</td><td>8</td><td>32</td></tr><tr><td></td><td></td><td>$53</td></tr></table> If 1 unit from each group is left, ending inventory is: $1 \times \$7 = \$ 7$ $+ 1 \times \ 8 = \ 8$ $\$15$ <table><tr><td>Cost of goods available for sale</td><td>−</td><td>Cost of ending inventory</td><td>=</td><td>Cost of goods sold</td></tr><tr><td>$53</td><td>−</td><td>$15</td><td>=</td><td>$38</td></tr></table>
Weighted-average method, p. 408	$\text{Weighted average unit cost} = \dfrac{\text{Total cost of goods available for sale}}{\text{Total number of units available for sale}}$	<table><tr><td></td><td>**Cost per unit**</td><td>**Total cost**</td></tr><tr><td>1/XX, 4 units at</td><td>$4</td><td>$16</td></tr><tr><td>5/XX, 2 units at</td><td>5</td><td>10</td></tr><tr><td>8/XX, 3 units at</td><td>6</td><td>18</td></tr><tr><td></td><td></td><td>$44</td></tr></table> $\text{Unit cost} = \dfrac{\$44}{9} = \$4.89$ If 5 units left, cost of ending inventory is $5 \text{ units} \times \$4.89 = \$24.45$
FIFO—first-in, first-out method, p. 408	Sell old inventory first. Ending inventory is made up of last merchandise brought into store.	Using example above: 5 units left: ↓ <table><tr><td>(Last into store)</td><td>3 units at $6</td><td>$18</td></tr><tr><td></td><td>2 units at $5</td><td>10</td></tr><tr><td>Cost of ending inventory</td><td></td><td>$28</td></tr></table>
LIFO—last-in, first-out method, p. 409	Sell last inventory brought into store first. Ending inventory is made up of oldest merchandise in store.	Using weighted-average example: 5 units left: ↓ <table><tr><td>(First into store)</td><td>4 units at $4</td><td>$16</td></tr><tr><td></td><td>1 unit at $5</td><td>5</td></tr><tr><td>Cost of ending inventory</td><td></td><td>$21</td></tr></table>

(continues)

Chapter Organizer and Reference Guide (concluded)

Topic	Key point, procedure, formula	Example(s) to illustrate situation
Retail method, p. 411	Ending inventory at cost equals: $\dfrac{\text{Cost of goods available at cost}}{\text{Cost of goods available at retail}} \times$ Ending inventory at retail (This is cost ratio.)	<table><tr><td></td><td>Cost</td><td>Retail</td></tr><tr><td>Beginning inventory</td><td>$52,000</td><td>$ 83,000</td></tr><tr><td>Net purchases</td><td>28,000</td><td>37,000</td></tr><tr><td>Cost of goods available for sale</td><td>$80,000</td><td>$120,000</td></tr><tr><td>Less net sales for month</td><td></td><td>80,000</td></tr><tr><td>Ending inventory at retail</td><td></td><td>$ 40,000</td></tr></table>Cost ratio $= \dfrac{\$80,000}{\$120,000} = .67 = 67\%$ Rounded to nearest percent. Ending inventory at cost, $26,800 (.67 × $40,000)
Gross profit method, p. 412	$\begin{array}{l}\text{Beginning} \\ \text{inventory}\end{array} + \begin{array}{l}\text{Net} \\ \text{purchases}\end{array} - \begin{array}{l}\text{Estimated} \\ \text{cost of} \\ \text{goods sold}\end{array} = \begin{array}{l}\text{Estimated} \\ \text{ending} \\ \text{inventory}\end{array}$	**Goods available for sale** Beginning inventory $30,000 Net purchases 3,000 Cost of goods available for sale $33,000 Less: Estimated cost of goods sold: Net sales at retail $18,000 Cost percentage (100% − 30%) .70 Estimated cost of goods sold 12,600 Estimated ending inventory $20,400
Inventory turnover at retail and at cost, p. 413	$\dfrac{\text{Net sales}}{\begin{array}{c}\text{Average inventory} \\ \text{at retail}\end{array}}$ or $\dfrac{\text{Cost of goods sold}}{\begin{array}{c}\text{Average inventory} \\ \text{at cost}\end{array}}$	Inventory, January 1 at cost $20,000 Inventory, December 31 at cost 48,000 Cost of goods sold 62,000 At cost: $\dfrac{\$62,000}{\dfrac{\$20,000 + \$48,000}{2}} = 1.82$ (inventory turnover at cost)
Distribution of overhead, p. 414	Based on floor space or sales volume, calculate: 1. Ratios of department floor space or sales to the total. 2. Multiply ratios by total amount of overhead to be distributed.	Total overhead to be distributed, $10,000 **Floor space** Department A 6,000 sq. ft. Department B 2,000 sq. ft. 8,000 sq. ft. Ratio A $= \dfrac{6,000}{8,000} = .75$ Ratio B $= \dfrac{2,000}{8,000} = .25$ Dept. A = .75 × $10,000 = $7,500 Dept. B = .25 × $10,000 = $2,500
Key terms	Average inventory, *p. 413* Distribution of overhead, *p. 414* First-in, first-out (FIFO) method, *p. 408* Gross profit method, *p. 412* Inventory turnover, *p. 413*	Just-in-time (JIT) inventory system, *p. 414* Last-in, first-out (LIFO) method, *p. 409* Overhead expenses, *p. 414* Periodic inventory system, *p. 406* Perpetual inventory system, *p. 406* Retail method, *p. 412* Specific identification method, *p. 407* Weighted-average method, *p. 408*

**Critical Thinking
Discussion Questions**

1. Explain how you would calculate the cost of ending inventory and cost of goods sold for specific identification, FIFO, LIFO, and weighted-average methods. Explain why during inflation, LIFO results in a tax savings for a business.

2. Explain the cost ratio in the retail method of calculating inventory. What effect will the increased use of computers have on the retail method?

3. What is inventory turnover? Explain the effect of a high inventory turnover during the Christmas shopping season.

4. How is the distribution of overhead calculated by floor space or sales? Give an example of why a store in your area cut back one department to expand another. Did it work?

DRILL PROBLEMS

18–1. Using the specific identification method, calculate **(a)** the cost of ending inventory and **(b)** the cost of goods sold given the following:

Date	Units purchased	Cost per scooter	Ending inventory
July 1	50 Razor scooters	$20	6 scooters from July 1
September 1	70 Razor scooters	30	9 scooters from September 1
November 1	90 Razor scooters	35	12 scooters from November 1

From the following, **(a)** calculate the cost of ending inventory (round the average unit cost to the nearest cent) and **(b)** cost of goods sold using the weighted-average method, FIFO, and LIFO (ending inventory shows 61 units).

	Number purchased	Cost per unit	Total
January 1 inventory	40	$4	$ 160
April 1	60	7	420
June 1	50	8	400
November 1	55	9	495

18–2. Weighted average:

18–3. FIFO:

18–4. LIFO:

From the following, calculate the cost of ending inventory and cost of goods sold for LIFO, FIFO, and the weighted-average methods (make sure to first find total cost to complete the table); ending inventory is 49 units:

	Beginning inventory and purchases	Units	Unit cost	Total dollar cost
18–5.	Beginning inventory, January 1	5	$2.00	
18–6.	April 10	10	2.50	
18–7.	May 15	12	3.00	
18–8.	July 22	15	3.25	
18–9.	August 19	18	4.00	
18–10.	September 30	20	4.20	
18–11.	November 10	32	4.40	
18–12.	December 15	16	4.80	

18–13. LIFO:

> **Cost of ending inventory**   **Cost of goods sold**

18–14. FIFO:

> **Cost of ending inventory**   **Cost of goods sold**

18–15. Weighted average:

> **Cost of ending inventory**   **Cost of goods sold**

18–16. From the following, calculate the cost ratio (round to the nearest hundredth percent) and the cost of ending inventory to the nearest cent under the retail method.

Net sales at retail for year	$40,000	Purchases—cost	$14,000
Beginning inventory—cost	27,000	Purchases—retail	19,000
Beginning inventory—retail	49,000		

18–17. Complete the following (round answers to the nearest hundredth):

a. Average inventory at cost	b. Average inventory at retail	c. Net sales	d. Cost of goods sold	e. Inventory turnover at cost	f. Inventory turnover at retail
$14,000	$21,540	$70,000	$49,800		

Complete the following (assume $90,000 of overhead to be distributed):

	Square feet	Ratio	Amount of overhead allocated
18–18. Department A	10,000		
18–19. Department B	30,000		

18–20. Given the following, calculate the estimated cost of ending inventory using the gross profit method.

| Gross profit on sales | 55% | Net purchases | $ 3,900 |
| Beginning inventory | $29,000 | Net sales at retail | 17,000 |

WORD PROBLEMS

18–21. A local Footlocker store made the following wholesale purchases of new Sketches running shoes: September 1, 14
Excel   pairs at $70.00; November 5, 16 pairs at $79.50; and December 4, 9 pairs at $82.99. An inventory taken last week
indicates that 20 pairs are still in stock. Calculate the cost of ending inventory by LIFO and calculate cost of goods
sold.

18–22. Marvin Company has a beginning inventory of 12 sets of paints at a cost of $1.50 each. During the year, the store
purchased 4 sets at $1.60, 6 sets at $2.20, 6 sets at $2.50, and 10 sets at $3.00. By the end of the year, 25 sets were
sold. Calculate **(a)** the number of paint sets in stock and **(b)** the cost of ending inventory under LIFO, FIFO, and
the weighted-average method. Round to nearest cent for the weighted average.

18–23. The May 2001 issue of *Tax Adviser* reported on tax consequences using LIFO versus FIFO methods. Mountain
State Ford used the LIFO inventory method for its parts and accessories (parts) inventory. The following purchases
were made: 60 spark plugs at $.70 each, 40 spark plugs at $.73 each, 45 spark plugs at $.75 each, and 30 spark
plugs at $.80 each. A recent inventory indicated 85 spark plugs were still in stock. What would be the cost of the
ending inventory using LIFO and FIFO?

18–24. Moose Company has a beginning inventory at a cost of $77,000 and an ending inventory costing $84,000. Sales
were $302,000. Assume Moose's markup rate is 37%. Based on the selling price, what is the inventory turnover at
cost? Round to the nearest hundredth.

18–25. May's Dress Shop's inventory at cost on January 1 was $39,000. Its retail value is $59,000. During the year, May purchased additional merchandise at a cost of $195,000 with a retail value of $395,000. The net sales at retail for the year were $348,000. Could you calculate May's inventory at cost by the retail method? Round the cost ratio to the nearest whole percent.

18–26. A sneaker shop has made the following wholesale purchases of new running shoes: 11 pairs at $24, 20 pairs at $2.50, and 16 pairs at $26.50. An inventory taken last week indicates that 17 pairs are still in stock. Calculate the cost of this inventory by FIFO.

18–27. Over the past 3 years, the gross profit rate for Jini Company was 35%. Last week a fire destroyed all Jini's inventory. Using the gross profit method, estimate the cost of inventory destroyed in the fire, given the following facts that were recorded in a fireproof safe:

Beginning inventory	$ 6,000
Net purchases	64,000
Net sales at retail	49,000

CHALLENGE PROBLEMS

18–28. Sandy Wise has purchased Fonar Corporation stock over several months in 2001. In May, she purchased 300 shares at $2.39 a share. In June, she purchased 200 shares at $2.50 a share. In July, she purchased 150 shares at $2.65 a share. After selling a portion of her stock, she now has 210 shares left. **(a)** What would be the value of her remaining shares using the LIFO, FIFO, and weighted-average methods? **(b)** If she sold each share at $3.10 a share (assume no commission involved), what would be her gain under each method?

18–29. Logan Company uses a perpetual inventory system on a FIFO basis. Assuming inventory on January 1 was 800 units at $8 each, what is the cost of ending inventory at the end of October 5?

Received			Sold	
Date	**Quantity**	**Cost per unit**	**Date**	**Quantity**
Apr. 15	220	$5	Mar. 8	500
Nov. 12	1,900	9	Oct. 5	200

SUMMARY PRACTICE TEST

1. E Toy has a beginning inventory of 13 sets of paints at a cost of $1.96 each. During the year, E Toy purchased 9 sets at $2.20, 10 sets at $2.26, 15 sets at $2.95, and 16 sets at $3.40. By the end of the year, 35 sets were sold. Calculate **(a)** the number of paint sets in stock and **(b)** the cost of ending inventory under LIFO, FIFO, and weighted-average method. *(pp. 407–409)*

2. Wally Company allocates overhead expenses to all departments on the basis of floor space (square feet) occupied by each department. The total overhead expenses for a recent year were $140,000. Department A occupied 6,000 square feet; Department B, 12,000 square feet; and Department C, 8,000 square feet. What is the overhead allocated to Department C? In your calculations, round to the nearest whole percent. *(p. 414)*

3. Books.com has a beginning inventory costing $82,000 and an ending inventory costing $84,500. Sales for the year were $330,000. Assume Books.com's markup rate on selling price is 75%. Based on the selling price, what is the inventory turnover at cost? Round to the nearest hundredth. *(p. 413)*

4. Dot's Dress Shop's inventory at cost on January 1 was $70,100. Its retail value is $91,500. During the year, Dot purchased additional merchandise at a cost of $225,000 with a retail value of $328,000. The net sales at retail for the year were $301,000. Calculate Dot's inventory at cost by the retail method. Round the cost ratio to the nearest whole percent. *(p. 411)*

5. On January 1, Ryan Company had an inventory costing $80,000. During January, Ryan had net purchases of $111,500. Over recent years, Ryan's gross profit in January has averaged 40% on sales. The company's net sales in January were $188,500. Calculate the estimated cost of ending inventory using the gross profit method. *(p. 412)*

● Bed Bath & Beyond's 350 superstores also serve as warehouses—saving time, cutting distribution costs and boosting the company's profit margins.

Bed Bath & Beyond says it has met or exceeded analysts' earnings forecasts for 36 straight quarters—or every quarter since it went public. The stock, recently at $21, sells at 25 times the calendar 2002 estimate of 83 cents per share. That's high for a retailer, but the company has a lot of growth to go. Curwin says that the Bed Bath & Beyond concept can support 850 locations in the U.S., which the company already has mapped out. That could keep the stock cooking for another ten years.

Business Math Issue

Bed Bath & Beyond probably uses periodic inventory.
1. List the key points of the article and information to support your position.
2. Write a group defense of your position using math calculations to support your view.

BUSINESS MATH SCRAPBOOK
WITH INTERNET APPLICATION

Putting Your Skills to Work

Minding the Store

Kimberly-Clark Keeps Costco in Diapers, Absorbing Costs Itself

Under New System, Supplier Stocks Retailer's Shelves And Boosts Bottom Lines

Averting a Huggies Squeeze

By EMILY NELSON
And ANN ZIMMERMAN
Staff Reporters of THE WALL STREET JOURNAL

One morning, a Costco store in Los Angeles began running a little low on size-one and size-two Huggies. Crisis loomed.

So what did Costco managers do? Nothing. They didn't have to, thanks to a special arrangement with Kimberly-Clark Corp., the company that makes the diapers.

Under this deal, responsibility for replenishing stock falls on the manufacturer, not Costco. In return, the big retailer shares detailed information about individual stores' sales. So, long before babies in Los Angeles would ever notice it, diaper dearth was averted by a Kimberly-Clark data analyst working at a computer hundreds of miles away in Neenah, Wis.

"When they were doing their own ordering, they didn't have as good a grasp" of inventory, says the Kimberly-Clark data analyst, Michael Fafnis. Now, a special computer link with Costco allows Mr. Fafnis to make snap decisions about where to ship more Huggies and other Kimberly-Clark products.

Just a few years ago, the sharing of such data between a major retailer and a key supplier would have been unthinkable. But the arrangement between Costco Wholesale Corp. and Kimberly-Clark underscores a sweeping change in American retailing. Across the country, powerful retailers from Wal-Mart Stores Inc. to Target Corp. to J.C. Penney Co. are pressuring their suppliers to take a more active role in shepherding products from the factory to store shelves.

PROJECT A
Do you think this was a good marketing strategy?

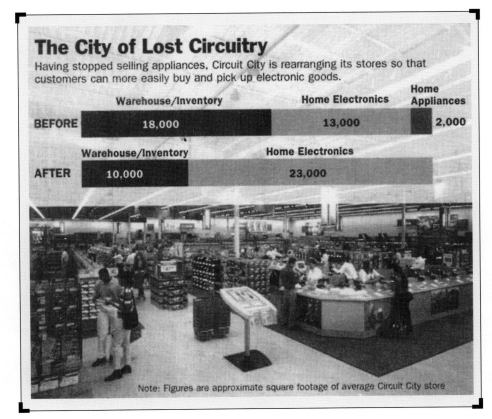

The City of Lost Circuitry

Having stopped selling appliances, Circuit City is rearranging its stores so that customers can more easily buy and pick up electronic goods.

	Warehouse/Inventory	Home Electronics	Home Appliances
BEFORE	18,000	13,000	2,000
AFTER	10,000	23,000	

Note: Figures are approximate square footage of average Circuit City store

PROJECT B
Go to the Circuit City home page on the Web to see if Circuit City has stopped selling appliances. Do you agree with this decision?

Internet Projects: See text website (www.mhhe.com/slater7e) and *The Business Math Internet Resource Guide.*

A PUMPKIN in its "natural grown state" is a "food product"; thus sales are exempt from Connecticut sales tax, the state says. But once something is "physically done" to "change its primary purpose from food to decoration," then "the pumpkin (or jack-o'-lantern) becomes taxable," the state says. Changes include "painting, carving, preserving, etc."

19

Sales, Excise, and Property Taxes

LU 19–1:   Sales and Excise Taxes

• Compute sales tax on goods sold involving trade and cash discounts and shipping charges *(pp. 428–29).*

• Explain and calculate excise tax *(p. 429).*

LU 19–2:   Property Tax

• Calculate the tax rate in decimal *(p. 430).*

• Convert tax rate in decimal to percent, per $100 of assessed value, per $1,000 of assessed value, and in mills *(p. 431).*

• Compute property tax due *(p. 431).*

Panel Focuses On Extending Web-Tax Ban

By GLENN R. SIMPSON
Staff Reporter of THE WALL STREET JOURNAL

WASHINGTON — Members of a badly divided federal commission on Internet-tax issues have begun to focus on a long-term extension of the current moratorium on new Internet taxes as one measure most of them can agree to recommend.

A multiyear moratorium is the centerpiece of a new compromise effort being floated by six companies with representatives on the commission. During the hiatus, state governments would be charged with simplifying their tax structures in exchange for enhanced power to tax interstate commerce conducted on the Web.

Several parts of the new proposal are contentious, and a number of people involved in the debate on both sides of the issue said they doubt it would be a successful compromise vehicle. Virginia Gov. James Gilmore, chairman of the commission, "has not found any consensus" favoring the compromise, spokesman Mark Miner said, "and doesn't believe that this policy represents a fixed or final position by the business leaders."

The moratorium, however, seems to have broad appeal. Advocates for the states say extending the moratorium would give states time to find ways to tax many transactions under existing law, while opponents of taxing Internet commerce are fairly content to let them try. The current moratorium expires in October 2001.

Commissioner Grover Norquist, a leader of the antitax forces, said he prefers a permanent ban on new Internet-tax measures but might settle for a three- to five-year moratorium, "because the number of Net users grows every year, and that strengthens the antitax position."

The broad outlines of the nascent compromise proposal, which is being pushed by representatives for **America Online** **Inc.**, **MCI WorldCom** Inc., **Charles Schwab** Corp., **AT&T** Corp., **Time Warner** Inc. and **Gateway** Inc., follow a proposed solution that emerged in December at a meeting of

Rachel Epstein/PhotoEdit

The above *Wall Street Journal* clipping discusses the debate occurring among the members of the federal commission on Internet tax issues as they consider how to tax Internet purchases. A multiyear moratorium on state income taxes seems to have broad appeal.

What does the greatest damage to your pocketbook, a sales tax, property tax, or state income tax? If you say "a state income tax," you are wrong. In no state does a state income tax do the greatest damage to your finances. The greatest damage is done by property taxes or sales taxes—and almost always both.

Sales tax rates vary from state to state. Four state capitals (Concord, New Hampshire; Dover, Delaware; Helena, Montana; and Salem, Oregon) do not impose a sales tax. However, if you live in California, Florida, Texas, or Washington, your combined state and local tax rate reaches 7% or more.

In Learning Unit 19–1 you will learn how sales taxes are calculated. This learning unit also discusses the excise tax that is collected in addition to the sales tax. Learning Unit 19–2 explains the use of property tax.

LEARNING UNIT 19–1 | SALES AND EXCISE TAXES

Today, many states have been raising their sales tax and excise tax. Also, states have been gradually dropping some of their sales tax exemptions. In Connecticut, a 6% sales tax was imposed on newspapers sold at newsstands but not through subscriptions. Connecticut also imposes a 6% sales tax at vending machines.

Sales Tax

In many cities, counties, and states, the sellers of certain goods and services collect **sales tax** and forward it to the appropriate government agency. Forty-five states have a sales tax. Of the 45 states, 28 states and the District of Columbia exempt food; 44 states and the District of Columbia exempt prescription drugs.

Sales taxes vary from 4% to 10.75%. Would consumers purchase more goods if they did not have to pay sales taxes? Read *The Wall Street Journal* article "New York Prepares to End Sales Tax on Clothing" in the Scrapbook (p. 437). It will be interesting to see if the end of this tax results in more sales of shoes and clothing items.

Sales taxes are usually computed electronically by the new cash register systems and scanners. However, it is important to know how sellers calculate sales tax manually. The following example of a car battery will show you how to manually calculate sales tax.

Amount of
sales tax
↓

P
($1.08)
─────────
B × R
($21.50) (.05)

$21.50 + $1.08 = $22.58
(sale)   (tax
          amount)

EXAMPLE

Selling price of a Sears battery	$32.00	Shipping charge	$3.50
Trade discount to local garage	10.50	Sales tax	5%

Manual calculation

$32.00 − $10.50 = $21.50 taxable
× .05
──────
$ 1.08 tax
+ 21.50 taxable
+ 3.50 shipping
──────
$26.08 total price with tax and shipping

Check

100% is base + 5% is tax = 105%
1.05 × $21.50 = $22.58
+ 3.50 shipping
──────
$26.08

In this example, note how the trade discount is subtracted from the selling price before any cash discounts are taken. If the buyer is entitled to a 6% cash discount, it is calculated as follows:

.06 × $21.50 = $1.29

Also, remember that we do not take cash discounts on the sales tax or shipping charges.

Calculating Actual Sales

Managers often use the cash register to get a summary of their total sales for the day. The total sales figure includes the sales tax. So the sales tax must be deducted from the total sales. To illustrate this, let's assume the total sales for the day were $40,000, which included a 7% sales tax. What were the actual sales?

Hint: $40,000 is 107% of actual sales

$$\text{Actual sales} = \frac{\text{Total sales}}{1 + \text{Tax rate}}$$

Total sales

$$\text{Actual sales} = \frac{\$40,000}{1.07} = \$37,383.18$$

100% sales
+ 7% tax
──────
107% → 1.07

Thus, the store's actual sales were $37,383.18. The actual sales plus the tax equal $40,000.

Check

$37,383.18 × .07 = $ 2,616.82 sales tax
+ 37,383.18 actual sales
──────────
$40,000.00 total sales including sales tax

Excise Tax

Governments (local, federal, and state) levy **excise tax** on particular products and services. This can be a sizable source of revenue for these governments.

Consumers pay the excise tax in addition to the sales tax. The excise tax is based on a percent of the *retail* price of a product or service. This tax, which varies in different states, is imposed on luxury items or nonessentials. Examples of products or services subject to the excise tax include airline travel, telephone service, alcoholic beverages, jewelry, furs, fishing rods, tobacco products, and motor vehicles. Although excise tax is often calculated as a percent of the selling price, the tax can be stated as a fixed amount per item sold. The following example calculates excise tax as a percent of the selling price.[1]

EXAMPLE On June 1, Angel Rowe bought a fur coat for a retail price of $5,000. Sales tax is 7% with an excise tax of 8%. Her total cost is as follows:

───────

[1]If excise tax were a stated fixed amount per item, it would have to be added to the cost of goods or services before any sales tax were taken. For example, a $100 truck tire with a $4 excise tax would be $104 before the sales tax was calculated.

$5,000
+   350 sales tax (.07 × $5,000)
+   400 excise tax (.08 × $5,000)
$5,750

Let's check your progress with a Practice Quiz.

LU 19-1 PRACTICE QUIZ

From the following shopping list, calculate the total sales tax (food items are excluded from sales tax, which is 8%):

| Chicken | $6.10 | Orange juice | $1.29 | Shampoo | $4.10 |
| Lettuce | $ .75 | Laundry detergent | $3.65 | | |

✓ **SOLUTION**

Shampoo $4.10
Laundry detergent   + 3.65
                                        $7.75 × .08 = $.62

LEARNING UNIT 19-2 | PROPERTY TAX

When you own property, you must pay property tax. In this unit we listen in on a conversation between a property owner and a tax assessor.

Defining Assessed Value

Bill Adams was concerned when he read in the local paper that the property tax rate had been increased. Bill knows that the revenue the town receives from the tax helps pay for fire and police protection, schools, and other public services. However, Bill wants to know how the town set the new rate and the amount of the new property tax.

Bill went to the town assessor's office to get specific details. The assessor is a local official who estimates the fair market value of a house. Before you read the summary of Bill's discussion, note the following formula:

Property Can Have Two Meanings

Both subject to property tax

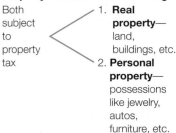

1. **Real property**— land, buildings, etc.
2. **Personal property**— possessions like jewelry, autos, furniture, etc.

Assessed value = Assessment rate × Market value

Bill: What does **assessed value** mean?

Assessor: *Assessed value* is the value of the property for purposes of computing property taxes. We estimated the market value of your home at $210,000. In our town, we assess property at 30% of the market value. Thus, your home has an assessed value of $63,000 ($210,000 × .30). Usually, assessed value is rounded to the nearest dollar.

Bill: I know that the **tax rate** multiplied by my assessed value ($63,000) determines the amount of my property tax. What I would like to know is how did you set the new tax rate?

Determining the Tax Rate

Assessor: In our town first we estimate the total amount of revenue needed to meet our budget. Then we divide the total of all assessed property into this figure to get the *tax rate*. The formula looks like this:

$$\text{Tax rate} = \frac{\text{Budget needed}}{\text{Total assessed value}[2]}$$

Our town budget is $125,000, and we have a total assessed property value of $1,930,000. Using the formula, we have the following:

$$\frac{\$125,000}{\$1,930,000} = \$.0647668 = .0648 \text{ tax rate per dollar}$$

Note that the rate should be rounded up to the indicated digit, *even if the digit is less than 5.* Here we rounded to the nearest ten thousandth.

---

[2]Remember that exemptions include land and buildings used for educational and religious purposes and the like.

How the Tax Rate Is Expressed

Assessor: We can express the .0648 tax rate per dollar in the following forms:

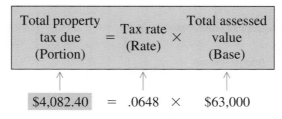

By percent	Per $100 of assessed value	Per $1,000 of assessed value	In mills
6.48% (Move decimal two places to right.)	$6.48 (.0648 × 100)	$64.80 (.0648 × 1,000)	64.80 $\left(\dfrac{.0648}{.001}\right)$

A **mill** is $\frac{1}{10}$ of a cent or $\frac{1}{1,000}$ of a dollar (.001). To represent the number of mills as a tax rate per dollar, we divide the tax rate in decimal by .001. Rounding practices vary from state to state. Colorado tax bills are now rounded to the thousandth mill. An alternative to finding the rate in mills is to multiply the rate per dollar by 1,000, since a dollar has 1,000 mills. In the problems in this text, we round the mills per dollar to nearest hundredth.

How to Calculate Property Tax Due[3]

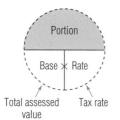

Assessor: The following formula will show you how we arrive at your **property tax:**

$$\text{Total property tax due (Portion)} = \text{Tax rate (Rate)} \times \text{Total assessed value (Base)}$$

$$\$4,082.40 = .0648 \times \$63,000$$

We can use the other forms of the decimal tax rate to show you how the property tax will not change even when expressed in various forms:

By percent	Per $100	Per $1,000	Mills
6.48% × $63,000 = $4,082.40	$\dfrac{\$63,000}{\$100} = 630$ 630 × $6.48 = $4,082.40	$\dfrac{\$63,000}{\$1,000} = 63$ 63 × $64.80 = $4,082.40	Property tax due = Mills × .001 × Assessed value = 64.80 × .001 × $63,000 = $4,082.40

Now it's time to try the Practice Quiz.

LU 19–2 PRACTICE QUIZ

From the following facts: (1) calculate assessed value of Bill's home; (2) calculate the tax rate for the community in decimal (to nearest ten thousandths); (3) convert the decimal to **(a)** %, **(b)** per $100 of assessed value, **(c)** per $1,000 of assessed value, and **(d)** in mills (to nearest hundredth); and (4) calculate the property tax due on Bill's home in decimal, per $100, per $1,000, and in mills.

Given

Assessed market value	40%	Total budget needed	$ 176,000
Market value of Bill's home	$210,000	Total assessed value	$1,910,000

✓ **SOLUTIONS**

1. .40 × $210,000 = $84,000

2. $\dfrac{\$176,000}{\$1,910,000}$ = .0922 per dollar

3. **a.** .0922 = 9.22%

   b. .0922 × 100 = $9.22

   c. .0922 × 1,000 = $92.20

   d. $\dfrac{.0922}{.001}$ = 9.20 mills (or .0922 × 1,000)

4. .0922 × $84,000 = $7,744.80

   $9.22 × 840 = $7,744.80

   $92.20 × 84 = $7,744.80

   92.20 × .001 × $84,000 = $7,744.80

---

[3]Some states have credits available to reduce what the homeowner actually pays. For example, 42 out of 50 states give tax breaks to people over age 65. In Alaska, the state's homestead exemption reduces the property tax of a $168,000 house from $1,512 to $253.

Chapter Organizer and Reference Guide

Topic	Key point, procedure, formula	Example(s) to illustrate situation
Sales tax, p. 428	Sales tax is not calculated on trade discounts. Shipping charges, etc., also are not subject to sales tax. $\text{Actual sales} = \dfrac{\text{Total sales}}{1 + \text{Tax rate}}$ Cash discounts are calculated on sale price before sales tax is added on.	Calculate sales tax: Purchased 12 bags of mulch at $59.40; 10% trade discount; 5% sales tax. $59.40 − $5.94 = $53.46 $53.46 × .05 Any cash discount would be calculated on $53.46. $2.67 sales tax

Excise tax, p. 429	Excise tax is calculated separately from sales tax and is an additional tax. It is based as a percent of the selling price. It could be stated as a fixed amount per item sold. In that case, the excise tax would be added to the cost of the item before any sales tax calculations. Rate for excise tax will vary.	Jewelry $4,000 retail price
		Sales tax 7%
		Excise tax 10%
		  $4,000
		+ 280 sales tax
		+ 400 excise tax
		  $4,680

Assessed value, p. 430	Assessment rate × Market value	$100,000 house; rate, 30%; $30,000 assessed value.
Tax rate, p. 430	$\dfrac{\text{Budget needed}}{\text{Total assessed value}} = \text{Tax rate}$ (Round rate up to indicated digit even if less than 5.)	$\dfrac{\$800,000}{\$9,200,000} = .08695 = .0870$ tax rate per $1
Expressing tax rate in other forms, p. 431	1. Percent: Move decimal two places to right. Add % sign. 2. Per $100: Multiply by 100. 3. Per $1,000: Multiply by 1,000. 4. Mills: Divide by .001.	1. .0870 = 8.7% 2. .0870 × 100 = $8.70 3. .0870 × 1,000 = $87 4. $\dfrac{.0870}{.001} = 87$ mills
Calculating property tax, p. 431	$\dfrac{\text{Total property}}{\text{tax due}} = \text{Tax rate} \times \dfrac{\text{Total assessed}}{\text{value}}$ Various forms: 1. Percent × Assessed value 2. Per $100: $\dfrac{\text{Assessed value}}{\$100} \times \text{Rate}$ 3. Per $1,000: $\dfrac{\text{Assessed value}}{\$1,000} \times \text{Rate}$ 4. Mills: Mills × .001 × Assessed value	*Example:* Rate, .0870 per $1; $30,000 assessed value 1. (.087)8.7% × $30,000 = $2,610 2. $\dfrac{\$30,000}{\$100} = 300 \times \$8.70 = \$2,610$ 3. $\dfrac{\$30,000}{\$1,000} = 30 \times \$87 = \$2,610$ 4. $\dfrac{.0870}{.001} = 87$ mills 87 mills × .001 × $30,000 = $2,610
Key terms	Assessed value, *p. 430* Personal property, *p. 430* Sales tax, *p. 428* Excise tax, *p. 429* Property tax, *p. 431* Tax rate, *p. 430* Mill, *p. 431* Real property, *p. 430*	

Critical Thinking Discussion Questions

1. Explain sales and excise taxes. Should all states have the same tax rate for sales tax?

2. Explain how to calculate actual sales when the sales tax was included in the sales figure. Is a sales tax necessary?

3. How is assessed value calculated? If you think your value is unfair, what could you do?

4. What is a mill? When we calculate property tax in mills, why do we use .001 in the calculation?

DRILL PROBLEMS

Calculate the following:

	Retail selling price	Sales tax (5%)	Excise tax (9%)	Total price including taxes
19–1.	$ 900			
19–2.	$1,500			

Calculate the actual sales since the sales and sales tax were rung up together; assume a 6% sales tax (round your answer to the nearest cent):

19–3.	$90,000	
19–4.	$26,000	

Calculate the assessed value of the following pieces of property:

	Assessment rate	Market value	Assessed value
19–5.	40%	$180,000	
19–6.	80%	$210,000	

Calculate the tax rate in decimal form to the nearest ten thousandth:

	Required budget	Total assessed value	Tax rate per dollar
19–7.	$920,000	$39,500,000	

Complete the following:

	Tax rate per dollar	In percent	Per $100	Per $1,000	Mills
19–8.	.0956				
19–9.	.0699				

Complete the amount of property tax due to the nearest cent for each situation:

	Tax rate	Assessed value	Amount of property tax due
19–10.	40 mills	$65,000	
19–11.	$42.50 per $1,000	105,000	
19–12.	$8.75 per $100	125,000	
19–13.	$94.10 per $1,000	180,500	

WORD PROBLEMS

19–14. Abby Kaminsky went to Precision Equipment and bought an $800 Stairmaster that is subject to a 5% sales tax and an 8% excise tax. What is the total amount Abby paid?

19–15. Don Chather bought a new computer for $1,995. This included a 6% sales tax. What is the amount of sales tax and the selling price before the tax?

19–16. On May 7, 2001, the *Boston Globe* reported on a proposed cigarette tax increase. If the bill becomes law, the Massachusetts tobacco excise tax would rise to $1.26 per pack. If a package of cigarettes sells for $3.00, what percent of this price is excise tax?

19–17. In the community of Revere, the market value of a home is $180,000. The assessment rate is 30%. What is the assessed value?

19–18. The January 8, 2001, issue of *Arkansas Business* reported on tax increases. The Arkansas sales and use tax rate increased from 4.625% to 5.125%. Claudia McClain recently purchased a Ford Explorer for $28,600. **(a)** What was the amount of sales tax Claudia paid? **(b)** How much would she have saved before the increase?

19–19. Lois Clark bought a ring for $6,000. She must still pay a 5% sales tax and a 10% excise tax. The jeweler is shipping the ring, so Lois must also pay a $40 shipping charge. What is the total purchase price of Lois's ring?

19–20. Blunt County needs $700,000 from property tax to meet its budget. The total value of assessed property in Blunt is $110,000,000. What is the tax rate of Blunt? Round to the nearest ten thousandth. Express the rate in mills.

19–21. Bill Shass pays a property tax of $3,200. In his community, the tax rate is 50 mills. What is Bill's assessed value?

19–22. The home of Bill Burton is assessed at $80,000. The tax rate is 18.50 mills. What is the tax on Bill's home?

19–23. On May 6, 2000, the *Daily Herald* reported on a school district losing funds on two local businesses because of proposed reduced property tax assessments. Bake Line Products is seeking to have its property reassessed from the $2.27 million, at which it's now valued, to $1.98 million. The owners of the Golf Center hope to have their property reassessed from $848,730 to $593,575. The current tax rate is .0725. How much will the district lose if both requests are granted? Round to the nearest ten thousands.

19–24. Bill Blake pays a property tax of $2,500. In his community, the tax rate is 55 mills. What is Bill's assessed value? Round to the nearest dollar.

19–25. On March 20, 2001, the *Saint Paul Pioneer Press* reported on property taxes based on square footage. A new comparative property tax study by the executive director of a Minneapolis group of landlords showed that the Wells Fargo Center in downtown Minneapolis pays four times the taxes of the Wells Fargo Center in downtown Denver. The property tax rate for Minneapolis is $8.73 per square foot, and the Denver rate is $2.14 a square foot. If 3,500 square feet is occupied at each location, what is the difference paid in property taxes?

CHALLENGE PROBLEMS

19–26. On June 15, 2001, the *Herald-Journal* reported on the property taxes of Wellford, South Carolina. The city council took the first step toward approving next year's budget, which will more than double property taxes for Wellford residents. A 40-mill tax increase will be required, taking the rate from 29 mills to 69 mills. The assessment rate is 40%. The total proposed budget for Wellford is $739,000, about 18% more than last year. **(a)** What would the owner of a $50,000 home pay in property taxes? **(b)** How much did the $50,000 homeowner pay in property taxes the previous year? **(c)** What was the amount of last year's budget to nearest dollar? **(d)** What is the total assessed value of Wellford's property this year?

19–27. Art Neuner, an investor in real estate, bought an office condominium. The market value of the condo was $250,000 with a 70% assessment rate. Art feels that his return should be 12% per month on his investment after all expenses. The tax rate is $31.50 per $1,000. Art estimates it will cost $275 per month to cover general repairs, insurance, and so on. He pays a $140 condo fee per month. All utilities and heat are the responsibility of the tenant. Calculate the monthly rent for Art. Round your answer to the nearest dollar (at intermediate stages).

SUMMARY PRACTICE TEST

1. Jay Brunner bought a new Gateway computer at Circuit City for $1,700. The price included a 5% sales tax. What are the sales tax and the selling price before the tax? *(p. 429)*

2. Shelley Katz bought a ring for $5,000 from Long's. She must pay a 5% sales tax and an 8% excise tax. Since the jeweler is shipping the ring, Jane must also pay a $15 shipping charge. What is the total purchase price of Shelley's ring? *(p. 429)*

3. The market value of a home in Portland, Oregon, is $210,000. The assessment rate is 40%. What is the assessed value? *(p. 430)*

4. Richland County needs $980,000 from its property tax to meet the budget. The total value of assessed property in Richland is $184,000,000. What is Richland's tax rate? Round to the nearest ten-thousandth. Express the rate in mills (to the nearest tenth). *(p. 430)*

5. The home of Jamie Clair is assessed at $299,000. The tax rate is 8.15 mills. What is the tax on Jamie's home? *(p. 431)*

6. BJ's Warehouse has a market value of $800,000. The property in BJ's area is assessed at 40% of the market value. The tax rate is $58.50 per $1,000 of assessed value. What is BJ's property tax? *(p. 431)*

SPENDING | With coffers bulging, states are declaring a temporary moratorium on collecting **SALES TAX** on low-priced clothing and footwear.

SHOP TILL YOU DROP

THE LATEST FAD among state legislatures wondering what to do with budget surpluses: sales-tax holidays.

By declaring a temporary moratorium on state sales taxes on certain items, politicians can score cheap points with voters yet easily return to business as usual if and when surpluses dry up. Florida, New York and Texas will repeat sales-tax holidays in 2000, and legislators in Georgia and Michigan are considering the idea. Texas comptroller Carole Keeton Rylander says taxpayers saved an estimated $32.6 million during Texas's first sales-tax holiday, which ran for three days last August.

Other states, especially those bordering states that declare holidays, may be forced to jump on the bandwagon. Vermont recently granted a permanent state sales-tax exemption for clothing priced at $110 or less, and similarly priced footwear will be exempt as of July 1, 2001. Beginning March 1, jurisdictions in neighboring New York State can decide whether they want to collect state sales tax on comparably priced shoes and clothes.

Tax-free days are generally planned for late summer or around Labor Day to coincide with back-to-school shopping. "Low- and middle-income families need help stretching their back-to-school dollars," says Michigan representative Nancy Cassis, chair of the House committee on tax policy.

TAX TAKES A HOLIDAY

States that have declared or are considering sales-tax holidays:

FLORIDA
One week in early August for clothes and shoes costing $100 or less.

MICHIGAN
Pending legislative approval, August 28 through September 11 for apparel up to $500.

NEW YORK
Week of January 15 for clothes and shoes priced under $500. Starting in March, jurisdictions can choose to ban sales taxes on clothes and shoes priced under $110.

TEXAS
First weekend in August for clothes and shoes priced under $100.

CHRISTOPHER ROBBINS

Business Math Issue

Sales tax holidays are unethical.
1. List the key points of the article and information to support your position.
2. Write a group defense of your position using math calculations to support your view.

BUSINESS MATH SCRAPBOOK
WITH INTERNET APPLICATION

Putting Your Skills to Work

New York Prepares to End Sales Tax on Clothing

ALBANY, N.Y. (AP)—Eliminating a state sales tax once seemed as unlikely in New York as pineapple on pizza, a friendly gesture from a motorist or adopting the state budget in the same season it's due.

Yet on Wednesday the state's 4% sales tax on shoes and clothing items valued at as much as $110 each will be history. It's a half-billion dollar present from Gov. George Pataki and the state legislature to New Yorkers, but some fear it's a gift that could keep on taking.

State officials had hoped county and city officials would join them by ending the local share of the tax that typically adds 3% to 4% to the purchase price. Yet just 14 of the state's 62 counties and two cities—its biggest (New York City) and its smallest (Sherrill)—are dropping their local sales taxes on the same purchases the state is.

"This is a lot more complicated than the state would lead you to believe," said Ken Crannell of the New York State Association of Counties.

A 1995 report partly funded by NYSAC concluded that eliminating sales tax doesn't spur sales nearly enough to offset the loss in tax revenue, and that even few "border counties" in New York lose many clothing sales to lower-taxing neighboring states.

"A family only has so much to spend on clothes," Mr. Crannell said. "From a political point of view, it's the greatest thing. But from an economic standpoint, what do

you get?"

The answer is already concerning some counties.

For most, there are few resources to compensate for the lost revenue—which in a small county like Tioga runs to $52,000 a year, and to $4 million a year in a bigger county like Rockland. And no studies seem to conclude that increased buying prompted by the elimination of the tax will compensate indirectly for the lost tax revenue.

At the 91-year-old Rudnick's clothing store in downtown Schenectady, the state's seven tax-free weeks since 1997 resulted in spikes in sales, but no year-end increase overall, said owner Linda Tolokonsky.

However, she said the state's permanent cut is welcomed, although she wishes Schenectady County would also drop its tax.

"It's probably one of the most positive things Gov. Pataki came in with, especially with us along the borders," she said of the $596 million consumers will save and the state loses each year. "I think we'll see a drastic difference."

Counties would most likely have to turn to property taxes to make up for the loss of sales tax, said Professor Emeritis Donald Reeb of the State University of New York at Albany and an authority on government finances. The state sales tax created during the Depression is being rescinded in the best of times and there's no telling when

the good new days will end, he said.

Under the law, counties have the option of cutting their sales taxes to conform to the state's action on a year-by-year basis.

"The governor doesn't want to dictate to the counties how to conduct their finances," said Marc Carey of the state Department of Taxation and Finance. "That's exactly why the governor wrote the legislation the way he did."

In Rockland County, on the state line with sales-tax-free New Jersey, the concern over the sales tax's effect on local property taxes is rising. The county is dropping its clothing and footwear sales taxes on purchases up to $110 starting Wednesday.

"Sales-tax growth that we've been experiencing in recent years appears to be leveling off," said Rockland County Executive C. Scott Vanderhoef. He said that trend, coupled with the revenue the county agreed to give up beginning Wednesday, "may give us a crunch . . . that is a concern."

"In a perfect world every county would want to get rid of the sales tax," said Steve Nelson, spokesman for Rensselaer County along New York's eastern border, an hour's drive from tax-free Vermont and Massachusetts. "But it isn't advisable or even possible."

PROJECT A

Do you think removing the tax will increase shoes and clothing sales in New York?

THE COMMONWEALTH OF MASSACHUSETTS
TOWN OF MARBLEHEAD   *** THIRD PAYMENT NOTICE ***
OFFICE OF THE COLLECTOR OF TAXES
FISCAL YEAR 199X REAL ESTATE TAX BILL
Based on assessments as of January 1, 199X your Real Estate Tax for the fiscal year beginning July 1, 199X and ending June 30, 199X on the parcel of real estate described below is as follows:

OFFICES AT: MARY ALLEY MUNICIPAL OFFICE BUILDING
MAIL TO: LOCKBOX 3, MARBLEHEAD, MA 01945
HOURS: WEEKDAYS 8 AM - 4:30 PM   BILL #
TAX COLLECTOR: WALTER STACKHOUSE   1673

TAX RATE	Class	Residential 1	Open Space 2	Commercial 3	Industrial 4
PER $1000.	Rate	10.94	10.94	10.94	10.94

Betterment or Lien Type	Amount	Committed Interest	Class	Description	Total Tax & Assessments	
			1	RESID.		2,908.95
					TOTAL PAID	1,369.26
					THIRD BILL AMOUNT	769.84
TOTAL ASSESSMENTS	.00			TOTAL VALUE	FOURTH BILL AMOUNT	769.85
				RESIDENTIAL EXEMPTION		
				TAXABLE VALUATION 265,900	AMOUNT NOW DUE ✓	769.84
				TOTAL TAX 2,908.95		

TOWN OF MARBLEHEAD
DEC 3 199X
COLLECTOR OF TAXES

JEFFREY SLATER
80 GARFIELD ST
MARBLEHEAD MA   01945

PAYMENTS MUST BE MADE TO THE TOWN OF MARBLEHEAD AND RECEIVED BY THE COLLECTOR BY 4:30 PM ON 2/ 1/9X

SCHOLARSHIP CONTRIBUTION

PROPERTY LOCATION	MAP	LOT	PLOT	BOOK	PAGE	CLASS	AREA	EQV.	ISSUED
80 GARFIELD ST	125	22		6985	081	101	10585		12/27/9X

INTEREST AT THE RATE OF 14% PER ANNUM WILL ACCRUE ON OVERDUE PAYMENTS FROM THE FIRST DAY THE PAYMENT IS DUE UNTIL PAYMENT IS MADE. SEE REVERSE SIDE FOR IMPORTANT INFORMATION.

PROJECT B

1. Check the total tax.
2. Check the assessed value of $265,900.
3. Check the tax rate of $10.94 per $1,000.

Internet Projects: See text website (www.mhhe.com/slater7e) and *The Business Math Internet Resource Guide.*

McDonald's Is Sued Over Its Use Of Beef Extract in French Fries

By Devon Spurgeon

Staff Reporter of The Wall Street Journal

After 11 years of touting its fries as cooked with 100% vegetable oil, **McDonald's** Corp. is conceding that the recipe also includes a very small amount of beef extract.

A consumer lawsuit filed Tuesday charges McDonald's with "fraudulently concealing the existence of beef in their french fries." The lawsuit, filed in King County Superior Court in Seattle, seeks an injunction against the use of beef tallow, which is made from the fat of cattle. McDonald's denies the existence of beef tallow in its french fries.

The plaintiffs are three vegetarians, including two Hindus who avoid meat for religious reasons. They claim they were "fraudulently induced to purchase and consume McDonald's french fries." Their suit seeks class-action status on behalf of all vegetarians who have eaten McDonald's french fries since 1990.

The french-fry category of the official McDonald's ingredient list makes no mention of beef tallow or beef extract. The top three ingredients in french fries are potatoes, partially hydrogenated soybean oil and natural flavor.

But McDonald's, Oak Brook, Ill., issued a statement Tuesday acknowledging the presence of beef flavoring in its fries. "The natural flavoring consists of a miniscule amount of beef extract," the statement said.

The lawsuit contends "a reasonable person would reasonably conclude the use of the term 'natural flavor' to mean flavors natural to the potatoes or vegetable oils in which the product is presumably cooked." McDonald's literature says its fries are cooked in hydrogenated soybean oils and corn oils.

In 1990, McDonald's made a big to-do of cooking its fries in 100% vegetable oil. The company and the plaintiffs disagree on whether that amounted to a claim that the fries were 100% vegetarian.

But the acknowledgment of the presence of beef extract could alienate vegetarians who had considered the fries to be untouched by meat.

Life, Fire, and Auto Insurance

LU 20–1: Life Insurance

- Explain the types of life insurance; calculate life insurance premiums *(pp. 440–42).*

- Explain and calculate cash value and other nonforfeiture options *(pp. 442–44).*

LU 20–2: Fire Insurance

- Explain and calculate premiums for fire insurance of buildings and their contents *(pp. 445–46).*

- Calculate refunds when the insured and the insurance company cancel fire insurance *(pp. 445–46).*

- Explain and calculate insurance loss when coinsurance is not met *(p. 446).*

LU 20–3: Auto Insurance

- Explain and calculate the cost of auto insurance *(pp. 447–50).*

It is not unusual to pay between $5,000 and $7,000 a month for nursing home care. As a result, nursing home insurance has become a big business. You can learn more about nursing home insurance and its costs by looking up websites on the Internet.

Regardless of the type of insurance you buy—nursing home, property, life, fire, or auto—be sure to read and understand the policy before you buy the insurance. It has been reported that half of the people in the United States who have property insurance have not read their policy and 60% do not understand their policy. Are you one of these statistics? If you are, this insurance chapter will help you become an informed policy reader. The chapter should answer many of your questions about life insurance, fire insurance, and auto insurance. We begin by studying life insurance.

Frank Siteman/PhotoEdit

LEARNING UNIT 20-1 | LIFE INSURANCE

Courtesy State Farm Insurance Companies.

Bob Brady owns Bob's Deli. He is 40 years of age, married, and has three children. Bob wants to know what type of life insurance protection will best meet his needs. Following is a discussion between an insurance agent, Rick Jones, and Bob.

Bob: I would like to buy a life insurance policy that will pay my wife $200,000 in the event of my death. My problem is that I do not have much cash. You know, bills, bills, bills. Can you explain some types of life insurance and their costs?

Rick: Let's begin by explaining some life insurance terminology. The **insured** is you—the **policyholder** receiving coverage. The **insurer** is the company selling the insurance policy. Your wife is the **beneficiary.** As the beneficiary, she is the person named in the policy to receive the insurance proceeds at the death of the insured (that's you, Bob). The amount stated in the policy, say, $200,000, is the **face amount** of the policy. The **premium** (determined by statisticians called *actuaries*) is the periodic payments you agree to make for the cost of the insurance policy. You can pay premiums annually, semiannually, quarterly, or monthly. The more frequent the payment, the higher the total cost due to increased paperwork, billing, and so on. Now let's look at the different types of insurance.

Types of Insurance

In this section Rick explains term insurance, straight life (ordinary life), 20-payment life, 20-year endowment, and universal life insurance.

Term Insurance

Rick: The cheapest type of life insurance is **term insurance,** but it only provides *temporary* protection. Term insurance pays the face amount to your wife (beneficiary) only if you die within the period of the insurance (1, 5, 10 years, and so on).

For example, let's say you take out a 5-year term policy. The insurance company automatically allows you to renew the policy at increased rates until age 70. A new policy called **level premium term** may be less expensive than an annual term policy since each year for, say, 50 years, the premium will be fixed.

The policy of my company lets you convert to other insurance types without a medical examination. To determine your rates under 5-year term insurance, check this table (Table 20.1). The annual premium at 40 years per $1,000 of insurance is $3.52. We use the following steps to calculate the total yearly premium.

TABLE 20.1

Life insurance rates for males (for females, subtract 3 years from the age)*

Age	Five-year term	Age	Straight life	Age	Twenty-payment life	Age	Twenty-year endowment
20	1.85	20	5.90	20	8.28	20	13.85
21	1.85	21	6.13	21	8.61	21	14.35
22	1.85	22	6.35	22	8.91	22	14.92
23	1.85	23	6.60	23	9.23	23	15.54
24	1.85	24	6.85	24	9.56	24	16.05
25	1.85	25	7.13	25	9.91	25	17.55
26	1.85	26	7.43	26	10.29	26	17.66
27	1.86	27	7.75	27	10.70	27	18.33
28	1.86	28	8.08	28	11.12	28	19.12
29	1.87	29	8.46	29	11.58	29	20.00
30	1.87	30	8.85	30	12.05	30	20.90
31	1.87	31	9.27	31	12.57	31	21.88
32	1.88	32	9.71	32	13.10	32	22.89
33	1.95	33	10.20	33	13.67	33	23.98
34	2.08	34	10.71	34	14.28	34	25.13
35	2.23	35	11.26	35	14.92	35	26.35
36	2.44	36	11.84	36	15.60	36	27.64
37	2.67	37	12.46	37	16.30	37	28.97
38	2.95	38	13.12	38	17.04	38	30.38
39	3.24	39	13.81	39	17.81	39	31.84
40	3.52	40	14.54	40	18.61	40	33.36
41	3.79	41	15.30	41	19.44	41	34.94
42	4.04	42	16.11	42	20.31	42	36.59
43	4.26	43	16.96	43	21.21	43	38.29
44	4.50	44	17.86	44	22.15	44	40.09

*Note that these tables are a sampling of age groups, premium costs, and insurance coverage that are available under 45 years of age.

Calculating Annual Life Insurance Premiums

Step 1. Look up the age of the insured and the type of insurance in Table 20.1 (for females, subtract 3 years). This gives the premium cost per $1,000.

Step 2. Divide the amount of coverage by $1,000 and multiply the answer by the premium cost per $1,000.

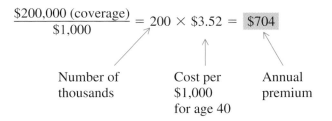

$$\frac{\$200,000 \text{ (coverage)}}{\$1,000} = 200 \times \$3.52 = \boxed{\$704}$$

Number of thousands   Cost per $1,000 for age 40   Annual premium

Airport flight insurance is a type of term insurance.

From this formula you can see that for $704 per year for the next 5 years, we, your insurance company, offer to pay your wife $200,000 in the event of your death. At the end of the 5th year, you are not entitled to any cash from your paid premiums. If you do not renew your policy (at a higher rate) and die in the 6th year, we will not pay your wife anything. Term insurance provides protection for only a specific period of time.

Bob: Are you telling me that my premium does not build up any cash savings that you call **cash value**?

Rick: The term insurance policy does not build up cash savings. Let me show you a policy that does build up cash value. This policy is straight life.

Straight Life (Ordinary Life)

Rick: Straight life insurance provides *permanent* protection rather than the temporary protection provided by term insurance. The insured pays the same premium each year or until death.[1] The premium for straight life is higher than that for term insurance

---

[1]In the following section on nonforfeiture values, we show how a policyholder in later years can stop making payments and still be covered by using the accumulated cash value built up.

because straight life provides both protection and a built-in cash savings feature. According to our table (Table 20.1, p. 441), your annual premium, Bob, would be:

Face value is usually the amount paid to the beneficiary at the time of insured's death.

$$\frac{\$200,000}{\$1,000} = 200 \times \$14.54 = \boxed{\$2,908} \text{ annual premium}$$

Bob: Compared to term, straight life is quite expensive.

Rick: Remember that term insurance has no cash value accumulating, as straight life does. Let me show you another type of insurance—20-payment life—that builds up cash value.

Twenty-Payment Life

Rick: A **20-payment life** policy is similar to straight life in that 20-payment life provides permanent protection and cash value, but you (the insured) pay premiums for only the first 20 years. After 20 years you own **paid-up insurance.** According to my table (Table 20.1), your annual premium would be:

$$\frac{\$200,000}{\$1,000} = 200 \times \$18.61 = \boxed{\$3,722} \text{ annual premium}$$

Bob: The 20-payment life policy is more expensive than straight life.

Rick: This is because you are only paying for 20 years. The shorter period of time does result in increased yearly costs. Remember that in straight life you pay premiums over your entire life. Let me show you another alternative that we call 20-year endowment.

Twenty-Year Endowment

Rick: The **20-year endowment** insurance policy is the most expensive. It is a combination of term insurance and cash value. For example, from age 40 to 60, you receive term insurance protection in that your wife would receive $200,000 should you die. At age 60, your protection *ends* and you receive the face value of the policy that equals the $200,000 cash value. Let's use my table again (Table 20.1) to see how expensive the 20-year endowment is:

$$\frac{\$200,000}{\$1,000} = 200 \times \$33.36 = \boxed{\$6,672} \text{ annual premium}$$

In summary, Bob, here is a review of the costs for the various types of insurance we have talked about:

	5-year term	Straight life	20-payment life	20-year endowment
Premium cost per year	$704	$2,908	$3,722	$6,672

Before we proceed, I have another policy that may interest you—universal life.

Universal Life Insurance

Rick: **Universal life** is basically a **whole-life** insurance plan with flexible premium schedules and death benefits. Under whole life, the premiums and death benefits are fixed. Universal has limited guarantees with greater risk on the holder of the policy. For example, if interest rates fall, the policyholder must pay higher premiums, increase the number of payments, or switch to smaller death benefits in the future.

Bob: That policy is not for me—too much risk. I'd prefer fixed premiums and death benefits.

Rick: OK, let's look at how straight life, 20-payment life, and 20-year endowment can build up cash value and provide an opportunity for insurance coverage without requiring additional premiums. We call these options **nonforfeiture values.**

Nonforfeiture Values

Rick: Except for term insurance, the other types of life insurance build up cash value as you pay premiums. These policies provide three options should you, the policyholder, ever want to cancel your policy, stop paying premiums, or collect the cash value. My company lists these options here (Figure 20.1).

For example, Bob, let's assume that at age 40 we sell you a $200,000 straight life policy. Assume that at age 55, after the policy has been in force for 15 years, you want to stop paying premiums. From this table (Table 20.2), I can show you the options that are available.

Let's assume your building has an insured value of $190,000 and is rated Class B, Area No. 2, and we insure your contents for $80,000. Then we calculate your total annual premium for building and contents as follows:

$$\text{Premium} = \frac{\text{Insured value}}{\$100} \times \text{Rate}$$

Building

$$\frac{\$190,000}{\$100} = 1,900 \times \$.50 = \$950$$

Contents

$$\frac{\$80,000}{\$100} = 800 \times \$.60 = \$480$$

Total premium = $950 + $480 = $1,430

For our purpose, we round all premiums to the nearest cent. In practice, the premium is rounded to the nearest dollar.

Canceling Fire Insurance

Alice: What if my business fails in 7 months? Do I get back any portion of my premium when I cancel?

Bob: If the insured—that's you, Alice—cancels or wants a policy for less than 1 year, we use this **short-rate table** (Table 20.4). The rates in the short-rate table will cost you more. For example, if you cancel at the end of 7 months, the premium cost is 67% of the annual premium. These rates are higher because it is more expensive to process a policy for a short time. We would calculate your refund as follows:

$$\text{Short-rate premium} = \text{Annual premium} \times \text{Short rate}$$

$$\$958.10 = \$1,430 \times .67$$

$$\text{Refund} = \text{Annual premium} - \text{Short-rate premium}$$

$$\$471.90 = \$1,430 - \$958.10$$

Alice: Let's say that I don't pay my premium or follow the fire codes. What happens if your insurance company cancels me?

Bob: If the insurance company cancels you, the company is *not* allowed to use the short-rate table. To calculate what part of the premium the company may keep,[2] you can prorate the premium based on the actual days that have elapsed. We can illustrate the amount of your refund by assuming you are canceled after 7 months:

For insurance company:

$$\text{Charge} = \$1,430 \text{ annual premium} \times \frac{7 \text{ months elapsed}}{12}$$

$$\text{Charge} = \$834.17$$

For insured:

$$\text{Refund} = \$1,430 \text{ annual premium} - \$834.17 \text{ charge}$$

$$\text{Refund} = \$595.83$$

Note that when the insurance company cancels the policy, the refund ($595.83) is greater than if the insured cancels ($471.90).

TABLE 20.4
Fire insurance short-rate and cancellation table

Time policy is in force		Percent of annual rate to be charged	Time policy is in force		Percent of annual rate to be charged
Days:	5	8%	Months:	5	52%
	10	10		6	61
	20	15		7	67
	25	17		8	74
Months:	1	19		9	81
	2	27		10	87
	3	35		11	96
	4	44		12	100

[2]Many companies use $\frac{\text{Days}}{365}$.

Coinsurance

Alice: My friend tells me that I should meet the coinsurance clause. What is coinsurance?

Bob: Usually, fire does not destroy the entire property. **Coinsurance** means that you and the insurance company *share* the risk. The reason for this coinsurance clause[3] is to encourage property owners to purchase adequate coverage.

Alice: What is adequate coverage?

Bob: In the fire insurance industry, the usual rate for coinsurance is 80% of the current replacement cost. This cost equals the value to replace what was destroyed. If your insurance coverage is 80% of the current value, the insurance company will pay all damages up to the face value of the policy.

Alice: Hold it Bob! Will you please show me how this coinsurance is figured?

Bob: Yes, Alice, I'll be happy to show you how we figure coinsurance. Let's begin by looking at the following steps so you can see what amount of the insurance the company will pay.

Calculating What Insurance Company Pays with Coinsurance Clause

Step 1.   Set up a fraction. The numerator is the actual amount of the insurance carried on the property. The denominator is the amount of insurance you should be carrying on the property to meet coinsurance (80% times the replacement value).

Step 2.   Multiply the fraction by the amount of loss (up to the face value of the policy).

Let's assume for this example that you carry $60,000 fire insurance on property that will cost $100,000 to replace. If the coinsurance clause in your policy is 80% and you suffer a loss of $20,000, your insurance company will pay the following:

Insurance coverage $\longrightarrow$ — Loss

$$\text{Step 1} \longrightarrow \frac{\$60,000}{\$80,000} \times \$20,000 = \boxed{\$15,000}\,[4]$$

What you should have carried — ($100,000 $\times$ .80)   **Step 2**

If you had had actual insurance coverage of $80,000, then the insurance company would have paid $20,000. Remember that if the coinsurance clause is met, the most an insurance company will pay is the face value of the policy.

You are now ready for the following Practice Quiz.

Although there are many types of property and homeowner's insurance policies, they usually include fire protection.

---

1.   Calculate the total annual premium of a warehouse that has an area rating of 2 with a building classification of B. The value of the warehouse is $90,000 with contents valued at $30,000.

2.   If insured cancels in Problem 1 at the end of month 9, what are the cost of the premium and the refund?

3.   Jones insures a building for $120,000 with an 80% coinsurance clause. The replacement value is $200,000. Assume a loss of $60,000 from fire. What will the insurance company pay? If the loss was $160,000 and coinsurance *was* met, what will the insurance company pay?

✓ SOLUTIONS

1. $\dfrac{\$90,000}{\$100} = 900 \times \$.50 = \$450$

$\dfrac{\$30,000}{\$100} = 300 \times \$.60 = \underline{\quad 180}$

$\boxed{\$630} \longleftarrow$ total premium

---

[3]In some states (including Wisconsin), the clause is not in effect for losses under $1,000.

[4]This kind of limited insurance payment for a loss is often called an **indemnity.**

2. $630 \times .81 =$ $510.30 \qquad 630 - 510.30 =$ $119.70

3. $\dfrac{\$120,000}{\$160,000} = \dfrac{3}{4} \times \$60,000 =$ $45,000

$\uparrow$

$(.80 \times \$200,000) \qquad \$160,000$ never more than face value

LEARNING UNIT 20–3 | AUTO INSURANCE

If you own an auto, you have had some experience purchasing auto insurance. Often, first-time auto owners do not realize that auto insurance can be a substantial expense. Also, the cost of auto insurance varies from state to state. According to statistics, the most expensive auto insurance is in New Jersey where the average annual premium was $1,094.56. Those living in Hawaii had an annual average premium of $1,078.32; in Rhode Island, the annual average premium was $1,034.46; and in Massachusetts, the annual average premium was $1,009.56. Wherever you live, you might be interested to know that the national average premium was $730.39.

Insurance rates often increase when a driver is involved in an accident. Some insurance companies give reduced rates to accident-free drivers—a practice that has encouraged drivers to be more safety conscious. For example, State Farm Insurance offers a discount to drivers who maintain a safety record. An important factor in safe driving is the use of a seat belt. Make it a habit to always put on your seat belt.

In this unit we follow Shirley as she learns about auto insurance. Shirley, who just bought a new auto, has never purchased auto insurance. So she called her insurance agent, Bob Long, who agreed to meet her for lunch. We will listen in on their conversation.

Shirley: Bob, where do I start?

Bob: Our state has two kinds of **liability insurance,** or **compulsory insurance,** that by law you must buy (regulations and requirements vary among states). Liability insurance covers any physical damages that you inflict on others or their property. You must buy liability insurance for the following:

Liability insurance includes
1. **Bodily injury**—injury or death to people in passenger car or other cars, etc.
2. **Property damage**—injury to other people's autos, trees, buildings, hydrants, etc.

1. **Bodily injury** to others: 10/20. This means that the insurance company will pay damages to people injured or killed by your auto up to $10,000 for injury to one person per accident or a total of $20,000 for injuries to two or more people per accident.

2. **Property damage** to someone else's property: 5. The insurance company will pay up to $5,000 for damages that you have caused to the property of others.

Now we leave Shirley and Bob for a few moments as we calculate Shirley's premium for compulsory insurance.

Calculating Premium for Compulsory Insurance[5]

The tables we use in this unit are for Territory 5. Other tables are available for different territories.

Insurance companies base auto insurance rates on the territory you live in, the class of driver (class 10 is experienced driver with driver training), whether auto is for business use, how much you drive the car, the age of the car, and the make of the car (symbol). Shirley lives in Territory 5 (suburbia). She is classified as 17 because she is an inexperienced operator licensed for less than 6 years. Her car is age 3 and symbol 4 (make of car). We use Table 20.5 to calculate Shirley's compulsory insurance. Note that the table rates in this unit are not representative of all areas of the country. In case of lawsuits, the minimum coverage may not be adequate. Some states add surcharges to the premium if the person has a poor driving record. The tables are designed to show how rates are calculated. From Table 20.5, we have the following:

	Bodily	$ 98
+	Property	160
		$258

Remember that the $258 premium represents minimum coverage. Assume Shirley hits two people and the courts award them $13,000 and $5,000, respectively. Shirley would be

---

[5]Some states may offer medical payment insurance (a supplement to policyholders' health and accident insurance) as well as personal injury protection against uninsured or underinsured motorists.

TABLE 20.5
Compulsory insurance (based on class of driver)

Bodily injury to others		Damage to someone else's property	
Class	10/20	Class	5M*
10	$ 55	10	$129
17	98	17	160
18	80	18	160
20	116	20	186

Explanation of 10/20 and 5

10	20	5
Maximum paid to one person per accident for bodily injury	Maximum paid for total bodily injury per accident	Maximum paid for property damage per accident

*M means thousands.

responsible for $3,000 because the insurance company would pay only up to $10,000 per person and a total of $20,000 per accident.

Although total damages of $18,000 are less than $20,000, the insurance company pays only $15,000.

$$
\begin{array}{ccc}
 & (1) & (2) \\
 & \$13,000 + \$5,000 = & \$18,000 \\
\text{Paid by insurance company} \longrightarrow & -\ 10,000 -\ \ 5,000 = & -15,000 \\
\text{Paid by Shirley} \longrightarrow & \$\ 3,000 + \$\ \ \ \ 0 = & \$\ 3,000
\end{array}
$$

We return to Shirley and Bob. Bob now shows Shirley how to calculate her optional insurance coverage. Remember that optional insurance coverages (Tables 20.6 to 20.10) are added to the costs in Table 20.5.

Calculating Optional Insurance Coverage

Bob: In our state, you can add optional bodily injury to the compulsory amount. If you finance your car, the lender may require specific amounts of optional insurance to protect its investment. I have two tables (Tables 20.6 and 20.7) here that we use to calculate the option of 250/500/50. This means that in an accident the insurance company will pay $250,000 per person, up to $500,000 per accident, and up to $50,000 for property damage.

Bob then explains the tables to Shirley. By studying the tables, you can see how insurance companies figure bodily injury and damage to someone else's property. Shirley is Class 17:

Bodily
250/500 = $228

Property
50M   = + 168

$396 premium for optional bodily injury and property damage

Note: These are additional amounts to compulsory.

TABLE 20.6
Bodily injury

Class	15/30	20/40	20/50	25/50	25/60	50/100	100/300	250/500	500/1,000
10	27	37	40	44	47	69	94	144	187
17	37	52	58	63	69	104	146	228	298
18	33	46	50	55	60	89	124	193	251
20	41	59	65	72	78	119	168	263	344

TABLE 20.7
Damage to someone else's property

Class	10M	25M	50M	100M
10	132	134	135	136
17	164	166	168	169
18	164	166	168	169
20	191	193	195	197

Collision and comprehensive are optional insurance types that pay only the insured. Note that Tables 20.8 and 20.9 are based on territory, age, and car symbol. The higher the symbol, the more expensive the car.

Shirley: Is that all I need?

Bob: No, I would recommend two more types of optional coverage: **collision** and **comprehensive.** Collision provides protection against damages to your car caused by a moving vehicle. It covers the cost of repairs less **deductibles** (amount of repair you cover first before the insurance company pays the rest) and depreciation.[6] In collision, insurance companies pay the resale or book value. So as the car gets older, after 5 or more years, it might make sense to drop the collision. The decision depends on how much risk you are willing to assume. Comprehensive covers damages resulting from theft, fire, falling objects, and so on. Now let's calculate the cost of these two types of coverage—assuming a $100 deductible for collision and a $200 deductible for comprehensive—with some more of my tables (Tables 20.8 and 20.9).

	Class	Age	Symbol	Premium	
Collision	17	3	4	$191 ($148 + $43)	Cost to reduce deductibles
Comprehensive	17	3	4	+ 56 ($52 + $4)	
				$247	

Total premium for collision and comprehensive

TABLE 20.8   Collision

Classes	Age group	Symbols 1–3 $300 ded.	Symbol 4 $300 ded.	Symbol 5 $300 ded.	Symbol 6 $300 ded.	Symbol 7 $300 ded.	Symbol 8 $300 ded.	Symbol 10 $300 ded.
10–20	1	180	180	187	194	214	264	279
	2	160	160	166	172	190	233	246
	3	148	148	154	166	183	221	233
	4	136	136	142	160	176	208	221
	5	124	124	130	154	169	196	208

These classes would use all this information.
To find the premium, use the age and symbol only.

Additional cost to reduce deductible

Class	From $300 to $200	From $300 to $100
10	13	27
17	20	43
18	16	33
20	26	55

TABLE 20.9   Comprehensive

Classes	Age group	Symbols 1–3 $300 ded.	Symbol 4 $300 ded.	Symbol 5 $300 ded.	Symbol 6 $300 ded.	Symbol 7 $300 ded.	Symbol 8 $300 ded.	Symbol 10 $300 ded.
10–25	1	61	61	65	85	123	157	211
	2	55	55	58	75	108	138	185
	3	52	52	55	73	104	131	178
	4	49	49	52	70	99	124	170
	5	47	47	49	67	94	116	163

Additional cost to reduce deductible: From $300 to $200 add $4

TABLE 20.10
Transportation and towing

Substitute transportation	$16
Towing and labor	4

---

[6]In some states, repair to glass has no deductible and many insurance companies now use a $500 deductible instead of $300.

TABLE 20.11

Worksheet for calculating Shirley's auto premium

Compulsory insurance	Limits	Deductible	Premium
Bodily injury to others	$10,000 per person $20,000 per accident	None	$ 98 (Table 20.5)
Damage to someone else's property	$5,000 per accident	None	$160 (Table 20.5)
Options			
Optional bodily injury to others	$250,000 per person $500,000 per accident	None	$228 (Table 20.6)
Optional property damage	$50,000 per accident	None	$168 (Table 20.7)
Collision	Actual cash value	$100	$191 (Table 20.8) ($148 + $43)
Comprehensive	Actual cash value	$200	$ 56 (Table 20.9) ($52 + $4)
Substitute transportation	Up to $12 per day or $300 total	None	$ 16 (Table 20.10)
Towing and labor	$25 per tow	None	$ 4 (Table 20.10)
			$921 Total premium

Shirley: Anything else?

Bob: I would also recommend that you buy towing and substitute transportation coverage. The insurance company will pay up to $25 for each tow. Under substitute transportation, the insurance company will pay you $12 a day for renting a car, up to $300 total. Again, from another table (Table 20.10), we find the additional premium for towing and substitute transportation is $20 ($16 + $4).

We leave Shirley and Bob now as we make a summary of Shirley's total auto premium in Table 20.11.

Premiums for collision, property damage, and comprehensive are not reduced by no fault.

No-Fault Insurance Some states have **no-fault insurance,** a type of auto insurance that was intended to reduce premium costs on bodily injury. With no fault, one forfeits the right to sue for *small* claims involving medical expense, loss of wages, and so on. Each person collects the bodily injury from his or her insurance company no matter who is at fault. In reality, no-fault insurance has not reduced premium costs, due to large lawsuits, fraud, and operating costs of insurance companies. Many states that were once considering no fault are no longer pursuing its adoption. Note that states with no-fault insurance require the purchase of *personal-injury protection (PIP).* The most successful no-fault law seems to be in Michigan, since it has tough restrictions on the right to sue along with unlimited medical and rehabilitation benefits.

It's time to take your final Practice Quiz in this chapter.

LU 20–3 PRACTICE QUIZ

Calculate the annual auto premium for Mel Jones who lives in Territory 5, is a driver classified 18, and has a car with age 4 and symbol 7. His state has compulsory insurance, and Mel wants to add the following options:

1. Bodily injury, 100/300.
2. Damage to someone else's property, 10M.
3. Collision, $200 deductible.
4. Comprehensive, $200 deductible.
5. Towing.

✓ SOLUTIONS

Compulsory

Bodily	$ 80	(Table 20.5)
Property	160	(Table 20.5)
Options		
Bodily	124	(Table 20.6)
Property	164	(Table 20.7)
Collision	192 ($176 + $16)	(Table 20.8)
Comprehensive	103 ($99 + $4)	(Table 20.9)
Towing	4	(Table 20.10)
Total annual premium	$827	

Chapter Organizer and Reference Guide

Topic	Key point, procedure, formula	Example(s) to illustrate situation
Life insurance, p. 440	Using Table 20.1, per $1,000: $\dfrac{\text{Coverage desired}}{\$1,000} \times \text{Rate}$ For females, subtract 3 years.	**Given** $80,000 of insurance desired; age 34; male. 1. Five-year term: $\dfrac{\$80,000}{\$1,000} = 80 \times \$2.08 \quad \boxed{\$166.40}$ 2. Straight life: $\dfrac{\$80,000}{\$1,000} = 80 \times \$10.71 = \boxed{\$856.80}$ 3. Twenty-payment life: $\dfrac{\$80,000}{\$1,000} = 80 \times \$14.28 \quad \boxed{\$1,142.40}$ 4. Twenty-year endowment: $\dfrac{\$80,000}{\$1,000} = 80 \times \$25.13 = \boxed{\$2,010.40}$
Nonforfeiture values, p. 442	**By Table 20.2** Option 1: Cash surrender value. Option 2: Reduced paid-up insurance policy continues for life at reduced face amount. Option 3: Extended term—original face policy continued for a certain period of time.	A $50,000 straight-life policy was issued to Jim Rose at age 28. At age 48 Jim wants to stop paying premiums. What are his nonforfeiture options? Option 1: $\dfrac{\$50,000}{\$1,000} = 50 \times \$265 = \boxed{\$13,250}$ Option 2: $50 \times \$550 = \boxed{\$27,500}$ Option 3: $\boxed{\text{21 years 300 days}}$
Fire insurance, p. 444	Per $100 $\text{Premium} = \dfrac{\text{Insurance value}}{\$100} \times \text{Rate}$ Rate can be for buildings or contents.	**Given** Area 3; Class B; building insured for $90,000; contents, $30,000. Building: $\dfrac{\$90,000}{\$100} = 900 \times \$.61 = \boxed{\$549}$ Contents: $\dfrac{\$30,000}{\$100} = 300 \times \$.65 = \boxed{\$195}$ Total: $\$549 + \$195 = \boxed{\$744}$
Canceling fire insurance—short-rate Table 20.4 (canceling by policyholder), p. 445	$\dfrac{\text{Short-rate}}{\text{premium}} = \dfrac{\text{Annual}}{\text{premium}} \times \dfrac{\text{Short}}{\text{rate}}$ Refund = Annual premium − Short-rate premium If insurance company cancels, do not use Table 20.4.	Annual premium is $400. Short rate is .35 (cancel end of 3 months). $\$400 \times .35 = \$140$ Refund = $\$400 - \$140 = \boxed{\$260}$
Canceling by insurance company, p. 445	$\text{Annual premium} \times \dfrac{\text{Months elapsed}}{12}$ (Refund is higher since company cancels.)	Using example above but if insurance company cancels at end of 3 months. $\$400 \times \tfrac{1}{4} = \$100$ Refund = $\$400 - \$100 = \boxed{\$300}$
Coinsurance, p. 446	Amount insurance company pays: $\dfrac{\substack{\text{Actual} \rightarrow \text{Insurance carried}\\ \text{insurance} \quad (\text{Face value})}}{\substack{\text{What coverage} \quad \text{Insurance required}\\ \text{should} \rightarrow \text{to meet coinsurance}\\ \text{have been} \quad (\text{Rate} \times \text{Replacement value})}} \times \text{Loss}$ Insurance company never pays more than the face value.	**Given** Face value, $30,000; replacement value, $50,000; coinsurance rate, 80%; loss, $10,000; insurance to meet required coinsurance, $40,000. $\dfrac{\$30,000}{\$40,000} \times \$10,000 = \boxed{\$7,500}$ paid by insurance company ($\$50,000 \times .80$)

(continues)

Chapter Organizer and Reference Guide (concluded)

Topic	Key point, procedure, formula	Example(s) to illustrate situation

Auto insurance, p. 447	**Compulsory** Required insurance.
	Optional Added to cost of compulsory.
	Bodily injury—pays for injury to person caused by insured.
	Property damage—pays for property damage (not for insured auto).
	Collision—pays for damages to insured auto.
	Comprehensive—pays for damage to insured auto for fire, theft, etc.
	Towing.
	Substitute transportation.
		Calculate the annual premium.
		Driver class 10; compulsory 10/20/5.
		Optional
		Bodily—100/300
		Property—10M
		Collision—age 3, symbol 10, $100 deductible
		Comprehensive—$300 deductible
		
		                        ($55 + $129)
		10/20/5 $184 Table 20.5
		Bodily 94 Table 20.6
		Property 132 Table 20.7
		                          ($233 + $27)
		Collision 260 Table 20.8
		Comprehensive 178 Table 20.9
		Total premium $848

Key terms	Beneficiary, *p. 440* Bodily injury, *p. 447* Cash value, *p. 441* Coinsurance, *p. 446* Collision, *p. 449* Comprehensive insurance, *p. 449* Compulsory insurance, *p. 447* Deductibles, *p. 449* Extended term insurance, *p. 443*	Face amount, *p. 440* Fire insurance, *p. 444* Indemnity, *p. 446* Insured, *p. 440* Insurer, *p. 440* Level premium term, *p. 446* Liability insurance, *p. 447* No-fault insurance, *p. 450* Nonforfeiture values, *p. 442* Paid-up insurance, *p. 442* Policyholder, *p. 440* Premium, *p. 444* Property damage, *p. 447* Reduced paid-up insurance, *p. 443* Short-rate table, *p. 445* Straight life insurance, *p. 441* Term insurance, *p. 440* 20-payment life, *p. 442* 20-year endowment, *p. 442* Universal life, *p. 442* Whole life, *p. 442*

Critical Thinking Discussion Questions

1. Compare and contrast term insurance versus whole-life insurance. At what age do you think people should take out life insurance?

2. What is meant by *nonforfeiture values?* If you take the cash value option, should it be paid in a lump sum or over a number of years?

3. How do you use a short-rate table? Explain why an insurance company gets less in premiums if it cancels a policy than if the insured cancels.

4. What is coinsurance? Do you feel that an insurance company should pay more than the face value of a policy if a catastrophe resulted?

5. Explain compulsory auto insurance, collision, and comprehensive. If your car is stolen, explain the steps you might take with your insurance company.

6. "Health insurance is not that important. It would not be worth the premiums." Please take a stand.

DRILL PROBLEMS

Calculate the annual premium for the following policies using Table 20.1 (for females subtract 3 years from the table).

	Amount of coverage (face value of policy)	Age and sex of insured	Type of insurance policy	Annual premium
20–1.	$70,000	26 F	Straight life	
20–2.	$90,000	40 M	20-payment life	
20–3.	$75,000	38 M	5-year term	
20–4.	$50,000	27 F	20-year endowment	

Calculate the following nonforfeiture options for Lee Chin, age 42, who purchased a $200,000 straight life policy. At the end of year 20, Lee stopped paying premiums.

20–5. Option 1: Cash surrender value

20–6. Option 2: Reduced paid-up insurance

20–7. Option 3: Extended term insurance

Calculate the total cost of a fire insurance premium for a building and contents given the following (round to nearest cent):

	Rating of area	Class	Building	Contents	Total premium cost
20–8.	3	B	$90,000	$40,000	

Calculate the short-rate premium and refund of the following:

	Annual premium	Canceled after	Short-rate premium	Refund
20–9.	$700	8 months by insured		
20–10.	$360	4 months by insurance company		

Complete the following:

	Replacement value of property	Amount of insurance	Kind of policy	Actual fire loss	Amount insurance company will pay
20–11.	$100,000	$60,000	80% coinsurance	$22,000	
20–12.	$60,000	$40,000	80% coinsurance	$42,000	

Calculate the annual auto insurance premium for the following:

20–13. Britney Sper, Territory 5
Class 17 operator
Compulsory, 10/20/5 _____

Optional

a. Bodily injury, 500/1,000 _____

b. Property damage, 25M _____

c. Collision, $100 deductible
Age of car is 2; symbol of car is 7 _____

d. Comprehensive, $200 deductible _____

Total annual premium _____

WORD PROBLEMS

20–14. On March 26, 2001, the *National Underwriter/Life & Health Financial Services* discussed buying term life insurance online. Online quotes from insurance firms may vary by as much as 160%, which could cost consumers hundreds of dollars each year. Based on a $100,000 policy for a 38-year-old male, annual premiums ranged from $194.00 to $371.52 a year. Using your text, what would be the annual premium?

20–15. Marc Sing, age 44, saw a Metropolitan Life Insurance advertisement stating that its $100,000 term policy costs $210 per year. Compare this to Table 20.1 in the text. How much would he save by going with Metropolitan?

20–16. Margie Rale, age 38, a well-known actress, decided to take out a limited-payment life policy. She chose this since she expects her income to decline in future years. Margie decided to take out a 20-year payment life policy with a coverage amount of $90,000. Could you advise Margie about what her annual premium will be? If she decides to stop paying premiums after 15 years, what will be her cash value?

20–17. Janette Raffa has two young children and wants to take out an additional $300,000 of 5-year term insurance. Janette is 40 years old. What will be her additional annual premium? In 3 years, what cash value will have been built up?

20–18. Roger's office building has a $320,000 value, a 2 rating, and a B building classification. The contents in the building are valued at $105,000. Could you help Roger calculate his total annual premium?

20–19. Abby Ellen's toy store is worth $400,000 and is insured for $200,000. Assume an 80% coinsurance clause and that a fire caused $190,000 damage. What is the liability of the insurance company?

20–20. The *TIAA-CREF Life Insurance Company 2001 Annual Life Insurance Review* listed the cost of term life insurance. The cost of a $50,000 policy on a 39-year-old male would be $110.75 a year, and a 39-year-old female would pay $99.50 a year. Compare the premium of TIAA-CREF with the premium in your text. **(a)** What is the difference for a male? **(b)** What is the difference for a female?

20–21. The March 26, 2001, issue of *National Underwriter/Life & Health Financial Services* reported that auto insurance quotes gathered online could vary by as much as 300% on the same risk. Variations from $947 to $1,558 were given via the Internet. A class 18 operator carries compulsory 10/20/5 insurance. He has the following optional coverage: bodily injury, 500/1,000; property damage, 50M; and collision, $200 deductible. His car is 1 year old, and the symbol of the car is 8. He has comprehensive insurance, with a $200 deductible. Using your text, what is the total annual premium?

20–22. Dan Miller insured his pizza shop for $100,000 for fire insurance at an annual rate per $100 of $.66. At the end of 11 months, Earl canceled the policy since his pizza shop went out of business. What was the cost of Earl's premium and his refund?

20–23. Warren Ford insured his real estate office with a fire insurance policy for $95,000 at a cost of $.59 per $100. Eight months later the insurance company canceled his policy because of a failure to correct a fire hazard. What did Warren have to pay for the 8 months of coverage? Round to the nearest cent.

20–24. The December 4, 2000, issue of *Time* ran an article titled "Will Your Insurance Policy Pay the Entire Cost to Rebuild Your Home? Better Check Now." Replacement costs vary by location, so it's important to make sure you have correctly estimated what it will cost to replace your home in the event of a fire. Replacement costs for the same two-story, 2,400 square feet, two-car-garage frame home are listed below.

San Francisco	$250,500
New York	245,800
Chicago	200,200
Boston	195,500

If the coinsurance clause in your policy is 80%, how much insurance must you carry in each location to be fully covered in the event of a loss?

20–25. Tina Grey bought a new Honda Civic and insured it with only 10/20/5 compulsory insurance. Driving up to her ski chalet one snowy evening, Tina hit a parked van and injured the couple inside. Tina's car had damage of $4,200, and the van she struck had damage of $5,500. After a lengthy court suit, the injured persons were awarded personal injury judgments of $16,000 and $7,900, respectively. What will the insurance company pay for this accident, and what is Tina's responsibility?

20–26. Rusty Reft, who lives in Territory 5, carries 10/20/5 compulsory liability insurance along with optional collision that has a $300 deductible. Rusty was at fault in an accident that caused $3,600 damage to the other auto and $900 damage to his own. Also, the courts awarded $15,000 and $7,000, respectively, to the two passengers in the other car for personal injuries. How much will the insurance company pay, and what is Rusty's share of the responsibility?

20–27. Marika Katz bought a new Blazer and insured it with only compulsory insurance 10/20/5. Driving up to her summer home one evening, Marika hit a parked car and injured the couple inside. Marika's car had damage of $7,500, and the car she struck had damage of $5,800. After a lengthy court suit, the couple struck were awarded personal injury judgments of $18,000 and $9,000, respectively. What will the insurance company pay for this accident, and what is Marika's responsibility?

CHALLENGE PROBLEMS

20–28. On August 6, 2000, the *Los Angeles Times* reported a change in the city of La Habra's fire-protection rating. This year's assessment for the La Habra Fire Department changed from a 2 rating to a 3. Marcia Nix owns a $225,000 building and has $35,000 in contents. The building has a B classification. **(a)** What will be the increase in premiums for the building? **(b)** What will be the increase in premiums for the contents? **(c)** What will be the total amount of premiums? **(d)** If the building had an A classification, what would be the total amount of premiums?

20–29. Bill, who understands the types of insurance that are available, is planning his life insurance needs. At this stage of his life (age 35), he has budgeted $200 a year for life insurance premiums. Could you calculate for Bill the amount of coverage that is available under straight life and for a 5-year term? Could you also show Bill that if he were to die at age 40, how much more his beneficiary would receive if he'd been covered under the 5-year term? Round to the nearest thousand.

SUMMARY PRACTICE TEST

1. Phil Kaminisky, age 39, an actor, expects his income to decline in future years. He decided to take out a 20-year payment life policy with a $90,000 coverage. What will be Phil's annual premium? If he decides to stop paying premiums after 15 years, what will be his cash value? *(pp. 441, 443)*

2. Bob Costas, age 35, bought a straight life insurance policy for $150,000. Calculate his annual premium. If after 20 years Bob no longer pays premiums, what nonforfeiture options will be available to him? *(p. 443)*

3. The property of Lee's Garage is worth $700,000. Lee has a $500,000 fire insurance policy that contains an 80% coinsurance clause. What will the insurance company pay on a fire that causes $450,000 damage? If Andy meets the coinsurance, how much will the insurance company pay? *(p. 446)*

4. Ginger Hunt insured her pizza shop with a $90,000 fire insurance policy at an $.88 annual rate per $100. At the end of 8 months, Ginger's pizza shop went out of business so she canceled the policy. What was the cost of Ginger's premium and her refund? *(p. 445)*

5. Larry Bird insured his real estate office with a $100,000 fire insurance policy at a $.78 annual rate per $100. Six months later the insurance company canceled his policy because Larry failed to correct a fire hazard. What was Larry's cost for the 6-month coverage? Round to the nearest cent. *(p. 445)*

6. Bill King, who lives in Territory 5, carries 10/20/5 compulsory liability insurance along with optional collision that has a $1,000 deductible. Bill was at fault in an accident that caused $3,800 damage to the other car and $6,100 damage to his own car. Also, the courts awarded $16,000 and $9,000, respectively, to the two passengers in the other car for personal injuries. How much does the insurance company pay, and what is Bill's share of the responsibility? *(pp. 447–50)*

INSURANCE | Adult children are buying **LONG-TERM-CARE**

POLICIES for their parents. *By Kimberly Lankford*

PROTECTING MOM

A FEW YEARS ago, Brenda Joiner of Jasper, Ga., noticed that her mother kept mentioning a nagging fear. At the time, Joiner's parents were in their early seventies, and her mother worried that at some point, she would have to go to a nursing home.

To allay her mother's fears, Joiner bought her a long-term-care insurance policy for Mother's Day two years ago. She explained that it would give her mother the freedom to pick whatever care she wanted, including care in her own home or in Joiner's.

"My mother never mentioned a nursing home again," she says.

Joiner now pays $2,710 a year for a GE Financial Assurance policy to provide her mother with $100 a day in coverage for three years. She considers it a small price to pay to put her parents at ease—and protect her own retirement plan. "Now I don't have to worry that I'd have to spend all my savings to take care of her, and she doesn't have to worry about becoming a burden," says Joiner.

Protect your savings. With the cost of nursing-home care averaging nearly $56,000 a year for a private room, according to the MetLife Mature Market Institute, the bills can quickly wipe out a retirement nest egg. Some adult children are buying long-term-care policies for their parents to protect their inheritances or their own resources from being spent on their parents' care.

Karen Dinwiddie of Alexandria, Va., decided it was well worth the money to buy a long-term-care policy for her mother, now 72, who lives in Michigan. She jumped at the chance

when her employer offered long-term care as part of its benefit plan and made it easy for employees to buy policies for their spouses and parents. Now she pays $140 a month for a policy that will provide three years' worth of coverage for her mom—who

● Karen Dinwiddie bought peace of mind with a long-term-care policy for her mother, Norma Jean Burch.

wouldn't have been able to afford the cost of the policy on her own. "It has taken a big worry off my shoulders," she says.

Dinwiddie's employer didn't offer a discount for parents, but many do—often knocking up to 15% off the cost of a policy for employees' parents and spouses, says Robert Pearson of Care-Quest, which administers group long-term-care plans. (Parents still need to provide medical records—and usually don't qualify for coverage if they are already in poor health.)

Raising the issue. Unfortunately, it can be tough to talk with your parents about long-term-care insurance, and

many people procrastinate until their parents' health becomes too bad to get a policy. "It's a simple concept, but there's a lot of emotional baggage that comes with it," says Marilee Driscoll, a consultant on long-term-care planning in Plymouth, Mass.

She knows about this from experience. Her husband, William, first broached the subject with his mother about ten years ago. "She was not quite 70 and didn't consider herself old," he says. "The idea of needing help hadn't crossed her mind—she's the one who gave the help."

But she liked the idea that the insurance could help her pay for care in her home for as long as possible. She bought a small policy, the value of which has diminished as the cost of care has skyrocketed. Four years ago, Driscoll and his four siblings bought an extra policy to fill in the gaps. Splitting the bill five ways makes it much more affordable and gives them all a sense of relief.

"We're spread all over the country, and this makes sense," he says. "It's really an important thing. If you're middle class, the cost of care can chew up all your resources and take away choices fast." **K** —*Reporter:* **COURTNEY MCGRATH**

Business Math Issue

Long-term health care is overrated.
1. List the key points of the article and information to support your position.
2. Write a group defense of your position using math calculations to support your view.

BUSINESS MATH SCRAPBOOK
WITH INTERNET APPLICATION

Putting Your Skills to Work

FULLY GUARANTEED Level Premium Term Life Insurance

Non-smoker Monthly Premiums*

Age**	$300,000 Coverage		$500,000 Coverage	
	25 Year Term	30 Year Term	25 Year Term	30 Year Term
25	$19.05	$21.40	$28.28	$32.19
30	$19.84	$22.19	$29.58	$33.50
35	$21.66	$24.80	$32.63	$37.85
40	$28.19	$33.67	$43.50	$52.64

* Monthly premiums available with SBLI's Electronic Funds Transfer.

** Age nearest birthday.

You may apply for a similar policy at the end of the term subject to underwriting and higher premiums. Coverage may be continued to age 85 at increasing yearly term rates without proof of insurability. You may obtain a buyer's guide and policy summary prior to delivery of your policy. Policy Form No. B-36.3

PROJECT A

Go to The Savings Bank Life Insurance Company of Massachusetts website at www.sbli.com and see if level premium term life insurance rates have changed.

Internet Projects: See text website (www.mhhe.com/slater7e) and *The Business Math Internet Resource Guide.*

Royal Caribbean Cruises Ltd.
More Ship Repairs to Trim Second-Quarter Earnings

For the third time in as many weeks, Royal Caribbean Cruises Ltd. warned that its second-quarter earnings would be hurt because of cancellations of cruises caused by ship repairs. An engine-room fire Saturday aboard the Nordic Empress off Bermuda forced the cancellation of sailings scheduled for June 17 and June 24. The Miami company, the second-largest in the cruise business, said the latest problems would trim three or four cents a share from its earnings. Less than two weeks ago, it warned earnings would be hurt by the cancellation of Alaska cruises on June 8 and 15 by its Celebrity Cruises ship Infinity, which would cut earnings three to four cents a share. Also this month, Celebrity canceled a 14-night European cruise on its Galaxy ship, which it said would trim its profit by four to five cents a share. Analysts had expected Royal Caribbean to post second-quarter earnings of 34 cents a share, according to Thomson Financial/First Call. At 4 p.m. in New York Stock Exchange composite trading, Royal Caribbean was down 25 cents at $19.15.

©2001 Dow Jones & Company, Inc.

21

Stocks, Bonds, and Mutual Funds

Agreement Is Made to Buy Purina Mills for $230 Million

Land O'Lakes Inc., a farmer-owned food and agricultural cooperative, said it agreed to acquire **Purina Mills** Inc., St. Louis, one of the nation's biggest makers of livestock feed, for about $230 million and the assumption of about $130 million in debt. Land O'Lakes, Arden Hills, Minn., said the deal, valued at $23 a share, adds to its dairy and beef-feed business Purina's strong horse-feed production. The deal further consolidated the animal-feed sector and ended speculation on who Purina had been in talks with. Pressed to explain why its stock jumped 75% in less than two weeks, the company in May said it was mulling a takeover offer from a suitor it refused to identify. Analysts and agriculture officials criticized Purina for taking too long to disclose the potential deal and questioned whether some investors had knowledge of the offer before it was made public. Brad Kerbs, president and chief executive of Purina, said yesterday that Land O'Lakes was the suitor the company was referring to in May. An attorney for Purina said Nasdaq is investigating trading during that stock climb.

©2001 Dow Jones & Company, Inc.

The Wall Street Journal clipping "Agreement Is Made to Buy Purina Mills for $230 Million" presents the need for strict secrecy when a company such as Purina is considering a takeover offer from an unannounced suitor. Note that in less than two weeks, Purina's stock jumped 75%. Could it be that some investors had knowledge of the proposed takeover before it was made public?

Before you become an investor, you should follow these general principles: (1) know your risk tolerance and the risk of the investments you are considering—determine whether you are a low-risk conservative investor or a high-risk speculative investor; (2) know your time frame—how soon you need your money; (3) know the liquidity of the investments you are considering—how easy it is to get your money; (4) know the return you can expect on your money—how much your money should earn; and (5) do not put "all your eggs in one basket"—diversify with a mixture of stocks, bonds, and cash equivalents. Most important, before you seek financial advice from others, go to the library, and/or the Internet and do some research so you can judge the advice you receive.

This chapter introduces you to the major types of investments—stocks, bonds, and mutual funds. These investments indicate the performance of the companies they represent and the economy of the country at home and abroad.

LEARNING UNIT 21–1 | STOCKS

We begin this unit with an introduction to the basic stock terms. Then we explain the reason why people buy stocks, newspaper stock quotations, dividends on preferred and common stocks, and return on investment.

Introduction to Basic Stock Terms

Companies sell shares of ownership in their company to raise money to finance operations, plan expansion, and so on. These ownership shares are called **stocks.** The buyers of the stock (**stockholders**) receive **stock certificates** (Figure 21.1) verifying the number of shares of stock they own.

FIGURE 21.1
Stock certificate

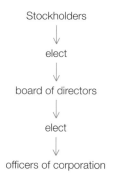

Stockholders
↓
elect
↓
board of directors
↓
elect
↓
officers of corporation

Amy Etra/PhotoEdit

If you own 50 shares of common stock, you are entitled to 50 votes in company elections. Preferred stockholders do not have this right.

The two basic types of stock are **common stock** and **preferred stock.** Common stockholders have voting rights. Preferred stockholders do not have voting rights, but they receive preference over common stockholders in **dividends** (payments from profit) and in the company's assets if the company goes bankrupt. **Cumulative preferred stock** entitles its owners to a specific amount of dividends in 1 year. Should the company fail to pay these dividends, the **dividends in arrears** accumulate. The company pays no dividends to common stockholders until the company brings the preferred dividend payments up to date.

Why Buy Stocks?

Some investors own stock because they think the stock will become more valuable, for example, if the company makes more profit, new discoveries, and the like. Other investors own stock to share in the profit distributed by the company in dividends (cash or stock).

For various reasons, investors at different times want to sell their stock or buy more stock. Strikes, inflation, or technological changes may cause some investors to think their stock will decline in value. These investors may decide to sell. Then the law of supply and demand takes over. As more people want to sell, the stock price goes down. Should more people want to buy, the stock price would go up. The following *Wall Street Journal* cartoon illustrates how people can buy or sell stock at anytime:

©2001 Dow Jones & Company, Inc.

How Are Stocks Traded?

Stock exchanges provide an orderly trading place for stock. You can think of these exchanges as an auction place. Only **stockbrokers** and their representatives are allowed to trade on the floor of the exchange. Stockbrokers charge commissions for stock trading—buying and selling stock for investors. As you might expect, in this age of the Internet, stock trades can also be made on the Internet. See the Scrapbook (p. 477) for the summary of online brokers who are trading on the Internet.

How to Read Stock Quotations in the Newspaper's Financial Section

We will use Circuit City stock to learn how to read the stock quotations found in your newspaper. Note the following newspaper listing of Circuit City stock:

YTD %CHG	52 WEEKS HI	52 WEEKS LO	STOCK (SYM)	DIV	YLD %	PE	VOL 100's	LAST	NET CHG
+ 45.0	38.69	8.69	CircCty CC	.07	.4	23	11187	16.68	+ 0.57

The highest price at which Circuit City stock traded during the past 52 weeks was $38.69 per share. This means that during the year someone was willing to pay $38.69 for a share of stock. Since January 1, the stock is up 45% (YTD).

The lowest price at which Circuit City stock traded during the year was $8.69 per share.

The newspaper lists the company name. The symbol that Circuit City uses for trading is CC. Circuit City paid $.07 per share to stock owners last year. So if you owned 100 shares, you received a **cash dividend** of $7 (100 shares × $.07).

The **stock yield** percent tells stockholders that the dividend per share is returning a rate of .4% to investors. This .4% is based on the closing price. The calculation is:

$$\text{Stock yield} = \frac{\text{Annual dividend per share}}{\text{Today's closing price per share}} = \frac{\$.07}{\$16.68} = .419\%, \text{ or } .4\%$$
(rounded to nearest tenth percent)

The .4% return may seem low to people who could earn a better return on their money elsewhere. Remember that if the stock price rises and you sell, your investment may result in a high rate of return.

The Circuit City stock is selling at $16.68; it is selling at 23 times its **earnings per share (EPS).** Earnings per share are not listed on the stock quote.

$$\text{Earnings per share} = \text{Annual earnings} \div \text{Total number of shares outstanding}$$

The **price-earnings ratio,** or **PE ratio,** measures the relationship between the closing price per share of stock and the annual earnings per share. For Circuit City we calculate the following price-earnings ratio. (Assume Circuit City earns $.73 per share. This is not listed in the newspaper.)

Round PE to the nearest whole number.

$$\text{PE ratio} = \frac{\text{Closing price per share of stock}}{\text{Annual earnings per share}} = \frac{\$16.68}{\$.73} = 23$$

If the PE ratio column shows ". . . ," this means the company has no earnings. The PE ratio will often vary depending on quality of stock, future expectations, economic conditions, and so on.

In the newspaper stock quotations for Circuit City, the number in the volume column is in 100s. Thus, to 11187, you add two zeros to get 1,118,700. This indicates that 1,118,700 shares were traded on this day. Remember that shares of stock need a buyer and a seller to trade.

The last trade of the day was at $16.68 per share.

On the *previous day,* the closing price was $16.11 (not given). The *new* close is $16.68. The result is that the closing price is up $.57 from the *previous day.*

Dividends on Preferred and Common Stocks

If you own stock in a company, the company may pay out dividends. (Not all companies pay dividends.) The amount of the dividend is determined by the net earnings of the company listed in its financial report.

Earlier we stated that cumulative preferred stockholders must be paid all past and present dividends before common stockholders can receive any dividends. Following is an example to illustrate the calculation of dividends on preferred and common stocks for 2003 and 2004.

EXAMPLE The stock records of Jason Corporation show the following:

Preferred stock issued: 20,000 shares.   In 2003, Jason paid no dividends.

Preferred stock cumulative at $.80 per share.   In 2004, Jason paid $512,000 in dividends.

Common stock issued: 400,000 shares.

Remember that common stockholders do not have the cumulative feature as preferred do.

Since Jason declared no dividends in 2003, the company has $16,000 (20,000 shares × $.80 = $16,000) dividends in arrears to preferred stockholders. The dividend of $512,000 in 2004 is divided between preferred and common stocks as follows:

	2003	**2004**
Dividends paid	0	$512,000
Preferred stockholders*	Paid: 0 Owe: Preferred, $16,000 (20,000 shares × $.80)	Paid for 2003 $ 16,000 (20,000 shares × $.80) Paid for 2004 16,000 $ 32,000
Common stockholders	0	Total dividend $512,000 Paid preferred for 2003 and 2004 − 32,000 To common $480,000 $\dfrac{\$480{,}000}{400{,}000 \text{ shares}} = \$1.20$ per share

*For a discussion of par value (arbitrary value placed on stock for accounting purposes) and cash and stock dividend distribution, check your accounting text.

Calculating Return on Investment

Now let's learn how to calculate a return on your investment of Circuit City stock, assuming the following:

> Bought 200 shares at $21.25.
> Sold at end of 1 year 200 shares at $27.50.
> 1% commission rate on buying and selling stock.
> Current $.07 dividend per share in effect.

Bought		**Sold**	
200 shares at $21.25	$4,250.00	200 shares at $27.50	$5,500.00
+ Broker's commission		− Broker's commission	
(.01 × $4,250)	+ 42.50	(.01 × $5,500)	− 55.00
Total cost	$4,292.50	Total receipt	$5,445.00

Note: A commission is charged on both the buying and selling of stock.

Total receipt	$5,445.00
Total cost	− 4,292.50
Net gain	$1,152.50
Dividends	+ 14.00 (200 shares × $.07)
Total gain	$1,166.50

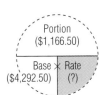

Portion $\dfrac{\$1{,}166.50}{\$4{,}292.50} =$ **27.18%** rate of return (to nearest hundredth percent)

Portion ($1,166.50)

Base × Rate
($4,292.50)   (?)

Base

It's time for another Practice Quiz.

LU 21–1 PRACTICE QUIZ

1. From the following Texaco stock quotation (**a**) explain the letters, (**b**) estimate the company's earnings per share, and (**c**) show how "YTD %" was calculated.

YTD	52 WEEKS				YLD		VOL		NET
% CHG	HI	LO	STOCK (SYM)	DIV	%	PE	100's	LAST	CHG
+ 16.3	73.90	48.25	Texaco TX	1.80	2.5	14	13020	72.25	+ 0.46
(A)	(B)	(C)	(D)	(E)	(F)	(G)	(H)	(I)	(J)

2. **Given** 30,000 shares of preferred cumulative stock at $.70 per share; 200,000 shares of common; 2003, no dividend; 2004, $109,000. How much is paid to each class of stock in 2004?

✓ **SOLUTIONS**

1. **a.** (A) Percent change since January 1.
   (B) Highest price traded in last 52 weeks.
   (C) Lowest price traded in past 52 weeks.
   (D) Name of corporation is Texaco (symbol TX).
   (E) Dividend per share per year is $1.80.
   (F) Yield for year is 2.5%.
   (G) Texaco stock sells at 14 times its earnings.
   (H) Sales volume for the day is 1,302,000 shares.
   (I) The last price (closing price for the day) is $72.25.
   (J) Stock is up $.46 from closing price yesterday.

   b. EPS $= \dfrac{\$72.25}{14} = \$5.16$ per share   **c.** $\dfrac{\$1.80}{\$72.25} = 2.5\%$

2. **Preferred:** 30,000 × $.70 = $21,000   Arrears 2003
                                 + 21,000   2004
                                 $42,000

   Common: $67,000 ($109,000 − $42,000)

LEARNING UNIT 21–2 │ BONDS

Have you heard of the Rule of 115? This rule is used as a rough measure to show how quickly an investment will triple in value. To use the rule, divide 115 by the rate of return your money earns. For example, if a bond earns 5% interest, divide 115 by 5. This measure estimates that your money in the bond will triple in 23 years.

This unit begins by explaining the difference between bonds and stocks. Then you will learn how to read bond quotations and calculate bond yields.

Reading Bond Quotations

Bond quotes are stated in percents of the face value of the bond and not in dollars as stock is. Interest is paid semiannually.

Sometimes companies raise money by selling bonds instead of stock. When you buy stock, you become a part owner in the company. To raise money, companies may not want to sell more stock and thus dilute the ownership of their current stock owners, so they sell bonds. **Bonds** represent a promise from the company to pay the face amount to the bond owner at a future date, along with interest payments at a stated rate.

Once a company issues bonds, they are traded as stock is. If a company goes bankrupt, bondholders have the first claim to the assets of the corporation—before stockholders. As with stock, changes in bond prices vary according to supply and demand. Brokers also charge commissions on bond trading. These commissions vary.

How to Read the Bond Section of the Newspaper

The bond section of the newspaper shows the bonds that are traded that day. The information given on bonds differs from the information given on stocks. The newspaper states bond prices in *percents of face amount, not in dollar amounts* as stock prices are stated. Also, bonds are usually in denominations of $1,000 (the face amount).

When a bond sells at a price below its face value, the bond is sold at a discount. Why? The interest that the bond pays may not be as high as the current market rate. When this happens, the bond is not as attractive to investors, and it sells for a **discount.** The opposite could, of course, also occur. The bond may sell at a **premium,** which means that the bond sells for more than its face value or the bond interest is higher than the current market rate.

Let's look at this newspaper information given for IBM bonds:

Bonds	Current yield	Vol.	Close	Net change
IBM 8⅜ 19	7.0	5	120½	+1

Note: Bond prices are stated as a percent of face amount.

The name of the company is IBM. It produces a wide range of computers. The interest on the bond is $8\frac{3}{8}\%$. The company pays the interest semiannually. The bond matures (comes due) in 2019. The total interest for the year is $83.75 (.08375 × $1,000). Remember that the face value of the bond is $1,000. Now let's show this with the following formula:

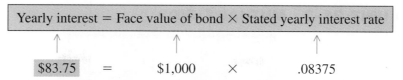

$$\boxed{\text{Yearly interest} = \text{Face value of bond} \times \text{Stated yearly interest rate}}$$

$$\$83.75 \quad = \quad \$1,000 \quad \times \quad .08375$$

We calculate the 7.0% yield by dividing the total annual interest of the bond by the total cost of the bond. (For our purposes, we will omit the commission cost.) All bond yields are rounded to the nearest tenth percent.

Note this bond is selling for more than $1,000 since its interest is very attractive compared to other new offerings.

$$\boxed{\frac{\text{Yearly interest}}{\begin{array}{c}\text{Cost of bond}\\\text{at closing}\end{array}}} = \frac{\$83.75 \ (.08375 \times \$1,000)}{\$1,205 \ (1.205 \times \$1,000)}$$

$$= 6.95\% = \boxed{7.0\%} \qquad \text{This is same as 120.5\%.}$$

Five $1,000 bonds were traded. Note that we do *not* add two zeros as we did to the sales volume of stock.

The last bond traded on this day was 120.5% of face value, or in dollars, $1,205 ($120\frac{1}{2}\% = 120.5\% = 1.205$).

The last trade of the day was up 1% of the face value from the last trade of yesterday. In dollars this is 1% = $10.

$$1\% = .01 \times \$1,000 = \$10$$

Thus, the closing price on this day, 120.5% − 1%, equals yesterday's close of 119.5% ($1,195). Note that *yesterday's close is not listed in today's quotations.*

Calculating Bond Yields

The IBM bond (selling at a premium) pays $8\frac{3}{8}\%$ interest when it is yielding investors 7%.

$$\boxed{\text{Bond yield} = \frac{\text{Total annual interest of bond}}{\text{Total current cost of bond at closing*}}}$$

*We assume this to be the buyer's purchase price.

The following example will show us how to calculate **bond yields.**

EXAMPLE   Jim Smith bought 5 bonds of IBM at the closing price of $120\frac{1}{2}$ (remember that in dollars $120\frac{1}{2}$ is $1,205). Jim's total cost excluding commission is:

$$5 \times \$1,205 = \$6,025$$

What is Jim's interest?

No matter what Jim pays for the bonds, he will still receive interest of $83.75 per bond (.08375 × $1,000). Jim bought the bonds at $1,205 each, resulting in a bond yield of 7%. Let's calculate Jim's yield to the nearest tenth percent:

The yield is 7% since Jim paid more for the bonds and still receives 8 3/8% of the face value.

$$\underset{(5 \text{ bonds} \times \$83.75 \text{ interest per bond per year})}{\frac{\$418.75}{\$6,025}} = 6.95\% = \boxed{7\%}$$

Now let's try another Practice Quiz.

LU 21–2 PRACTICE QUIZ

Bonds	Yield	Sales	Close	Net change
Aetna $6\frac{3}{8}$ 03	6.4	20	$100\frac{3}{8}$	$+\frac{7}{8}$

From the above bond quotation, **(1)** calculate the cost of 5 bonds at closing (disregard commissions) and **(2)** check the current yield of 6.4%.

✓ **SOLUTIONS**

1. $100\frac{3}{8}\% = 100.375\% = 1.00375 \times \$1,000 = \$1,003.75 \times 5 = \boxed{\$5,108.75}$
2. $6.375\% = .06375 \times \$1,000 = \$63.75$ annual interest

$$\frac{\$63.75}{\$1,003.75} = 6.35\% = \boxed{6.4\%}$$

LEARNING UNIT 21-3 | MUTUAL FUNDS

Mark Richards/PhotoEdit

In recent years, mutual funds have increased dramatically and people in the United States have invested billions in mutual funds. Investors can choose from several fund types—stock funds, bond funds, international funds, balanced (stocks and bonds) funds, and so on. This learning unit tells you why investors choose mutual funds and discusses the net asset value of mutual funds, mutual fund commissions, and how to read a mutual fund quotation.

Why Investors Choose Mutual Funds

The main reasons investors choose mutual funds are the following:

1. **Diversification.** When you invest in a mutual fund, you own a small portion of many different companies. This protects you against the poor performance of a single company but not against a sell-off in the market (stock and bond exchanges) or fluctuations in the interest rate.
2. **Professional management.** You are hiring a professional manager to look after your money when you own shares in mutual funds. The success of a particular fund is often due to the person(s) managing the fund.
3. **Liquidity.** Most funds will buy back your fund shares whenever you decide to sell.
4. **Low fund expenses.** Competition forces funds to keep their expenses low to maximize their performance. Because stocks and bonds in a mutual fund represent thousands of shareholders, funds can trade in large blocks, reducing transaction costs.
5. **Access to foreign markets.** Through mutual funds, investors can conveniently and inexpensively invest in foreign markets.

Net Asset Value

Investing in a **mutual fund** means that you buy shares in the fund's portfolio (group of stocks and/or bonds). The value of your mutual fund share is expressed in the share's **net asset value (NAV),** which is the dollar value of one mutual fund share. You calculate the NAV by subtracting the fund's current liabilities from the current market value of the fund's investments and dividing this by the number of shares outstanding.

$$NAV = \frac{\text{Current market value of fund's investments} - \text{Current liabilities}}{\text{Number of shares outstanding}}$$

The NAV helps investors track the value of their fund investment. After the market closes on each business day, the fund uses the closing prices of the investments it owns to find the dollar value of one fund share, or NAV. This is the price investors receive if they sell fund shares on that day or pay if they buy fund shares on that day.

Commissions When Buying Mutual Funds

The following table is a quick reference for the cost of buying mutual fund shares. Commissions vary from 0% to $8\frac{1}{2}$%, depending on how the mutual fund is classified.

Classification	Commission charge*	Offer price to buy
No-load (NL) fund	No sales charge	NAV (buy directly from investment company)
Low-load (LL) fund	3% or less	NAV + commission % (buy directly from investment company or from a broker)
Load fund	$8\frac{1}{2}$% or less	NAV + commission % (buy from a broker)

*On a front-end load, you pay commission when you purchase the fund shares, while on a back-end load, you pay when you redeem or sell. In general, if you hold the shares for more than 5 years, you pay no commission charge.

The offer price to buy a share for a low-load or load fund is the NAV plus the commission. Now let's look at how to read a mutual fund quotation.

How to Read a Mutual Fund Quotation

We will be studying the Putnam Mutual Funds. Cindy Joelson has invested in the Growth and Income Fund with the hope that over the years this will provide her with financial security when she retires. On May 1, Cindy turns to *The Wall Street Journal* and looks up the Putnam Growth Income Fund quotation.

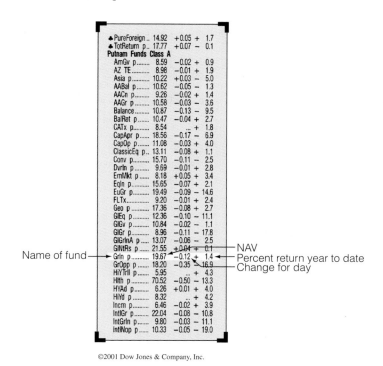

Name of fund ——→ Grln p
NAV
Percent return year to date
Change for day

The name of the fund is Growth and Income, which has the investment objective of growth and income securities as set forth in the fund's prospectus (document giving information about the fund). Note that this is only one fund in the Putnam family of funds.

- The $19.67 figure is the NAV plus the sales commission.
- The fund has lost $.12 from the NAV quotation of the previous day.
- The fund has a 1.4% return this year (January through June 11). This assumes reinvestments of all distributions. Sales charges are not reflected.

Note: In some newspapers you can see the amount a fund has returned for more than 1 year.

LU 21–3 PRACTICE QUIZ

From the mutual fund quotation of the Smith Barney Aggressive Growth Fund shown below, complete the following:

1. NAV

   _____

2. NAV change

   _____

3. Total return, YTD

   _____

✓ **SOLUTIONS**

1. 103.51
2. − 1.26
3. + 5%

Grlnc 1	15.65	−0.14 −	3.6
LgCpCo1	20.91	−0.18 −	5.3
Smith Barney A			
AdjGvA p	9.82	... +	3.3
AgGrA p	103.51	−1.26 +	5.0
ApprA p	14.93	−0.12 +	2.6
BalancA p	13.25	−0.09 −	5.2
CaMuA p	16.56	−0.01 +	1.2
DvLgCpA	16.28	−0.19 −	6.1
DvsInA p	6.85	−0.01 +	1.8
FdValA p	15.10	−0.10 +	2.7
GlGvtA p	10.43	−0.01 +	2.5
Grlnc A p	15.64	−0.13 −	3.7
GvScA	9.41	−0.02 +	1.8
HilncA t	8.04	−0.02 +	2.0
InAgGrA p	27.46	−0.31 −	21.9
InAlCpGrA p	15.32	−0.10 −	16.0
IntNYA	8.68	... +	2.3
InvGdA	11.94	−0.03 +	4.5
LgCapGA p	21.75	−0.32 −	5.1
LgCapV A p	17.62	−0.06 +	0.5
LgCpCoA p	20.80	−0.18 −	5.5
MdCpCoA p	21.13	−0.22 −	2.9

Chapter Organizer and Reference Guide

Topic	Key point, procedure, formula	Example(s) to illustrate situation
Stock yield, p. 464	$$\frac{\text{Annual dividend per share}}{\text{Today's closing price per share}}$$ (Round yield to nearest tenth percent.)	Annual dividend, $.72 Today's closing price, $42\frac{3}{8}$ $$\frac{\$.72}{\$42.375} = \boxed{1.7\%}$$
Price-earnings ratio, p. 464	$$PE = \frac{\text{Closing price per share of stock}}{\text{Annual earnings per share}}$$ (Round answer to nearest whole number.)	From example above: Closing price, $42\frac{3}{8}$ Annual earnings per share, $4.24 $$\frac{\$42.375}{\$4.24} = 9.99 = \boxed{10}$$

Dividends with cumulative preferred, p. 464	Cumulative preferred stock is entitled to all dividends in arrears before common stock receives dividend.	2003 dividend omitted; in 2004, $400,000 in dividends paid out. Preferred is cumulative at $.90 per share; 20,000 shares of preferred issued and 100,000 shares of common issued.
		To preferred:
		  20,000 shares × $.90 = $18,000
		In arrears 2003:
		  20,000 shares × .90 = <u>18,000</u>
		    Dividend to preferred <u>$36,000</u>
		To common: $364,000 ($400,000 − $36,000)
		$$\frac{\$364,000}{100,000 \text{ shares}} = \begin{array}{l}\$3.64 \text{ dividend to common}\\ \text{per share}\end{array}$$

Cost of a bond, p. 466	Bond prices are stated as a percent of the face value. Bonds selling for less than face value result in bond discounts. Bonds selling for more than face value result in bond premiums.	Bill purchases 5 $1,000, 12% bonds at closing price of $103\frac{1}{4}$. What is his cost (omitting commissions)? $103\frac{1}{4}$% = 103.25% = 1.0325 in decimal 1.0325 × $1,000 bond = $\boxed{\$1,032.50 \text{ per bond}}$ 5 bonds × $1,032.50 = $\boxed{\$5,162.50}$
Bond yield, p. 467	$$\frac{\text{Total annual interest of bond}}{\text{Total current cost of bond at closing}}$$ (Round to nearest tenth percent.)	Calculate bond yield from last example on one bond. ($1,000 × .12) $$\frac{\$120}{\$1,032.50} = \boxed{11.6\%}$$
NAV, p. 468	$$NAV = \frac{\begin{array}{l}\text{Current market value}\\ \text{of fund's investment}\end{array} - \begin{array}{l}\text{Current}\\ \text{liabilities}\end{array}}{\text{Number of shares outstanding}}$$	The NAV of the Scudder Income Bond Fund was $12.84. The NAV change was 0.01. What was the NAV yesterday? $\boxed{\$12.83}$
Key terms	Bonds, *p. 466* Bond yield, *p. 467* Cash dividend, *p. 464* Common stocks, *p. 463* Cumulative preferred stock, *p. 463* Discount, *p. 466*	Dividends, *p. 464* Dividends in arrears, *p. 463* Earnings per share (EPS), *p. 464* Mutual fund, *p. 468* Net asset value (NAV), *p. 468* PE ratio, *p. 464* Preferred stock, *p. 463* Premium, *p. 466* Price-earnings ratio, *p. 464* Stockbrokers, *p. 463* Stock certificate, *p. 462* Stockholders, *p. 462* Stocks, *p. 462* Stock yield, *p. 464*

Critical Thinking Discussion Questions

1. Explain how to read a stock quotation. What are some of the red flags of buying stock?

2. What is the difference between odd and round lots? Explain why the commission on odd lots could be quite expensive.

3. Explain how to read a bond quote. What could be a drawback of investing in bonds?

4. Compare and contrast stock yields and bond yields. As a conservative investor, which option might be better? Defend your answer.

5. Explain what NAV means. What is the difference between a load and a no-load fund? How safe are mutual funds?

END-OF-CHAPTER PROBLEMS

Name _____ Date _____

DRILL PROBLEMS

Calculate the cost (omit commission) of buying the following shares of stock:

21–1. 600 shares of America Online at $37.66.

21–2. 400 shares of eBay at $42.66.

Calculate the yield of each of the following stocks (round to the nearest tenth percent):

	Company	Yearly dividend	Closing price per share	Yield
21–3.	Boeing	$.68	$64.63	
21–4.	Circuit City	$.07	$ 9.56	

Calculate the earnings per share, price-earnings ratio (to nearest whole number), or stock price as needed:

	Company	Earnings per share	Closing price per share	Price-earnings ratio
21–5.	BellSouth	$3.15	$ 40.13	_____
21–6.	American Express	$3.85	_____	26

21–7. Calculate the total cost of buying 400 shares of CVS at $59.38. Assume a 2% commission.

21–8. If in Problem 21–1 the 600 shares of America Online stock were sold at $32.66, what would be the loss? Commission is omitted.

21–9. Given: 20,000 shares cumulative preferred stock ($2.25 dividend per share): 40,000 shares common stock. Dividends paid: 2003, $8,000; 2004, 0; and 2005, $160,000. How much will preferred and common receive each year?

For each of these bonds, calculate the total dollar amount you would pay at the quoted price (disregard commission or any interest that may have accrued):

	Company	Bond price	Number of bonds purchased	Dollar amount of purchase price
21–10.	Petro	$87\frac{3}{4}$	3	_____
21–11.	Wang	114	2	_____

For the following bonds, calculate the total annual interest, total cost, and current yield (to the nearest tenth percent):

Bond	Number of bonds purchased	Selling price	Total annual interest	Total cost	Current yield
21–12. Sharn $11\frac{3}{4}$ 09	2	115	_____	_____	_____
21–13. Wang $6\frac{1}{2}$ 07	4	$68\frac{1}{8}$	_____	_____	_____

21–14. From the following calculate the net asset values. Round to the nearest cent.

	Current market value of fund investment	Current liabilities	Number of shares outstanding	NAV
a.	$ 5,550,000	$770,000	600,000	_____
b.	$13,560,000	$780,000	840,000	_____

21–15. From the following mutual fund quotation, complete the blanks:

	Inv. obj.	NAV	NAV chg.	Total return YTD	4 wks.	1 yr.	R
EuGr	ITL	12.04	−0.06	+8.2	+0.9	+9.6	A

NAV _____   NAV change _____

Total return, 1 year _____   Rating _____

WORD PROBLEMS

21–16. Harriet Kaminsky bought 600 shares of Mattel at $12.72 per share. Assume a commission of 2% of the purchase price. What is the total cost to Harriet?

21–17. Assume in Problem 21–16 that Harriet sells the stock for $18.15 with the same 2% commission rate. What is the bottom line for Harriet?

21–18. Jim Corporation pays its cumulative preferred stockholders $1.60 per share. Jim has 30,000 shares of preferred and 75,000 shares of common. In 2003, 2004, and 2005, due to slowdowns in the economy, Jim paid no dividends. Now in 2006, the board of directors decided to pay out $500,000 in dividends. How much of the $500,000 does each class of stock receive as dividends?

21–19. Maytag Company earns $4.80 per share. Today the stock is trading at $59.25. The company pays an annual dividend of $1.40. Calculate **(a)** the price-earnings ratio (round to the nearest whole number) and **(b)** the yield on the stock (to the nearest tenth percent).

21–20. The April 30, 2001, issue of *Forbes* reported on interest earned on investment-grade corporate bonds. They yield meaningful premiums over Treasurys. This attraction, however, doesn't offset either the added risks in the heavily indebted corporate sector or, for many investors, the state income tax owed on corporate interest. Frank White has 3 corporate bonds yielding 5.5% return. Frank resides in a state with a 3% state income tax. How much tax must Frank pay to the state each year?

21–21. The following bond was quoted in *The Wall Street Journal:*

Bonds	Curr. yld.	Vol.	Close	Net chg.
NY Tel $7\frac{1}{4}$ 11	7.2	10	$100\frac{7}{8}$	$+1\frac{1}{8}$

Five bonds were purchased yesterday, and 5 bonds were purchased today. How much more did the 5 bonds cost today (in dollars)?

21–22. On April 2, 2001, *U.S. News & World Report* reported on bond interest. In 1981, when inflation and deficit spending were rampant, yields on a 10-year bond hit a record of 15.3%. Bonds this year are paying about 4.8%. On a thousand-dollar investment, what is the difference in the amount of this year's interest?

21–23. Ron bought a bond of Bee Company for $79\frac{1}{4}$. The original bond was $5\frac{3}{4}$ 08. Ron wants to know the current yield (to the nearest tenth percent). Please help Ron with the calculation.

21–24. Abby Sane decided to buy corporate bonds instead of stock. She desired to have the fixed-interest payments. She purchased 5 bonds of Meg Corporation $11\frac{3}{4}$ 09 at $88\frac{1}{4}$. As the stockbroker for Abby (assume you charge her a $5 commission per bond), please provide her with the following: **(a)** the total cost of the purchase, **(b)** total annual interest to be received, and **(c)** current yield (to nearest tenth percent).

21–25. Mary Blake is considering whether to buy stocks or bonds. She has a good understanding of the pros and cons of both. The stock she is looking at is trading at $59.25, with an annual dividend of $3.99. Meanwhile, the bond is trading at $96\frac{1}{4}$, with an annual interest rate of $11\frac{1}{2}\%$. Calculate for Mary her yield (to the nearest tenth percent) for the stock and the bond.

21–26. The June 2001 issue of *Bloomberg Personal Finance* reported the price-earnings ratios of Cisco Systems and Qualcomm. Cisco was selling at $17.58—22 times its earnings. Qualcomm was selling at $61.48 with average earnings per share of $1.46. **(a)** What are the average earnings per share for Cisco? **(b)** What is the price-earnings ratio for Qualcomm? Round to the nearest whole number.

21–27. Louis Hall read in the paper that Fidelity Growth Fund has a NAV of $16.02. He called Fidelity and asked them how the NAV was calculated. Fidelity gave him the following information:

Current market value of fund investment	$8,550,000
Current liabilities	$ 860,000
Number of shares outstanding	480,000

Did Fidelity provide Louis with the correct information?

21–28. Lee Ray bought 130 shares of a mutual fund with a NAV of $13.10. This fund also has a load charge of $8\frac{1}{2}\%$. **(a)** What is the offer price and **(b)** what did Lee pay for his investment?

21–29. Ron and Madeleine Couple received their 2001 Form 1099-DIV (dividends received) in the amount of $1,585. Ron and Madeleine are in the 28% bracket. What would be their tax liability on the dividends received?

 CHALLENGE PROBLEMS

21–30. The October 30, 2000, issue of *Business Week* reported on the investment potential of the Krispy Kreme Doughnut Corporation. When the stock became public in April 2000, it sold at $21 a share; then it shot past $103. Margie Browning, a wise investor, purchased 500 shares at $21 and sold the 500 at $103. She paid a 2% commission before and after the sale. She will have to pay a 20% capital gain. How much is Margie's tax liability?

21–31. On September 6, Irene Westing purchased one bond of Mick Corporation at $98\frac{1}{2}$. The bond pays $8\frac{3}{4}$ interest on June 1 and December 1. The stockbroker told Irene that she would have to pay the accrued interest and the market price of the bond and a $6 brokerage fee. What was the total purchase price for Irene? Assume a 360-day year (each month is 30 days) in calculating the accrued interest. (*Hint:* Final cost = Cost of bond + Accrued interest + Brokerage fee. Calculate time for accrued interest.)

SUMMARY PRACTICE TEST

1. Brenna Clark bought 400 shares of Cisco Systems stock at $36.25 per share. Assume a commission of 3% of the purchase price. What is the total cost to Brenna? *(p. 463)*

2. Hertz Company earns $3.50 per share. Today, the stock is trading at $33.81. The company pays an annual dividend of $.20. Calculate **(a)** the price-earnings ratio (to the nearest whole number), and **(b)** the yield on the stock (to the nearest tenth percent). *(p. 464)*

3. The stock of Goodyear is trading at $19.38. The price-earnings ratio is 19 times earnings. Calculate the earnings per share (to the nearest cent) for Goodyear. *(p. 464)*

4. Angel Rice bought 7 bonds of SRY Company $5\frac{3}{4}$ 03 at 92 and 5 bonds of Litte Company $6\frac{3}{4}$ 03 at 82. Assume the commission on the bonds is $3 per bond. What was the total cost of all the purchases? *(p. 466)*

5. Sue Ring bought one bond of Lane Company for 141. The original bond was $6\frac{3}{4}$ 04. Sue wants to know the current yield to the nearest tenth percent. Help Sue with the calculation. *(p. 467)*

6. Cumulative preferred stockholders of Lee Company receive $.80 per share. The company has 80,000 shares outstanding. For the last 6 years, Lee paid no dividends. This year, Lee paid $310,000 in dividends. What is the amount of dividends in arrears that is still owed to preferred stockholders? *(p. 465)*

7. Louis Short bought 700 shares of a mutual fund with a NAV of $14.22. This fund has a load charge of 3%. **(a)** What is the offer price and **(b)** what did Louis pay for the investment? *(p. 468)*

STOCKS | **KRISPY KREME**'s doughnuts have achieved cult status. Unfortunately, so have its shares. *By Brian P. Knestout*

THE SWEET SMELL OF EXCESS

FAMOUS FOR their light consistency and sweet, crackly glaze, Krispy Kreme doughnuts draw rave reviews from calorically oblivious consumers. The company receives 5,000 e-mails a month from sugar-loving fans. Krispy Kreme aficionados turn up in droves for new-store openings. Company artifacts are on display at the Smithsonian's Museum of American History (but not the original 1937 recipe, which has remained unchanged over the years and is locked in a fireproof vault at the company's Winston-Salem, N.C., dough-mixing plant).

This cultlike devotion has carried over to the stock. Since going public in April 2000 at a split-adjusted price of $10 a share, it has rocketed to $38, giving **Krispy Kreme Doughnuts** a market value of $2 billion. At that level, the stock (symbol KKD; 877-447-5736) sells at 96 times the consensus earnings estimate of 40 cents a share for the year ending next January. For would-be investors, such a rich price leaves a sour taste.

Room to grow. That's not to suggest that the case for Krispy Kreme is entirely full of holes. The company has a proven product and an enviable brand name. Sales of doughnuts, beverages and other merchandise accounted for more than two-thirds of the company's $300 million in revenues last year. Franchise fees and sales of doughnut-

processing equipment and supplies that all Krispy Kreme stores must use (including the proprietary dough mix, made only in Winston-Salem) account for the rest.

MICHEAL McLAUGHLIN

What's whetted investors' appetites most is Krispy Kreme's growth potential; including franchised shops, Krispy Kreme has only 185 stores in 30 states. So the company is expanding aggressively. It rolled out 36 new outlets in the U.S. last year, and expects to launch an additional 250 stores over the next five years. Krispy Kreme is also considering expanding overseas.

As a result, Krispy is growing much faster than either a typical food processor or restaurant chain. Earnings grew 75% last year, to 28 cents a share, and, says First Call/Thomson Financial, analysts see profits expanding 25% a year over the next three to five years.

High-caloric shares. That brings us back to the issue most likely to give investors indigestion: the share price. Krispy's price-earnings ratio is nearly four times the expected long-term growth rate. That seems excessive. Merrill Lynch's Peter Oakes questions the company's ability to keep sales at older stores growing quickly enough to justify the high price. He rates the stock a near-term sell. Analyst Ken Shea of Standard & Poor's also has a sell rating, figuring that the company is worth only $25 to $30 a share. Short sellers betting on a decline hold a staggering 44% of the company's traded shares.

One shareholder who's taken advantage of the stock's run-up is chairman and chief executive Scott Livengood. He recently sold 95,000 shares, about 5% of his holdings. If you have the good fortune of already being a shareholder, you might want to follow his lead and take some profits. If you're interested in the stock, we suggest waiting for a lower price. Meantime, have a doughnut. At 60 cents or so a pop, it's a cheaper—and tastier—way to go. **K** —*Reporter:* **DANIELLE GIOVANNELLI**

DOUGHNUTS | The hole story

3 MILLION
Number of doughnuts produced daily.

TWO
Number of times the annual production of Krispy Kreme doughnuts would circle the earth if laid end to end.

90 MILLION
Pounds of sugar used per year.

25 CENTS
Price of a dozen doughnuts in 1937, when Krispy Kreme was founded.

$4.50
Price of a dozen doughnuts in 2001.

Business Math Issue

Krispy Kreme really has no room to grow . . . the competition will react quickly.
1. List the key points of the article and information to support your position.
2. Write a group defense of your position using math calculations to support your view.

BUSINESS MATH SCRAPBOOK
WITH INTERNET APPLICATION

Putting Your Skills to Work

Online Options

How big online brokers compare in some key categories

BROKER	WEB SITE	ASSETS TO OPEN ACCOUNT [1]	WEB TRADING COMMISSION [3]	WIRELESS TRADING OFFERED?	MARKETSHARE OF ONLINE BROKERAGE ASSETS [4]
Charles Schwab	schwab.com	$5,000	$29.95 for trades up to 1,000 shares	Yes	38.5%
Fidelity Investments	fidelity.com	$2,500	$25 for up to 1,000 shares	Yes	30.6%
TD Waterhouse	tdwaterhouse.com	$1,000	$12 for up to 5,000 shares	Yes	10.5%
E*Trade	etrade.com	$1,000	$14.95 for up to 5,000 shares on New York Stock Exchange and American Stock Exchange stocks, $19.95 for Nasdaq Stock Market stocks	Yes	5.6%
Ameritrade	ameritrade.com	$2,000	$8 for unlimited shares	Yes	3.3%
DLJdirect	dljdirect.com	No initial funds required [2]	$20 for up to 1,000 shares	Yes	2.5%
Datek Online	datek.com	No initial funds required [2]	$9.99 for up to 5,000 shares	No	1.4%
National Discount Brokers	ndb.com	No initial funds required [2]	$14.75 for unlimited shares on Nasdaq stocks and up to 5,000 shares on NYSE and Amex stocks.	Yes	1.0%

[1] Assets needed to open a basic online trading account. May not reflect promotional offers. [2] Depending on the firm, funds would have to be deposited before or soon after making a trade. [3] Per-share fees usually apply past limit. Brokers also often levy special fees on limit orders, which are orders to buy or sell stock at no worse than a set price. Note that these prices are standard commissions and may not reflect discounts for active traders or special promotions. [4] As of end of the third quarter.

Sources: Chase H&Q; Company Web sites.

©2001 Dow Jones & Company, Inc.

PROJECT A
Visit the above websites today to see how the commissions have changed.

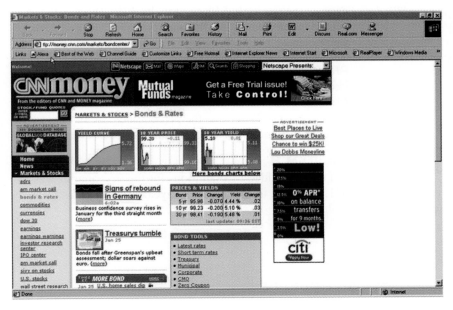

PROJECT B
Go to http://cnnfn.com/markets/bondcenter. Look up the cost and rate on a 10-year Treasury bond. Use that to calculate the yearly interest on the bond and the stated yearly interest rate.

Internet Projects: See text website (www.mhhe.com/slater7e) and *The Business Math Internet Resource Guide.*

VIDEO CASE

Federal Signal Corporation

Federal Signal Corporation began its operations in 1901. The company is a manufacturer and worldwide supplier of safety, signaling, and communications equipment; hazardous area lighting; fire rescue vehicles; vehicle-mounted aerial access platforms; and street sweeping and vacuum loader vehicles. The four major operating groups are Safety Products, Tool, Environmental Products, and Fire Rescue.

U.S. fire departments buy 3,000 to 4,000 fire trucks every year, priced from $110,000 for a small pumper to more than $600,000 for an elaborate aerial ladder. Federal Signal, a publicly held corporation, is one of the largest national players with an estimated 20% of the U.S. market, but its share of the crowded international market is still only about 20%.

While the economic downshift has hurt most manufacturers of trucks and heavy equipment, it appears to have helped Federal Signal by making available the raw materials the company needs. Four years ago, Federal Signal was struggling to

get enough chassis to manufacture a growing backlog of fire truck orders at its three North American fire truck plants. The chassis shortage pulled down profits for the company's Fire Rescue Group. Federal Signal began turning the corner on the chassis shortage, primarily because of its suppliers' bad fortune.

Now the market for big trucks is oversaturated. That's bad news for truck manufacturers but good news for Federal Signal, which is whittling down some of its backorders for fire trucks and, as a result, picking up its bottom line and stock price.

One factor that protects Federal Signal during economic downturns is municipal budgeting. Generally, municipalities have longer lead time for spending on bigger capital equipment. Since Federal Signal is not dependent on private industry for business, the future does look as bright as Federal's warning lights.

PROBLEM 1
The Fire Rescue Group is Federal Signal's biggest sales generator with revenue of $310 million, followed by the Safety Products Group with $262 million and the Environment Products Group with $247 million. What percent are the sales of the Fire Rescue Group to the total sales? Round to the nearest hundredth percent.

PROBLEM 2
With Federal Signal stock selling at $23.22, there were 58,200 shares traded in one day on the New York Stock Exchange. What was the total value of the stock traded?

PROBLEM 3
Federal Signal's current assets were as follows:

Cash and cash equivalents	$ 15,336
Trade accounts receivable	162,878
Inventories	176,892
Prepaid expenses	10,745

Current liabilities totaled $362,457. What is Federal Signal's current ratio? Round to the nearest hundredth.

PROBLEM 4
With a share price of $23.22 for Federal Signal stock: **(a)** What would be the price of 300 shares with a 2% commis-

sion? **(b)** Earnings per share (EPS) are $1.23; what would be the price-earnings (PE) ratio? Round to the nearest whole number.

PROBLEM 5
With a $23.22 closing price and an annual dividend of $.78, what would be Federal Signal's dividend yield? Round to the nearest hundredth percent.

PROBLEM 6
Federal Signal has a quarterly EPS of $.26. The company expects the quarterly EPS to grow by 14%. What is the expected dollar amount for the quarterly EPS? Round to the nearest cent.

PROBLEM 7
Federal Signal's interest expense increased to $7.8 million from $7.0 million, largely as a result of increased financial services assets. What was the percent increase in interest expense? Round to the nearest hundredth percent.

PROBLEM 8
Net cash provided by operations for the first quarter was $21.9 million, up 30% from last year. What was last year's cash flow?

Behind the Music

MCA Spent Millions On Carly Hennessy— Haven't Heard of Her?

Pop Hopeful's Washout Is All-Too-Familiar Tune; Album Sells 378 Copies

Limo Rides, Dinner at Spago

By Jennifer Ordoñez
Staff Reporter of The Wall Street Journal

MARINA DEL REY, Calif.—Eighteen-year-old recording artist Carly Hennessy is packing up her small apartment. Her promotional posters will go into storage, and the beige rental couch will be returned. A weight-control message that the slender teen scrawled in marker on the refrigerator—"NO, U R FAT"—will be wiped clean.

For two years, Vivendi Universal SA's MCA Records paid the rent here while Ms. Hennessy prepared for pop stardom. And that's not all: the label so far has spent about $2.2 million to make and market her new album, an upbeat pop recording called "Ultimate High." "Some people just struggle," she says. "I was very, very lucky."

Not lucky enough. "Ultimate High" was released in stores nationwide three months ago. So far, it has sold only 378 copies—amounting to about $4,900 at its suggested retail price.

In many other industries, this would be considered an extraordinary bomb. But in today's troubled music business, it's routine. Of the thousands of albums released in the U.S. each year by the five major record companies, fewer than 5% become profitable, music executives say.

Business Statistics

Michael Newman/PhotoEdit

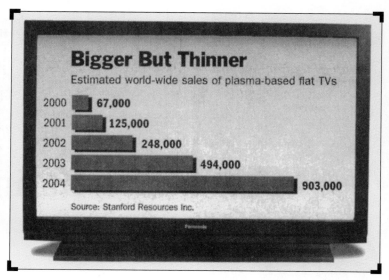

©2000 Dow Jones & Company, Inc.

Business statistics can be important in predicting future sales. Note how *The Wall Street Journal* clipping "Bigger But Thinner" predicts the increased sales of plasma-based flat TVs in the future. TV dealers could use this prediction to guide them in determining the amount of plasma-based flat TVs they should stock for future customers.

In this chapter we look at various techniques that analyze and graphically represent business statistics. Learning Unit 22–1 discusses the mean, median, and mode. Learning Unit 22–2 explains how to gather data by using frequency distributions and to express these data visually in graphs. Emphasis is placed on whether graphs are indeed giving accurate information. The chapter concludes with an introduction to index numbers—an application of statistics—and an optional learning unit on measures of dispersion.

LEARNING UNIT 22–1 │ MEAN, MEDIAN, AND MODE

Companies frequently use averages and measurements to guide their business decisions. The mean and median are the two most common averages used to indicate a single value that represents an entire group of numbers. The mode can also be used to describe a set of data.

Mean

The accountant of Bill's Sport Shop told Bill, the owner, that the average daily sales for the week were $150.14. The accountant stressed that $150.14 was an average and did not represent specific daily sales. Bill wanted to know how the accountant arrived at $150.14.

The accountant went on to explain that he used an arithmetic average, or **mean** (a measurement), to arrive at $150.14 (rounded to the nearest hundredth). He showed Bill the following formula:

$$\text{Mean} = \frac{\text{Sum of all values}}{\text{Number of values}}$$

The accountant used the following data:

	Sun.	Mon.	Tues.	Wed.	Thur.	Fri.	Sat.
Sport Shop sales	$400	$100	$68	$115	$120	$68	$180

To compute the mean, the accountant used these data:

$$\text{Mean} = \frac{\$400 + \$100 + \$68 + \$115 + \$120 + \$68 + \$180}{7} = \boxed{\$150.14}$$

When values appear more than once, businesses often look for a **weighted mean.** The format for the weighted mean is slightly different from that for the mean. The concept, however, is the same except that you weight each value by how often it occurs (its frequency). Thus, considering the frequency of the occurrence of each value allows a weighting of each day's sales in proper importance. To calculate the weighted mean, use the following formula:

$$\text{Weighted mean} = \frac{\text{Sum of products}}{\text{Sum of frequencies}}$$

Let's change the sales data for Bill's Sport Shop and see how to calculate a weighted mean:

	Sun.	Mon.	Tues.	Wed.	Thur.	Fri.	Sat.
Sport Shop sales	$400	$100	$100	$80	$80	$100	$400

Value	Frequency	Product
$400	2	$ 800
100	3	300
80	2	160
		$1,260

The weighted mean is $\dfrac{\$1,260}{7} = \boxed{\$180}$

Note how we multiply each value by its frequency of occurrence to arrive at the product. Then we divide the sum of the products by the sum of the frequencies.

When you calculate your grade point average (GPA), you are using a weighted average. The following formula is used to calculate GPA:

$$\text{GPA} = \frac{\text{Total points}}{\text{Total credits}}$$

Now let's show how Jill Rivers calculated her GPA to the nearest tenth.

Given   A = 4; B = 3; C = 2; D = 1; F = 0

Courses	Credits attempted	Grade received	Points (Credits × Grade)
Introduction to Computers	4	A	16 (4 × 4)
Psychology	3	B	9 (3 × 3)
English Composition	3	B	9 (3 × 3)
Business Law	3	C	6 (2 × 3)
Business Math	3	B	9 (3 × 3)
	16		49 $\dfrac{49}{16} = 3.1$

When high or low numbers do not significantly affect a list of numbers, the mean is a good indicator of the center of the data. If high or low numbers do have an effect, the median may be a better indicator to use.

Median

Who the Buyers Are

Demographics of buyers of entry-level Mercedeses and BMWs*

CATEGORY	MERCEDES	BMW
Median Age	51	40
Median Household Income	$98,900	$98,200
Percent Male	49%	61%
Percent Married	71%	59%
Use the Internet	77%	92%

*Figures are for buyers of model-year 2000 Mercedes C-Class and BMW 3-Series cars. Source: Strategic Vision

The Wall Street Journal clipping "Who the Buyers Are" gives the statistics of median entry-level buyers of Mercedes and BMWs for the model year 2000. The **median** is another measurement that indicates the center of the data. An average that has one or more extreme values is not distorted by the median. For example, let's look at the yearly salaries of the employees of Rusty's Clothing Shop:

Alice Knight	$95,000	Jane Wang	$67,000
Jane Hess	27,000	Bill Joy	40,000
Joel Floyd	32,000		

Note how Alice's salary of $95,000 will distort an average calculated by the mean:

$$\frac{\$95,000 + \$27,000 + \$32,000 + \$67,000 + \$40,000}{5} = \boxed{\$52,200}$$

The $52,200 average salary is considerably more than the salary of three of the employees. So it is not a good representation of the store's average salary. Let's use the following steps to find the median.

Finding the Median of a Group of Values

Step 1. Orderly arrange values from the smallest to the largest.

Step 2. Find the middle value.

    a. *Odd number of values:* Median is the middle value. You find this by first dividing the total number of numbers by 2. The next-higher number is the median.

    b. *Even number of values:* Median is the average of the two middle values.

For Rusty's Clothing Shop, we find the median as follows:

1. Arrange values from smallest to largest:
    $27,000; $32,000; $40,000; $67,000; $95,000

2. Since the middle value is an odd number, $40,000 is the median. Note that half of the salaries fall below the median and half fall above ($5 \div 2 = 2\frac{1}{2}$—next number is the median).

    If Jane Hess ($27,000) were not on the payroll, we would find the median as follows:

1. Arrange values from smallest to largest:
    $32,000; $40,000; $67,000; $95,000

2. Average the two middle values:
    $$\frac{\$40,000 + \$67,000}{2} = \boxed{\$53,500}$$

Note that the median results in two salaries below and two salaries above the average.
Now we'll look at another measurement tool—the mode.

Mode

The **mode** is a measurement that also records values. In a series of numbers, the value that occurs most often is the mode. If all the values are different, there is no mode. If two or more numbers appear most often, you may have two or more modes. Note that we do not have to arrange the numbers in the lowest-to-highest order, although this could make it easier to find the mode.

EXAMPLE   3, 4, 5, 6, 3, 8, 9, 3, 5, 3

    3 is the mode since it is listed 4 times.

Now let's check your progress with a Practice Quiz.

LU 22–1 PRACTICE QUIZ

Barton Company's sales reps sold the following last month:

Sales rep	Sales volume	Sales rep	Sales volume
A	$16,500	C	$12,000
B	15,000	D	48,900

Calculate the mean and the median. Which is the better indicator of the center of the data? Is there a mode?

✓ **SOLUTIONS**

$$\text{Mean} = \frac{\$16{,}500 + \$15{,}000 + \$12{,}000 + \$48{,}900}{4} = \boxed{\$23{,}100}$$

$$\text{Median} = \frac{\$15{,}000 + \$16{,}500}{2} = \boxed{\$15{,}750}$$

$12,000, $\boxed{\$15{,}000, \$16{,}500,}$
$48,900. Note how we arrange numbers from smallest to highest to calculate median.

Median is the better indicator since in calculating the mean, the $48,900 puts the average of $23,100 much too high. There is no mode.

LEARNING UNIT 22–2 | FREQUENCY DISTRIBUTIONS AND GRAPHS

In this unit you will learn how to gather data and illustrate these data. Today, computer software programs can make beautiful color graphics. But how accurate are these graphics? This *Wall Street Journal* clipping gives an example of graphics that did not agree with the numbers beneath them. The clipping reminds all readers to check the numbers illustrated by the graphics.

What's Wrong With this Picture? Utility's Glasses Are Never Empty

By KATHLEEN DEVENY
Staff Reporter of THE WALL STREET JOURNAL

When Les Waas, an investor in Philadelphia Suburban Corp., paged through the company's 1994 annual report, he was impressed by what he saw.

The water utility had used a series of charts to represent its revenues, net income and book value per share, among other results. Each figure was represented by the level of water in a glass. Each chart showed strong growth.

Then Mr. Waas looked a little more carefully. The bars in the chart seemed to indicate far more impressive growth than the numbers beneath them. A chart showing the growth in the number of Philadelphia Suburban's water customers, for ex-

Number of Metered Water Customers (thousands)

| | 1990 | 1991 | 1992 | 1993 | 1994 |
| | 235 | 237 | 245 | 247 | 250 |

ample, seemed to indicate the company's customer base had more than tripled since 1990. But the numbers actually increased only 6.4%.

The reason for the disparity: The charts don't begin at zero. Even an empty glass in the accompanying chart would represent a customer base of 230,000.

©1995 Dow Jones & Company, Inc.

Collecting raw data and organizing the data is a prerequisite to presenting statistics graphically. Let's illustrate this by looking at the following example.

A computer industry consultant wants to know how much college freshmen are willing to spend to set up a computer in their dormitory rooms. After visiting a local college dorm, the consultant gathered the following data on the amount of money 20 students spent on computers:

$1,000 $7,000 $4,000 $1,000 $ 5,000 $1,000 $3,000
5,000 2,000 3,000 3,000 3,000 8,000 9,000
3,000 6,000 6,000 1,000 10,000 1,000

Note that these raw data are not arranged in any order. To make the data more meaningful, the consultant made the **frequency distribution** table at the left. Think of this distribution table as a way to organize a list of numbers to show the patterns that may exist.

As you can see, 25% ($\frac{5}{20} = \frac{1}{4} = 25\%$) of the students spent $1,000 and another 25% spent $3,000. Only four students spent $7,000 or more.

Now let's see how we can use bar graphs.

Price of computer	Tally	Frequency
$ 1,000	ＪＨＴ	5
2,000	I	1
3,000	ＪＨＴ	5
4,000	I	1
5,000	II	2
6,000	II	2
7,000	I	1
8,000	I	1
9,000	I	1
10,000	I	1

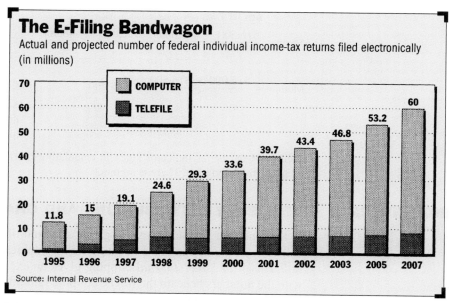

© 1997 Dow Jones & Company, Inc.

Bar Graphs

Bar graphs help readers see the changes that have occurred over a period of time. This is especially true when the same type of data is repeatedly studied. The above *Wall Street Journal* clipping uses a bar graph to show the actual and projected number of federal individual income-tax returns filed electronically (in millions).

Let's return to our computer consultant example and make a bar graph of the computer purchases data collected by the consultant. Note that the height of the bar represents the frequency of each purchase. Bar graphs can be vertical or horizontal.

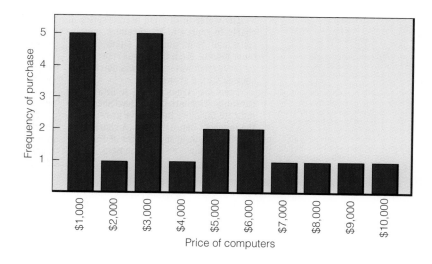

We can simplify this bar graph by grouping the prices of the computers. The grouping, or *intervals,* should be of equal sizes.

Class	Frequency
$1,000–$ 3,000.99	11
3,001– 5,000.99	3
5,001– 7,000.99	3
7,001– 9,000.99	2
9,001– 11,000.99	1

A bar graph for the grouped data follows.

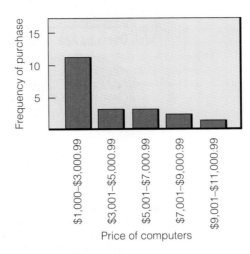

Next, let's see how we can use line graphs.

Line Graphs

A **line graph** shows trends over a period of time. Often separate lines are drawn to show the comparison between two or more trends.

The Wall Street Journal clipping "Ford Builds a Car to Suit India's Tastes" uses a line graph to show the projected number of cars and commercial vehicles sold (in thousands of units). Note the "Even Faster Than Elsewhere" table at the right showing India with the greatest projected compound annual growth.

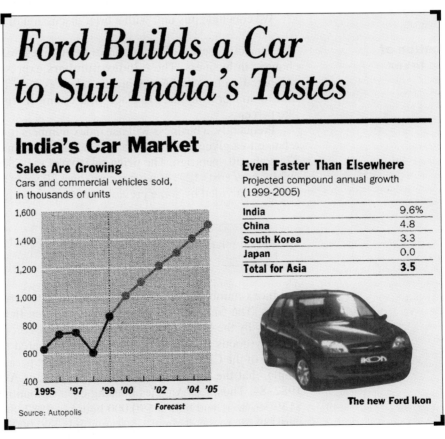

We conclude our discussion of graphics with the use of the circle graph.

Circle Graphs

Circle graphs, often called *pie charts,* are especially helpful for showing the relationship of parts to a whole. The entire circle represents 100%, or 360°; the pie-shaped pieces represent the subcategories. Note how the circle graph in *The Wall Street Journal* clipping "Age and Activity" on the following page shows Web users by age.

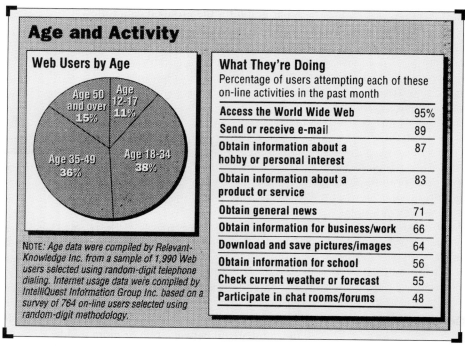

© 1998 Dow Jones & Company, Inc.

.15 × 360° =   54.0
.11 × 360° =   39.6
.36 × 360° = 129.6
.38 × 360° = 136.8
                  360.0

An Application of Statistics: Index Numbers

To draw a circle graph (or pie chart), begin by drawing a circle. Then take the percentages and convert each percentage to a decimal. Next multiply each decimal by 360° to get the degrees represented by the percentage. Circle graphs must total 360°.

We conclude this unit with a brief discussion of index numbers.

The financial section of a newspaper often gives different index numbers describing the changes in business. These **index numbers** express the relative changes in a variable compared with some base, which is taken as 100. The changes may be measured from time to time or from place to place. Index numbers function as percents and are calculated like percents.

Frequently, a business will use index numbers to make comparisons of a current price relative to a given year. For example, a calculator may cost $9 today relative to a cost of $75 some 30 years ago. The **price relative** of the calculator is $\frac{\$9}{\$75} \times 100 = 12\%$. The calculator now costs 12% of what it cost some 30 years ago. A price relative, then, is the current price divided by some previous year's price—the base year—multiplied by 100.

$$\text{Price relative} = \frac{\text{Current price}}{\text{Base year's price}} \times 100$$

Index numbers can also be used to estimate current prices at various geographic locations. The frequently quoted Consumer Price Index (CPI), calculated and published monthly by the U.S. Bureau of Labor Statistics, records the price relative percentage cost of many goods and services nationwide compared to a base period. Table 22.1 gives a portion of the CPI that uses 1982–84 as its base period. Note that the table shows, for example, that the price relative for housing in Los Angeles is 139.3% of what it cost in 1982–84. Thus, Los Angeles housing costs amounting to $100.00 in 1982–84 now cost $139.30. So if you built a $90,000 house in 1982–84, it is worth $125,370 today. (Convert 139.3% to the decimal 1.393; multiply $90,000 by 1.393 = $125,370.)

Once again, we complete the unit with a Practice Quiz.

TABLE 22.1

Consumer Price Index (in percent)

Expense	Atlanta	Chicago	New York	Los Angeles
Food	131.9	130.3	139.6	130.9
Housing	128.8	131.4	139.3	139.3
Clothing	133.8	124.3	121.8	126.4
Medical care	177.6	163.0	172.4	163.3

LU 22–2 PRACTICE QUIZ

DVD

1. The following is the number of sales made by 20 salespeople on a given day. Prepare a frequency distribution and a bar graph. Do not use intervals for this example.

5	8	9	1	4	4	0	3	2	8
8	9	5	1	9	6	7	5	9	10

2. Assuming the following market shares for diapers 5 years ago, prepare a circle graph:

Pampers	32%	Huggies	24%
Luvs	20%	Others	24%

3. Today a new Explorer costs $30,000. In 1991 the Explorer cost $19,000. What is the price relative? Round to the nearest tenth percent.

✓ **SOLUTIONS**

1.

Number of sales	Tally	Frequency
0	I	1
1	II	2
2	I	1
3	I	1
4	II	2
5	III	3
6	I	1
7	I	1
8	III	3
9	IIII	4
10	I	1

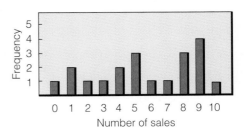

2.

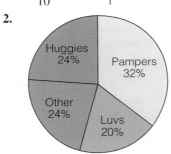

$.32 \times 360° = 115.20°$
$.20 \times 360° = 72.00°$
$.24 \times 360° = 86.40°$
$.24 \times 360° = 86.40°$

3. $\dfrac{\$30,000}{\$19,000} \times 100 = 157.9$

LEARNING UNIT 22–3 | MEASURES OF DISPERSION (OPTIONAL)

In Learning Unit 22–1 you learned how companies use the mean, median, and mode to indicate a single value, or number, that represents an entire group of numbers, or data. Often it is valuable to know how the information is scattered (spread or dispersed) within a data set. A **measure of dispersion** is a number that describes how the numbers of a set of data are spread out or dispersed.

This learning unit discusses three measures of dispersion—range, standard deviation, and normal distribution. We begin with the range—the simplest measure of dispersion.

Range

The **range** is the difference between the two extreme values (highest and lowest) in a group of values or a set of data. For example, often the actual extreme values of hourly temperature readings during the past 24 hours are given but not the range or difference between the high and low readings. To find the range in a group of data, subtract the lowest value from the highest value.

> Range = Highest value − Lowest value

Thus, if the high temperature reading during the past 24 hours was 90° and the low temperature reading was 60°, the range is 90° − 60°, or 30°.

The difficulty in using the range is that this measure depends only on the values of the extremes and does not consider any other values in the data set. Also, the range depends on the number of values on which it is based; that is, the larger the number of values, the larger the range is apt to be. The range gives only a general idea of the spread of the values in a set of data.

EXAMPLE   Find the range of the following values: 83.6, 77.3, 69.2, 93.1, 85.4, 71.6.

Range = 93.1 − 69.2 = 23.9

Standard Deviation

Since the **standard deviation** is intended to measure the spread of data around the mean, the first step in finding the standard deviation of a set of data is to determine its mean. The following diagram shows two sets of data—A and B. Note that, as shown in the diagram, the means of these two data are equal. Now look at how the data in both sets are spread or dispersed.

Data set A	Data set B
x x x x x	x x x x x
0 1 2 3 4 5 6 7 8 9 10 11 12 13	0 1 2 3 4 5 6 7 8 9 10 11 12 13
Mean = (1 + 2 + 5 + 10 + 12) ÷ 5 = 6	Mean = (4 + 4 + 5 + 8 + 9) ÷ 5 = 6

You can see that although the means of data sets A and B are equal, data set A is clearly more widely dispersed; therefore, the data in set B will have a smaller standard deviation than the data in set A.

To find the standard deviation of an ungrouped set of data, use the following steps:

Finding the Standard Deviation

Step 1. Find the mean of the set of data.

Step 2. Subtract the mean from each piece of data to find each deviation.

Step 3. Square each deviation (multiply the deviation by itself).

Step 4. Sum all squared deviations.

Step 5. Divide the sum of the squared deviations by $n - 1$, where n equals the number of pieces of data.

Step 6. Find the square root ($\sqrt{\ }$) of the number obtained in Step 5 (use a calculator). This is the standard deviation. (The square root is a number that when multiplied by itself equals the amount shown inside the square root symbol.)

Two additional points should be made. First, Step 2 sometimes results in negative numbers. Since the sum of the deviations obtained in Step 2 should always be zero, we would not be able to find the average deviation. This is why we square each deviation—to generate positive quantities only. Second, the standard deviation we refer to is used with *sample* sets of data, that is, a collection of data from a population. The population is the *entire* collection of data. When the standard deviation for a population is calculated, the sum of the squared deviations is divided by n instead of by $n - 1$. In all problems that follow, sample sets of data are being examined.

EXAMPLE   Calculate the standard deviations for the sample data sets A and B given in the diagram above. Round the final answer to the nearest tenth. Note that Step 1—find the mean—is given in the diagram.

Standard deviation of data sets A and B: The table on the left uses Steps 2 through 6 to find the standard deviation of data set A, and the table on the right uses Steps 2 through 6 to find the standard deviation of data set B.

Data	Step 2 Data − Mean	Step 3 (Data − Mean)²	Data	Step 2 Data − Mean	Step 3 (Data − Mean)²
1	1 − 6 = −5	25	4	4 − 6 = −2	4
2	2 − 6 = −4	16	4	4 − 6 = −2	4
5	5 − 6 = −1	1	5	5 − 6 = −1	1
10	10 − 6 = 4	16	8	8 − 6 = 2	4
12	12 − 6 = 6	36	9	9 − 6 = 3	9
	Total 0	94 **(Step 4)**		Total 0	22 **(Step 4)**

Step 5: Divide by $n − 1$: $\dfrac{94}{5 − 1} = \dfrac{94}{4} = 23.5$

Step 6: The square root of $\sqrt{23.5}$ is 4.8 (rounded). The standard deviation of data set A is 4.8.

Step 5: Divide by $n − 1$: $\dfrac{22}{5 − 1} = \dfrac{22}{4} = 5.5$

Step 6: The square root of $\sqrt{5.5}$ is 2.3. The standard deviation of data set B is 2.3.

As suspected, the standard deviation of data set B is less than that of set A. The standard deviation value reinforces what we see in the diagram.

Normal Distribution

One of the most important distributions of data is the **normal distribution.** In a normal distribution, data are spread *symmetrically* about the mean. A graph of such a distribution looks like the bell-shaped curve in Figure 22.1. Many data sets are normally distributed. Examples are the life span of automobile engines, women's heights, and intelligence quotients.

In a normal distribution, the data are spread out symmetrically—50% of the data lie above the mean, and 50% of the data lie below the mean. Additionally, if the data are normally distributed, 68% of the data should be found within one standard deviation above and below the mean. About 95% of the data should be found within two standard deviations above and below the mean. Figure 22.1 illustrates these facts.

EXAMPLE   Assume that the mean useful life of a particular lightbulb is 2,000 hours and is normally distributed with a standard deviation of 300 hours. Calculate the useful life of the lightbulb with **(a)** one standard deviation of the mean and **(b)** two standard deviations of the mean; also **(c)** calculate the percent of lightbulbs that will last 2,300 hours or longer.

a. The useful life of the lightbulb one standard deviation from the mean is one standard deviation above *and* below the mean.

2,000 ± 300 = 1,700 and 2,300 hours

The useful life is somewhere between 1,700 and 2,300 hours.

b. The useful life of the lightbulb within two standard deviations of the mean is within two standard deviations above *and* below the mean.

2,000 ± 2(300) = 1,400 and 2,600 hours

FIGURE 22.1

Standard deviation and the normal distribution

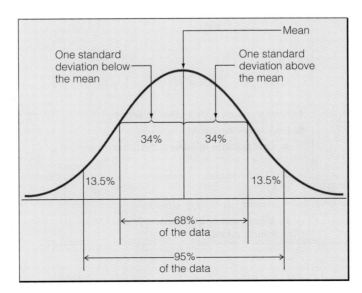

c. Since 50% of the data in a normal distribution lie below the mean and 34% represent the amount of data one standard deviation above the mean, we must calculate the percent of data that lies beyond one standard deviation above the mean.

$$100\% - (50\% + 34\%) = \boxed{16\%}$$

So 16% of the bulbs should last 2,300 hours or longer.

It's time for another Practice Quiz.

LU 22–3 PRACTICE QUIZ

1. Calculate the range for the following data: 58, 13, 17, 26, 5, 41.
2. Calculate the standard deviation for the following sample set of data: 113, 92, 77, 125, 110, 93, 111. Round answers to the nearest tenth.

✓ **SOLUTIONS**

1. $58 - 5 = \boxed{53}$ range

2.

Data	Data − Mean	(Data − Mean)²
113	113 − 103 = 10	100
92	92 − 103 = −11	121
77	77 − 103 = −26	676
125	125 − 103 = 22	484
110	110 − 103 = 7	49
93	93 − 103 = −10	100
111	111 − 103 = 8	64
	Total	1,594

$$1,594 \div (7 - 1) = 265.6666667$$
$$\sqrt{265.6666667} = \boxed{16.3} \text{ standard deviation}$$

Chapter Organizer and Reference Guide

Topic	Key point, procedure, formula	Example(s) to illustrate situation
Mean, p. 482	Sum of all values / Number of values	Age of basketball team: 22, 28, 31, 19, 15 Mean = $\dfrac{22 + 28 + 31 + 19 + 15}{5}$ = $\boxed{23}$
Weighted mean, p. 482	Sum of products / Sum of frequencies	**S.** **M.** **T.** **W.** **Th.** **F.** **S.** Sales $90 $75 $80 $75 $80 $90 $90 **Value** **Frequency** **Product** $90 3 $270 75 2 150 80 2 160 7 $580 Mean = $\dfrac{\$580}{7}$ = $\boxed{\$82.86}$
Median, p. 483	1. Arrange values from smallest to largest. 2. Find the middle value. **a. Odd number of values:** median is middle value. $\left(\dfrac{\text{Total number of numbers}}{2}\right)$ Next-higher number is median. **b. Even number of values:** average of two middle values.	12, 15, 8, 6, 3 **1.** 3 6 8 12 15 **2.** $\dfrac{5}{2} = 2.5$ Median is third number, $\boxed{8.}$

(continues)

Chapter Organizer and Reference Guide (continued)

Topic	Key point, procedure, formula	Example(s) to illustrate situation
Frequency distribution, p. 485	Method of listing numbers or amounts not arranged in any particular way by columns for numbers (amounts), tally, and frequency	Number of sodas consumed in one day: 1, 5, 4, 3, 4, 2, 2, 3, 2, 0 **Number of sodas**	**Tally**	**Frequency** 0 | 1 1 | 1 2 ||| 3 3 || 2 4 || 2 5 | 1
Bar graphs, p. 486	Height of bar represents frequency. Bar graph used for grouped data. Bar graphs can be vertical or horizontal.	From soda example above:
Line graphs, p. 487	Shows trend. Helps to put numbers in order.	**Sales** 2003 $1,000 2004 2,000 2005 3,000
Circle graphs, p. 487	Circle = 360° % × 360° = Degrees of pie to represent percent Total should = 360°	60% favor diet soda 40% favor sugared soda .60 × 360° = 216° .40 × 360° = 144° $\overline{}$ 360°
Price relative, p. 488	Price relative = $\dfrac{\text{Current price}}{\text{Base year's price}} \times 100$	A station wagon's sticker price was $8,799 in 1982. Today it is $14,900. Price relative = $\dfrac{\$14,900}{\$8,799} \times 100 =$ 169.3 (rounded to nearest tenth percent)
Range (optional), p. 489	Range = Highest value − Lowest value	Calculate range of the data set consisting of 5, 9, 13, 2, 8 Range = 13 − 2 = 11

(continues)

Chapter Organizer and Reference Guide (concluded)		
Topic	**Key point, procedure, formula**	**Example(s) to illustrate situation**
Standard deviation (optional), p. 490	1. Calculate mean. 2. Subtract mean from each piece of data. 3. Square each deviation. 4. Sum squares. 5. Divide sum of squares by $n - 1$, where n = number of pieces of data. 6. Take square root of number obtained in Step 5, to find the standard deviation.	Calculate the standard deviation of this set of data: 7, 2, 5, 3, 3. 1. Mean = $\dfrac{20}{5}$ = 4 2. $7 - 4 = 3$ $\quad 2 - 4 = -2$ $\quad 5 - 4 = 1$ $\quad 3 - 4 = -1$ $\quad 3 - 4 = -1$ 3. $\quad (3)^2 = 9$ $\quad (-2)^2 = 4$ $\quad (1)^2 = 1$ $\quad (-1)^2 = 1$ $\quad \underline{(-1)^2 = 1}$ 4. $\qquad 16$ 5. $16 \div 4 = 4$ 6. Standard deviation = $\boxed{2}$
Key terms	Bar graph, *p. 486* Circle graph, *p. 487* Frequency distribution, *p. 485* Index numbers, *p. 488* Line graph, *p. 487*	Mean, *p. 482* Measure of dispersion, *p. 489* Median, *p. 483* Mode, *p. 484* Normal distribution, *p. 491* Price relative, *p. 488* Range, *p. 489* Standard deviation, *p. 490* Weighted mean, *p. 482*

Critical Thinking Discussion Questions

1. Explain the mean, median, and mode. Give an example that shows you must be careful when you read statistics in an article.

2. Explain frequency distributions and the types of graphs. Locate a company annual report and explain how the company shows graphs to highlight its performance. Does the company need more or fewer of these visuals? Could price relatives be used?

3. Explain the statement that standard deviations are not accurate.

Name _____ Date _____

DRILL PROBLEMS (*Note:* Problems for optional Learning Unit 22–3 follow the Challenge Problem 22–24, page 499.)

Calculate the mean (to the nearest hundredth):

22–1. 6, 9, 7, 4

22–2. 8, 11, 19, 17, 15

22–3. $55.83, $66.92, $108.93

22–4. $1,001, $68.50, $33.82, $581.95

22–5. Calculate the grade-point average: A = 4, B = 3, C = 2, D = 1, F = 0 (to nearest tenth).

Courses	Credits	Grade
Computer Principles	3	B
Business Law	3	C
Logic	3	D
Biology	4	A
Marketing	3	B

22–6. Find the weighted mean (to the nearest tenth):

Value	Frequency	Product
4	7	
8	3	
2	9	
4	2	

Find the median:

22–7. 55, 10, 19, 38, 100, 25

22–8. 95, 103, 98, 62, 31, 15, 82

Find the mode:

22–9. 8, 9, 3, 4, 12, 8, 8, 9

22–10. 22, 19, 15, 16, 18, 18, 5, 18

22–11. Given: Truck cost 2004 $30,000
          Truck cost 2001 $21,000

Calculate the price relative (round to the nearest tenth percent).

22–12. Given the following sales of Lowe Corporation, prepare a line graph (run sales from $5,000 to $20,000).

2003	$ 8,000
2004	11,000
2005	13,000
2006	18,000

22–13. Prepare a frequency distribution from the following weekly salaries of teachers at Moore Community College. Use the following intervals:

$200–$299.99
300– 399.99
400– 499.99
500– 599.99

$210	$505	$310	$380	$275
290	480	550	490	200
286	410	305	444	368

22–14. Prepare a bar graph from the frequency distribution in Problem 22–13.

22–15. How many degrees on a pie chart would each be given from the following?

Wear digital watch	42%
Wear traditional watch	51%
Wear no watch	7%

WORD PROBLEMS

22–16. The June 18, 2001, issue of *Advertising Age* reported on the April 2001 top 10 multichannel Internet retailers ranked by visitors. From the following information, find the mean and median visits:

1. ticketmaster.com	4,824,000	6. hp.com	3,347,000
2. barnesandnoble.com	4,509,000	7. mcafee.com	3,331,000
3. dell.com	4,050,000	8. intuit.com	2,993,000
4. hallmark.com	3,683,000	9. sears.com	2,959,000
5. apple.com	3,588,000	10. bluelight.com	2,823,000

22–17. The March 20, 2000, issue of *Industry Week/IW* reported on the latest interest yields. United States interest rates were compared to European Union rates. From the following information, prepare a line graph comparing the United States and European Union:

	Latest	3 months ago	6 months ago	12 months ago
USA	6.59%	6.75%	6.50%	6.20%
European Union	5.56	5.30	5.40	5.50

22–18. On June 21, 2001, the *Los Angeles Times* reported on the market share of record companies. The latest weekly market shares are based on current albums sold. This is an indicator of music-company performance. Market shares were: Universal, 31.4%; WEA, 18.2%; Sony, 15.0%; BMG, 12.0%; EMD, 8.2%; and others, 15.2%. From this information, construct a circle graph of these market shares.

22–19. Bill Small, a travel agent, provided Alice Hall with the following information regarding the cost of her upcoming vacation:

Transportation	35%
Hotel	28%
Food and entertainment	20%
Miscellaneous	17%

Construct a circle graph for Alice.

22–20. Jim Smith, a marketing student, observed how much each customer spent in a local convenience store. Based on the following results, prepare **(a)** a frequency distribution and **(b)** a bar graph. Use intervals of $0–$5.99, $6.00–$11.99, $12.00–$17.99, and $18.00–$23.99.

$18.50	$18.24	$ 6.88	$9.95
16.10	3.55	14.10	6.80
12.11	3.82	2.10	
15.88	3.95	5.50	

22–21. Angie's Bakery bakes bagels. Find the weighted mean (to the nearest whole bagel) given the following daily production for June:

200	150	200	150	200
150	190	360	360	150
190	190	190	200	150
360	400	400	150	200
400	360	150	400	360
400	400	200	150	150

22–22. Melvin Company reported sales in 2005 of $300,000. This compared to sales of $150,000 in 2004 and $100,000 in 2003. Construct a line graph for Melvin Company.

CHALLENGE PROBLEMS

22–23. On June 15, 2001, the *San Francisco Business Times* reported on the annual revenue of the largest travel agencies in the Bay Area. The results are as follows

AAA Travel Agency	$86,700,000
Riser Group	63,200,000
Casto Travel	62,900,000
Balboa Travel	36,200,000
Hunter Travel Managers	36,000,000

(a) What would be the mean and the median? **(b)** What is the total revenue percent of each agency? **(c)** Prepare a circle graph depicting the percents.

22–24. The following circle graph is a suggested budget for Ron Rye and his family for a month:

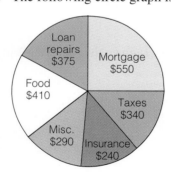

Ron would like you to calculate the percent (to the hundredth) for each part of the circle graph along with the appropriate number of degrees.

LEARNING UNIT 22–3 OPTIONAL ASSIGNMENTS Name _____ Date _____

DRILL PROBLEMS

1. Calculate the range for the following set of data: 117, 98, 133, 52, 114, 35.

Calculate the standard deviation for the following sample sets of data. Round the final answers to the nearest tenth.

2. 83.6, 92.3, 56.5, 43.8, 77.1, 66.7

3. 7, 3, 12, 17, 5, 8, 9, 9, 13, 15, 6, 6, 4, 5

4. 41, 41, 38, 27, 53, 56, 28, 45, 47, 49, 55, 60

WORD PROBLEMS

5. The mean useful life of car batteries is 48 months. They have a standard deviation of 3. If the useful life of batteries is normally distributed, calculate (a) the percent of batteries with a useful life of less than 45 months and (b) the percent of batteries that will last longer than 54 months.

6. The average weight of a particular box of crackers is 24.5 ounces with a standard deviation of 0.8 ounce. The weights of the boxes are normally distributed. What percent of the boxes (a) weigh more than 22.9 ounces and (b) weigh less than 23.7 ounces?

7. An examination is normally distributed with a mean score of 77 and a standard deviation of 6. Find the percent of individuals scoring as indicated below.

   a. Between 71 and 83
   b. Between 83 and 65
   c. Above 89
   d. Less than 65
   e. Between 77 and 65

8. Listed below are the sales figures in thousands of dollars for a group of insurance salespeople. Calculate the mean sales figure and the standard deviation.

$117	$350	$400	$245	$420
223	275	516	265	135
486	320	285	374	190

9. The time in seconds it takes for 20 individual sewing machines to stitch a border onto a particular garment is listed below. Calculate the mean stitching time and the standard deviation to the nearest hundredth.

67	69	64	71	73
58	71	64	62	67
62	57	67	60	65
60	63	72	56	64

SUMMARY PRACTICE TEST

1. In June, Logan Realty sold 10 homes at the following prices: $135,000; $170,000; $90,000; $98,000; $185,000; $150,000; $108,000; $114,000; $142,000; and $250,000. Calculate the mean and median. *(pp. 482, 483)*

2. Sears Hardware Store counted the number of customers entering the store for a week. The results were 1,300; 950; 1,300; 1,700; 880; 920; and 1,210. What is the mode? *(p. 484)*

3. This semester Lee Win took four 3-credit courses at Middlesex Community College. She received an A in accounting and Bs in history, psychology, and algebra. What is her cumulative grade-point average (assume A = 4 and B = 3) to the nearest hundredth? *(p. 483)*

4. Ron's Sub Shop reported the following sales for the first 20 days of June. *(p. 485)*

$200	$400	$600	$400	$600
300	600	300	500	700
200	600	200	500	200
100	600	100	700	700

Prepare a frequency distribution for Ron.

5. Star Company produced the following number of maps during the first 5 weeks of last year. Prepare a bar graph. *(p. 486)*

Week	Maps
1	800
2	700
3	300
4	750
5	400

6. Leser Corporation reported record profits of 10%. It stated in the report that the cost of sales was 40% with expenses of 50%. Prepare a circle graph for Leser. *(p. 488)*

7. Today a new Land Rover costs $39,000. In 1990, the Rover cost $22,000. What is the price relative to the nearest tenth percent? *(p. 488)*

*8. Calculate the standard deviation for the following set of data: 20, 32, 45, 26, 35, 42, 40. Round final answer to nearest tenth. *(p. 490)*

*Optional problem.

STOCKS | Its new boss is restoring luster to **TOYS "R" US**. *By Steven T. Goldberg*

RETAILING'S COMEBACK KID

STEVEN RUBIN

BY THE TIME veteran retail executive John Eyler took over two years ago, Toys "R" Us was in decline. Its stores were dirty, dark and shabby. With prices too low to beat, Wal-Mart Stores was eating away at the toy chain's dominant market share. In fact, Wal-Mart now sells more toys than Toys "R" Us.

Eyler, 54, is pushing Toys "R" Us away from its discount roots. He's remodeling stores and improving service, which should result in higher sales and profit margins. "We are beginning to see positive results from our strategic investments," Eyler says. If Eyler succeeds in rejuvenating the company, the stock—which at $22 is down nearly 50% from its all-time high and sells at just 15 times expected 2002 profits—looks like a bargain. Goldman Sachs analyst Matthew Fassler calls Toys "a powerful turnaround opportunity."

New partnerships. One of Eyler's first moves was to introduce more products with the Toys "R" Us label. Sales of

private-label brands, which carry higher profit margins than other toymakers' products, are expected to quadruple from two years ago—bringing them to 20% of revenues. Eyler has also established partnerships with other firms. For example, Toys "R" Us is the only place where you can buy the hot Harley-Davidson Barbie dolls or Home Depot tools for kids.

Toys "R" Us has already remodeled 60% of its 703 U.S. stores to make them more contemporary and inviting. In the second quarter, sales were 7% higher at the remodeled stores than they were at older outlets. The company has also replaced almost 30% of its store managers and launched new training programs for remaining employees. "Toys was notorious for bad service," says James Leach, analyst for Strong Discovery, which owns the stock. "Customer-satisfaction scores [based on surveys] have improved at rates never seen before in this company," Eyler says.

Christmas crunch. Toys "R" Us lost money in the first two quarters of

2001 because of the remodeling costs and the sluggish economy, and it expects more red ink in the third quarter. The make-or-break Christmas quarter, which usually accounts for 50% of sales and 70% of profits annually, is especially crucial this year.

One fund manager who's confident that Eyler and his team are on track is Mark Greenberg, who runs Invesco Leisure. He says that Toys "R" Us will soon regain its mantle as *the* place to go for toys and that the company should have a big Christmas. (The chain, with nearly 500 stores overseas, also owns Babies "R" Us, Kids "R" Us and half of Toys "R" Us–Japan.) Moreover, says Greenberg, Toys should prosper even if the economy continues to grow slowly—or not at all, even in the wake of the terrorist attacks. Consumers, he says, are more likely to cut back spending on themselves rather than on their children. Says Greenberg: "People will still buy toys, and that's why Toys is going to come through with good earnings numbers for quite a while." **K** —*Reporter:* **CHRISTINE PULFREY**

SPOTLIGHT | Toys "R" Us

- **Symbol:** TOY
- **Headquarters:** Montvale, N.J.
- **Earnings per share: 2001** $0.95
  2002: $1.17e **2003:** $1.52e
- **Web site:** www.toysrus.com
- **Shareholder services:** 800-785-8697

WEEKLY CLOSING PRICES

2001

S O N D J F M A M J J A S*

*consensus of analysts' estimates for fiscal years ending January 31 *to September 17

SOURCES: First Call/Thomson Financial; Yahoo!

Business Math Issue

Toys "Я" Us strategy is too late in today's Internet society.
1. List the key points of the article and information to support your position.
2. Write a group defense of your position using math calculations to support your view.

BUSINESS MATH SCRAPBOOK
WITH INTERNET APPLICATION
Putting Your Skills to Work

GETTING GOING ◇ *By Jonathan Clements*

The Many Ways to Play the Averages

IF YOU WANT to understand why most folks live longer than the life-expectancy tables suggest, why the typical family doesn't give a hoot about stocks and why most portfolio managers fail to beat the market, cast your mind back to grade school.

You might recall learning that there was more than one way to calculate an average. Most times, you add up all the observations, divide by the number of observations and get the "mean."

But as your math teacher no doubt explained, occasionally it makes more sense to use the "median," which you get by arraying the observations from highest to lowest and then picking the one in the middle. That way, you get an average that isn't skewed by a few unusually high or unusually low numbers.

But this stuff isn't just for kids. The mean and median diverge all the time—sometimes with intriguing financial implications.

One Life to Live: How long will you live? Consider some statistics from William Huff, an actuary at Seattle insurer Safeco Corp. According to one of Safeco's life-expectancy tables, the average male life expectancy is 80.1 years.

But this average is a mean, which gets dragged down by folks who die young because of accidents and disease. What if you aren't so unfortunate? You may want to take your cue from the median, which is 83 years. Half of men will die by this age and half after. Similarly, among women, the mean is 84.3 years, but the median is 87.

"If you want enough money to make it to death, you're going to have to plan for a higher age than the mean," Mr. Huff says. But even the median life expectancy should only be a starting point, he adds, because half of all people will live longer.

Unshared Wealth: "If you look at the aggregate data, households have more invested in stocks than in real estate," says Joseph Tracy, a vice president at the Federal Reserve Bank of New York. "But when you look at the typical household, they have very little in stocks and much more in real estate."

The reason: Stock ownership is concentrated in the hands of the wealthy. As of 1995, the median household—halfway down the wealth spectrum—had 66% of total assets in real estate and nothing in stocks.

Haves and Have Nots: Based on U.S. Census Bureau data, the mean household income was $51,855 in 1998, but the medi-

an was just $38,885. Meanwhile, according to the January 2000 Federal Reserve Bulletin, the mean family net worth was $282,500 in 1998, while the median was $71,600.

Why these big gaps? Because the wealthiest have so much money and the highest earners garner such big incomes, it skews the means upward, so that the means are much higher than the levels enjoyed by the typical family.

This imbalance can be seen in federal tax returns, says Frank Levy, a professor of urban economics at Massachusetts Institute of Technology. The top 0.3% of tax returns, he notes, accounts for some 12% of all adjusted gross income.

Missing the Boat: Most years, a majority of portfolio managers trail the market. A big reason is the drag from investment costs, including management fees and trading expenses.

Dusan Petricic

But the pattern of stock returns also plays a role. The market average (which is a weighted mean) tends to be driven higher each year by a fistful of stocks that post huge gains, so that the median stock lags behind the market.

Result? Each year, you end up with a minority of money managers who hold the year's hottest stocks and thus earn fabulous returns, while the rest miss out on the big winners and therefore trail the index.

The solution is to diversify even more. "The more names you hold, the greater the probability that you'll hold some of the big winners and so your returns will at least keep up the market," says David Ikenberry, a finance professor at Rice University's Jones Graduate School of Management in Houston.

Frenzied Few: Recent statistics suggest that folks are buying and selling stocks like crazy. But it turns out that this trading frenzy is largely confined to a small group of investors.

For instance, according to a study of trading through a large discount-brokerage firm over a six-year period, households turned over 75% of their stock portfolios each year, as measured by the mean. But the median turnover was just 32%, according to the study, which will appear in the April issue of the Journal of Finance.

"Yes, the tremendous turnover comes from a small group that trades a lot," says one of the study's authors, Terrance Odean, a finance professor at the University of California at Davis. "But even the average person appears to be trading more than they did five years ago."

PROJECT A
Summarize the key points of this article and go to the Web to find an example to support the data found in the article.

Internet Projects: See text website (www.mhhe.com/slater7e) and *The Business Math Internet Resource Guide.*

Additional Homework Assignments by Learning Unit

LEARNING UNIT 1–1 ▌ READING, WRITING, AND ROUNDING WHOLE NUMBERS

DRILL PROBLEMS

1. Express the following numbers in verbal form:

   a. 7,954 _____

   _____

   b. 160,501 _____

   _____

   c. 2,098,767 _____

   _____

   d. 58,003 _____

   _____

   e. 50,025,212,015 _____

   _____

2. Write in numeric form:

   a. Eighty thousand, one hundred eighty-one _____

   b. Fifty-eight thousand, three _____

   c. Two hundred eighty thousand, five _____

   d. Three million, ten _____

   e. Sixty-seven thousand, seven hundred sixty _____

3. Round the following numbers:

   a. To the nearest ten:

   42 _____   379 _____   855 _____   5,981 _____   206 _____

   b. To the nearest hundred:

   9,664 _____   2,074 _____   888 _____   271 _____   75 _____

   c. To the nearest thousand:

   21,486 _____   621 _____   3,504 _____   9,735 _____

4. Round off each number to the nearest ten, nearest hundred, nearest thousand, and round all the way. (Remember that you are rounding the original number each time.)

		Nearest ten	Nearest hundred	Nearest thousand	Round all the way
a.	4,752	_____	_____	_____	_____
b.	70,351	_____	_____	_____	_____
c.	9,386	_____	_____	_____	_____
d.	4,983	_____	_____	_____	_____
e.	408,119	_____	_____	_____	_____
f.	30,051	_____	_____	_____	_____

5. Name the place position (place value) of the underlined digit.

   a. 8,348 _____

   b. 9,734 _____

   c. 347,107 _____

   d. 723 _____

   e. 28,200,000,121 _____

   f. 706,359,005 _____

   g. 27,563,530 _____

WORD PROBLEMS

6. Ken Lawler was shopping for a computer. He went to three different websites and found the computer he wanted at three different prices. At website A the price was $2,115, at website B the price was $1,990, and at website C the price was $2,050. What is the approximate price Ken will have to pay for the computer? Round to the nearest thousand. (Just one price.)

7. Amy Parker had to write a check at the bookstore when she purchased her books for the new semester. The total cost of the books was $384. How will she write this amount in verbal form on her check?

8. Matt Schaeffer was listening to the news and heard that steel production last week was one million, five hundred eighty-seven thousand tons. Express this amount in numeric form.

9. Jackie Martin is the city clerk and must go to the aldermen's meetings and take notes on what is discussed. At last night's meeting, they were discussing repairs for the public library, which will cost three hundred seventy-five thousand, nine hundred eighty-five dollars. Write this in numeric form as Jackie would.

10. A government survey revealed that 25,963,400 people are employed as office workers. To show the approximate number of office workers, round the number all the way.

11. Bob Donaldson wished to present his top student with a certificate of achievement at the end of the school year in 2004. To make it appear more official, he wanted to write the year in verbal form. How did he write the year?

12. Nancy Morrissey has a problem reading large numbers and determining place value. She asked her brother to name the place value of the 4 in the number 13,542,966. Can you tell Nancy the place value of the 4? What is the place value of the 3?

    The 4 is in the _____ place.

    The 3 is in the _____ place.

LEARNING UNIT 1-2 | ADDING AND SUBTRACTING WHOLE NUMBERS

DRILL PROBLEMS

1. Add by totaling each separate column:

	a.	b.	c.	d.	e.	f.	g.	h.
	599	43	493	36	716	535	751	75,730
	142	58	826	76	458	107	378	48,531
		96		43	397	778	135	15,797
				24	139	215	747	
					478	391	368	

2. Estimate by rounding all the way, then add the actual numbers:

a.	b.	c.
580	1,470	475
971	7,631	837
548	4,383	213
430		775
506		432

d.	e.	f.
442	2,571	10,928
609	3,625	9,321
766	4,091	12,654
410	928	15,492
128		

3. Estimate by rounding all the way, then subtract the actual numbers:

a.	b.	c.
81	91	68
− 42	− 33	− 59

d.	e.	f.
981	622	1,125
− 283	− 328	− 913

4. Subtract and check:

a.	b.	c.
4,947	3,724	474,820
− 4,362	− 2,138	− 85,847

d.	e.	f.
50,000	65,003	15,715
− 21,762	− 24,987	− 3,503

5. In the following sales report, total the rows and the columns, then check that the grand total is the same both horizontally and vertically.

Salesperson	Region 1	Region 2	Region 3	Total
a. Becker	$ 5,692	$ 7,403	$ 3,591	
b. Edwards	7,652	7,590	3,021	
c. Graff	6,545	6,738	4,545	
d. Jackson	6,937	6,950	4,913	
e. Total				

WORD PROBLEMS

6. Bill Blue owes $5,299 on his car loan, plus interest of $462. How much will it cost him to pay off this loan?

7. Sales at Rich's Convenience Store were $3,587 on Monday, $3,944 on Tuesday, $4,007 on Wednesday, $3,890 on Thursday, and $4,545 on Friday. What were the total sales for the week?

8. Poor's Variety Store sold $5,000 worth of lottery tickets in the first week of August; it sold $289 less in the second week. How much were the lottery ticket sales in the second week of August?

9. A truck weighed 9,550 pounds when it was empty. After being filled with rubbish, it was driven to the dump where it weighed in at 22,347 pounds. How much did the rubbish weigh?

10. Lynn Jackson had $549 in her checking account when she went to the bookstore. Lynn purchased an accounting book for $62, the working papers for $28, a study guide for $25, and a mechanical pencil for $5. After Lynn writes a check for the entire purchase, how much money will remain in her checking account?

11. A new hard-body truck is advertised with a base price of $6,986 delivered. However, the window sticker on the truck reads as follows: tinted glass, $210; automatic transmission, $650; power steering, $210; power brakes, $215; safety locks, $95; air conditioning, $1,056. Estimate the total price, including the accessories, by rounding all the way and *then* calculating the exact price.

12. Four different stores are offering the same make and model of camcorder:

Store A	Store B	Store C	Store D
$1,285	$1,380	$1,440	$1,355

Find the difference between the highest price and the lowest price. Check your answer.

13. A Xerox XC830 copy machine has a suggested retail price of $1,395. The net price is $649. How much is the discount on the copy machine?

LEARNING UNIT 1–3 | MULTIPLYING AND DIVIDING WHOLE NUMBERS

DRILL PROBLEMS

1. In the following problems, first estimate by rounding all the way, then work the actual problems and check:

	Actual	Estimate	Check
a.	151 $\times$ 14		
b.	4,216 $\times$ 45		
c.	52,376 $\times$ 309		
d.	3,106 $\times$ 28		

2. Multiply (use the shortcut when applicable):

a. 4,072
   $\times$ 100

b. 5,100
   $\times$ 40

c. 76,000
   $\times$ 1,200

d. 93 $\times$ 100,000

3. Divide by rounding all the way; then do the actual calculation and check showing the remainder as a whole number.

	Actual	Estimate	Check

a. 8)7,709

b. 26)5,910

	Actual	Estimate	Check

c. $151\overline{)3{,}783}$

d. $46\overline{)19{,}550}$

4. Divide by the shortcut method:

a. $200\overline{)5{,}400}$ **b.** $50\overline{)5{,}650}$

c. $1{,}200\overline{)43{,}200}$ **d.** $17{,}000\overline{)510{,}000}$

WORD PROBLEMS

5. Jeanne Francis sells state lottery tickets in her variety store. If Jeanne's Variety Store sells 385 lottery tickets per day, how many tickets will be sold in a 7-day period?

6. Arlex Oil Company employs 100 people who are eligible for profit sharing. The financial manager has announced that the profits to be shared amount to $64,000. How much will each employee receive?

7. John Duncan's employer withheld $4,056 in federal taxes from his pay for the year. If equal deductions are made each week, what is John's weekly deduction?

8. Anne Domingoes drives a Volvo that gets 32 miles per gallon of gasoline. How many miles can she travel on 25 gallons of gas?

9. How many 8-inch pieces of yellow ribbon can be cut from a spool of ribbon that contains 6 yards (1 yard = 36 inches)?

10. The number of commercials aired per day on a local television station is 672. How many commercials are aired in 1 year?

11. The computer department at City College purchased 18 computers at a cost of $2,400 each. What was the total price for the computer purchase?

12. Net income for Goodwin's Partnership was $64,500. The five partners share profits and losses equally. What was each partner's share?

13. Ben Krenshaw's supervisor at the construction site told Ben to divide a load of 1,423 bricks into stacks containing 35 bricks each. How many stacks will there be when Ben has finished the job? How many "extra" bricks will there be?

LEARNING UNIT 2–1 | TYPES OF FRACTIONS AND CONVERSION PROCEDURES

DRILL PROBLEMS

1. Identify the type of fraction—proper, improper, or mixed number:

   a. $\dfrac{14}{9}$ b. $\dfrac{26}{27}$ c. $\dfrac{29}{27}$

   d. $9\dfrac{3}{11}$ e. $\dfrac{18}{5}$ f. $\dfrac{30}{37}$

2. Convert to a mixed number:

   a. $\dfrac{29}{4}$ b. $\dfrac{137}{8}$ c. $\dfrac{27}{5}$

   d. $\dfrac{29}{9}$ e. $\dfrac{71}{8}$ f. $\dfrac{43}{6}$

3. Convert the mixed number to an improper fraction:

   a. $7\dfrac{1}{5}$ b. $12\dfrac{3}{11}$

   c. $4\dfrac{3}{7}$ d. $20\dfrac{4}{9}$

   e. $10\dfrac{11}{12}$ f. $17\dfrac{2}{3}$

4. Tell whether the fractions in each pair are equivalent or not:

   a. $\dfrac{3}{4}$ $\dfrac{9}{12}$ _____   b. $\dfrac{2}{3}$ $\dfrac{12}{18}$ _____   c. $\dfrac{7}{8}$ $\dfrac{15}{16}$ _____

   d. $\dfrac{4}{5}$ $\dfrac{12}{15}$ _____   e. $\dfrac{3}{2}$ $\dfrac{9}{4}$ _____   f. $\dfrac{5}{8}$ $\dfrac{7}{11}$ _____

   g. $\dfrac{7}{12}$ $\dfrac{7}{24}$ _____   h. $\dfrac{5}{4}$ $\dfrac{30}{24}$ _____   i. $\dfrac{10}{26}$ $\dfrac{12}{26}$ _____

5. Find the greatest common divisor by the step approach and reduce to lowest terms:

   a. $\dfrac{36}{42}$

   b. $\dfrac{30}{75}$

   c. $\dfrac{74}{148}$

   d. $\dfrac{15}{600}$

   e. $\dfrac{96}{132}$

f. $\dfrac{84}{154}$

6. Convert to higher terms:

a. $\dfrac{8}{10} = \dfrac{}{70}$

b. $\dfrac{2}{15} = \dfrac{}{30}$

c. $\dfrac{6}{11} = \dfrac{}{132}$

d. $\dfrac{4}{9} = \dfrac{}{36}$

e. $\dfrac{7}{20} = \dfrac{}{100}$

f. $\dfrac{7}{8} = \dfrac{}{560}$

WORD PROBLEMS

7. Ken drove to college in $3\frac{1}{4}$ hours. How many quarter-hours is that? Show your answer as an improper fraction.

8. Mary looked in the refrigerator for a dozen eggs. When she found the box, only 5 eggs were left. What fractional part of the box of eggs was left?

9. At a recent meeting of a local Boosters Club, 17 of the 25 members attending were men. What fraction of those in attendance were men?

10. By weight, water is two parts out of three parts of the human body. What fraction of the body is water?

11. Three out of 5 students who begin college will continue until they receive their degree. Show in fractional form how many out of 100 beginning students will graduate.

12. Tina and her friends came in late to a party and found only $\frac{3}{4}$ of a pizza remaining. In order for everyone to get some pizza, she wanted to divide it into smaller pieces. If she divides the pizza into twelfths, how many pieces will she have? Show your answer in fractional form.

13. Sharon and Spunky noted that it took them 35 minutes to do their exercise routine. What fractional part of an hour is that? Show your answer in lowest terms.

14. Norman and his friend ordered several pizzas, which were all cut into eighths. The group ate 43 pieces of pizza. How many pizzas did they eat? Show your answer as a mixed number.

LEARNING UNIT 2–2 | ADDING AND SUBTRACTING FRACTIONS

DRILL PROBLEMS

1. Find the least common denominator (LCD) for each of the following groups of denominators using the prime numbers:

   a. 8, 16, 32   **b.** 9, 15, 20

   c. 12, 15, 32   **d.** 7, 9, 14, 28

2. Add and reduce to lowest terms or change to a mixed number if needed:

   a. $\dfrac{2}{7} + \dfrac{3}{7}$ **b.** $\dfrac{5}{12} + \dfrac{8}{15}$

   c. $\dfrac{7}{8} + \dfrac{5}{12}$ **d.** $7\dfrac{2}{3} + 5\dfrac{1}{4}$

   e. $\dfrac{2}{3} + \dfrac{4}{9} + \dfrac{1}{4}$

3. Subtract and reduce to lowest terms:

   a. $\dfrac{5}{9} - \dfrac{2}{9}$ **b.** $\dfrac{14}{15} - \dfrac{4}{15}$ **c.** $\dfrac{8}{9} - \dfrac{5}{6}$ **d.** $\dfrac{7}{12} - \dfrac{9}{16}$

   e. $33\dfrac{5}{8} - 27\dfrac{1}{2}$ **f.** $9 - 2\dfrac{3}{7}$ **g.** $15\dfrac{1}{3} - 9\dfrac{7}{12}$

   h. $92\dfrac{3}{10} - 35\dfrac{7}{15}$ **i.** $93 - 57\dfrac{5}{12}$ **j.** $22\dfrac{5}{8} - 17\dfrac{1}{4}$

WORD PROBLEMS

4. Dan Lund took a cross-country trip. He drove $5\frac{3}{8}$ hours on Monday, $6\frac{1}{2}$ hours on Tuesday, $9\frac{3}{4}$ hours on Wednesday, $6\frac{3}{8}$ hours on Thursday, and $10\frac{1}{4}$ hours on Friday. Find the total number of hours Dan drove in the first 5 days of his trip.

5. Sharon Parker bought 20 yards of material to make curtains. She used $4\frac{1}{2}$ yards for one bedroom window, $8\frac{3}{5}$ yards for another bedroom window, and $3\frac{7}{8}$ yards for a hall window. How much material did she have left?

6. Molly Ring visited a local gym and lost $2\frac{1}{4}$ pounds the first weekend and $6\frac{1}{8}$ pounds in week 2. What is Molly's total weight loss?

7. Bill Williams had to drive $46\frac{1}{4}$ miles to work. After driving $28\frac{5}{6}$ miles he noticed he was low on gas and had to decide whether he should stop to fill the gas tank. How many more miles does Bill have to drive to get to work?

8. Albert's Lumber Yard purchased $52\frac{1}{2}$ cords of lumber on Monday and $48\frac{3}{4}$ cords on Tuesday. It sold $21\frac{3}{8}$ cords on Friday. How many cords of lumber remain at Albert's Lumber Yard?

9. At Arlen Oil Company, where Dave Bursett is the service manager, it took $42\frac{1}{3}$ hours to clean five boilers. After a new cleaning tool was purchased, the time for cleaning five boilers was reduced to $37\frac{4}{9}$ hours. How much time was saved?

LEARNING UNIT 2–3 | MULTIPLYING AND DIVIDING FRACTIONS

DRILL PROBLEMS

1. Multiply (use cancellation technique):

a. $\dfrac{6}{13} \times \dfrac{26}{12}$

b. $\dfrac{3}{8} \times \dfrac{2}{3}$

c. $\dfrac{5}{7} \times \dfrac{9}{10}$

d. $\dfrac{3}{4} \times \dfrac{9}{13} \times \dfrac{26}{27}$

e. $6\dfrac{2}{5} \times 3\dfrac{1}{8}$

f. $2\dfrac{2}{3} \times 2\dfrac{7}{10}$

g. $45 \times \dfrac{7}{9}$

h. $3\dfrac{1}{9} \times 1\dfrac{2}{7} \times \dfrac{3}{4}$

i. $\dfrac{3}{4} \times \dfrac{7}{9} \times 3\dfrac{1}{3}$

j. $\dfrac{1}{8} \times 6\dfrac{2}{3} \times \dfrac{1}{10}$

2. Multiply (do not use canceling; reduce by finding the greatest common divisor):

a. $\dfrac{3}{4} \times \dfrac{8}{9}$

b. $\dfrac{7}{16} \times \dfrac{8}{13}$

3. Multiply or divide as indicated:

a. $\dfrac{25}{36} \div \dfrac{5}{9}$

b. $\dfrac{18}{8} \div \dfrac{12}{16}$

c. $2\dfrac{6}{7} \div 2\dfrac{2}{5}$

d. $3\dfrac{1}{4} \div 16$

e. $24 \div 1\dfrac{1}{3}$

f. $6 \times \dfrac{3}{2}$

g. $3\dfrac{1}{5} \times 7\dfrac{1}{2}$

h. $\dfrac{3}{8} \div \dfrac{7}{4}$

i. $9 \div 3\dfrac{3}{4}$

j. $\dfrac{11}{24} \times \dfrac{24}{33}$

k. $\dfrac{12}{14} \div 27$

l. $\dfrac{3}{5} \times \dfrac{2}{7} \div \dfrac{3}{10}$

WORD PROBLEMS

4. Mary Smith plans to make 12 meatloafs to store in her freezer. Each meatloaf requires $2\dfrac{1}{4}$ pounds of ground beef. How much ground beef does Mary need?

5. Judy Carter purchased a real estate lot for $24,000. She sold it 2 years later for $1\dfrac{5}{8}$ times as much as she had paid for it. What was the selling price?

6. Lynn Clarkson saw an ad for a camcorder that cost $980. She knew of a discount store that would sell it to her for a markdown of $\dfrac{3}{20}$ off the advertised price. How much is the discount she can get?

7. To raise money for their club, the members of the Marketing Club purchased 68 bushels of popcorn to resell. They plan to repackage the popcorn in bags that hold $\dfrac{2}{21}$ of a bushel each. How many bags of popcorn will they be able to fill?

8. Richard Tracy paid a total of $375 for stocks costing $9\dfrac{3}{8}$ per share. How many shares did he purchase?

9. While training for a marathon, Kristin Woods jogged $7\dfrac{3}{4}$ miles per hour for $2\dfrac{2}{3}$ hours. How many miles did Kristin jog?

10. On a map, 1 inch represents 240 miles. How many miles are represented by $\dfrac{3}{8}$ of an inch?

11. In Massachusetts, the governor wants to allot $\dfrac{1}{6}$ of the total sales tax collections to public education. The total sales tax collected is $2,472,000; how much will go to education?

LEARNING UNIT 3–1 | ROUNDING; FRACTION AND DECIMAL CONVERSIONS

DRILL PROBLEMS

1. Write in decimal:

    a. Forty-three hundredths _____

    b. Seven tenths _____

    c. Nine hundred fifty-three thousandths _____

    d. Four hundred one thousandths _____

    e. Six hundredths _____

2. Round each decimal to the place indicated:

    a. .4326 to the nearest thousandth _____

    b. .051 to the nearest tenth _____

    c. 8.207 to the nearest hundredth _____

    d. 2.094 to the nearest hundredth _____

    e. .511172 to the nearest ten thousandth _____

3. Name the place position of the underlined digit:

    a. .8$\underline{2}$6 _____

    b. .91$\underline{4}$ _____

    c. 3.$\underline{1}$169 _____

    d. 53.17$\underline{5}$ _____

    e. 1.017$\underline{4}$ _____

4. Convert to fractions (do not reduce):

    a. .83 _____   **b.** .426 _____   **c.** 2.516 _____

    d. .62$\frac{1}{2}$ _____   **e.** 13.007 _____   **f.** 5.03$\frac{1}{4}$ _____

5. Convert to fractions and reduce to lowest terms:

    a. .4   **b.** .44

    c. .53   **d.** .336

    e. .096   **f.** .125

    g. .3125   **h.** .008

    i. 2.625   **j.** 5.75

    k. 3.375   **l.** 9.04

6. Convert the following fractions to decimals and round your answer to the nearest hundredth:

    a. $\frac{1}{8}$ **b.** $\frac{7}{16}$

    c. $\frac{2}{3}$ **d.** $\frac{3}{4}$

e. $\dfrac{9}{16}$

f. $\dfrac{5}{6}$

g. $\dfrac{7}{9}$

h. $\dfrac{38}{79}$

i. $2\dfrac{3}{8}$

j. $9\dfrac{1}{3}$

k. $11\dfrac{19}{50}$

l. $6\dfrac{21}{32}$

m. $4\dfrac{83}{97}$

n. $1\dfrac{2}{5}$

o. $2\dfrac{2}{11}$

p. $13\dfrac{30}{42}$

WORD PROBLEMS

7. Alan Angel got 2 hits in his first 7 times at bat. What is his average to the nearest thousandths place?

8. Bill Breen earned $1,555, and his employer calculated that Bill's total FICA deduction should be $118.9575. Round this deduction to the nearest cent.

9. At the local college, .566 of the students are men. Convert to a fraction. Do not reduce.

10. The average television set is watched 2,400 hours a year. If there are 8,760 hours in a year, what fractional part of the year is spent watching television? Reduce to lowest terms.

11. On Saturday, the employees at the Empire Fish Company work only $\frac{1}{3}$ of a day. How could this be expressed as a decimal to nearest thousandths?

12. The North Shore Cinema has 610 seats. At a recent film screening there were 55 vacant seats. Show as a fraction the number of filled seats. Reduce as needed.

13. Michael Sullivan was planning his marketing strategy for a new product his company had produced. He was fascinated to discover that Rhode Island, the smallest state in the United States, was only twenty thousand, five hundred seven ten millionths the size of the largest state, Alaska. Write this number in decimal.

14. Bull Moose Company purchased a new manufacturing plant, located on an acre of land, for a total price of $2,250,000. The accountant determined that $\frac{3}{7}$ of the total price should be allocated as the price of the building. What decimal portion is the price of the building? Round to the nearest thousandth.

LEARNING UNIT 3–2 | ADDING, SUBTRACTING, MULTIPLYING, AND DIVIDING DECIMALS

DRILL PROBLEMS

1. Rearrange vertically and add:

    a. $4.83 + 6.2 + 12.005 + 1.84$ **b.** $1.0625 + 4.0881 + .0775$

    c. $.903 + .078 + .17 + .1 + .96$ **d.** $3.38 + .175 + .0186 + .2$

2. Rearrange and subtract:

    a. $.86 - .43$ **b.** $.885 - .069$

    c. $11.67 - .935$ **d.** $261.2 - 8.08$

3. Multiply and round to the nearest tenth:

    a. $13.6 \times .02$ **b.** $1.73 \times .069$

    c. 400×3.7 **d.** 0.025×5.6

4. Divide and round to the nearest hundredth:

    a. $13.869 \div .6$ **b.** $1.0088 \div .14$ **c.** $18.7 \div 2.16$

    d. $15.64 \div .34$

5. Complete by the shortcut method:
    a. $6.87 \times 1,000$
    d. $.21 \times 1,000$
    g. $.0021 \div 10$
    j. $23.0109 \div 100$

    b. $927,530 \div 100$
    e. 347×100
    h. $85.44 \times 10,000$

    c. $27.2 \div 1,000$
    f. $347 \div 100$
    i. 83.298×100

WORD PROBLEMS (Use *Business Math Handbook* Tables as Needed.)

6. John Sampson noted his odometer reading of 17,629.3 at the beginning of his vacation. At the end of his vacation the reading was 20,545.1. How many miles did he drive during his vacation?

7. Jeanne Allyn purchased 12.25 yards of ribbon for a craft project. The ribbon cost 37¢ per yard. What was the total cost of the ribbon?

8. Leo Green wanted to find out the gas mileage for his company truck. When he filled the gas tank, he wrote down the odometer reading of 9,650.7. The next time he filled the gas tank the odometer reading was 10,112.2. He looked at the gas pump and saw that he had taken 18.5 gallons of gas. Find the gas mileage per gallon for Leo's truck. Round to the nearest tenth.

9. At Halley's Rent-a-Car, the cost per day to rent a medium-size car is $35.25 plus 37¢ a mile. What would be the charge to rent this car for 1 day if you drove 205.4 miles?

10. A trip to Mexico costs 6,000 pesos. What is this in U.S. dollars? Check your answer.

11. If a commemorative gold coin weighs 7.842 grams, find the number of coins that can be produced from 116 grams of gold. Round to the nearest whole number.

LEARNING UNIT 4–1 | THE CHECKING ACCOUNT; CREDIT CARD TRANSACTIONS

DRILL PROBLEMS

1. The following is a deposit slip made out by Fred Young of the F. W. Young Company.

   a. How much cash did Young deposit?   _____

   b. How many checks did Young deposit?   _____

   c. What was the total amount deposited?   _____

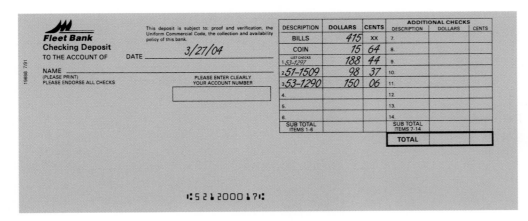

DESCRIPTION	DOLLARS	CENTS	ADDITIONAL CHECKS DESCRIPTION	DOLLARS	CENTS
BILLS	415	XX	7.		
COIN	15	64	8.		
LIST CHECKS 1. 53-1297	188	44	9.		
2. 51-1509	98	37	10.		
3. 53-1290	150	06	11.		
4.			12.		
5.			13.		
6.			14.		
SUB TOTAL ITEMS 1-6			SUB TOTAL ITEMS 7-14		
			TOTAL		

Fleet Bank — Checking Deposit. TO THE ACCOUNT OF. DATE 3/27/04. NAME (PLEASE PRINT). PLEASE ENDORSE ALL CHECKS. This deposit is subject to: proof and verification, the Uniform Commercial Code, the collection and availability policy of this bank. PLEASE ENTER CLEARLY YOUR ACCOUNT NUMBER.
⑆5212000 17⑆

2. Blackstone Company had a balance of $2,173.18 in its checking account. Henry James, Blackstone's accountant, made a deposit that consisted of 2 fifty-dollar bills, 120 ten-dollar bills, 6 five-dollar bills, 14 one-dollar bills, $9.54 in change, plus two checks they had accepted, one for $16.38 and the other for $102.50. Find the amount of the deposit and the new balance in Blackstone's checking account.

3. Answer the following questions using the illustration:

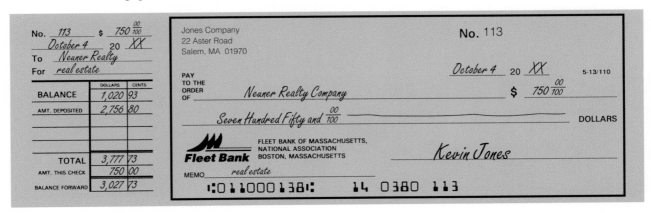

No. 113 $ 750 00/100. October 4 20 XX. To Neuner Realty. For real estate.

	DOLLARS	CENTS
BALANCE	1,020	93
AMT. DEPOSITED	2,756	80
TOTAL	3,777	73
AMT. THIS CHECK	750	00
BALANCE FORWARD	3,027	73

Jones Company / 22 Aster Road / Salem, MA 01970. No. 113. October 4 20 XX. 5-13/110. PAY TO THE ORDER OF Neuner Realty Company $ 750 00/100. Seven Hundred Fifty and 00/100 DOLLARS. FLEET BANK OF MASSACHUSETTS, NATIONAL ASSOCIATION, BOSTON, MASSACHUSETTS. Kevin Jones. MEMO real estate. ⑆011000138⑆ 14 0380 113

   a. Who is the payee?   _____

   b. Who is the drawer?   _____

   c. Who is the drawee?   _____

   d. What is the bank's identification number?   _____

   e. What is Jones Company's account number?   _____

f. What was the balance in the account on September 30? _____

g. For how much did Jones write Check No. 113? _____

h. How much was deposited on October 1? _____

i. How much was left after Check No. 113 was written? _____

4. Write each of the following amounts in verbal form as you would on a check:

    a. $25 _____

    b. $245.75 _____

    c. $3.98 _____

    d. $1,205.05 _____

    e. $3,013 _____

    f. $510.10 _____

5. From the following credit card transactions, calculate the net deposit that would be recorded on the merchant batch summary slip for the day.

MasterCard sales	Returns
$22.95	$ 4.09
18.51	16.50
16.92	

LEARNING UNIT 4–2 | BANK STATEMENT AND RECONCILIATION PROCESS; TRENDS IN BANKING

WORD PROBLEMS

1. Find the bank balance on January 31.

Date	Checks and payments			Deposits	Balance
January 1					401.17
January 2	108.64				_____
January 5	116.50			432.16	_____
January 6	14.92	150.00	10.00		_____
January 11	12.29			633.89	_____
January 18	108.64	18.60			_____
January 25	43.91	23.77		657.22	_____
January 26	75.00				_____
January 31	6.75 sc				_____

2. Joe Madruga, of Madruga's Taxi Service, received a bank statement for the month of May showing a balance of $932.36. His records show that the bank had not yet recorded two of his deposits, one for $521.50 and the other for $98.46. There are outstanding checks in the amounts of $41.67, $135.18, and $25.30. The statement also shows a service charge of $3.38. The balance in the check register is $1,353.55. Prepare a bank reconciliation for Madruga's as of May 31.

3. In reconciling the checking account for Nasser Enterprises, Beth Accomando found that the bank had collected a $3,000 promissory note on the company's behalf and had charged a $15 collection fee. There was also a service charge of $7.25. What amount should be added/subtracted from the checkbook balance to bring it up to date?

   Add: _____   Deduct: _____

4. In reconciling the checking account for Colonial Cleaners, Steve Papa found that a check for $34.50 had been recorded in the check register as $43.50. The bank returned an NSF check in the amount of $62.55. Interest income of $8.25 was earned and a service charge of $10.32 was assessed. What amount should be added/subtracted from the checkbook balance to bring it up to date?

   Add: _____   Deduct: _____

5. Matthew Stokes was completing the bank reconciliation for Parker's Tool and Die Company. The check register balance was $1,503.67. Matthew found that a $76.00 check had been recorded in the check register as $67.00; that a note for $1,500 had been collected by the bank for Parker's and the collection fee was $12.00; that $15.60 interest was earned on the account; and that an $8.35 service charge had been assessed. What should the check register balance be after Matthew updates it with the bank reconciliation information?

6. Long's Video Shop had the following MasterCard sales: $44.18, $66.10, $12.50, and $24.95. Returns for the day were $13.88 and $12.99. What will be the amount of the net deposit for Long's Video Shop on the merchant batch summary slip?

7. Consumers, community activists, and politicians are decrying the new line of accounts because several include a $3 service charge for some customers who use bank tellers for transactions that can be done through an automated teller machine. Bill Wade banks at a local bank that charges this fee. He was having difficulty balancing his checkbook because he did not notice this fee on his bank statement. His bank statement showed a balance of $822.18. Bill's checkbook had a balance of $206.48. Check No. 406 for $116.08 and Check No. 407 for $12.50 were outstanding. A $521 deposit was not on the statement. Bill has his payroll check electronically deposited to his checking account—the payroll check was for $1,015.12 (Bill's payroll checks vary each month). There are also a $1 service fee and a teller fee of $6. Complete Bill's bank reconciliation.

8. At First National Bank in San Diego, some customers have to pay $25 each year as an ATM card fee. John Levi banks at First National Bank and just received his bank statement showing a balance of $829.25; his checkbook balance is $467.40. The bank statement shows an ATM card fee of $25.00, teller fee of $9.00, interest of $1.80, and John's $880 IRS refund check, which was processed by the IRS and deposited to his account. John has two checks that have not cleared—No. 112 for $620.10 and No. 113 for $206.05. There is also a deposit in transit for $1,312.10. Prepare John's bank reconciliation.

LEARNING UNIT 5–1 | SOLVING EQUATIONS FOR THE UNKNOWN

DRILL PROBLEMS

1. Write equations for the following situations. Use N for the unknown number. Do not solve the equations.

   a. Three times a number is 70.

   b. A number increased by 13 equals 25.

   c. Seven less than a number is 5.

   d. Fifty-seven decreased by 3 times a number is 21.

   e. Fourteen added to one-third of a number is 18.

   f. Twice the sum of a number and 4 is 32.

   g. Three-fourths of a number is 9.

   h. Two times a number plus 3 times the same number plus 8 is 68.

2. Solve for the unknown number:

   a. $B + 12 = 38$ **b.** $29 + M = 44$ **c.** $D - 77 = 98$

   d. $7N = 63$ **e.** $\dfrac{X}{12} = 11$ **f.** $3Q + 4Q + 2Q = 108$

   g. $H + 5H + 3 = 57$ **h.** $2(N - 3) = 62$ **i.** $\dfrac{3R}{4} = 27$

   j. $E - 32 = 41$ **k.** $5(2T - 2) = 120$ **l.** $12W - 5W = 98$

   m. $49 - X = 37$ **n.** $12(V + 2) = 84$ **o.** $7D + 4 = 5D + 14$

   p. $7(T - 2) = 2T - 9$

Name _____   Date _____

LEARNING UNIT 5–2 | SOLVING WORD PROBLEMS FOR THE UNKNOWN

WORD PROBLEMS

1. A blue denim shirt at the Gap was marked down $15. The sale price was $30. What was the original price?

Unknown(s)	Variable(s)	Relationship

2. Goodwin's Corporation found that $\frac{2}{3}$ of its employees were vested in their retirement plan. If 124 employees are vested, what is the total number of employees at Goodwin's?

Unknown(s)	Variable(s)	Relationship

3. Eileen Haskin's utility and telephone bills for the month totaled $180. The utility bill was 3 times as much as the telephone bill. How much was each bill?

Unknown(s)	Variable(s)	Relationship

4. Ryan and his friends went to the golf course to hunt for golf balls. Ryan found 15 more than $\frac{1}{3}$ of the total number of golf balls that were found. How many golf balls were found if Ryan found 75 golf balls?

Unknown(s)	Variable(s)	Relationship

5. Linda Mills and Sherry Somers sold 459 tickets for the Advertising Club's raffle. If Linda sold 8 times as many tickets as Sherry, how many tickets did each one sell?

Unknown(s)	Variable(s)	Relationship

6. Jason Mazzola wanted to buy a suit at Giblee's. Jason did not have enough money with him, so Mr. Giblee told him he would hold the suit if Jason gave him a deposit of $\frac{1}{5}$ of the cost of the suit. Jason agreed and gave Mr. Giblee $79. What was the price of the suit?

Unknown(s)	Variable(s)	Relationship

7. Peter sold watches ($7) and necklaces ($4) at a flea market. Total sales were $300. People bought 3 times as many watches as necklaces. How many of each did Peter sell? What were the total dollar sales of each?

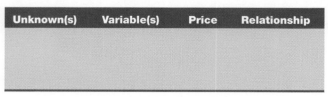

Unknown(s)	Variable(s)	Price	Relationship

8. Peter sold watches ($7) and necklaces ($4) at a flea market. Total sales for 48 watches and necklaces were $300. How many of each did Peter sell? What were the total dollar sales of each?

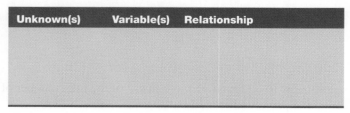

Unknown(s)	Variable(s)	Price	Relationship

9. A 3,000 piece of direct mailing cost $1,435. Printing cost is $550, about $3\frac{1}{2}$ times the cost of typesetting. How much did the typesetting cost? Round to the nearest cent.

Unknown(s)	Variable(s)	Relationship

10. In 2003, Tony Rigato, owner of MRM, saw an increase in sales to $13.5 million. Rigato states that since 2000, sales have more than tripled. What were his sales in 2000?

Unknown(s)	Variable(s)	Relationship

LEARNING UNIT 6–1 | CONVERSIONS

DRILL PROBLEMS

1. Convert the following to percents (round to the nearest tenth of a percent if needed):

   a. .08 _____ %   b. .875 _____ %

   c. .009 _____ %   d. 8.3 _____ %

   e. 5.26 _____ %   f. 6 _____ %

   g. .0105 _____ %   h. .1180 _____ %

   i. 5.0375 _____ %   j. .862 _____ %

   k. .2615 _____ %   l. .8 _____ %

   m. .025 _____ %   n. .06 _____ %

2. Convert the following to decimals (do not round):

   a. 37% _____   b. .09% _____

   c. 4.7% _____   d. 9.67% _____

   e. .2% _____   f. $\frac{1}{4}\%$ _____

   g. .76% _____   h. 110% _____

   i. $12\frac{1}{2}\%$ _____   j. 5% _____

   k. .004% _____   l. $7\frac{5}{10}\%$ _____

   m. $\frac{3}{4}\%$ _____   n. 1% _____

3. Convert the following to percents (round to the nearest tenth of a percent if needed):

   a. $\frac{7}{10}$ _____ %   b. $\frac{1}{5}$ _____ %

   c. $1\frac{5}{8}$ _____ %   d. $\frac{2}{7}$ _____ %

   e. 2 _____ %   f. $\frac{14}{100}$ _____ %

   g. $\frac{1}{6}$ _____ %   h. $\frac{1}{2}$ _____ %

   i. $\frac{3}{5}$ _____ %   j. $\frac{3}{25}$ _____ %

   k. $\frac{5}{16}$ _____ %   l. $\frac{11}{50}$ _____ %

   m. $4\frac{3}{4}$ _____ %   n. $\frac{3}{200}$ _____ %

4. Convert the following to fractions in simplest form:

   a. 40% _____   b. 15% _____

   c. 50% _____   d. 75% _____

   e. 35% _____   f. 85% _____

   g. $12\frac{1}{2}\%$ _____   h. $37\frac{1}{2}\%$ _____

   i. $33\frac{1}{3}\%$ _____   j. 3% _____

   k. 8.5% _____   l. $5\frac{3}{4}\%$ _____

   m. 100% _____   n. 10% _____

5. Complete the following table by finding the missing fraction, decimal, or percent equivalent:

Fraction	Decimal	Percent	Fraction	Decimal	Percent
a. _____	.25	25%	h. $\frac{1}{6}$	$.16\overline{6}$	_____
b. $\frac{3}{8}$	_____	$37\frac{1}{2}\%$	i. _____	$.083\overline{3}$	$8\frac{1}{3}\%$
c. $\frac{1}{2}$	.5	_____	j. $\frac{1}{9}$	_____	$11\frac{1}{9}\%$
d. $\frac{2}{3}$	_____	$66\frac{2}{3}\%$	k. _____	.3125	$31\frac{1}{4}\%$
e. _____	.4	40%	l. $\frac{3}{40}$	.075	_____
f. $\frac{3}{5}$	.6	_____	m. $\frac{1}{5}$	_____	20%
g. $\frac{7}{10}$	_____	70%	n. _____	1.125	$112\frac{1}{2}\%$

WORD PROBLEMS

6. In 2004, Mutual of New York reported an overwhelming 70% of its new sales came from existing clients. What fractional part of its new sales came from existing clients? Reduce to simplest form.

7. Six hundred ninety corporations and design firms competed for the Industrial Design Excellence Award (IDEA) in 2004. Twenty were selected as the year's best and received gold awards. Show the gold award winners as a fraction; then show what percent of the entrants received gold awards. Round to the nearest tenth of a percent.

8. In the first half of 2004, stock prices in the Standard & Poor's 500-stock index rose 17.5%. Show the increase in decimal.

9. In the recent banking crisis, many banks were unable to cover their bad loans. Citicorp, the nation's largest real estate lender, was reported as having only enough reserves to cover 39% of its bad loans. What fractional part of its loan losses was covered?

10. Dave Mattera spent his vacation in Las Vegas. He ordered breakfast in his room, and when he went downstairs to the coffee shop, he discovered that the same breakfast was much less expensive. He had paid 1.884 times as much for the breakfast in his room. What was the percent of increase for the breakfast in his room?

11. Putnam Management Company of Boston recently increased its management fee by .09%. What is the increase as a decimal? What is the same increase as a fraction?

12. Joel Black and Karen Whyte formed a partnership and drew up a partnership agreement, with profits and losses to be divided equally after each partner receives a $7\frac{1}{2}\%$ return on his or her capital contribution. Show their return on investment as a decimal and as a fraction. Reduce.

Name _____ Date _____

LEARNING UNIT 6–2 ▌ APPLICATION OF PERCENTS—PORTION FORMULA

DRILL PROBLEMS

1. Fill in the amount of the base, rate, and portion in each of the following statements:

a. The Johnsons spend $1,000 a month on food, which is $12\frac{1}{2}$% of their monthly income of $8,000.

Base _____   Rate _____   Portion _____

b. Rocky Norman got a $15 discount when he purchased a new camera. This was 20% off the sticker price of $75.

Base _____   Rate _____   Portion _____

c. Mary Burns got a 12% senior citizens discount when she bought a $7.00 movie ticket. She saved $0.84.

Base _____   Rate _____   Portion _____

d. Arthur Bogey received a commission of $13,500 when he sold the Brown's house for $225,000. His commission rate is 6%.

Base _____   Rate _____   Portion _____

e. Leo Davis deposited $5,000 in a certificate of deposit (CD). A year later he received an interest payment of $450 which was a yield of 9%.

Base _____   Rate _____   Portion _____

f. Grace Tremblay is on a diet that allows her to eat 1,600 calories per day. For breakfast she had 600 calories, which is $37\frac{1}{2}$% of her allowance.

Base _____   Rate _____   Portion _____

2. Find the portion; round to the nearest hundredth if necessary:

a. 7% of 74 _____   **b.** 12% of 205 _____   **c.** 16% of 630 _____

d. 7.5% of 920 _____   **e.** 25% of 1,004 _____   **f.** 10% of 79 _____

g. 103% of 44 _____   **h.** 30% of 78 _____   **i.** .2% of 50 _____

j. 1% of 5,622 _____   **k.** $6\frac{1}{4}$% of 480 _____   **l.** 150% of 10 _____

m. 100% of 34 _____   **n.** $\frac{1}{2}$% of 27 _____

3. Find the rate; round to the nearest tenth of a percent as needed:

a. 30 is what percent of 90? _____   **b.** 6 is what percent of 200? _____

c. 275 is what percent of 1,000? _____   **d.** .8 is what percent of 44? _____

e. 67 is what percent of 2,010? _____   **f.** 550 is what percent of 250? _____

g. 13 is what percent of 650? _____   **h.** $15 is what percent of $455? _____

i. .05 is what percent of 100? _____   **j.** $6.25 is what percent of $10? _____

4. Find the base; round to the nearest tenth as needed:

a. 63 is 30% of _____   **b.** 60 is 33% of _____   **c.** 150 is 25% of _____

d. 47 is 1% of _____   **e.** $21 is 120% of _____   **f.** 2.26 is 40% of _____

g. 75 is $12\frac{1}{2}$% of _____   **h.** 18 is 22.2% of _____   **i.** $37.50 is 50% of _____

j. 250 is 100% of _____

5. Find the percent of increase or decrease. Round to nearest tenth percent as needed:

	Last year	This year	Amount of change	Percent of change
a.	5,962	4,378	_____	_____
b.	$10,995	$12,250	_____	_____
c.	120,000	140,000	_____	_____
d.	120,000	100,000	_____	_____

WORD PROBLEMS

6. A machine that originally cost $2,400 was sold for $600 at the end of 5 years. What percent of the original cost is the selling price?

7. Joanne Byrne invested $75,000 in a candy shop and is making 12% per year on her investment. How much money per year is she making on her investment?

8. There was a fire in Bill Porper's store that caused 2,780 inventory items to be destroyed. Before the fire, 9,565 inventory items were in the store. What percent of inventory was destroyed? Round to nearest tenth percent.

9. Elyse's Dress Shoppe makes 25% of its sales for cash. If the cash receipts on January 21 were $799, what were the total sales for the day?

10. The YMCA is holding a fund-raiser to collect money for a new gym floor. So far it has collected $7,875, which is 63% of the goal. What is the amount of the goal? How much more money must the YMCA collect?

11. Leslie Tracey purchased her home for $51,500. She sold it last year for $221,200. What percent profit did she make on the sale? Round to nearest tenth percent.

12. Maplewood Park Tool & Die had an annual production of 375,165 units this year. This is 140% of the annual production last year. What was last year's annual production?

LEARNING UNIT 7–1 | TRADE DISCOUNTS—SINGLE AND CHAIN*

DRILL PROBLEMS

1. Calculate the trade discount amount for each of the following items:

Item	List price	Trade discount	Trade discount amount
a. Gateway	$1,200	40%	_____
b. Flat screen TV	$1,200	30%	_____
c. Suit	$ 500	10%	_____
d. Bicycle	$ 800	$12\frac{1}{2}\%$	_____
e. David Yurman bracelet	$ 950	40%	_____

2. Calculate the net price for each of the following items:

Item	List price	Trade discount amount	Net price
a. Home Depot table	$600	$250	_____
b. Bookcase	$525	$129	_____
c. Rocking chair	$480	$ 95	_____

3. Fill in the missing amount for each of the following items:

Item	List price	Trade discount amount	Net price
a. Sears electric saw	_____	$19	$56.00
b. Electric drill	$90	_____	$68.50
c. Ladder	$56	$15.25	_____

4. For each of the following, find the percent paid (complement of trade discount) and the net price:

List price	Trade discount	Percent paid	Net price
a. $45	15%	_____	_____
b. $195	12.2%	_____	_____
c. $325	50%	_____	_____
d. $120	18%	_____	_____

5. In each of the following examples, find the net price equivalent rate and the single equivalent discount rate:

Chain discount	Net price equivalent rate	Single equivalent discount rate
a. 25/5	_____	_____
b. 15/15	_____	_____
c. 15/10/5	_____	_____
d. 12/12/6	_____	_____

_____
*Freight problems to be shown in LU 7–2 material.

6. In each of the following examples, find the net price and the trade discount:

	List price	Chain discount	Net price	Trade discount
a.	$5,000	10/10/5	_____	_____
b.	$7,500	9/6/3	_____	_____
c.	$898	20/7/2	_____	_____
d.	$1,500	25/10	_____	_____

7. The list price of a handheld calculator is $19.50, and the trade discount is 18%. Find the trade discount amount.

8. The list price of a silver picture frame is $29.95, and the trade discount is 15%. Find the trade discount amount and the net price.

9. The net price of a set of pots and pans is $65, and the trade discount is 20%. What is the list price?

10. Jennie's Variety Store has the opportunity to purchase candy from three different wholesalers; each of the wholesalers offers a different chain discount. Company A offers 25/5/5, Company B offers 20/10/5, and Company C offers 15/20. Which company should Jennie deal with? *Hint:* Choose the company with the highest single equivalent discount rate.

11. The list price of a television set is $625. Find the net price after a series discount of 30/20/10.

12. Mandy's Accessories Shop purchased 12 purses with a total list price of $726. What was the net price of each purse if the wholesaler offered a chain discount of 25/20?

13. Kransberg Furniture Store purchased a bedroom set for $1,097.25 from Furniture Wholesalers. The list price of the set was $1,995. What trade discount rate did Kransberg receive?

14. Susan Monk teaches second grade and receives a discount at the local art supply store. Recently she paid $47.25 for art supplies after receiving a chain discount of 30/10. What was the regular price of the art supplies?

LEARNING UNIT 7–2 | CASH DISCOUNTS, CREDIT TERMS, AND PARTIAL PAYMENTS

DRILL PROBLEMS

1. Complete the following table:

	Date of invoice	Date goods received	Terms	Last day of discount period	End of credit period
a.	February 8		2/10, n/30	_____	_____
b.	August 26		2/10, n/30	_____	_____
c.	October 17		3/10, n/60	_____	_____
d.	March 11	May 10	3/10, n/30, ROG	_____	_____
e.	September 14		2/10, EOM	_____	_____
f.	May 31		2/10, EOM	_____	_____

2. Calculate the cash discount and the net amount paid.

	Invoice amount	Cash discount rate	Discount amount	Net amount paid
a.	$75	3%	_____	_____
b.	$1,559	2%	_____	_____
c.	$546.25	2%	_____	_____
d.	$9,788.75	1%	_____	_____

3. Use the complement of the cash discount to calculate the net amount paid. Assume all invoices are paid within the discount period.

	Terms of invoice	Amount of invoice	Complement	Net amount paid
a.	2/10, n/30	$1,125	_____	_____
b.	3/10, n/30 ROG	$4,500	_____	_____
c.	2/10, EOM	$375.50	_____	_____
d.	1/15, n/45	$3,998	_____	_____

4. Calculate the amount of cash discount and the net amount paid.

	Date of invoice	Terms of invoice	Amount of invoice	Date paid	Cash discount	Amount paid
a.	January 12	2/10, n/30	$5,320	January 22	_____	_____
b.	May 28	2/10, n/30	$975	June 7	_____	_____
c.	August 15	2/10, n/30	$7,700	August 26	_____	_____
d.	March 8	2/10, EOM	$480	April 10	_____	_____
e.	January 24	3/10, n/60	$1,225	February 3	_____	_____

5. Complete the following table:

	Total invoice	Freight charges included in invoice total	Date of invoice	Terms of invoice	Date of payment	Cash discount	Amount paid
a.	$852	$12.50	3/19	2/10, n/30	3/29	_____	_____
b.	$669.57	$15.63	7/28	3/10, EOM	9/10	_____	_____
c.	$500	$11.50	4/25	2/10, n/60	6/5	_____	_____
d.	$188	$9.70	1/12	2/10, EOM	2/10	_____	_____

6. In the following table, assume that all the partial payments were made within the discount period.

	Amount of invoice	Terms of invoice	Partial payment	Amount to be credited	Balance outstanding
a.	$481.90	2/10, n/30	$90.00	_____	_____
b.	$1,000	2/10, EOM	$500.00	_____	_____
c.	$782.88	3/10, n/30, ROG	$275.00	_____	_____
d.	$318.80	2/15, n/60	$200.00	_____	_____

WORD PROBLEMS

7. Northwest Chemical Company received an invoice for $12,480, dated March 12, with terms of 2/10, n/30. If the invoice was paid March 22, what was the amount due?

8. On May 27, Trotter Hardware Store received an invoice for trash barrels purchased for $13,650 with terms of 3/10, EOM; the freight charge, which is included in the price, is $412. What are **(a)** the last day of the discount period and **(b)** the amount of the payment due on this date?

9. The Glass Sailboat received an invoice for $930.50 with terms 2/10, n/30 on April 19. On April 29, it sent a payment of $430.50. **(a)** How much credit will be given on the total due? **(b)** What is the new balance due?

10. Dallas Ductworks offers cash discounts of 2/10, 1/15, n/30 on all purchases. If an invoice for $544 dated July 18 is paid on August 2, what is the amount due?

11. The list price of a DVD player is $299.90 with trade discounts of 10/20 and terms of 3/10, n/30. If a retailer pays the invoice within the discount period, what amount must the retailer pay?

12. The invoice of a sneaker supplier totaled $2,488.50, was dated February 7, and offered terms 2/10, ROG. The shipment of sneakers was received on March 7. What are **(a)** the last date of the discount period and **(b)** the amount of the discount that will be lost if the invoice is paid after that date?

13. Starburst Toy Company receives an invoice amounting to $1,152.30 with terms of 2/10, EOM and dated November 6. If a partial payment of $750 is made on December 8, what are **(a)** the credit given for the partial payment and **(b)** the balance due on the invoice?

14. Todd's Sporting Goods received an invoice for soccer equipment dated July 26 with terms 3/10, 1/15, n/30 in the amount of $3,225.83, which included shipping charges of $375.50. If this bill is paid on August 5, what amount must be paid?

LEARNING UNIT 8–1 | MARKUPS BASED ON COST (100%)

DRILL PROBLEMS

1. Fill in the missing numbers:

	Cost	Dollar markup	Selling price
a.	$9.20	$1.59	_____
b.	$8.32	_____	$11.04
c.	$25.27	_____	$29.62
d.	_____	$75.00	$165.00
e.	$86.54	$29.77	_____

2. Calculate the markup based on cost (round to the nearest cent).

	Cost	Markup (percent of cost)	Dollar markup
a.	$425.00	30%	_____
b.	$1.52	20%	_____
c.	$9.90	$12\frac{1}{2}\%$	_____
d.	$298.10	50%	_____
e.	$74.25	38%	_____
f.	$552.25	100%	_____

3. Calculate the dollar markup and rate of the markup as a percent of cost (round percents to nearest tenth percent). Verify your result, which may be slightly off due to rounding.

	Cost	Selling price	Dollar markup	Markup (percent of cost)	Verify
a.	$2.50	$4.50	_____	_____	
b.	$12.50	$19.00	_____	_____	
c.	$0.97	$1.25	_____	_____	
d.	$132.25	$175.00	_____	_____	
e.	$65.00	$89.99	_____	_____	

4. Calculate the dollar markup and the selling price.

	Cost	Markup (percent of cost)	Dollar markup	Selling price
a.	$2.20	40%	_____	_____
b.	$2.80	16%	_____	_____
c.	$840.00	$12\frac{1}{2}\%$	_____	_____
d.	$24.36	30%	_____	_____

5. Calculate the cost (round to the nearest cent).

	Selling price	Rate of markup based on cost	Cost
a.	$1.98	30%	_____
b.	$360.00	60%	_____
c.	$447.50	20%	_____
d.	$1,250.00	100%	_____

6. Find the missing numbers. Round money to the nearest cent and percents to the nearest tenth percent.

	Cost	Dollar markup	Percent markup on cost	Selling price
a.	$72.00	_____	40%	_____
b.	_____	$7.00	_____	$35.00
c.	$8.80	$1.10	_____	_____
d.	_____	_____	28%	$19.84
e.	$175.00	_____	_____	$236.25

WORD PROBLEMS

7. The cost of an office chair is $159 and the markup rate is 24% of the cost. What are **(a)** the dollar markup and **(b)** the selling price?

8. If Barry's Furniture Store purchased a floor lamp for $120 and plans to add a markup of $90, **(a)** what will the selling price be and **(b)** what is the markup as a percent of cost?

9. If Lesjardin's Jewelry Store is selling a gold bracelet for $349, which includes a markup of 35% on cost, what are **(a)** Lesjardin's cost and **(b)** the amount of the dollar markup?

10. Toll's Variety Store sells an alarm clock for $14.75. The alarm clock cost Toll's $9.90. What is the markup amount as a percent of cost? Round to the nearest whole percent.

11. Swanson's Audio Supply marks up its merchandise by 40% on cost. If the markup on a cassette player is $85, what are **(a)** the cost of the cassette player and **(b)** the selling price?

12. Brown's Department Store is selling a shirt for $55. If the markup is 70% on cost, what is Brown's cost (to the nearest cent)?

13. Ward's Greenhouse purchased tomato flats for $5.75 each. Ward's has decided to use a markup of 42% on cost. Find the selling price.

LEARNING UNIT 8–2 | MARKUPS BASED ON SELLING PRICE (100%)

DRILL PROBLEMS

1. Calculate the markup based on the selling price.

	Selling price	Markup (percent of selling price)	Dollar markup
a.	$12.00	40%	_____
b.	$230.00	25%	_____
c.	$81.00	42.5%	_____
d.	$72.88	$37\frac{1}{2}\%$	_____
e.	$1.98	$7\frac{1}{2}\%$	_____

2. Calculate the dollar markup and the markup as a percent of selling price (to the nearest tenth percent). Verify your answer, which may be slightly off due to rounding.

	Cost	Selling price	Dollar markup	Markup (percent of selling price)	Verify
a.	$2.50	$4.25	_____	_____	
b.	$16.00	$24.00	_____	_____	
c.	$45.25	$85.00	_____	_____	
d.	$0.19	$0.25	_____	_____	
e.	$5.50	$8.98	_____	_____	

3. Given the *cost* and the markup as a percent of *selling price,* calculate the selling price.

	Cost	Markup (percent of selling price)	Selling price
a.	$5.90	15%	_____
b.	$600	32%	_____
c.	$15	50%	_____
d.	$120	30%	_____
e.	$0.29	20%	_____

4. Given the selling price and the percent markup on selling price, calculate the cost.

	Cost	Markup (percent of selling price)	Selling price
a.	_____	40%	$6.25
b.	_____	20%	$16.25
c.	_____	19%	$63.89
d.	_____	$62\frac{1}{2}\%$	$44.00

5. Calculate the equivalent rate of markup (round to the nearest hundredth percent).

Markup on cost	Markup on selling price		Markup on cost	Markup on selling price
a. 40%	_____		**b.** 50%	_____
c. _____	50%		**d.** _____	35%
e. _____	40%			

WORD PROBLEMS

6. Fisher Equipment is selling a Wet/Dry Shop Vac for $49.97. If Fisher's markup is 40% of the selling price, what is the cost of the Shop Vac?

7. Gove Lumber Company purchased a 10-inch table saw for $225 and will mark up the price 35% on the selling price. What will the selling price be?

8. To realize a sufficient gross margin, City Paint and Supply Company marks up its paint 27% on the selling price. If a gallon of Latex Semi-Gloss Enamel has a markup of $4.02, find **(a)** the selling price and **(b)** the cost.

9. A Magnavox 20-inch color TV cost $180 and sells for $297. What is the markup based on the selling price? Round to the nearest hundredth percent.

10. Bargain Furniture sells a five-piece country maple bedroom set for $1,299. The cost of this set is $700. What are **(a)** the markup on the bedroom set, **(b)** the markup percent on cost, and **(c)** the markup percent on the selling price? Round to the nearest hundredth percent.

11. Robert's Department Store marks up its sundries by 28% on the selling price. If a 6.4-ounce tube of toothpaste costs $1.65, what will the selling price be?

12. To be competitive, Tinker Toys must sell the Nintendo Control Deck for $89.99. To meet expenses and make a sufficient profit, Tinker Toys must add a markup on the selling price of 23%. What is the maximum amount that Tinker Toys can afford to pay a wholesaler for Nintendo?

13. Nicole's Restaurant charges $7.50 for a linguini dinner that costs $2.75 for the ingredients. What rate of markup is earned on the selling price? Round to the nearest hundredth percent.

LEARNING UNIT 8–3 | MARKDOWNS AND PERISHABLES

DRILL PROBLEMS

1. Find the dollar markdown and the sale price.

	Original selling price	Markdown percent	Dollar markdown	Sale price
a.	$80	20%	_____	_____
b.	$2,099.98	25%	_____	_____
c.	$729	30%	_____	_____

2. Find the dollar markdown and the markdown percent on original selling price.

	Original selling price	Sale price	Dollar markdown	Markdown percent
a.	$19.50	$9.75	_____	_____
b.	$250	$175	_____	_____
c.	$39.95	$29.96	_____	_____

3. Find the original selling price.

	Sale price	Markdown percent	Original selling price
a.	$328	20%	_____
b.	$15.85	15%	_____

4. Calculate the final selling price.

	Original selling price	First markdown	Second markdown	Final markup	Final selling price
a.	$4.96	25%	8%	5%	_____
b.	$130	30%	10%	20%	_____

5. Find the missing amounts.

Number of units	Unit cost	Total cost	Estimated* spoilage	Desired markup (percent of cost)	Total selling price	Selling price per unit
a. 72	$3	_____	12%	50%	_____	_____
b. 50	$0.90	_____	16%	42%	_____	_____

*Round to the nearest whole unit as needed.

WORD PROBLEMS

6. Windom's is having a 30%-off sale on their box springs and mattresses. A queen-size, back-supporter mattress is priced at $325. What is the sale price of the mattress?

7. Murray and Sons sell a personal fax machine for $602.27. It is having a sale, and the fax machine is marked down to $499.88. What is the percent of the markdown?

8. Coleman's is having a clearance sale. A lamp with an original selling price of $249 is now selling for $198. Find the percent of the markdown. Round to the nearest hundredth percent.

9. Johnny's Sports Shop has advertised markdowns on certain items of 22%. A soccer ball is marked with a sale price of $16.50. What was the original price of the soccer ball?

10. Sam Grillo sells seasonal furnishings. Near the end of the summer a five-piece patio set that was priced $349.99 had not been sold, so he marked it down by 12%. As Labor Day approached, he still had not sold the patio set, so he marked it down an additional 18%. What was the final selling price of the patio set?

11. Calsey's Department Store sells their down comforters for a regular price of $325. During its white sale the comforters were marked down 22%. Then, at the end of the sale, Calsey's held a special promotion and gave a second markdown of 10%. When the sale was over, the remaining comforters were marked up 20%. What was the final selling price of the remaining comforters?

12. The New Howard Bakery wants to make a 60% profit on the cost of its pies. To calculate the price of the pies, it estimated that the usual amount of spoilage is 5 pies. Calculate the selling price for each pie if the number of pies baked each day is 24 and the cost of the ingredients for each pie is $1.80.

13. Sunshine Bakery bakes 660 loaves of bread each day and estimates that 10% of the bread will go stale before it is sold and will have to be discarded. The owner of the bakery wishes to realize a 55% markup on cost on the bread. If the cost to make a loaf of bread is $0.46, what should the owner sell each loaf for?

LEARNING UNIT 9-1 | CALCULATING VARIOUS TYPES OF EMPLOYEES' GROSS PAY

DRILL PROBLEMS

1. Fill in the missing amounts for each of the following employees. Do not round the overtime rate in your calculations and round your final answers to the nearest cent.

Employee	Total hours	Rate per hour	Regular pay	Overtime pay	Gross pay
a. Ben Badger	40	_____	_____	_____	_____
b. Casey Guitare	43	_____	_____	_____	_____
c. Norma Harris	37	_____	_____	_____	_____
d. Ed Jackson	45	_____	_____	_____	_____

2. Calculate each employee's gross from the following data. Do not round the overtime rate in your calculation but round your final answers to the nearest cent.

Employee	S	M	Tu	W	Th	F	S	Total hours	Rate per hour	Regular pay	Overtime pay	Gross pay
a. L. Adams	0	8	8	8	8	8	0	_____	$8.10	_____	_____	_____
b. M. Card	0	9	8	9	8	8	4	_____	$11.35	_____	_____	_____
c. P. Kline	2	$7\frac{1}{2}$	$8\frac{1}{4}$	8	$10\frac{3}{4}$	9	2	_____	$10.60	_____	_____	_____
d. J. Mack	0	$9\frac{1}{2}$	$9\frac{3}{4}$	$9\frac{1}{2}$	10	10	4	_____	$9.95	_____	_____	_____

3. Calculate the gross wages of the following production workers.

Employee	Rate per unit	No. of units produced	Gross pay
a. A. Bossie	$0.67	655	_____
b. J. Carson	$0.87\frac{1}{2}$	703	_____

4. Using the given differential scale, calculate the gross wages of the following production workers.

Units produced	Amount per unit
From 1–50	$.55
From 51–100	.65
From 101–200	.72
More than 200	.95

Employee	Units produced	Gross pay
a. F. Burns	190	_____
b. B. English	210	_____
c. E. Jackson	200	_____

5. Calculate the following salespersons' gross wages.

    a. Straight commission:

Employee	Net sales	Commission	Gross pay
M. Salley	$40,000	13%	_____

b. Straight commission with draw:

Employee	Net sales	Commission	Draw	Commission minus draw
G. Gorsbeck	$38,000	12%	$600	_____

c. Variable commission scale:

Up to $25,000	8%
Excess of $25,000 to $40,000	10%
More than $40,000	12%

Employee	Net sales	Gross pay
H. Lloyd	$42,000	_____

d. Salary plus commission:

Employee	Salary	Commission	Quota	Net sales	Gross pay
P. Floyd	$2,500	3%	$400,000	$475,000	_____

WORD PROBLEMS

For all problems with overtime, be sure to round only the final answer.

6. In the first week of December, Dana Robinson worked 52 hours. His regular rate of pay is $11.25 per hour. What was Dana's gross pay for the week?

7. Davis Fisheries pays its workers for each box of fish they pack. Sunny Melanson receives $.30 per box. During the third week of July, Sunny packed 2,410 boxes of fish. What is Sunny's gross pay?

8. Maye George is a real estate broker who receives a straight commission of 6%. What would her commission be for a house that sold for $197,500?

9. Devon Company pays Eileen Haskins a straight commission of $12\frac{1}{2}\%$ on net sales. In January, Devon gave Eileen a draw of $600. She had net sales that month of $35,570. What was Eileen's commission minus draw?

10. Parker and Company pays Selma Stokes on a variable commission scale. In a month when Selma had net sales of $155,000, what was her gross pay based on the following schedule?

Net sales	Commission rate
Up to $40,000	5%
Excess of $40,000 to $75,000	5.5%
Excess of $75,000 to $100,000	6%
More than $100,000	7%

11. Marsh Furniture Company pays Joshua Charles a monthly salary of $1,900 plus a commission of $2\frac{1}{2}\%$ on sales over $12,500. Last month, Joshua had net sales of $17,799. What was Joshua's gross pay for the month?

12. Amy McWha works at Lamplighter Bookstore where she earns $7.75 per hour plus a commission of 2% on her weekly sales in excess of $1,500. Last week, Amy worked 39 hours and had total sales of $2,250. What was Amy's gross pay for the week?

LEARNING UNIT 9-2 | COMPUTING PAYROLL DEDUCTIONS FOR EMPLOYEES' PAY; EMPLOYERS' RESPONSIBILITIES

DRILL PROBLEMS

Use tables in the *Business Math Handbook* (assume FICA rates in text).

Employee	Allowances and marital status	Cumulative earnings	Salary per week	Taxable earnings S.S.	Medicare
1. Pete Small	M—3	$79,000	$2,300	a. _____	b. _____
2. Alice Hall	M—1	$78,000	$1,100	c. _____	d. _____
3. Jean Rose	M—2	$90,000	$990	e. _____	f. _____

4. What is the tax for Social Security and Medicare for Pete in Problem 1?

5. Calculate Pete's FIT by the percentage method.

6. What would employees contribute for this week's payroll for SUTA and FUTA?

WORD PROBLEMS

7. Cynthia Pratt has earned $79,200 thus far this year. This week she earned $3,500. Find her total FICA tax deduction (Social Security and Medicare).

8. If Cynthia (Problem 7) earns $1,050 the following week, what will be her new total FICA tax deduction?

9. Roger Alley, a service dispatcher, has weekly earnings of $750. He claimed four allowances on his W-4 form and is married. Besides his FIT and FICA deductions, he has deductions of $35.16 for medical insurance and $17.25 for union dues. Calculate his net earnings for the third week in February. Use the percentage method.

10. Nicole Mariotte is unmarried and claimed one withholding allowance on her W-4 form. In the second week of February, she earned $707.35. Deductions from her pay included federal withholding, Social Security, Medicare, health insurance for $47.75, and $30.00 for the company meal plan. What is Nicole's net pay for the week? Use the percentage method.

11. Gerald Knowlton had total gross earnings of $80,100 in the last week of November. His earnings for the first week in December were $804.70. His employer uses the percentage method to calculate federal withholding. If Gerald is married, claims two allowances, and has medical insurance of $52.25 deducted each week from his pay, what is his net pay for the week?

LEARNING UNIT 10–1 | CALCULATION OF SIMPLE INTEREST AND MATURITY VALUE

DRILL PROBLEMS

1. Find the simple interest for each of the following loans:

	Principal	Rate	Time	Interest
a.	$2,000	9%	1 year	_____
b.	$3,000	12%	3 years	_____
c.	$18,000	$8\frac{1}{2}\%$	10 months	_____

2. Find the simple interest for each of the following loans; use the exact interest method. Use the days-in-a-year calendar in the text when needed.

	Principal	Rate	Time	Interest
a.	$700	14%	30 days	_____
b.	$4,290	8%	250 days	_____
c.	$1,500	8%	Made March 11 Due July 11	_____

3. Find the simple interest for each of the following loans using the ordinary interest method (Banker's Rule).

	Principal	Rate	Time	Interest
a.	$5,250	$7\frac{1}{2}\%$	120 days	_____
b.	$700	12%	70 days	_____
c.	$2,600	11%	Made on June 15 Due October 17	_____

WORD PROBLEMS

4. On October 17, Nina Verga borrowed $3,136 at a rate of 12%. She promised to repay the loan in 10 months. What are **(a)** the amount of the simple interest and **(b)** the total amount owed upon maturity?

5. Marjorie Folsom borrowed $5,500 to purchase a computer. The loan was for 9 months at an annual interest rate of $12\frac{1}{2}\%$. What are **(a)** the amount of interest Marjorie must pay and **(b)** the maturity value of the loan?

6. Eric has a loan for $1,200 at an ordinary interest rate of 9.5% for 80 days. Julie has a loan for $1,200 at an exact interest rate of 9.5% for 80 days. Calculate **(a)** the total amount due on Eric's loan and **(b)** the total amount due on Julie's loan.

7. Roger Lee borrowed $5,280 at $13\frac{1}{2}\%$ on May 24 and agreed to repay the loan on August 24. The lender calculates interest using the exact interest method. How much will Roger be required to pay on August 24?

8. On March 8, Jack Faltin borrowed $10,225 at $9\frac{3}{4}\%$. He signed a note agreeing to repay the loan and interest on November 8. If the lender calculates interest using the ordinary interest method, what will Jack's repayment be?

9. Dianne Smith's real estate taxes of $641.49 were due on November 1, 2004. Due to financial difficulties, Dianne was unable to pay her tax bill until January 15, 2005. The penalty for late payment is $13\frac{3}{8}\%$ ordinary interest. What is the penalty Dianne will have to pay, and what is Dianne's total payment on January 15?

10. On August 8, Rex Eason had a credit card balance of $550, but he was unable to pay his bill. The credit card company charges interest of $18\frac{1}{2}\%$ annually on late payments. What amount will Rex have to pay if he pays his bill 1 month late?

11. An issue of *Your Money* discussed average consumers who carry a balance of $2,000 on one credit card. If the yearly rate of interest is 18%, how much are consumers paying in interest per year?

12. AFBA Industrial Bank of Colorado Springs, Colorado, charges a credit card interest rate of 11% per year. If you had a credit card debt of $1,500, what would your interest amount be after 3 months?

LEARNING UNIT 10-2 | FINDING UNKNOWN IN SIMPLE INTEREST FORMULA

DRILL PROBLEMS

1. Find the principal in each of the following. Round to the nearest cent. Assume 360 days. *Calculator hint:* Do denominator calculation first, do not round; when answer is displayed, save it in memory by pressing [M+]. Now key in the numerator (interest amount), [÷], [MR], [=] for the answer. Be sure to clear memory after each problem by pressing [MR] again so that the M is no longer in the display.

	Rate	Time	Interest	Principal
a.	8%	70 days	$68	_____
b.	11%	90 days	$125	_____
c.	9%	120 days	$103	_____
d.	$8\frac{1}{2}$%	60 days	$150	_____

2. Find the rate in each of the following. Round to the nearest tenth of a percent. Assume 360 days.

	Principal	Time	Interest	Rate
a.	$7,500	120 days	$350	_____
b.	$975	60 days	$25	_____
c.	$20,800	220 days	$910	_____
d.	$150	30 days	$2.10	_____

3. Find the time (to the nearest day) in each of the following. Assuming ordinary interest, use 360 days.

	Principal	Rate	Interest	Time (days)	Time (years) (Round to nearest hundredth)
a.	$400	11%	$7.33	_____	_____
b.	$7,000	12.5%	$292	_____	_____
c.	$1,550	9.2%	$106.95	_____	_____
d.	$157,000	10.75%	$6,797.88	_____	_____

4. Complete the following. Assume 360 days for all examples.

	Principal	Rate (nearest tenth percent)	Time (nearest day)	Simple interest
a.	$345	_____	150 days	$14.38
b.	_____	12.5%	90 days	$46.88

c. $750	12.2%	_____	$19.06
d. $20,260	16.7%	110 days	_____

WORD PROBLEMS

Use 360 days.

5. In June, Becky opened a $20,000 bank CD paying 6% interest, but she had to withdraw the money in a few days to cover one child's college tuition. The bank charged her $600 in penalties for the withdrawal. What percent of the $20,000 was she charged?

6. Dr. Vaccarro invested his money at $12\frac{1}{2}\%$ for 175 days and earned interest of $760. How much money did Dr. Vaccarro invest?

7. If you invested $10,000 at 5% interest in a 6-month CD compounding interest daily, you would earn $252.43 in interest. How much would the same $10,000 invested in a bank paying simple interest earn?

8. Thomas Kyrouz opened a savings account and deposited $750 in a bank that was paying 7.2% simple interest. How much were his savings worth in 200 days?

9. Mary Millitello paid the bank $53.90 in interest on a 66-day loan at 9.8%. How much money did Mary borrow? Round to the nearest dollar.

10. If Anthony Lucido deposits $2,400 for 66 days and makes $60.72 in interest, what interest rate is he receiving?

11. Find how long in days David Wong must invest $23,500 of his company's cash at 8.4% in order to earn $652.50 in interest.

LEARNING UNIT 10–3 | U.S. RULE—MAKING PARTIAL NOTE PAYMENTS BEFORE DUE DATE

DRILL PROBLEMS

1. A merchant borrowed $3,000 for 320 days at 11% (assume a 360-day year). Use the U.S. Rule to complete the following table:

Payment number	Payment day	Amount paid	Interest to date	Principal payment	Adjusted balance
					$3,000
1	75	$500	_____	_____	_____
2	160	$750	_____	_____	_____
3	220	$1,000	_____	_____	_____
4	320	_____	_____	_____	_____

2. Use the U.S. Rule to solve for total interest costs, balances, and final payments (use ordinary interest).

   Given
   Principal, $6,000, 5%, 100 days
   Partial payments on 30th day, $2,000
                     on 70th day, $1,000

WORD PROBLEMS

3. John Joseph borrowed $10,800 for 1 year at 14%. After 60 days, he paid $2,500 on the note. On the 200th day, he paid an additional $5,000. Use the U.S. Rule and ordinary interest to find the final balance due.

4. Doris Davis borrowed $8,200 on March 5 for 90 days at $8\frac{3}{4}$%. After 32 days, Doris made a payment on the loan of $2,700. On the 65th day, she made another payment of $2,500. What is her final payment if you use the U.S. Rule with ordinary interest?

5. David Ring borrowed $6,000 on a 13%, 60-day note. After 10 days, David paid $500 on the note. On day 40, David paid $900 on the note. What are the total interest and ending balance due by the U.S. Rule? Use ordinary interest.

LEARNING UNIT 11-1 | STRUCTURE OF PROMISSORY NOTES; THE SIMPLE DISCOUNT NOTE

DRILL PROBLEMS

1. Identify each of the following characteristics of promissory notes with an **I** for simple interest note, a **D** for simple discount note, or a **B** if it is true for both.
   ___ Interest is computed on face value, or what is actually borrowed.
   ___ A promissory note for a loan usually less than 1 year.
   ___ Borrower receives proceeds = Face value − Bank discount.
   ___ Maturity value = Face value + Interest.
   ___ Maturity value = Face value.
   ___ Borrower receives the face value.
   ___ Paid back by one payment at maturity.
   ___ Interest computed on maturity value, or what will be repaid, and not on actual amount borrowed.

2. Find the bank discount and the proceeds for the following (assume 360 days):

	Maturity value	Discount rate	Time (days)	Bank discount	Proceeds
a.	$7,000	9%	60	_____	_____
b.	$4,550	8.1%	110	_____	_____
c.	$19,350	12.7%	55	_____	_____
d.	$63,400	10%	90	_____	_____
e.	$13,490	7.9%	200	_____	_____
f.	$780	$12\frac{1}{2}\%$	65	_____	_____

3. Find the effective rate of interest for each of the loans in Problem 2. Use the answers you calculated in Problem 2 to solve these problems (round to the nearest tenth percent).

	Maturity value	Discount rate	Time (days)	Effective rate
a.	$7,000	9%	60	_____
b.	$4,550	8.1%	110	_____
c.	$19,350	12.7%	55	_____
d.	$63,400	10%	90	_____

| e. $13,490 | 7.9% | 200 | _____ |
| f. $780 | $12\frac{1}{2}$% | 65 | _____ |

WORD PROBLEMS

Assume 360 days.

4. Mary Smith signed a $7,500 note for 135 days at a discount rate of 13%. Find the discount and the proceeds Mary received.

5. The Salem Cooperative Bank charges an $8\frac{3}{4}$% discount rate. What are the discount and the proceeds for a $16,200 note for 60 days?

6. Bill Jackson is planning to buy a used car. He went to City Credit Union to take out a loan for $6,400 for 300 days. If the credit union charges a discount rate of $11\frac{1}{2}$%, what will the proceeds of this loan be?

7. Mike Drislane goes to the bank and signs a note for $9,700. The bank charges a 15% discount rate. Find the discount and the proceeds if the loan is for 210 days.

8. Flora Foley plans to have a deck built on the back of her house. She decides to take out a loan at the bank for $14,300. She signs a note promising to pay back the loan in 280 days. If the note was discounted at 9.2%, how much money will Flora receive from the bank?

9. At the end of 280 days, Flora (Problem 8) must pay back the loan. What is the maturity value of the loan?

10. Dave Cassidy signed a $7,855 note at a bank that charges a 14.2% discount rate. If the loan is for 190 days, find **(a)** the proceeds and **(b)** the effective rate charged by the bank (to the nearest tenth percent).

11. How much money must Dave (Problem 10) pay back to the bank?

LEARNING UNIT 11–2 | DISCOUNTING AN INTEREST-BEARING NOTE BEFORE MATURITY

DRILL PROBLEMS

1. Calculate the maturity value for each of the following promissory notes (use 360 days):

	Date of note	Principal of note	Length of note (days)	Interest rate	Maturity value
a.	April 12	$4,800	135	10%	_____
b.	August 23	$15,990	85	13%	_____
c.	December 10	$985	30	11.5%	_____

2. Find the maturity date and the discount period for the following; assume no leap years. *Hint:* See Exact Days-in-a-Year Calendar, Chapter 7.

	Date of note	Length of note (days)	Date of discount	Maturity date	Discount period
a.	March 11	200	June 28	_____	_____
b.	January 22	60	March 2	_____	_____
c.	April 19	85	June 6	_____	_____
d.	November 17	120	February 15	_____	_____

3. Find the bank discount for each of the following (use 360 days):

	Date of note	Principal of note	Length of note	Interest rate	Bank discount rate	Date of discount	Bank discount
a.	October 5	$2,475	88 days	11%	9.5%	December 10	_____
b.	June 13	$9,055	112 days	15%	16%	August 11	_____
c.	March 20	$1,065	75 days	12%	11.5%	May 24	_____

4. Find the proceeds for each of the discounted notes in Problem 3.

a. _____

b. _____

c. _____

WORD PROBLEMS

5. Connors Company received a $4,000, 90-day, 10% note dated April 6 from one of its customers. Connors Company held the note until May 16, when the company discounted it at a bank at a discount rate of 12%. What were the proceeds that Connors Company received?

6. Souza & Sons accepted a 9%, $22,000, 120-day note from one of its customers on July 22. On October 2, the company discounted the note at Cooperative Bank. The discount rate was 12%. What were (a) the bank discount and (b) the proceeds?

7. The Fargate Store accepted an $8,250, 75-day, 9% note from one of its customers on March 18. Fargate's discounted the note at Parkside National Bank at $9\frac{1}{2}$% on March 29. What proceeds did Fargate receive?

8. On November 1, Marjorie's Clothing Store accepted a $5,200, $8\frac{1}{2}$%, 90-day note from Mary Rose in granting her a time extension on her bill. On January 13, Marjorie discounted the note at Seawater Bank, which charged a 10% discount rate. What were the proceeds that Majorie received?

9. On December 3, Duncan's Company accepted a $5,000, 90-day, 12% note from Al Finney in exchange for a $5,000 bill that was past due. On January 29, Duncan discounted the note at The Sidwell Bank at 13.1%. What were the proceeds from the note?

10. On February 26, Sullivan Company accepted a 60-day, 10% note in exchange for a $1,500 past-due bill from Tabot Company. On March 28, Sullivan Company discounted at National Bank the note received from Tabot Company. The bank discount rate was 12%. What are (a) the bank discount and (b) the proceeds?

11. On June 4, Johnson Company received from Marty Russo a 30-day, 11% note for $720 to settle Russo's debt. On June 17, Johnson discounted the note at Eastern Bank whose discount rate was 15%. What proceeds did Johnson receive?

12. On December 15, Lawlers Company went to the bank and discounted a 10%, 90-day, $14,000 note dated October 21. The bank charged a discount rate of 12%. What were the proceeds of the note?

LEARNING UNIT 12–1 | COMPOUND INTEREST (FUTURE VALUE)—THE BIG PICTURE

DRILL PROBLEMS

1. In the following examples, calculate manually the amount at year-end for each of the deposits, assuming that interest is compounded annually. Round to the nearest cent each year.

	Principal	Rate	Number of years	Year 1	Year 2	Year 3	Year 4
a.	$530	8%	2	_____	_____		
b.	$1,980	12%	4	_____	_____	_____	_____

2. In the following examples, calculate the simple interest, the compound interest, and the difference between the two. Round to the nearest cent; do not use tables.

	Principal	Rate	Number of years	Simple interest	Compound interest	Difference
a.	$4,600	10%	2	_____	_____	_____
b.	$18,400	9%	4	_____	_____	_____
c.	$855	$7\frac{1}{5}\%$	3	_____	_____	_____

3. Find the future value and the compound interest using the Future Value of $1 at Compound Interest table or the Compound Daily table. Round to the nearest cent.

	Principal	Investment terms	Future value	Compound interest
a.	$10,000	6 years at 8% compounded annually	_____	_____
b.	$10,000	6 years at 8% compounded quarterly	_____	_____
c.	$8,400	7 years at 12% compounded semiannually	_____	_____
d.	$2,500	15 years at 10% compounded daily	_____	_____
e.	$9,600	5 years at 6% compounded quarterly	_____	_____
f.	$20,000	2 years at 6% compounded monthly	_____	_____

4. Calculate the effective rate (APY) of interest using the Future Value of $1 at Compound Interest table.

Investment terms	Effective rate (annual percentage yield)
a. 12% compounded quarterly	_____
b. 12% compounded semiannually	_____
c. 6% compounded quarterly	_____

WORD PROBLEMS

5. John Mackey deposited $5,000 in his savings account at Salem Savings Bank. If the bank pays 6% interest compounded quarterly, what will be the balance of his account at the end of 3 years?

6. Pine Valley Savings Bank offers a certificate of deposit at 12% interest, compounded quarterly. What is the effective rate (APY) of interest?

7. Jack Billings loaned $6,000 to his brother-in-law Dan, who was opening a new business. Dan promised to repay the loan at the end of 5 years, with interest of 8% compounded semiannually. How much will Dan pay Jack at the end of 5 years?

8. Eileen Hogarty deposits $5,630 in City Bank, which pays 12% interest, compounded quarterly. How much money will Eileen have in her account at the end of 7 years?

9. If Kevin Bassage deposits $3,500 in Scarsdale Savings Bank, which pays 8% interest, compounded quarterly, what will be in his account at the end of 6 years? How much interest will he have earned at that time?

10. Arlington Trust pays 6% compounded semiannually. How much interest would be earned on $7,200 for 1 year?

11. Paladium Savings Bank pays 9% compounded quarterly. Find the amount and the interest on $3,000 after three quarters. Do not use a table.

12. David Siderski bought a $7,500 bank certificate paying 16% compounded semiannually. How much money did he obtain upon cashing in the certificate 3 years later?

13. An issue of *Your Money* showed that the more frequently the bank compounds your money, the better. Just how much better is a function of time. A $10,000 investment for 6% in a 5-year certificate of deposit at three different banks can result in different interest being earned.
   a. Bank A (simple interest, no compounding)
   b. Bank B (quarterly compounding)
   c. Bank C (daily compounding)
   What would be the interest for each bank?

LEARNING UNIT 12-2 ❘ PRESENT VALUE—THE BIG PICTURE

DRILL PROBLEMS

1. Use the *Business Math Handbook* to find the table factor for each of the following:

	Future value	Rate	Number of years	Compounded	Table value
a.	$1.00	10%	5	Annually	_____
b.	$1.00	12%	8	Semiannually	_____
c.	$1.00	6%	10	Quarterly	_____
d.	$1.00	12%	2	Monthly	_____
e.	$1.00	8%	15	Semiannually	_____

2. Use the *Business Math Handbook* to find the table factor and the present value for each of the following:

	Future value	Rate	Number of years	Compounded	Table value	Present value
a.	$1,000	14%	6	Semiannually	_____	_____
b.	$1,000	16%	7	Quarterly	_____	_____
c.	$1,000	8%	7	Quarterly	_____	_____
d.	$1,000	8%	7	Semiannually	_____	_____
e.	$1,000	8%	7	Annually	_____	_____

3. Find the present value and the interest earned for the following:

	Future value	Number of years	Rate	Compounded	Present value	Interest earned
a.	$2,500	6	8%	Annually	_____	_____
b.	$4,600	10	6%	Semiannually	_____	_____
c.	$12,800	8	10%	Semiannually	_____	_____
d.	$28,400	7	8%	Quarterly	_____	_____
e.	$53,050	1	12%	Monthly	_____	_____

4. Find the missing amount (present value or future value) for each of the following:

	Present value	Investment terms	Future value
a.	$3,500	5 years at 8% compounded annually	_____
b.	_____	6 years at 12% compounded semiannually	$9,000
c.	$4,700	9 years at 14% compounded semiannually	_____

WORD PROBLEMS

Solve for future value or present value.

5. Paul Palumbo assumes that he will need to have a new roof put on his house in 4 years. He estimates that the roof will cost him $18,000 at that time. What amount of money should Paul invest today at 8%, compounded semiannually, to be able to pay for the roof?

6. Tilton, a pharmacist, rents his store and has signed a lease that will expire in 3 years. When the lease expires, Tilton wants to buy his own store. He wants to have a down payment of $35,000 at that time. How much money should Tilton invest today at 6% compounded quarterly to yield $35,000?

7. Brad Morrissey loans $8,200 to his brother-in-law. He will be repaid at the end of 5 years, with interest at 10% compounded semiannually. Find out how much he will be repaid.

8. The owner of Waverly Sheet Metal Company plans to buy some new machinery in 6 years. He estimates that the machines he wishes to purchase will cost $39,700 at that time. What must he invest today at 8% compounded semiannually to have sufficient money to purchase the new machines?

9. Paul Stevens's grandparents want to buy him a car when he graduates from college in 4 years. They feel that they should have $27,000 in the bank at that time. How much should they invest at 12% compounded quarterly to reach their goal?

10. Gilda Nardi deposits $5,325 in a bank that pays 12% interest, compounded quarterly. Find the amount she will have at the end of 7 years.

11. Mary Wilson wants to buy a new set of golf clubs in 2 years. They will cost $775. How much money should she invest today at 9% compounded annually so that she will have enough money to buy the new clubs?

12. Jack Beggs plans to invest $30,000 at 10% compounded semiannually for 5 years. What is the future value of the investment?

13. Ron Thrift has a 1991 Honda that he expects will last 3 more years. Ron does not like to finance his purchases. He went to First National Bank to find out how much money he should put in the bank to purchase a $20,300 car in 3 years. The bank's 3-year CD is compounded quarterly with a 4% rate. How much should Ron invest in the CD?

14. The Downers Grove YMCA had a fund-raising campaign to build a swimming pool in 6 years. Members raised $825,000; the pool is estimated to cost $1,230,000. The money will be placed in Downers Grove Bank, which pays daily interest at 6%. Will the YMCA have enough money to pay for the pool in 6 years?

LEARNING UNIT 13–1 | ANNUITIES: ORDINARY ANNUITY AND ANNUITY DUE (FIND FUTURE VALUE)

DRILL PROBLEMS

1. Find the value of the following ordinary annuities (calculate manually):

	Amount of each annual deposit	Interest rate	Value at end of year 1	Value at end of year 2	Value at end of year 3
a.	$1,000	8%	_____	_____	_____
b.	$2,500	12%	_____	_____	_____
c.	$7,200	10%	_____	_____	_____

2. Use the Ordinary Annuity Table: Compound Sum of an Annuity of $1 to find the value of the following ordinary annuities:

	Annuity payment	Payment period	Term of annuity	Interest rate	Value of annuity
a.	$650	Semiannually	5 years	6%	_____
b.	$3,790	Annually	13 years	12%	_____
c.	$500	Quarterly	1 year	8%	_____

3. Find the annuity due (deposits are made at beginning of period) for each of the following using the Ordinary Annuity Table:

	Amount of payment	Payment period	Interest rate	Time (years)	Amount of annuity
a.	$900	Annually	7%	6	_____
b.	$1,200	Annually	11%	4	_____
c.	$550	Semiannually	10%	9	_____

4. Find the amount of each annuity:

	Amount of payment	Payment period	Interest rate	Time (years)	Type of annuity	Amount of annuity
a.	$600	Semiannually	12%	8	Ordinary	_____
b.	$600	Semiannually	12%	8	Due	_____
c.	$1,100	Annually	9%	7	Ordinary	_____

WORD PROBLEMS

5. At the end of each year for the next 9 years, D'Aldo Company will deposit $25,000 in an ordinary annuity account paying 9% interest compounded annually. Find the value of the annuity at the end of the 9 years.

6. David McCarthy is a professional baseball player who expects to play in the major leagues for 10 years. To save for the future, he will deposit $50,000 at the beginning of each year into an account that pays 11% interest compounded annually. How much will he have in this account at the end of 10 years?

7. Tom and Sue plan to get married soon. Because they hope to have a large wedding, they are going to deposit $1,000 at the end of each month into an account that pays 24% compounded monthly. How much will they have in this account at the end of 1 year?

8. Chris Dennen deposits $15,000 at the end of each year for 13 years into an account paying 7% interest compounded annually. What is the value of her annuity at the end of 13 years? How much interest will she have earned?

9. Amanda Blinn is 52 years old today and has just opened an IRA. She plans to deposit $500 at the end of each quarter into her account. If Amanda retires on her 62nd birthday, what amount will she have in her account if the account pays 8% interest compounded quarterly?

10. Jerry Davis won the citywide sweepstakes and will receive a check for $2,000 at the beginning of each 6 months for the next 5 years. If Larry deposits each check in an account that pays 8% compounded semiannually, how much will he have at the end of 5 years?

11. Mary Hynes purchased an ordinary annuity from an investment broker at 8% interest compounded semiannually. If her semiannual deposit is $600, what will be the value of the annuity at the end of 15 years?

LEARNING UNIT 13-2 | PRESENT VALUE OF AN ORDINARY ANNUITY (FIND PRESENT VALUE)

DRILL PROBLEMS

1. Use the Present Value of an Annuity of $1 table to find the amount to be invested today to receive a stream of payments for a given number of years in the future. Show the manual check of your answer. (Check may be a few pennies off due to rounding.)

	Amount of expected payments	Payment period	Interest rate	Term of annuity	Present value of annuity
a.	$1,500	Yearly	9%	2 years	_____
b.	$2,700	Yearly	13%	3 years	_____
c.	$2,700	Yearly	6%	3 years	_____

2. Find the present value of the following annuities. Use the Present Value of an Annuity of $1 table.

	Amount of each payment	Payment period	Interest rate	Time (years)	Compounded	Present value of annuity
a.	$2,000	Year	7%	25	Annually	_____
b.	$7,000	Year	11%	12	Annually	_____
c.	$850	6 months	12%	5	Semiannually	_____
d.	$1,950	6 months	14%	9	Semiannually	_____
e.	$500	Quarter	12%	10	Quarterly	_____

WORD PROBLEMS

3. Tom Hanson would like to receive $200 each quarter for the 4 years he is in college. If his bank account pays 8% compounded quarterly, how much must he have in his account when he begins college?

4. Jean Reith has just retired and will receive a $12,500 retirement check every 6 months for the next 20 years. If her employer can invest money at 12% compounded semiannually, what amount must be invested today to make the semiannual payments to Jean?

5. Tom Herrick will pay $4,500 at the end of each year for the next 7 years to pay the balance of his college loans. If Tom can invest his money at 7% compounded annually, how much must he invest today to make the annual payments?

6. Helen Grahan is planning an extended sabbatical for the next 3 years. She would like to invest a lump sum of money at 10% interest so that she can withdraw $6,000 every 6 months while on sabbatical. What is the amount of the lump sum that Helen must invest?

7. Linda Rudd has signed a rental contract for office equipment, agreeing to pay $3,200 at the end of each quarter for the next 5 years. If Linda can invest money at 12% compounded quarterly, find the lump sum she can deposit today to make the payments for the length of the contract.

8. Sam Adams is considering lending his brother John $6,000. John said that he would repay Sam $775 every 6 months for 4 years. If money can be invested at 8%, calculate the equivalent cash value of the offer today. Should Sam go ahead with the loan?

9. The State Lotto Game offers a grand prize of $1,000,000 paid in 20 yearly payments of $50,000. If the state treasurer can invest money at 9% compounded annually, how much must she invest today to make the payments to the grand prize winner?

10. Thomas Martin's uncle has promised him upon graduation a gift of $20,000 in cash or $2,000 every quarter for the next 3 years. If money can be invested at 8%, which offer will Thomas accept? (Thomas is a business major.)

11. Paul Sasso is selling a piece of land. He has received two solid offers. Jason Smith has offered a $60,000 down payment and $50,000 a year for the next 5 years. Kevin Bassage offered $35,000 down and $55,000 a year for the next 5 years. If money can be invested at 7% compounded annually, which offer should Paul accept? (To make the comparison, find the equivalent cash price of each offer.)

12. Abe Hoster decided to retire to Spain in 10 years. What amount should Abe invest today so that he will be able to withdraw $30,000 at the end of each year for 20 years after he retires? Assume he can invest money at 8% interest compounded annually.

LEARNING UNIT 13–3 | SINKING FUNDS (FIND PERIODIC PAYMENTS)

DRILL PROBLEMS

1. Given the number of years and the interest rate, use the Sinking Fund Table based on $1 to calculate the amount of the periodic payment.

Frequency of payment	Length of time	Interest rate	Future amount	Sinking fund payment
a. Annually	19 years	5%	$125,000	_____
b. Annually	7 years	10%	$205,000	_____
c. Semiannually	10 years	6%	$37,500	_____
d. Quarterly	9 years	12%	$12,750	_____
e. Quarterly	6 years	8%	$25,600	_____

2. Find the amount of each payment into the sinking fund and the amount of interest earned.

Maturity value	Interest rate	Term (years)	Frequency of payment	Sinking fund payment	Interest earned
a. $45,500	5%	13	Annually	_____	_____
b. $8,500	10%	20	Semiannually	_____	_____
c. $11,000	8%	5	Quarterly	_____	_____
d. $66,600	12%	7 1/2	Semiannually	_____	_____

WORD PROBLEMS

3. To finance a new police station, the town of Pine Valley issued bonds totaling $600,000. The town treasurer set up a sinking fund at 8% compounded quarterly in order to redeem the bonds in 7 years. What is the quarterly payment that must be deposited into the fund?

4. Arlex Oil Corporation plans to build a new garage in 6 years. To finance the project, the financial manager established a $250,000 sinking fund at 6% compounded semianually. Find the semiannual payment required for the fund.

5. The City Fisheries Corporation sold $300,000 worth of bonds that must be redeemed in 9 years. The corporation agreed to set up a sinking fund to accumulate the $300,000. Find the amount of the periodic payments made into the fund if payments are made annually and the fund earns 8% compounded annually.

6. Gregory Mines Corporation wishes to purchase a new piece of equipment in 4 years. The estimated price of the equipment is $100,000. If the corporation makes periodic payments into a sinking fund with 12% interest compounded quarterly, find the amount of the periodic payments.

7. The Best Corporation must buy a new piece of machinery in $4\frac{1}{2}$ years that will cost $350,000. If the firm sets up a sinking fund to finance this new machine, what will the quarterly deposits be assuming the fund earns 8% interest compounded quarterly?

8. The Lowest-Price-in-Town Company needs $75,500 in 6 years to pay off a debt. The company makes a decision to set up a sinking fund and make semiannual deposits. What will their payments be if the fund pays 10% interest compounded semiannually?

9. The WIR Company plans to renovate their offices in 5 years. They estimate that the cost will be $235,000. If they set up a sinking fund that pays 12% quarterly, what will their quarterly payments be?

LEARNING UNIT 14–1 | COST OF INSTALLMENT BUYING

DRILL PROBLEMS

1. For the following installment problems, find the amount financed and the finance charge.

	Sale price	Down payment	Number of monthly payments	Monthly payment	Amount financed	Finance charge
a.	$1,500	$300	24	$58	_____	_____
b.	$12,000	$3,000	30	$340	_____	_____
c.	$62,500	$4,700	48	$1,500	_____	_____
d.	$4,975	$620	18	$272	_____	_____
e.	$825	$82.50	12	$67.45	_____	_____

2. For each of the above purchases, find the deferred payment price.

	Sale price	Down payment	Number of monthly payments	Monthly payment	Deferred payment price
a.	$1,500	$300	24	$58	_____
b.	$12,000	$3,000	30	$340	_____
c.	$62,500	$4,700	48	$1,500	_____
d.	$4,975	$620	18	$272	_____
e.	$825	$82.50	12	$67.45	_____

3. Use the Annual Percentage Rate Table per $100 to calculate the estimated APR for each of the previous purchases.

	Sale price	Down payment	Number of monthly payments	Monthly payment	Annual percentage rate
a.	$1,500	$300	24	$58	_____
b.	$12,000	$3,000	30	$340	_____
c.	$62,500	$4,700	48	$1,500	_____
d.	$4,975	$620	18	$272	_____
e.	$825	$82.50	12	$67.45	_____

4. Given the following information, calculate the monthly payment by the loan amortization table.

	Amount financed	Interest rate	Number of months of loan	Monthly payment
a.	$12,000	10%	18	_____
b.	$18,000	11%	36	_____
c.	$25,500	13.50%	54	_____

WORD PROBLEMS

5. Jill Walsh purchases a bedroom set for a cash price of $3,920. The down payment is $392, and the monthly installment payment is $176 for 24 months. Find (a) the amount financed, (b) the finance charge, and (c) the deferred payment price.

6. An automaker promotion loan on a $20,000 automobile and a down payment of 20% are being financed for 48 months. The monthly payments will be $367.74. What will be the APR for this auto loan? Use the table in the *Business Math Handbook*.

7. David Nason purchased a recreational vehicle for $25,000. David went to City Bank to finance the purchase. The bank required that David make a 10% down payment and monthly payments of $571.50 for 4 years. Find **(a)** the amount financed, **(b)** the finance charge, and **(c)** the deferred payment that David paid.

8. Calculate the estimated APR that David (Problem 7) was charged per $100 using the Annual Percentage Rate Table.

9. Young's Motors advertised a new car for $16,720. They offered an installment plan of 5% down and 42 monthly payments of $470. What are **(a)** the deferred payment price and **(b)** the estimated APR for this car (use the table)?

10. Angie French bought a used car for $9,000. Angie put down $2,000 and financed the balance at 11.50% for 36 months. What is her monthly payment? Use the loan amortization table.

LEARNING UNIT 14–2 | PAYING OFF INSTALLMENT LOAN BEFORE DUE DATE

DRILL PROBLEMS

1. Find the balance of each loan outstanding and the total finance charge.

	Amount financed	Monthly payment	Number of payments	Payments to date	Balance of loan outstanding	Finance charge
a.	$1,500	$125	15	10	_____	_____
b.	$21,090	$600	40	24	_____	_____
c.	$895	$60	18	10	_____	_____
d.	$4,850	$150	42	30	_____	_____

2. For the loans in Problem 1, find the number of payments remaining and calculate the rebate amount of the finance charge (use Rebate Fraction Table Based on Rule of 78).

	Amount financed	Monthly payment	Number of payments	Payments to date	Number of payments remaining	Finance charge rebate
a.	$1,500	$125	15	10	_____	_____
b.	$21,090	$600	40	24	_____	_____
c.	$895	$60	18	10	_____	_____
d.	$4,850	$150	42	30	_____	_____

3. For the loans in Problems 1 and 2, show the remaining balance of the loan and calculate the payoff amount to retire the loan at this time.

	Amount financed	Monthly payment	Number of payments	Payments to date	Balance of loan outstanding	Final payoff
a.	$1,500	$125	15	10	_____	_____
b.	$21,090	$600	40	24	_____	_____
c.	$895	$60	18	10	_____	_____
d.	$4,850	$150	42	30	_____	_____

4. Complete the following; show all the steps.

	Loan	Months of loan	Monthly payment	End of month loan is repaid	Final payoff
a.	$6,200	36	$219	24	_____
b.	$960	12	$99	8	_____

WORD PROBLEMS

5. Maryjane Hannon took out a loan for $5,600 to have a swimming pool installed in her backyard. The note she signed required 21 monthly payments of $293. At the end of 15 months, Maryjane wants to know the balance of her loan outstanding and her total finance charge.

6. After calculating the above data (Problem 5), Maryjane is considering paying off the rest of the loan. To make her decision, Maryjane wants to know the finance charge rebate she will receive and the final payoff amount.

7. Ben Casey decided to buy a used car for $7,200. He agreed to make monthly payments of $225 for 36 months. What is Ben's total finance charge?

8. After making 20 payments, Ben (Problem 7) wants to pay off the rest of the loan. What will be the amount of Ben's final payoff?

9. Jeremy Vagos took out a loan to buy a new boat that cost $12,440. He agreed to pay $350 a month for 48 months. After 24 monthly payments, he calculates that he has paid $8,400 on his loan and has 24 payments remaining. Jeremy's friend Luke tells Jeremy that he will pay off the rest of the loan (in a single payment) if he can be half owner of the boat. What is the amount that Luke will have to pay?

LEARNING UNIT 14-3 | REVOLVING CHARGE CREDIT CARDS

DRILL PROBLEMS

1. Use the U.S. Rule to calculate the outstanding balance due for each of the following independent situations:

Monthly payment number	Outstanding balance due	$1\frac{1}{2}\%$ interest payment	Amount of monthly payment	Reduction in balance due	Outstanding balance due
a. 1	$9,000.00	_____	$600	_____	_____
b. 5	$5,625.00	_____	$1,000	_____	_____
c. 4	$926.50	_____	$250	_____	_____
d. 12	$62,391.28	_____	$1,200	_____	_____
e. 8	$3,255.19	_____	$325	_____	_____

2. Complete the missing data for a $6,500 purchase made on credit. The annual interest charge on this revolving charge account is 18%, or $1\frac{1}{2}\%$ interest on previous month's balance. Use the U.S. Rule.

Monthly payment number	Outstanding balance due	$1\frac{1}{2}\%$ interest payment	Amount of monthly payment	Reduction in balance due	Outstanding balance due
1	$6,500	_____	$700	_____	_____
2	_____	_____	$700	_____	_____
3	_____	_____	$700	_____	_____

3. Calculate the average billing daily balance for each of the monthly statements for the following revolving credit accounts (assume a 30-day billing cycle):

Billing date	Previous balance	Payment date	Payment amount	Charge date(s)	Charge amount(s)	Average daily balance
a. 4/10	$329	4/25	$35	4/29	$56	_____
b. 6/15	$573	6/25	$60	6/26	$25	
				6/30	$72	_____
c. 9/15	$335.50	9/20	$33.55	9/25	$12.50	
				9/26	$108	_____

4. Find the finance charge for each monthly statement (Problem 3) if the annual percentage rate is 15%.

    a. _____   b. _____   c. _____

WORD PROBLEMS

5. Niki Marshall is going to buy a new bedroom set at Scottie's Furniture Store, where she has a revolving charge account. The cost of the bedroom set is $5,500. Niki does not plan to charge anything else to her account until she has completely paid for the bedroom set. Scottie's Furniture Store charges an annual percentage rate of 18%, or $1\frac{1}{2}\%$ per month. Niki plans to pay $1,000 per month until she has paid for the bedroom set. Set up a schedule for Niki to show her outstanding balance at the end of each month after her $1,000 payment and also the amount of her final payment. Use the U.S. Rule.

6. Frances Dollof received her monthly statement from Brown's Department Store. The following is part of the information contained on that statement. Finance charge is calculated on the average daily balance.

Date	Reference	Department	Description	Amount
Dec. 15	5921	359	Petite sportswear	84.98
Dec. 15	9612	432	Footwear	55.99
Dec. 15	2600	126	Women's fragrance	35.18
Dec. 23	6247	61	Ralph Lauren towels	20.99
Dec. 24	0129	998	Payment received—thank you	100.00CR

Previous balance		Annual percentage rate	Billing date
719.04	12/13	18%	JAN 13

- -

Brown's Charge Account Terms

Payment is required in monthly installments upon receipt of monthly statement in accordance with Brown's payment terms.

When my new balance is:	My minimum required payment is:	When my new balance is:	My minimum required payment is:
Up to $20.00	New Balance	$350.01 to $400.00	$40.00
$ 20.01 to $200.00	$20.00	$400.01 to $450.00	$45.00
$200.01 to $250.00	$25.00	$450.01 to $500.00	$50.00
$250.01 to $300.00	$30.00	More than $500.00	$50.00 plus
$300.01 to $350.00	$35.00		$10.00 for each $50.00 (or fraction thereof) of New Balance over $500.00

a. Calculate the average daily balance for the month.

b. What is Ms. Dollof's finance charge?

c. What is the new balance for Ms. Dollof's account?

d. What is the minimum payment Frances is required to pay according to Brown's payment terms?

7. What is the finance charge for a Brown's customer who has an average daily balance of $3,422.67?

8. What is the minimum payment for a Brown's customer with a new balance of $522.00?

9. What is the minimum payment for a Brown's customer with a new balance of $325.01?

10. What is the new balance for a Brown's customer with a previous balance of $309.35 whose purchases totaled $213.00, given that the customer made a payment of $75.00 and the finance charge was $4.65?

RECAP OF WORD PROBLEMS IN LU14-1

11. A home equity loan on a $20,000 automobile with a down payment of 20% is being financed for 48 months. The interest is tax deductible. The monthly payments will be $401.97. What is the APR on this loan? Use the table in the *Business Math Handbook*. If the person is in the 28% income tax bracket, what will be the tax savings with this type of a loan?

12. An automobile with a total transaction price of $20,000 with a down payment of 20% is being financed for 48 months. Banks and credit unions require a monthly payment of $400.36. What is the APR for this auto loan? Use the table in the *Business Math Handbook*.

13. Assume you received a $2,000 rebate that brought the price of a car down to $20,000; the financing rate was for 48 months, and your total interest was $3,279. Using the table in the *Business Math Handbook*, what was your APR?

LEARNING UNIT 15-1 | TYPES OF MORTGAGES AND THE MONTHLY MORTGAGE PAYMENT

DRILL PROBLEMS

1. Use the table in the *Business Math Handbook* to calculate the monthly payment for principal and interest for the following mortgages:

	Price of home	Down payment	Interest rate	Term in years	Monthly payment
a.	$200,000	15%	$6\frac{1}{2}\%$	25	_____
b.	$200,000	15%	$10\frac{1}{2}\%$	30	_____
c.	$450,000	10%	$11\frac{3}{4}\%$	30	_____
d.	$450,000	10%	11%	30	_____

2. For each of the mortgages in Problem 1, calculate the amount of interest that will be paid over the life of the loan.

	Price of home	Down payment	Interest rate	Term in years	Total interest paid
a.	$200,000	15%	$6\frac{1}{2}\%$	25	_____
b.	$200,000	15%	$10\frac{1}{2}\%$	30	_____
c.	$450,000	10%	$11\frac{3}{4}\%$	30	_____
d.	$450,000	10%	11%	30	_____

3. Calculate the increase in the monthly mortgage payments for each of the rate increases in the following mortgages. Also calculate what percent of change the increase represents (round to the tenth percent).

	Mortgage amount	Term in years	Interest rate	Increase in interest rate	Increase in monthly payment	Percent change
a.	$175,000	22	9%	1%	_____	_____
b.	$300,000	30	$11\frac{3}{4}\%$	$\frac{3}{4}\%$	_____	_____

4. Calculate the increase in total interest paid for the increase in interest rates in Problem 3.

	Mortgage amount	Term in years	Interest rate	Increase in interest rate	Increase in total interest paid
a.	$175,000	22	9%	1%	_____
b.	$300,000	30	$11\frac{3}{4}\%$	$\frac{3}{4}\%$	_____

WORD PROBLEMS

5. The Counties are planning to purchase a new home that costs $329,000. The bank is charging them $10\frac{1}{2}\%$ interest and requires a 20% down payment. The Counties are planning to take a 25-year mortgage. How much will their monthly payment be for principal and interest?

6. The MacEacherns wish to buy a new house that costs $299,000. The bank requires a 15% down payment and charges $11\frac{1}{2}\%$ interest. If the MacEacherns take out a 15-year mortgage, what will their monthly payment for principal and interest be?

7. Because the monthly payments are so high, the MacEacherns (Problem 6) want to know what the monthly payments would be for **(a)** a 25-year mortgage and **(b)** a 30-year mortgage. Calculate these two payments.

8. If the MacEacherns choose a 30-year mortgage instead of a 15-year mortgage, **(a)** how much money will they "save" monthly and **(b)** how much more interest will they pay over the life of the loan?

9. If the MacEacherns choose the 25-year mortgage instead of the 30-year mortgage, **(a)** how much more will they pay monthly and **(b)** how much less interest will they pay over the life of the loan?

10. Larry and Doris Davis plan to purchase a new home that costs \$415,000. The bank that they are dealing with requires a 20% down payment and charges $12\frac{3}{4}$%. The Davises are planning to take a 25-year mortgage. What will the monthly payment be?

11. How much interest will the Davises (Problem 10) pay over the life of the loan?

LEARNING UNIT 15–2 | AMORTIZATION SCHEDULE—BREAKING DOWN THE MONTHLY PAYMENT

DRILL PROBLEMS

1. In the following, calculate the monthly payment for each mortgage, the portion of the first monthly payment that goes to interest, and the portion of the payment that goes toward the principal.

	Amount of mortgage	Interest rate	Term in years	Monthly payment	Portion to interest	Portion to principal
a.	\$170,000	8%	22	_____	_____	_____
b.	\$222,000	$11\frac{3}{4}$%	30	_____	_____	_____
c.	\$167,000	$10\frac{1}{2}$%	25	_____	_____	_____
d.	\$307,000	13%	15	_____	_____	_____
e.	\$409,500	$12\frac{1}{2}$%	20	_____	_____	_____

2. Prepare an amortization schedule for the first 3 months of a 25-year, 12% mortgage on \$265,000.

Payment number	Monthly payment	Portion to interest	Portion to principal	Balance of loan outstanding
1	_____	_____	_____	_____
2	_____	_____	_____	_____
3	_____	_____	_____	_____

3. Prepare an amortization schedule for the first 4 months of a 30-year, $10\frac{1}{2}$% mortgage on \$195,500.

Payment number	Monthly payment	Portion to interest	Portion to principal	Balance of loan outstanding
1	_____	_____	_____	_____
2	_____	_____	_____	_____
3	_____	_____	_____	_____
4	_____	_____	_____	_____

WORD PROBLEMS

4. Jim and Janice Hurst are buying a new home for \$235,000. The bank which is financing the home requires a 20% down payment and charges a $13\frac{1}{2}$% interest rate. Janice wants to know **(a)** what the monthly payment for the principal and interest will be if they take out a 30-year mortgage and **(b)** how much of the first payment will be for interest on the loan.

5. The Hursts (Problem 4) thought that a lot of their money was going to interest. They asked the banker just how much they would be paying for interest over the life of the loan. Calculate the total amount of interest that the Hursts will pay.

6. The banker told the Hursts (Problem 4) that they could, of course, save on the interest payments if they took out a loan for a shorter period of time. Jim and Janice decided to see if they could afford a 15-year mortgage. Calculate how much more the Hursts would have to pay each month for principal and interest if they took a 15-year mortgage for their loan.

7. The Hursts (Problem 4) thought that they might be able to afford this, but first wanted to see **(a)** how much of the first payment would go to the principal and **(b)** how much total interest they would be paying with a 15-year mortgage.

8.

	1980	**2002**
Cost of median-priced new home	$44,200	$136,600
10% down payment	$4,420	
Fixed-rate, 30-year mortgage		
Interest rate	8.9%	$7\frac{1}{2}\%$
Total monthly principal and interest	$316	

Complete the 2002 year.

9. You can't count on your home mortgage lender to keep you from getting in debt over your head. The old standards of allowing 28% of your income for mortgage debt (including taxes and insurance) usually still apply. If your total monthly payment is $1,033, what should be your annual income to buy a home?

10. Assume that a 30-year fixed-rate mortgage for $100,000 was 9% at one date as opposed to 7% the previous year. What is the difference in monthly payments for these 2 years?

11. If you had a $100,000 mortgage with $7\frac{1}{2}\%$ interest for 25 years and wanted a $7\frac{1}{2}\%$ loan for 35 years, what would be the change in monthly payments? How much more would you pay in interest?

LEARNING UNIT 16-1 | BALANCE SHEET—REPORT AS OF A PARTICULAR DATE

DRILL PROBLEMS

1. Complete the balance sheet for David Harrison, Attorney, and show that

Assets = Liabilities + Owner's equity

Account totals are as follows: accounts receivable, $4,800; office supplies, $375; building (net), $130,000; accounts payable, $1,200; notes payable, $137,200; cash, $2,250; prepaid insurance, $1,050; office equipment (net), $11,250; land, $75,000; capital, $85,900; and salaries payable, $425.

DAVID HARRISON, ATTORNEY Balance Sheet December 31, 2004		
Assets		
Current assets:		
Cash	_____	
Accounts receivable	_____	
Prepaid insurance	_____	
Office supplies	_____	
Total current assets		_____
Plant and equipment:		
Office equipment (net)	_____	
Building (net)	_____	
Land	_____	
Total plant and equipment		_____
Total assets		_____
Liabilities		
Current liabilities:		
Accounts payable	_____	
Salaries payable	_____	
Total current liabilities		_____
Long-term liabilities:		
Notes payable	_____	
Total liabilities		_____
Owner's Equity		
David Harrison, capital, December 31, 2004		_____
Total liabilities and owner's equity		_____

2. Given the amounts in each of the accounts of Fisher-George Electric Corporation, fill in these amounts on the balance sheet to show that

Assets = Liabilities + Stockholders' equity

Account totals are as follows: cash, $2,500; merchandise inventory, $1,325; automobiles (net), $9,250; common stock, $10,000; accounts payable, $275; office equipment (net), $5,065; accounts receivable, $300; retained earnings, $6,895; prepaid insurance, $1,075; salaries payable, $175; and mortgage payable, $2,170.

FISHER-GEORGE ELECTRIC CORPORATION
Balance Sheet
December 31, 2004

Assets

Current assets:
Cash _____
Accounts receivable _____
Merchandise inventory _____
Prepaid insurance _____
  Total current assets _____

Plant and equipment:
Office equipment (net) _____
Automobiles (net) _____
  Total plant and equipment _____
Total assets _____

Liabilities

Current liabilities:
Accounts payable _____
Salaries payable _____
  Total current liabilities _____

Long-term liabilities:
Mortgage payable _____
  Total liabilities _____

Stockholders' Equity

Common stock _____
Retained earnings _____
  Total stockholders' equity _____
Total liabilities and stockholders' equity _____

3. Complete a vertical analysis of the following partial balance sheet (round all percents to the nearest hundredth percent).

THREEMAX, INC.
Comparative Balance Sheet Vertical Analysis
At December 31, 2003 and 2004

	2004		2003	
	Amount	Percent	Amount	Percent
Assets				
Cash	$ 8,500	_____	$ 10,200	_____
Accounts receivable (net)	11,750	_____	15,300	_____
Merchandise inventory	55,430	_____	54,370	_____
Store supplies	700	_____	532	_____
Office supplies	650	_____	640	_____
Prepaid insurance	2,450	_____	2,675	_____
Office equipment (net)	12,000	_____	14,300	_____
Store equipment (net)	32,000	_____	31,000	_____
Building (net)	75,400	_____	80,500	_____
Land	200,000	_____	150,000	_____
Total assets	$398,880	_____	$359,517	_____

4. Complete a horizontal analysis of the following partial balance sheet (round all percents to the nearest hundredth percent).

THREEMAX, INC. Comparative Balance Sheet Horizontal Analysis At December 31, 2003 and 2004				
	2004	2003	Change	Percent
Assets				
Cash	$ 8,500	$ 10,200	_____	_____
Accounts receivable (net)	11,750	15,300	_____	_____
Merchandise inventory	55,430	54,370	_____	_____
Store supplies	700	532	_____	_____
Office supplies	650	640	_____	_____
Prepaid insurance	2,450	2,675	_____	_____
Office equipment (net)	12,000	14,300	_____	_____
Store equipment (net)	32,000	31,000	_____	_____
Building (net)	75,400	80,500	_____	_____
Land	200,000	150,000	_____	_____
Total assets	$398,880	$359,517		

LEARNING UNIT 16–2 | INCOME STATEMENT—REPORT FOR A SPECIFIC PERIOD OF TIME

DRILL PROBLEMS

1. Complete the income statement for Foley Realty, doing all the necessary addition. Account totals are as follows: office salaries expense, $15,255; advertising expense, $2,400; rent expense, $18,000; telephone expense, $650; insurance expense, $1,550; office supplies, $980; depreciation expense, office equipment, $990; depreciation expense, automobile, $2,100; sales commissions earned, $98,400; and management fees earned, $1,260.

FOLEY REALTY Income Statement For the Year Ended December 31, 2004	
Revenues:	
Sales commissions earned	_____
Management fees earned	_____
Total revenues	_____
Operating expenses:	
Office salaries expense	_____
Advertising expense	_____
Rent expense	_____
Telephone expense	_____
Insurance expense	_____
Office supplies expense	_____
Depreciation expense, office equipment	_____
Depreciation expense, automobile	_____
Total operating expenses	_____
Net income	_____

2. Complete the income statement for Toll's, Inc., a merchandising concern, doing all the necessary addition and subtraction. Sales were $250,000, sales returns and allowances were $1,400, sales discounts were $2,100, merchandise inventory, December 31, 2003, was $42,000, purchases were $156,000, purchases returns and allowances were $1,100, purchases discounts were $3,000, merchandise inventory, December 31, 2004, was $47,000, selling expenses were $37,000, and general and administrative expenses were $29,000.

TOLL'S, INC.
Income Statement
For the Year Ended December 31, 2004

Revenues:
  Sales
    Less: Sales return and allowances _____
       Sales discounts _____ _____
  Net sales _____

Cost of goods sold:
  Merchandise inventory, December 31, 2003 _____
  Purchases
    Less: Purchases returns and allowances _____
       Purchase discounts _____ _____
  Cost of net purchases
  Goods available for sale _____
  Merchandise inventory, December 31, 2004 _____
    Total cost of goods sold _____
Gross profit from sales _____

Operating expenses:
  Selling expenses _____
  General and administrative expenses _____
    Total operating expenses _____
Net income _____

3. Complete a vertical analysis of the following partial income statement (round all percents to the nearest hundredth percent). Note net sales are 100%.

THREEMAX, INC.
Comparative Income Statement Vertical Analysis
For Years Ended December 31, 2003 and 2004

	2004		2003	
	Amount	Percent	Amount	Percent
Sales	$795,450		$665,532	
Sales returns and allowances	−6,250		−5,340	
Sales discounts	−6,470		−5,125	
Net sales	$782,730		$655,067	
Cost of goods sold:				
Beginning inventory	$ 75,394		$ 81,083	
Purchases	575,980		467,920	
Purchases discounts	−4,976		−2,290	
Goods available for sale	$646,398		$546,713	
Less ending inventory	−66,254		−65,712	
Total costs of goods sold	$580,144		$481,001	
Gross profit	$202,586		$174,066	

4. Complete a horizontal analysis of the following partial income statement (round all percents to the nearest hundredth percent).

THREEMAX, INC. Comparative Income Statement Horizontal Analysis For Years Ended December 31, 2004 and 2003				
	2004	**2003**	**Change**	**Percent**
Sales	$795,450	$665,532	_____	_____
Sales returns and allowances	−6,250	−5,340	_____	_____
Sales discounts	−6,470	−5,125	_____	_____
Net sales	$782,730	$655,067	_____	_____
Cost of goods sold:				
Beginning inventory	$ 75,394	$ 81,083	_____	_____
Purchases	575,980	467,920	_____	_____
Purchases discounts	−4,976	−2,290	_____	_____
Goods available for sale	$646,398	$546,713	_____	_____
Less ending inventory	−66,254	−65,712	_____	_____
Total cost of goods sold	$580,144	$481,001	_____	_____
Gross profit	$202,586	$174,066	_____	_____

LEARNING UNIT 16–3 | TREND AND RATIO ANALYSIS

DRILL PROBLEMS

1. Express each amount as a percent of the base-year (2001) amount. Round to the nearest tenth percent.

	2004	**2003**	**2002**	**2001**
Sales	$562,791	$560,776	$588,096	$601,982
Percent	_____	_____	_____	_____
Gross profit	$168,837	$196,271	$235,238	$270,891
Percent	_____	_____	_____	_____
Net income	$67,934	$65,927	$56,737	$62,762
Percent	_____	_____	_____	_____

2. If current assets = $42,500 and current liabilities = $56,400, what is the current ratio (to the nearest hundredth)?

3. In Problem 2, if inventory = $20,500 and prepaid expenses = $9,750, what is the quick ratio, or acid test (to the nearest hundredth)?

4. If accounts receivable = $36,720 and net sales = $249,700, what is the average day's collection (to the nearest whole day)?

5. If total liabilities = $243,000 and total assets = $409,870, what is the ratio of total debt to total assets (to the nearest hundredth percent)?

6. If net income = $55,970 and total stockholders' equity = $440,780, what is the return on equity (to the nearest hundredth percent)?

7. If net sales = $900,000 and total assets = $1,090,000, what is the asset turnover (to the nearest hundredth)?

8. In Problem 7, if the net income is $36,600, what is the profit margin on net sales (to the nearest hundredth percent)?

WORD PROBLEMS

9. Calculate trend percentages for the following items using 2003 as the base year. Round to the nearest hundredth percent.

	2006	2005	2004	2003
Sales	$298,000	$280,000	$264,000	$249,250
Cost of goods sold	187,085	175,227	164,687	156,785
Accounts receivable	29,820	28,850	27,300	26,250

10. According to the balance sheet for Ralph's Market, current assets = $165,500 and current liabilities = $70,500. Find the current ratio (to the nearest hundredth).

11. On the balance sheet for Ralph's Market (Problem 10), merchandise inventory = $102,000. Find the quick ratio (acid test).

12. The balance sheet of Moses Contractors shows cash of $5,500, accounts receivable of $64,500, an inventory of $42,500, and current liabilities of $57,500. Find Moses' current ratio and acid test ratio (both to the nearest hundredth).

13. Moses' income statement shows gross sales of $413,000, sales returns of $8,600, and net income of $22,300. Find the profit margin on net sales (to the nearest hundredth percent).

14. **Given:**

Cash	$ 39,000	Retained earnings	$194,000
Accounts receivable	109,000	Net sales	825,000
Inventory	150,000	Cost of goods sold	528,000
Prepaid expenses	48,000	Operating expenses	209,300
Plant and equipment (net)	487,000	Interest expense	13,500
Accounts payable	46,000	Income taxes	32,400
Other current liabilities	43,000	Net income	41,800
Long-term liabilities	225,000		
Common stock	325,000		

Calculate (to nearest hundredth or hundredth percent as needed):

a. Current ratio.   b. Quick ratio.   c. Average day's collection.

d. Total debt to total assets.   e. Return on equity.   f. Asset turnover.

g. Profit margin on net sales.

15. The Vale Group lost $18.4 million in profits for the year 2003 as sales dropped to $401 million. Sales in 2002 were $450.6 million. What percent is the decrease in Vale's sales? Round to the nearest hundredth percent.

LEARNING UNIT 17-1 | CONCEPT OF DEPRECIATION AND THE STRAIGHT-LINE METHOD

DRILL PROBLEMS

1. Find the annual straight-line rate of depreciation, given the following estimated lives.

Life	Annual rate	Life	Annual rate
a. 25 years	_____	b. 4 years	_____
c. 10 years	_____	d. 5 years	_____
e. 8 years	_____	f. 30 years	_____

2. Find the annual depreciation using the straight-line depreciation method (round to the nearest whole dollar).

	Cost of asset	Residual value	Useful life	Annual depreciation
a.	$2,460	$400	4 years	_____
b.	$24,300	$2,000	6 years	_____
c.	$350,000	$42,500	12 years	_____
d.	$17,325	$5,000	5 years	_____
e.	$2,550,000	$75,000	30 years	_____

3. Find the annual depreciation and ending book value for the first year using the straight-line depreciation method. Round to the nearest dollar.

	Cost	Residual value	Useful life	Annual depreciation	Ending book value
a.	$6,700	$600	3 years	_____	_____
b.	$11,600	$500	6 years	_____	_____
c.	$9,980	–0–	5 years	_____	_____
d.	$36,950	$2,500	12 years	_____	_____
e.	$101,690	$3,600	27 years	_____	_____

4. Find the first-year depreciation to nearest dollar for the following assets, which were only owned for part of a year. Round to the nearest whole dollar the annual depreciation for in-between calculations.

	Date of purchase	Cost of asset	Residual value	Useful life	First year depreciation
a.	April 8	$10,500	$1,200	4 years	_____
b.	July 12	$23,900	$3,200	6 years	_____
c.	June 19	$8,880	$800	3 years	_____
d.	November 2	$125,675	$6,000	17 years	_____
e.	May 25	$44,050	–0–	9 years	_____

WORD PROBLEMS

5. North Shore Grinding purchased a lathe for $37,500. This machine has a residual value of $3,000 and an expected useful life of 4 years. Prepare a depreciation schedule for the lathe using the straight-line depreciation method.

6. Colby Wayne paid $7,750 for a photocopy machine with an estimated life of 6 years and a residual value of $900. Prepare a depreciation schedule using the straight-line depreciation method. Round to nearest whole dollar. (Last year's depreciation may have to be adjusted due to rounding.)

7. The Leo Brothers purchased a machine for $8,400 that has an estimated life of 3 years. At the end of 3 years the machine will have no value. Prepare a depreciation schedule for this machine.

8. Fox Realty bought a computer table for $1,700. The estimated useful life of the table is 7 years. The residual value at the end of 7 years is $370. Find (a) the annual rate of depreciation to the nearest hundredth percent, (b) the annual amount of depreciation, and (c) the book value of the table at the end of the *third* year using the straight-line depreciation method.

9. Cashman, Inc., purchased an overhead projector for $560. It has an estimated useful life of 6 years, at which time it will have no remaining value. Find the book value at the end of 5 years using the straight-line depreciation method. Round the annual depreciation to the nearest whole dollar.

10. Shelley Corporation purchased a new machine for $15,000. The estimated life of the machine is 12 years with a residual value of $2,400. Find **(a)** the annual rate of depreciation to the nearest hundredth percent, **(b)** the annual amount of depreciation, **(c)** the accumulated depreciation at the end of 7 years, and **(d)** the book value at the end of 9 years.

11. Wolfe Ltd. purchased a supercomputer for $75,000 on July 7, 2003. The computer has an estimated life of 5 years and will have a residual value of $15,000. Find **(a)** the annual depreciation amount, **(b)** the depreciation amount for 2003, **(c)** the accumulated depreciation at the end of 2004, and **(d)** the book value at the end of 2005.

LEARNING UNIT 17–2 | UNITS-OF-PRODUCTION METHOD

DRILL PROBLEMS

1. Find the depreciation per unit for each of the following assets. Round to three decimal places.

Cost of asset	Residual value	Estimated production	Depreciation per unit
a. $3,500	$800	9,000 units	_____
b. $309,560	$22,000	1,500,000 units	_____
c. $54,890	$6,500	275,000 units	_____

2. Find the annual depreciation expense for each of the assets in Problem 1.

Cost of asset	Residual value	Estimated production	Depreciation per unit	Units produced	Amount of depreciation
a. $3,500	$800	9,000 units	_____	3,000	_____
b. $309,560	$22,000	1,500,000 units	_____	45,500	_____
c. $54,890	$6,500	275,000 units	_____	4,788	_____

3. Find the book value at the end of the first year for each of the assets in Problems 1 and 2.

Cost of asset	Residual value	Estimated production	Depreciation per unit	Units produced	Book value
a. $3,500	$800	9,000 units	_____	3,000	_____
b. $309,560	$22,000	1,500,000 units	_____	45,500	_____
c. $54,890	$6,500	275,000 units	_____	4,788	_____

4. Calculate the accumulated depreciation at the end of year 2 for each of the following machines. Carry out the unit depreciation to three decimal places.

Cost of machine	Residual value	Estimated life	Hours used during year 1	Hours used during year 2	Accumulated depreciation
a. $67,900	$4,300	19,000 hours	5,430	4,856	_____
b. $3,810	$600	33,000 hours	10,500	9,330	_____
c. $25,000	$4,900	80,000 hours	7,000	12,600	_____

WORD PROBLEMS

5. Prepare a depreciation schedule for the following machine: The machine cost $63,400; it has an estimated residual value of $5,300 and expected life of 290,500 units. The units produced were:

Year 1	95,000 units
Year 2	80,000 units
Year 3	50,000 units
Year 4	35,500 units
Year 5	30,000 units

6. Forsmann & Smythe purchased a new machine that cost $46,030. The machine has a residual value of $2,200 and estimated output of 430,000 hours. Prepare a units-of-production depreciation schedule for this machine (round the unit depreciation to three decimal places). The hours of use were:

Year 1   90,000 hours
Year 2   150,000 hours
Year 3   105,000 hours
Year 4   90,000 hours

7. Young Electrical Company depreciates its vans using the units-of-production method. The cost of its new van was $24,600, the useful life is 125,000 miles, and the trade-in value is $5,250. What are (a) the depreciation expense per mile (to three decimal places) and (b) the book value at the end of the first year if it drives 29,667 miles?

8. Tremblay Manufacturing Company purchased a new machine for $52,000. The machine has an estimated useful life of 185,000 hours and a residual value of $10,000. The machine was used for 51,200 hours the first year. Find (a) the depreciation rate per hour (round to three decimal places), (b) the depreciation expense for the first year, and (c) the book value of the machine at the end of the first year.

LEARNING UNIT 17–3 | SUM-OF-THE-YEARS'-DIGITS METHOD

DRILL PROBLEMS

1. Find the sum-of-the-years'-digits depreciation rate as a fraction for each year of life for the following assets:

Useful life	Year 1	Year 2	Year 3	Year 4	Year 5	Year 6	Year 7	Year 8
a. 5 years	____	____	____	____	____			
b. 3 years	____	____	____					
c. 8 years	____	____	____	____	____	____	____	____

2. Find the first year depreciation amount for the following assets using the sum-of-the-years'-digits depreciation method. Round to the nearest whole dollar.

	Cost of asset	Residual value	Useful life	First year depreciation
a.	$2,460	$400	4 years	_____
b.	$24,300	$2,000	6 years	_____
c.	$350,000	$42,500	12 years	_____
d.	$17,325	$5,000	5 years	_____
e.	$2,550,000	$75,000	30 years	_____

3. Find the depreciation expense and ending book value for the first year using the sum-of-the-years'-digits depreciation method. Round to the nearest dollar (depreciation expense as well as ending book value).

	Cost	Residual value	Useful life	First year depreciation	Ending book value
a.	$6,700	$600	3 years	_____	_____
b.	$11,600	$500	6 years	_____	_____
c.	$9,980	–0–	5 years	_____	_____
d.	$36,950	$2,500	12 years	_____	_____
e.	$101,690	$3,600	27 years	_____	_____

WORD PROBLEMS

4. North Shore Grinding purchased a lathe for $37,500. This machine has a residual value of $3,000 and an expected useful life of 4 years. Prepare a depreciation schedule for the lathe using the sum-of-the-years'-digits depreciation method.

5. Colby Wayne paid $7,750 for a photocopy machine with an estimated life of 6 years and a residual value of $900. Prepare a depreciation schedule using the sum-of-the-years'-digits depreciation method. Round all amounts to the nearest whole dollar.

6. Leo Brothers purchased a machine for $8,400 that has an estimated life of 3 years. At the end of 3 years, the machine will have no value. Prepare a depreciation schedule for this machine.

7. Fox Realty bought a computer table for $1,700. The estimated useful life of the table is 7 years. The residual value at the end of 7 years is $370. Find **(a)** the sum-of-the-years' denominator, **(b)** the amount of depreciation at the end of the *third* year, and **(c)** the book value of the table at the end of the *third* year using the sum-of-the-years'-digits depreciation method.

8. Cashman, Inc., purchased an overhead projector for $560. It has an estimated useful life of 6 years, at which time it will have no remaining value. Find the book value at the end of 5 years using the sum-of-the-years'-digits depreciation method. Round to the nearest whole dollar.

LEARNING UNIT 17–4 | DECLINING-BALANCE METHOD

DRILL PROBLEMS

1. Find the declining-balance rate of depreciation, given the following estimated lives.

Life	Declining rate
a. 25 years	_____
b. 10 years	_____
c. 8 years	_____

2. Find the first year depreciation amount for the following assets using the declining-balance depreciation method. Round to the nearest whole dollar.

Cost of asset	Residual value	Useful life	First year depreciation
a. $2,460	$400	4 years	_____
b. $24,300	$2,000	6 years	_____
c. $350,000	$42,500	12 years	_____
d. $17,325	$5,000	5 years	_____
e. $2,550,000	$75,000	30 years	_____

3. Find the depreciation expense and ending book value for the first year, using the declining-balance depreciation method. Round to the nearest dollar.

Cost	Residual value	Useful life	First year depreciation	Ending book value
a. $6,700	$600	3 years	_____	_____
b. $11,600	$500	6 years	_____	_____
c. $9,980	–0–	5 years	_____	_____
d. $36,950	$2,500	12 years	_____	_____
e. $101,690	$3,600	27 years	_____	_____

WORD PROBLEMS

4. North Shore Grinding purchased a lathe for $37,500. This machine has a residual value of $3,000 and an expected useful life of 4 years. Prepare a depreciation schedule for the lathe using the declining-balance depreciation method. Round to the nearest whole dollar.

5. Colby Wayne paid $7,750 for a photocopy machine with an estimated life of 6 years and a residual value of $900. Prepare a depreciation schedule using the declining-balance depreciation method. Round to the nearest whole dollar.

6. The Leo Brothers purchased a machine for $8,400 that has an estimated life of 3 years. At the end of 3 years, the machine will have no value. Prepare a depreciation schedule for this machine. Round to the nearest whole dollar.

7. Fox Realty bought a computer table for $1,700. The estimated useful life of the table is 7 years. The residual value at the end of 7 years is $370. Find **(a)** the declining depreciation rate to the nearest hundredth percent, **(b)** the amount of depreciation at the end of the *third* year, and **(c)** the book value of the table at the end of the *third* year using the declining-balance depreciation method. Round to the nearest whole dollar.

8. Cashman, Inc., purchased an overhead projector for $560. It has an estimated useful life of 6 years, at which time it will have no remaining value. Find the book value at the end of 5 years using the declining-balance depreciation method. Round to the nearest whole dollar.

9. Shelley Corporation purchased a new machine for $15,000. The estimated life of the machine is 12 years with a residual value of $2,400. Find **(a)** the declining-balance depreciation rate as a fraction and as a percent (hundredth percent), **(b)** the amount of depreciation at the end of the first year, **(c)** the accumulated depreciation at the end of 7 years, and **(d)** the book value at the end of 9 years. Round to the nearest dollar.

LEARNING UNIT 17–5 | MODIFIED ACCELERATED COST RECOVERY SYSTEM (MACRS) WITH INTRODUCTION TO ACRS

DRILL PROBLEMS

1. Using the MACRS method of depreciation, find the recovery rate, first-year depreciation expense, and book value of the asset at the end of the first year. Round to the nearest whole dollar.

Cost of asset	Recovery period	Recovery rate	Depreciation expense	End-of-year book value
a. $2,500	3 years	_____	_____	_____
b. $52,980	3 years	_____	_____	_____
c. $4,250	5 years	_____	_____	_____
d. $128,950	10 years	_____	_____	_____
e. $13,775	5 years	_____	_____	_____

2. Find the accumulated depreciation at the end of the second year for each of the following assets. Round to the nearest whole dollar.

Cost of asset	Recovery period	Accumulated depreciation at end of 2nd year using MACRS	Book value at end of 2nd year using MACRS
a. $2,500	3 years	_____	_____
b. $52,980	3 years	_____	_____
c. $4,250	5 years	_____	_____
d. $128,950	10 years	_____	_____
e. $13,775	5 years	_____	_____

WORD PROBLEMS

3. Colby Wayne paid $7,750 for a photocopy machine that is classified as equipment and has a residual value of $900. Prepare a depreciation schedule using the MACRS depreciation method. Round all calculations to the nearest whole dollar.

4. Fox Realty bought a computer table for $1,700. The table is classified as furniture. The residual value at the end of the table's useful life is $370. Using the MACRS depreciation method, find **(a)** the amount of depreciation at the end of the *third* year, **(b)** the total accumulated depreciation at the end of year 3, and **(c)** the book value of the table at the end of the *third* year. Round all calculations to the nearest dollar.

5. Cashman, Inc., purchased an overhead projector for $560. It is classified as office equipment and will have no residual value. Find the book value at the end of 5 years using the MACRS depreciation method. Round to the nearest whole dollar.

6. Shelley Corporation purchased a new machine for $15,000. The machine is comparable to equipment used for two-way exchange of voice and data with a residual value of $2,400. Find **(a)** the amount of depreciation at the end of the first year, **(b)** the accumulated depreciation at the end of 7 years, and **(c)** the book value at the end of 9 years. Round to the nearest dollar.

7.* Wolfe Ltd. purchased a supercomputer for $75,000 at the beginning of 1996. The computer is classified as a 5-year asset and will have a residual value of $15,000. Using MACRS, find **(a)** the depreciation amount for 1996, **(b)** the accumulated depreciation at the end of 1997, **(c)** the book value at the end of 1998, and **(d)** the last year that the asset will be depreciated.

8.* Cummins Engine Company uses a straight-line depreciation method to calculate the cost of an asset of $1,200,000 with a $200,000 residual value and a life expectancy of 15 years. How much would Cummins have for depreciation expense for each of the first 2 years? Round to the nearest dollar for each year.

9. An article in an issue of *Management Accounting* stated that Cummins Engine Company changed its depreciation. The cost of its asset was $1,200,000 with a $200,000 residual value (with a life expectancy of 15 years) and an estimated productive capacity of 864,000 products. Cummins produced 59,000 products this year. What would it write off for depreciation using the units-of-production method?

---

*These problems are placed here for a quick review.

LEARNING UNIT 18–1 | ASSIGNING COSTS TO ENDING INVENTORY—SPECIFIC IDENTIFICATION; WEIGHTED AVERAGE; FIFO; LIFO

DRILL PROBLEMS

1. Given the value of the beginning inventory, purchases for the year, and ending inventory, find the cost of goods available for sale and the cost of goods sold.

	Beginning inventory	Purchases	Ending inventory	Cost of goods available for sale	Cost of goods sold
a.	$1,000	$4,120	$2,100	_____	_____
b.	$52,400	$270,846	$49,700	_____	_____
c.	$205	$48,445	$376	_____	_____
d.	$78,470	$2,788,560	$100,600	_____	_____
e.	$965	$53,799	$2,876	_____	_____

2. Find the missing amounts; then calculate the number of units available for sale and the cost of the goods available for sale.

Date	Category	Quantity	Unit cost	Total cost
January 1	Beginning inventory	1,207	$45	_____
February 7	Purchase	850	$46	_____
April 19	Purchase	700	$47	_____
July 5	Purchase	1,050	$49	_____
November 2	Purchase	450	$52	_____
Goods available for sale		_____		_____

3. Using the *specific identification* method, find the ending inventory and cost of goods sold for the merchandising concern in Problem 2.

Remaining inventory	Unit cost	Total cost
20 units from beginning inventory	_____	_____
35 units from February 7	_____	_____
257 units from July 5	_____	_____
400 units from November 2	_____	_____
Cost of ending inventory		_____
Cost of goods sold		_____

4. Using the *weighted-average* method, find the average cost per unit (to the nearest cent) and the cost of ending inventory.

	Units available for sale	Cost of goods available for sale	Units in ending inventory	Weighted-average unit cost	Cost of ending inventory
a.	2,350	$120,320	1,265	_____	_____
b.	7,090	$151,017	1,876	_____	_____
c.	855	$12,790	989	_____	_____
d.	12,964	$125,970	9,542	_____	_____
e.	235,780	$507,398	239,013	_____	_____

5. Use the *FIFO* method of inventory valuation to determine the value of ending inventory, which consists of 40 units, and the cost of goods sold.

Date	Category	Quantity	Unit cost	Total cost
January 1	Beginning inventory	37	$219.00	_____
March 5	Purchases	18	230.60	_____
June 17	Purchases	22	255.70	_____
October 18	Purchases	34	264.00	_____
Goods available for sale		___		_____

Ending inventory = _____   Cost of goods sold = _____

6. Use the *LIFO* method of inventory valuation to determine the value of the ending inventory, which consists of 40 units, and the cost of goods sold.

Date	Category	Quantity	Unit cost	Total cost
January 1	Beginning inventory	37	$219.00	_____
March 5	Purchases	18	230.60	_____
June 17	Purchases	22	255.70	_____
October 18	Purchases	34	264.00	_____
Goods available for sale		___		_____

Ending inventory = _____   Cost of goods sold = _____

WORD PROBLEMS

7. At the beginning of September, Green's of Gloucester had 13 yellow raincoats in stock. These raincoats cost $36.80 each. During the month, Green's purchased 14 raincoats for $37.50 each and 16 raincoats for $38.40 each, and they sold 26 raincoats. Calculate **(a)** the average unit cost (round to the nearest cent) and **(b)** the ending inventory value using the weighted-average method.

8. If Green's of Gloucester (Problem 7) used the FIFO method, what would the value of the ending inventory be?

9. If Green's of Gloucester (Problem 7) used the LIFO method, what would the value of the ending inventory be?

10. Hobby Caterers purchased recycled-paper sketch pads during the year as follows:

January	350 pads for $.27 each
March	400 pads for $.31 each
July	200 pads for $.36 each
October	850 pads for $.26 each
November	400 pads for $.31 each

At the end of the year, the company had 775 of these sketch pads in stock. Find the ending inventory value using **(a)** the weighted-average method (round to the nearest cent), **(b)** the FIFO method, and **(c)** the LIFO method.

11. On March 1, Sandler's Shoe Store had the following sports shoes in stock:

13 pairs running shoes for $33 a pair
22 pairs walking shoes for $29 a pair
35 pairs aerobic shoes for $26 a pair
21 pairs cross-trainers for $52 a pair

During the month Sandler's sold 10 pairs of running shoes, 15 pairs of walking shoes, 28 pairs of aerobic shoes, and 12 pairs of cross-trainers. Use the specific identification method to find **(a)** the cost of the goods available for sale, **(b)** the value of the ending inventory, and **(c)** the cost of goods sold.

LEARNING UNIT 18–2 | RETAIL METHOD; GROSS PROFIT METHOD; INVENTORY TURNOVER; DISTRIBUTION OF OVERHEAD

DRILL PROBLEMS

1. Given the following information, calculate **(a)** the goods available for sale at cost and retail, **(b)** the cost ratio (to the nearest thousandth), **(c)** the ending inventory at retail, and **(d)** the cost of the March 31 inventory (to the nearest dollar) by the retail inventory method.

	Cost	Retail
Beginning inventory, March 1	$57,300	$95,500
Purchases during March	$28,400	$48,000
Sales during March		$79,000

2. Given the following information, use the gross profit method to calculate **(a)** the cost of goods available for sale, **(b)** the cost percentage, **(c)** the estimated cost of goods sold, and **(d)** the estimated cost of the inventory as of April 30.

Beginning inventory, April 1	$30,000
Net purchases during April	81,800
Sales during April	98,000
Average gross profit on sales	40%
Inventory, April 1	_____
Net purchases	_____

3. Given the following information, find the average inventory.

Merchandise inventory, January 1, 200A	$82,000
Merchandise inventory, December 31, 200A	$88,000

4. Given the following information, find the inventory turnover for the company in Problem 3 to the nearest hundredth.

Cost of goods sold (12/31/0A) $625,000

5. Given the following information, calculate the **(a)** average inventory at retail, **(b)** average inventory at cost, **(c)** inventory turnover at retail, and **(d)** inventory turnover at cost. Round to the nearest hundredth.

	Cost	Retail
Merchandise inventory, January 1	$ 250,000	$ 355,000
Merchandise inventory, December 31	$ 235,000	$ 329,000
Cost of goods sold	$1,525,000	
Sales		$2,001,000

6. Given the floor space for the following departments, find the entire floor space and the percent each department represents.

		Percent of floor space
Department A	15,000 square feet	_____
Department B	25,000 square feet	_____
Department C	10,000 square feet	_____
Total floor space	50,000 square feet	_____

7. If the total overhead for all the departments (Problem 6) is $200,000, how much of the overhead expense should be allocated to each department?

Overhead/department	
Department A	_____
Department B	_____
Department C	_____

WORD PROBLEMS

8. During the accounting period, Ward's Greenery sold $290,000 of merchandise at marked retail prices. At the end of the period, the following information was available from Ward's records:

	Cost	Retail
Beginning inventory	$ 53,000	$ 79,000
Net purchases	$204,000	$280,000

Use the retail method to estimate Ward's ending inventory at cost. Round the cost ratio to the nearest thousandth.

9. On January 1, Benny's Retail Mart had a $49,000 inventory at cost. During the first quarter of the year, Benny's made net purchases of $199,900. Benny's records show that during the past several years, the store's gross profit on sales has averaged 35%. If Benny's records show $275,000 in sales for the quarter, estimate the ending inventory for the first quarter, using the gross profit method.

10. On April 4, there was a big fire and the entire inventory of R. W. Wilson Company was destroyed. The company records were salvaged. They showed the following information:

Sales (January 1 through April 4)	$127,000
Merchandise inventory, January 1	16,000
Net purchases	71,250

On January 1, the inventory was priced to sell for $38,000 and additional items bought during the period were priced to sell for $102,000. Calculate the cost of the inventory that was destroyed by the fire using the retail method. Round the cost ratio to the nearest thousandth.

11. During the past 4 years, the average gross margin on sales for R. W. Wilson Company was 36% of net sales. Using the data in Problem 10, calculate the cost of the ending inventory destroyed by fire using the gross profit method.

12. Chase Bank has to make a decision on whether to grant a loan to Sally's Furniture store. The lending officer is interested in how often Sally's inventory is turned over. Using selected information from Sally's income statement, calculate the inventory turnover for Sally's Furniture Store (to the nearest hundredth).

Merchandise inventory, January 1, 200A	$ 43,000
Merchandise inventory, December 31, 200A	55,000
Cost of goods sold	128,000

13. Wanting to know more about a business he was considering buying, Jake Paige studied the business's books. He found that beginning inventory for the previous year was $51,000 at cost and $91,800 at retail, ending inventory was $44,000 at cost and $72,600 at retail, sales were $251,000, and cost of goods sold was $154,000. Using this information, calculate for Jake the inventory turnover at cost and the inventory turnover at retail.

14. Ralph's Retail Outlet has calculated its expenses for the year. Total overhead expenses are $147,000. Ralph's accountant must allocate this overhead to four different departments. Given the following information regarding the floor space occupied by each department, calculate how much overhead expense should be allocated to each department.

Department W	12,000 square feet
Department X	9,000 square feet
Department Y	14,000 square feet
Department Z	7,000 square feet

15. How much overhead would be allocated to each department of Ralph's Retail Outlet (Problem 14) if the basis of allocation were the sales of each department? Sales for each of the departments were:

Department W	$110,000
Department X	$120,000
Department Y	$170,000
Department Z	$100,000

LEARNING UNIT 19–1 | SALES AND EXCISE TAXES

DRILL PROBLEMS

1. Calculate the sales tax and the total amount due for each of the following:

Total sales	Sales tax rate	Sales tax	Total amount due
a. $536	5%	_____	_____
b. $11,980	6%	_____	_____
c. $3,090	$8\frac{1}{4}\%$	_____	_____
d. $17.65	$5\frac{1}{2}\%$	_____	_____
e. $294	7.42%	_____	_____

2. Find the amount of actual sales and amount of sales tax on the following total receipts:

Total receipts	Sales tax rate	Actual sales	Sales tax
a. $27,932.15	5.5%	_____	_____
b. $35,911.53	7%	_____	_____
c. $115,677.06	$6\frac{1}{2}\%$	_____	_____
d. $142.96	$5\frac{1}{4}\%$	_____	_____
e. $5,799.24	4.75%	_____	_____

3. Find the sales tax, excise tax, and total cost for each of the following items:

Retail price	Sales tax, 5.2%	Excise tax, 11%	Total cost
a. $399	_____	_____	_____
b. $22,684	_____	_____	_____
c. $7,703	_____	_____	_____

4. Calculate the amount, subtotal, sales tax, and total amount due of the following:

Quantity	Description	Unit price	Amount
3	Taxable item	$4.30	_____
2	Taxable item	$5.23	_____
4	Taxable item	$1.20	_____
		Subtotal	_____
		5% sales tax	_____
		Total	_____

5. Given the sales tax rate and the amount of the sales tax, calculate the price of the following purchases (before tax was added):

Tax rate	Tax amount	Price of purchase
a. 7%	$71.61	_____
b. $5\frac{1}{2}\%$	$3.22	_____

6. Given the sales tax rate and the total price (including tax), calculate the price of the following purchases (before the tax was added):

Tax rate	Total price	Price of purchase
a. 5%	$340.20	_____
b. 6%	$1,224.30	_____

WORD PROBLEMS

7. In a state with a 4.75% sales tax, what will be the sales tax and the total price of a video game marked $110?

8. Browning's invoice included a sales tax of $38.15. If the sales tax rate is 6%, what was the total cost of the taxable goods on the invoice?

9. David Bowan paid a total of $2,763 for a new computer. If this includes a sales tax of 5.3%, what was the marked price of the computer?

10. After a 5% sales tax and a 12% excise tax, the total cost of a leather jacket was $972. What was the selling price of the jacket?

11. A customer at the RDM Discount Store purchased four tubes of toothpaste priced at $1.88 each, six toothbrushes for $1.69 each, and three bottles of shampoo for $2.39 each. What did the customer have to pay if the sales tax is $5\frac{1}{2}$%?

12. Bill Harrington purchased a mountain bike for $875. Bill had to pay a sales tax of 6% and an excise tax of 11%. What was the total amount Bill had to pay for his mountain bike?

13. Donna DeCoff received a bill for $754 for a new chair she had purchased. The bill included a 6.2% sales tax and a delivery charge of $26. What was the selling price of the chair?

LEARNING UNIT 19–2 | PROPERTY TAX

DRILL PROBLEMS

1. Find the assessed value of the following properties (round to the nearest whole dollar):

	Market value	Assessment rate	Assessed value
a.	$195,000	35%	_____
b.	$1,550,900	50%	_____
c.	$75,000	75%	_____
d.	$2,585,400	65%	_____
e.	$349,500	85%	_____

2. Find the tax rate for each of the following municipalities (round to the nearest tenth of a percent):

	Budget needed	Total assessed value	Tax rate
a.	$2,594,000	$44,392,000	_____
b.	$17,989,000	$221,900,000	_____
c.	$6,750,000	$47,635,000	_____
d.	$13,540,000	$143,555,500	_____
e.	$1,099,000	$12,687,000	_____

3. Express each of the following tax rates in all the indicated forms:

	By percent	Per $100 of assessed value	Per $1,000 of assessed value	In mills
a.	7.45%	_____	_____	_____
b.	_____	$14.24	_____	_____
c.	_____	_____	_____	90.8
d.	_____	_____	$62.00	_____

4. Calculate the property tax due for each of the following:

Total assessed value	Tax rate	Total property tax due
a. $12,900	$6.60 per $100	_____
b. $175,400	43 mills	_____
c. $320,500	2.7%	_____
d. $2,480,000	$17.85 per $1,000	_____
e. $78,900	59 mills	_____
f. $225,550	$11.39 per $1,000	_____
g. $198,750	$2.63 per $100	_____

WORD PROBLEMS

5. The county of Chelsea approved a budget of $3,450,000, which had to be raised through property taxation. If the total assessed value of properties in the county of Chelsea was $37,923,854, what will the tax rate be? The tax rate is stated per $100 of assessed valuation.

6. Linda Tawse lives in Camden and her home has a market value of $235,000. Property in Camden is assessed at 55% of its market value, and the tax rate for the current year is $64.75 per $1,000. What is the assessed valuation of Linda's home?

7. Using the information in Problem 6, find the amount of property tax that Linda will have to pay.

8. Mary Faye Souza has property with a fair market value of $219,500. Property in Mary Faye's city is assessed at 65% of its market value and the tax rate is $3.64 per $100. How much is Mary Faye's property tax due?

9. Cagney's Greenhouse has a fair market value of $1,880,000. Property is assessed at 35% by the city. The tax rate is 6.4%. What is the property tax due for Cagney's Greenhouse?

10. In Chester County, property is assessed at 40% of its market value, the residential tax rate is $12.30 per $1,000, and the commercial tax rate is $13.85 per $1,000. What is the property tax due on a home that has a market value of $205,000?

11. Using the information in Problem 10, find the property tax due on a grocery store with a market value of $5,875,000.

12. Bob Rose's home is assessed at $195,900. Last year the tax rate was 11.8 mills, and this year the rate was raised to 13.2 mills. How much more will Bob have to pay in taxes this year?

LEARNING UNIT 20-1 | LIFE INSURANCE

DRILL PROBLEMS

1. Use the table in the *Business Math Handbook* to find the annual premium per $1,000 of life insurance and calculate the annual premiums for each policy listed. Assume the insureds are males.

	Face value of policy	Type of insurance	Age at issue	Annual premium per $1,000	Number of $1,000s in face value	Annual premium
a.	$25,000	Straight life	31	_____	_____	_____
b.	$40,500	20-year endowment	40	_____	_____	_____
c.	$200,000	Straight life	44	_____	_____	_____
d.	$62,500	20-payment life	25	_____	_____	_____
e.	$12,250	5-year term	35	_____	_____	_____
f.	$42,500	20-year endowment	42	_____	_____	_____

2. Use Table 20.1 to find the annual premium for each of the following life insurance policies. Assume the insured is a 30-year-old male.

	Face value of policy	Five-year term policy	Straight life policy	Twenty-payment life policy	Twenty-year endowment
a.	$50,000	_____	_____	_____	_____
b.	$1,000,000	_____	_____	_____	_____
c.	$250,000	_____	_____	_____	_____
d.	$72,500	_____	_____	_____	_____

3. Use the table in the *Business Math Handbook* to find the annual premium for each of the following life insurance policies. Assume the insured is a 30-year-old female.

	Face value of policy	Five-year term policy	Straight life policy	Twenty-payment life policy	Twenty-year endowment
a.	$50,000	_____	_____	_____	_____
b.	$1,000,000	_____	_____	_____	_____
c.	$250,000	_____	_____	_____	_____
d.	$72,500	_____	_____	_____	_____

4. Use the table in the *Business Math Handbook* to find the nonforfeiture options for the following policies:

	Years policy in force	Type of policy	Face value	Cash value	Amount of paid-up insurance	Extended term
a.	10	Straight life	$25,000	_____	_____	_____
b.	20	20-year endowment	$500,000	_____	_____	_____
c.	5	20-payment life	$2,000,000	_____	_____	_____
d.	15	Straight life	$750,000	_____	_____	_____
e.	5	20-year endowment	$93,500	_____	_____	_____

WORD PROBLEMS

5. If Mr. Davis, aged 39, buys a $90,000 straight life policy, what is the amount of his annual premium?

6. If Miss Jennie McDonald, age 27, takes out a $65,000 20-year endowment policy, what premium amount will she pay each year?

7. If Gary Thomas decides to cash in his $45,000 20-payment life insurance policy after 15 years, what cash surrender value will he receive?

8. Mary Allyn purchased a $70,000 20-year endowment policy when she was 26 years old. Ten years later, she decided that she could no longer afford the premiums. If Mary decides to convert her policy to paid-up insurance, what amount of paid-up insurance coverage will she have?

9. Peter and Jane Rizzo are both 28 years old and are both planning to take out $50,000 straight life insurance policies. What is the difference in the annual premiums they will have to pay?

10. Paul Nasser purchased a $125,000 straight life policy when he was 30 years old. He is now 50 years old. Two months ago, he slipped in the bathtub and injured his back; he will not be able to return to his regular job for several months. Due to a lack of income, he feels that he can no longer continue to pay the premiums on his life insurance policy. If Paul decides to surrender his policy for cash, how much cash will he receive?

11. If Paul Nasser (Problem 10) chooses to convert his policy to paid-up insurance, what will the face value of his new policy be?

LEARNING UNIT 20–2 | FIRE INSURANCE

DRILL PROBLEMS

1. Use the tables in the *Business Math Handbook* to find the premium for each of the following:

	Rating of area	Building class	Building value	Value of contents	Total annual premium
a.	3	A	$80,000	$32,000	_____
b.	2	B	$340,000	$202,000	_____
c.	2	A	$221,700	$190,000	_____
d.	1	B	$96,400	$23,400	_____
e.	3	B	$65,780	$62,000	_____

2. Use the tables in the *Business Math Handbook* to find the short-term premium and the amount of refund due if the insured cancels.

	Annual premium	Months of coverage	Short-term premium	Refund due
a.	$1,860	3	_____	_____
b.	$650	7	_____	_____
c.	$1,200	10	_____	_____
d.	$341	12	_____	_____
e.	$1,051	4	_____	_____

3. Find the amount to be paid for each of the following losses:

	Property value	Coinsurance clause	Insurance required	Insurance carried	Amount of loss	Insurance company pays (indemnity)
a.	$85,000	80%	_____	$70,000	$60,000	_____
b.	$52,000	80%	_____	$45,000	$50,000	_____
c.	$44,000	80%	_____	$33,000	$33,000	_____
d.	$182,000	80%	_____	$127,400	$61,000	_____

WORD PROBLEMS

4. Mary Rose wants to purchase fire insurance for her building, which is rated as Class B; the rating of the area is 2. If her building is worth $225,000 and the contents are worth $70,000, what will her annual premium be?

5. Janet Ambrose owns a Class A building valued at $180,000. The contents of the building are valued at $145,000. The territory rating is 3. What is her annual fire insurance premium?

6. Jack Altshuler owns a building worth $355,500. The contents are worth $120,000. The classification of the building is B, and the rating of the area is 1. What annual premium must Jack pay for his fire insurance?

7. Jay Viola owns a store valued at $460,000. His fire insurance policy (which has an 80% coinsurance clause) has a face value of $345,000. A recent fire resulted in a loss of $125,000. How much will the insurance company pay?

8. The building that is owned by Tally's Garage is valued at $275,000 and is insured for $225,000. The policy has an 80% coinsurance clause. If there is a fire in the building and the damages amount to $220,000, how much of the loss will be paid for by the insurance company?

9. Michael Dannon owns a building worth $420,000. He has a fire insurance policy with a face value of $336,000 (there is an 80% coinsurance clause). There was recently a fire that resulted in a $400,000 loss. How much money will he receive from the insurance company?

10. Rice's Rent-A-Center business is worth $375,000. He has purchased a $250,000 fire insurance policy. The policy has an 80% coinsurance clause. What will Rice's reimbursement be (a) after a $150,000 fire and (b) after a $330,000 fire?

11. If Maria's Pizza Shop is valued at $210,000 and is insured for $147,000 with a policy that contains an 80% coinsurance clause, what settlement is due after a fire that causes (a) $150,000 in damages and (b) $175,000 in damages?

LEARNING UNIT 20–3 | AUTO INSURANCE

DRILL PROBLEMS

1. Calculate the annual premium for compulsory coverage for each of the following.

Driver classification	Bodily	Property	Total premium
a. 17	_____	_____	_____
b. 20	_____	_____	_____
c. 10	_____	_____	_____

2. Calculate the amount of money the insurance company and the driver should pay for each of the following accidents, assuming the driver carries compulsory insurance only.

Accident and court award	Insurance company pays	Driver pays
a. Driver hit one person and court awarded $15,000.	_____	_____
b. Driver hit one person and court awarded $12,000 for personal injury.	_____	_____
c. Driver hit two people; court awarded first person $9,000 and the second person $12,000.	_____	_____

3. Calculate the additional premium payment for each of the following options.

Optional insurance coverage	Addition to premium
a. Bodily injury 50/100/25, driver class 20	_____
b. Bodily injury 25/60/10, driver class 17	_____
c. Collision insurance, driver class 10, age group 3, symbol 5, deductible $100	_____
d. Comprehensive insurance, driver class 10, age group 3, symbol 5, deductible $200	_____
e. Substitute transportation, towing, and labor; driver class 10, age group 3, symbol 5	_____

4. Compute the annual premium for compulsory insurance with optional liability coverage for bodily injury and damage to someone else's property.

Driver classification	Bodily coverage	Premium
a. 17	50/100/25	_____
b. 20	100/300/10	_____
c. 10	25/60/25	_____
d. 18	250/500/50	_____
e. 20	25/50/10	_____

5. Calculate the annual premium for each of the following drivers with the indicated options. All drivers must carry compulsory insurance.

Driver classification	Car age	Car symbol	Bodily injury	Collision	Comprehensive	Transportation and towing	Annual premium
a. 10	2	4	50/100/10	$100 deductible	$300 deductible	Yes	_____
b. 18	3	2	25/60/25	$200 deductible	$200 deductible	Yes	_____

WORD PROBLEMS

6. Ann Centerino's driver classification is 10. She carries only compulsory insurance coverage. What annual insurance premium must she pay?

7. Gary Hines is a class 18 driver. He wants to add optional bodily injury and property damage of 250/500/50 to his compulsory insurance coverage. What will be Gary's total annual premium?

8. Sara Goldberg wants optional bodily injury coverage of 50/100/25 and collision coverage with a deductible of $300 in addition to the compulsory coverage her state requires. Sara is a class 17 driver and has a symbol 4 car that is 2 years old. What annual premium must Sara pay?

9. Karen Babson has just purchased a new car with a symbol of 8. She wants bodily injury and property liability of 500/1,000/100, comprehensive and collision insurance with a $200 deductible, and transportation and towing coverage. If Karen is a class 10 driver, what will be her annual insurance premium? There is no compulsory insurance requirement in her state. Assume age group 1.

10. Craig Haberland is a class 18 driver. He has a 5-year-old car with a symbol of 4. His state requires compulsory insurance coverage. In addition, he wishes to purchase collision and comprehensive coverage with the maximum deductible. He also wants towing insurance. What will Craig's annual insurance premium be?

11. Nancy Poland has an insurance policy with limits of 10/20. If Nancy injures a pedestrian and the judge awards damages of $18,000, **(a)** how much will the insurance company pay and **(b)** how much will Nancy pay?

12. Peter Bell carries insurance with bodily injury limits of 25/60. Peter is in an accident and is charged with injuring four people. The judge awards damages of $10,000 to each of the injured parties. How much will the insurance company pay? How much will Peter pay?

13. Jerry Greeley carries an insurance policy with bodily injury limits of 25/60. Jerry is in an accident and is charged with injuring four people. If the judge awards damages of $20,000 to each of the injured parties, **(a)** how much will the insurance company pay and **(b)** how much will Jerry pay?

14. An issue of *Your Money* reported that the Illinois Department of Insurance gave a typical premium for a brick house in Chicago built in 1950, assuming no policy discounts and a replacement cost estimated at $100,000. With a $100 deductible, the annual premium will be $653. Using the rate in your textbook, with a rating area 3 and class B, what would be the annual premium? (This problem reviews fire insurance.)

15. An issue of *Money* ran a story on cutting car insurance premiums. Raising the car insurance deductible to $500 will cut the collision premium 15%. Theresa Mendex insures her car; her age group is 5 and symbol is 5. What would be her reduction if she changed her policy to a $500 deductible? What would the collision insurance now cost?

16. Robert Stuono lost his life insurance when he was downsized from an investment banking company early this year. So Stuono, age 44, enlisted the help of an independent agent who works with several insurance companies. His goal is $350,000 in term coverage with a level premium for 5 years. What will Robert's annual premium be for term insurance? (This problem reviews life insurance.)

LEARNING UNIT 21–1 | STOCKS

DRILL PROBLEMS

52 weeks					Yld		Vol				Net
Hi	Lo	Stocks	SYM	Div	%	PE	100s	High	Low	Close	chg
43.88	25.51	Disney	DIS	.21	.8	49	49633	27.69	26.50	27.69	+0.63

1. From the listed information for Disney, complete the following:
   a. _____ was the highest price at which Disney stock traded during the year.
   b. _____ was the lowest price at which Disney stock traded during the year.
   c. _____ was the amount of the dividend Disney paid to shareholders last year.
   d. _____ is the dividend amount a shareholder with 100 shares would receive.
   e. _____ is the rate of return the stock yielded to its stockholders.
   f. _____ is how many times the earnings per share the stock is selling for.
   g. _____ is the number of shares traded on the day of this stock quote.
   h. _____ is the highest price paid for Disney stock on this day.
   i. _____ is the lowest price paid for Disney stock on this day.
   j. _____ is the change in price from yesterday's closing price.

2. Use the Disney information to show how the yield percent was calculated.

3. What was the price of the last trade of Disney stock yesterday?

WORD PROBLEMS

4. Assume a stockbroker's commission of 2%. What will it cost to purchase 200 shares of Saplent Corporation at $10.75?

5. In Problem 4, the stockbroker's commission for selling stock is the same as that for buying stock. If the customer who purchased 200 shares at $10.75 sells the 200 shares of stock at the end of the year at $18.12, what will be the gain on investment?

6. Holtz Corporation's records show 80,000 shares of preferred stock issued. The preferred dividend is $2 per share, which is cumulative. The records show 750,000 shares of common stock issued. In 2003, no dividends were paid. In 2004, the board of directors declared a dividend of $582,500. What are (a) the total amount of dividends paid to preferred stockholders, (b) the total amount of dividends paid to common stockholders, and (c) the amount of the common dividend per share?

7. Melissa Tucker bought 300 shares of Delta Air Lines stock listed at $61.22 per share. What is the total amount she paid if the stockbroker's commission is 2.5%?

8. A year later, Melissa (Problem 7) sold the stock she had purchased. The market price of the stock at this time was $72.43. Delta Air Lines had paid its shareholders a dividend of $1.20 per share. If the stockbroker's commission to sell stock is 2.5%, what gain did Melissa realize?

9. The board of directors of Parker Electronics, Inc., declared a $539,000 dividend. If the corporation has 70,000 shares of common stock outstanding, what is the dividend per share?

DRILL PROBLEMS

Bond	Current yield	Sales	Close	Net change
IBM $10\frac{1}{4}$ 04	10.0	11	$102\frac{1}{2}$	$+\frac{1}{8}$

1. From the bond listing above complete the following:
   a. _____ is the name of the company.
   b. _____ is the percent of interest paid on the bond.
   c. _____ is the year in which the bond matures.
   d. _____ is the total interest for the year.
   e. _____ was yesterday's close on the IBM bond.

2. Show how to calculate the current yield of 10.0% for IBM. (Trade commissions have been omitted.)

3. Use the information for the IBM bonds to calculate (a) the amount the last bond traded for on this day and (b) the amount the last bond traded for yesterday.

4. What will be the annual interest payment (a) to the bondholder assuming he paid $101\frac{3}{4}$ and (b) to the bondholder who purchased the bond for $102\frac{1}{2}$?

5. If Terry Gambol purchased three IBM bonds at this day's closing price, (a) what will be her total cost excluding commission and (b) how much interest will she receive for the year?

6. Calculate the bond yield (to the nearest tenth percent) for each of the following:

Bond interest rate	Purchase price	Bond yield
a. 7%	97	_____
b. $9\frac{1}{2}\%$	$101\frac{5}{8}$	_____
c. $13\frac{1}{4}\%$	$104\frac{1}{4}$	_____

7. For each of the following, state whether the bond sold at a premium or a discount and give the amount of the premium or discount.

Bond interest rate	Purchase price	Premium or discount
a. 7%	97	_____
b. $9\frac{1}{2}\%$	$101\frac{5}{8}$	_____
c. $13\frac{1}{4}\%$	$104\frac{1}{4}$	_____

WORD PROBLEMS

8. Rob Morrisey purchased a $1,000 bond that was quoted at $102\frac{1}{4}$ and paying $8\frac{7}{8}\%$ interest. (a) How much did Rob pay for the bond? (b) What was the premium or discount? (c) How much annual interest will he receive?

9. Jackie Anderson purchased a bond that was quoted at $62\frac{1}{2}$ and paying interest of $10\frac{1}{2}\%$. (a) How much did Jackie pay for the bond? (b) What was the premium or discount? (c) What interest will Jackie receive annually? (d) What is the bond's current annual yield (to the nearest tenth percent)?

10. Swartz Company issued bonds totaling $2,000,000 in order to purchase updated equipment. If the bonds pay interest of 11%, what is the total amount of interest the Swartz Company must pay semiannually?

11. The RJR and ACyan companies have both issued bonds that are paying $7\frac{3}{8}\%$ interest. The quoted price of the RJR bond is $94\frac{1}{8}$, and the quoted price of the ACyan bond is $102\frac{7}{8}$. Find the current annual yield on each (to the nearest tenth percent).

12. Mary Rowe purchased 25 bonds of Chrysler Corporation $8\frac{3}{8}\%$ bonds of 2004. The bonds closed at $93\frac{1}{4}$. Find **(a)** the total purchase price and **(b)** the amount of the first semiannual interest payment Mary will receive.

13. What is the annual yield (to the nearest hundredth percent) of the bonds Mary Rowe purchased?

14. Mary Rowe purchased a $1,000 bond listed as ARch $10\frac{7}{8}$ 05 for $122\frac{3}{4}$. What is the annual yield of this bond (to the nearest tenth percent)?

LEARNING UNIT 21-3 | MUTUAL FUNDS

DRILL PROBLEMS

From the following, calculate the NAV. Round to the nearest cent.

Current market value of fund investments	Current liabilities	Number of shares outstanding	NAV
1. $6,800,000	$850,000	500,000	___
2. $11,425,000	$690,000	810,000	___
3. $22,580,000	$1,300,000	1,400,000	___

Complete the following using this information:

NAV	Net change	Fund name	Inv. obj.	YTD %Ret	Total return 1 Yr R
$23.48	+.14	EuroA	Eu	+37.3	+7.6 E

4. NAV ___

5. NAV change ___

6. Total return year to date ___

7. Return for the last 12 months ___

8. What does an E rating mean? ___

Calculate the commission (load) charge and the offer to buy.

NAV	% commission (load) charge	Dollar amount of commission (load) charge	Offer price
9. $17.00	$8\frac{1}{2}\%$	___	___
10. $21.55	6%	___	___
11. $14.10	4%	___	___

WORD PROBLEMS

12. Paul wanted to know how his Fidelity mutual fund $14.33 NAV in the newspaper was calculated. He called Fidelity, and he received the following information:

Current market value of fund investment	$7,500,000
Current liabilities	$910,000
Number of shares outstanding	460,000

Please calculate the NAV for Paul. Was the NAV in the newspaper correct?

13. Jeff Jones bought 150 shares of Putnam Vista Fund. The NAV of the fund was $9.88. The offer price was $10.49. What did Jeff pay for these 150 shares?

14. Pam Long purchased 300 shares of the no-load Scudder's European Growth Company Fund. The NAV is $12.61. What did Pam pay for the 300 shares?

15. Assume in Problem 14 that 8 years later Pam sells her 300 shares. The NAV at the time of sale was $12.20. What is the amount of her profit or loss on the sale?

16. Financial planner J. Michael Martin recommended that Jim Kelly choose a long-term bond because it gives high income while Kelly waits for better stock market opportunities down the road. The bond Martin recommended matures in 2005 and was originally issued at $8\frac{1}{2}\%$ interest and the current yield is 7.9%. What would be the current selling price for this bond and how would that price appear in the bond quotations?

17.

Bonds	Vol.	Close	Net chg.
Comp USA $9\frac{1}{2}$ 03	70	$102\frac{3}{8}$	$-\frac{1}{8}$
GMA 7 05	5	$101\frac{5}{8}$	$-1\frac{1}{4}$

From the above information, compare the two bonds for:

a. When the bonds expire.

b. The yield of each bond.

c. The current selling price.

d. Whether the bond is selling at a discount or premium.

e. Yesterday's bond close.

LEARNING UNIT 22–1 | MEAN, MEDIAN, AND MODE

Note: Optional problems for LU 22–3 are found on page 499.

DRILL PROBLEMS

1. Find the mean for the following lists of numbers. Round to the nearest hundredth.
   a. 12, 16, 20, 25, 29   Mean _____
   b. 80, 91, 98, 82, 68, 82, 79, 90   Mean _____
   c. 9.5, 12.3, 10.5, 7.5, 10.1, 18.4, 9.8, 6.2, 11.1, 4.8, 10.6   Mean _____

2. Find the weighted mean for the following. Round to the nearest hundredth.
   a. 4, 4, 6, 8, 8, 13, 4, 6, 8   Weighted mean _____
   b. 82, 85, 87, 82, 82, 90, 87, 63, 100, 85, 87   Weighted mean _____

3. Find the median for the following:
   a. 56, 89, 47, 36, 90, 63, 55, 82, 46, 81   Median _____
   b. 59, 22, 39, 47, 33, 98, 50, 73, 54, 46, 99   Median _____

4. Find the mode for the following:
   24, 35, 49, 35, 52, 35, 52   Mode _____

5. Find the mean, median, and mode for each of the following:
   a. 72, 48, 62, 54, 73, 62, 75, 57, 62, 58, 78
   Mean _____   Median _____   Mode _____
   b. $0.50, $1.19, $0.58, $1.19, $2.83, $1.71, $2.21, $0.58, $1.29, $0.58
   Mean _____   Median _____   Mode _____
   c. $92, $113, $99, $117, $99, $105, $119, $112, $95, $116, $102, $120
   Mean _____   Median _____   Mode _____
   d. 88, 105, 120, 119, 105, 128, 160, 151, 90, 153, 107, 119, 105
   Mean _____   Median _____   Mode _____

WORD PROBLEMS

6. The sales for the year at the 8 Bed and Linen Stores were $1,442,897, $1,556,793, $1,703,767, $1,093,320, $1,443,984, $1,665,308, $1,197,692, and $1,880,443. Find the mean earnings for a Bed and Linen Store for the year.

7. To avoid having an extreme number affect the average, the manager of Bed and Linen Stores (Problem 6) would like you to find the median earnings for the 8 stores.

8. The Bed and Linen Store in Salem sells many different towels. Following are the prices of all the towels that were sold on Wednesday: $7.98, $9.98, $9.98, $11.49, $11.98, $7.98, $12.49, $12.49, $11.49, $9.98, $9.98, $16.00, and $7.98. Find the mean price of a towel.

9. Looking at the towel prices, the Salem manager (Problem 8) decided that he should have calculated a weighted mean. Find the weighted mean price of a towel.

10. The manager of the Salem Bed and Linen Store above would like to find another measure of the central tendency called the *median*. Find the median price for the towels sold.

11. The manager at the Salem Bed and Linen Store would like to know the most popular towel among the group of towels sold on Wednesday. Find the mode for the towel prices for Wednesday.

DRILL PROBLEMS

1. A local dairy distributor wants to know how many containers of yogurt health club members consume in a month. The distributor gathered the following data:

17	17	22	14	26	23	23	15	18	16
18	15	23	18	29	20	24	17	12	15
18	19	18	20	28	21	25	21	26	14
16	18	15	19	27	15	22	19	19	13
20	17	13	24	28	18	28	20	17	16

Construct a frequency distribution table to organize this data.

2. Construct a bar graph for the Problem 1 data. The height of each bar should represent the frequency of each amount consumed.

3. To simplify the amount of data concerning yogurt consumption, construct a relative frequency distribution table. The range will be from 1 to 30 with five class intervals: 1–6, 7–12, 13–18, 19–24, and 25–30.

4. Construct a bar graph for the grouped data.

5. Prepare a pie chart to represent the above data.

WORD PROBLEMS

6. The women's department of a local department store lists its total sales for the year: January, $39,800; February, $22,400; March, $32,500; April, $33,000; May, $30,000; June, $29,200; July, $26,400; August, $24,800; September, $34,000; October, $34,200; November, $38,400; December, $41,100. Draw a line graph to represent the monthly sales of the women's department for the year. The vertical axis should represent the dollar amount of the sales.

7. The following list shows the number of television sets sold in a year by the sales associates at Souza's TV and Appliance Store.

115	125	139	127	142	153	169	126	141
130	137	150	169	157	146	173	168	156
140	146	134	123	142	129	141	122	141

Construct a relative frequency distribution table to represent the data. The range will be from 115 to 174 with intervals of 10.

8. Use the data in the distribution table for Problem 7 to construct a bar graph for the grouped data.

9. Expenses for Flora Foley Real Estate Agency for the month of June were as follows: salaries expense, $2,790; utilities expense, $280; rent expense, $2,000; commissions expense, $4,800; and other expenses, $340. Present this data in a circle graph. (First calculate the percent relationship between each item and the total, then determine the number of degrees that represents each item.)

10. Today a new Jeep costs $25,000. In 1970, the Jeep cost $4,500. What is the price relative? (Round to nearest tenth percent.)

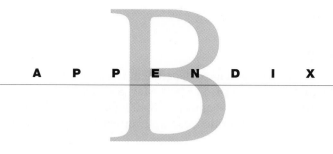

Check Figures

Odd-Numbered Drill and Word Problems for End-of-Chapter Problems.

Challenge Problems.

Summary Practice Tests (all).

Cumulative Reviews (all).

Odd-Numbered Additional Assignments by Learning Unit from Appendix A.

CHECK FIGURES TO DRILL AND WORD PROBLEMS (ODDS), CHALLENGE PROBLEMS, SUMMARY PRACTICE TESTS, AND CUMULATIVE REVIEWS

CHAPTER 1

End-of-Chapter Problems

1–1. 112
1–3. 198
1–5. 13,580
1–7. 113,690
1–9. 38
1–11. 1,700
1–13. 1,074
1–15. 31,110
1–17. 340,531
1–19. 126,000
1–21. 90
1–23. 86 R4
1–25. 187
1–27. 1,616
1–29. 24,876
1–31. 17,989; 18,000
1–33. 80
1–35. 104
1–37. 216
1–39. 19 R21
1–41. 2,227
1–43. 15,589
1–45. 2,162,000
1–47. 850
1–49. 12 R600; 12 R610
1–51. $2,971,700,000
1–53. $24,115
1–55. $26,390
1–57. 2,980 shares; $154,960
1–59. 84
1–61. 1 mile per gallon
1–63. 922; $54,398
1–65. 7,050
1–67. $182,090
1–69. $28,745
1–71. $1,250
1–73. $9,922
1–75. 54,506
1–77. $24
1–79. $7,294,702; $1,105,298
1–80. $12,000 difference

Summary Practice Test

1. 8,022,200
2. Seven million, nine hundred forty-four thousand, five hundred eighty-one
3. **a.** 60 **b.** 600 **c.** 8,000 **d.** 20,000
4. 18,000; 18,648
5. 5,600,000; 5,995,352
6. 844,582,000
7. 260 R20
8. 100
9. $72
10. $700; no
11. $350

CHAPTER 2

End-of-Chapter Problems

2–1. Proper
2–3. Improper
2–5. $61\frac{2}{5}$
2–7. $\frac{59}{3}$
2–9. $\frac{11}{13}$
2–11. 60 $(2 \times 2 \times 3 \times 5)$
2–13. 96 $(2 \times 2 \times 2 \times 2 \times 2 \times 3)$
2–15. $\frac{13}{21}$
2–17. $15\frac{5}{12}$
2–19. $\frac{5}{6}$
2–21. $7\frac{4}{9}$
2–23. $\frac{5}{16}$
2–25. $\frac{3}{25}$
2–27. $\frac{1}{3}$
2–29. $\frac{7}{18}$
2–31. $1\frac{7}{12}$ yards needed
2–33. $25
2–35. $1,200
2–37. $63\frac{1}{4}$ inch; $11\frac{1}{12}$ inch remain
2–39. $2\frac{1}{2}$ miles below average
2–41. $6\frac{1}{2}$ gallons
2–43. $525
2–45. $\frac{23}{36}$
2–47. $25
2–49. $3\frac{3}{4}$ lb apple; $8\frac{1}{8}$ cups flour; $\frac{5}{8}$ cup marg.; $5\frac{15}{16}$ cups of sugar; 5 teaspoon cin.
2–51. 400 people
2–53. 92 pieces
2–55. 5,800 books
2–57. $200
2–59. $35\frac{7}{16}$ ft; $4\frac{9}{16}$ ft left
2–61. $62,500,000
2–63. $\frac{3}{8}$
2–65. $2\frac{3}{5}$ hours
2–67. 60 sandwiches
2–68. $261\frac{3}{4}$ inch; 4 boards
2–69. **a.** 400 homes **b.** $320,000 **c.** 3,000 people; 2,500 people **d.** $112.50 **e.** $8,800,000

Summary Practice Test

1. Mixed number
2. Proper
3. Improper
4. $27\frac{3}{5}$
5. $\frac{31}{4}$
6. $14; \frac{7}{10}$
7. 88
8. 28 $(2 \times 7 \times 2)$
9. $5\frac{17}{18}$
10. $\frac{3}{14}$
11. $6\frac{4}{19}$
12. $\frac{1}{4}$
13. $6\frac{4}{5}$ hours
14. 12,555 chairs
15. **a.** 24,000 soy **b.** 36,000 reg.
16. $36\frac{1}{4}$ hours
17. $15

CHAPTER 3

End-of-Chapter Problems

3–1. Thousandths
3–3. .9; .95; .948
3–5. 6.9; 6.92; 6.925
3–7. 6.6; 6.56; 6.556
3–9. $2,011.67
3–11. .07
3–13. .09
3–15. .64
3–17. 14.91
3–19. $\frac{62}{100}$
3–21. $\frac{125}{10,000}$

3–23. $\dfrac{825}{1,000}$

3–25. $\dfrac{7,065}{10,000}$

3–27. $28\dfrac{48}{100}$

3–29. .004

3–31. .0085

3–33. 818.1279

3–35. 3.4

3–37. 2.32

3–39. 1.2; 1.26791

3–41. 4; 4.0425

3–43. 24,526.67

3–45. 161.29

3–47. 6,824.15

3–49. .04

3–51. .63

3–53. 2.585

3–55. .0086

3–57. 486

3–59. 3.950

3–61. 7,913.2

3–63. .545

3–65. $14.61

3–67. $1.40

3–69. $119.47

3–71. $8.97

3–73. $77

3–75. $399.16

3–77. $105.08

3–79. $204

3–81. $73.52

3–83. $3.15 diff.

3–85. $6,465.60

3–87. $160.31

3–88. $560.45

Summary Practice Test

1. 764.126
2. .6
3. .06
4. .006
5. $\dfrac{4}{10}$
6. $8\dfrac{95}{100}$
7. $\dfrac{951}{1,000}$
8. .14
9. .29
10. 4.63
11. .13
12. 288.8342
13. 10.3
14. 109.59
15. 22,453.6
16. 86,330

17. 705,518,978.1
18. $19.59
19. $531.56
20. $220.96
21. A $.145
22. $6.75
23. $2.30

Cumulative Review 1, 2, 3

1. $405
2. 200,000
3. 50,560,000
4. $10
5. $225,000 savings from Boston
6. 1¢: $500

   $1\dfrac{1}{2}$¢: $750
7. $369.56
8. $130,000,000
9. $47.73; $15.91; $63.64

CHAPTER 4

End-of-Chapter Problems

4–1. $1,572.87

4–3. $463.40

4–5. $844.10

4–7. $388.44

4–9. $2,038.56

4–11. $577.95

4–13. $998.86

4–14. $1,850.04

4–15. $3,061.67

Summary Practice Test

1. $199.88
2. $8,617.34
3. $7,685
4. $2,095.55
5. $6,976.70

CHAPTER 5

End-of-Chapter Problems

5–1. $H = 55$

5–3. $N = 240$

5–5. $Y = 15$

5–7. $Y = 12$

5–9. $P = 25$

5–11. $M = \$80,000$

5–13. Hugh 50; Joe 250

5–15. 50 shorts; 200 T-shirts

5–17. $B = 70$

5–19. $N = 63$

5–21. $Y = 7$

5–23. $P = \$429.50$

5–25. Pete = 90; Bill = 450

5–27. 48 boxes pens; 240 batteries

5–29. $B = 119$

5–31. $M = 60$

5–33. $D = \$134.9$ million

5–35. $W = 129$

5–37. Shift 1: 3,360; shift 2: 2,240

5–39. 22 cartons of hammers
18 cartons of wrenches

5–40. 150 Michele; 300 Jack

5–41. $B = 10$; $6B = 30$

Summary Practice Test

1. $300.99
2. $54,000
3. Circuit City, 30; Best Buy 180
4. Flo,180; Joy 720
5. 20 dishes; 80 pots
6. 600 hamburgers; 700 pizzas

CHAPTER 6

End-of-Chapter Problems

6–1. 74%

6–3. 70%

6–5. 356.1%

6–7. .04

6–9. .643

6–11. 1.19

6–13. 8.3%

6–15. 87.5%

6–17. $\dfrac{1}{20}$

6–19. $\dfrac{19}{60}$

6–21. $\dfrac{27}{400}$

6–23. 7.2

6–25. 102.5

6–27. 156.6

6–29. 114.88

6–31. 16.2

6–33. 141.67

6–35. 10,000

6–37. 17,777.78

6–39. 108.2%

6–41. 110%

6–43. 400%

6–45. 59.40

6–47. 1,100

6–49. 40%

6–51. −6%

6–53. 75%

6–55. $10,000

6–57. $105

6–59. 677.78%

6–61. $28,175

6–63. 90%

6–65. 157%

6–67. 39.94%

6–69. 12.8%

6–71. 1,000

6–73. $400

6–75. 25%

6–77. $44,444,400

6–79. 1,747,758
6–81. 13.3%
6–83. 40%
6–85. $1,160,000
6–87. $24,000
6–89. 29.79%
6–91. $41,176
6–93. 40%
6–95. 585,000
6–96. $146,300,000; 331,100,000; .84%
6–97. $55,429

Summary Practice Test
1. 68.2%
2. 80%
3. 1,547%
4. 800%
5. .42
6. .0569
7. 6.0
8. .0025
9. 16.7%
10. 12.5%
11. $\dfrac{63}{400}$
12. $\dfrac{9}{125}$
13. $540,000
14. 2,166,667
15. 95%
16. 11.25%
17. $423.08
18. $426
19. $200,000

CHAPTER 7

End-of-Chapter Problems
7–1. .9114; .0886; $35.35; $363.65
7–3. .893079; .106921; $28.76; $240.24
7–5. $369.70; $80.30
7–7. $1,392.59; $457.41
7–9. June 28; July 18
7–11. June 15; July 5
7–13. July 10; July 30
7–15. $138; $6,862
7–17. $2; $198
7–19. $408.16; $291.84
7–21. $48.38; $72.57
7–23. 9.80%
7–25. $576.06; $48.94
7–27. $5,100; $5,250
7–29. $5,850
7–31. $8,571.43
7–33. $8,173.20
7–35. $8,333.33; $11,666.67
7–37. $99.99
7–39. $489.90; $711.10
7–41. $4,658.97

7–43. $1,083.46; $116.54
7–45. $5,008.45
7–47. Save $4.27 with Verizon
7–49. $1,764; $252; 12.5%; $1,728.72
7–50. $4,794.99

Summary Practice Test
1. $210
2. $300
3. $284.23; $14.77
4. **a.** Oct 17; Nov 6
   b. Aug 16; Sept 5
   c. June 10; June 30
   d. May 10; May 30
5. $270; $630
6. $11,960
7. B: 27.2%
8. $1,530.61; $4,469.39
9. $6,566.26

CHAPTER 8

End-of-Chapter Problems
8–1. $40; $140
8–3. $4,285.71
8–5. $6.90; 45.70%
8–7. $65.70; $153.30
8–9. $110.83
8–11. $34.20; 69.8%
8–13. 11%
8–15. $3,830.40; $1,169.60; 23.39%
8–17. $3,000; 75%
8–19. $14.29
8–21. $11.4 million; 6%
8–23. $84
8–25. 42.86%
8–27. $3.56
8–29. $1,275
8–31. 26.47%
8–33. $14; 350%; 77.78%
8–35. $2.56
8–37. $899; 40%; 28.57%
8–38. 31.01%; $3.43; $3.02
8–39. $94.98; $20.36; loss

Summary Practice Test
1. $448
2. 65.26%
3. $781.25; $468.75
4. $90; 38.9%
5. $228.57
6. $419.30
7. 37.42%
8. $80
9. 41.2%
10. $.68

Cumulative Review 6, 7, 8
1. 650,000
2. $296.35
3. $133

4. $2,562.14
5. $48.75
6. $259.26
7. $1.96; $1.89

CHAPTER 9

End-of-Chapter Problems
9–1. 35; $231
9–3. $12.00; $452
9–5. $1,071
9–7. $60
9–9. $13,000
9–11. $4,500
9–13. $11,900; $6,900; $138; $388
9–15. $31; $27.55
9–17. $161.37; $74.40; $17.40; $946.83
9–19. $752.60; $113.60
9–21. $45.83; $10.72
9–23. $297
9–25. $825
9–27. $1,029.78
9–29. $357; $56
9–31. $4,166.67; $258.33; $60.42; $754.89
9–32. Difference $143.34

Summary Practice Test
1. 47; $454.50
2. $506
3. $14,200
4. $644.80; $217.50
5. $99.67
6. $7,800 SUTA; $112 FUTA; no tax in quarter 2

CHAPTER 10

End-of-Chapter Problems
10–1. $390; $9,390
10–3. $336.88; $7,336.88
10–5. $28.23; $613.23
10–7. $20.38; $1,020.38
10–9. $73.78; $1,273.78
10–11. $1,904.76
10–13. $4,390.61
10–15. $4,000; $84,000
10–17. $2,377.70
10–19. 4.7 years
10–21. $21,596.11
10–23. $714.87; $44.87
10–25. $4.20; $5.60
10–27. $2,608.65
10–29. $18,720.12
10–31. 12.37%
10–33. 72 days
10–35. 5.6%
10–36. C. $280; $1,400
10–37. $7.82; $275.33

Summary Practice Test
1. $32.67; $1,853.17
2. $235,200
3. $8,591.11
4. $8,583.01
5. $23,351.01
6. $106.06; $5,106.06

CHAPTER 11

End-of-Chapter Problems
11–1. $451.25; $17,548.75
11–3. 25 days
11–5. $51,451.39; 57; $733.18; $50,718.21
11–7. 6.09%
11–9. $8,537.50; 9.8%
11–11. $8,937
11–13. 4.04%
11–15. $5,133.33; 56; $71.87; $5,061.46
11–17. $4,836.44
11–18. $90.13; $177.50; 3.64%; 3.61%
11–19. $2,127.66; 9.57%

Summary Practice Test
1. $130,000
2. $110.83; $6,889.17; $7,000; 6.1%
3. $30,297.77
4. $40,388.05
5. $19,333.33; 7.8%
6. 5.58%

CHAPTER 12

End-of-Chapter Problems
12–1. 4; 3%; $787.86; $87.86
12–3. $10,404; $404
12–5. 12.55%
12–7. 12; 2%; .7885; $2,050.10
12–9. 28; 3%; .4371; $7,692.96
12–11. 2.2879 × $7,692.96
12–13. $19,961.20
12–15. Mystic $4,775
12–17. $25,734.40
12–19. $3,807
12–21. 5.06%
12–23. $37,644
12–25. Yes, $17,908 (compounding) or $8,376 (p. v.)
12–27. $3,739.20
12–29. $13,883.30
12–31. $143,923,500 int.
12–32. $689,125; $34,125 Bank B

Summary Practice Test
1. $20,861.10
2. $22,078
3. $121,193.74
4. No, $16,252.50 (compounding) or $11,505.60 (p. v.)
5. 9.2%

6. $18,324
7. $104,150
8. $39,837.60

CHAPTER 13

End-of-Chapter Problems
13–1. $110,095
13–3. $111,196
13–5. $3,118.59
13–7. End of first year $2,405.71
13–9. $1,410
13–11. $7,788.60
13–13. $1,004,370.50
13–15. $65,121.24
13–17. $900.655
13–19. $33,444
13–21. $13,838.25
13–23. Annuity $12,219.11
13–25. $3,625.60
13–27. $111,013.29
13–29. $404,313.97
13–30. $69,302; $36,508.29
13–31. $120,747.09

Summary Practice Test
1. $78,518.86
2. $33,914.88 or $33,913.57
3. $78,803.40
4. $2,320
5. $2,604
6. $148,908
7. $38,747.10
8. $118,591.68
9. $486,607.14
10. $404,095.78

Cumulative Review 10, 11, 12, 13
1. Annuity $2,058.62 or $2,058.59
2. $5,118.70
3. $116,963.02
4. $3,113.92
5. $5,797.92
6. $18,465.20
7. $29,632.35
8. $55,251

CHAPTER 14

End-of-Chapter Problems
14–1. Finance charge $2,100
14–3. Finance charge $1,279.76; 12.75%–13%
14–5. $119.39; $119.37
14–7. $295.14; $5,164.86
14–9. $2,741
14–11. 7.75% to 8%
14–13. a. $4,050 b. $1,656 c. $5,756 d. 14.25% to 14.50% e. $95.10
14–15. $59,155; $11,165

14–17. 8.75% to 9%
14–19. $218.31 outstanding balance
14–20. $4,285.86
14–21. 15.48%

Summary Practice Test
1. $24,500; $2,500
2. $31.75
3. 7.25% to 7.50%
4. $3,431.16
5. $1,743.20; $8,256.80
6. $405

CHAPTER 15

End-of-Chapter Problems
15–1. $1,007.24
15–3. $1,764
15–5. $173,141.60
15–7. $1,679.04; $1,656.25; $22.79; $158,977.21
15–9. $222 more
15–11. $771.93; $196,894.80
15–13. Payment 3, $119,857.38
15–15. $179,270.66
15–17. Almost 25 months
15–18. $1,690.15; $415,954

Summary Practice Test
1. $695.75; $622.92; $114,927.17
2. $509.04; $80,712
3. a. $486.72; $74,016
   b. $509.04; $80,712
   c. $532.08; $87,624
   d. $555.84; $94,752
4. $1,008
5. $182,400

CHAPTER 16

End-of-Chapter Problems
16–1. Total assets $36,000
16–3. Inventory −16.67%; mortgage note +13.79%
16–5. Depreciation 13.62%; 5.94%
16–7. Depreciation $100; + 16.67%
16–9. 1.43; 1.79
16–11. .20; .23
16–13. .06; .08
16–15. $4,000,000
16–17. 87.74%; 34.43%
16–19. 2006 68% sales
16–20. 6.93%; 386.67%
16–21. 3.5; 2.3

Summary Practice Test
1. a. $113,000 b. $95,700 c. $17,300 d. $56,700
2. Acc. rec. 12%; $25.23
3. Cash $8,000; +133.33%
4. 2006, 111%

5. Total assets $135,000
6. a. .88 **b.** .61 **c.** 42.75 days
d. 1.03 **e.** .21

CHAPTER 17

End-of-Chapter Problems
17–1. Book value (end of year) $45,000
17–3. Book value (end of year) $35,000
17–5. Book value (end of year) $25,000
17–7. Book value (end of year) $15,000
17–9. Book value (end of year) $7,000
17–11. Book value (end of year) $2,000
17–13. Book value (end of year) $15,000
17–15. Book value (end of year) $5,400
17–17. $1,400
17–19. $18,000; $18,000
17–21. $30,000; $24,000
17–23. $18,800; $30,080
17–25. $13,000; $3,750
17–27. $4,750; $9,500
17–29. $18,642
17–31. $5,000; $8,333.33; $7,800
17–32. $2,431.25; $14,662.50

Summary Practice Test
1. Book value end of year 2: $10,800
2. $1,142.40
3. Depreciation expense, $15,000; $12,000; $9,000; $6,000; $3,000
4. $5,000 difference
5. −$2,273 difference

CHAPTER 18

End-of-Chapter Problems
18–1. $810; $5,440
18–3. $543; $932
18–5. $10
18–7. $36
18–9. $72
18–11. $140.80
18–13. $147.75; $345.60
18–15. $188.65; $304.70
18–17. 3.56; 3.25
18–19. .75; $67,500
18–21. $1,457; $1,541.91
18–23. $60.25; $65.05
18–25. $55,120
18–27. $38,150
18–28. $501.90; $547.50; $520.80; gain $251.40
18–29. $1,900

Summary Practice Test
1. a. 28 **b.** $58.84; $89.80; $73.92
2. $43,400
3. .99
4. $82,950
5. $78,400

CHAPTER 19

End-of-Chapter Problems
19–1. $1,026
19–3. $84,905.66
19–5. $72,000
19–7. $.0233
19–9. 6.99%; $6.99; $69.90; 69.90
19–11. $4,462.50
19–13. $16,985.05
19–15. $112.92
19–17. $54,000
19–19. $6,940
19–21. $64,000
19–23. $40,000 loss of taxes
19–25. $23,065 more in Minn.
19–26. $1,380; $580; $626,271
19–27. $979

Summary Practice Test
1. $1,691.05; $80.95
2. $5,665
3. $84,000
4. 5.3 mills
5. $2,436.85
6. $18,720

CHAPTER 20

End-of-Chapter Problems
20–1. $462
20–3. $221.25
20–5. $53,000
20–7. 21 years, 300 days
20–9. $518; $182
20–11. $16,500
20–13. $1,067
20–15. $240 cheaper
20–17. $801
20–19. $118,750
20–21. $1,100
20–23. $373.67
20–25. $22,900; $10,700
20–27. $24,000; $16,300
20–28. $247.50; $17.50; $1,097.50
20–29. $72,000

Summary Practice Test
1. $1,602.90; $28,530
2. $1,689; $39,750; $82,500; 21 years 300 days
3. $401,785.71; $450,000
4. $792; $205.92
5. $390
6. Insurance company pays $27,900; Bill pays $7,000

CHAPTER 21

End-of-Chapter Problems
21–1. $22,596
21–3. 1.1%

21–5. 13
21–7. $24,227.04
21–9. 2003   preferred $8,000
         2004   0
         2005   preferred $127,000
                 common $33,000
21–11. $2,280
21–13. $260; $2,725; 9.5%
21–15. $12.04; $−.06; 9.6%; A
21–17. Gain $2,887.56
21–19. 12; 2.4%
21–21. $5,043.75; $56.25
21–23. 7.3%
21–25. Stock 6.7%; bond 11.9%
21–27. Yes, $16.02
21–29. $443.80
21–30. $7,952
21–31. $1,014.33

Summary Practice Test
1. $14,935
2. 10; .6%
3. $1.02
4. $10,576
5. 4.8%
6. $138,000 in arrears
7. $14.65; $10,255

CHAPTER 22

End-of-Chapter Problems
22–1. 6.50
22–3. $77.23
22–5. 2.7
22–7. 31.5
22–9. 8
22–11. 142.9
22–13. $200–$299.99 ⲦⲎ
22–15. Traditional watch 183.6°
22–17.

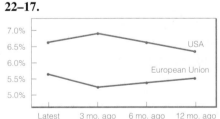

22–19. Transportation   126°
         Hotel   100.8°
         Food   72°
         Miscellaneous   61.2°

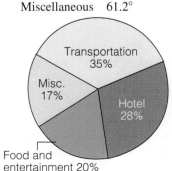

22–21. 250

22–23. 57,000,000 mean; Hunter 12.63%

22–24. 24.94%

Optional Assignment

1. 98
3. 4.3
5. 16%; 2.5%
7. 68%; 81.5%; 2.5%; 2.5%; 47.5%
9. 5.02

Summary Practice Test

1. $144,200; $138,500
2. 1,300
3. 3.25
4. 400; II; 2

5. Bar 3 on horizontal axis goes up to 300 on vertical axis

6. Profits 36°
   Cost of sales 144°
   Expense 180°

7. 177.3%
8. 9.0 standard deviation

CHECK FIGURES (ODDS) TO ADDITIONAL ASSIGNMENTS BY LEARNING UNIT FROM APPENDIX A

LU 1–1

1. **a.** Seven thousand, nine hundred fifty-four
   d. Fifty-eight thousand, three
3. **a.** 40; 380; 860; 5,980; 210
   c. 21,000; 1,000; 4,000; 10,000
5. **a.** Hundreds place
   c. Ten thousands place
   e. Billions place
7. Three hundred eighty-four
9. $375,985
11. Two thousand, four

LU 1–2

1. **a.** 741 **c.** 1,319 **d.** 179
3. **a.** Estimated 40; 39
   c. Estimated 10; 9
5. $71,577
7. $19,973
9. 12,797 lbs
11. Estimated $9,400; $9,422
13. $746 discount

LU 1–3

1. **a.** Estimated 2,000; actual 2,114
   c. Estimated 15,000,000; actual 16,184,184
3. **a.** Estimated 1,000; actual 963 R5
   c. Estimated 20; actual 25 R8
5. 2,695
7. $78
9. 27
11. $43,200
13. 40 stacks and 23 "extra" bricks

LU 2–1

1. **a.** Improper **b.** Proper
   c. Improper **d.** Mixed number
   e. Improper **f.** Proper
3. **a.** $\frac{36}{5}$ **c.** $\frac{31}{7}$ **f.** $\frac{53}{3}$

5. **a.** $6; \frac{6}{7}$ **b.** $15; \frac{2}{5}$ **e.** $12; \frac{8}{11}$

7. $\frac{13}{4}$

9. $\frac{17}{25}$

11. $\frac{60}{100}$

13. $\frac{7}{12}$

LU 2–2

1. **a.** 32 **b.** 180 **c.** 480
   d. 252
3. **a.** $\frac{1}{3}$ **b.** $\frac{2}{3}$ **e.** $6\frac{1}{8}$ **h.** $56\frac{5}{6}$
5. $3\frac{1}{40}$ yards
7. $17\frac{5}{12}$ miles
9. $4\frac{8}{9}$ hours

LU 2–3

1. **a.** $\overset{1}{\underset{1}{\cancel{6}}}{\cancel{13}} \times \overset{\overset{2}{\cancel{26}}}{\underset{\underset{1}{\cancel{12}}}{}} = 1$

3. **a.** $1\frac{1}{4}$ **b.** 3 **g.** 24 **l.** $\frac{4}{7}$
5. $39,000
7. 714
9. $20\frac{2}{3}$ miles
11. $412,000

LU 3–1

1. **a.** .43 **b.** .7 **c.** .953
   d. .401 **e.** .06
3. **a.** Hundredths place
   d. Thousandths place

5. **a.** $\frac{2}{5}$ **b.** $\frac{11}{25}$
   g. $\frac{5}{16}$ **l.** $9\frac{1}{25}$
7. .286
9. $\frac{566}{1,000}$
11. .333
13. .0020507

LU 3–2

1. **a.** 24.875 **b.** 5.2281 **d.** 3.7736
3. **a.** .3 **b.** .1 **c.** 1,480.0 **d.** .1
5. **a.** 6,870 **c.** .0272
   e. 34,700 **i.** 8,329.8
7. $4.53
9. $111.25
11. 15

LU 4–1

1. **a.** $430.64 **b.** 3 **c.** $867.51
3. **a.** Neuner Realty Co.
   b. Kevin Jones
   h. $2,756.80
5. $37.79

LU 4–2

1. $1,435.42
3. Add $3,000; deduct $22.25
5. $2,989.92
7. $1,214.60

LU 5–1

1. **a.** $3N = 70$ **e.** $14 + \frac{N}{3} = 18$
   h. $2N + 3N + 8 = 68$

LU 5–2

1. $45
3. $45 telephone; $135 utility
5. 51 tickets—Sherry;
   408 tickets—Linda
7. 12 necklaces ($48);
   36 watches ($252)
9. $157.14

LU 6–1

1. **a.** 8% **b.** 87.5%
   i. 503.8% **l.** 80%
3. **a.** 70% **c.** 162.5%
   h. 50% **n.** 1.5%
5. **a.** $\frac{1}{4}$ **b.** .375 **c.** 50%
   d. .66$\overline{6}$ **n.** $1\frac{1}{8}$
7. 2.9%
9. $\frac{39}{100}$
11. $\frac{9}{10,000}$

LU 6–2

1. **a.** $8,000; $12\frac{1}{2}$%; $1,000
   c. $7.00; 12%; $.84
3. **a.** 33.3% **b.** 3% **c.** 27.5%
5. **a.** −1,584; −26.6%
   d. −20,000; −16.7%
7. $9,000
9. $3,196
11. 329.5%

LU 7–1

1. **a.** $480 **b.** $360 **c.** $50
   d. $100 **e.** $380
3. **a.** $75 **b.** $21.50; $40.75
5. **a.** .7125; .2875 **b.** .7225; .2775
7. $3.51
9. $81.25
11. $315
13. 45%

LU 7–2

1. **a.** February 18; March 10
   d. May 20; June 9
   e. October 10; October 30
3. **a.** .98; $1,102.50
   c. .98; $367.99
5. **a.** $16.79; $835.21
7. $12,230.40
9. **a.** $439.29 **b.** $491.21
11. $209.45
13. **a.** $765.31 **b.** $386.99

LU 8–1

1. **a.** $10.79 **b.** $2.72
   c. $4.35 **d.** $90 **e.** $116.31
3. **a.** $2; 80% **b.** $6.50; 52%
   c. $.28; 28.9%
5. **a.** $1.52 **b.** $225
   c. $372.92 **d.** $625
7. **a.** $38.16 **b.** $197.16
9. **a.** $258.52 **b.** $90.48
11. **a.** $212.50 **b.** $297.50
13. $8.17

LU 8–2

1. **a.** $4.80 **b.** $57.50
   c. $34.43 **d.** $27.33 **e.** $.15
3. **a.** $6.94 **b.** $882.35 **c.** $30
   d. $171.43
5. **a.** 28.57% **b.** 33.33%
   d. 53.85%
7. $346.15
9. 39.39%
11. $2.29
13. 63.33%

LU 8–3

1. **a.** $16.00; $64
   b. $525; $1,574.98
3. **a.** $410 **b.** $18.65
5. **a.** $216; $324; $5.14
   b. $45; $63.90; $1.52
7. 17%
9. $21.15
11. $273.78
13. $.79

LU 9–1

1. **a.** $304; 0; $304
   b. $360; $40.50; $400.50
3. **a.** $438.85 **b.** $615.13
5. **a.** $5,200 **b.** $3,960
   c. $3,740 **d.** $4,750
7. $723.00
9. $3,846.25
11. $2,032.48

LU 9–2

1. **a.** $1,400; $2,300
3. 0; $990
5. $457.04
7. $125.15
9. $579.77
11. $636.81

LU 10–1

1. **a.** $180 **b.** $1,080
   c. $1,275
3. **a.** $131.25 **b.** $16.33
   c. $98.51
5. **a.** $515.63 **b.** $6,015.63
7. **a.** $5,459.66
9. $659.36
11. $360

LU 10–2

1. **a.** $4,371.44 **b.** $4,545.45
   c. $3,433.33
3. **a.** 60; .17 **b.** 120; .33 **c.** 270; .75
   d. 145; .40
5. 3%
7. $250
9. $3,000
11. 119 days

LU 10–3

1. **a.** $2,568.75; $1,885.47; $920.04
3. $4,267.59
5. $4,715.30; $115.30

LU 11–1

1. I; B; D; I; D; I; B; D
3. **a.** 9.1% **c.** 13%
5. $15,963.75
7. $848.75; $8,851.25
9. $14,300
11. $7,855

LU 11–2

1. **a.** $4,980 **b.** $16,480.80
   c. $994.44
3. **a.** $14.76 **b.** $223.25 **c.** $3.49
5. $4,031.67
7. $8,262.74
9. $5,088.16
11. $721.45

LU 12–1

1. **a.** $618.19 year 2
   b. $3,115.57 year 4
3. **a.** $15,869; $5,869
   b. $16,084; $6,084
5. $5,980
7. $8,881.20
9. $2,129.40
11. $3,207.09; $207.09
13. $3,000; $3,469; $3,498

LU 12–2

1. **a.** .6209 **b.** .3936 **c.** .5513
3. **a.** $1,575,50; $924.50
   b. $2,547.02; $2,052.98
5. $13,152.60
7. $13,356.98
9. $16,826.40
11. $652.32
13. $18,014.22

LU 13–1

1. **a.** $1,000; $2,080; $3,246.40
3. **a.** $6,888.60 **b.** $6,273.36
5. $325,525
7. $13,412
9. $30,200.85
11. $33,650.94

LU 13–2

1. **a.** $2,638.65 **b.** $6,375.24;
   $7,217.10
3. $2,715.54
5. $24,251.85
7. $47,608
9. $456,425
11. Accept Jason $265,010

LU 13–3

1. **a.** $4,087.50
3. $16,200
5. $24,030
7. $16,345
9. $8,742

LU 14–1

1. **a.** $1,200; $192
   b. $9,000; $1,200
3. **a.** 14.75%   **b.** 10%
   c. 11.25%
5. **a.** $3,528   **b.** $696
   c. $4,616
7. **a.** $22,500   **b.** $4,932
   c. $29,932
9. **a.** $20,576   **b.** 12.75%

LU 14–2

1. **a.** $625; $375
   b. $9,600; $2,910
3. **a.** $625; $578.12
5. $1,758; $553
7. $900
9. $7,287.76

LU 14–3

1. **a.** $465; $8,535
   b. $915.62; $4,709.38
3. **a.** $332.03   **b.** $584.83
   c. $384.28
5. Final payment $784.39
7. $51.34
9. $35
11. $922.49
13. 7.50% to 7.75%

LU 15–1

1. **a.** $1,149.20   **b.** $1,555.50;
   $4,090.50; $3,859.65
3. **a.** $117.25, 7.7%
   b. $174, 5.7%
5. $2,487.24
7. $2,584.71; $2,518.63
9. **a.** $66.08   **b.** $131,293.80
11. $773,560

LU 15–2

1. **a.** $1,371.90; $1,133.33; $238.57
3. #4 balance outstanding $195,183.05
5. $587,612.80
7. $327.12; $251,581.60
9. $44,271.43
11. $61,800

LU 16–1

1. Total assets $224,725
3. Merch. inventory 13.90%; 15.12%

LU 16–2

1. Net income $57,765
3. Purchases 73.59%; 71.43%

LU 16–3

1. Sales 2004, 93.5%; 2003, 93.2%
3. .22
5. 59.29%
7. .83
9. COGS 119.33%; 111.76%; 105.04%
11. .90
13. 5.51%
15. 11.01%

LU 17–1

1. **a.** 4%   **b.** 25%   **c.** 10%
   d. 20%
3. **a.** $2,033; $4,667
   b. $1,850; $9,750
5. $8,625 depreciation per year
7. $2,800 depreciation per year
9. $95
11. **a.** $12,000   **b.** $6,000
    c. $18,000   **d.** $45,000

LU 17–2

1. **a.** $.300   **b.** $.192   **c.** $.176
3. **a.** $.300, $2,600
   b. $.192, $300,824
5. $5,300 book value end of year 5
7. **a.** $.155   **b.** $20,001.61

LU 17–3

1. **a.** $\frac{5}{15}, \frac{4}{15}, \frac{3}{15}, \frac{2}{15}, \frac{1}{15}$
3. **a.** $3,050; $3,650
   b. $3,171; $8,429
5. $900 book value end of year 6
7. **a.** 28   **b.** $237.50   **c.** $845

LU 17–4

1. **a.** 8%   **b.** 20%   **c.** 25%
3. **a.** $4,467; $2,233
   b. $3,867; $7,733
5. $121, year 6
7. **a.** 28.57%   **b.** $248   **c.** $619
9. **a.** 16.67%   **b.** $2,500
   c. $10,814   **d.** $2,907

LU 17–5

1. **a.** 33%; $825; $1,675
3. Depreciation year 8, $346
5. $125
7. **a.** $15,000   **b.** $39,000
   c. $21,600   **d.** 2001
9. $68,440

LU 18–1

1. **a.** $5,120; $3,020
   b. $323,246; $273,546
3. $35,903; $165,262
5. $10,510.20; $16,345
7. $37.62; $639.54
9. $628.40
11. $3,069; $952; $2,117

LU 18–2

1. **a.** $85,700; $143,500; .597;
   $64,500; $38,507
3. $85,000
5. $342,000; $242,500; 5.85; 6.29
7. $60,000; $100,000; $40,000
9. $70,150
11. $5,970
13. 3.24; 3.05
15. $32,340; $35,280; $49,980;
    $29,400

LU 19–1

1. **a.** $26.80; $562.80
   b. $718.80; $12,698.80
3. **a.** $20.75; $43.89; $463.64
5. Total is **(a)** $1,023; **(b)** $58.55
7. $5.23; $115.23
9. $2,623.93
11. $26.20
13. $685.50

LU 19–2

1. **a.** $68,250   **b.** $775,450
3. **a.** $7.45; $74.50; 74.50
5. $9.10
7. $8,368.94
9. $42,112
11. $32,547.50

LU 20–1

1. **a.** $9.27; 25; $231.75
3. **a.** $93.00; $387.50; $535.00;
   $916.50
5. $1,242.90
7. $14,265
9. $47.50 more
11. $68,750

LU 20–2

1. **a.** $488   **b.** $2,912
3. **a.** $68,000; $60,000
   b. $41,600; $45,000
5. $1,463
7. $117,187.50
9. $336,000
11. **a.** $131,250
    b. $147,000

LU 20–3

1. **a.** $98; $160; $258
3. **a.** $312 **b.** $233 **c.** $181
   d. $59; $20
5. **a.** $647 **b.** $706
7. $601
9. $781
11. $10,000; $8,000
13. $60,000; $20,000
15. $19.50; $110.50

LU 21–1

1. **a.** $43.88 **f.** 49
3. $27.06
5. $1,358.52 gain
7. $18,825.15
9. $7.70

LU 21–2

1. **a.** IBM **b.** $10\frac{1}{4}$ **c.** 2004
   d. $102.50 **e.** $102\frac{3}{8}$

3. **a.** $1,025 **b.** $1,023.75
5. **a.** $3,075 **b.** $307.50
7. **a.** $30 discount **b.** $16.25 premium **c.** $42.50 premium
9. **a.** $625 **b.** $375 discount **c.** $105 **d.** 16.8%
11. 7.8%; 7.2%
13. 8.98%

LU 21–3

1. $11.90
3. $15.20
5. +$.14
7. 7.6%
9. $1.45; $18.45
11. $.56; $14.66
13. $1,573.50
15. $123.00 loss
17. **a.** 2003; 2005
    b. 9.3% Comp USA
    6.9% GMA
    c. $1,023.75 Comp USA
    $1,016.25 GMA

d. Both at premium
e. $1,025 Comp USA
$1,028.75 GMA

LU 22–1

1. **a.** 20.4 **b.** 83.75 **c.** 10.07
3. **a.** 59.5 **b.** 50
5. **a.** 63.7; 62; 62
7. $1,500,388.50
9. $10.75
11. $9.98

LU 22–2

1. 18: ̷Ht II 7
3. 25–30: ̷Ht III 8
5. 7.2°
7. 145–154: IIII 4
9. 98.4°; 9.9°; 70.5°; 169.2°; 11.9°

C

Glossary

The Glossary contains a comprehensive list of the key terms used in the text. In many cases, examples are also included in the definitions. Recall that key terms and their page references are listed in the Chapter Organizer and Reference Guide for each chapter.

Accelerated Cost Recovery System (ACRS) Tax law enacted in 1981 for assets put in service from 1981 through 1986.

Accelerated depreciation method Computes more depreciation expense in the early years of the asset's life than in the later years.

Accounts payable Amounts owed to creditors for services or items purchased.

Accounts receivable Amount owed by customers to a business from previous sales.

Accumulated depreciation Amount of depreciation that has accumulated on plant and equipment assets.

Acid test Current assets less inventory less prepaid expenses divided by current liabilities.

Addends Numbers that are combined in the addition process. *Example:* 8 + 9 = 17, of which 8 and 9 are the addends.

Adjustable rate mortgage Rate of mortgage is lower than a fixed rate mortgage. Rates adjusted without refinancing. Caps available to limit how high rate can go for each adjustment period over term of loan.

Adjusted bank balance Current balance of checkbook after reconciliation process.

Amortization Process of paying back a loan (principal plus interest) by equal periodic payments (see **amortization schedule**).

Amortization schedule Shows monthly payment to pay back loan at maturity. Payment also includes interest. Note payment is fixed at same amount each month.

Amount financed Cash price less down payment.

Annual percentage rate (APR) True or effective annual interest rate charged by sellers. Required to be stated by Truth in Lending Act.

Annual percentage rate (APR) table Effective annual rate of interest on a loan or installment purchase as shown by table lookup.

Annual percentage yield (APY) Truth in savings law forced banks to report actual interest in form of APY. Interest yield must be calculated on actual number of days bank has the money.

Annuities certain Annuities that have stated beginning and ending dates.

Annuity Stream of equal payments made at periodic times.

Annuity due Annuity that is paid (or received) at the beginning of the time period.

Assessed value Value of a property that an assessor sets (usually a percent of property's market value) that is used in calculating property taxes.

Asset cost Amount company paid for the asset.

Assets Things of value owned by a business.

Asset turnover Net sales divided by total assets.

ATM Automatic teller machine that allows customers of a bank to transfer funds and make deposits or withdrawals.

Average daily balance Sum of daily balances divided by number of days in billing cycle.

Average inventory Total of all inventories divided by number of times inventory taken.

Balance sheet Financial report that lists assets, liabilities, and equity. Report reflects the financial position of the company as of a particular date.

Bank discount The amount of interest charged by a bank on a note. (Maturity value × Bank discount rate × Number of days bank holds note) ÷ 360.

Bank discount rate Percent of interest.

Banker's Rule Time is exact days/360 in calculating simple interest.

Bank reconciliation Process of comparing the bank balance to the checkbook balance so adjustments can be made regarding checks outstanding, deposits in transit, and the like.

Bank statement Report sent by the bank to the owner of the checking account indicating checks processed, deposits made, and so on, along with beginning and ending balances.

Bar graph Visual representation using horizontal or vertical bars to make comparison or to show relationship on items of similar makeup.

Base Number that represents the whole 100%. It is the whole to which something is being compared. Usually follows word *of.*

Beneficiary Person(s) designated to receive the face value of the life insurance when insured dies.

Biweekly Every 2 weeks (26 times in a year).

Biweekly mortgage Mortgage payments made every 2 weeks rather than monthly. This payment method takes years off the life of the mortgage and substantially reduces the cost of interest.

Blank endorsement Current owner of check signs name on back. Whoever presents checks for payment receives the money.

Bodily injury Auto insurance that pays damages to people injured or killed by your auto.

Bond discount Bond selling for less than the face value.

Bond premium Bond selling for more than the face value.

Bonds Written promise by a company that borrows money usually with fixed-interest payment until maturity (repayment time).

Bond yield Total annual interest divided by total cost.

Book value Cost less accumulated depreciation.

Cancellation Reducing process that is used to simplify the multiplication and division of fractions. *Example:*

$$\frac{\overset{1}{\cancel{4}}}{8} \times \frac{1}{\underset{1}{\cancel{4}}}$$

Capital Owners' investment in the business.

Cash advance Money borrowed by holder of credit card. It is recorded as another purchase and is used in the calculation of the average daily balance.

Cash discount Savings that result from early payment by taking advantage of discounts offered by the seller; discount is not taken on freight or taxes.

Cash dividend Cash distribution of company's profit to owners of stock.

Cash value Except for term insurance, this indicates the value of the policy when terminated. Options fall under the heading of nonforfeiture values.

Centi- Prefix indicating .01 of a basic metric unit.

Chain or series discount Two or more trade discounts that are applied to the balance remaining after the previous discount is taken. Often called a **series discount.**

Check register Recordkeeping device that records checks paid and deposits made by companies using a checking account.

Checks Written documents signed by appropriate person that directs the bank to pay a specific amount of money to a particular person or company.

Check stub Provides a record of checks written. It is attached to the check.

Circle graph A visual representation of the parts to the whole.

Closing costs Costs incurred when property passes from seller to buyer such as for credit reports, recording costs, points, and so on.

CM Abbreviation for **credit memorandum.** The bank is adding to your account. The CM is found on the bank statement. *Example:* Bank collects a note for you.

Coinsurance   Type of fire insurance in which the insurer and insured share the risk. Usually there is an 80% coinsurance clause.

Collision   Optional auto insurance that pays for the repairs to your auto from an accident after deductible is met. Insurance company will only pay for repairs up to the value of the auto (less deductible).

Commissions   Payments based on established performance criteria.

Common denominator   To add two or more fractions, denominators must be the same.

Common stocks   Units of ownership called shares.

Comparative statement   Statement showing data from two or more periods side by side.

Complement   100% less the stated percent. *Example:* 18% → 82% is the complement (100% − 18%).

Compounding   Calculating the interest periodically over the life of the loan and adding it to the principal.

Compound interest   The interest that is calculated periodically and then added to the principal. The next period the interest is calculated on the adjusted principal (old principal plus interest).

Comprehensive insurance   Optional auto insurance that pays for damages to the auto caused by factors other than from collision (fire, vandalism, theft, and the like).

Compulsory insurance   Insurance required by law—standard coverage.

Constants   Numbers that have a fixed value such as 3 or −7. Placed on right side of equation; also called *knowns*.

Contingent annuities   Beginning and ending dates of the annuity are uncertain (not fixed).

Contingent liability   Potential liability that may or may not result from discounting a note.

Conversion periods   How often (a period of time) the interest is calculated in the compounding process. *Example:* Daily—each day; monthly—12 times a year; quarterly—every 3 months; semiannually—every 6 months.

Corporation   Company with many owners or stockholders. Equity of these owners is called stockholders' equity.

Cost   Price retailers pay to manufacturer or supplier to bring merchandise into store.

Cost of merchandise (goods) sold   Beginning inventory + Net purchases − Ending inventory.

Credit card   A piece of plastic that allows you to buy on credit.

Credit memo (CM)   Transactions of bank that increase customer's account.

Credit period (end)   Credit days are counted from date of invoice. Has no relationship to the discount period.

Cumulative preferred stock   Holders of preferred stock must receive current year and any dividends in arrears before any dividends are paid out to the holders of common stock.

Current assets   Assets that are used up or converted into cash within 1 year or operating cycle.

Current liabilities   Obligations of a company due within 1 year.

Current ratio   Current assets divided by current liabilities.

Daily balance   Calculated to determine customer's finance charge: Previous balance + Any cash advances + Purchases − Payments.

Daily compounding   Interest calculated on balance each day.

Debit card   Transactions result in money being immediately deducted from customer's checking account.

Debit memo (DM)   A debit transaction bank does for customers.

Deca-   Prefix indicating 10 times basic metric unit.

Deci-   Prefix indicating .1 of basic metric unit.

Decimal equivalent   Decimal represents the same value as the fraction. *Example:*

$$.05 = \frac{5}{100}$$

Decimal fraction   Decimal representing a fraction; the denominator has a power of 10.

Decimal point   Center of the decimal system—located between units and tenths. Numbers to left are *whole numbers;* to the right are *decimal numbers.*

Decimal system   The U.S. base 10 numbering system that uses the 10 single-digit numbers shown on a calculator.

Decimals   Numbers written to the right of a decimal point. *Example:* 5.3, 18.22.

Declining-balance method   Accelerated method of depreciation. The depreciation each year is calculated by book value beginning each year times the rate.

Deductibles   Amount insured pays before insurance company pays. Usually the higher the deductible, the lower the premium will be.

Deductions   Amounts deducted from gross earnings to arrive at net pay.

Deferred payment price   Total of all monthly payments plus down payment.

Denominator   The number of a common fraction below the division line (bar). *Example:*

$\frac{8}{9}$, of which 9 is the denominator

Deposits in transit   Deposits not received or processed by bank at the time the bank statement is prepared.

Deposit slip   Document that shows date, name, account number, and items making up a deposit.

Depreciation   Process of allocating the cost of an asset (less residual value) over the asset's estimated life.

Depreciation causes   Normal use, product obsolescence, aging, and so on.

Depreciation expense   Process involving asset cost, estimated useful life, and residual value (salvage or trade-in value).

Depreciation schedule   Table showing amount of depreciation expense, accumulated depreciation, and book value for each period of time for a plant asset.

Difference   The resulting answer from a subtraction problem. *Example:* Minuend less subtrahend equals difference.

$$215 - 15 = 200$$

Differential pay schedule   Pay rate is based on a schedule of units completed.

Digit   Our decimal number system of 10 characters from 0 to 9.

Discounting a note   Receiving cash from selling a note to a bank before the due date of a note. Steps to discount include: (1) calculate maturity value, (2) calculate number of days bank waits for money, (3) calculate bank discount, and (4) calculate proceeds.

Discount period   Amount of time to take advantage of a cash discount.

Distribution of overhead   Companies distribute overhead by floor space or sales volume.

Dividend   Number in the division process that is being divided by another. *Example:* 5)15, in which 15 is the dividend.

Dividends   Distribution of company's profit in cash or stock to owners of stock.

Dividends in arrears   Dividends that accumulate when a company fails to pay dividends to cumulative preferred stockholders.

Divisor   Number in the division process that is dividing into another. *Example:* 5)15, in which 5 is the divisor.

DM   Abbreviation for **debit memorandum.** The bank is charging your account. The DM is found on the bank statement. *Example:* NSF.

Dollar markdown   Original selling price less the reduction to price. Markdown may be stated as a percent of the original selling price. *Example:*

$$\frac{\text{Dollar markdown}}{\text{Original selling price}}$$

Dollar markup Selling price less cost. Difference is the amount of the markup. Markup is also expressed in percent.

Down payment Amount of initial cash payment made when item is purchased.

Drafts Written orders like checks instructing a bank, credit union, or savings and loan institution to pay your money to a person or organization.

Draw The receiving of advance wages to cover business or personal expenses. Once wages are earned, drawing amount reduces actual amount received.

Drawee One ordered to pay the check.

Drawer One who writes the check.

Due date Maturity date or when the note will be repaid.

Earnings per share Annual earnings ÷ Total number of shares outstanding.

Effective rate True rate of interest. The more frequent the compounding, the higher the effective rate.

Electronic deposits Credit card run through terminal which approves (or disapproves) the amount and adds it to company's bank balance.

Electronic funds transfer (EFT) A computerized operation that electronically transfers funds among parties without the use of paper checks.

Employee's Withholding Allowance Certificate (W-4) Completed by employee to indicate allowance claimed to determine amount of FIT that is deducted.

End of credit period Last day from date of invoice when customer can take cash discount.

End of month—EOM (also **proximo**) Cash discount period begins at the end of the month invoice is dated. After the 25th discount period, one additional month results.

Endorse Signing the back of the check; thus ownership is transferred to another party.

Endowment life Form of insurance that pays at maturity a fixed amount of money to insured or to the beneficiary. Insurance coverage would terminate when paid—similar to term life.

Equation Math statement that shows equality for expressions or numbers, or both.

Equivalent (fractional) Two or more fractions equivalent in value.

Escrow account Lending institution requires that each month $\frac{1}{12}$ of the insurance cost and real estate taxes be kept in a special account.

Exact interest Calculating simple interest using 365 days per year in time.

Excise tax Tax that government levies on particular products and services. Tax on specific luxury items or nonessentials.

Expression A meaningful combination of numbers and letters called *terms.*

Extended term insurance Resulting from nonforfeiture, it keeps the policy for the full face value going without further premium payments for a specific period of time.

Face amount Dollar amount stated in policy.

Face value Amount of insurance that is stated on the policy. It is usually the maximum amount for which the insurance company is liable.

Fair Credit and Charge Card Disclosure Act of 1988 Act that tightens controls on credit card companies soliciting new business.

Fair Labor Standards Act Federal law has minimum wage standards and the requirement of overtime pay. There are many exemptions for administrative personnel and for others.

Federal income tax (FIT) withholding Federal tax withheld from paycheck.

Federal Insurance Contribution Act (FICA) Percent of base amount of each employee's salary. FICA taxes used to fund retirement, disabled workers, Medicare, and so on. FICA is now broken down into Social Security and Medicare.

Federal Unemployment Tax Act (FUTA) Tax paid by employer. Current rate is .8% on first $7,000 of earnings.

Federal withholding tax See **Income tax.**

Finance charge Total payments − Actual loan cost.

Fire insurance Stipulated percent (normally 80%) of value that is required for insurance company to pay to reimburse one's losses.

First-in, first-out (FIFO) method This method assumes the first inventory brought into the store will be the first sold. Ending inventory is made up of goods most recently purchased.

Fixed rate mortgage Monthly payment fixed over number of years, usually 30 years.

FOB destination Seller pays cost of freight in getting goods to buyer's location.

FOB shipping point Buyer pays cost of freight in getting goods to his location.

Formula Equation that expresses in symbols a general fact, rule, or principle.

Fraction Expresses a part of a whole number. *Example:*

$\frac{5}{6}$ expresses 5 parts out of 6

Freight terms Determine how freight will be paid. Most common freight terms are **FOB shipping point** and **FOB destination.**

Frequency distribution Shows by table the number of times event(s) occurs.

Full endorsement This endorsement identifies the next person or company to whom the check is to be transferred.

Future value (FV) Final amount of the loan or investment at the end of the last period. Also called *compound amount.*

Future value of annuity Future dollar amount of a series of payments plus interest.

Graduated-payment mortgage Borrower pays less at beginning of mortgage. As years go on, the payments increase.

Graduated plans In beginning years, mortgage payment is less. As years go on, monthly payments rise.

Gram Basic unit of weight in metric system. An ounce equals about 28 grams.

Greatest common divisor The largest possible number that will divide evenly into both the numerator and denominator.

Gross pay Wages before deductions.

Gross profit Difference between cost of bringing goods into the store and selling price of the goods.

Gross profit from sales Net sales − Cost of goods sold.

Gross profit method Used to estimate value of inventory.

Gross sales Total earned sales before sales returns and allowances or sales discounts.

Hecto- Prefix indicating 100 times basic metric unit.

Higher terms Expressing a fraction with a new numerator and denominator that is equivalent to the original. *Example:*

$$\frac{2}{9} \rightarrow \frac{6}{27}$$

Home equity loan Cheap and readily accessible lines of credit backed by equity in your home; tax-deductible; rates can be locked in.

Horizontal analysis Method of analyzing financial reports where each total this period is compared by amount of percent to the same total last period.

Improper fraction Fraction that has a value equal to or greater than 1; numerator is equal to or greater than the denominator. *Example:*

$$\frac{6}{6}, \frac{14}{9}$$

Income statement Financial report that lists the revenues and expenses for a specific period of time. It reflects how well the company is performing.

Income tax or FIT Tax that depends on allowances claimed, marital status, and wages earned.

Indemnity Insurance company's payment to insured for loss.

Index numbers Express the relative changes in a variable compared with some base, which is taken as 100.

Individual retirement account (IRA) An account established for retirement planning.

Installment cost Down payment + (Number of payments × Monthly payment). Also called deferred payment.

Installment loan Loan paid off with a series of equal periodic payments.

Installment purchases Purchase of an item(s) that requires periodic payments for a specific period of time with usually a high rate of interest.

Insured Customer or policyholder.

Insurer The insurance company that issues the policy.

Interest Principal × Rate × Time.

Interest-bearing note Maturity value of note is greater than amount borrowed since interest is added on.

Inventory turnover Ratio that indicates how quickly inventory turns:

$$\frac{\text{Cost of goods sold}}{\text{Average inventory at cost}}$$

Invoice Document recording purchase and sales transactions.

Just-in-time (JIT) inventory system System that eliminates inventories. Suppliers provide materials daily as manufacturing company needs them.

Kilo- Prefix indicating 1,000 times basic metric unit.

Last-in, first-out (LIFO) method This method assumes the last inventory brought into the store will be the first sold. Ending inventory is made up of the oldest goods purchased.

Least common denominator (LCD) Smallest nonzero whole number into which all denominators will divide evenly. *Example:*

$$\frac{2}{3} \text{ and } \frac{1}{4} \qquad \text{LCD} = 12$$

Level premium term Insurance premium that is fixed, say, for 50 years.

Liabilities Amount business owes to creditors.

Liability insurance Insurance for bodily injury to others and damage to someone else's property.

Like fractions Proper fractions with the same denominators.

Like terms Terms that are made up with the same variable:

$$A + 2A + 3A = 6A$$

Limited payment life (20-payment life) Premiums are for 20 years (a fixed period) and provide paid-up insurance for the full face value of the policy.

Line graphs Graphical presentation that involves a time element. Shows trends, failures, backlogs, and the like.

Line of credit Provides immediate financing up to an approved limit.

Liquid assets Cash or other assets that can be converted quickly into cash.

List price Suggested retail price paid by customers.

Liter Basic unit of measure in metric, for volume.

Loan amortization table Table used to calculate monthly payments.

Long-term liabilities Debts or obligations that company does not have to pay within 1 year.

Lowest terms Expressing a fraction when no number divides evenly into the numerator and denominator except the number 1. *Example:*

$$\frac{5}{10} \rightarrow \frac{1}{2}$$

Maker One who writes the note.

Manual deposit Salesperson fills out charge slip and completes merchant batch header slip at end of business day.

Margin Difference between cost of bringing goods into store and selling price of goods

Markdowns Reductions from original selling price caused by seasonal changes, special promotions, and so on.

Markup Amount retailers add to cost of goods to cover operating expenses and make a profit.

Markup percent calculation Markup percent on cost × Cost = Dollar markup; or Markup percent on selling price × Selling price = Dollar markup.

Maturity date Date the principal and interest are due.

Maturity value Principal plus interest (if interest is charged). Represents amount due on the due date.

Maturity value of note Amount of cash paid on the due date. If interest-bearing maturity, value is greater than amount borrowed.

Mean Statistical term that is found by:

$$\frac{\text{Sum of all figures}}{\text{Number of figures}}$$

Measure of dispersion Number that describes how the numbers of a set of data are spread out or dispersed.

Median Statistical term that represents the central point or midpoint of a series of numbers.

Merchandise inventory Cost of goods for resale.

Merchant batch header slip Slip used by company to list and attach charge slips.

Meter Basic unit of length in metric system. A meter is a little longer than a yard.

Metric system A decimal system of weights and measures. The basic units are meters, grams, and liters.

Mill $\frac{1}{10}$ of a cent or $\frac{1}{1,000}$ of a dollar. In decimal, it is .001. *In application:*

$$\frac{\text{Property}}{\text{tax due}} = \frac{\text{Mills} \times .001 \times}{\text{Assessed valuation}}$$

Milli- Prefix indicating .001 of basic metric unit.

Minuend In a subtraction problem, the larger number from which another is subtracted. *Example:*

$$50 - 40 = 10$$

Mixed decimal Combination of a whole number and decimal, such as 59.8, 810.85.

Mixed number Sum of a whole number greater than zero and a proper fraction:

$$2\frac{1}{4}, 3\frac{3}{9}$$

Mode Value that occurs most often in a series of numbers.

Modified Accelerated Cost Recovery System (MACRS) Part of Tax Reform Act of 1986 that revised depreciation schedules of ACRS. Tax Bill of 1989 updates MACRS.

Monthly Some employers pay employees monthly.

Mortgage Cost of home less down payment.

Mortgage note payable Debt owed on a building that is a long-term liability; often the building is the collateral.

Multiplicand The first or top number being multiplied in a multiplication problem. *Example:*

$$\begin{array}{ccccc} \text{Product} & = & \text{Multiplicand} & \times & \text{Multiplier} \\ 40 & = & 20 & \times & 2 \end{array}$$

Multiplier The second or bottom number doing the multiplication in a problem. *Example:*

$$\begin{array}{ccccc} \text{Product} & = & \text{Multiplicand} & \times & \text{Multiplier} \\ 40 & = & 20 & \times & 2 \end{array}$$

Mutual fund Investors buy shares in the fund's portfolio (group of stocks and/or bonds).

Net asset value (NAV)   The dollar value of one mutual fund share; calculated by subtracting current liabilities from current market value of fund's investments and dividing this by number of shares outstanding.

Net deposits   Credit card sales less returns.

Net income   Gross profit less operating expenses.

Net pay   See **Net wages.**

Net price   List price less amount of trade discount. The net price is before any cash discount.

Net price equivalent rate   When multiplied times the list price, this rate or factor produces the actual cost to the buyer. Rate is found by taking the complement of each term in the discount and multiplying them together (do not round off).

Net proceeds   Maturity value less bank discount.

Net profit (net income)   Gross profit − Operating expenses.

Net purchases   Purchases − Purchase discounts − Purchase returns and allowances.

Net sales   Gross sales − Sales discounts − Sales returns and allowances.

Net wages   Gross pay less deductions.

Net worth   Assets less liabilities.

No-fault insurance   Involves bodily injury. Damage (before a certain level) that is paid by an insurance company no matter who is to blame.

Nominal rate   Stated rate.

Nonforfeiture values   When a life insurance policy is terminated (except term), it represents (1) the available cash value, (2) additional extended term, or (3) additional paid-up insurance.

Noninterest-bearing note   Note where the maturity value will be equal to the amount of money borrowed since no additional interest is charged.

Nonsufficient funds (NSF)   Drawer's account lacked sufficient funds to pay written amount of check.

Normal distribution   Data is spread symmetrically about the mean.

Numerator   Number of a common fraction above the division line (bar). *Example:*

$\dfrac{8}{9}$, in which 8 is the numerator

Omnibus Budget Reconciliation Act of 1989   An update of MACRS. Unless business use of equipment is greater than 50%, straight-line depreciation is required.

Open-end credit   Set payment period. Also, additional credit amounts can be added up to a set limit. It is a revolving charge account.

Operating expenses (overhead)   Regular expenses of doing business. These are not costs.

Ordinary annuities   Annuity that is paid (or received) at end of the time period.

Ordinary dating   Cash discount is available within the discount period. Full amount due by end of credit period if discount is missed.

Ordinary interest   Calculating simple interest using 360 days per year in time.

Ordinary life insurance   See **Straight life insurance.**

Outstanding balance   Amount left to be paid on a loan.

Outstanding checks   Checks written but not yet processed by the bank before bank statement preparation.

Overdraft   Occurs when company or person wrote a check without enough money in the bank to pay for it (NFS check).

Overhead expenses   Operating expenses *not* directly associated with a specific department or product.

Override   Commission that managers receive due to sales by people that they supervise.

Overtime   Time-and-a-half pay for more than 40 hours of work.

Owner's equity   See **Capital.**

Paid-up insurance   A certain level of insurance can continue, although the premiums are terminated. This results from the nonforfeiture value (except term). Result is a reduced paid-up policy until death.

Partial products   Numbers between multiplier and product.

Partial quotient   Occurs when divisor doesn't divide evenly into the dividend.

Partnership   Business with two or more owners.

Payee   One who is named to receive the amount of the check.

Payroll register   Multicolumn form to record payroll data.

Percent   Stands for hundredths. *Example:*

4% is 4 parts of one hundred, or $\dfrac{4}{100}$

Percentage method   A method to calculate withholdings. Opposite of wage bracket method.

Percent decrease   Calculated by decrease in price over original amount.

Percent increase   Calculated by increase in price over original amount.

Percent markup on cost   Dollar markup divided by the cost; thus, markup is a percent of the cost.

Percent markup on selling price   Dollar markup divided by the selling price; thus, markup is a percent of the selling price.

Periodic inventory system   Physical count of inventory taken at end of a time period. Inventory records are not continually updated.

Periods   Number of years times the number of times compounded per year (see **Conversion period**).

Perishables   Goods or services with a limited life.

Perpetual inventory system   Inventory records are continually updated; opposite of periodic.

Personal property   Items of possession, like cars, home, furnishings, jewelry, and so on. These are taxed by the property tax (don't forget real property is also taxed).

Piecework   Compensation based on the number of items produced or completed.

Place value   The digit value that results from its position in a number.

Plant and equipment   Assets that will last longer than 1 year.

Point of sale   Terminal that accepts cards (like those used at ATMs) to purchase items at retail outlets. No cash is physically exchanged.

Points   Percentage(s) of mortgage that represents an additional cost of borrowing. It is a one-time payment made at closing.

Policy   Written insurance contract.

Policyholder   The insured.

Portion   Amount, part, or portion that results from multiplying the base times the rate. Not expressed as a percent; it is expressed as a number.

Preferred stock   Type of stock that has a preference regarding a corporation's profits and assets.

Premium   Periodic payments that one makes for various kinds of insurance protection.

Premium rates (payroll)   Higher rates based on a quota system.

Prepaid expenses   Items a company buys that have not been used are shown as assets.

Prepaid rent   Rent paid in advance.

Present value of annuity   Amount of money needed today to receive a specified stream (annuity) of money in the future.

Present value (PV)   How much money will have to be deposited today (or at some date) to reach a specific amount of maturity (in the future).

Price-earnings (PE) ratio Closing price per share of stock divided by earnings per share.

Price relative The quotient of the current price divided by some previous year's price—the base year—multiplied by 100.

Prime numbers Whole number greater than 1 that is only divisible by itself and 1. *Examples:* 2, 3, 5.

Principal Amount of money that is originally borrowed, loaned, or deposited.

Proceeds Maturity value less the bank charge.

Product Answer of a multiplication process, such as:

$$\begin{array}{ccccc} \text{Product} & = & \text{Multiplicand} & \times & \text{Multiplier} \\ 50 & = & 5 & \times & 10 \end{array}$$

Promissory note Written unconditional promise to pay a certain sum (with or without interest) at a fixed time in the future.

Proper fractions Fractions with a value less than 1; numerator is smaller than denominator, such as $\frac{5}{9}$.

Property damage Auto insurance covering damages that are caused to the property of others.

Property tax Tax that raises revenue for school districts, cities, counties, and the like.

Property tax due Tax rate × Assessed valuation

Proximo (prox) Same as end of month.

Purchase discounts Savings received by buyer for paying for merchandise before a certain date.

Purchase returns and allowances Cost of merchandise returned to store due to damage, defects, and so on. An *allowance* is a cost reduction that results when buyer keeps or buys damaged goods.

Pure decimal Has no whole number(s) to the left of the decimal point, such as .45.

Quick assets Current assets − Inventory − Prepaid expenses.

Quick ratio (Current assets − Inventory − Prepaid expenses) ÷ Current liabilities.

Quotient The answer of a division problem.

Range Difference between the highest and lowest values in a group of values or set of data.

Rate Percent that is multiplied times the base that indicates what part of the base we are trying to compare to. Rate is not a whole number.

Rate of interest Percent of interest that is used to compute the interest charge on a loan for a specific time.

Ratio analysis Relationship of one number to another.

Real property Land, buildings, and so on, which are taxed by the property tax.

Rebate Finance charge that a customer receives for paying off a loan early.

Rebate fraction Sum of digits based on number of months to go divided by sum of digits based on total number of months of loan.

Receipt of goods (ROG) Used in calculating the cash discount period; begins the day that the goods are received.

Reciprocal of a fraction The interchanging of the numerator and the denominator. Inverted number is the reciprocal. *Example:*

$$\frac{6}{7} \rightarrow \frac{7}{6}$$

Reduced paid-up insurance Insurance that uses cash value to buy protection, face amount is less than original policy, and policy continues for life.

Remainder Leftover amount in division.

Repeating decimals Decimal numbers that repeat themselves continuously and thus do not end.

Residual value Estimated value of a plant asset after depreciation is taken (or end of useful life).

Restrictive endorsement Check must be deposited to the payee's account. This restricts one from cashing it.

Retail method Method to estimate cost of ending inventory. The cost ratio times ending inventory at retail equals the ending cost of inventory.

Retained earnings Amount of earnings that is kept in the business.

Return on equity Net income divided by stockholders' equity.

Revenues Total earned sales (cash or credit) less any sales discounts, returns, or allowances.

Reverse mortgage Federal Housing Administration makes it possible for older homeowners to live in their homes and get cash or monthly income.

Revolving charge account Charges for a customer are allowed up to a specified maximum, a minimum monthly payment is required, and interest is charged on balance outstanding.

ROG Receipt of goods; cash discount period begins when goods are received, not ordered.

Rounding decimals Reducing the number of decimals to an indicated position, such as 59.59 ⟶ 59.6 to the nearest tenth.

Rounding whole numbers all the way Process to estimate actual answer. When rounding all the way, only one nonzero digit is left. Rounding all the way gives the least degree of accuracy. *Example:* 1,251 to 1,000; 2,995 to 3,000.

Rule of 78 Method to compute rebates on consumer finance loans. How much of finance charge are you entitled to? Formula or table lookup may be used.

Safekeeping Bank procedure whereby a bank does not return checks. Canceled checks are photocopied.

Salaries payable Obligations that a company must pay within 1 year for salaries earned but unpaid.

Sales (not trade) discounts Reductions in selling price of goods due to early customer payment.

Sales returns and allowances Reductions in price or reductions in revenue due to goods returned because of product defects, errors, and so on. When the buyer keeps the damaged goods, an allowance results.

Sales tax Tax levied on consumers for certain sales of merchandise or services by states, counties, or various local governments.

Salvage value Cost less accumulated depreciation.

Selling price Cost plus markup equals selling price.

Semiannually Twice a year.

Semimonthly Some employees are paid twice a month.

Series discount See chain discount.

Short-rate table Fire insurance rate table used when insured cancels the policy.

Short-term policy Fire insurance policy for less than 1 year.

Signature card Information card signed by person opening a checking account.

Simple discount note A note in which bank deducts interest in advance.

Simple interest Interest is only calculated on the principal. In $I = P \times R \times T$, the interest plus original principal equals the maturity value of an interest-bearing note.

Simple interest formula

$$\text{Interest} = \text{Principal} \times \text{Rate} \times \text{Time}$$

$$\text{Principal} = \frac{\text{Interest}}{\text{Rate} \times \text{Time}}$$

$$\text{Rate} = \frac{\text{Interest}}{\text{Principal} \times \text{Time}}$$

$$\text{Time} = \frac{\text{Interest}}{\text{Principal} \times \text{Rate}}$$

Single equivalent discount rate Rate or factor as a single discount that calculates the amount of the trade discount by multiplying the rate times the list price. This single equivalent discount replaces a series of chain discounts. The single equivalent rate is (1 − Net price equivalent rate).

Single trade discount Company gives only one trade discount.

Sinking fund An annuity in which the stream of deposits with appropriate interest will equal a specified amount in the future.

Sliding scale commissions Different commission. Rates depend on different levels of sales.

Sole proprietorship A business owned by one person.

Specific identification method This method calculates the cost of ending inventory by identifying each item remaining to invoice price.

Standard deviation Measures the spread of data around the mean.

State unemployment tax (SUTA) Tax paid by employer. Rate varies depending on amount of unemployment the company experiences.

Stockbrokers People who with their representatives do the trading on the floor of the stock exchange.

Stock certificate Piece of paper that shows certificate of ownership in a company.

Stockholder One who owns stock in a company.

Stockholders' equity Assets less liabilities.

Stocks Ownership shares in the company sold to buyers, who receive stock certificates.

Stock yield percent Dividend per share divided by the closing price per share.

Straight commission Wages calculated as a percent of the value of goods sold.

Straight life insurance (whole or ordinary) Protection (full value of policy) results from continual payment of premiums by insured. Until death or retirement, nonforfeiture values exist for straight life.

Straight-line method Method of depreciation that spreads an equal amount of depreciation each year over the life of the assets.

Straight-line rate (rate of depreciation) One divided by number of years of expected life.

Subtrahend In a subtraction problem smaller number that is being subtracted from another. *Example:* 30 in

150 − 30 = 120

Sum Total in the adding process.

Sum-of-the-years'-digits method Accelerated method of depreciation. Depreciation each year is calculated by multiplying cost (less residual value) times a fraction. Numerator is number of years of useful life remaining. Denominator is the sum of the years of estimated life.

Tax rate $\dfrac{\text{Budget needed}}{\text{Total assessed value}}$

Term life insurance Inexpensive life insurance that provides protection for a specific period of time. No nonforfeiture values exist for term.

Term policy Period of time that the policy is in effect.

Terms of the sale Criteria on invoice showing when cash discounts are available, such as rate and time period.

Time Expressed as years or fractional years, used to calculate the simple interest.

Trade discount Reduction off original selling price (list price) not related to early payment.

Trade discount amount List price less net price.

Trade discount rate Trade discount amount given in percent.

Trade-in (scrap) Estimated value of a plant asset after depreciation is taken (or end of useful life).

Treasury bill Loan to the federal government for 91 days (13 weeks), 182 days (26 weeks), or 1 year.

Trend analysis Analyzing each number as a percentage of a base year.

Truth in Lending Act Federal law that requires sellers to inform buyers, in writing, of (1) the finance charge and (2) the annual percentage rate. The law doesn't dictate what can be charged.

Twenty-payment life Provides permanent protection and cash value, but insured pays premiums for first 20 years.

Twenty-year endowment Most expensive life insurance policy. It is a combination of term insurance and cash value.

Unemployment tax Tax paid by the employer that is used to aid unemployed persons.

Units-of-production method Depreciation method that estimates amount of depreciation based on usage.

Universal life Whole life insurance plan with flexible premium and death benefits. This life plan has limited guarantees.

Unknown The variable we are solving for.

Unlike fractions Proper fractions with different denominators.

Useful life Estimated number of years the plant asset is used.

U.S. Rule Method that allows the borrower to receive proper interest credits when paying off a loan in more than one payment before the maturity date.

U.S. Treasury bill A note issued by federal government to investors.

Value of an annuity Sum of series of payments and interest (think of this as the maturity value of compounding).

Variable commission scale Company pays different commission rates for different levels of net sales.

Variable rate Home mortgage rate is not fixed over its lifetime.

Variables Letters or symbols that represent unknowns.

Vertical analysis Method of analyzing financial reports where each total is compared to one total. *Example:* Cash is a percent of total assets.

W-4 See **Employee's Withholding Allowance Certificate.**

Wage bracket method Tables used in Circular E to compute FIT withholdings.

Weekly Some employers pay employees weekly.

Weighted-average method Calculates the cost of ending inventory by applying an average unit cost to items remaining in inventory for that period of time.

Weighted mean Used to find an average when values appear more than once.

Whole life insurance See **Straight life insurance.**

Whole number Number that is 0 or larger and doesn't contain a decimal or fraction, such as 10, 55, 92.

Withholding Amount of deduction from one's paycheck.

Workers' compensation Business insurance covering sickness or accidental injuries to employees that result from on-the-job activities.

Metric System

Metric System Seems To Be Moving Ahead

WITH MANY STATES lowering their resistance, a plan to convert highway signs to the metric system is inching forward.

For decades, outcries from motorists and state officials have squelched efforts to switch from miles to kilometers. This month, however, the Federal Highway Administration is reviewing a new batch of comments on a proposed switch, and only a few states say they're opposed to metric. Moreover, most states say a fast conversion would be better than replacing mileage signs as they wear out (too confusing), or posting signs with both miles and kilometers for a few years (too expensive).

"We're a bit surprised to find the states as forthcoming and responsive as they've been," Rodney Slater, federal highway administrator, says. His agency may require kilometer signs as soon as 1996 to satisfy a five-year-old law requiring use of the metric system by anyone receiving federal funds.

John Sullivan: Angie, I drove into the gas station last night to fill the tank up. Did I get upset! The pumps were not in gallons but in liters. This country (U.S.) going to metric is sure making it confusing.

Angie Smith: Don't get upset. Let me first explain the key units of measure in metric, and then I'll show you a convenient table I keep in my purse to convert metric to U.S. (also called customary system), and U.S. to metric. Let's go on.

The metric system is really a decimal system in which each unit of measure is exactly 10 times as large as the previous unit. In a moment, we will see how this aids in conversions. First, look at the middle column (Units) of this to see the basic units of measure:

U.S.	Thousands	Hundreds	Tens	Units	Tenths	Hundredths	Thousandths
Metric	Kilo- 1,000	Hecto- 100	Deka- 10	Gram Meter Liter 1	Deci- .1	Centi- .01	Milli- .001

- Weight: Gram (think of it as $\frac{1}{30}$ of an ounce).
- Length: Meter (think of it for now as a little more than a yard).
- Volume: Liter (a little more than a quart).

To aid you in looking at this, think of a decimeter, a centimeter, or a millimeter as being "shorter" (smaller) than a meter, whereas a dekameter, hectometer, and kilometer are "larger" than a meter. For example:

1 centimeter $= \frac{1}{100}$ of a meter; or 100 centimeters equals 1 meter.

1 millimeter $= \frac{1}{1,000}$ meter; or 1,000 millimeters equals 1 meter.

1 hectometer $= 100$ meters.

1 kilometer $= 1,000$ meters.

Remember we could have used the same setup for grams or liters. Note the summary here.

Length	Volume	Mass
1 meter:	1 liter:	1 gram:
= 10 decimeters	= 10 deciliters	= 10 decigrams
= 100 centimeters	= 100 centiliters	= 100 centigrams
= 1,000 millimeters	= 1,000 milliliters	= 1,000 milligrams
= .1 dekameter	= .1 dekaliter	= .1 dekagram
= .01 hectometer	= .01 hectoliter	= .01 hectogram
= .001 kilometer	= .001 kiloliter	= .001 kilogram

Practice these conversions and check solutions.

PRACTICE QUIZ 1

Convert the following:
1. 7.2 meters to centimeters
2. .89 meter to millimeters
3. 64 centimeters to meters
4. 350 grams to kilograms
5. 7.4 liters to centiliters
6. 2,500 milligrams to grams

✓ **SOLUTIONS**

1. 7.2 meters = 7.2 × 100 = 720 centimeters (remember, 1 meter = 100 centimeters)
2. .89 meters = .89 × 1,000 = 890 millimeters (remember, 1 meter = 1,000 millimeters)
3. 64 centimeters = 64/100 = .64 meters (remember, 1 meter = 100 centimeters)
4. 350 grams = $\frac{350}{1,000}$ = .35 kilograms (remember 1 kilogram = 1,000 grams)
5. 7.4 liters = 7.4 × 100 = 740 centiliters (remember, 1 liter = 100 centiliters)
6. 2,500 milligrams = $\frac{2,500}{1,000}$ = 2.5 grams (remember, 1 gram = 1,000 milligrams

Angie: Look at the table of conversions and I'll show you how easy it is. Note how we can convert liters to gallons. Using the conversion from meters to U.S. (liters to gallons), we see that you multiply numbers of liters by .26, or 37.95 × .26 = 9.84 gallons.

Common conversion factors for English/metric					
A. To convert from U.S. to	**Metric**	**Multiply by**	**B. To convert from metric to**	**U.S.**	**Multiply by**
Length:			*Length:*		
Inches (in)	Meters (m)	.025	Meters (m)	Inches (in)	39.37
Feet (ft)	Meters (m)	.31	Meters (m)	Feet (ft)	3.28
Yards (yd)	Meters (m)	.91	Meters (m)	Yards (yd)	1.1
Miles	Kilometers (km)	1.6	Kilometers (km)	Miles	.62
Weight:			*Weight:*		
Ounces (oz)	Grams (g)	28	Grams (g)	Ounces (oz)	.035
Pounds (lb)	Grams (g)	454	Grams (g)	Pounds (lb)	.0022
Pounds (lb)	Kilograms (kg)	.45	Kilograms (kg)	Pounds (lb)	2.2
Volume or capacity:			*Volume or capacity:*		
Pints	Liters (L)	.47	Liters (L)	Pints	2.1
Quarts	Liters (L)	.95	Liters (L)	Quarts	1.06
Gallons (gal)	Liters (L)	3.8	Liters (L)	Gallons	.26

John: How would I convert 6 miles to kilometers?

Angie: Take the number of miles times 1.6, thus 6 miles × 1.6 = 9.6 kilometers.

John: If I weigh 120 pounds, what is my weight in kilograms?

Angie: 120 times .45 (use the conversion table) equals 54 kilograms.

John: OK. Last night, when I bought 16.6 liters of gas, I really bought 4.3 gallons (16.6 liters times .26).

PRACTICE QUIZ 2

Convert the following:

1. 10 meters to yards
2. 110 quarts to liters
3. 78 kilometers to miles
4. 52 yards to meters
5. 82 meters to inches
6. 292 miles to kilometers

✓ **SOLUTIONS**

1. 10 meters × 1.1 = 11 yards
2. 110 quarts × .95 = 104.5 liters
3. 78 kilometers × .62 = 48.36 miles
4. 52 yards × .91 = 47.32 meters
5. 82 meters × 39.37 = 3,228.34 inches
6. 292 miles × 1.6 = 467.20 kilometers

APPENDIX D | PROBLEMS

DRILL PROBLEMS

Convert:

1. 65 centimeters to meters

2. 7.85 meters to centimeters

3. 44 centiliters to liters

4. 1,500 grams to kilograms

5. 842 millimeters to meters

6. 9.4 kilograms to grams
7. .854 kilograms to grams
8. 5.9 meters to millimeters
9. 8.91 kilograms to grams
10. 2.3 meters to millimeters

Convert (round off to nearest tenth):
11. 50.9 kilograms to pounds
12. 8.9 pounds to grams
13. 395 kilometers to miles
14. 33 yards to meters
15. 13.9 pounds to grams
16. 594 miles to kilometers
17. 4.9 feet to meters
18. 9.9 feet to meters
19. 100 yards to meters
20. 40.9 kilograms to pounds
21. 895 miles to kilometers
22. 1,000 grams to pounds
23. 79.1 meters to yards
24. 12 liters to quarts
25. 2.92 meters to feet
26. 5 liters to gallons
27. 8.7 meters to feet
28. 8 gallons to liters
29. 1,600 grams to pounds
30. 310 meters to yards

WORD PROBLEM

31. **Given:** A metric ton is 39.4 bushels of corn. Calculate number of bushels purchased from metric tons to bushels of corn.
    Problem: Soviets bought 450,000 metric tons of U.S. corn, valued at $58 million, for delivery after September 30.

STUDENT DVD-ROM

This student DVD-ROM contains the following assets designed to help you succeed in the business math course:

- **Videos** bring the author to you, where Jeff Slater carefully walks you through a review of each of the Learning Unit Practice Quizzes, with brief real applications to introduce each chapter segment.
- **Video Cases** applying business math concepts to real companies tied to information and assignments in the text.
- **Excel Spreadsheet Templates** to assist in solving end-of-chapter exercises that are indicated by an Excel logo.
- **PowerPoint** lecture slides walk you through the chapter concepts.
- **Practice Quizzes** covering key concepts in each chapter and giving you quick feedback on your responses.
- **Business Math Software Tutorials** for each chapter in the book in true/false, multiple-choice, interactive, and key terms formats.
- **Internet Resource Guide** providing information on using the Internet and useful websites for use with each chapter.
- **Web Link** to the Practical Business Math Procedures text website, which contains additional material to help you.

Help File for the WinDVD Web Edition DVD Player

The WinDVD player should launch automatically and play the Slater 7/E DVD content. The help files are no longer active, so here are some operating tips:

Right-clicking on the WinDVD interface will pop up a menu with two choices:

1. **View full screen**
   Checking this will increase the size of the video screen to maximum screen; unchecking will return to previous state.
2. **Remote: Vertical-Horizontal**
   Checking Vertical orients the player controls vertically on the left of the video screen; checking Horizontal (default) will place the player controls at the bottom of the video screen.

Player controls:
(If you hover over the button, you will see the name of the button appear)

The only player controls that work with this title are:

Play—no need to use this unless title is paused
Pause—this will pause playback (pressing play will continue playback)
Stop—this will stop playback (pressing play will return you to main menu)

Fast Forward—scans forward
Rewind—rewinds to beginning of title and starts playback

Root Menu—returns to the previous selected menu or to previously playing title
Title Menu—returns to the main menu

Left-Right-Down-Up—used to navigate onscreen buttons
Select Current Button—used to select onscreen buttons
(mouse is the preferred navigator device)

To quit, press ALT + F4 keys simultaneously.